MY MEXICO

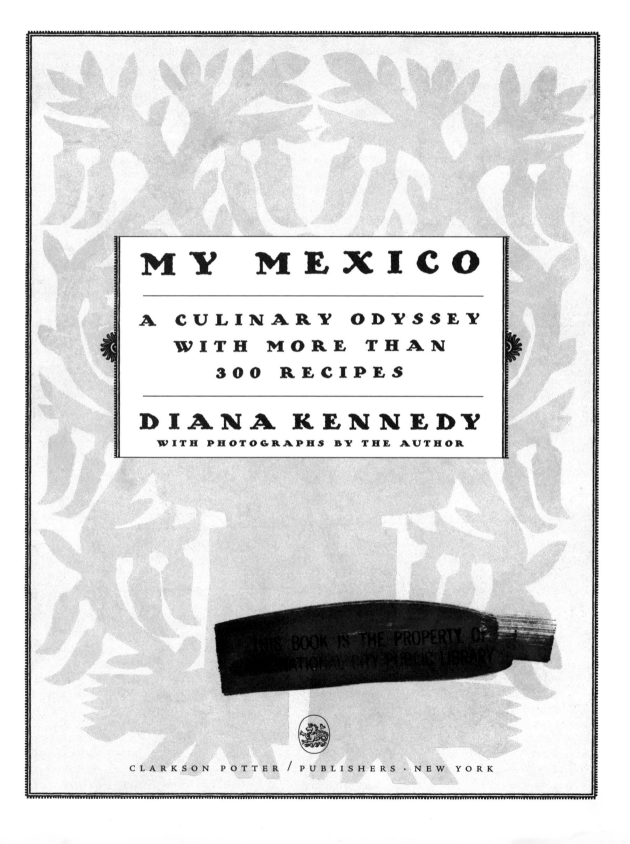

MY MEXICO

A CULINARY ODYSSEY
WITH MORE THAN
300 RECIPES

DIANA KENNEDY

WITH PHOTOGRAPHS BY THE AUTHOR

CLARKSON POTTER / PUBLISHERS · NEW YORK

ACKNOWLEDGEMENTS

❁

MY SINCERE THANKS TO: *Lauren Shakely and Roy Finamore at Clarkson Potter; Frances McCullough, my editor; Susan Lescher, my agent; Chris Benton, my copyeditor; Louise Fili, my designer; Merri Ann Morrell, my typesetter.*

MY GREAT INDEBTEDNESS TO THOSE WHO ENCOURAGED ME, CONTRIBUTED RECIPES, OR HELPED ME AS I JOURNEYED ONCE AGAIN AROUND MEXICO, ESPECIALLY: *Violet Gershenson; Carmen Ramírez Degollado; María Dolores Torres Yzabal; Pina Hamilton de Córdoba, Oaxaca; Oscar Kaufman, Campeche; Fernando del Moral Muriel, Aguascalientes; María Redondo de Williams; Guadalupe López de Lara de Zorilla; Lic. Antonio Tiro y Sra.*

The bark paper cutouts from San Pablito, State of Puebla, which appear as illustrations throughout this book, are used to invoke spirits of fruits and vegetables to ensure a good harvest. FRONTIS: *Frijoles (beans).*

Published by Clarkson N. Potter, Inc., 201 East 50th Street, New York, New York, 10022. Member of the Crown Publishing Group.

Random House, Inc. New York, Toronto, London, Sydney, Auckland
www.randomhouse.com

CLARKSON N. POTTER, POTTER, and colophon are trademarks of Clarkson N. Potter, Inc.

Printed in the United States of America

Design by Louise Fili, Ltd.

Library of Congress Cataloging-in-Publication Data
Kennedy, Diana
My Mexico: a culinary odyssey with more than 300 recipes / by Diana Southwood Kennedy. — 1st ed.
Includes index.
1. Cookery, Mexican. 2. Mexico—Social life and customs. I. Title.
TX716.M4K467   1998
641.5972—dc21   98-9181
CIP
ISBN 0-609-60247-0
10 9 8 7 6 5 4 3 2 1
First Edition

CONTENTS

✺

INTRODUCTION

✳

WHY *MY* MEXICO? IT SOUNDS RATHER ARROGANT AND POSSESSIVE, DOESN'T IT? WELL, THE TITLE CAME TO ME IN A FLASH — AND THE MORE I THOUGHT ABOUT IT, THE MORE APPROPRIATE IT SEEMED. AFTER ALL, THIS BOOK IS about the Mexico I know. It is a highly personal, somewhat lopsided view from other people's kitchens, where I seem to have spent an awful lot of time talking about food or actually cooking and eating with the families I visit.

When I first came to Mexico in 1957, I didn't come as an anthropologist or to study the costumes, dances, fiestas, or pyramids that continue to fascinate and attract people from other lands. I came to get married to a foreign correspondent based in Mexico. The plan was to live there for a few years before moving on to some other beat. I brought with me no particular talent, just a love of good food and an abounding curiosity and restlessness. I was immediately enthralled by the markets and the exotic ingredients; very soon I fell under the spell of the incredible beauty of the countryside that produced such a wealth of foods. I could never get enough of those early journeys into remote parts of the country and still cannot, even today. Soon I had to admit to a very strong addiction to Mexico.

Ever since, my life in Mexico has for the most part been, or has seemed to be, a series of fascinating adventures, most of them culinary. Of course I have had my disappointments, my surprises and delights, and many fruitless journeys during those years, but it has never been boring. There has never been a moment that I can remember in which I didn't have plans for yet another search for some unrecorded recipe, fabled regional cook, or elusive herb or chile.

I am never happier than when I am off somewhere in my truck discovering new things, for long ago I came to the realization that the wealth of Mexican foodstuffs and the variety of ways in which they are prepared are inexhaustible. And the more I travel, the more I realize that most families, even in the smallest communities, have a culinary history: recipes and methods handed down from one generation to another. If all this had been recorded over the years, it would reveal a lot about the changes in these societies through good times and bad, changes in climate and therefore agriculture, and the effects of the political and social influences brought about by workers coming and going between the larger cities and the United States. There is also a great deal of creativity among the cooks (usually women), using their skill and imagination to transform the monotony of the daily basic foods and, when the budget allows it, adding a few delicacies to make the occasional meal more festive. I am always urging cooks I meet to write down (if they can write) the basics of their recipes and demonstrate them to a younger member of the family who can take more detailed notes, so that this knowledge is not lost in the changes that are beginning to infiltrate, and that I fear will invade, Mexico.

When I first started writing my Mexican cookbooks at the beginning of the seventies, there was still a rather small, specialized audience for such exotic-sounding recipes calling for practically unknown ingredients, many of them hard, if not impossible, to find. But now the floodgates have opened: immigration and tourism have brought about greater exchanges both ways across the border. This process has been accelerated by NAFTA and by a group of young, energetic chefs eager to bring new seasonings and tastes to their eclectic foods.

This is my sixth book, all but one devoted entirely to Mexican food, so I suppose it is inevitable that I am constantly asked: What is this one about? And how does it differ from the other books? You could say that this one is a natural extension of the others because I learn something every time I travel, talk to cooks, and even cook with them. It is not a "compleat" gastronomic journey through Mexico, every region nicely balanced with recipes of every type. This is a more eccentric book, a record of my more recent wanderings, often comparing them with memories I had stored away from previous trips. I have included some recipes that have never (to my knowledge) been written down, others that appeared in books published a century or more ago and have now been largely forgotten. But surely it is not only the recipes that count but the people that keep them alive and their surrounding countryside, which provides the very special ingredients that distinguish one area from another. So this book offers a deeper and more personal look into the foods of this complex and fascinating country.

Although I have traveled the length and breadth of Mexico and around much of the coast, as you will see from the chapters that follow, I have focused much more on the central and southern regions, perhaps because, very generally speaking, change has come more slowly there and local traditions are held in greater respect.

The assembling of this disparate material has not been easy: Mexico is a huge country with vastly different cultures, climates, and vegetation. I have memories of so many past trips during the thirty-eight years that I have been visiting or living there, and I am overwhelmed with the changes I have seen during those years. Finally, my editor and I decided on a series of geographical blocks that follow the natural sequence of my journeys throughout the country.

I begin with San Pancho, near Zitácuaro, Michoacán, where I have had a home for the last eighteen years. From there I would travel to Morelia, occasionally to Tacámbaro, but more frequently to Jalisco and briefly up to Nayarit.

Although I have visited San Miguel many times, less often Aguascalientes and Zacatecas, it was my journey north to Chihuahua that incorporated all of these regions in a totally different pattern of food and eating from, say, that of the states bordering the Gulf of Mexico. The Central Hub, covering food experiences in the states surrounding Mexico City, also seemed logical: Hidalgo, Morelos, the State of Mexico, and a little more distant Puebla, through which I have traveled since my first days in Mexico City in 1957.

The grouping of the areas on the Gulf of Mexico (with the exception of Yucatán, whose foods I have included in my books) seemed natural considering their exuberant tropical environments and dedication to their traditional foods, preserved in particular by the indigenous groups of those areas. Finally there are the southern Pacific coast states of Oaxaca and Guerrero, through which I have traveled on countless occasions throughout my time in Mexico. The richness of their folklore and the variety of their natural ingredients makes them, Oaxaca above all, outstanding in their contribution to the gastronomy of Mexico.

Last of all, the Miscellany gathers up the fascinating odds and ends of my gastronomic wanderings: articles I have done on the disappearing recipes for insects, wild plants, including dried cuitlacoche and mushrooms, the influence of medieval Spain in the *Matanzas* of Puebla, and finally delving into old cookbooks, to find recipes that are still viable today and to learn of their attitudes toward food and their advice to the cooks.

All these have contributed to my world of food here in Mexico, to which I have dedicated the main part of my life.

So, in this rather unconventional cookbook I have tried to include recipes that will appeal to a wide audience as well as accounts of my culinary wanderings for those who read my cookbooks (or so they tell me) like novels.

There are some very simple recipes for the fairly inexperienced cook — don't miss the new *guacamoles* or the addictive chilatas. There are more complicated ones for aficionados who have cooked from my other books and already know the intricacies of the ingredients and methods. And then I have included quite a bit for the curious, adventurous cooks and chefs who have traveled extensively in Mexico and want to reproduce some of the more exotic foods they have tried in their own travels. Last, but by no means least, this book is intended for Mexican expatriates who are nostalgic for their native regions and traditional foods.

In a recent television interview I was asked how I would describe Mexican food. I found myself floundering hopelessly and helplessly — where to begin, what to encompass? The interviewers graciously tried to hide their impatience. Little did they realize what an impossible question that was to answer even in one hour, let alone two minutes. To do justice to the foods of this extraordinarily complex country would take many lifetimes of research and travel. For complex Mexico is. It stretches for seven thousand kilometers from north to south in the form of a cornucopia, three quarters of it just below the Tropic of Cancer. It is bordered for the most part by two cordilleras (mountain ranges) that slope down to the Gulf of Mexico to the east and the Pacific Ocean to the west, with a vast high central plateau, thus creating many geographical zones and microclimates. The accidents of history — highly developed ancient civilizations, foreign invasions and influences, and diverse indigenous cultures, many of which still survive today — have all played a part in this complexity.

It is an eternal project to record not only the wealth of culinary knowledge and folklore but also the fascinating human stories behind it all. I feel very much at home among the people I meet along the highways, and in the streets and marketplaces, for food is a language all its own that transcends mere words or actions. It was this feeling that gave me the title for this book, which in many ways will never really come to an end.

THE WESTERN CENTER AND ITS PACIFIC COAST

❀

Chayote (vegetable pear)

MICHOACÁN

San Pancho—How I Got There

IT IS THE BEGINNING OF MAY, AND THE HOTTEST MONTH OF ALL, AS I SIT DOWN TO WRITE THIS BOOK IN MY ECOLOGICAL HOUSE IN SAN FRANCISCO COATEPEC DE MORELOS, KNOWN LOCALLY AS San Pancho. The sky is hazy with heat and the dust stirred up by the sudden gusts of high winds, with occasional palls of smoke from a forest fire in the mountains to the east. Often these fires are purposely started by clandestine agents scouting timber for the greedy timber merchants who can then go in to clear and to cut or by farmers' unattended burning of last year's stubble to prepare the land for planting. The hills to the south and west are brown and bare in sharp contrast to the brilliant green valley, where the dam provides irrigation to the low fields around it. This is the month when tempers flare and explode, when young blades and old machos drink up a storm and give primeval screams or shoot off their rounds of ammunition as they saunter through the lanes of San Pancho. There is a heaviness in the air and a sense of foreboding. Will the rains come on time? The signs are anxiously awaited. Heriberto, my nearest neighbor, says he has seen the first *aludas*, winged ants, that are a sure sign, but the *mayates*, june bugs, hovering around the lamps and bombarding me at night are still too small. André down at the hotel says the swifts have not yet finished their nests (of course it is hard to know, since he drives them away with a broom because their droppings offend his sense of order—inherited from his French colonialist father). ☀ Occasionally the sky will threaten rain toward evening, and the next morning there is a delicious scent of damp undergrowth from the tree-clad mountains above. But when the bullfrogs begin their first intermittent raspings, you know that rain is near. On the other hand, if the rainy season starts too early, the last of the coffee berries will burst and spoil, the tomatoes will rot and never ripen, and too often August, the month in which the ears of corn are filling out, will be dry. At this time of year I bless my adobe house, despite all its drawbacks. It keeps pleasantly cool while the water from the solar collector gives me piping-hot showers. ☀ People who live in harsher climates tend to think that there are no seasons here in the semitropics of 5,900 feet. Yes, there's no snow, and just a very occasional frost or brief, gusty hailstorm. January is a bare month, cool and sunny, and if we are in favor with the gods, the first days of February bring welcome rains, *cabañuelas*, which encourage the plums and peaches to bloom and help top up the tanks for the hot, dry months ahead. ☀ The weeks that follow bring the most brilliant-hued flowers of the year: bougainvilleas of all shades, geraniums, amaryllis, cacti and tropical climbers contrasting with the pale blue masses of plumbago, while citrus blossoms perfume the air and my bees are satiated with these aromas. The vegetable garden is at its best. The first delicate peas and fava beans are harvested, and the nopal cactus rows come alive, shooting out their tender and succulent paddles. Carlos, who is in charge outside, cuts the vegetables and collects the blackberries and strawberries a little too early, but, as he explains, we have a host of eager and cunning winged sharecroppers who would leave me nothing if they had their way.

Yesterday he brought in the freshly winnowed crop of wheat. Not much—it was planted on a small patch of poor land—but it's enough for my whole-wheat loaves for the year. Every month brings its own modest harvest, and as the last picking of coffee is completed the small, black indigenous avocados are ready.

The orioles and red throats are scrapping over the mulberries, while the decorative maracua vine outside my study window is alive with its white passion flowers, all facing straight up to the sky with their green "antennae" to attract the attention of the hummingbirds, butterflies, and bees. The lime tree is heavy with fruit, while the oranges and tangerines are just forming for the summer crop. The stone walls around the house are bedecked with the showy white cereus blossoms of the *pitahayas*—that most exotic of fruits with shiny, shocking pink skin, pale green "hooks," and deep magenta flesh, specked with myriad tiny black seeds.

The little red and yellow plums will ripen in the next months, next to the brilliant-colored tamarillos and the last of the citrons. As May draws to an end, it is the time to plant the corn and ask for the irrigation water that flows down through a maze of open canals through the orchards and pastures of my neighbors. The water comes from springs in land owned higher up by a nearby village and is shared between them, my neighbors, and the community lands down by the dam. I shall never forget the magical sound of the water gushing through the channels at four in the morning: it was a sound that always woke me up before high stone walls and extra trees were planted to muffle the sound. I used to help with the irrigating in those early days. It is compelling, almost addictive work as you direct the water into one channel between the rows of corn. At first it is absorbed by the dry soil, a trickle turns into a flow, and the plant straightens up and glows. You make a small dike and then start the next row.

That sound of water is music, just like the first drops of rain that drum at night on the hot, dry tiles of the roof and resound against the pine shingles of my bedroom ceiling. I always pray to my pantheistic gods that it will drum long enough to freshen the plants and not just evaporate on the hard, dry soil. I often get up and open the terrace doors early the next morning and breathe in the air, alive with scents of pine, cedar, avocado leaves, and the damp undergrowth that smells of sage. With those first rains a certain cosmic tension is released and I find myself turning over and sleeping more at peace.

Weeds and lilies grow up between the flagstones of the kitchen terrace, and the gray stone walls gradually come alive with mosses, lichens, ferns, and miniature flowers that had laid dormant in the crevices. The hills around turn from burnt umber and ochre to many shades of green as they take part in this incredible metamorphosis.

We plant small patches of corn, all types and colors, that I bring back from my travels around the country. After the first weeding, beans and pumpkins are planted to accompany them.

As the rains progress, the high mesa to the south buzzes with activity long before dawn for the very brief spell when the first tender little field mushrooms appear. This is the time for the light green pear-shaped squash from a plant that creeps along the ground (all the year in Oaxaca) and provides not only the squash itself but also tender shoots for cooking and the largest and most fragrant yellow flowers of all the squash varieties. The *chayotes* are forming: dark green and prickly, long and pear shaped, and small cream colored. The tips of their long, curling vines can also be cooked and mixed with scrambled eggs or in a soup. Later in the year, when the plant has dried and the leaves fallen, the bulbous root is unearthed, cooked, and eaten just as it is or made into small fritters. My neighbors can be seen carrying these long light brown tubers cooked, to be sold in the market or along the sidewalks or bartered with the chauffeur of the large van carrying them into town. Later still, when the plume at the top of the corn plant, the male flower, is just bursting open, we gather them, dry them in the sun, and winnow them for the anthers, later to be toasted for *tamales de espiga* (page 10).

In the fall the sweet potatoes are dug up and put out to "season" in the sun for three days before being baked so that their natural sugar exudes. As the days progress, a second crop of oranges, both sweet and bitter, and tangerines ripen and the *granadillas (Granada china)* whose vines have swarmed over the avocado trees begin to ripen, turning from purplish green to orangey yellow. As October advances, the land around my house as well as the meadows and fields are covered with a haze of yellow and pink wildflowers; as November approaches we are surrounded by clouds of white flowering shrubs that light up the land in contrast to the brilliant red of the poinsettias. If the year has been a fruitful one, there is always something to cook: blackberries from the forests higher up or large, juicy cultivated ones for ices and jams, quinces in July and guavas in December for *ates* (fruit pastes), passion fruit for ices, bitter oranges for marmalade, citrons and peaches for candy, and calamondins for preserves, enough to last for a year or more.

I have to keep these things firmly in my mind as changes are occurring: our lanes are not as quiet now, with passenger vans making their macho roar, garbage strewn at night along the entrance to the village, and the booming music of recurring local fiestas in Zitácuaro, all symptomatic of the mindless and raucous elements of any society that invade and destroy, with no thought for the future and what they are not leaving for future generations.

I am so often asked how I came to settle on San Pancho in the first place. Well, almost twenty years ago now an English acquaintance, who had built himself a charming house there and knew I was looking for land, invited me for the weekend to see the area. I too fell in love with the place just as he had done years earlier. He was a meticulous person, so when he was searching for a place to build a weekend house, he methodically visited all the likely spots within a radius of one hundred miles around Mexico City. He came to know Zitácuaro when he stayed at Rancho San Cayetano, the small hotel owned and run by an elderly American lady. It is situated on the Huetamo highway, about three kilometers from Zitácuaro, precisely at the point where a roughly surfaced lane turns off to San Pancho. From there it is exactly one kilometer to the center of this sprawling village and its late-sixteenth-century Franciscan church.

In front of the church is a public garden—*el jardin*, which used to be the graveyard—with a small bandstand in the center. It used to be shadowed by towering jacaranda trees. Every spring they bloomed, forming a magnificent cloud of purply blue. Imagine that against an azure sky with the salmon-pink church in the background. As the weeks progressed you would walk on a thick carpet of blue that hid the bare earth. But one day the local *políticos*, who would easily find any pretext to get drunk, decided that the blossoms made a mess, and besides, they wanted a garden with flowers and less shade—or so they said. The trees were felled over my shrill protestations, which prompted the *jefe del pueblo* to inform me that prisons were built for women too, and I told him to go to hell . . . well, I have already written about that in my personal cookbook *Nothing Fancy*. The sale of the firewood kept them all in booze for weeks; it was one long bacchanalia.

Most of the houses are built in traditional style with white-painted adobe walls, earth red around the base to camouflage the mud splashed up from the streets in the heavy rains. The gently sloping roofs are covered with thick tiles that have mellowed to all shades of red and brown over the years. Each house has its piece of land and orchard at the back, and until recently fruit was still picked in bulk and sent daily to the local and Mexico City markets. But in that seemingly peaceful place there was discord: Catholics against Protestants, old political caciques against those who dared to oppose them, whole families closely interrelated, pitted against their relatives, even brothers and sisters at loggerheads. The causes were the normal ones: past or present feuds over inheritances, debts, or what you will.

The young people of the more affluent families were sent off to study for academic or professional careers, and very soon their parents joined them in the city. The village was almost dead except during holidays and feast days, weddings and funerals, though a few families managed to make a living from the lands and orchards that they stayed on and had twelve children each.

Many orchards were abandoned during those years, many of the sons went off as migrant workers to the United States, and irrigation water was not plentiful. The village above San Pancho, San Miguel, which controls most of the springs that bring water from the mountains, was growing too fast; people were dividing up their lands, and indiscriminate tree felling was taking its toll. Everything seemed to be contributing to the gradual disintegration of this once-beautiful place.

When I was thinking seriously of buying near Zitácuaro, I remembered what a friend and well-known Náhuatl scholar, who had studied the history of that area, had said: "Don't buy there; there's a lot of witchcraft around." And I also remembered what a very wise friend, a renowned forestry expert and one of the first serious British ecologists, said when he heard of my infatuation with the place: "Beware of the ideal." I thought of that again when a neighbor blocked my narrow entranceway, saying it was only for men walking or donkeys and not for trucks carrying building materials. A politician who was a friend of my late husband helped me regain my access rights and when I nearly gave up in despair said, "Diana, never let go of a dream." For by then my plans had built themselves into a dream.

I wanted a house of locally made materials that would address itself to the resources of the area and be in tune with the restrictions with which my neighbors had to live, and had survived, for many years. I wanted a center for my studies of Mexican foods, a place where I could not only plant chiles and herbs from different parts of the country but also plant trees and help the earth around come alive again after so many years of neglect.

To this day I don't really know why I hung on to this dream—which threatened many times to become a nightmare—so tenaciously and against all odds. I was told by one of the taciturn, unfriendly men of the main family controlling most of the lands around me that San Pancho was a *pueblo fantasmo* (ghost village): people came but never stayed. I often thought of those words in the early days before I had a car, as I walked across the village in the early afternoons of those hot spring days. There was no sound of human life, only the braying of a donkey, the crowing of a misguided rooster, and the dry rustle of coffee bushes and avocado trees. The silence was eerie.

In those days I was known as *la gringa loca*, who had bought land without water. The story of getting that irrigation water by insisting on my rights as a bona fide landholder and then finally getting my one hour of dubious drinking water daily could itself fill a book. Gratefully, I have almost erased from my memory those arduous days, and when I do think fleetingly about them I try to rationalize it all as "building character" (a little late in life) or "adding to worldly experience," shutting out the thought—much nearer the truth—that I was just plain stupid and stubborn in attempting what many others had tried and failed to do.

The small orchards around San Pancho are bordered by loose stone walls, bare and gray in the dry months and gloriously multicolored soon after the rains: with pale pink begonias and little red and purple trumpets. Today I can still see neighbors striding along the way to their fields, their curved machetes like extensions of their right arms and their faces shaded by wide-brimmed sombreros that have small tassels swaying from the back. There are donkeys laden with dried kindling for the local bakers, pattering surefootedly over the uneven rocky surface along the lane, and the occasional horseman erect and moving in rhythm with his mount, acknowledging another presence with a grudging *"Buenos días."* Occasionally I meet opposition to my little truck from heavily plodding oxen—still used for plowing here—or a herd of Holsteins ambling along, as though they have all day to reach their pastures on the mesa that rises and extends along the southern limits of the village holdings.

Nowadays, despite the defacing Pepsi signs and carelessly thrown litter, the blaring of portable radios and noisy Volkswagen vans carrying people to and from Zitácuaro, some vestiges of the past remain in the memories of the older people, in the beliefs, the myths, and the food. Sra. Catalina, the mother of Carlos, my *capataz,* and eight other children (who now works for the Italian priests who have come to live here and from whom she learned to make spaghetti bolognese) is proud of her recipe for *tamales de espiga.* A few days after she had come to make them with me, she appeared with her husband at the entrance to my land, smiling and waving a piece of paper. On it her mother had written in a shaky hand, *"Tamales de espiga datan de 1770 que tienen conocimiento y son originarios de San Francisco Coatepec de Morelos."* (*Tamales de espiga* date from 1770, when they were known, and originated in San Francisco Coatepec de Morelos.)

TAMALES DE ESPIGA

✸

[MAKES 60 TAMALES]

TAMALES DE ESPIGA ARE TRADITIONALLY MADE FOR THE SEPTEMBER INDE-
PENDENCE FESTIVITIES, BUT SRA. CATALINA BEGINS TO PREPARE FOR THEM
toward the end of July, when the male flower of the corn cultivated during the rainy season
(not from irrigated corn in the dry months because Sra. Catalina says this does not have such
a strong flavor) is just bursting out of its green sheath, as the local saying goes: *"cuando la milpa
está bandereando"* (when the cornfield is bedecked with flags).

I had heard about these unique *tamales* from neighbors and must confess that the first
time I tried one I was unimpressed, but then I hadn't tried Sra. Catalina's. It was then that I
began to appreciate their delicate malty/honey flavor and spongy texture. The dough itself is
made of white flour leavened with *pulque* and flavored with the dried toasted anthers or
pollen sacs of the male flowers that crown the cornstalk and sweetened with *piloncillo*, the
dark colored cones of raw sugar. The *tamales* are steamed in dried corn husks and traditionally eaten for breakfast or supper accompanied by a glass of milk.

The flowers themselves are made up of many (I have counted up to eighteen) strands. You
have to reach up and, holding the bunch in your fist, lift them out of their sheathlike socket.
We did this late one afternoon and immediately wrapped them in a piece of dry toweling until
the following morning. The next day, about ten o' clock, when the sun was warm, they were
spread out in one layer on a piece of cotton (not toweling) in the sun to dry. At noon they were
turned over and again at two-thirty in the afternoon before they were wrapped once again in
the toweling at about four o' clock, when the sun was beginning to lose its strength.

This whole process was repeated the following day since the *espigas* generally need two
sunnings *(dos soles)*. To test if they have been dried out enough, tap one of the strands and the
anthers *(anteras)* or pollen sacs (erroneously referred to in my village as *pistilos*, or pistils) that
resemble light green threads about half a centimeter long, and if they fall easily from their
husks, the sprays are ready to be threshed.

Doña Catalina ordered a switch made of peach wood, about one and a half meters long, which should be flexible and stripped of its bark. Her son Carlos provided exactly what she had asked for. She started beating the sprays with a gentle rhythmic motion, then stopped and complained that the switch was too long. It was cut down to a more manageable size of one meter, and the work proceeded until she was satisfied that as many of the anthers as possible had been separated. The dried stalks were removed and the winnowing began.

The winnowing was not, as one might suspect, done with the wind or by tossing it in the air but by drawing the fringe of a *rebozo* slowly over the surface so that the husks adhered to the fabric. But it wasn't quite as easy as that. Catalina said she had forgotten to bring her *rebozo*—actually she had lent it to her daughter, who had lost it. We sent across to some neighbors to borrow one. Elena, who had two, we were told, sent back word that she couldn't find hers; Esther had just laundered her *rebozo*, and it was still damp. I produced a woolen one and thought it worked quite well, but it did not pass Catalina's stringent test. The most efficient fringe for their work, so it turns out, is that of an ordinary *rebozo de hilo* (a common *rebozo* made of a more commercial thread).

The cleaned anthers, mixed with some of the brilliant yellow pollen that had been shaken from them, were a luminous pale green but needed to be dried for two extra days. At this point they could be stored in an airtight container for future use. (I have actually used them after one year, and they still retained their aroma and flavor.) Now to the recipe:

4½ pounds (2 generous kg) all-purpose flour (about 18 cups)
1 quart (1 l) fresh pulque (see box, below)
2⅛ pounds (1 kg) piloncillo or dark brown sugar
approximately 3 cups (750 ml) water
½ cup (125 ml) anthers
60 dried corn husks, soaked

Put one quarter of the flour into a wide bowl. Add the *pulque* and, after making the sign of the cross (even I as a pantheist do it), mix to a loose, rather lumpy batter. As an added assurance against mishaps, place two twigs in the form of a cross on top of the bowl and then cover

[CONTINUED]

PULQUE

PULQUE IS THE FERMENTED *sap of the century plant* (Agave atrovirens, A. Americana). *Rich in amino acids, with minerals, salts, and natural sugar, not only does it provide a healthful, slightly alcoholic drink, but it was also one of the principal elements—with corn and chiles —in the diet of the indigenous people of central Mexico from pre-Columbian times.*

Pulque is often curado, *flavored with fruits—strawberries, pineapples, tunas (fruits of certain cacti), among others—and sold in* pulquerías *or* cantinas *and even canned for consumption both at home and abroad.*

It has a rather sour, earthy, fruity flavor and slightly slimy consistency and is very much an acquired taste. More acceptable to most "outsiders" is the lighter, frothy aguamiel from which it is made. When the maguey or agave matures, anywhere from seven to nine years, and is about to send up its thick stalk crowned with flowers, the center is scraped to form a bowl into which the sap, or aguamiel, drains. This liquid is drawn off with a special gourd twice daily (like milking a cow). Timing has to be exact and all utensils and hands cleaned scrupulously to prevent the aguamiel from spoiling. It is then added to the vat of mature pulque to be transformed through fermentation into pulque within a few hours.

Not only is pulque consumed as a drink, but it is also used for leavening bread, for rustic table sauces (salsa borracha, etc.), for grinding dried chiles, for seasoning pastes for barbecued meats, for stews or adding with piloncillo (cones of brown unrefined sugar) to make a fermented tepache (a drink more often made with pineapple).

In recipes light beer makes an acceptable substitute.

with a towel. Set aside to proof at about 75°F (24°C) for about 4 hours; it should be bubbly and well fermented with a thin crust over the surface.

Meanwhile, break the *piloncillo* into small pieces and add it, or the sugar, to the water in a small pan. Dissolve over low heat and set aside to cool.

Put the anthers into an ungreased pan and stir over low heat until they begin to toast to a golden brown and a delicious malty aroma emanates from them. Grind them to a powder in an electric spice/coffee grinder (traditionally they are ground on a *metate*, which is then brushed down with an *escobetilla*, or little brush formed out of a bundle of dried roots).

Distribute the remaining flour evenly around the edge of the fermented starter. Sift the ground anthers into the middle and pour the syrup over them to form a central pool. Again, bless the mixture with the sign of the cross before beginning to fold the flour into the other ingredients with your hand. You must always fold in with a counterclockwise motion, turning the bowl gradually as you go.

When the ingredients are all well incorporated, the dough should be fairly stiff (if too stiff, add a little more water by degrees) and sticky and the color of *cafe con leche*.

Turn the mixture out onto a flat surface, form it into a round cushion shape, cover loosely with a cloth, and leave overnight or for not more than 14 hours, at room temperature (about 60°F/15°C).

The next day fill the bottom of a *tamale* steamer with water and a few coins that will rattle around as the water boils. If the rattling slows down or stops completely, you know that more boiling water should be added immediately. The steamer should then be set over a wood or charcoal fire; according to Sra. Catalina, this adds the authentic touch to the flavor of the *tamal.*

To form the *tamales,* start by cutting a strip of the dough about 2½ inches (6.5 cm) wide and divide it into pieces about 2 inches (5 cm) long. Make only 10 or so to begin with. Place a piece of the dough into the corn husks, leaving about 2 inches (5 cm) of space between the cupped end of the husk and the dough to allow for expansion. Holding the edges of the cup loosely over the dough, fold the tip over to completely cover the dough, again very loosely.

When you have prepared the 10 *tamales,* open up the steamer (the water should be boiling) and bless it with a double sign of the cross. Start by placing the *tamales* in one layer around the edge of the steamer with one in the middle to complete the layer, or *tendida.* Cover the steamer with a tight lid and steam the *tamales* for about 7 minutes so that they are just beginning to set (*para que se sancochen*—although this literally means to parboil) before adding another layer, then after 5 minutes add the next layer and subsequent layers at each 5-minute interval until they are packed loosely into the steamer.

The *tamales* should take about 1 hour to cook. To test, remove one, unwrap it, and make

[CONTINUED]

sure that it is spongy to the touch and that the dough comes easily away from the warm husk. Then, just to make sure, break one open to ensure the dough is cooked all the way through. Serve immediately.

FRUTAS EN TACHA—PRESERVED FRUITS

There are three stands in the Zitácuaro market that sell *frutas en tacha*—fruits cured in a solution of lime or wood ash and cooked to a brown stickiness in raw sugar. The bitter oranges, citrons, figs, pumpkins, and *chilacayotes* are grown locally. During Holy Week, street stands do a brisk trade in selling these fruits stuffed into white bread rolls: the standard breakfast for most families who still observe traditional ways of eating.

You don't have to drive very far south of Zitácuaro to reach the hot country, where there are still remains of haciendas and the *ingenios,* sugar mills, that belonged to them. Before the Revolution and land reforms, extensive areas there were planted with sugarcane. After the partition of these lands to the *campesinos,* a few of them elected to continue cultivating cane but, of course, on a much smaller scale. Up until about six years ago, every year at the end of January I used to drive down with one or two neighbors to a village about thirty kilometers away to buy my year's supply of the large, dark brown cones of unrefined sugar. Sadly, all the small mills have now disappeared. I always enjoyed those morning drives. The village stood several kilometers back from the highway on a rough narrow road that wound through a steep canyon. The sweet smell of the crushed cane met you as you neared the first houses and *trapiche,* a rustic sugar mill, but we always went on through the village on a bumpy track that finally led to a wide opening in the cane fields.

DURAZNOS EN TACHA

PRESERVED PEACHES

❁

[MAKES 50 PEACHES]

SEVERAL YEARS AGO A GOVERNOR OF THE STATE CAME TO LUNCH AND I PROUDLY SHOWED HIM MY VERY INTERESTING BUT POOR LAND. REMEMBER-ing that it was mostly neglected orchard, he thoughtfully sent me a truckload of fruit trees. I distributed them through the village as a gesture of goodwill, and we all had ten trees each. The rascally old *jefe de pueblo*, the authority in our village, who was an inveterate drunk, kept sending people who did not own land to try to get more trees for himself than the allotted amount. We caught on very fast.

There were peach trees among those sent that produce a firm fruit with crisp orange-colored flesh. They are not only delicious to eat but ideal just before they become too ripe, to preserve in the traditional way, *tachados*.

When my peach trees first started to fruit, I decided that now was the time to learn the recipe. I had eaten them from the market, from a local restaurant, and finally from a neighbor. I tried their recipes but somehow wasn't satisfied. The subject came up one day when chatting with Sra. Lola, who also lives in the village, and I invited her to try my first efforts. . . . "No," she said, "these are too *correoso*," coarse and chewy. "My mother knows how to make them much better." I checked every step of the recipe with Sra. Lucinda, but when it came to "How long do they take to cook?" she replied: "They will let you know." I think I cooked about one hundred that first time and it took eight hours! If the rains do not extend into the fall for too long, the peaches will dry out nicely and will last for up to two years. They get drier, less sweet, and a little more chewy.

Don't be put off by the cooking time. Get a fascinating book or invite a talkative person to keep you company. If you hurry the peaches, they boil so fast they will not cook right through evenly and have a tougher skin. Be sure to pick peaches that are still underripe.

50 small underripe peaches, about 4 pounds (1 kg)
approximately 3 quarts (3 l) cold water
just over ¼ cup (63 ml) wood ash, ground and sifted (see Note)
4 pounds (3 kg 600 g) granulated sugar
5 cups (1.25 l) water

NOTE: *The amount of ash given is for hard wood; if you are using soft wood ash like pine, increase the amount by almost double.*

Rinse the peaches, removing any remains of the stalk. Prick each peach with a fork three times, making sure that the tines reach down to the pit. [CONTINUED]

Put the 3 quarts (3 l) water into a glass, stainless-steel, or hard-baked stoneware crock. Stir the wood ash into the water and allow the gray particles to settle to the bottom. This will take about 20 minutes.

Place the peaches carefully in the water, which should cover them, and leave them to soak overnight. While they are soaking and while you are still awake, gently tilt the pan from side to side to make sure the peaches are soaking evenly.

The following day, remove the peaches, rinse them well in fresh water, and gently rub the downy surface from the skin. Meanwhile, put the sugar and 5 cups (1.25 l) water in a preserving pan, bring to a boil, lower the heat, and stir until the sugar has melted. Add the peaches. Now the water should come only three quarters of the way up the fruit. Cook uncovered over low heat, so that the peaches just simmer until the syrup begins to thicken and the skin of the peaches takes on a greenish hue. As the syrup thickens, it will coat the peaches and penetrate the flesh. They are done when the peaches and the flesh inside are a deep brown color and the sugar hangs in a thick strand from the spoon. This may take 4 to 5 hours or more! Transfer to a drying rack to drain and dry them off in a dry, airy place—in the sun if you don't have beehives around. Store in a dry, well-ventilated place to avoid mold.

CHILAQUILES EN SALSA VERDE DE SRA. JUANA

SRA. JUANA'S *CHILAQUILES* IN GREEN SAUCE

❁

[SERVES 4]

FRIENDS WHO STAY AT RANCHO SAN CAYETANO, THE SMALL HOTEL ABOUT A MILE FROM WHERE I LIVE, ALWAYS RAVE ABOUT JUANA'S *CHILAQUILES* IN green sauce that are served at breakfast time. *Chilaquiles* means "broken up old sombrero" but is in fact stale corn tortillas broken up and served with a lavish topping of cream cheese, chopped onion, and sometimes *chorizo* or shredded chicken. It is a very popular breakfast dish in central Mexico in particular, and each area has its own, slightly different version. Here in the eastern part of Michoacán the tortilla pieces are fried crisp and remain al dente when the sauce has been added; elsewhere they are often cooked to a softer consistency.

Since Juana has to provide for late risers who amble into the breakfast room throughout the morning, she cooks the sauce separately and adds it to the fried tortillas just before serving.

THE SAUCE

12 ounces (340 g) tomates verdes, about 14 medium,
husks removed and rinsed

4 serrano chiles or to taste

1 garlic clove, roughly chopped

1 tablespoon vegetable oil

salt to taste

oil for frying

8 5-inch (13-cm) corn tortillas, cut into ½-inch (13-mm) squares
and left to dry overnight

½ cup (125 ml) finely chopped white onion

THE TOPPING

⅔ cup (164 ml) roughly chopped cilantro

¾ cup (188 ml) crumbled queso fresco *or substitute (page 525)*

⅓ cup (83 ml) crème fraîche or sour cream thinned with a little milk

Put the *tomates verdes* and chiles into a small pan, cover with water, and cook over low heat until soft but not falling apart. Drain off all but ⅓ cup (83 ml) of the cooking water. Transfer to a blender jar with the garlic and blend until smooth.

Heat 1 tablespoon oil in a skillet, add the sauce with salt to taste, and cook over medium heat, stirring from time to time, until slightly reduced and seasoned—about 5 minutes. Keep warm.

Heat oil to a depth of about ¼ inch (7 mm) in a deep skillet, add the tortilla pieces, a few at a time, and fry until crisp and light gold. Drain on paper toweling and continue with the remaining pieces. Drain off all but ¼ cup (63 ml) of the oil in the pan. Add the tortilla pieces and the onion, cover, and fry over low heat, shaking the pan from time to time, until the onion is translucent; it should not be browned. [CONTINUED]

Add the warm sauce and cook, stirring to mix well for about 5 minutes. Serve immediately, topping each portion with a generous amount of *cilantro*, cheese, and cream.

ENSALADA DE NOPALITOS ESTILO SAN PANCHO

NOPAL SALAD, SAN PANCHO

❁

[MAKES ENOUGH FOR 12 TACOS OR 4 MAIN-DISH SALADS]

BOTH JUANA, ONE OF THE COOKS AT THE HOTEL, AND MY HOUSEKEEPER, CON-SUELO, PREPARE A CACTUS SALAD IN THIS WAY. IT IS SLIGHTLY DIFFERENT from those published in my other books. They steam the cactus pieces, while I always cook mine *al vapor*, in their own juice. Here the salad is often served with *chicharrón* scattered over the top as part of a mixed *botana* with drinks, although it can, of course, be served as a dinner salad or as a stuffing for tacos.

1 tablespoon vegetable oil

4 cups (1 l) cactus pieces, cut into squares of just over ¼ inch (7 mm)

¼ cup (63 ml) water

salt to taste

2 tablespoons finely chopped white onion

½ cup (125 ml) finely chopped tomatoes

*½ cup (125 ml) loosely packed finely chopped
cilantro leaves and small stems*

1½ tablespoons fresh lime juice

3 serrano chiles or to taste, finely chopped

1 additional tablespoon light olive oil or vegetable oil

*3 ounces (85 g) chicharrón, broken into
1-inch (2.5-cm) pieces (optional)*

In a heavy skillet, heat 1 tablespoon vegetable oil over medium heat, add the cactus pieces, water, and salt, cover the pan, and cook over medium heat for about 5 minutes. By then the cactus will be juicy and slimy (if it is fresh enough). Remove the lid and continue cooking, scraping the bottom of the pan from time to time to prevent sticking, until all the moisture has evaporated and the viscosity is absorbed back into the cactus, about 10 minutes. The quantity will have reduced by about half. Set aside to cool.

Mix in the rest of the ingredients and set aside to season for at least 30 minutes. Just before serving, scatter the top with the *chicharrón*.

BOTANA DE CHILACAS

CHILACAS WITH CREAM AND CHEESE

Sra. Consuelo Mendoza

✺

[MAKES APPROXIMATELY 1¼ CUPS (313 ML)—8 BOTANAS]

THERE ARE FOODS IN ANY CUISINE THAT I CAN EAT OVER AND OVER AGAIN, AND NEVER TIRE OF THE TASTE OR TEXTURE. THE CHILACA, THAT LONG, skinny dark green chile, is one of them, either fresh or in its dried form as pasilla chile. It has a delicious flavor and, although generally mildly picante, it can surprise you at times with its fierceness.

Chilacas, occasionally found in New Mexico and California, are popular in the cooking of this part of Michoacán and around Morelia, I suppose because they are grown extensively in the fertile lands around Queréndaro in the valley farther east. When you drive through that little town in the fall, you can see the crop of chilacas and poblanos spread out on *petates* (mats) to dry along the main avenue alongside little stands selling honey and the local bread from the nearby pottery town of Zinapécuaro.

My housekeeper admits that she is not a good cook, although she does provide daily meals for her family and the relatives that are continually dropping by unannounced. Obviously having worked for me for several years, she knows the dishes that I more or less routinely (although there is not much of a routine in my house) prepare and those that I bring back from my travels, but occasionally she suggests something that her sisters-in-law have picked up. The following two recipes came from those welcome suggestions.

This delicious snack is eaten at room temperature with freshly made corn tortillas to accompany drinks before a meal.

8 chilacas, peeled and cleaned, or 7 small poblano chiles
2 tablespoons fresh lime juice
2 tablespoons finely chopped white onion
3 tablespoons finely crumbled queso fresco or substitute (page 525)
salt to taste

Tear (remember, this chile is often referred to as *chile para deshebrar*, or "chile to shred") the chilacas into very thin strips, or cut the poblanos into very thin strips. Mix the chiles with the rest of the ingredients and set aside to season for at least 30 minutes before serving with fresh tortillas.

HABITAS GUISADAS PARA BOTANA

FAVA BEAN SNACK

Consuelo Mendoza

❋

[MAKES 3½ TO 4 CUPS (875 ML TO 1 L)]

LAST SPRING I HAD AN ABUNDANCE OF TENDER AND DELICIOUS FAVA BEANS. I HAD COOKED THEM IN EVERY WAY POSSIBLE AND WAS SEARCHING FOR A new way of preparing them when my housekeeper, Consuelo, came up with this recipe. It was actually passed on to her from a sister-in-law who comes from a village near Toluca, where fava beans are a major crop. In fact, both fresh and dried fava beans are used extensively there. It is important to have tender beans. I have always had bad luck in the U.S. with favas since they are so often picked far too late, when they are large and starchy.

Serve this as a *botana* with drinks or as an appetizer, either warm or at room temperature.

3½ cups (875 ml) hulled tender fava beans, inner skin left on
⅓ cup (83 ml) vegetable oil
2 cups (500 ml) thinly sliced white onion
3 garlic cloves, finely chopped
3 manzano or jalapeño chiles, seeds and veins removed,
cut into thin strips
salt to taste

¼ cup (63 ml) water
3 large sprigs epazote, roughly chopped
1 teaspoon dried oregano, crumbled

Shave off a small portion of the skin at the point where the beans were attached to the pod to enable the flavors to penetrate and prick with a fork on both sides. Heat the oil in a skillet, add the onion, garlic, and chiles, and cook gently without browning until the onion is translucent.

Add the beans, salt, and water, cover the pan, and continue cooking, shaking the pan from time to time to prevent sticking, for about 10 minutes. Add the *epazote* and cook for 5 minutes more, stirring in the oregano just before the end of the cooking time.

CALDO DE HONGO Y FLOR

BROTH WITH MUSHROOMS AND SQUASH FLOWERS

❀

[SERVES 6]

THIS CALDO IS THE INEVITABLE SOUP COURSE IN MY MENUS AS THE RAINY SEASON ADVANCES AND THERE ARE STILL SOME OF THE DELICATE LITTLE mushrooms called *clavitos (Leophyllum decastes)*—crudely called "fried chicken mushrooms" in the U.S.—and the squash flowers are large and fragrant. Of course, any tender mushroom may be substituted. The balance of ingredients could vary according to taste and availability of ingredients, but the base should be a good, flavorful, but not too strong chicken broth. I prefer to cook some of the vegetables separately to intensify their flavor before adding them to the broth—more trouble, but it is worth it.

Very sweet American corn won't do here; look for field corn at a farmer's market or farmstand.

3½ tablespoons vegetable oil
1 medium white onion, finely chopped
3 garlic cloves, finely chopped

[CONTINUED]

4 ounces (115 g) zucchini, finely diced, 1 cup (250 ml) loosely packed

salt to taste

¾ cup (188 ml) fresh corn kernels, not sweet

12 ounces (340 g) squash flowers, 4 cups (1 l) very tightly packed,
sepals removed and roughly chopped

8 ounces (225 g) juicy mushrooms, tips of stems removed, rinsed

2 large sprigs epazote

5 cups (1.25 l) chicken broth

2 poblano chiles, charred, peeled, seeds and veins removed,
and cut into strips

Heat 2 tablespoons of the oil in a skillet over medium heat, add two thirds of the onion and garlic, and cook without browning until translucent. Add the zucchini, sprinkle with salt, cover the pan, and cook for about 3 minutes. Add the corn and continue cooking for 3 more minutes. Add the squash flowers and cook, uncovered, until all the vegetables are just tender but not too juicy, about 10 minutes. If they are juicy, raise the heat for a few minutes.

Chop the larger mushrooms, leaving the smaller ones whole. Heat 1 tablespoon of the remaining oil in a skillet over medium heat, add the remaining onion and garlic, and cook until translucent. Add the mushrooms and cook over fairly high heat for about 5 minutes. Add the *epazote* and cook for 2 minutes more.

Add the mushrooms and vegetables to the broth in a saucepan. Bring the broth up to a simmer and continue simmering for about 10 minutes or until the flavors have mingled.

Heat the remaining ½ tablespoon oil, add the chile strips with a sprinkle of salt, and cook for 1 minute. Serve on top of the broth.

Mexico City to Zitácuaro, Michoacán

Returning to San Pancho from Mexico City in those first years when the roads were still lightly traveled, I would often stop to take photographs or just gaze at the landscape that unfolded with every turn in the road—mountains, plains, and forests—always marveling at their beauty, the colors, the brilliance of the light, and the variety of wildflowers. You could listen to the silence then, broken now and again by birdsong.

No longer. I now think of that drive as a lesson in survival as trailers, trucks, and buses of enormous dimensions rush past and what I guess to be minor bureaucrats or traveling sales-men swing out wide around the bends and overtake on blind curves. The devil himself seems to be behind the wheel or snapping at their heels. Surely one is permitted some nostalgia for those less frenetic days!

The journey starts by driving out of Mexico City on Highway 15, which leads due west, climbing steeply up along the edge of the Desierto de los Leones, a thickly wooded national park. As you reach the highest point, a pass of about 9,000 feet, the road begins to drop in wide curves down to the valley of the Río Lerma. It is dominated to the southwest by an extinct volcano, the Nevado de Toluca, whose slopes around the crater are periodically cov-ered with snow or wreathed in cloud. But before you reach Toluca, the next large town, you pass through La Marquesa, intersecting valleys mostly providing pastureland for sheep but now partly given over to an immense recreation area where go-cart tracks, football pitches, and hundreds of small shacks cater to the thousands of *capitalinos* who disgorge from the city every weekend or on national holidays to escape the smog. About twenty kilometers farther on, the broad highway becomes a divided boulevard, Paseo de Tollocan, lined with grassy banks and shaded by weeping willows—the only remaining traces of its former natural splendor as the marshy lakelands of the Río Lerma. Until it was drained to provide water for a profligate Mexico City, the whole area was traversed by hundreds of waterways that pro-vided fish, shrimplike *acociles*, frogs, and many types of wildfowl for the local inhabitants who fished from small crafts and were known long ago as "the Venetians of Mexico." It is now an industrial strip.

It takes much longer now to pass through the city of Toluca, the capital of the State of Mexico, despite the modern overpasses. Its immense and rapidly growing urban develop-ment stretches out and engulfs many of the surrounding villages and their cornfields which a few farmers stubbornly refuse to sell.

Once past the city limits you find yourself in an expanse of cleared land given over exclu-sively to the cultivation of corn. I was told that about fifty years ago this area was heavily forested with pines of enormous girth, which may be only partially true, allowing for the fact that in colonial times it was recognized as the principal area in the country for growing first-quality corn. Nowadays the corn always looks short and sometimes rather sad, because it is often ravaged by the sudden hailstorms that sweep across the valley in the rainy season. Planting the same single crop year after year and overgenerously using chemicals must have taken their toll on the thin topsoil.

This is a barren landscape in the winter, but as early as March there is a fuzz of green over the recently plowed land as the tips of the corn push up through the earth. The rains start earlier here at this high altitude, and by June the corn is standing high. But the days of late summer and early fall are those I wait for, when the land comes alive with flowers of different colors and as far as the eye can see there are odd patches of pink cosmos and yellow margaritas. The roadsides are bordered with these delicate flowers swaying in the breeze.

A few miles farther on, rounding a high bend in the road, you can see one gently curving valley after another of grasslands where sheep and cattle graze. Under the vigilance of two large haciendas that spread themselves low and comfortably over a rise in the land, on either side there are some well-ordered stands of trees . . . but too few. There are distant views, range upon range of foothills and the mountains beyond. All this is under a clear blue sky after the rains, its expanse broken only by billowing white clouds. You breathe a sigh of relief: at last, a space uninhibited and untrammeled by tires or feet. What a beautiful and varied highway this is, as you drive on through plantations of pine and cedar, some well cared for by the local communities, others partially destroyed by fire and beyond revival.

As you pass the junction of the Valle de Bravo road through another valley and yet another village, you come to Bosencheve, where the tall skinny pines bend perilously over the road and then enter a shaded canyon. This is my favorite part of the drive. Every leaf and pine needle seems to shine, and there is a resinous scent in the air and damp undergrowth. Not so very long ago the whole area was thickly forested, but now only a narrow fringe remains.

As the road winds up and up through the canyon, you reach the boundary between the State of Mexico and that of Michoacán. Here and there are large patches of clear-cut areas that soon become scars worn bare of all vegetation. I concentrate on the road, which begins its winding descent into the eastern part of Michoacán. As you round each curve you get a different-angled view of the land that drops off steeply below: a patchwork of cornfields with only a fringe of trees left here and there to hold back the soil. Finally, the panorama broadens out. The peaks of Mil Cumbres are straight ahead, and to the west the beginning of the hot country. It was on one of these journeys on a winter's afternoon that I had an unforgettable sight—a fiery ball of the setting sun perched directly on top of an isolated volcanic peak, El Coyote, against a background of misty gray. As the curves extend and finally flatten out, you can see Zitácuaro in the distance.

Perhaps my preoccupation with what is happening here is exaggerated, but witnessing the disdain for beauty and order in the rough-and-tumble effort to survive with uncontrolled population growth and more and more mouths to feed, you cannot help wondering just how far the earth can be desecrated without giving up or fighting back.

ZITÁCUARO

In one of the very Mexican areas of Los Angeles, I was amused to see a bumper sticker with the usual red heart and "I love Zitácuaro." I began to wonder why I couldn't say the same, having had a house near there for so many years. But Three Times Heróica Zitácuaro is not a lovable place.

When I first came to Mexico in 1957, I remember passing through what was then a quiet little town. The paved highway stopped as it entered the town and started again at the other side, Avenida Revolución, which ran through it, was unpaved but divided by a line of old shady trees. The local houses, typical of the region, were of adobe brick with gently sloping roofs of thick tiles. Many of them still had their *solares*, a plot of land at the back covering a square block planted with fruit trees, vegetables, and herbs, with hens pecking around and often a cow grazing contentedly. As the timber merchants, cattle ranchers, truck owners, and merchants of Lebanese descent grew rich from the surrounding countryside and the people living in it, the tranquillity was gradually broken. The main avenue was widened, paved, and stripped of its trees in the name of progress by some aspiring local politician. Only today, some thirty years later, have trees been replanted. Nearly all the old houses have been swept away to make room for ugly buildings, cement blocks of bizarre design and colors, the fantasies of the architects, the engineers, and their clients.

Alas, it is now a raucous town. Machos of all ages in fancy trucks, status symbols *par excel-*

lence, or driving the local transport in noisy Volkswagen vans without their mufflers, blare and rattle their way through the narrow streets. On practically every street corner the indolent young and deaf lounge disinterested by their stands, playing music cassettes through enormous loudspeakers. The streets are lined with people selling the same cheap merchandise: shoes, clothes, toys, but also chicken, bread, and vegetables. The peasants who come down from the surrounding hills are relegated to sitting on the sidewalks with small piles of their wares before them. It is there that I go first.

These country people provide a fascinating seasonal array: blackberries, mushrooms, and little wild orchids, squash flowers, quince, citrus blossoms, and herbs for any ailment. There are large orange-colored dried shrimp and dried fish brought up from the coasts, a seven-hour drive to the west, coconuts from the South, and pecans from the North. For Good Friday there are woven palm crosses with sprays of bay leaves and, as the Christmas season approaches, lengths of sugarcane, crab apples, *limas*, and slightly charred, unshelled peanuts for all the *piñatas*. There are piles of gray stringy and green velvety mosses to decorate the nativity cribs.

Zitácuaro is known for its hearty eating. As you stroll through the market any morning of the year, the small stands offer steaming *menudo* from large *cazuelas*. Don Lacho, who has a monopoly on heads of the slaughtered cattle from the *rastro*, offers you a sample of his succulent barbecued meat (*el rostro* as it is known locally) prized from the cheek. If you feel squeamish, just shut your eyes and eat. It is delicious. Profy, another local purveyor, who prides himself on his culinary skills, pushes a little cart through the center of the market and parks conveniently next to the women selling their homemade tortillas. You buy two tortillas, either white or blue corn, to wrap around his succulent pork or deftly seasoned chicken.

As I pass farther on to buy bones for the dogs, the savory smell of *rellena* (filling, or it can mean blood sausage) meets me. There are always the same two women sitting there behind their pots of rich stew of pig's blood and intestines seasoned with herbs and whole yellow *perón* chiles (sometimes it's made with chicken blood and intestines—see the recipe in *The Art of Mexican Cooking*).

By nine-thirty literally everyone who has arrived early to work in the market is standing around these eateries, *refresco* (bottled drink) in one hand, a taco in the other held above the mouth at just the right angle to catch any dripping goodness, while a line of patient dogs sit alert for any scraps that just might miss their target.

The streets too have their food stands, which become more numerous and more varied by the day. Large oval *huaraches*, made of corn masa smeared with beans, sauce, crumbled cheese, or whatever you choose, have been a regular favorite for some time. Breakfast dishes of eggs and *nopales* (cactus pieces), *chorizo* and potato, and thin seared and chopped steaks take over the cool damp mornings from the genteel little jelly and custard forms or even the baked sweet potatoes covered with shiny syrup.

Housewives can be seen, some still with their hair curlers in, hurrying home early from the market. A few still carry their decorative baskets, but alas, too many stuff their purchases in a limply swinging plastic bag.

But if the town is not *limpia y amable*—clean and pleasant, says the slogan on ubiquitous signs posted by some well-meaning municipal president (much to the amusement of a well-known magazine writer who dubbed Zitácuaro one of the ugliest towns in Mexico)—there are many wonderful people there who have helped me through the years and generously shared their culinary knowledge. Some of their recipes are recorded here and others in *The Art of Mexican Cooking.*

SALSA RANCHERA

RANCH SAUCE

Sra. Consuelo G. del Valle

✸

[SERVES 4 TO 6]

ONE AFTERNOON I HAD JUST FINISHED MAKING SOME *JALAPEÑOS EN ESCABECHE* AND FOUND I HAD STILL QUITE A LOT OF CHILES LEFT. I SUDDENLY REMEMbered having seen this recipe in a little book put together in Zitácuaro by the local Lions Club wives. Although Sra. del Valle now lives in Zitácuaro, she is originally from Jalisco, and most probably the recipe comes from that area or northern Michoacán, where there are many *minguichis*—variations on the theme of chiles, cream, and cheese.

Traditionally this is served with meats, especially broiled meats, but I like to serve it as a snack or first course with a nonpicante sauce of Mexican green tomatoes and corn tortillas—but it is only for those who simply love chiles.

3 tablespoons vegetable oil

2 garlic cloves, finely chopped

8 ounces (225 g) jalapeño chiles, seeds and veins removed,
cut into very fine strips, about 2 cups (500 ml) firmly packed

8 ounces (225 g) white onions, sliced as finely as possible,
about 2 cups (500 ml)

1 cup (250 ml) chicken or beef broth

salt to taste

8 ounces (225 g) queso fresco, Muenster, or mild Cheddar,
cut into thin strips

Heat the oil in a skillet or chafing dish. Add the garlic and cook briefly without browning. Add the chiles and onions and continue cooking gently until the onion is just turning a pale caramel color. Add the broth, taste for salt, and cook over medium heat until the onions and chiles are thoroughly cooked. Place the cheese over the top, lower the heat, cover the pan or put under a not-too-hot broiler, and serve as soon as the cheese has melted.

BOCOLES DE FRIJOL NEGRO

BLACK BEAN AND MASA SNACKS

Sra. Hortensia Fagoaga

❋

[MAKES 8 2½-INCH (6.5-CM) BOCOLES]

I INCLUDE THIS RECIPE IN THIS SECTION BECAUSE IT WAS GIVEN TO ME BY MY NEIGHBOR AND GREAT COOK HORTENSIA FAGOAGA. IT WAS GIVEN TO HER by a friend who lives in Monterrey but is probably originally from the Tampico area. There are any number of *antojitos* and *tamales* coming from the eastern part of Mexico, variations on the theme of black beans and *masa*. They are all delicious. These *bocoles* I fell for at first bite.

I know the recipe looks complicated with all its various parts, but the snacks can be prepared in stages and ahead—once assembled, they have to be eaten immediately.

THE MASA

8 ounces (225 g) tortilla masa *(page 530),*
about 1 scant cup (245 ml), as dry as possible

½ cup (125 ml) bean paste (page 295)

½ teaspoon baking powder (optional)

salt to taste

lard or oil for frying

HAVE READY

the pork filling (recipe follows)

the tomato sauce (recipe follows)

1½ cups (375 ml) finely shredded cabbage or romaine lettuce

4 heaped tablespoons finely grated queso añejo *or Romano*

½ cup (125 ml) thinned crème fraîche or sour cream

Mix the *masa*, bean paste, baking powder, and salt together well. Divide the dough into 8 equal balls about 1½ inches (4 cm) in diameter. Flatten each ball into a round about 2½ inches (6.5 cm) across and just over ¼ inch (7 mm) thick.

In a large skillet, melt enough lard or heat oil to a depth of about ⅛ inch (3 mm). Add the *bocoles* and cook over low heat for about 7 minutes on each side; they should be slightly crisp on the outside and the dough soft but cooked inside. Drain on absorbent paper.

While they are still warm, make a pocket by cutting almost halfway around the edge. Lifting up the dough, stuff with a little of the pork and 2 teaspoons of the sauce and place on a bed of cabbage or lettuce. Sprinkle with some of the cheese and a spoonful of the cream.

[CONTINUED]

PORK FILLING

[MAKES I CUP (250 ML)]

8 ounces (225 g) boneless stewing pork or pork shoulder,
cut into ¾-inch (2-cm) cubes

¼ medium white onion, roughly sliced

salt to taste

Cover the pork with water, add the onion and salt, and bring to a simmer. Continue simmering until the pork is tender, about 25 minutes. Set aside to cool off in the broth. Drain the meat and shred it, reserving the broth for another dish or soup.

TOMATO SAUCE

[MAKES I SCANT CUP (240 ML)]

8 ounces (225 g) tomatoes, broiled

1 small garlic clove, roughly chopped

2 serrano chiles, broiled

1 tablespoon vegetable oil

salt to taste

Put the tomatoes, garlic, and chiles into a blender jar and blend until smooth, adding only a little water if necessary. Heat the oil in a small skillet, add the blended ingredients and the salt, and cook until slightly reduced and well seasoned, about 5 minutes.

CARNE DE PUERCO CON RAJAS

PORK COOKED WITH CHILACAS AND TOMATOES

Sra. Irma Castrellón de Olivares

Ciudad Hidalgo, Michoacán

✸

[SERVES 6]

THIS IS A VERY SIMPLE BUT VERY TASTY RECIPE, AN EXAMPLE OF THE ONE-POT STEWS TYPICAL OF THE REGION. IT WAS GIVEN TO ME ONE HOT AND hazy day when I went to visit a small *balneario* just about one hour's drive from Zitácuaro, famous for its curative hot waters. It lies fifteen kilometers off the main road to Morelia near Ciudad Hidalgo. The owner's sister is the wife of the architect who built my ecological house. Both she and her sister love cooking, an interest inherited from their grandmother. She came from a Spanish family who settled in the area and bought up great tracts of land before the Revolution. One of her excellent recipes, *Cuñete de Pollo*, appears in *The Art of Mexican Cooking*. As we ate a simple but delicious meal of rice, followed by thin steaks of excellent quality cooked in a pasilla sauce, she gave me these two recipes.

This dish is traditionally served with tortillas and *corundas* (a recipe is given in *The Art of Mexican Cooking*), the regional *tamales* wrapped in a long corn leaf.

> 2¼ pounds (1 generous kg) pork, half country-style spareribs and
> half boneless stewing pork with some fat cut into 1½-inch (4-cm) cubes
>
> 6 garlic cloves, peeled
>
> 2 peppercorns
>
> 1 tablespoon salt or to taste
>
> 1¼ pounds (565 g) tomatoes
>
> 3 tomates verdes, husks removed, rinsed
>
> 3 serrano chiles or more to taste
>
> about 6 medium chilacas or 3 poblano chiles, charred, peeled, seeds and
> veins removed, and torn or cut into narrow strips

Put the pork into a wide pan, cover with water, and set over medium heat. Crush the garlic with the peppercorns and salt and add to the pan. Cover and cook for about 15 minutes. Add the whole tomatoes, *tomates verdes*, and chiles and continue cooking until the chiles are soft but not falling apart—about 10 minutes.

Transfer the tomatoes, *tomates verdes*, and chiles to the blender jar with 1 cup (250 ml) of the meat broth and blend to a textured puree. Take out a second cup of the broth and reserve.

Remove the cover and continue to cook the pork until it is just tender—about 10 minutes. Remove any remaining broth and reserve. Continue to cook the meat over low heat until the

[CONTINUED]

fat renders out; there should be about 3 tablespoons—remove or make up to that amount with lard. Lightly brown the meat, add the blended ingredients, and fry over fairly high heat, stirring and scraping the bottom of the pan to prevent sticking, for about 5 minutes. Add the chile strips and the reserved broth—there should be about 2 cups (500 ml). If not, make up to that amount with water. Taste for salt and cook for 5 more minutes.

CARNE DE PUERCO EN PIPIÁN DE CHILE PASILLA

PORK IN A PASILLA CHILE AND PUMPKIN SEED SAUCE

Sra. Irma Castrellón de Olivares

Ciudad Hidalgo, Michoacán

❁

[SERVES 6]

THE PASILLA CHILE, WHICH IS THE DRIED CHILACA, IS USED A GREAT DEAL IN THIS PART OF MICHOACÁN SINCE IT IS GROWN IN THE NEXT VALLEY, AROUND Queréndaro and Maravatío.

This is a simple *pipián*, but so totally unlike that of other regions. It is a personal favorite of mine. It is traditionally served with local *tamales* called *corundas* (see the recipe in *The Art of Mexican Cooking*).

The pork used here would be meaty ribs and boneless shoulder, so I have suggested country-style pork ribs and stewing pork in equal quantities.

2¼ pounds (1 generous kg) pork, half country-style spareribs and half stewing pork with some fat, cut into 1½-inch (4-cm) cubes

approximately 2 quarts (2 l) water

6 garlic cloves, peeled and crushed

1 tablespoon salt or to taste

4 ounces (115 g) pasilla chiles, about 15, wiped clean, veins and seeds removed, and seeds reserved (with seeds from other large chiles, if necessary, to make ½ cup/125 ml)

1 tablespoon lard or vegetable oil

1 cup (250 ml) hulled raw pumpkin seeds

2 small garlic cloves, peeled and chopped

2 peppercorns

2 allspice

2 cloves

Put the pork into a wide casserole (in which you can cook and serve the *pipián*), cover with the water, add the smashed garlic and salt, cover, and cook over medium heat until the pork is just half cooked—about 20 minutes. Remove 1 quart (1 l) of the water and reserve.

Continue cooking the pork until it is tender. By this time the cooking water should have evaporated. If not, remove the broth and continue cooking the pork over medium heat until the fat renders out and lightly browns the meat. Leave 3 tablespoons fat in the pot.

Meanwhile, toast the chiles lightly on both sides in a dry skillet over medium-high heat, taking care not to burn the flesh, or the sauce will be bitter. Rinse and soak in 2 cups (500 ml) of the reserved broth for about 15 minutes.

Toast the chile seeds until they change to a pale brown color. Grind them in a spice grinder or blender.

Heat the lard in a skillet and gently fry the pumpkin seeds until they begin to swell up and pop around. Add them, along with the whole spices and peeled garlic, to the blender jar with the ground seeds. Add 1½ cups (375 ml) of the reserved broth and blend the ingredients together to a slightly textured puree. Add this to the meat frying in the casserole.

Blend the soaked chiles with the broth in which they were soaked and add to the pan. Continue cooking for about 5 minutes. Add any remaining broth and salt to taste and continue cooking over low heat for 5 more minutes.

The sauce should be fairly thick—coating the back of a wooden spoon—but you may need to add more liquid for the required consistency.

Señora Elvira

Sra. Elvira is in charge of the large parking lot where I park my truck on the days that I go into town. She is a plump, pretty little woman, the widow of a laconic, pessimistic little man who recently died of a sudden heart attack at a relatively early age, leaving her with two of the children still to educate and bring up. She lives in a compact and immaculately clean little house at the back of the lot and makes the most delicious hand-patted tortillas on an impro-vised wood-burning stove next to the cars.

One day she saw me return to the car with a basket full of large and fragrant squash flowers and asked how I was going to prepare them. A long conversation ensued with an exchange of recipes. Almost daily she prepares the main meal of the day for herself and the family, her brother, and his two children—eight or sometimes nine in all. When the budget is tight, the meal consists of *tacos sudados* or *quesadillas* of squash flowers, shredded meat with chiles, or just potatoes and chiles. They all sounded, although simple, most delicious. I went back to the market to buy the extra ingredients, went home, and made them. The recipes follow.

FLOR DE CALABAZA GUISADO CON JITOMATE

SQUASH FLOWERS COOKED WITH TOMATOES

Sra. Elvira Frutis Rivas, Zitácuaro

❁

[MAKES APPROXIMATELY 2 CUPS (500 ML)]

BECAUSE THIS FILLING IS RATHER MOIST, SHE PREFERS TO USE IT FOR *QUE-SADILLAS* OF CORN MASA THAT ARE THEN FRIED CRISP; SHE SERVES THEM sprinkled with finely grated *queso añejo* and some cream.

2 tablespoons vegetable oil

⅓ cup (83 ml) finely chopped white onion

1 garlic clove, finely chopped

1 cup (250 ml) finely chopped tomatoes

*2 chilacas or poblano chiles, charred, peeled, seeds and veins removed,
and torn or cut into narrow strips*

salt to taste

*8 ounces (225 g) cleaned squash flowers (stalks and stringy green sepals
removed), roughly chopped, about 3 cups (750 ml) tightly packed
(see* The Art of Mexican Cooking, *pages 150–151)*

Heat the oil in a heavy skillet, add the onion and garlic, and cook for a few seconds without browning. Add the tomatoes, chiles, and salt and cook over medium heat for about 5 minutes or until the juice has been reduced. Add the flowers and continue cooking, stirring the mixture from time to time, for about 10 minutes, until moist but not too juicy. Adjust the seasoning.

TACOS SUDADOS

STEAMED TACOS

✳

I AM VERY PARTIAL TO THE SOFT TEXTURE OF THESE TACOS, LIKE THOSE OF TACOS DE CANASTA THAT ARE OFTEN SOLD IN THE MARKETPLACES. FRESHLY made tortillas are rolled around fillings of various types (see the following recipes) and placed in a basket lined with a heavy cloth. Thickly covered on top, they arrive warm and steaming at their destination.

Tacos sudados are best made with smaller corn tortillas—4 inches (10 cm) in diameter is ideal.

Prepare the steamer or an improvised one with a rack set into a fairly shallow pan with hot water up to the level of the rack or just below. Line the space above with a tea towel or cloth with sufficient overlap at the top to cover the surface of the tacos.

Put one large spoonful of the mixture into each tortilla, double over, and secure with a toothpick. You may, if you wish, pass each tortilla quickly through hot oil and then fill it. This is a matter of choice. Sra. Elvira prefers to do it that way.

Place the tacos in overlapping layers in the top of the steamer, cover with the cloth and a lid, and steam until they are all piping hot—about 5 minutes. Yes, I am afraid the bottom layer—and sometimes in between, depending on the quality of the tortillas—sticks, but my neighbors say, "Well, yes" and shrug their shoulders.

CARNE DESHEBRADA PARA TACOS SUDADOS

SHREDDED MEAT FILLING FOR STEAMED TACOS

Sra. Elvira Frutis Rivas, Zitácuaro

✸

[MAKES 2 CUPS (500 ML)]

ALTHOUGH PORK AND CHICKEN BREAST COULD BE USED FOR THIS RECIPE, I THINK BEEF WORKS BETTER WITH THE PASILLA CHILE. YOU WILL NEED I pound (450 g) of boneless meat or two small chicken breasts for 2 cups (500 ml) of shredded meat, and the cooking time will vary according to the cut. Although it's not traditional, I like to serve this taco with a green tomato sauce.

1 pound (450 g) skirt steak, cut into 1-inch (2.5-cm) cubes

¼ medium white onion

salt to taste

2 garlic cloves, roughly chopped

¼ white onion, roughly chopped

*4 pasilla chiles, veins and seeds removed,
soaked in hot water for 10 minutes*

3 tablespoons vegetable oil

Barely cover the meat with water, add the onion and salt, and bring to a simmer. Cook until the meat is tender but not too soft, about 35 minutes. Set aside to cool off in the broth. Strain, reserving the broth, and shred to a medium texture—if the meat is too finely shredded, it will lose some of its flavor.

Put ¼ cup (63 ml) of the reserved broth into a blender, add the garlic and chopped onion, and blend for a few seconds. Add the drained chiles with ¾ cup (188 ml) reserved broth and blend until smooth, adding more broth if necessary to loosen the blades of the blender.

Heat the oil in a skillet, add the sauce, and fry, stirring and scraping the bottom of the pan from time to time to prevent sticking, until it is well seasoned and reduced a little, about 5 minutes. Add the shredded meat and salt if needed and continue cooking for about 5 more minutes. The mixture should be almost dry.

SALSA VERDE (CRUDA)

RAW GREEN TOMATO SAUCE

✺

[MAKES 2 CUPS (500 ML)]

1 pound (450 g), tomatoes verdes, about 22 medium,
husks removed and rinsed
4 serrano chiles or to taste, roughly chopped
1 cup loosely packed roughly chopped cilantro
1 large garlic clove, roughly chopped
salt to taste

THE TOPPING FOR THE TACOS (OPTIONAL)
finely chopped white onion
roughly chopped cilantro

Put the *tomates verdes* into a small pan, barely cover with water, bring to a simmer, and simmer until soft but not falling apart—they will become a washed-out green color—about 10 minutes. Drain and reserve a little of the cooking water.

Put ½ cup (125 ml) of the cooking water into a blender with the chiles, *cilantro*, and garlic and blend until almost smooth. Gradually add the cooked *tomates verdes* and blend briefly after each addition. The sauce should have a slightly rough-textured appearance. Add salt. The sauce will thicken as it stands and may need to be diluted with a little more water.

PAPAS GUISADAS PARA TACOS SUDADOS

POTATO FILLING FOR STEAMED TACOS

✸

[MAKES 1½ CUPS (375 ML)]

1 pound (450 g) waxy potatoes, peeled and cut into ½-inch (13-mm) cubes

salt to taste

approximately 3 tablespoons vegetable oil

2 tablespoons finely chopped white onion

*3 chilacas or poblano chiles, charred, peeled, veins and seeds removed,
and torn or cut into narrow strips*

about 6 ounces (180 g) tomatoes, finely chopped, about 1 cup (250 ml)

Barely cover the potatoes with water, add salt, and cook over medium heat for about 10 minutes—they should be half cooked. Drain and set aside.

Heat the oil in a heavy skillet, add the drained potatoes, and fry, turning them over so that they brown evenly. Add the onion and chiles and continue frying for 1 minute more. Add the tomatoes and continue cooking until the mixture is well seasoned and fairly dry—about 5 minutes.

CARNE DE PUERCO EN PIPIÁN

PORK IN A PUMPKIN SEED SAUCE

Sra. Hortensia Fagoaga

✸

[SERVES 6 TO 8]

THIS IS A VERY SIMPLE BUT DELICIOUS DISH WITH A COARSE, NUTTY TEXTURE TO THE SAUCE. THE PORK IS USUALLY COMBINED WITH *CHILACAYOTE*, A large cucurbit (page 50) when it is small and tender and the skin has not hardened into a rind.

Any one of the many varieties of wild mushrooms are often used in this *pipián* instead of, or as well as, the *chilacayote*. Of course, any green or zucchini squash could be substituted but cooked for a shorter time.

When you are cleaning the larger dried chiles for any other recipe, save the seeds. You will need extra for this sauce (or for the Oaxacan *pipián* in *The Art of Mexican Cooking*, for instance).

This dish is served, like a mole, with a lot of the sauce—which in this case is of a thinner consistency—and corn tortillas.

2 pounds (900 g) small pork ribs, cut into 2-inch (5-cm) pieces,
or country-style spareribs

½ medium white onion

salt to taste

1½ pounds (675 g) chilacayote or zucchini, cut into 1-inch (2.5-cm)
cubes, about 7 cups (1.75 l)

6 ancho chiles, veins and seeds removed

2 chipotle mora *chiles* or to taste or 3 canned chipotles en adobo

⅔ cup (164 ml) chile seeds (see note above)

⅔ cup (164 ml) hulled raw pumpkin seeds

¼ cup (63 ml) sesame seeds

3 large sprigs epazote

Cover the pork well with water, add the onion and salt, cover, and cook over medium heat for about 20 minutes. Add the *chilacayote* and cook until both are tender—about 20 minutes more. Drain and reserve the broth.

Toast the chiles lightly on both sides, cover with hot water, and leave to soak for about 15 minutes.

Put 1 cup (250 ml) of the reserved meat broth into a blender. In a dry skillet, toast first the chile seeds until they turn a deep golden color, then the pumpkin seeds until they swell and begin to pop about, and last the sesame seeds until they turn a pale golden color. Transfer to the blender and blend to a textured puree, adding a little more of the broth if necessary.

Strain the chiles and transfer to the blender jar with 1 more cup (250 ml) of the broth and blend all together to a thick-textured consistency. Pour the mixture into the pan with the meat and *chilacayote* and the rest of the broth and continue cooking over low heat for about 10 minutes. Adjust salt, add the *epazote*, and cook for 5 more minutes.

Journey to Morelia

IT WAS IN THE LOCAL POST OFFICE THAT I FIRST HEARD I WAS
TO BE ONE OF THE JUDGES AT THE MORELIA FAIR TO CHOOSE
THE BEST REGIONAL DISH. THAT VERY MORNING I CALLED A
friend in Morelia just to make sure. She said, "Yes, come right away, the judging
begins early tomorrow." ☀ It is always a joy to drive to Morelia, about two and a half
hours away, especially if you take the longer route via Mil Cumbres (a thousand
peaks). The road, in fact, runs along the western edge of the central mountainous
mass of Mexico. Once heavily forested, the area has been ravaged in recent years by
indiscriminate felling with no reforestation to follow. For a great part of the way the
highway itself is sheltered by at least a fringe of trees, a rich variety of hardwoods and
conifers. Driving along, you get an occasional breathtaking view, a seemingly neverending panorama of the hot country below, dotted by serried peaks and, as far as the
eye can see, the foothills of the Sierra Madre del Sur, which separates the interior of
Michoacán from the hot coastal plains of the Pacific. ☀ There is very little traffic,

since most drivers choose the more direct route through Queréndaro. You pass through only one little village spread along the highway at its highest point, and the only other signs of life are occasional *rancherías*, or settlements, with their small plantations of corn during the rainy season or children guarding the cattle grazing on the few patches of pastureland between the stands of trees. ☀ No time of year is without its colorful display of wildflowers—spectacular pink and red thistles, flowering bushes, and then many species of cacti on the otherwise bare wall of rock as the road descends. The scent of the pines, the silence broken only by birdsong—and the occasional roar of an out-of-condition bus—and the sheer beauty of it all make you wish it would continue for another hundred miles. Only too soon you drop down into the valley to meet small shanty-town settlements—and the accompanying garbage—within hailing distance of Morelia. ☀ That beautiful and dignified city of Morelia—included by UNESCO as part of the Patrimony of Humanity—has some lovely broad, tree-lined boulevards, but the city is now choked by uncontrolled growth around its periphery, while the center is clogged and the gorgeous architecture partially hidden behind endless street stands. ☀ The next morning there was chaotic activity at the fairground as cooks and their family helpers came to represent their villages' special foods. They were laden with benches, tables, small charcoal-burning stoves, huge *cazuelas* and *ollas*, the traditional earthen cooking pots, squawking chickens, turkeys, sides of pork, and hunks of beef. As the morning wore on, the aromas became tantalizing: smoking wood, resinous pine, and charcoal mixed in with charring of chiles. It was a memorable day. I still have some of the recipes, but many of the best were spirited away by a cunning local gastronome. Few had the ingredient amounts, and instructions were terse: two sheep, two cases of beer, and a liter of tequila for Drunken Sheep. There was *chiripo* and *atapacua* from San Juan Parangaricutiro (both beef stews), *birria de chivo* (a goat stew) from Briseñas, and *guajalote irimbence*, turkey from Irimbo—richly flavored and hearty rustic fare. Judging was almost impossible. I know I heartily disagreed with the majority of the well-shod Mexico City judges. I wanted to give every one of those cooks a prize for their patience and generosity, coming from so far, preparing so much, and serving with smiles the hundreds who filed by.

It was on that occasion and many more like it that I got to know a great Morelian cook and restaurateuse, Livier Ruiz, who has become a cherished friend. I have published a few of her recipes before and here is one of hers and two simple ones from the food fair.

CHULETAS DE PUERCO EN AGRIDULCE

PORK CHOPS IN A SWEET-SOUR SAUCE

Sra. Livier Ruiz de Suárez, Morelia

✺

[SERVES 6]

THIS IS AN UNUSUAL AND SAVORY WAY OF COOKING PORK CHOPS, WHICH NORMALLY TEND TO BE RATHER DRY. YOU CAN, OF COURSE, SUBSTITUTE VEAL FOR the pork. A dish of this kind is best served with plain white rice.

6 guajillo chiles
approximately 3 tablespoons lard or vegetable oil
6 loin pork chops about ½ inch (13 mm) thick, slightly flattened
salt to taste
¾ cup (188 ml) fresh orange juice
juice of ½ lime
1-inch (2.5-cm) cinnamon stick
4 allspice
4 cloves

2 garlic cloves, roughly chopped
2 medium white onions, thinly sliced
3 thick pineapple slices, cut into 1-inch (2.5-cm) cubes

Slit the chiles open, remove the seeds and veins, cover with hot water, and set aside to soak for about 20 minutes.

Heat the lard in a heavy pan and lightly brown the chops, sprinkled with salt, on both sides —do a few at a time so they do not touch in the pan. Remove from the fat and set aside.

Put the juices into a blender, add the spices and garlic, and blend until smooth. Add this with the onions and pineapple to the pan and cook over high heat, scraping the bottom of the pan for about 3 minutes to prevent sticking.

Put the drained chiles into the blender with ⅓ cup (83 ml) fresh water and blend as smoothly as possible. Add this to the pan, pressing the puree through a fine strainer, extracting as much as possible of the juice and flesh. Discard the debris. Cook over fairly high heat, scraping the bottom of the pan to prevent sticking, for about 3 minutes.

Add the pork chops and salt to taste. Cover the pan with a tight lid and cook over very low heat, shaking the pan from time to time, until the meat is tender, 30 to 40 minutes. Or bake the dish in a 325°F (165°C) oven for about 45 minutes.

CALABACITAS MICHOACANAS

ZUCCHINI MICHOACÁN STYLE

Sra. Cirena Arias Miranda

❁

[SERVES 6]

THIS IS A DELICIOUS WAY OF PREPARING SQUASH, TYPICAL OF THE REGION, WITH PLENTIFUL CREAM AND CHEESE. IT MAKES A GOOD VEGETARIAN DISH, a first course, or an accompaniment for broiled meat.

3 tablespoons vegetable oil
2 pounds (900 g) zucchini, trimmed and cut into small cubes,
about 8 cups (2 l)

[CONTINUED]

salt to taste

approximately ½ cup (125 ml) water

2 garlic cloves, roughly chopped

1 medium white onion, roughly chopped

⅓ cup (83 ml) loosely packed roughly chopped cilantro,
small stalks included

*4 poblano chiles, charred, peeled, seeds and veins removed,
and roughly chopped*

1 cup (250 ml) crème fraîche or sour cream

½ cup (125 ml) finely grated queso añejo, Muenster, or mild Cheddar

Heat the oil in a flameproof casserole or heavy skillet. Add the squash, sprinkle with salt, and cook over medium heat, stirring from time to time, until partially cooked but not soft—about 5 minutes.

Put the water into a blender, add the garlic, onion, and *cilantro*, and blend until smooth. Gradually add the chiles and continue blending until smooth. Add to the squash in the pan, stirring in well. Cover the pan and cook over medium heat, stirring from time to time to prevent sticking, for about 10 minutes. If the mixture seems dry, add a little more water. It should be moist, but not too juicy.

Stir in the cream, bring to a simmer, and cook for 5 minutes more. Adjust the seasoning, sprinkle the *queso añejo* over the top, and serve.

NOTE: *If you're using Muenster or Cheddar, sprinkle it over the top and cover or put under the broiler just until it melts but does not brown.*

POZOLILLO

❋

[SERVES 6 TO 8]

POZOLILLO IS THE DIMINUTIVE OF POZOLE, THE PORK AND HOMINY SOUP/ STEW. THE MAIN DIFFERENCE IS THE USE OF FRESH CORN INSTEAD OF THE large, dry white corn kernels used in *pozole*. The recipe was given to me by a family in Querétaro who thought it originated in the States of Mexico and Michoacán, and indeed, there are similar recipes there. Both dishes are traditionally accompanied by *raspadas* or *tostadas*—fried tortillas that have had a layer of the *masa* scraped off to make them thinner, or ordinary tortillas fried crisp.

It is very important not to use supersweet corn, like so much of that produced in the United States nowadays.

12 ounces (340 g) stewing pork, cut into ¾-inch (2-cm) cubes

10 cups (2.5 l) water

salt to taste

1 whole chicken breast, with skin and bone,
cut into quarters

7 cups (1.75 l) corn kernels, not supersweet

4 poblano chiles, seeds and veins removed, roughly chopped

1 cup (250 ml) loosely packed roughly chopped cilantro

½ large white onion, roughly chopped

3 large sprigs epazote

TO SERVE

12 tostadas

1 cup (250 ml) finely chopped white onion

⅓ cup (83 ml) finely chopped serrano chiles

lime quarters

Put the pork, water, and salt in a large pot. Bring to a simmer and cook for about 15 minutes. Add the chicken breast and cook for 10 more minutes. Add 5 cups (1.25 l) of the corn kernels.

Put 1 cup (250 ml) of the broth into a blender, add the remaining corn, and blend until smooth. Add the chiles, *cilantro*, and onion and blend again until almost smooth. Add to the pot and continue cooking for 20 more minutes or until the meats are tender.

Remove the chicken breast and, when cool, shred thoroughly and keep warm. Add the *epazote* and simmer the *pozolillo* for 5 more minutes.

Fill each soup bowl with some of the shredded chicken and plenty of broth and pass the accompaniments separately.

Tacámbaro Cookbook

Sr. Raúl Ramírez, Zitácuaro

Whenever I go to Morelia I have to wander through the *ex-convento* of San Francisco, which is now a center for the handicrafts of the State of Michoacán. The imagination and creativity of the artisans from many areas of the state is expressed vividly in the diversity and high quality of the pieces on sale there.

On one visit I happened to notice some particularly intricate silver jewelry made by a resident of Zitácuaro, Sr. Raúl Ramírez. On my return I decided to look him up. After a brief inspection of his small workshop I found myself engaged in an animated conversation about food. He gave me some chiles and *tamales* from his native Hidalgo and told me how delicious the grubs were inside those cunningly made bags of web and leaves hanging from my avocado tree. I regret not having taken more assiduous notes on our conversations at that time.

On several occasions after that I went to see him and then one day found he had disappeared. On one of those last visits he handed me a sheaf of closely typed (by himself) pages —copies of two small cookbooks in manuscript that had been lent to him by an old family in Tacámbaro, Michoacán.

A couple of the recipes appear in *The Art of Mexican Cooking*, but these four unusual, simple, and delicious recipes are new.

POLLO EN PULQUE

CHICKEN IN *PULQUE*

❋

[SERVES 6]

THIS IS A SURPRISINGLY DELICATELY FLAVORED AND DELICIOUS DISH. ALTHOUGH IN THE ORIGINAL RECIPE THE CHICKEN WAS FRIED IN LARD, I USE rendered chicken fat. Please use chicken with the skin on; you needn't eat it, but you need it for its flavor.

3 tablespoons rendered chicken fat
2½ pounds (1.125 kg) extra-large chicken pieces
salt to taste
1 quart (1 l) pulque (page 12) or light beer
2 sprigs fresh thyme or ¼ teaspoon dried
2 sprigs fresh marjoram or ½ teaspoon dried
2 bay leaves
4 peppercorns
6 large scallions, both white and green parts, thickly sliced
4 garlic cloves, roughly chopped

TO SERVE
serrano chiles or jalapeños en escabeche
green olives
salsa macho (page 490)
corn tortillas

Heat the fat in a heavy casserole, liberally sprinkle the chicken pieces with salt, and fry a few pieces at a time so that they are not touching in the pan, until the skin is golden and crisp.

Drain off the fat and reserve. Add the *pulque* or beer and herbs and peppercorns, cover, and cook over medium heat for about 15 minutes from the time it comes up to a simmer.

Heat the reserved fat in a small skillet, add the scallions and garlic, and fry until they just start to change color. Add to the chicken in the pan with 2 tablespoons of the fat and continue cooking uncovered over medium heat until the chicken is tender and the broth reduced by about half. (Rather than overcook the chicken, if the broth has not been reduced sufficiently, drain it off and boil it down separately—about 15 minutes.) Serve the chicken with some of the broth, topped with the chile strips and olives. Pass the *salsa macho* and tortillas separately.

NOTE: *The original recipe says to strain off the chicken broth before serving. I prefer to serve the chicken with some of the reduced broth, because it is wonderfully savory.*

CHICHARRÓN EN NARANJA

CHICHARRÓN IN AN ORANGE SAUCE

✺

[SERVES 4]

"IMPREGNATE THE PIECES OF *CHICHARRÓN* WITH ORANGE JUICE. SEPARATELY TAKE A CHILE WITH GROUND TOMATOES AND ONION AND FRY IT. ADD TO IT the pieces of *chicharrón* and more orange juice." This is a literal translation of a very unusual Tacámbaro recipe from a family cookbook.

I am sure it has happened to all of us who love to cook: when you read a recipe that sounds wonderful, sometimes it just doesn't come off—but what a surprise when it does, especially when it introduces you to a new combination of flavors! This is one of those surprising recipes to delight those who permit themselves to eat *chicharrón*.

1⅓ cups (333 ml) fresh orange juice

4 ounces (115 g) chicharrón, broken into pieces
about 1 to 1½ inches (2.5 to 4 cm)

3 cups (750 ml) roughly chopped tomatoes

1 garlic clove, roughly chopped

1 tablespoon vegetable oil

½ small white onion, thinly sliced

2 jalapeño chiles or to taste, seeds removed
and cut into narrow strips

salt to taste

Pour 1 cup (250 ml) of the orange juice over the *chicharrón* and leave to soak and soften for about 30 minutes. (If the *chicharrón* is not very well made and rather tough, it may take longer.)

In a blender, grind the tomatoes with the garlic. Heat the oil in a skillet, add the onion, chile strips, and salt, and cook for a few seconds without browning. Add the tomato puree and cook over high heat to reduce—about 5 minutes. Add the *chicharrón* and remaining ⅓ cup (83 ml) orange juice, salt as necessary if the *chicharrón* has not been presalted, and cook until it is well impregnated with the sauce (which should be neither too juicy nor too dry)— about 5 minutes.

CHILACAYOTES EN NATAS

CHILACOYOTE IN CREAM

✸

[SERVES 4 TO 6]

NATAS ARE MADE OF THE LAYER OF THICK CREAM THAT FORMS OVER RAW MILK WHEN IT IS SCALDED: A PARTICULARLY RICH VERSION IS THE CLOTTED cream of Devon, Cornwall, and Somerset in southwestern England. They give a delicious flavor and slightly textured—almost as if curdled—appearance to the sauce. It is important, however, not to let the sauce boil once it has been added; it should just come to a simmer, or the proteins form into tough particles. An acceptable substitute would be crème fraîche or any thick cream, which can, of course, be cooked for a longer period.

This recipe and the one that follows can be served either as a first course or to accompany a meat dish.

1 pound (450 g) chilacayote or squash (see page 50),
cut into ¼-inch (7-mm) rounds

boiling water to cover

salt to taste

THE SAUCE

12 ounces (340 g) tomatoes, roughly chopped, about 2 scant cups (450 ml)

½ medium white onion, roughly chopped

1 garlic clove, roughly chopped

2 tablespoons pork lard, butter, or oil

¾ cup (188 ml) natas or crème fraîche

Cover the *chilacayote* with the boiling water in a saucepan and add salt. Cook until just tender, about 10 minutes, drain, and set aside. In a blender, blend the tomatoes, onion, and garlic to a textured puree. Heat the lard, add the puree, and fry over high heat with a little salt until reduced by about half—about 5 minutes. Add the *chilacayote* and cook for about 5 minutes, then stir in the *natas* and bring to a simmer. Serve immediately.

CHILACAYOTE

CHILACAYOTE IS THE FRUIT of a climbing plant of the Cucurbitaceae family, a native plant of Mexico, with a brilliant yellow flower similar to those of most squashes and pumpkins. When the fruit is small and tender—up to about 7 inches (18 cm) in length—it is a pale green color flecked with cream and is prepared as a vegetable. It is most commonly cooked unpeeled, either with or without meat in pipián—sauces of pumpkin seed.

Chilacayotes can grow up to 12 inches (30 cm) long and 9 inches (22.5 cm) wide. As it matures, the skin hardens to a rind and the color changes to a dark green flecked with a lighter color. When the rind is completely hard, both the thick flesh and spaghettilike strands inside, dotted with flat black seeds, are candied. The strands are cooked in a syrup and served as cabello de angel, angel hair, a highly esteemed, textured but flavorless dessert.

Chilacayotes grow wild in my area of the country and have climbed and spread over the high trees in the orchard with their immense fruits hanging down as though ready to attack any passersby. They present a dramatic sight in the late fall.

Quite recently in the local market I saw a sack of what appeared to be dark green flat, wide pepitas, or pumpkin seeds. In fact they were hulled chilacayote seeds and were delicious toasted.

While the chilacayote is not a favorite of mine—it too much resembles the watery, flavorless vegetable marrow of my youth—I use it because I have a fresh, organic supply and am always looking for new methods of preparing it. I came across the two recipes—one preceding this, the other following—in the old Tacámbaro cookbook, and they are delicious. Zucchini or any fresh squash could be used as a substitute.

CHILACAYOTES PUNCHUCHES

❂

[SERVES 4]

2 tablespoons lard or vegetable oil

½ cup (125 ml) finely chopped white onion

salt to taste

1 pound (450 g) tomatoes, finely chopped, about 2⅔ cups (664 ml)

2 chipotle chiles en adobo, canned or homemade

1 tablespoon mild vinegar

¾ pound (340 g) chilacayotes (see opposite), zucchini, or green squash,
cut into strips ¼ inch (7 mm) thick

½ teaspoon dried oregano, crumbled

½ cup (125 ml) water

Heat the lard in a skillet, add the onion with a sprinkle of salt, and fry without browning until translucent for about 1 minute. Add the tomatoes and cook until the juice has evaporated a little. Add the remaining ingredients and cook uncovered until tender—about 15 to 20 minutes. The mixture should be moist but not too juicy.

JALISCO

A MERE MENTION OF JALISCO, THE STATE, OR GUADALAJARA, ITS CAPITAL, CONJURES UP (APART FROM TEQUILA) VISIONS OF *CHARROS*—GENTLEMEN HORSEMEN DRESSED IN SPLEN-did riding habits lavishly studded with silver ornaments and their wide-brimmed *sombreros*—as well as *mariachis,* their musical counterparts, in almost equally elegant attire. They are unique to Jalisco, manifestations of a cultural and social life that evolved in the days of prosperous hacienda life before the Revolution. They have now spread to many parts of Mexico. ❁ I have been traveling in different parts of Jalisco as long as I have been in Mexico, but it had never really come together for me as an entity, perhaps because its boundaries wander so much and I have approached it at so many different points. Nayarit is its West Coast neighbor to the north; Jalisco almost engulfs Colima to the south; fingers of its land penetrate Zacatecas to the northwest; and its arid lands join those of Aguascalientes. Its most extensive boundaries to the south and southeast are with Michoacán. With the beautiful lake of Chapala and its string of minor lakes to the south and a coastline of over 200 kilometers, it has attracted many foreigners who make their permanent home there. ❁ To the northeast of Guadalajara, beyond the extensive central plain, is the area known as Los Altos, the Heights, where many people have retained their Spanish traditions—and appearance for that matter, tall with pale skin and dark hair. The architectural jewel of Los Altos is Lagos de Moreno, declared by ex-president Salinas as a colonial monument. It is a delightful place with elegant houses, squares, and parks that reflect the affluent life there in the late nineteenth century. (Another architecturally beautiful town that I pass through on my way from Michoacán to the Colima coast is Mazamitla, set high in pine forests where you think you have walked onto a scene from a Spanish movie set in the eighteenth century.) ❁ Much of the western mass of Jalisco is high sierra, crossed by only two tortuous highways (and a new, straighter toll road to the north) that take you down to the coast. Prosperous mines attracted miners and prospectors from Europe, many from England and Ireland, to this area in the eighteenth century. After the decline of these mines during the Revolution many of the families stayed on, and generations later you can still meet fair or red-headed O'Higginses, O'Reillys, and O'Gormans. ❁ Despite these outside influences and geographical differences, there is not great divergence in the popular, everyday food of Jalisco (many years ago I was severely reprimanded by a young American archaeologist for saying this), as there is for instance in Oaxaca, the prime example, Puebla, or Chiapas. While the coastal towns have naturally seen changes in eating habits due to tourism, the average Mexican family there will still go out for the evening *pozole* and *gorditas*. Signs advertising *birria* (a meat stew typical of Jalisco) will be displayed at every little eating establishment in town and along the highways.

Jalisciences can be proud of the quality of their cheese, fish, and meats and the variety of their breads and sweetmeats. But let's not forget the colorful and practical clay pots and plates, both rustic and sophisticated, in which they are prepared and served—these are made in Tlaquepaque and Tonalá on the edge of Guadalajara.

Puerto Vallarta and Points North

It often takes only a chance remark about a new recipe, or rather one I have never heard of before, to send me off in pursuit. It happened again recently when a friend from Mexico City mentioned some very special sweetmeats made in Mascota, a small town in the Sierras above Puerto Vallarta. So of course I had to go and try them.

I never take the shortest routes via toll highways but map out my way along roads I haven't already traveled. I like to see the countryside and what is grown there, the villages and their regional architecture, and the changes that are taking place, often far too fast.

This time I drove north through Michoacán into Jalisco and then west past Chapala. I had forgotten how beautiful the lake is. It was especially so on that dull morning of the rainy season, and so serene, not a ripple on its pale blue-gray surface with the misty gray mountainous mass looming behind protectively. The narrow twisting road is one of the main arteries down to the coast, and traffic was constant and sporadically heavy, unnervingly so as we dipped down into canyons with unguarded edges.

It was a long and tiring drive, hot and very dry in parts, and many fields lay uncultivated for the lack of rain. After a night spent in the little coastal town of Melaque, I drove off early the next morning north through the mostly scrubby land, gray and lifeless except for the occasional flowering shrub. Where the soil was deeper and more suitable for cultivation or cattle, the only trees had been felled and ugly black scars dotted the landscape. Only occasionally was there a glimpse of the sea or a distant house revealing the whereabouts of the almost hidden small resorts that dot the coastline.

Halfway on my journey I stopped for breakfast at a clean, airy little restaurant under a large *palapa* that offered an amazing array of seafood dishes for breakfast, lunch, or supper, whatever the hour of the day. The shrimp catch had just been brought in, so why not! I sat down to a large plate, *para pelar*, to peel, still warm, accompanied by my own filtered coffee, which travels with me everywhere.

The landscape did not change much as the road passed through small *rancherías*, or settlements, with their small plantations of bananas, limes, and coconut palms, that seemed isolated and forgotten. Suddenly the tropical vegetation became more luxuriant as the land began to rise on either side and higher up still the road wound through rich stands of pines, oaks, and other hardwoods, so far mercifully spared by the large sawmill a short distance away.

At last the highway began its steep descent toward the coast through a narrow canyon; you could see the bay, dominated by Puerto Vallarta. Another ten kilometers down I was in Mismaloya, now almost totally built up along the coastal road.

Puerto Vallarta brings back many memories of sporadic visits in years gone by. I first went there when Paul, my late husband, was writing a piece for the *New York Times* on John Huston and his production of *The Night of the Iguana*. There were no paved highways then, and one had to fly in, the plane descending abruptly from the high, forested Sierra Madre Occidental to the narrow coastal plain. The small port, almost totally undeveloped at the time, was jumping with intrigue and temperament, and I shall always remember Richard Burton, after a few drinks, imitating his father's precise Welsh diction of "The Verb To Be." Years later, after the death of my husband, when I started teaching Mexican cooking in New York, another talented member of that cast, Grayson Hall, came to my very first classes and reminded me of those rather crazy days.

Change was coming. The renowned (and now lamented) Posada Vallarta was in its first stages of development. It was to become a wonderful training ground for chefs and hotel staff under the guidance of Violet and Suna Gershenson, who introduced sophisticated food into that burgeoning little coastal resort.

Up until then the food had been very limited in scope, because of difficult transport. Everyone on the beach tried the freshly caught fish impaled on sticks and broiled over mangrovewood. It no longer exists; instead, *pescado sarandeado*, fish opened up and grilled by turning over several times in a light metal frame, is the order of the day. I was told in Nayarit, farther north, that this method of cooking fish was invented on the "island on the lake" of Mexcaltitán. Now everyone has his own version, with condiments and hot sauces of different types used with varying degrees of success.

The weather had been turbulent that year, and the unpaved road we were to have taken up into the Sierra Cacoma was partially washed out and dangerous, so that trip to Mascota for the sweetmeats had to be postponed until the late fall. Instead, I stayed for a few days in Puerto Vallarta and under the guidance of friends who live there tried the local specialties, new and old.

POZOLE DE CAMARÓN

SHRIMP POZOLE

Sra. Rafaela Villaseñor

✺

[MAKES APPROXIMATELY 12 CUPS (3 L), 8 SERVINGS]

THE MOST POPULAR SUPPER DISH BY FAR IN THE WESTERN STATES OF MEX-ICO FROM NAYARIT DOWN THROUGH GUERRERO, ESPECIALLY IN THE HOT country and coastal areas—with a few exceptions of course—is *pozole*. *Pozole* is a brothy stew of large white corn kernels and pork. Guerrero lays claim to it, and curiously, there white *pozole* is served in the morning and green *pozole* midday on Thursdays.

The preparation of the corn remains much the same, but the toppings vary slightly from one region to another, and occasionally you will find chicken cooked with the pork.

For local residents of Puerto Vallarta there is no *pozole* to compare with that of Señora Rafaela Villaseñor. Many years ago, to support a growing family, she sold her *pozole* and *gorditas de res* on the street corner just below where she lived. Now, apart from her growing take-out business, she will prepare large quantities to order for special occasions.

For the devout who shun meat during Lent she prepares a red *pozole* with shrimp both fresh and dried. While this *pozole* is made in many communities along the coast of Colima and Jalisco, it was her recipe that I found most satisfying.

1 pound (450 g) prepared corn for pozole (see page 58)

2 quarts (2 l) plus 1¼ cups (313 ml) or more water as needed

4 ancho chiles

4 guajillo chiles

4 cloves

⅛ teaspoon cumin seeds

4 garlic cloves, roughly chopped

3 tablespoons olive oil

8 ounces (225 g) fresh medium shrimp (see preparation at end of recipe)

3 ounces (85 g) dried shrimp (see preparation at end of recipe)

salt to taste

TO SERVE

finely chopped white onion

thinly sliced radishes

thinly shredded cabbage

dried oregano

lime quarters

Cover the corn with 2 quarts (2 l) of the water in a large saucepan and set over medium heat to cook until the kernels open up or "flower"—about 3 hours (50 minutes or more at a high altitude, in a pressure cooker). Set aside.

Remove the stems, veins, and seeds from the chiles separately and put them in two individual piles. Cover them *separately* with hot water and cook over low heat for about 5 minutes. Set aside to soak for about 10 minutes to soften and become fleshy. Drain, discarding the cooking water.

Put ¼ cup (63 ml) of the water into a blender, add the cloves, cumin, and garlic, and blend thoroughly. Add another ½ cup (125 ml) of the water and a few of the anchos, then blend until smooth. Add the rest of the anchos and blend again, adding only enough water to release the blades of the blender. The sauce should be quite thick.

Heat the olive oil in a heavy pan in which you are going to cook the *pozole*. Add the ancho

[CONTINUED]

sauce and fry for about 3 minutes, scraping the bottom of the pan from time to time to prevent sticking.

Add another ½ cup (125 ml) of the water to the blender and add the guajillos gradually, blending thoroughly after each addition. Add this puree through a fine strainer to the pan, thoroughly pressing out the debris of tough skins.

Cook the puree of chiles over low heat, scraping the pan to prevent sticking, for about 5 minutes.

Add the corn and the water in which it was cooked and the cheesecloth bag with the shrimp heads and shells. Cook slowly for about 15 minutes. Add the dried and fresh shrimp and cook for another 10 minutes. Taste for salt. Remove the cheesecloth bag, squeezing it well to extract as much liquid as possible.

Serve the *pozole* with plenty of the broth and pass the accompaniments separately.

NOTE: *If the broth is too strong for your taste, add more hot water to dilute.*

PREPARATION OF THE SHRIMP

DRIED: See box, page 393. Choose the largest you can find with head and tail intact—or at least in the same bag. Soak in hot water for 5 minutes to remove excess salt. Drain and then remove the heads and feet, leaving the skin and tail intact for texture and flavor. Reserve the heads.

FRESH: Medium shrimp are best for this dish, but try to buy them with heads still intact if possible for better flavor. Remove the heads and reserve them; peel and devein the shrimp. Put the dried and fresh shrimp heads along with the fresh shells into a piece of cheesecloth and tie tightly.

GORDITAS DE RES

Sra. Rafaela Villaseñor

❁

[SERVES 6]

WHEN SHOWING ME THIS RECIPE, SEÑORA VILLASEÑOR MADE SMALL TORTILLAS— DE DOS MORDIDAS, OF TWO BITES.

HAVE READY

12 ounces (340 g) masa for tortillas (page 530),
about 1⅓ cups (333 ml)

lard or oil for frying

⅔ cup (164 ml) bean paste from refried beans

2 cups (500 ml) loosely packed finely shredded cabbage

⅔ cup (164 ml) finely grated queso añejo or Romano

THE MEAT

8 ounces (225 g) skirt steak

salt to taste

2 tablespoons vegetable oil

⅓ medium white onion, finely chopped

6 ounces (180 g) tomatoes, finely chopped,
about 1 cup (250 ml)

THE SAUCE

3 ancho chiles, veins and seeds removed

4 black peppercorns

3 cloves

[CONTINUED]

Cut the steak into 1½-inch (4-cm) squares, cover with water in a saucepan, add salt, and bring to a simmer. Continue simmering until the meat is tender, about 40 minutes. Leave the meat in the broth to cool, then strain, reserving the broth, and shred, not too finely. You should have about 1 heaped cup (275 ml) meat.

Heat the oil, add the onion, and fry briefly until translucent. Add the tomatoes and cook over medium heat until it has reduced and seasoned—about 4 minutes. Add the shredded meat, season as necessary, and cook until the mixture is almost dry—about 5 minutes. Set aside and keep warm.

Cover the chiles with hot water and leave to soak for about 15 minutes or until soft and fleshy. Put ½ cup (125 ml) of the reserved meat broth into a blender. Add the peppercorns and cloves and blend until smooth. Gradually add the drained chiles and another ½ cup (125 ml) of the broth and blend until smooth. The sauce should be of medium consistency and coat the back of a wooden spoon. Add more broth if necessary to obtain this consistency and test for salt.

Divide the *masa* into 12 pieces. Roll each piece into a ball about 1½ inches (4 cm) in diameter. Cover the balls with a cloth while you work. Press a ball of the dough out to a not-too-thin tortilla 4 inches (10 cm) in diameter. Cook as you would any tortilla, on an ungreased *comal* or griddle, pinching up the edges to form a low rim. Set aside. Continue with the rest of the dough.

Heat lard or oil in a skillet to a depth of about ⅛ inch (3 mm). Dip a few of the tortillas in the raw sauce—it should cover them well on both sides—and fry in the hot fat for about 2 minutes on each side. Add more fat as necessary. Drain on paper toweling. Spread 1 heaped teaspoon of the bean paste over the *gordita,* then a small pile of the shredded meat, finishing off with shredded cabbage and plenty of the cheese. Serve immediately—this is pan-to-mouth food.

PULPO EN SALSA GUAJILLO

OCTOPUS IN GUAJILLO CHILE SAUCE

Jose Ruiz Muñoz Restaurant Tampico

❂

[SERVES 8 AS A FIRST COURSE, 6 AS A MAIN COURSE]

SR. RUIZ PREPARES BOTH OCTOPUS AND SQUID IN THIS SAUCE, WHICH IS SIM-PLE AND DELICIOUS, IN HIS AIRY AND ATTRACTIVE RESTAURANT IN PUERTO Vallarta. Like many restaurateurs in resort areas that cater to many foreign tourists as well as Mexicans, Sr. Ruiz is always finding and inventing new ways of preparing seafood, such as the very delicate dish of strips of a white-fleshed fish in a sauce made of squash flowers that he serves.

In many better-known seafood restaurants along the coasts of Mexico the tendency is to rob octopus of all the texture and flavor by using a pressure cooker or cooking it too long. If you use small octopus, it is usually unnecessary to precook it for this type of dish; stir-frying and a short simmering in its juice will do it. However, Sr. Ruiz told me that the octopus from that area of the coast tends to be tougher than Gulf Coast octopus and needs longer cooking. Indeed, an octopus I bought recently did have a very dark-colored, tougher skin. In any case, always look for those that are under 2 pounds.

Since this is a rather strongly flavored sauce, I prefer to serve this dish in small quantities as a first course with some corn tortillas or crusty, French-type bread. As a main course it can be served with plain white rice—I particularly like the simple way of cooking rice in Tabasco (page 326).

2 small octopus, about 2 pounds (900 g) each, cleaned
3 tablespoons olive oil
½ large white onion, thinly sliced
8 garlic cloves, thinly sliced
salt to taste

[CONTINUED]

4 ounces (115 g) guajillo chiles
1 pound (450 g) unskinned tomatoes, broiled (page 527)
5 peppercorns
1 teaspoon dried oregano
5 cloves
2 tablespoons olive oil
salt to taste

Rinse the octopus well and cut it into small pieces. Heat the oil in a heavy pan, add the onion and garlic with a sprinkle of salt, and cook over high heat for about 5 minutes. Cover the pan and cook over medium heat, shaking the pan from time to time for about 10 minutes or until tender.

Slit the chiles open and remove the stems, seeds, and veins. Toast briefly on a warm *comal* (not too hot or the chiles will burn and make the sauce bitter) on both sides. Cover with hot water and set aside to soak for about 15 minutes.

Meanwhile, put 2 of the broiled tomatoes and some of the juice that has exuded into a blender. Add the peppercorns, oregano, and cloves and blend until smooth. Add the rest of the tomatoes and blend again.

Heat the olive oil in a deep skillet, add the sauce, and reduce over fairly high heat for about 5 minutes.

Put ¾ cup (188 ml) water into the blender, add the chiles a few at a time, blending well after each addition, and blend as smoothly as possible. (Add more water only if necessary to release the blades of the blender.) Add the chile sauce to the pan through a fine strainer, pressing down hard on the chiles to extract as much of the flesh and juice as possible. Discard the debris.

Cook the sauce over fairly high heat for 5 more minutes or until reduced and well seasoned. Add salt.

Add the octopus to the pan and cook in the sauce over high heat, scraping the bottom of the pan to avoid sticking, until it is a thick consistency and coats the octopus well—about 10 minutes. If the octopus is still a little chewy, add 1 cup water, cover the pan, and cook for about 1 hour over low heat, testing for correct texture from time to time.

This dish can be cooked ahead and reheated.

TINO'S CEVICHE

Restaurant Tino, Puerto Vallarta

✸

[MAKES APPROXIMATELY 2½ CUPS (625 ML)]

THIS WAY OF MAKING *CEVICHE* IS APPEALING FOR PEOPLE (LIKE ME) WHO DO NOT LIKE TO EAT VERY LARGE CUBES OF RAW FISH. THE RECIPE COMES FROM the lively, airy restaurant called Tino's in Puerto Vallarta, where it's served as a topping for *tostadas*. Although *sierra* is generally used for this *ceviche*, any white nonfatty fish could be substituted. Make sure that there are no very small bones running down the middle of the fillets before freezing.

12 ounces (340 g) fillets of sierra (king mackerel)
1 medium carrot, trimmed and scraped
⅓ cup (83 ml) fresh lime juice
2 tablespoons very finely chopped white onion
1 jalapeño chile, seeds removed
2 heaped tablespoons very finely chopped cilantro
1 small tomato, very finely chopped,
⅛ teaspoon dried oregano, crumbled
salt to taste

Put the fish into the freezer until it is partially frozen and firm to the touch. Chop roughly together with the carrot and put into a food processor. Process sporadically until the mixture has a fairly fine texture but is not reduced to a paste. Turn out into a nonreactive bowl and stir the lime juice into it well.

Set aside to "cook" for 30 minutes, no longer. Transfer to a fine strainer or, better still, a piece

[CONTINUED]

of cheesecloth and press or squeeze to extract the moisture. Mix in the rest of the ingredients and set aside to season for at least 1 hour before serving. Don't keep this more than 6 hours; it will lose its fresh taste.

CAPIROTADA DE DOÑA ROSA

DOÑA ROSA'S BREAD PUDDING

✺

[SERVES 8]

SRA. ROSA, WHO COMES A FEW DAYS A WEEK TO A FRIEND'S HOME IN PUERTO VALLARTA TO COOK, IS WELL KNOWN FOR HER *CAPIROTADA.* HER RECIPE IS unlike the more common ones in Mexico: rounds of bread fried crisp and soaked in a syrup with nuts and raisins or other regional elaborations. Hers is more like a bread pudding moistened with custard.

The bread Doña Rosa uses is called *picón,* a round raised semisweet egg/yeast bread about 5 inches (13 cm) in diameter. I suggest you substitute challah or even stale brioche. She also uses evaporated milk diluted with water, which I can't stand, so I use whole milk and add some grated lime peel.

The ideal dish for this amount is an ovenproof one about 8½ inches (21.5 cm) in diameter and at least 3 inches (8 cm) deep. It is lined on the bottom and a little way up the sides with fried corn tortillas so that the custard does not seep down and stick to the base of the casserole.

7 cups (1.75 l) whole milk
2-inch (5-cm) cinnamon stick
½ cup (125 ml) sugar
1½ tablespoons cornstarch
2 egg yolks
½ teaspoon vanilla extract
vegetable oil for frying
6 5-inch (13-cm) corn tortillas

1 ripe plantain, about 1 pound (450 g)

approximately 16 small slices of dried bread (see note above)
½ inch (13 mm) thick

10 ounces (285 g) dried prunes, soaked until slightly softened and pits
removed

heaped ½ cup (135 ml) roughly chopped pecans

½ cup (125 ml) raisins

Warm the milk with the cinnamon and sugar in a saucepan. Put the cornstarch into a small bowl, add a little of the warmed milk, and mix with a wooden spoon until smooth. Add some more of the milk, stir well, and then return it to the pan. Mix the egg yolks—just to break them up, not beat them—add a little of the warmed milk, and quickly mix until smooth. Add more of the milk and then return it to the pan. Cook over low heat, stirring from time to time and scraping the bottom of the pan to prevent sticking, until the mixture begins to thicken slightly. Stir in the vanilla and set aside.

Heat the oven to 350°F (177°C).

Heat about ⅛ inch (3 mm) of oil in a skillet and fry the tortillas on both sides until they are leathery, not crisp. Add a little more oil as necessary. Blot them well and line the bottom of the mold (see note above). Peel the plantain and cut into slices. Fry the slices on both sides in the oil until golden brown, blot, and set aside.

Put a layer of the bread over the tortillas, sprinkle with a third of the drained prunes, nuts, and raisins, and add a third of the plantain. Remove the cinnamon stick from the custard.

Very slowly pour 1½ cups (375 ml) of the custard over the first layer, a little at a time, allowing the bread to absorb the liquid—if you pour it too fast, it will all just sink to the bottom of the dish. Repeat with a second layer and then finish off with the third layer of bread, etc., and the remaining milk.

Bake in the top of the oven until most of the liquid has been absorbed—about 40 minutes. Set aside for about 20 minutes before serving so that the remaining liquid is absorbed. Serve lukewarm with crème fraîche or whipped cream.

Some friends familiar with the area and I were on our way to Aticama, a small fishing community renowned for its spectacular array of seafood cocktails. Each little restaurant there, housed in open *palapas* along the water's edge, displayed these cocktails prominently to tempt passersby. They were all lined up, each type of seafood in its bulbous goblet of thick glass along a counter colorfully decorated with fruits and flowers.

A local specialty was smoked *lisa*, grilled while you waited over a mangrovewood fire— not delicious, but interesting.

In Puerto Vallarta we had been asked to look for beet bread made in a neighboring community on the way. It was curious to see large signs outside practically every house announcing "*pan de calabacita, pan de zanahoria, pan de plátano*" (zucchini, carrot, and banana breads) but nowhere beet. As our search took us from house to house, we found out that a visitor from the United States who had stayed there for a period had introduced these cakelike breads and they had provided a modest income from sales to visitors who came from as far away as Puerto Vallarta, about a two-hour drive.

On our way, I had noticed in the village of El Llano what appeared to be stunted trees with thick leaves and large pendulous fruits with dark green knobbly skin. On our return I stopped to take a photograph. They were unfortunately not ripe, but farther along in an open shop there they were for sale. The ripe fruit known as *yaca* had a strongly perfumed orange flesh. Sra. Villegas was also selling the pulp of the fruit in plastic bags.

The fruit, a native of Brazil, flourished in that area and has been incorporated into the local food. The firm flesh is sometimes used in the following recipe instead of the fried plantains, but *yaca* not being generally available, we'll stick to plantains.

POLLO EN BLANCO

CHICKEN IN WHITE SAUCE

Sra. María Villegas, El Llano, Nayarit

❋

[SERVES 6]

WELL, THIS IS NOT EXACTLY A WHITE SAUCE AS WE KNOW IT, BUT THE NAME INDICATES THAT IT IS NOT A COLORED CHILE SAUCE. THE RECIPE WAS GIVEN to me by María Villegas—who is actually from Guadalajara but married someone from this village of El Llano. We passed through it on our way along a quiet road leading down to the coast of Nayarit and eventually on to San Blas.

1 large chicken, cut into serving pieces, plus 1 extra whole breast
chicken broth or water to cover
salt to taste
6 medium carrots, trimmed and scraped
6 small new potatoes
1 small chayote, cut into strips about 1 inch (2.5 cm) thick
2 small zucchini, quartered lengthwise
1 pound (450 g) tomatoes
⅛ teaspoon cumin seeds
6 black peppercorns
1 heaped teaspoon dried oregano
3 tablespoons vegetable oil or the rendered chicken fat
1 plantain, about 12 ounces (340 g), peeled and sliced lengthwise
1½ tablespoons all-purpose flour
1½ tablespoons vinegar
⅓ cup (83 ml) raisins

In a large pan, cover the chicken with broth or water with salt to taste and simmer until tender, approximately 25 minutes. Drain and return the broth to the pan. Set the chicken aside. Bring the broth to a simmer, add the carrots and potatoes, and cook for 10 minutes. Add

[CONTINUED]

the *chayote* and zucchini and cook for another 10 minutes or until the vegetables are just tender. Remove the vegetables from the broth and cut into large cubes. Set aside.

Put the tomatoes whole into the hot broth and simmer until soft but not falling apart—about 15 minutes. Remove and reserve the broth.

Put ½ cup (125 ml) of the broth into a blender, add the cumin, peppercorns, and oregano, and blend until smooth. Gradually add the tomatoes and blend until smooth. Set aside.

Heat the oil in a heavy skillet, add the plantain, and fry until golden on both sides. Drain well and reserve.

Measure 2 tablespoons of the oil into the pot in which you are going to cook the stew. Add the flour, stirring well to eliminate any lumps, and cook to a deep golden color. Add the tomato puree, stirring well to make a smooth sauce, and cook over low heat, scraping the bottom of the pan to prevent sticking, for about 3 minutes. Add the vinegar and raisins and cook until the sauce thickens very slightly, about 3 minutes more.

Add 2 cups (500 ml) of the chicken broth, the chicken, and the vegetables and cook again over low heat for about 5 minutes. Adjust the salt. Five minutes before serving, add the fried plantain and just heat through.

Puerto Vallarta to Nayarit

I decided to continue up the coast at a more leisurely pace and visit Compostela and Tepic, neither of which I had seen before. The narrow highway wound between belts of tropical growth broken by clearings for cattle or corn or lush plantations of mango and papaya.

There were also occasional fields of tobacco, with the cut leaves hung up to dry in bunches sheltered under long, narrow roofs. Nayarit, like Veracruz, is one of the main tobacco producers in Mexico. Like many other crops, it is diminishing with the vagaries of demand in foreign markets and a lack of coherent and stable agricultural policies.

The land began to climb and twist through foothills until there was a sudden, magnificent view of a huge valley to the north and east that stretched as far as the eye could see, transversed by rivers, streams, and lakes with towering mountains in the distance. I had never realized that Nayarit was so richly endowed with this abundance of water, apparently not yet contaminated by the effluence of uncontrolled industry.

Tepic, the capital of the State of Nayarit, is one of those nondescript towns that have grown with no regard to any architectural harmony with the few remaining colonial houses and buildings. Not surprisingly, the market too offered hardly anything of interest. The food-stuffs were predictable, and the space for the most part was invaded by small stands selling cheap clothes and shoes.

The small but interesting archaeological museum saved the day with some fascinating regional pieces of great beauty and imposing size. The renowned local seafood restaurant where every visitor is sent turned out to be a disappointment. I was immediately suspicious on receiving a menu without prices; I can only assume that they were fixed at the whim of the waitress or the fierce-looking lady presiding over the cash register. I was to eat far better local special-ties—*sopes, empanadas,* and grilled fish—at a very simple coastal restaurant the next day.

The following morning I drove on to the little town of Santiago Ixcuintla—the name derives from the edible hairless dogs, now almost extinct, that were so often portrayed in the pre-Hispanic artifacts of the area.

Santiago, a little agricultural town in the western part of Nayarit, must have been quite prosperous in its day if one can judge by the rather elaborate church and public buildings. No longer. I eschewed the seedy-looking hotels in the center in favor of a slightly better-kept motel on extensive grounds at the edge of town. No sooner was I installed than I realized that this establishment served a double purpose: on one side were the "decent" rooms; on the other the entrance doors were concealed inside the curtained garages that hid the license plates of the car owners occupying the rooms with their *movidas* (sexual partners).

But it could have been worse: the other side was busy during the day, and we were left to sleep relatively undisturbed at night apart from the occasional and inevitable roar of the engine of a latecomer's truck. As in so many of these little hostelries off the beaten track of tourists, the rooms were ugly and bare with a television chained to the wall almost at ceiling level. The shower head flooded the closet-sized bathroom—you had to wade across to the lavatory—and the thin lumpy mattresses were covered with threadbare sheets and pillows stuffed to bursting with squeaking plastic.

Wandering around this sad little town, I came across a street vendor selling shrimp *tamales*, which I had heard about for years and never had a chance to try. They are in fact a specialty of Esquinapa in the neighboring State of Sinaloa. The dough was roughly textured and heavy with lard. It was filled with a whole shrimp: the head with feelers, legs, shell, and tail, which made for a rather abrasive mouthful. I was not impressed and hurried off to the market for some of my standby foods—delicious juicy mangoes, sweet ripe pineapples, and a tempting variety of bananas, all grown locally.

Supper too was a disappointment. A little *birrería*—a modest eating place serving *birria* exclusively (page 83)—opposite the bus station had been recommended to me. The meat was mushily overcooked and the broth tasteless. I left after the first mouthful and thought of it again only when I was eating the most delicious *birria* in Mascota some months later. On such occasions I keep telling myself that, gastronomically speaking, it is always hit or miss when charting new territory, but all the same, there had been rather too many misses on that trip. Surely my planned visit to Camichín the next day would turn up something more exciting.

The Boca de Camichín lies due east of Santiago, and it is where the Río San Pedro enters the Pacific Ocean. On the southern bank of the river lies a small fishing settlement: a group of rather flimsy dwellings and little restaurants or *ramadas* where the tables are sheltered by palm fronds slung across rustic wooden scaffolding. The people living there support themselves by fishing in the local waters and collecting oysters from the extensive beds lying just offshore. On weekends they cater to the townspeople who come out to eat the specialties: *chivichangas* and *sopes* of oysters.

Although the *palapas* were practically indistinguishable—many without names—it did not take long to find that of Sra. María Cruz de López. Her restaurant had been recommended by her nephew, a young fisherman whom I had given a ride to the coast. A fresh basket of oysters had just been brought in with a large *pargo* (Pacific snapper) that was flopping around on the table.

After a warm welcome, the López family agreed to prepare their local specialties for me and set to work, with the help of two fishermen friends, shucking the oysters and starting the fire of mangrovewood under the grill. One of the men deftly cut the fish into two fillets, with the head and skin intact. The open sides of the fillets were smeared with a strong paste of salt, garlic, and hot chiles, ready to be grilled or *sarandeado*—meaning that the fish is turned over at very brief intervals so that it is never dry. The morning wore on slowly and pleasantly as we cooked and sampled, washing the food down with plenty of cold beer.

I promised to go back and take their boat through the inland lagoons to the mysterious island of Mexcaltitán—legendary departure point of the Nahuas who founded Tenochtítlan (now part of Mexico City) in 1325.

SOPES DE OSTIONES

SOPES TOPPED WITH OYSTERS

Sra. María Cruz de López

✹

[MAKES 12 3-INCH (8-CM) SOPES]

I IMAGINE THAT THE VERY THOUGHT OF DOING THIS TO OYSTERS IS LAUGH-ABLE IN MOST PEOPLE'S BOOK, BUT THERE ARE SMALL OYSTERS GALORE IN Boca de Camichín, and the cooks there are always thinking up new ways of using them for regular visitors. Of course the little Olympia oysters would be perfect—if it weren't for the price. It surprises me to hear myself recommending a can, but . . . I've made this recipe using a can of miniature clams, using the liquid for the *masa* as well. They worked very well, and I was also tempted to use smoked oysters—it made for a very tasty and economical *botana*, a change from the usual shredded meat topping.

THE MASA

*1 cup (250 ml) masa for tortillas (page 530), 9½ ounces (265 g),
preferably rather dry*

¼ cup (63 ml) oyster or clam juice

approximately 2 tablespoons lard or vegetable oil

THE TOPPINGS

¾ cup (188 ml) cooked, drained, and mashed bayo or pinto beans

1 cup (250 ml) small oysters or canned clams, drained (see note above)

[CONTINUED]

1 cup (250 ml) cooked cubed carrot

1 cup (250 ml) cooked cubed potato

*1 heaped cup (265 ml) finely shredded lettuce seasoned
with a little salt and lime juice*

⅓ cup (83 ml) finely chopped white onion

1 cup (250 ml) tomato sauce (recipe follows)

¼ cup (63 ml) very finely grated queso añejo or Romano

crumbled dried oregano

Mix the *masa* with the oyster juice. Divide into 12 balls about 1¼ inches (3 cm) in diameter and set aside. If you are making double the amount or more, keep the other batches of *masa* under a damp cloth while you work with the first batch.

Press the balls out gently in a baggie-lined tortilla press to about 3½ inches (9 cm) in diameter, no larger. Cook on an ungreased *comal* or griddle as if you were making tortillas.

While still hot, press the dough up around the edge to form a rim—you will probably burn your thumbs, but don't let the dough get cold. Cover with a cloth to keep the *sopes* slightly warm and flexible.

Spread each one with a little of the bean paste, cover with a scant tablespoon of the oysters, a tablespoon of the carrots and potatoes mixed, a little shredded lettuce, chopped onion, a tablespoon of the tomato sauce, and a liberal sprinkling of the cheese and oregano.

Heat the lard or oil in a pan or *comal* and just heat the bottoms of the *sopes* through for a minute or two before serving.

TOMATO SAUCE

[MAKES 2 CUPS (500 ML)]

1 pound (450 g) tomatoes

1 jalapeño chile or more to taste, roughly chopped

2 small garlic cloves, roughly chopped

1 tablespoon vegetable oil

½ cup (125 ml) water or juice from the oysters

salt to taste

finely crumbled dried oregano

Cover the tomatoes with hot water in a saucepan and simmer until soft but not falling apart—about 10 minutes. Drain, saving the hot water for the vegetables. Put the tomatoes, chile, and garlic into a blender and blend until smooth.

Heat the oil in a small skillet and cook the sauce over high heat for about 2 minutes. Add the water with salt if necessary and cook for another 2 minutes.

If using this as a table sauce, sprinkle the oregano on top just before serving. If using it on the *sopes*, sprinkle the oregano on top of the *sopes*.

CHIVICHANGAS DE OSTIONES

OYSTER *CHIVICHANGAS*

Sra. María Cruz de López

✸

[MAKES 6 *CHIVICHANGAS* ABOUT 5 INCHES (13 CM) LONG]

12 ounces (340 g) masa *for tortillas (page 530), about 1⅓ cups (333 ml)*

salt to taste

1 tablespoon salsa de chile cora (page 75)

2 dozen medium oysters, more or less, depending on size

3 tablespoons vegetable oil plus oil for frying

3 heaped tablespoons finely chopped white onion

1 jalapeño chile, finely chopped

4 ounces (115 g) tomatoes, finely chopped, about ⅔ cup (164 ml)

Mix the *masa* with a little salt and the hot sauce. Divide the dough into 6 equal pieces and roll each into a ball about 1¾ inches (4.5 cm) in diameter. Cover with a damp cloth.

Drain the oysters well. Heat the 3 tablespoons oil in a skillet, add the onion and chile, and fry without browning for about 1 minute. Add the tomato and fry until almost dry. Add the drained oysters and salt to taste and stir-fry rapidly for about 2 minutes. Set aside to cool slightly and then drain off the excess juice.

Heat ½ inch (13 mm) of oil in a skillet. Press one of the balls of dough out in a baggie-lined

[CONTINUED]

tortilla press to a very thin circle about 6 inches (15.5 cm) in diameter. Put a few of the oysters along the center. Fold one side of the dough over the filling, leaving about 1 inch (2.5 cm) of dough exposed on the opposite side. Fold this over and fold the ends up about ½ inch (13 mm) to seal in the filling. Fry in very hot oil on both sides until the dough is crisp on the outside and a deep golden color. Drain well on paper toweling and serve immediately, opening up one end to add a little of the hot sauce.

Don't expect the dough to be crisp all the way through. It will be soft but cooked around the filling.

If you are not serving informally straight from the pan, as they are best, then as the *chivichangas* are cooked, place them on an oven tray lined with absorbent paper and reheat in a 400°F (205°C) oven. This will also help extract some of the excess oil.

EMPANADAS DE CAMARÓN

SHRIMP EMPANADAS

Sra. María Cruz de López, Boca de Camichín, Nayarit

❋

[MAKES 12 EMPANADAS]

THE FILLING
1½ cups (375 ml) peeled raw shrimp
2 tablespoons vegetable oil
2 tablespoons finely chopped white onion
1 jalapeño chile, chopped
salt to taste
2 small tomatoes, finely chopped, about ⅔ cup (164 ml)
2 heaped tablespoons finely chopped cilantro

THE MASA
vegetable oil for frying
1 pound (450 g) masa for tortillas (page 528), about 1¾ cups (438 ml)
1 teaspoon salsa de chile cora (see opposite)

Roughly chop the shrimp. Heat the oil in a skillet, add the onion and chile with a sprinkle of salt, and fry without browning for a few seconds. Add the tomatoes and cook for about 2 minutes or until some of the juice has evaporated. Stir in the shrimp and stir-fry until just opaque, about 3 minutes. Taste for salt, stir in the *cilantro*, and set aside. Heat about ¼ inch (7 mm) of oil in a skillet.

Mix the *masa* with the hot sauce and a little salt. Divide the masa into 12 pieces and form into balls about 1½ inches (4 cm) in diameter. Using a baggie-lined tortilla press, press one of the balls out to about 5 inches (13 cm), put a very heaped tablespoon of filling in the center of the dough, double it over, and carefully lift it off the plastic bag lining the tortilla press. Carefully set into the hot oil.

Fry on both sides until crisp and lightly browned. Drain on paper toweling and eat immediately.

SALSA DE CHILE CORA

CHILE CORA SAUCE

✳

[MAKES APPROXIMATELY 1½ CUPS (375 ML)]

THIS IS A TYPICAL TABLE SAUCE—USED AS A CONDIMENT—FROM NAYARIT. THE RECIPE WAS GIVEN TO ME IN THE SMALL MARKET TOWN OF COMPOSTELA. The chile is grown locally and named for the indigenous people living nearby. It is a shiny, dark red triangular chile usually used in its dried state. I have seen it elsewhere labeled *chile catarino.*

Like any sauce made with dried chiles of this type it will keep for a few days in the refrigerator.

8 ounces (225 g) tomates verdes, about 9 medium
7 dried cora or cascabel chiles
2 tablespoons lard or vegetable oil
2 garlic cloves, roughly chopped

[CONTINUED]

⅓ cup (83 ml) water

salt to taste

Remove the husks from the *tomates verdes*, rinse, cover with water in a saucepan, and simmer until soft but not falling apart—about 10 minutes. Wipe the chiles clean with a damp cloth and remove the stems. Heat the lard in a skillet and fry the chiles, turning them so that they do not burn (or the sauce will be bitter) for about 2 minutes. Remove with a slotted spoon and when cool crumble into a blender.

Add the garlic and water and blend to a slightly textured consistency. Add the drained *tomates verdes* and salt to taste, then blend again to a fairly smooth consistency.

Mascota and San Sebastián

Fall had come and almost gone before my friend Violet called to say that the trip to Mascota, where they make luscious candied fruits, had been arranged. A friend of hers who had contacts there would be our guide, and her brother would drive a high, comfortable vehicle since a standard car could not make it.

It was only 115 kilometers but would take about six and a half hours. In 1974 the *Guide Bleu* stated "the road is mediocre," and that was an overstatement—especially for the French!

Our friends immediately told us—this was Saturday morning—that they had to be back by Sunday night and were sorry but there wouldn't be time enough to see San Sebastián. They had, however, seen to it that I would get all the information I needed and try the food and fruits. I had been told sometime before to be sure not to miss San Sebastián. Ah well, you never know what fate has in store, I thought, having been in Mexico for such a long time, and settled back to enjoy the ride.

Those first three hours seemed endless, as fascinating as the journey was, as we found our way slowly up a loose dirt track—sending clouds of dust up behind us, crossing through streams, over rocky little riverbeds through a constantly changing landscape as we gained altitude. Thick tropical vegetation thinned out to semitropical and finally was dotted with stunted pines and scrubby oaks with occasional narrow views of the valleys and coastal plain below. We saw hardly a soul, and small herds of cattle would stop their grazing and turn to stare as we went by. There was an occasional farmstead with crumbling adobe house, and the silence was broken once in a while by the roar of a truck or the coughing sputter from the exhaust of an old bus descending in the opposite direction with unaccustomed precaution.

We passed a sign pointing to San Sebastián—ten kilometers, what a pity we didn't have time to stop—but we had to get to Mascota for a late lunch and well before the light began to fade. Less than two kilometers farther on we rounded a curve too tightly, skidded on the loose surface, and hit a small, oncoming truck that had swung out a fraction too wide. Water poured from their radiator, and the engine died. The couple in the truck were from San Sebastián, so it was decided that we should go back there to get help.

We returned to the signpost and took a narrow road that wound up through pine forests and past drying fields of corn and cattle grazing until we came to an avenue of majestic elm and walnut trees that formed a high arch, as if welcoming us to the little town. While the woman who had come back with us was negotiating for a tow truck and reporting the incident to the local transit authority—a young man casually dressed in a T-shirt and baggy pants—we hurriedly bought fruit to appease our hunger and walked back slowly to the car, admiring the elegant little town sitting in isolation in a basin (or so it seemed) in the foothills of the surrounding sierras. The houses and public buildings were in simple Spanish colonial style, with white painted walls and low sloping roofs covered with reddish tiles mottled with age. Then and there we decided to stay on the way back.

We returned to the scene of the accident with the transit chief and a promise of help from the mechanic in San Sebastián, but despite the deposit of a tidy sum to cover the repairs (and our friend's driver's license), the authority insisted we go back again immediately to sign an official document. It would take him several hours to type it up. Couldn't we sign on the way back tomorrow? With tempers still hot, the negotiations stalled, and when they resumed it all became so convoluted that I decided it was time for the women to take over. I just happened to have one of my books in Spanish with rather a ludicrous photograph of me on the back in sombrero and serape. Our friend explained that we had an important mission: the *presidente municipal* was waiting for us, and we were very late, and besides, I was a distinguished visitor who had the Order of the Aztec Eagle. We were soon on our way!

Those last two and a half hours were by far the worst. At first the road was shaded by trees along a small river and there were some homesteads and a few children playing while their fathers gossiped over a beer. Surprisingly there was also a field, beyond an imposing gateway with a hundred little triangular shelters, each with a number, to house fighting cocks that were pecking around outside. I could only think of the noise at dawn and what would happen if they all started fighting together! Unfortunately there was no one in sight to ask, and in any case we were already very late. We were held up twice by huge machines trying to clear the road of a recent fall of rocks and earth and then began a precarious descent when the road narrowed considerably as it hugged the side of the steep slope. The loose stony surface made it slippery, and the bends were closed and blind. Luckily our driver seemed unconcerned as the drivers of the occasional truck that served as collective transport for the area sped around at an alarming speed for those conditions and glared at us as though we had no right to be taking up the space.

As we descended, we had a distant view of the broad valley below and soon caught sight of the tiled roofs of Mascota, *la Esmeralda de la Sierra*, the Emerald of the Sierra, as it is known locally.

It was by then late afternoon: the restaurant that we had heard so much about was closed for a wedding party, so we hurried along to the lady who was famous for her conserves. She had gone to Mass, a long one, her son said, but he finally took pity on us and showed us in to buy her much acclaimed wares.

Where were the stuffed peaches that we had particularly come to buy? There was no peach harvest this year. Nobody had them! Similar incidents flashed through my mind: I had arrived on the wrong day, in the wrong season, there had been a drought, too much rain. . . . It was always a risk one took when setting off on these gastronomic trails.

But what a variety of sweets there were: *ates*, called *cajetas*, of local fruits—pears, apples, guavas, and *tejocotes*, a type of crab apple, thin layers of fruit conserve rolled up with a coating of sugar, the most delicious being a pale green color and sharper than the others, made of steamed green mangoes. There were little bags of *arrayan*, small wild guavas cooked with and rolled in sugar, with the delicious acidic taste of tamarind but with all the little seeds included. To console us for the lack of peaches, he did still have some boxes of stuffed guavas. The guavas had been left in a lime solution overnight, cooked in a syrup, then dried in the sun, all of which had given them an intense flavor and special texture. They were then stuffed with a *cajeta* of the same fruit. They were unique, and one could see why the lady-who-had-gone-to-Mass was so renowned in the region and even as far as Guadalajara.

After downing some lavishly topped *tostadas* and generously trimmed *gorditas*, we went off to see Sra. Carolina. She and her daughter Lilia were respected and dedicated local teachers and, apart from that, enthusiastic traditional cooks. Lilia's daughter Bertha, the third generation, has carried on that tradition and become a very talented cook, devoting herself to making cheeses, *jocoqui* (a delicious soured raw milk, page 80), and butter and to raising special chickens while her husband works his family's ranch.

The hours flew by as they all volunteered recipes—many carefully written down—with tips and advice all given so generously.

The men were dragged from the game on television when supper was announced: delicious sweet and savory *tamales, gordas de harina* (page 91), *arepas* (page 92), *atole*, and hot creamy milk.

We finally fell into bed, happily tired, in the immaculately clean but spartan hotel in the center of the town.

Mascota has extremely broad streets, one of which continues for more than a block, shearing off at an unexpected angle, leaving one bewildered and temporarily lost. A good memory and a great sense of direction are necessary to avoid the circular tours that we took that morning to find Lilia's house for a late breakfast.

When we arrived, Lilia was grilling strips of beef on what she called an *asador de echazo*, a grill made of junk. It was a metal plate set on top of an old wide tire rim, the fire underneath neatly confined by the metal. Bertha, or Bety as she prefers to be known, was beating the *jocoqui* and patiently described to me how it was made.

It wasn't so much the choice of food at that breakfast that was so exceptional as the quality of it and the care with which each item had been prepared. The tortillas of white corn were some of the finest I had had in a long time: light and mealy, spread with that fresh *jocoqui*, and sprinkled with salt. It was the epitome of simple but delicious Mexican fare. There was *chicharrón* (fried pork skin) still hot from the frying vat, locally grown yellow Peruano beans (although not Peruvian) in their broth, two sauces, and a freshly made *panela* cheese. The meat, although delicious, was almost superfluous.

Farewells were prolonged as we were given cheese, a little pot of what they call *oregano de maceta*—a cultivated oregano that is used fresh, while the fragrant dried oregano of the region is collected wild—*jocoqui*, and for me 2 pounds of butter. I put off thinking how I would get it back to Mexico City the next day. We then had to stop for gas, for a large supply of that very special dried oregano and some packages of *tortitas* (page 87), a must if a friend knew you had visited Mascota.

We were finally off and starting up that dreaded track with a crumbling, unguarded edge. I tried not to look or exclaim too loudly as the opposition came hurtling down!

Somehow we arrived in record time at San Sebastián, and there, waiting for us in the central plaza, was our transit official, this time in his neatly pressed official uniform, holding up a spottily typed document. Our friends signed the paper and continued on their way, promising to freeze our perishable goods while we stayed behind in the primitive rooms of the only little rooming house in town.

JOCOQUI

Sra. Bertha Elena Moreno de Gonzalez

❁

[MAKES 5 CUPS (1.25 L)]

IN SOME PARTS OF MEXICO *JOCOQUI* REFERS TO NATURALLY SOURED CREAM— THE SAME AS THE CRÈME FRAÎCHE OF FRANCE—AND IN OTHERS IT IS yogurt. Here in Jalisco, where it is used a lot, *jocoqui* means naturally soured milk that has been drained of some of the whey.

I have never tasted such delicious *jocoqui* as that in Mascota, prepared by a young and very capable cook, Bertha Elena, or Bety. Of course, it does help to have superb raw milk straight from the morning's milking at their ranch nearby.

It may seem absurd to urbanites, or suburbanites for that matter, to include a recipe for *jocoqui*, but there is always someone who wants to know how or who can actually get raw milk and make it. The Moreno family likes to eat *jocoqui* when it is absolutely fresh, smeared onto a corn tortilla with a little salt, nothing else. When it is a day old, it is relegated to sauces, like that for *taquitos* (recipe follows).

Set 2 quarts of raw milk to sour in an unglazed clay pot or plastic container, cover loosely, and set aside in a warm place for 2 days. Skim the cream from the top and set aside in the refrigerator. Leave the milk for 2 or 3 more days, depending on the time it takes to sour and become bubbly—*se hacen bombitas* is the local expression. Skim off and discard the filmy layer that forms over the top of the milk and put the rest into a cheesecloth bag to drain.

Bety says to leave it to drain until it becomes fairly dry, like ricotta, and then beat it with a little milk and then the reserved cream. I actually left it to drain for 2 hours, which got rid of most of the whey, beat it smooth, and then beat in the reserved cream. I did not need the extra milk. It is silky smooth, pleasantly acid, and creamy.

Jocoqui substitute: Leave some not-too-sour whole-milk yogurt to drain for 3 hours, then beat with a little cream.

TACOS DE JOCOQUI

TACOS FILLED WITH CHILE STRIPS IN *JOCOQUI* SAUCE

Bertha Elena Moreno

❀

[MAKES 12 6-INCH (15.5-CM) TACOS]

THIS IS WITHOUT DOUBT ONE OF MY FAVORITE DISHES. THE FILLING IS USU-ALLY (AND MOST DELICIOUSLY) MADE WITH CHILE STRIPS AND CHEESE, although the tacos can also be filled with carrot and potato. As an alternative I suggest using the filling of various vegetables such as that for *quesadillas de verduras* from Chilapa, Guerrero (page 382).

Everything can be prepared ahead of time, but the tacos should be assembled at the last moment before baking. These tacos make an excellent main vegetarian course for four servings, a first course for six, or an accompaniment to broiled or roasted meat.

oil for frying
12 6-inch (15.5-cm) tortillas

THE SAUCE

1 pound (450 g) tomatoes, finely chopped, about 2 rounded cups (550 ml)
⅓ medium white onion, roughly chopped
1 tablespoon vegetable oil
1½ cups (375 ml) jocoqui (recipe precedes) or substitute

THE FILLING

10 ounces (285 g) queso fresco, panela, or Muenster, cut into strips
1½ cups (375 ml) rajas of poblano chile,
fried with a little onion (see The Art of Mexican Cooking*)*

Have ready a well-greased ovenproof dish, or dishes, into which the tacos will just fit in one layer—2 ovenproof glass 8-inch (20-cm) square dishes are just right.

Put the tomatoes and onions in a blender and puree. Heat the oil in a skillet, add the sauce, and cook, stirring and scraping the bottom of the pan to prevent sticking from time to time, until the juice has been reduced and the sauce begins to sizzle around the edges of the pan— about 4 minutes. Transfer to the blender, add the *jocoqui*, and blend until smooth.

Heat the oven to 375°F (190°C).

In another skillet, heat a little oil, just enough to cover the surface of the pan, and fry each tortilla lightly, just to soften; they should not be crisp around the edges. Blot on paper toweling. Put a few strips of cheese and plenty of chile strips along the center, roll the tortillas loosely, and set aside in the prepared dishes. Pour the sauce as evenly as possible over the top of the tacos (decorate if desired with some of the chile strips and/or cheese), lightly cover with foil, and bake until the sauce is bubbling and the filling heated through (stick a clean finger in to test)—about 15 minutes. Serve immediately.

BIRRIA ESTILO MASCOTA

Familia Moreno

☼

[SERVES 12]

AFTER TRAVELING EXTENSIVELY IN JALISCO AND PART OF NAYARIT, ONE TENDS TO BECOME HEARTILY TIRED OF THE SOUPY, STRINGY MEAT THAT passes for *birria* in most little restaurants and *cenadurías*, supper places, so it was with some reluctance that I talked about *birria* with the Moreno family. Then I found myself writing it down with enthusiasm.

They use various meats for their *birria*, depending on which one is most plentiful at the time—mutton, pork, beef, even chicken. After a long steaming, which means you have a delicious broth, the meat is then given a brief roasting in the oven to give it a more appetizing appearance and improve its texture and flavor.

Rice is usually served first in this meal, then the meat in shallow bowls with plenty of the broth topped with finely shredded cabbage and chopped onion. A very hot sauce of *chile de árbol* is served separately, and afterward some *frijoles de olla*. If you have any of the broth left over, it makes a delicious, rich soup.

A stew like *birria* has to be made in fairly large quantities so that you have rich broth. The cuts of meat should include some bone and fat—you can always skim the fat off afterward. I like to use beef brisket, breast of lamb or mutton, or pork shoulder. I find the taste of goat too strong, and chicken falls apart too quickly without absorbing the flavors.

Start this recipe a day ahead.

THE SEASONING PASTE

4 ancho chiles, veins and seeds removed

*1 cup (250 ml) pineapple vinegar or ½ cup (125 ml) wine vinegar and
½ cup (125 ml) rice vinegar*

4 garlic cloves, roughly chopped

4 1½-inch (4-cm) cinnamon sticks

½ teaspoon cumin seeds, crushed

[CONTINUED]

½ teaspoon peppercorns, crushed

2 teaspoons dried oregano, crumbled

*1½ ounces (45 g/½ small round tablet) Mexican drinking chocolate,
crumbled*

salt to taste

THE MEAT

*6½ pounds (3 kg) meat such as brisket (see note above),
cut into large pieces*

FOR THE BROTH

1 pound (450 g) tomatoes

TO SERVE

finely shredded cabbage

finely chopped white onion

lime quarters

sauce for birria *(recipe follows)*

Start one day ahead.

Cover the ancho chiles with hot water in a saucepan, simmer for 5 minutes, and set aside to soak for 5 minutes more. Drain.

Put the vinegar into a blender, add the garlic, spices, and oregano, and blend until smooth. Gradually add the chiles and chocolate and blend until smooth—you may need to add a little water to release the blender blade, but do not dilute too much because the loose paste should coat the meat well. Add plenty of salt and coat the pieces of meat. Cover and leave in a cool place or in the bottom of the refrigerator overnight.

Prepare a *tamale* steamer (page 522), or improvise one with a rack that stands about 4 inches (10 cm) above the water line. Fill the bottom with about 2 quarts (2 l) water. Set the pieces of meat into the top of the steamer and cover tightly with plastic wrap so very little steam can escape. Steam the meat until tender but not too soft—about 4 hours. Put some small coins in the water; as they cease rattling around, add more boiling water.

Heat the oven to 400°F (205°C). Transfer the meat to a roasting pan and roast for about 30 minutes, turning it over once, or until the meat is shiny and slightly crusty.

Meanwhile, cook the whole tomatoes in the broth from the bottom of the steamer, transfer to the blender, and blend until smooth. Return to the broth and heat through.

Serve the *birria* with the toppings (see note above). Any leftover meat can be used shredded for tacos or as a topping for *tostadas* and the broth served as a soup.

SALSA PARA BIRRIA

SAUCE FOR BIRRIA

Mascota, Jalisco

✺

[MAKES ABOUT ½ CUP (125 ML)]

THIS SAUCE IS SERVED AS A CONDIMENT WITH BIRRIA. IT IS VERY HOT INDEED, THIN AND BRILLIANT RED. IT IS BEST LEFT TO SEASON FOR A FEW hours before serving.

20 chiles de árbol
½ cup (125 ml) mild vinegar or half rice vinegar and half wine vinegar
scant ½ teaspoon dried oregano, crumbled
2 garlic cloves, roughly chopped
4 peppercorns, crushed
salt to taste

Cover the chiles with water in a saucepan, bring to a simmer, and continue simmering for about 10 minutes. Set aside to soak for 10 more minutes. Drain and discard the water. Remove the stems and tear the chiles with seeds into small pieces.

Add the chiles to a blender along with the vinegar and blend as smooth as possible. Gradually add the oregano, garlic, and peppercorns, and blend again.

Transfer the sauce to a nonreactive bowl, pressing it through a fine strainer to extract as much of the juice as possible. Stir in salt to taste and set aside to season for a few hours.

CHILAQUILES

Sra. Carolina de López, Mascota

❋

[SERVES 4]

THE SAUCE

12 ounces (340 g) tomatoes

4 chiles de árbol, lightly toasted in a dry skillet

1 tablespoon vegetable oil

salt to taste

THE CHILAQUILES

approximately ¼ cup (63 ml) vegetable oil

*6 5-inch (13-cm) tortillas, cut into 1-inch (2.5-cm) squares
and left to dry overnight*

4 eggs

salt to taste

FOR THE TOPPING

⅓ cup (83 ml) finely chopped white onion

*1 cup (250 ml) loosely packed grated Muenster or crumbled queso fresco
(in Jalisco, adobera)*

1 scant teaspoon crumbled dried oregano

For the sauce: Cover the tomatoes with water in a saucepan and bring to a simmer. Continue simmering until soft right through but not falling apart, about 10 minutes. Drain and transfer to a blender. Crumble the toasted chiles in with the tomatoes and blend until smooth. Heat the tablespoon of oil in a skillet, add the sauce with salt, and fry over medium heat until reduced and seasoned, about 3 minutes. Set aside.

For the chilaquiles: Heat a little of the oil in a skillet and add a few pieces of tortilla. Fry until golden and partially crisp (do not crowd the pan). Transfer with a slotted spoon to a strainer, shake off any excess oil, and then drain on paper toweling. Continue with the rest of the pieces, adding a little oil as necessary.

Beat the eggs lightly with salt to taste. Drain off all but 2 tablespoons of oil from the pan in which the tortillas were fried. Return the tortilla pieces to the pan, then pour the eggs over them and stir until the eggs are just set.

To serve: Stir in the tomato sauce and mix well, stirring continuously for about 3 minutes. Turn the chilaquiles out onto a warmed serving dish, sprinkle the onion, cheese, and oregano over the top, and serve immediately.

HONGOS GUISADOS CON YERBABUENA

MUSHROOMS COOKED WITH MINT

Sra. Carolina de López

✺

[MAKES APPROXIMATELY 2 CUPS (500 ML)]

ALTHOUGH WILD MUSHROOMS ARE USED FOR THIS RECIPE, CULTIVATED ONES —EITHER OYSTER OR SHIITAKE—MAY BE SUBSTITUTED. BUTTER IS USED IN Mascota, but I prefer to use half butter and half vegetable oil.

A whole clove of garlic is always added when cooking wild mushrooms in Mexico. If it discolors badly, then there is a poisonous mushroom among them; pitch them out.

> 2 tablespoons vegetable oil
> 2 tablespoons unsalted butter
> ¼ cup (63 ml) finely chopped white onion
> 3 serrano chiles or to taste, finely chopped
> 1 garlic clove if using wild mushrooms (see note above)
> salt to taste
> 4 ounces (115 g) tomatoes, finely chopped, about ⅔ cup (164 ml)
> 1 pound (450 g) wild, oyster, or shiitake mushrooms,
> wiped clean and thinly sliced
> 2 tablespoons roughly chopped mint leaves

Heat the oil and butter in a heavy skillet. Add the onion, chiles, garlic, and a sprinkle of salt. Cook over low heat for about 1 minute without browning. Add the tomatoes and continue

[CONTINUED]

cooking over medium heat until the juice has been absorbed—about 3 minutes. Add the mushrooms and cook, adding more salt if necessary until they are well cooked through and well seasoned, stirring in the mint after 5 minutes and continuing to cook for another 5 minutes. Cover and set aside for about 10 minutes before serving.

TORTITAS DE REGALO

GIFT COOKIES

Sra. Carolina de López

❋

[MAKES 40 SMALL COOKIES]

THESE SHORT AND SUGARY LITTLE COOKIES ARE A GREAT FAVORITE IN MAS-COTA. PORK LARD IS USED ABUNDANTLY HERE, AND IT IS INDISPENSABLE FOR the correct texture and flavor. The cookies are cut out with a circular, fluted cutter and then cut in half again. Once baked, they're coated with a seven-minute frosting.

The cookies keep very well stored in an airtight container.

THE DOUGH

½ cup (125 ml) water

¼ teaspoon anise seeds

8 ounces (225 g) all-purpose flour, about 2 scant cups (450 ml)

1 teaspoon baking powder

5 ounces (140 g) sugar, about ½ cup plus 2 tablespoons (135 ml)

¼ teaspoon salt

3½ ounces (100 g) pork lard, about ⅓ cup plus 2 tablespoons (115 ml)

1 egg yolk, lightly beaten with ½ egg white

THE FROSTING

½ cup (125 ml) sugar

1 egg white

⅛ teaspoon cream of tartar

2 tablespoons cold water

¼ teaspoon vanilla extract or ½ tablespoon fresh lime juice

Put the water into a small saucepan, add the anise seeds, and simmer for about 5 minutes. Set aside to cool. Mix the flour with the baking powder, 5 ounces (140 g) sugar, and salt. Lightly rub in the lard with the tips of your fingers, then stir in the beaten egg with a metal spoon. Moisten the dough with about ¼ cup (63 ml) of the strained anise water and mix until you have a malleable but not too soft dough. Add a little more water if necessary.

Heat the oven to 350°F (177°C). (If the weather is hot and the dough unmanageable, refrigerate it for an hour or so.) Roll out the dough ¼ inch (7 mm) thick and cut to the desired shape, about 2½ inches (6.5 cm) in diameter. Carefully transfer the cookies to ungreased sheets and bake to a pale golden color—about 15 minutes Allow to cool a little before transferring to a wire rack to cool off completely and become crisp.

To prepare the frosting, put all the ingredients into a double-boiler and stir well. When the sugar has dissolved, beat the mixture over medium heat for about 7 minutes. Coat the cookies with the frosting and decorate as desired.

ROLLOS DE MANGO VERDE

GREEN MANGO ROLL

Mascota

❋

[MAKES 4 10-INCH (25-CM) MANGO PASTE ROLLS]

OF ALL THE FRUIT CONFECTIONS I HAVE COOKED AND EATEN IN MEXICO, THIS TOPS THE LIST. IT WAS ONE OF THOSE SURPRISES THAT I WAS LED TO BY my friend Violet, who has known about the Mascota sweetmeats for many years.

I dedicate this recipe to my fans, who I know will search out the meanest-looking, hard little green mangoes in Latin American fruit stores and make this delectable fruit paste. You are aiming at about four sheets of fruit paste just less than ¼ inch (7 mm) thick—any thicker, and they will break when you roll them. If this happens, cut the paste into squares and just dust with sugar; nobody will know the difference.

6 pounds (2.7 kg) green mangoes
1¾ pounds (800 g) granulated sugar, just over 3½ cups (875 ml)
¼ cup (63 ml) fresh lime juice
confectioners' or fine granulated sugar for dusting

Have ready 4 cookie sheets measuring at least 10 by 8 inches (25 by 20 cm).

Peel the mangoes, taking care to remove all the tough skin, and put into the top of a steamer. Cover tightly and cook until the flesh is perfectly soft—about 25 minutes (some of the mangoes may burst open and resemble mashed potato). Set aside to cool.

When cool enough to handle, scrape all the flesh from the pits and put into a food processor. Process to a smooth pulp—a few slightly harder pieces will always remain—adding a little water only if necessary.

Now weigh or measure the pulp; there should be about 3 pounds (1.35 kg)—yes, believe it or not!—or about 5¾ cups (1.44 l). Put the pulp in a very heavy pan along with the granulated sugar and the lime juice and stir over low heat until the sugar has melted. Increase the heat until the mixture begins to bubble and continue cooking for exactly 20 minutes, making sure that you continue stirring and scraping the bottom of the pan because these dense mixtures scorch easily.

Sprinkle the surface of the cookie sheets with water and tip them to drain off any excess water. Spread the mixture out to about 3/16 inch (5 mm), and set aside to cool and dry over the next few days. The drying time will vary, depending on your climate. In Arizona it will take about 3 days to become a rather tough sheet and in damper climates up to 7 to 9 days.

Sprinkle the confectioners' sugar on both sides of the paste and roll loosely so that you have four rolls, each 10 inches (25 cm) long.

When serving this paste, slice through the roll at ¼-inch (7-mm) intervals—thinner if you want to decorate a dessert with shreds of the paste, which will now have a yellow-greenish tone.

TURCO

[SERVES 12 TO 16]

THE *DICCIONARIO DE COCINA* SIMPLY SAYS OF *TURCO*: "A TIMBAL OF CORN." IT IS IN FACT A TYPE OF PIE WITH A THICK CRUST THAT CAN BE MADE OF CORN *masa*, chickpeas, or rice, either sweet or savory and often with filling. This recipe, given to me in Mascota, Jalisco, is made with a semisweet flour dough with a thin layer of savory stuffing in the middle. It is served either as part of the main course or, more often than not, with the desserts.

My friend María Dolores, whose mother came from Sonora, has the family *turco* mold shaped like a turban. Now for easy serving on festive occasions it is more prosaically presented in a large glass or other ovenproof dish. Turco is a sine qua non for weddings and baptisms in particular.

I am afraid I find it rather boring and have been known to serve it with tomato sauce and strips of pickled jalapeño, much to the chagrin of my traditional friends from Jalisco.

THE FILLING

12 ounces (340 g) ground stewing pork with a little fat

salt to taste

6 ounces (180 g) tomates verdes, *about 7 medium, husks removed,
rinsed, and finely chopped*

⅓ cup (83 ml) finely chopped white onion

½-inch (13-mm) cinnamon stick

4 peppercorns

½ teaspoon dried oregano, crumbled

4 ounces (115 g) potatoes, cooked, peeled, and roughly mashed,
about 1 scant cup (240 ml)

2 tablespoons raisins

[CONTINUED]

½ cup (125 ml) water

6 ounces (180 g) grated piloncillo or dark brown sugar, about 1 cup

4 eggs

4 egg yolks

14 ounces (400 g) lard, 1¾ cups (438 ml)

2 pounds (900 g) all-purpose flour, about 7 cups (1.75 l)

2 teaspoons baking powder

¼ teaspoon baking soda

approximately ½ teaspoon salt

4 ounces (115 g) granulated sugar, ½ cup (125 ml)

Have ready an ovenproof dish, ideally 13 by 9 inches (33 by 23 cm) and at least 2½ to 3 inches (6.5 to 8 cm) deep.

Put the pork into a heavy skillet, sprinkle with salt, and set over low heat until the moisture from the meat has been absorbed and the fat rendered out. Add the rest of the ingredients and continue cooking over medium heat until well seasoned—15 minutes. Adjust the salt and set the filling aside to cool before using.

Put the water to heat in a small pan, stir in the *piloncillo*, and continue stirring until it has dissolved. Set aside to cool and then strain.

Heat the oven to 350°F (177°C).

Beat the eggs and yolks together lightly and add with the lard to the syrup.

Sift together the flour, baking powder, soda, and salt and stir in the egg mixture. Form the dough into a cohesive mass with the tips of your fingers and divide it into 2 parts. Roll each piece lightly into the shape of the dish. Spread one along the bottom and cover with an even layer of the filling, then cover with the other half of the dough and sprinkle the top with the granulated sugar. Bake until spongy to the touch and browned on top—about 45 minutes to 1 hour. It is best served soon after it has been baked.

GORDAS DE HARINA

Sra. Carolina de López

❁

[MAKES 40 5-INCH (13-CM) COOKIES]

GORDAS—FAT ONES—IS A STRANGE NAME FOR THESE WAFERLIKE DISKS THAT ARE SERVED WITH COFFEE. SEÑORA CAROLINA SAYS THAT AFTER MUCH experimenting she finds that the three fats are best to use in this recipe, since each one contributes to the flavor or consistency.

It is best to cook *gordas* very slowly—on an iron griddle, or better still soapstone, rather than a thin *comal*. These *gordas* keep well if stored in an airtight container in a cool place.

2½ ounces (75 g) vegetable shortening, about ⅓ cup (83 ml)
2½ ounces (75 g) pork lard, about ⅓ cup plus 2 teaspoons (93 ml)
2½ ounces (75 g) natas, about a scant ⅓ cup (81 ml) or
5 tablespoons unsalted butter
½ cup (125 ml) sugar
4 teaspoons salt
2 large eggs
1 pound (450 g) all-purpose flour

Cream the fats together well and gradually beat in the sugar, salt, and eggs with 1 tablespoon of the flour. Gradually work in the remaining flour and mix to a soft, malleable consistency. Divide the dough into about 40 balls about 1¼ inches (3 cm) in diameter and cover them loosely with plastic wrap while you work with a few at a time.

Line a tortilla press with plastic baggies and proceed as if you were going to make tortillas. Flatten one ball of the dough out to about 5 inches (13 cm) in diameter, lift off the top baggie, place the dough (still on the second baggie) on the inside of your hand, and carefully lay the dough onto a warm griddle. The heat should be low at all times so that the fat in the dough does not scorch. Cook until the underside is mottled with light golden brown—about 5 minutes. (The second side is never as attractive as the first, so don't expose it when serving the *gordas*.) Cool on a rack so that they become quite crisp.

AREPAS

[MAKES 16 3-INCH (8-CM) COOKIES]

AREPAS IN MASCOTA ARE CRISP, SEMISWEET STAR-SHAPED COOKIES SERVED WITH COFFEE AT EITHER BREAKFAST OR SUPPERTIME. TRADITIONALLY THEY are baked in a wood oven, which of course gives a very special texture and flavor. But they are still very good cooked in a domestic oven.

½ cup (125 ml) water

peel of 1 orange

6 ounces (180 g) grated piloncillo or dark brown sugar, 1 cup (250 ml)
firmly packed

2 ounces (60 g) vegetable shortening, ⅓ cup (83 ml)

a scant 4 ounces (115 g) pork lard, a scant ½ cup (115 ml)

¾ teaspoon baking powder

½ teaspoon baking soda

¼ teaspoon salt

2 tablespoons fresh lime juice

2 eggs, lightly beaten

1½ pounds (675 g) all-purpose flour, about 5½ cups (1.375 l)

THE GLAZE

1 egg yolk

1 tablespoon milk

⅓ cup (83 ml) granulated sugar

Put the water into a saucepan with the orange peel and brown sugar. Cook over medium heat, stirring, until the sugar has completely melted. Continue boiling until the mixture starts to thicken and forms a thin thread when dropped from a spoon. Stir in the fats and set aside to cool a little. Don't worry if the sugar stiffens; it will dissolve when beaten with the other ingredients.

When cool, add the baking powder and soda, salt, lime juice, and eggs with 1 tablespoon of the flour. Beat well, then stir in—do not beat in—the flour and work the dough with your hands to a stiff cohesive mass. Add a little water if necessary to obtain this texture.

Have ready 2 ungreased baking sheets. Heat the oven to 350°F (177°C).

Flatten the dough onto a lightly floured board to just over ¼ inch (7 mm) thick. Cut out the cookies with a star- or flower-shaped cutter about 3 inches (8 cm) across and set about 1 inch (2.5 cm) apart (they do not spread much) on the cookie sheets. Beat the egg yolk and milk together and brush over the top of the *arepas*. Sprinkle with the granulated sugar and bake until crisp and lightly browned—25 to 35 minutes. Cool on a rack. *Arepas* keep very well in an airtight container.

SALSA DE LIMA AGRIA

SOUR LIMA SAUCE

✸

[MAKES ABOUT 2 CUPS (500 ML)]

THE SOUR *LIMA* (A CITRIC FRUIT AS SHARP AS ITS NAME) LENDS ITS UNIQUE FLAVOR TO THE TRADITIONAL YUCATECAN *SOPA DE LIMA* AND ALSO ACCOM-panies the red *mole* of Chilapa, Guerrero. I was surprised to come across it in this part of Jalisco and in a quite different form: the flesh and juice combined with other ingredients are used in a very refreshing, acidy relish. Here it is served with *pacholas* (see *The Art of Mexican Cooking*), thin "steaks" of ground beef, and many of the other local dishes.

Given time, I am sure that some enterprising person will either import or grow this sour *lima* in the United States, but meanwhile I suggest a not-too-sweet white grapefruit with lime juice as a substitute. I have tried it, and it is very good.

3 whole limas, *peeled and segments cleaned from the pithy skin,*
or 1 cup (250 ml) cleaned grapefruit segments
¼ cup (63 ml) juice of limas *or fresh lime juice*
¼ cup (63 ml) pineapple vinegar or rice vinegar
1 teaspoon salt or to taste
2 tablespoons sugar

[CONTINUED]

⅓ cup (83 ml) finely chopped white onion

½ teaspoon dried oregano, crumbled

2 jalapeño chiles en escabeche, finely diced

2 tablespoons juice from canned chiles

1¼ cups (313 ml) finely diced cucumber with seeds and inner pulp

Mix all the ingredients together and allow to stand for about 10 minutes before serving.

ENCHILADAS DE MASCOTA

Sra. Carolina de López

✸

[MAKES 12 ENCHILADAS]

THESE ENCHILADAS ARE USUALLY SERVED WITH A SALSA DE LIMA AGRIA (PAGE 94), A PERFECT FOIL FOR THE MILD SAUCE. IF YOU DON'T HAVE THE SALSA prepared, then substitute jalapeños *en escabeche.*

THE SAUCE

1 large ancho chile, veins and seeds removed

10 dried prunes, pitted

1 to 1¼ cups (250 to 313 ml) water

4 ounces (115 g) tomatoes, simmered until soft, about 10 minutes

1½ ounces (45 g) Mexican drinking chocolate

¼-inch (scant 1-cm) cinnamon stick

1 slice white onion, roughly chopped

2 tablespoons mild vinegar or half rice vinegar and half wine vinegar

salt to taste

1 tablespoon sesame seeds, lightly toasted

THE TORTILLAS

approximately ½ cup (125 ml) vegetable oil for frying

12 5-inch (13-cm) corn tortillas

THE FILLING

¾ cup (188 ml) finely chopped white onion
1½ cups (375 ml) finely crumbled queso fresco or substitute (page 525)
½ teaspoon dried oregano, finely crumbled

Cover the chile and prunes with hot water in a saucepan and simmer for 5 minutes. Set aside to soak for 10 more minutes. Drain. Put 1 cup (250 ml) of the water into a blender, add the chile torn into pieces, the prunes, and the rest of the ingredients and blend until smooth, adding water as necessary to release the blender blade. The sauce should be of medium consistency and cover a tortilla well. Add more water to dilute if necessary. Have ready a warmed serving dish.

Heat a little oil in the bottom of a skillet, dip one of the tortillas into the raw sauce, and fry for a few seconds on both sides. Hold the *enchilada* over the pan for a few seconds for the excess oil to run off (you can't drain on paper toweling, or the sauce will adhere to the paper). Fill with 1 tablespoon of the onion, 2 tablespoons of the cheese, and a sprinkle of oregano, sprinkle with salt if necessary, roll the *enchilada* up loosely, and place on the serving dish. Continue with the rest of the tortillas.

If you have any leftover sauce, dilute with a little water, bring to a boil in the skillet, and pour over the enchiladas. Sprinkle the top with the remaining cheese and onion and serve immediately.

ALTERNATE METHOD: Heat the *enchiladas* in a 375°F (190°C) oven for about 10 minutes, no longer, and then serve.

SAN SEBASTIÁN

"San Sebastián, legendary in the past: famous yesterday and forgotten today." ". . . crowned with pine-covered hills, the silence is only broken by the murmuring of the streams in the rains and the warbling of blackbirds, mockingbirds, thrush and finch that welcome the dawn and say farewell to the day; the orange trees and coffee bushes perfume the air with their flowers in May and June."

A priest wrote that in a little book in which he had collected historical notes from the town's archives. His love for nature was evident as well in the patio of the house that he had occupied until fairly recently: it was alive with flowers. It must have been a sad blow for him and his parishioners when after fifteen years he was sent off to another church, some distance away.

Indeed the town does seem forgotten today except for the few devotees from Puerto Vallarta who come at weekends to the cool of the mountains and stay within those white walls and under the tiled roofs that by local law cannot be changed. Most of the young and able-bodied men and women go elsewhere to work, and those who arrive from the ranches around buy supplies and hurry away.

We were fascinated by the largest and most active of the stores that carry a miscellany of goods from rope, candles, axes, cookies, and sugar bulging from bags, boxes, and string bundles that cover the walls in total disarray. There is one refrigerator full to bursting with soft drinks with some local cheeses stuffed in between the bottles as an afterthought. Near a basket of disintegrating dried chiles, and almost concealed, are large cubes of the most delicious crab apple *cajeta* brought in from the small nearby communities that still exist despite the closing of the mines. They live off their land, their fruit trees, a few cows, and a patch of corn and beans. There were boxes of oranges, tomatoes, and onions softly moldering by the door.

Surprisingly, there are two dress stores with very up-to-date models, one owned by the couple who helped cause the crash (page 77), the other housing the only telephone where idlers sit around eavesdropping, hoping for a juicy bit of gossip.

Magnificent tortillas were the saving grace of the meal we ate that day of chicken in *pipián* in a little restaurant, or rather kitchen, that had been recommended to us. We had been directed to a house set on a steep rise not far from the center. We were seated on the balcony at an improvised table of wooden boards against the wall of the house with our backs to the magnificent view across to the west. The hardworking owner was enthusiastic enough about what she was doing, but even the beans were insipid. She did not have *sazón*, we concluded, despite the appetizing aromas coming from the pots on her hand-formed *adobe*, wood-burning stove.

Sra. Soledad, the owner of the small *posada* where we had left our luggage, was sitting on her terrace overlooking the main plaza when we returned. We gave her a report on what we had eaten. She took us into her kitchen, which was appetizingly cluttered with large pans of milk sitting around simmering or souring for *jocoqui* or the cheese most favored in that area, *panela*. She let us try the rich, thick soured cream on a tortilla and shared two of her recipes with me: rice with chile and *panela* and a roll of pork, both of which follow. She spends a lot of time in her kitchen (when she is not in church), sending a steady supply of her local specialties to her daughter, who works in Guadalajara. The stories of her life, of her family and the neighbors would make fascinating material for a nonsuburban soap opera, with the changes she has witnessed there through good, but many more bad, times.

Before leaving the next day we went to look up the woman who is renowned for her *cajetas* and rolls of fruit pastes. Part of her porch was piled high with *tejocotes*, a type of crab apple, that had just been picked. More were cooking with sugar in huge pots on the stove, and the first batches, in brick shapes or from molds in the form of small pumpkins, were drying out in the sun. Left alone in the world, she ekes out a living making these sweetmeats, working a greater part of the year as each type of fruit is harvested. We bought as much as we could carry and were just about to leave when our chauffeur arrived from Puerto Vallarta.

The transit official came to wish us well, Sra. Soledad waved us good-bye, even our crash victims managed a salute. We had been quite ready to leave but as we swerved down toward the coast we knew we would be back, just to make sure it hadn't been all a dream—this San Sebastián, a ghost of its former self.

As the priest, Gabriel Pulido, wrote in his little book: "Guadalajara had its eyes fixed on you in Viceregal times [for the riches of its mines]. Today it does not even know you, nor who you are, nor where you are."

ARROZ BLANCO CON RAJAS Y PANELA

WHITE RICE WITH CHILE STRIPS AND *PANELA* CHEESE

Sra. Soledad García Ríos

✹

[SERVES 4]

1 cup (250 ml) long-grain white rice, not precooked or unconverted

¼ cup (63 ml) vegetable oil

salt to taste

¼ white onion, roughly sliced

1½ cups (375 ml) water

½ cup (125 ml) milk

2 poblano chiles, charred, peeled, veins and seeds removed, and
cut into narrow strips

4 ounces (115 g) queso panela or Muenster, thinly sliced

Cover the rice with hot water, rinse well in cold water, and shake off all the excess liquid. Heat the oil in a heavy casserole, stir in the rice so that it becomes well covered with the oil, sprinkle with salt, and fry for about 5 minutes. Stir in the onion and continue frying until the rice sounds brittle. Before it browns, drain off the excess oil (use it for another batch of rice, for example). Add the water and milk and stir in the chile strips.

Cook uncovered over medium heat until all the water has been absorbed and holes appear in the surface of the rice. Cover, lower the heat, and cook for about 5 minutes more or until the rice is tender. Set the rice aside for 15 more minutes to absorb all the moist steam and expand. Cover the surface with the cheese and gently heat through (better in the oven) until the cheese has melted.

LOMO RELLENO

STUFFED PORK ROLL

Sra. Soledad García Ríos

✸

[SERVES 6]

SRA. SOLEDAD DOES THE FIRST STAGE OF THE COOKING IN A PRESSURE COOKER TO RETAIN THE MOISTURE IN THE MEAT, SINCE THE LOIN TENDS TO be compact and rather dry. However, you can use a heavy pot with tight lid. Have your butcher, preferably a Mexican one who will understand what this is all about, make a thin sheet, *cecina*, out of the boned loin. One pound should be about 8 inches (20 cm) of the loin. I find it easier to make two smaller rolls each 8 inches long, so divide the meat in two.

*1 pound boneless pork loin, butterflied and cut into 2 8-inch-wide
(20-cm-wide) pieces*

salt to taste

freshly ground black pepper to taste

2 tablespoons mild vinegar

1 cup (250 ml) water

THE FILLING

8 ounces (225 g) chorizo, skinned and crumbled

*8 ounces (225 g) potatoes, cooked, peeled, and roughly mashed,
about 1 scant cup (240 ml)*

½ medium white onion, finely chopped

salt to taste

1 egg, lightly beaten

THE SAUCE

3 ancho chiles, veins and seeds removed

2 cups (500 ml) water

½ cup (125 ml) mild vinegar

1 garlic clove, roughly chopped

2 peppercorns

[CONTINUED]

1 clove, crushed

⅛ teaspoon cumin seeds

¼ teaspoon dried oregano, crumbled

2 tablespoons sesame seeds, toasted in a dry pan

1 small slice French bread

2 tablespoons lard or vegetable oil

Season the pork on both sides, sprinkle with the vinegar, roll each piece up, and set aside to season for 1 hour. Meanwhile, prepare the filling: Put the *chorizo* into a skillet and cook over low heat until all the fat has rendered out. Discard all but 2 tablespoons of the fat. Stir in the potatoes and onion and cook over low heat for about 2 minutes. Add salt as necessary. Set aside to cool and then mix with the beaten egg. You should have about 2½ cups (625 ml).

Divide the filling into half and spread each of the pieces of meat with it. Roll each piece of meat and tie firmly—but not too tightly or the stuffing will extrude.

If not using a pressure cooker, place the meat in a heavy pan, closely seal the lid, and cook over low heat, shaking the pot from time to time, for about 45 minutes. The meat should be just tender.

Meanwhile, make the sauce: Put the chiles and 1 cup (250 ml) of the water plus the vinegar into a small pan, bring to a simmer, and cook for 5 minutes. Set aside to soak for 5 more minutes. Put ½ cup (125 ml) of the water into a blender, add the garlic, spices, oregano, and sesame seeds, and blend as smoothly as possible. Add the remaining ½ cup (125 ml) water, a few of the chiles, and the bread and blend until fairly smooth. Add the remaining chiles and again blend as smooth as possible. The sauce should be thick—don't dilute further unless absolutely necessary to release the blender blade.

Remove the meat from the broth, reserving the broth for the sauce. Heat the lard in a heavy casserole, add the meat rolls, and brown them lightly, rolling them over from time to time. Add the sauce and reduce over fairly high heat, scraping the bottom of the pan to prevent sticking, then add the reserved broth and continue cooking over fairly high heat, adding salt as necessary until the meat has absorbed the flavors of the sauce—about 15 minutes. Remove the string, slice the meat, and serve with plenty of the sauce.

A JOURNEY NORTH:
THE BAJÍO TO
THE NORTHERN PLAINS

❋

Tuna (prickly pear)

GUANAJUATO, SAN MIGUEL DE ALLENDE, COMONFORT

LAST FALL THE TIME HAD FINALLY ARRIVED WHEN I COULD ACCEPT A LONG-STANDING INVITATION TO VISIT THE CATTLE RANCH OF SOME FRIENDS OF MINE IN CHIHUAHUA. I SET OFF IN the last days of September, when the countryside is at its most glorious after the rains, stopping off in Guanajuato and Aguascalientes, in the very center of Mexico, the Bajío, and finally through Coahuila to Chihuahua. ☀ I had made the first part of this journey several times in recent years, but there is always something more to discover: another regional cook, a new recipe, or something I had not seen before in the markets. ☀ It was a four-hour drive to my first stop, Comonfort, across the agricultural heart of Michoacán and the State of Guanajuato. It took me through many little towns: Maravatío, with its elegant little theater, now a relic of the past, and its beautifully proportioned central plaza; Acámbaro, which developed around a Franciscan monastery built in 1526 and later flourished with the coming of the railroads; and Salvatierra, a stopping point for the heavy trucks that ply the route between Celaya and Morelia. Not so many years ago, when my journeys to San Miguel de Allende were more frequent, I enjoyed this tranquil journey, fascinated by the scenes of activity in these small agricultural centers where people from the countryside converged with their produce. But now it is the same chaotic traffic scene one meets throughout the larger regional towns of Mexico, with few exceptions. ☀ I always breathe a sigh of relief as I head out into the country once more, wondering at what point some sanity and order will return and reverse the ever-present noise and pollution here and in the world at large. ☀ San Miguel and Comonfort lie directly to the north of Celaya, and one has to drive right through it. Traffic is slow, giving one time to admire the order and lushness of the central *jardín* bordered by dense *laureles de la India* (a type of bay), which provide shelter for the shoe-shiners and the men idling away the hours on the rococo metal benches. ☀ It is here in Celaya that the architect Francisco Eduardo Tresguerras was born in 1759; he was renowned for his stylized churches, especially altars. If I have time to stop, I often wander into the churches of San Francisco and Nuestra Señora del Carmen. ☀ Celaya is an important agricultural center and famous to many outsiders for its *cajeta de Celaya*, a thick caramelized confection made partially with goat's milk. ☀ My first stop was for lunch at a friend's ranch a few kilometers to the west of Comonfort. The land borders an extensive valley given over to intensive agriculture, much of the produce destined for markets in the United States. The area has been claimed, with the help of irrigation, from the scrubby, natural wilderness still evident in the low hills behind the ranch. When I was there, the black soil was spiked with green, the tender shoots of onions and garlic and brilliant green stretches of *cilantro* perfuming the air.

A group of ladies who meet weekly to discuss various topics—among them, of course, food and recipes—had been invited. Each had brought along a local dish for the abundant *botana* to accompany the drinks. It was more than enough for a complete meal, but I had been forewarned that there was *pozolillo* (a *pozole* made with fresh corn) to follow as the main course. There were *papas locas*, small, unpeeled new potatoes cooked with onions and olive oil and seasoned with lime juice and *chile de árbol*. Our host offered red-ripened poblano chiles —charred, peeled, and cooked with a lot of onion—and was particularly proud he had grown the chiles right there and invented the dish. There was a bowl of well-seasoned mushrooms, *chicharrón*, and a wonderfully refreshing guacamole made with seasonal, local fruits. Although the quince trees around the house were in season, not one had been left by the workers, who have a passion for the raw fruit sprinkled with the extremely picante *chile de árbol*. The very thought of it makes most people's mouths pucker!

GUACAMOLE CHAMACUERO

Sra. Leticia Sánchez, Comonfort, Guanajuato

❋

[MAKES APPROXIMATELY 3 CUPS]

BETWEEN CELAYA AND SAN MIGUEL DE ALLENDE LIES THE LITTLE TOWN OF COMONFORT, FORMERLY KNOWN AS CHAMACUERO AND RENAMED AFTER THE former Mexican president Comonfort, who died in the area.

This unusual *guacamole* is an old family recipe given to me by Sra. Sánchez. It is made in late summer and fall, when the peaches, grapes, and pomegranates are ripe in the local orchards. This *guacamole* lends itself to many inauthentic innovations.

2 heaped tablespoons finely chopped white onion
2 to 3 serrano chiles, finely chopped
salt to taste
2 cups (500 ml) roughly crushed avocado pulp

¾ cup (188 ml) peeled and finely diced firm but ripe peaches
½ cup (125 ml) halved seedless grapes
1½ tablespoons fresh lime juice
⅓ cup (83 ml) pomegranate seeds

Crush the onion, chiles, and salt together to a paste. Stir in the avocado pulp, peaches, grapes, lime juice, and half the pomegranate seeds. Mix well, sprinkle the surface with the remaining seeds, and serve at room temperature.

BOTANA DE PAPAS LOCAS

"CRAZY" POTATO SNACK

✺

[MAKES 1 POUND]

ALTHOUGH SMALL RED-SKINNED POTATOES WERE SERVED THAT DAY AT THE RANCH, THE WORD *LOCA* REFERS TO THE VERY SMALL, LIGHT-SKINNED POTA-toes that grow wild in the hills in the northern part of the Bajío: Zacatecas, San Luis Potosí, and part of Guanajuato.

1 pound (450 g) very small new potatoes
salt to taste
¼ cup (63 ml) mild vinegar
¼ cup (63 ml) olive oil
2 medium white onions, thinly sliced
2 teaspoons powdered chile de árbol or pulla
3 tablespoons fresh lime juice

Put the potatoes into a heavy pan, cover with water, add salt and vinegar, bring to a boil, and cook covered over medium heat until just tender—about 20 minutes. Drain.

Heat the olive oil in a skillet, add the potatoes, and fry until slightly browned—about 5 minutes. Add the onions and chile powder and continue frying, stirring them from time to time, taking care that the onions do not burn—about 5 minutes. Add the lime juice and serve still warm with toothpicks.

San Miguel de Allende

I have known San Miguel de Allende since the late fifties, when it was idyllic. Many of its streets and houses were in a state of benign neglect. You could hear the soft patter of donkeys' hooves as they carried their burdens of firewood down the steep cobbled streets. I remember masses of vivid jacaranda blossoms vying with a cloudless azure sky and the brilliance of the light across the plains to the west and the distant mountains beyond.

In those days it was easier to stand and appreciate the facades of the elegant buildings that graced San Miguel and conjure up a picture of its golden age in the eighteenth century, when many of the churches, palaces, and stately homes were built.

San Miguel was founded in 1542 (some say '48) by a Franciscan friar, Juan, and thirteen years later was recognized by the viceroy as San Miguel el Grande. The town grew up around a constantly flowing spring (alas nowadays reduced to a trickle and then only in the rainy season), which made it possible to have mills and a weaving industry. It gradually became an important center, a focal point for trade, serving the many large haciendas with their herds of cattle. It was also a center for tanning, leatherwork, and iron for implements and weapons, as well as to embellish the local architecture with decorative balconies.

San Miguel also became a center for culture and learning in the eighteenth century; it attracted rich mine owners and influential trading families, who became patrons of the arts and architecture. Later it gave birth to many distinguished and brave men; in fact, to those who planned and initiated the struggle for independence. Sadly, a result of that struggle was the gradual decline of the town and the riches of the area with the destruction of the factories and cruel reprisals. During the Revolution and the Christero War many families fled, losing their lands, homes, and livelihoods.

The revitalization of the town really started in the early fifties, when foreign artists, mostly from the United States and Canada, attracted by its beauty, tranquillity, and climate, came there to live and collaborated with local families in helping to turn the fortunes of this very special place around. Many of the neglected houses were gradually restored, often for foreign residents, and, as a result, a market began to grow for local artisan talent.

I have been a fairly regular visitor since those early days, but for some reason I could never fathom I did not take a very deep interest in the local food until a few years ago when a friend invited a group of the local ladies to meet me. Our lively discussion on their families' food has never really finished but has continued on every visit since. What amazed me was their faithful adherence to their traditional recipes, many with strong Spanish roots, that have been passed down from their great-grandmothers through succeeding generations. I was shown manuscript cookbooks dating back to the early 1800s, or even farther, still used today, and I was generously given handwritten copies of some of those recipes.

In the Redondo household, for special occasions, a galantine of turkey was prepared with the finest ingredients from the grandfather's well-stocked post-Revolution larder. For a week before the killing the turkey was fed on corn, wheat, and milk and then, to ensure that the neck skin remained intact for stuffing, the bird was suffocated with a huge dose of alcohol. Sra. MariLu Redondo de Lambarri, an expert cook, will still prepare the exact galantine recipe for special occasions. For the Day of the Dead, the traditional dish is her *fiambre, muy sanmiguelense,* with three meats: chicken, tongue, and pig's feet, smothered with sliced fruits and a light oil and vinegar dressing.

Sra. Celia Hoyos de Tellez showed me her printed cookbook dated 1845, given to her by an aunt who taught her how to make the cold almond punch—the delicious and inevitable drink for saint's days and birthdays, with eight egg yolks and a large quantity of almonds. When the bishop came to lunch, there was invariably *sopa de gota* to start, followed by a fairly elaborate series of dishes: he was, as the local phrase goes, *"muy chocolatado"* (literally, well-chocolated), as his figure no doubt bore witness.

A recipe for *helado fingido,* false ice cream, made of shredded coconut with lime rind in a sugar syrup and served cold, dates back to 1790 and came from her great-grandmother. Señora Celia had written out two recipes for *tumbagones,* tubes of wafer-thin dough fried and dusted with confectioners' sugar. I was told that they were typical of San Miguel and made only there, but later this was disputed hotly by a cook in Dolores Hidalgo who claimed them for her town some thirty kilometers away. There were recipes for *pollos cardenales*—chicken cooked in a sauce reddened with beets—or *enmostados,* surprisingly in a sauce of mustard greens, and an intriguing and complicated version of meatballs, *albóndigas reales.* The ground meat was mixed with ancho chiles, saffron, and wine vinegar, and they were stuffed with raisins, almonds, ham or egg, and parsley. Another distinguished lady who loved to cook had typed up for me her grandmother's recipe for the most delicate *buñuelos: buñuelos de abue Emma,* calling for eighteen egg yolks to produce three hundred wispy little *buñuelos.* I actually did make fifty using one sixth of the egg yolks!

Most of these recipes reflect the Spanish roots of families who have lived in San Miguel for generations, and culinary traditions are still preserved by many of those families, especially for family gatherings or religious festivals.

ENSALADA DE TOMATE VERDE

MEXICAN GREEN TOMATO SALAD

Sra. María Redondo de Williams

✹

[SERVES 6 TO 8 AS A BOTANA]

THIS IS A MOST SURPRISINGLY DELICIOUS AND CRISP SALAD. MARÍA WILLIAMS SAID SHE DID NOT KNOW THE ORIGIN OF THE RECIPE BUT SHE HAD enriched it with trimmings to her taste. I think it is best served—as it was to a friend of mine on a ranch near San Miguel de Allende—as a *botana* with drinks and a pile of hot corn tortillas.

1 pound (450 g) tomates verdes
2 serrano chiles or to taste, finely chopped
2 tablespoons finely chopped white onion
¾ cup (188 ml) roughly chopped cilantro
2 to 3 tablespoons olive oil
salt to taste

THE TOPPING
½ cup (125 ml) queso fresco, crumbled, queso añejo,
or finely grated Romano
2 ounces (60 g) chicharrón, broken into small pieces
1 large avocado, diced

Remove the husks from the *tomates verdes*, rinse well, and dry before chopping them roughly. Mix with the rest of the ingredients. Just before serving, top with the cheese, *chicharrón*, and avocado.

TACOS SUDADOS DE FIDEO

STEAMED TACOS FILLED WITH VERMICELLI

Sra. MariLu Redondo de Lambarrí

❋

[MAKES 12 TACOS]

I WAS AS SURPRISED WHEN I FIRST HEARD OF THIS RECIPE FROM MARILU AS A FRIEND OF MINE WAS ON HEARING, MANY YEARS AGO, OF A SPAGHETTI SAND-wich in Australia.

I think these tacos are delicious, but don't expect them to be *picante*. I like to accompany them with a *guacamole verde* (*The Art of Mexican Cooking*) or *Estado de Mexico green sauce*.

THE MEAT
12 ounces (340 g) stewing pork, cut into ½-inch (13-mm) cubes
1 medium white onion, sliced
1 garlic clove, peeled
salt to taste

THE CHILE SAUCE
8 cascabel chiles or 4 large guajillo chiles
2 garlic cloves, roughly chopped
⅛ teaspoon cumin seeds
2 tablespoons lard or vegetable oil

THE PASTA
3 tablespoons vegetable oil
2 ounces (60 g) angel hair pasta
4 ounces (115 g) roughly chopped tomatoes, about ⅔ cup (164 ml)

[CONTINUED]

¼ small white onion

1 garlic clove, roughly chopped

12 5-inch (13-cm) tortillas

Have ready toothpicks and a shallow steamer (vegetable steamer or other improvisation in a shallow pot with about 1½ inches [4 cm] of water in the bottom).

THE MEAT: In a saucepan, cover the pork with water, add the onion, garlic, and salt, and cook over medium heat until tender. Drain the meat, reserving the broth, and set the meat aside to cool. Shred the meat, removing any fat or gristle.

THE CHILE SAUCE: Cover the chiles with hot water and soak for about 20 minutes. Put ½ cup (125 ml) of the reserved meat broth into a blender with the garlic and cumin seeds and blend well. Gradually add the drained chiles and blend until smooth. (*Note:* If using guajillo chiles, you will need to strain the sauce to remove any hard pieces of skin.)

Heat the oil in a skillet, add the meat, and fry for about 1 minute. Add the chile sauce with salt to taste and cook over fairly high heat, scraping the bottom of the pan to prevent sticking, until the sauce has been reduced and coats the meat—about 5 minutes.

THE PASTA: Heat the oil in a skillet, add the pasta, and fry, turning it over from time to time to fry evenly to a deep golden color. Drain off any excess oil. Blend the tomatoes with the onion and garlic and add to the pan, stirring well to prevent sticking. When the sauce has reduced and coats the pasta, add ½ cup (125 ml) of the reserved meat broth, adjust the salt, and cook covered over low heat until the pasta is just tender. Stir in the meat mixture and keep warm.

Meanwhile, heat the water in the bottom of the steamer. Put 1 very heaped tablespoon of the filling in each tortilla, double it over, and secure with a toothpick. Place in overlapping layers on the steamer rack, cover, and heat through for about 5 minutes. (If the tortillas are extra-thick, they may need a longer time.) Remove carefully with a broad spatula and serve immediately.

CHILES RELLENOS DE PAPA Y SARDINAS

CHILES STUFFED WITH POTATO AND SARDINES

Sra. María Redondo de Williams

❀

[SERVES 6]

THIS IS A VERY UNUSUAL AND DELICIOUS WAY OF PREPARING POBLANO CHILES THAT CAN BE SERVED AS EITHER A FIRST-COURSE SALAD OR A MAIN-COURSE vegetarian dish—leaving out the sardines for strict vegetarians.

6 medium poblano chiles, charred, peeled, seeds and veins removed,
but left whole

THE MARINADE

3 tablespoons vegetable oil

1 small white onion, sliced

4 garlic cloves, sliced

2 small carrots, peeled and thinly sliced

3 sprigs fresh thyme or ¼ teaspoon dried

3 sprigs fresh marjoram or ¼ teaspoon dried

1 bay leaf, Mexican if possible, torn into pieces

5 peppercorns

1½ cups (375 ml) mild vinegar or half rice vinegar and half wine vinegar

salt to taste

THE STUFFING

12 ounces (340 g) new potatoes, cooked, peeled, and roughly mashed,
about 1½ cups (375 ml)

1 small can sardines packed in olive oil, mashed, about ½ cup (125 ml)

finely chopped white onion

TO SERVE

lettuce leaves

approximately ¼ cup (63 ml) olive oil (optional)

[CONTINUED]

THE MARINADE: Heat the oil, add the onion, garlic, and carrots, and fry gently without browning for about 2 minutes. Add the rest of the ingredients and bring to a simmer. Continue cooking for about 3 minutes. Set aside to cool a little. Pour the marinade over the chiles and set aside at room temperature for about 2 hours.

THE STUFFING: Meanwhile, mix the roughly mashed potato—it should have some texture —with the sardines and onion with salt to taste. Drain the chiles and stuff each one with about ⅓ cup (83 ml) of the stuffing or until it looks very fat and appetizing.

Line the serving dish with lettuce leaves, arrange the chiles over them, and pour the marinade over them with olive oil on top.

CHILES PASILLAS RELLENOS DE PAPA

PASILLA CHILES STUFFED WITH POTATO

Sra. María Redondo de Williams

❋

[SERVES 12]

SEÑORA WILLIAMS SAYS THIS IS AN OLD FAMILY RECIPE THAT POSSIBLY GOES BACK SOME 200 YEARS.

12 pasilla *chiles*
1 pound (450 g) new potatoes, cooked, peeled, and roughly mashed
6 ounces (180 g) queso fresco or cream cheese crumbled (see note)
salt to taste
⅓ cup (83 ml) vegetable oil

THE SAUCE
2 pounds (900 g) tomates verdes, husks removed and rinsed
2 tablespoons roughly chopped onion
2 garlic cloves, roughly chopped
1 heaped tablespoon dark brown sugar
½ cup (125 ml) chicken broth or water

Carefully slit the chiles open and remove the seeds and veins, leaving the top intact. Cover with hot water and leave to soak until just soft—about 10 minutes. (Time will, of course, depend on how dry the chiles were in the first place.) Drain.

Mix together the potatoes and cheese with salt if necessary and fill the chiles—the cut edges should almost meet.

Heat the oil in a skillet and fry the chiles, rolling them over so they fry evenly, for about 5 minutes. Remove and drain.

Heat the oven to 350°F (177°C).

Cover the *tomates verdes* with water in a saucepan and simmer until soft—about 10 minutes. Drain and transfer to a blender. Add the onion and garlic and blend until smooth.

Reheat the oil in which the chiles were fried and fry the sugar for a few seconds. Add the blended ingredients with salt to taste and continue cooking the sauce over fairly high heat until slightly reduced—about 5 minutes. Add the broth to dilute to a medium consistency. Pour over the chiles, cover, and heat through in the oven until the sauce is bubbling and the potato filling well heated through—about 15 minutes.

Serve the chiles with plenty of the sauce and corn tortillas.

NOTE: *To crumble cream cheese, freeze it briefly first.*

POLLO EN MENUDENCIAS

CHICKEN IN GIBLET SAUCE

Sra. Celia Hoyos de Tellez

✸

[SERVES 4 TO 6]

THIS RECIPE WAS PASSED ALONG TO SRA. CELIA HOYOS DE TELLEZ BY HER COMADRE (GODMOTHER), ANGELINA, WHO CALCULATES THAT IT IS AT LEAST one hundred years old.

This is a strong, rich sauce that I prefer to accompany with plain boiled potatoes with strips of red pepper on top to add a patch of color. The dish can be prepared ahead of time.

4 chicken gizzards
4 chicken hearts
¼ medium white onion, roughly sliced
1 garlic clove, roughly chopped
salt to taste
4 chicken livers
3 tablespoons olive oil or rendered chicken fat
1 large chicken, about 4 pounds (1.8 kg), cut into serving pieces
5 small garlic cloves, roughly chopped
¼ cup (63 ml) fresh lime juice
rounded ¼ teaspoon cumin seeds
⅓ cup (83 ml) red wine
freshly ground pepper to taste
1½ to 2 cups (375 to 500 ml) water

Barely cover the gizzards and hearts with water in a saucepan, add the onion, the clove of garlic, and salt and cook over medium heat for about 20 minutes or until almost tender. Add the livers and cook for another 10 minutes. Transfer the giblets and the broth in which they were cooked to a blender and blend until smooth. Set aside.

Heat the oil in a deep skillet and add a few of the chicken pieces in one layer—they should not touch each other. Sprinkle well with salt and fry until they are a deep golden color. Remove and fry the rest of the chicken.

Return the chicken pieces to the pan. Blend together the 5 garlic cloves, lime juice, and cumin until smooth. Add to the pan and cook over high heat for 1 minute. Add the blended giblets, wine, salt and pepper, and water. Cover the pan and cook over low heat, turning the chicken pieces over so they are cooked evenly, stirring and scraping the bottom of the pan to prevent sticking, for about 25 minutes or until the chicken is tender. The sauce should be of medium consistency and lightly cover the back of a wooden spoon. Serve as suggested in the headnote.

AGUASCALIENTES

The Journey North

CONTINUING THE JOURNEY NORTH FROM SAN MIGUEL AND ONCE PAST THE AGRICULTURAL FRINGES OF LAND AROUND DOLORES HIDALGO, YOU PASS ONLY THE OCCAsional *ranchería*, a small settlement nearly always situated near some source of water: springs that feed a small pond or narrow stream. The land is poor and scrubby, dotted with the occasional mesquite tree and intersected by towering sheer and craggy rock formations. The sky was an intense blue that morning, except for some billowing clouds casting shadows that heightened the horizontal and brilliant ribbons of color: greens and yellows of all shades. Dotted over the landscape and bordering the highway were shimmering patches of gold as if some diaphanous mantle had been cast over the land in expectation of All Saints and All Souls, when the funereal yellow *cempazuchil* (Mexican marigolds) abound. At a bend in the road outside a small cottage was a bank of cosmos of all shades of color from white to deep purple. Cars and trucks flashed past me on the road, their drivers grim faced and determined to outpace each other, too familiar with their accustomed route to be moved by that unfolding scene.

Aguascalientes

Aguascalientes is one of the smallest states and the physical center of Mexico. It proudly proclaims its motto: *Agua clara, claro cielo, buena tierra, gente buena* (Clear water, clear sky, good land, good people). Aguascalientes, hot waters, is the name of both the state and the capital city, owing to the numerous hot springs that still provide a continuous supply of thermal water to many of the houses in the older part of the city and to the elegant public baths that were built in the last century.

Although the city was founded in 1575, a small settlement of Spaniards had arrived nine years earlier. It became an important and strategic stopping place for the mule trains carrying silver and other precious metals along what was known as the Silver Trail for the mines in the north, mainly in Zacatecas and Durango, to Mexico City. Later, as haciendas were established to control and cultivate their large tracts of land, Aguascalientes became an important center of agriculture and commerce.

Many traces of its past have now been lost in the urban mass, but some elegant colonial houses still exist, mostly to house institutions: museums and the cultural center. But the architectural jewel of this city is the state government palace on the main square. It has a striking, almost severe facade of mulberry-colored volcanic rock; inside there is a wonderful feeling of light and space created by a series of decorative supporting arches on both floors.

Apart from this historic area and the now almost-historic Hotel Francia—whose bar and restaurant is a famous meeting place for bullfighters and their followers from all over the country—the city is hardly recognizable from my first visit twenty-five years ago. It has extended way beyond its former limits to house newly attracted and nonpolluting industries and, surprisingly, for the preponderance of semiarid lands, an important dairying center. Perhaps it is better known as the largest producer of guavas in Mexico, concentrated in the broad valley around Calvillo to the west, which has an ideal climate for year-round harvest.

To many Mexicans, Aguascalientes is better known for its colorful fair, *La Feria de San Marcos*, held yearly in the San Marcos gardens for two weeks in the latter part of April, and for its fine embroidery and drawn thread works on linen and cotton tablecloths, mats, napkins, and even baby clothes.

"You go to Aguascalientes to eat well," I overheard at a recent gathering. This sentiment was echoed during a lively *fandango*—a traditional wedding celebration—in Oaxaca of all places. Somebody I had just met was talking about her travels in the Bajío, and we simultaneously concurred that the *Cenaduría San Antonio* in Aguascalientes was the epitome of *cenadurías*—popular evening eating places. Its appearance is unprepossessing with no frills, but is the liveliest center of activity in the town, always crowded with families from all walks of life. Conversation is loud and enthusiastic until the generously served plates arrive, piled high with the local specialties: *tostadas* swamped under masses of shredded chicken, topped with tomato, shredded lettuce, and the best of local cheese and cream, small fried tacos filled with potato, *enchiladas*, pickled pig's feet and soft pork rinds, *guacamole*, and vegetables cured in vinegar. There are *atoles*, gruel thickened with corn *masa*, of every imaginable flavor and their very special *tamales*—savory ones filled with meat and sauce or cheese, chile strips, and green sauce, which are my favorites. Nowhere else in Mexico will you find such a variety of sweet *tamales*—their own concoctions—flavored with *rompope* (Mexican eggnog), peanuts and candied cactus, and *cajeta* (a goat's milk caramel sauce). But most in demand, certainly from visitors from out of town, is the *Platillo Hidrocalido* (literally Hot Water Plate), a take-off on Aguascalientes. There is a generous helping of practically everything on the menu and a choice of *tamales* to boot; it's certainly enough for two very large or three more modest helpings.

Many of the items are innovations on a traditional theme by one of the brothers who own the business, the rotund Jesús Romo. When you talk to him about his restaurant, as I did at length, you immediately sense his complete dedication to good food and attention to detail, most notable when explaining his meticulous preparation of *masa* for *tamales*. He is a generous host, and his clientele knows it and keeps coming back for more.

If you like *menudo* as I do, particularly as a boost on a breakfastless morning, then you have to visit Menudo Toña. It was founded forty years ago by the present owner's grandmother in a smaller locale. It is open daily, Good Fridays excepted, in the mornings from seven until midday and, of course, much earlier during the fair, when it is unthinkable to wind up the early morning revelries without visiting Toña's for a large bowl of *menudo*. I always order a small portion to make room for the simple but delicious *cuajadillas*. As the name suggests, it is the part of the tripe known as *cuajo* from which the enzyme is extracted for clabbering milk in country areas. Seasoned with *guajillo* chiles (confusingly called *cascabel*), it is cooked with the rest of the ingredients: cow's foot and all parts of the animal's stomach —not just the boring honeycomb you will always find in the United States, except in the Mexican meat markets. The *cuajo* is chopped roughly, put into a small tortilla, and moistened with a little of the fat that gathers on the top of the broth. The tortilla is doubled over and then reheated on the *comal*. Chopped onion and *cilantro* are all you need to complete the snack. It makes me hungry just writing about it. There are no real secrets to this *menudo*, except that it is cooked in large quantities for a very long time and the basic ingredients are of the very best quality.

When I am in Aguascalientes, I always make time to visit the main market, Mercado Terán, in the center of the city. It is clean and orderly, and the people there are polite and helpful, despite my endless questions. On the upper level, the cream, cheese, and ricotta are excellent and the eating stands downstairs offer very fresh and appetizing food with huge containers of *chile bola* (round chile *cascabel* when dried), round, yellow chiles pickled in brine and vinegar. The fish stands always sell finely ground boneless fish for the local *ceviche*, an interesting variation—especially for those who do not like raw fish in lumps despite its "cooking" in lime juice. It is then seasoned with the usual tomato, onion, chiles, and *cilantro*.

Outside in the street at one corner of the market a young woman is usually selling *tamales* and *condoches* or *gorditas de horno*, which her mother and grandmother still make in their adobe oven. The traditional ovens for *condoches* are shaped like elongated cones and known in some areas as *coceres*. *Condoches* are slightly flattened cakes of corn dough enriched with lard, or *coco de aceite* (page 125). There are sweet ones and those mixed with *jocoqui* (page 80), which lends a pleasant acidy taste to the dough. The savory ones (recipe, page 125) are sometimes filled with a mixture of beans and chiles and then baked, or slit open and stuffed after cooking.

Aguascalientes is a twenty-four-hour eating city. Taquería Max is open all night, and the trays of freshly cooked stews are constantly filled to keep up with the steady flow of customers who come to take out their well-stuffed tacos, pass the time of day, or gossip with the jovial Max while they eat.

Throughout the day and evening the women cooking at Gorditas Victoria make their large *masa gordas* to order, cooking them in the front of the restaurant on large *comales* and stuffing them with whatever you choose from the variety of savory fillings: potatoes and chile strips or *chorizo*, *nopales* or shredded meats in one of many chile sauces.

Whether you are an ice cream fancier or not, you have to go, at least to look—actually, you will not be able to resist trying—at the amazing range of ices and ice creams in the *nevería* El As, many of which are made of fresh fruit purees alone or in combinations so diverse that you will be in a complete dilemma about what to choose.

Pasquelito's *taquería was* a disappointment. Of course, I should have been more realistic, but that wonderful eating experience there twenty-five years ago, which I mentioned in *The Cuisines of Mexico*, is indelible in my memory. The sight of that young pig, roasted to perfection, being carried in at precisely five o'clock in the afternoon, and the aroma and taste of those tacos stuffed with succulent fatty meat is unforgettable. This time the far-too-chopped-up meat had lost its sheen on a warming pan, while the sight of two young employees glued to the blaring television, oblivious to customers, made me hurry away, still hungry.

On that first visit, Sra. Ana de Andrea—she and her husband own the Hotel Francia in Aguascalientes and a restaurant and catering business that bears their name in Mexico City—generously shared two recipes that had made her innovative catering menu such a success: guavas stuffed with coconut and chicken cooked with grapes, both included in *The Cuisines of Mexico*. On this last visit they invited me to an elegant lunch, and she gave me her recipe for ancho chiles stuffed with *picadillo* (recipe follows) in a crème fraîche that bears the Andrea hallmark and has already become famous among the dishes she caters in both Mexico City and Aguascalientes.

One cannot talk about Aguascalientes without mentioning that great cooking teacher and author of the forties and fifties, Señora Josefina Velázques de Léon, who was, I believe, the first woman to travel around the country teaching and collecting recipes from the local cooks for her invaluable series of books on regional Mexican cuisines. Although not born there, she spent much of her youth with relatives in Aguascalientes and says that her cooking apprenticeship started there in the homes of her aunts. She had a very warm spot indeed in her gastronomic heart for Aguascalientes.

CHILES ANCHOS RELLENOS DE LOS ANDREA

THE ANDREA FAMILY'S STUFFED ANCHO CHILES

✸

[SERVES 6]

THE CHILES

6 large ancho chiles

3 tablespoons vinegar

3 tablespoons grated piloncillo or soft dark brown sugar

THE FILLING

2 tablespoons vegetable oil

1 small white onion, finely chopped

2 garlic cloves, finely chopped

12 ounces (340 g) ground pork, including a little fat

12 ounces (340 g) lean ground beef

salt to taste

8 ounces (225 g) tomatoes, finely chopped, about 1⅓ cups (333 ml)

4 peppercorns

2 cloves

½-inch (13-mm) cinnamon stick

2 sprigs fresh thyme, finely chopped, or ⅛ teaspoon dried

2 sprigs fresh marjoram, finely chopped, or ⅛ teaspoon dried

scant ⅓ cup (80 ml) raisins

2 heaped tablespoons slivered almonds or pine nuts

1 tablespoon vinegar

1½ cups (375 ml) crème fraîche, diluted with a little milk
6 sprigs flat-leaf parsley
pomegranate seeds or halved peeled grapes

THE CHILES: Slit the chiles open carefully, to leave them whole and intact and remove the seeds and veins. Barely cover with water in a saucepan, stir in the vinegar and sugar, and bring to a simmer. Simmer for 5 minutes and set aside to soak until the chiles are fleshy and the skin soft—about 30 minutes, depending on how dry the chiles were in the first place. Drain and set aside in a colander while you prepare the filling.

THE FILLING: Heat the vegetable oil in a skillet, add the onion and garlic, and fry without browning until translucent—about 30 seconds. Add the meats and salt and fry, turning the meat over and pressing out any lumps so that it will cook evenly, for about 3 minutes. Add the tomatoes, cover the pan, and cook over medium heat for about 5 minutes—shaking the pan from time to time to prevent sticking.

Crush the spices together roughly and add to the pan with the herbs. Cook uncovered, stirring from time to time, for about 3 minutes. Add the raisins, almonds, and vinegar and continue cooking over medium heat, scraping the bottom of the pan to prevent sticking, until the meat is well cooked and seasoned, moist but not juicy, and shiny. Set aside to cool off a little.

TO SERVE: Stuff the chiles until they are very fat—about ½ cup (125 ml) per chile. Set each chile in the middle of a large dinner plate, pour about ⅓ cup (83 ml) of the cream around it, and decorate with the parsley and pomegranate seeds or grapes. Serve at room temperature.

ENCHILADAS ROJAS DE AGUASCALIENTES

RED *ENCHILADAS* FROM AGUASCALIENTES

Doña Petra

❀

[MAKES 12 SMALL ENCHILADAS]

THIS IS ONE VERSION OF THE MANY RED *ENCHILADA* RECIPES THAT ARE TYPICAL OF AGUASCALIENTES. THEY ARE SIMPLE AND VERY TASTY. SUBSTITUTING oil for lard and omitting the chicken makes this a good vegetarian dish. Since *enchiladas* and their (often fried) accompaniments in whatever form tend to be rather greasy, I have modified the cooking method to reduce some of the fat.

THE SAUCE

4 large ancho chiles, stems, veins, and seeds removed

1 garlic clove, roughly chopped

2 cups (500 ml) water

1 tablespoon lard or vegetable oil

salt to taste

THE ENCHILADAS

6 ounces (180 g) potatoes, cooked, peeled, and sliced

oil for frying

6 portions poached chicken

12 small corn tortillas—4 inches (10 cm) in diameter is ideal

½ cup (125 ml) finely chopped onion, lightly salted

¼ cup (63 ml) crème fraîche or sour cream

¼ cup (63 ml) finely grated queso añejo or Romano

strips of jalapeño chiles en escabeche

Have ready a shallow ovenproof dish into which the *enchiladas* will just fit in one layer.

Cover the chiles with hot water in a saucepan, bring to a simmer, and continue simmering for 5 minutes. Leave to soak for 5 more minutes or until soft. Drain the chiles, tear into pieces, and put into a blender. Add the garlic and 1 cup (250 ml) water and blend until smooth.

Heat the tablespoon of lard or oil in a skillet, add the sauce, and fry over medium heat, stirring and scraping the bottom of the pan to prevent sticking, for about 5 minutes. Stir in the rest of the water and salt and cook for another 3 minutes. Set aside and keep it warm.

Brush both sides of the potato slices with oil and brown slightly under a hot broiler. Transfer to a warm oven.

Spread a coating of the sauce over the chicken pieces with a little of the oil and broil until slightly crisp on the outside. Keep the chicken warm in the oven while you prepare the *enchiladas*.

Add about ¼ inch (7 mm) (no more) oil to another skillet and fry the tortillas on both sides until well heated through (sometimes they puff up) but not crisp. Drain well on absorbent paper.

Put a little of the chopped onion across the middle of each tortilla, roll them up loosely, and place side by side in an ovenproof dish. Pour on the crème fraîche, sprinkle liberally with the cheese, and heat through, either in the oven or under the broiler for a few minutes. Serve immediately with the pieces of chicken on the side and the potatoes as a final topping, with strips of jalapeños *en escabeche*.

CONDOCHES

❁

[MAKES APPROXIMATELY 12 3-INCH (8-CM) GORDITAS]

IT IS NOT EASY TO FIND *CONDOCHES*, OR *GORDITAS DE HORNO* AS THEY ARE SOMETIMES KNOWN, IN URBAN AGUASCALIENTES, WITH THE EXCEPTION OF those sold outside the central market. Every morning María del Refugio Martínez sends her daughter to sell them fresh from her oven in a small village just outside the city. There are sweet ones enriched with, curiously enough, *coco de aceite*, the small oleaginous kernel of the palm fruit (*Acrocomia mexicana*, known also as *coyol* in the south of Mexico). Nobody can tell me how that came about! Sweet also are those *de maiz*, made of corn that has been softened —with the usual lime—and ground to a textured consistency. The ones I prefer (but you have to wait until after one o'clock) are salty and slightly acidy from the *jocoqui*. Often they are plain, but sometimes filled with a bean and chile mixture.

A thin, acidic yogurt can be used instead of the *jocoqui*. I prefer to make the dough the night before to increase the acidity.

1 teaspoon baking soda

½ teaspoon salt

⅓ to ½ cup (83 to 125 ml) jocoqui (page 80) or yogurt

1¼ pounds (565 g) masa for tortillas (page 528), as dry as possible,
about 2¼ cups (563 ml)

2 ounces (60 g) lard, softened, about ⅓ cup (83 ml)

Mix the baking soda and salt into the *jocoqui*. Gradually add the *masa* and the lard and beat for as long as you can (Sra. Martínez says 15 minutes, about 5 minutes with an electric mixer). The dough should be fairly loose and sticky. Leave in a warm place for several hours or overnight (see above).

Heat the oven to 350°F (177°C). Divide the dough into 12 parts and place them in rough mounds about 2 inches (5 cm) apart on ungreased baking sheets. Bake until firm to the touch—just to make sure, sacrifice one and break it open to see if the dough is cooked right through—about 35 minutes.

FRIJOLES PARA CONDOCHES

BEAN FILLING FOR *CONDOCHES*

❉

[MAKES ENOUGH FOR 24 CONDOCHES]

2 guajillo chiles, veins and seeds removed

1 garlic clove

2 peppercorns

⅛ teaspoon cumin seeds

2 tablespoons lard or vegetable oil

1 cup (250 ml) cooked and mashed bayo, canario,
or pinto beans

salt to taste

Toast the chiles on a *comal*, taking care not to let them burn. Cover with hot water and soak for about 10 minutes. Crush the garlic, peppercorns, and cumin together in a *molcajete*. Drain the chiles, tear them into small pieces, and grind to a rough texture with the garlic mixture.

Heat the lard in a small skillet, add the chile mixture, and fry for a few seconds. Gradually mash in the beans with a bean masher. Add salt and cook for about 3 minutes. Set aside to cool.

Split the *condoches* open and stuff with the bean paste.

HUEVOS CON NOPALES Y CILANTRO

EGGS WITH CACTUS PIECES AND *CILANTRO*

Sra. Antonia Hernández de Gutiérrez

❋

[SERVES 3]

YOLANDA GUTIÉRREZ, MY "GASTRONOMIC GUIDE" IN AGUASCALIENTES, PASSED THIS RECIPE ALONG TO ME. IT IS HER MOTHER'S WAY OF COOKING eggs with *nopales* and *cilantro*, which has become a firm favorite with the family. If *nopales* are not available, use cooked, chopped green beans.

2 tablespoons vegetable oil

*1 cebolla de rabo or 1 large or 4 small scallions,
both green and white parts*

2 garlic cloves, finely chopped

salt to taste

*1 very heaped cup (265 ml) cooked cactus pieces (page 19)
or sliced green beans*

½ teaspoon dried Mexican oregano, crushed

4 eggs, lightly beaten with salt to taste

½ cup (125 ml) firmly packed roughly chopped cilantro

Heat the oil in a skillet. Add the onion, garlic, and a sprinkle of salt and fry without browning for about 30 seconds. Add the cactus and oregano and cook for 1 minute more.

[CONTINUED]

Pour the eggs over the mixture, cover the pan, and cook over low heat, shaking the pan from time to time, until the eggs are almost set.

Sprinkle the *cilantro* over the surface of the eggs, cover the pan again, and cook for 1 minute more. Serve immediately with corn tortillas.

LOMO DE PUERCO EN SALSA DE GUAYABA

PORK LOIN IN GUAVA SAUCE

Cenaduría San Antonio, Aguascalientes

❂

[SERVES 4]

ALTHOUGH THIS RECIPE ORIGINALLY CALLED FOR BONED LOIN OF PORK CUT INTO FOUR PIECES, I PREFER TO USE EITHER SMALL PORK CHOPS WITH A LITtle fat left on or country-style spareribs. The sauce is an unusual and delicious one that can also be used with chicken.

1½ pounds (675 g) pork chops or country-style spareribs
salt and freshly ground pepper to taste
4 medium guavas, about 12 ounces (340 g),
ripe but still firm
2¾ cups (688 ml) water
¼ medium white onion, roughly chopped
2 garlic cloves, roughly chopped
2 whole cloves
1 bay leaf, Mexican if possible
1 pound (450 g) tomatoes, broiled until soft (page 527)
1 tablespoon lard or vegetable oil
1 tablespoon sugar

Season the pork well with salt and pepper and set aside for about 1 hour. Cut the guavas into halves lengthwise; scrape out the seeds and the viscous flesh surrounding them and reserve. Chop 3 of the guavas roughly, then cut the fourth into narrow strips and set aside.

Put ½ cup (125 ml) of the water into a blender, add the guava seeds, and blend at low speed briefly. Remove from the blender and set aside.

Put ¼ cup (63 ml) of the water into the blender, add the onion, garlic, cloves, and bay leaf, and blend until smooth. Gradually add the tomatoes with the chopped guavas, blending well after each addition until smooth.

Heat the lard in a heavy nonreactive pan in which you are going to cook the dish (or the sauce will discolor). Add a few of the pork chops, taking care that they do not touch in the pan, and fry until well browned on both sides. Remove and continue with the rest. Remove and set aside.

Drain off or add to the fat in the pan to make 2 tablespoons. Add the blended ingredients and fry, scraping the bottom of the pan to prevent sticking, for about 5 minutes. Add the meat with the remaining 2 cups water and the sugar, cover the pan, and cook over medium heat, stirring from time to time, until the meat is just tender—about 35 minutes.

Press the blended guava seeds into a fine strainer until as much as possible of the juice is extracted. Add the extracted liquid to the pan along with the sliced guavas. Adjust the salt and cook uncovered for 5 to 10 minutes. The sauce should be of medium consistency.

TAMALES SABOR A CHOCOLATE

CHOCOLATE-FLAVORED *TAMALES*

Sr. Jesús Romo, Aguascalientes

✺

[MAKES APPROXIMATELY 36 TAMALES]

SEÑOR ROMO'S SWEET TAMALES ARE ORIGINAL, BUT I THINK HIS CHOCOLATE ONES ARE OUTSTANDING, ALTHOUGH I MUST ADMIT TO TAMPERING A LITTLE with his recipe—and I think for the best. Instead of mixing the fruit into the dough, I fill the *tamales* with the raisins and nuts moistened with a little Kahlúa.

Traditionally *tamales*, either sweet or savory, are accompanied by *atole*, or hot chocolate, for supper or reheated for breakfast. I like to serve these as a dessert with some *crème anglaise* or *rompope* (Mexican eggnog).

1½ cups (375 ml) raisins

2 tablespoons Kahlúa

10 ounces (285 g) unsalted butter or 7 ounces (200 g) butter and
3 ounces (85 g) lard, about 1¼ cups (313 ml)

1½ teaspoons baking powder

¼ teaspoon salt

1 cup (250 ml) granulated sugar

1 teaspoon vanilla extract

1 teaspoon ground cinnamon

3 heaped tablespoons unsweetened cocoa powder

2 pounds (900 g) fairly dry masa for tamales (page 528),
about 5⅓ cups (1.333 l)

½ to 1 cup (125 to 250 ml) whole milk

1 heaped cup (265 ml) roughly chopped pecans

40 dried corn husks, soaked for about 1 hour and patted dry

Have ready a *tamale* steamer with water and coins in the bottom. Mix the raisins with the Kahlúa and set aside.

In a mixing bowl, beat the butter with the baking powder until thick and creamy. Gradually beat in the salt, sugar, vanilla, cinnamon, and cocoa powder. When they are all well incorporated, start adding the *masa* alternately with the milk. Do not add all the milk until you see the consistency of the *masa*—it should be light and thick so that it barely plops off the spoon and a small ball floats in a glass of water.

Mix the nuts in with the raisins. Spread 2 tablespoons of the dough, not too thin and not too thick, over the inside of a corn husk. Put a few of the raisins and nuts down the center of the dough and fold the leaf over in the usual way so that the dough covers, or almost covers, the filling. Stack vertically in the *tamale* steamer, firmly but not tightly, and steam for about 1½ hours or until the dough comes cleanly away from the husk when tested. Serve as described above.

ZACATECAS

The Journey North—Aguascalientes to Zacatecas

THE MAIN HIGHWAY DUE NORTH FROM AGUASCALIENTES IS UNSPECTACULAR, PASSING THROUGH SOME SMALL TOWNS AND FIELDS CULTIVATED WITH VINES, BEANS, CORN, AND chiles. The land is flat and mostly treeless but always framed by distant mountains. Some say the journey to Zacatecas, less than two hours away, is more colorful when the chiles are ripening in the fields, casting a reddish glow over the countryside. At the halfway point the land begins to rise gradually until you reach the colonial mining town of Zacatecas, set below the dramatic, abruptly rising *Cerro de la Bufa.* ❂ I visited Zacatecas for the first time in 1970. It was a joy to wander through the uneven streets connected to each other with alleyways of steep flights of stone steps and discover small tranquil plazas and gardens. A feeling of mystery hung over some of the old houses; no door was opened at a knock without a face peering out cautiously through the *postigo*—a small hatchway at eye level—to see if the caller was welcome. I was taken back to those days recently when reading *Recuerdos de Mi*

Barranca (Ruben Flores Villagrana's *Recollections of My Neighborhood*, although *barranca* means "a rugged area of ravines and gorges"), true legends of dramatic happenings in the streets named *Callejon del Indio Triste* (the Alley of the Sad Indian), *El Callejon del Mono Prieto* (the Alley of the Black Monkey), *La Calle del Deseo* (the Street of Desire), and *El Puente de los Ahogados* (the Bridge of the Drowned Ones), which exist to the present day in Zacatecas. It was, and still is, a devout city, but then the hidden public emerged from their houses, it seemed, only at the beck and call of the cathedral bells.

I have been back to Zacatecas several times recently, not only to learn something of the food but also drawn irresistibly by the newly restored beauty of the town, with its reddish-hued stone buildings that glow in the clear light of that altitude. It is not difficult to believe that this was the most important mining center of the colonial period, along with Guanajuato and Querétaro, when you see the ornate and graceful buildings that stand witness to the riches mined in the seventeenth and eighteenth centuries from the country around. Zacatecas was referred to as the *Civilizadora del Norte* (the Civilizer of the North). Although indigenous settlements existed there before the Conquest, the first Spaniards arrived in 1531, and from 1546 on its importance grew with the rush for gold and other precious metals.

This heritage has been protected by local architects and citizens who enlisted the help of the federal government for the restoration of the town in general and architectural jewels in particular, many of which have now been converted into museums. In fact, Zacatecas is now the most museumed city outside Mexico City.

The food market has been ousted from its central position and relegated to a side street, while the elegant building in which it was housed has been given a face-lift and turned into a small mall of boutiques.

On my first visit I was not greatly impressed with the food I tried. I remember the delicious regional *gorditas* that tasted of well-prepared corn, and very fresh cheeses and chiles, but there was a general lack of variety in the food offered by the small restaurants and *cenadurías*. At that time it was impossible to break down the conventional barriers and meet the more well-to-do families in their homes to learn more about their traditional and festive recipes.

This time it was somewhat different. Through the kindness of the Tourist Department I was not only guided through the Jeréz market but also introduced to some local cooks there.

Sr. Montes and his wife, the owners of Bar/Restaurant El Paraíso, which serves some delicious regional appetizers, were welcoming and informative, and I have included some of their recipes. Most important, I met Sra. María Guadalupe (Lupita) López de Lara de Zorilla. She interrupted her busy schedule—attending to her fascinating store of antiques, local handcrafts, and curiosities, in between looking after her family of eight—to talk to me at length. Her reminiscences about her grandparents, who had one of the largest cattle ranches in northern Mexico, were fascinating, as were the tales about her aunts, great cooks who now lead a secluded life, seeing only a few family friends and, of course, the clergy, rarely leaving their house.

The family recipes she gave me have been handed down, like so many in Mexico, from generation to generation. They relied on simple ingredients grown or available locally, enriched with others imported from Spain.

Caldo de res, a brothy beef stew with lots of vegetables, is a constant throughout the country, except, of course, in very remote, poor areas. It differs slightly from region to region, depending on the local vegetables available and the herbs or seasonings used or grown in that particular area. The crisp trimmings or sauces also differ from one place to another. Lupita's family adds the tiny, rosy-cheeked pears called *San Juaneras* because they appear around the end of June. Chickpeas and rice are also added. Marrow bones are a must; apart from the meat, the cooked marrow is smeared onto thick tortillas, or they are topped with the fat that floats on the top of the broth called *suegras* (mothers-in-law or dried crust of bread). It makes me hungry just writing about it because beef marrow is one of those wickedly unctuous foods—like *foie de canard*, if the French will forgive my mentioning them in the same breath.

She also gave me a very unusual version of *capirotada*, a bread pudding moistened not with custard but with a gruel of chickpeas and enriched with candied biznaga cactus, coconut, and cheese: a hot punch of unstrained guavas, served with a good shot of mezcal to keep out the cold.

Her grandfather always added honey to his beans, and the predictable ending to his meals was a *chorreada*, a flour tortilla doubled over a piece of *asadero* cheese and *queso de tuna*, a thick paste of red tunas, and toasted until the cheese and paste melt together. It is so simple but so delicious! The aunts contributed a refreshing drink of watermelon and red wine.

I extended my trip day by day to visit with Lupita and go to the little mining town of Vetagrande and its incipient mining museum and art gallery and, of course, the Sunday market of Jeréz.

CHORREADAS

❀

[MAKES 12 CHORREADAS]

SEÑORA MONTES OF EL PARAÍSO GRILL SAYS SHE INVENTED THE NAME CHOR-READA FOR THIS SIMPLE, TRADITIONAL DESSERT ON THEIR MENU. HOWEVER, they use a thick syrup of *tuna*, rather than the more substantial *queso de tuna*, which resembles an *ate* or fruit paste.

> 6 ounces (180 g) queso fresco or substitute (page 525), cut into strips
> 6 ounces (180 g) queso de tuna or guava
> or quince paste, cut into narrow strips
> 12 4- to 5-inch (10- to 13-cm) flour tortillas

Put a strip of the cheese and fruit along the center of each tortilla, double it over to cover the filling, and toast on an ungreased *comal* or skillet. Serve when the tortilla is slightly browned and the filling melted.

PAPAS PASTORES

SHEPHERD POTATOES

Sra. María Guadalupe de Zorilla

❁

[SERVES 4 AS A SIDE DISH, 6 TO 8 AS A SNACK]

IN THE DRY WINTER MONTHS IN THE MARKETS OF ZACATECAS, SAN LUIS POTOSÍ, AND SOME POINTS FARTHER SOUTH, YOU CAN SOMETIMES FIND THE tiniest—some less than 1 inch (2.5 cm) long—potatoes with light brown skins. They have several names, depending on the area: *güeros* (blondes), *locos* (mad), or *silvestres* and *cimarrónes* (both meaning wild). They do grow wild. The recipe I was given calls for the potatoes to be cooked in a pressure cooker; however, a heavy pot with a tight lid will do equally well.

Cooked in this way, they are generally eaten as a *botana* (snack) but are excellent with broiled meats or fish. The smallest new potatoes should be used, the waxier the better.

Of all the recipes for cooking these potatoes I collected traveling through the Bajío and north, this is my out-and-out favorite. In the original recipe the ingredients were ground together, but I think the texture is more interesting this way.

2 tablespoons olive oil
1 pound (450 g) very small new potatoes, rinsed and dried
salt to taste
⅓ cup (83 ml) finely chopped white onion
1 garlic clove, finely chopped
3 serrano chiles (or to taste), finely chopped
½ cup (125 ml) loosely packed roughly chopped cilantro
3 tablespoons fresh lime juice
1 cup (250 ml) water (½ cup/125 ml if using pressure cooker)

Heat the oil in a heavy pan, add the whole potatoes, sprinkle with salt, and fry, stirring them from time to time until the skins begin to wrinkle and brown. Add the onion, garlic, and chiles and fry for 3 minutes longer. Add the *cilantro* and lime juice and continue frying for

[CONTINUED]

1 minute more. Add the water, cover the pan, and cook over low heat until the liquid has almost all been absorbed, the flavors concentrated, and the potatoes tender.

NOTE: *If using the pressure cooker, cook the potatoes at low pressure for about 6 minutes with all the ingredients. Cool the pressure cooker quickly in a bowl of cold water, remove the lid, and continue cooking over high heat until the liquid has been absorbed.*

HUEVOS EN BATURILLO

EGGS WITH PARSLEY AND LIME JUICE

❀

[SERVES 2]

I WAS LEAFING THROUGH SOME OF THE OLD COOKBOOKS IN LUPITA'S COLLECTION AND FOUND ONE ENTITLED *MANUAL DE COCINERO Y COCINERA*—FOR BOTH men and women cooks. It was published in Puebla in 1849, the recipes taken from a literary magazine called *La Risa* (*The Laugh*). It was amusingly dedicated *"Al bello secso de Puebla"* (to the fair sex of Puebla). Another was printed in Durango in 1898, like many others, to raise money for charity, in this case for the sisters of St. Vincent de Paul.

Two recipes caught my eye: the one printed below and *Chiles Polcos*, quite different from those of Guanajuato—chiles stuffed with sardines and smothered with sliced bananas, peaches, pears, avocados, and cooked squash with more chile strips and a vinaigrette. But this one—eggs cooked with *natas* (the layer of cream formed on the top of scalded raw milk), parsley, and lime juice—I found delicious.

The word *baturilla* comes from *baturo*, a *gachupin* rancher. *Gachupin* was the name given to Spanish settlers in Latin America. I prefer to make egg dishes like this one in small quantities; you can control the balance of flavors and the setting point better.

Naturally the *natas* give a richer flavor, but crème fraîche makes an acceptable substitute, making up in richness what is lost in flavor.

4 large eggs
⅓ cup (83 ml) natas or crème fraîche
salt to taste

3 heaped tablespoons roughly chopped flat-leaf parsley
1 tablespoon lard or vegetable oil
1½ tablespoons fresh lime juice

Beat the eggs together with the *natas* and salt. Stir in the parsley. Beat the lard in a medium skillet, add the mixture, and stir over medium-high heat until almost set.

Stir in the lime juice and serve.

CHORIZO PARA TOSTADAS

CHORIZO COOKED WITH CABBAGE FOR *TOSTADAS*

Sra. María Guadalupe de Zorilla

❁

[MAKES APPROXIMATELY 1½ TO 2 CUPS (375 TO 500 ML)]

ALTHOUGH THIS RECIPE WAS GIVEN TO ME AS A TOPPING FOR *TOSTADAS*, IT MAKES A VERY GOOD FILLING FOR TACOS AS WELL. MUCH, OF COURSE, WILL depend on the quality of the *chorizo*. The most sought after in Zacatecas are not the more familiar links but homemade *chorizos* tied into small balls, sold in the little town of Malpaso on the way to Jeréz.

If the *chorizos* are rather dry and it is difficult to skin them easily, rub the outside with dampened hands; that'll do it. However, this trick doesn't apply if you buy *chorizos* in plastic casings—and I hope you don't.

8 ounces (225 g) chorizo
8 ounces (225 g) cabbage, very finely shredded and then chopped
salt if necessary

Remove the skin from the *chorizo* and crumble into a skillet. Cook over low heat until some of the fat renders out, stirring the *chorizo* from time to time, until just beginning to change color—about 5 minutes. Remove any excess fat. Add the cabbage and continue cooking over medium heat, stirring from time to time until the cabbage is just cooked. Season as necessary.

ENCHILADAS ZACATECANAS

ZACATECAS ENCHILADAS

Sra. María Guadalupe de Zorilla

❈

[MAKES 12 ENCHILADAS]

THE SAUCE

4 large ancho chiles, veins and seeds removed

2 cups (500 ml) whole milk

2 garlic cloves, roughly chopped

1 heaped tablespoon roughly chopped epazote leaves

vegetable oil for frying

1 tablespoon sugar

12 5-inch (13-cm) corn tortillas, freshly made if possible, kept warm

THE FILLING

*8 ounces (225 g) queso fresco or substitute (page 525),
crumbled, about 1¾ cups (438 ml)*

¾ cup (188 ml) finely chopped white onion

salt to taste

Have ready a warmed serving dish into which the *enchiladas* will just fit in one layer.

Cover the chiles with hot water and leave to soak until softened and reconstituted—about 15 minutes. Drain, tear into pieces, and put into a blender. Add the milk, garlic, and *epazote* and blend until smooth.

Heat 2 tablespoons of oil in a small skillet, add the blended ingredients, and fry, adding the sugar and salt to taste until slightly reduced and thickened so as to coat the tortillas well. Set aside and keep warm.

Add a thin layer of oil to a skillet, add the tortillas one by one, and heat through, rather than fry, for a few seconds on each side. "Blot" the fried tortilla on the next one to absorb some of the oil and drain again on paper toweling. Add a little more oil to the pan as necessary.

When all the tortillas have been fried, dip them into the sauce, put 1 heaped tablespoon of the cheese and onion, mixed together and salted if necessary, across the middle, roll up loosely, and set side by side in the serving dish. Pour any remaining sauce over the top, sprinkle with the rest of the filling, and serve immediately.

NOTE: *Do not assemble this dish ahead of time, or the tortillas will become soggy. When assembled, it can be reheated in a 350°F (177°C) oven for about 10 minutes.*

CHAYOTES CON NATAS

VEGETABLE PEARS WITH CREAM

Sra. María Guadalupe de Zorilla

✺

[MAKES 4 TO 6 SMALL SERVINGS]

WITH FEW EXCEPTIONS, CHAYOTES ARE RATHER INSIPID, BUT I WAS SURPRISED AT HOW DELICIOUS THEY COULD BE WHEN COOKED WITH NATAS (THE LAYER of cream that forms on the top of scalded raw milk). I have slightly embellished the recipe with onion and garlic. This dish is best left to stand for about 15 minutes before serving for the flavors to combine well.

1 tablespoon vegetable oil
2 heaped tablespoons thinly sliced white onion
2 small garlic cloves, finely chopped
1 serrano chile, finely chopped
salt to taste
*1 pound (450 g) chayotes, peeled and thinly sliced
with center core and "almond"*
freshly ground pepper to taste
⅔ cup (164 ml) water
¾ cup (188 ml) natas or crème fraîche

Choose a wide skillet in which the *chayote* slices will fit in no more than 2 layers. Heat the oil, add the onion, garlic, and chile with a sprinkle of salt, and cook without browning for a few

[CONTINUED]

seconds. Add the *chayote* slices, pepper, water, and a little more salt if necessary. Cover and cook over fairly high heat for about 8 minutes. The *chayote* should still be firm and most of the water evaporated—if still juicy, then drain off most of the liquid. Stir in the *natas*, cover the pan again, and cook over medium heat until the *chayote* is tender and coated with the *natas*.

Set aside, covered, for about 15 minutes before serving.

ASADO DE BODAS JEREZANO

WEDDING *MOLE* FROM JERÉZ

❁

[SERVES 6]

ALTHOUGH THIS IS A DISH TRADITIONALLY SERVED AT WEDDINGS, IT IS ALWAYS ON THE MENU OF RESTAURANT DORADO DEL RÍO IN JERÉZ, ZACATECAS.

2 pounds (900 g) stewing pork with a little fat,
cut into 1½-inch (4-cm) cubes

3 garlic cloves

salt to taste

THE SAUCE

36 guajillo chiles, 7 ounces (200 g) if large and pliable,
4 to 5 ounces (115 to 140 g) if small and very dry

¼ cup (63 ml) pork lard

3 thick rounds French bread, dried

3 garlic cloves, roughly chopped

3 bay leaves

2 tablespoons sugar

thickly peeled rind of 1 orange

1 ounce (30 g) Mexican drinking chocolate

salt to taste

In a saucepan, cover the pork with water, add the garlic and salt, and cook over medium heat until tender, about 40 minutes. Drain the meat, reserving the broth. Add water to make up to—or reduce to—4½ cups (1.125 l).

Meanwhile, slit open the chiles, remove seeds and veins, and lightly toast on a warm *comal* or skillet, taking care not to burn them. Cover with hot water and leave to soak for about 20 minutes. Drain, discarding the soaking water.

Put ½ cup (125 ml) of the broth into a blender, add a few of the chiles, and blend as smoothly as possible. Add the rest of the chiles a little at a time and blend until smooth, adding more broth only if necessary to release the blender blade.

Pass the chile puree through a fine strainer, pressing down hard to extract as much of the flesh and juice as possible. Discard the debris.

Heat 2 tablespoons of the lard in a heavy pan in which you will be cooking the *mole*, add the bread slices, and fry on both sides until crisp and brown. Add the bread and garlic with 1 cup of the meat broth to the blender and blend until smooth.

Add the rest of the lard to the pan and brown the meat lightly. Add the bread puree and fry for 1 minute longer, then add the blended chiles, bay leaves, sugar, orange rind, and chocolate and cook over medium heat, scraping the bottom of the pan to prevent sticking. Add the remaining broth, salt to taste, and cook for about 15 minutes more. The *mole* should be of medium thickness, lightly covering the back of a wooden spoon when finished.

FIGADETE PARA BOTANA

PORK RIND SNACK

❉

[MAKES APPROXIMATELY 1½ CUPS (375 ML)]

ONE OF THE SEVEN *CAZUELAS* TO ACCOMPANY *ASADO DE BODAS* (PAGE 140) IS *FIGADETE*, MADE OF THE SMALL FATTY PIECES OF PORK RIND THAT COLLECT AT the bottom of the vats in which the sheets of *chicharrón* have been fried; these are pressed into a block. *Chicharrón prensado* may be available in some Mexican markets: if not, buy some fatty *chicharrón*, break it into small pieces, and cook it in the oven until it is well browned and the fat rendered out.

Figadete is often served as a snack and filling for small corn tortillas. It is sometimes served hot mixed with cooked potatoes. Small pickled yellow chiles, either triangular or round, *güeros* or *bolitos*, are used in Zacatecas, but jalapeños *en escabeche* can be substituted.

However you prepare it, it *is* fatty—so I dedicate the recipe to homesick Zacatecans.

½ pound (225 g) chicharrón prensado, *chopped (see note above)*
½ medium white onion, thinly sliced
½ teaspoon dried oregano, crumbled
⅓ cup (83 ml) mild vinegar
4 güero *chiles (see note above) or jalapeño chiles* en escabeche
salt to taste
3 ounces (85 g) queso fresco, *cut into small cubes, or mild feta*

Mix all the ingredients except the cheese together and set aside to season for about 2 hours. Just before serving, mix in the cheese.

GUACAMOLE JEREZANO

GUACAMOLE OF JERÉZ

Srita. Teresa Galván

❋

[MAKES APPROXIMATELY 2¾ CUPS (688 ML)]

SOUR CREAM IN GUACAMOLE?—WELL, AT LEAST IT DOESN'T HAVE GARLIC AND LIME JUICE—YOU KNOW WHAT I'VE SAID ALL ALONG ABOUT GUACAMOLE WITH cream. And here it is in Jeréz, Zacatecas, Mexico, not Spain. I keep wondering whether the cream crept in with influences from north of the border, since a great percentage of men from that area go to work in the United States, although Srita. Galván seems to be traditional in her approach to the local food. This version of *guacamole* is delicious without the cream, and the acidity of the *tomate verde* prevents it from turning color quickly.

Of course, she wouldn't think of making it in anything but a *molcajete*—nor would I generally, but I must admit that in this case the blender is far faster, because the chiles tend to be toughish. But be careful not to overblend the avocado.

4 ounces (115 g) tomates verdes, about 8 small,
husks removed and halved

2 serrano chiles

2 Anaheim chiles, charred, peeled, veins and seeds removed

2 poblano chiles, charred, peeled, veins and seeds removed

salt to taste

½ cup (125 ml) loosely packed roughly chopped cilantro

1½ cups (375 ml) avocado pulp

⅓ cup (83 ml) crème fraîche or sour cream

¼ cup (63 ml) finely chopped white onion

Put the *tomates verdes* and serranos into a small saucepan, do not quite cover with water, bring to a simmer, and continue simmering until soft—about 10 minutes. Set aside to cool and then transfer to a blender with ¾ cup (188 ml) of the cooking water.

Chop the remaining chiles roughly and add to the blender with salt to taste and 1 heaped tablespoon of the *cilantro*. Blend to a fairly rough consistency. Crush the avocado pulp to a lumpy consistency and stir in the blended ingredients, cream, onion, and remaining *cilantro*. Adjust the salt and serve.

RAJAS DE CHILE ANCHO VERDE

CHILE STRIP RELISH

Professor Raúl Escobedo Galván

❂

[MAKES ABOUT 1 HEAPED CUP (265 ML)]

PROFESSOR RAÚL ESCOBEDO IS A YOUNG AND ENTHUSIASTIC MEMBER OF THE TOURISM DEPARTMENT'S STAFF IN ZACATECAS WHO ACTED AS MY VERY knowledgeable guide when I went to Jeréz, Zacatecas. This recipe came from his mother, who is a good cook. It is a rather sharp relish to serve on top of rice or with broiled meats. Once prepared, it is best seasoned for at least 2 hours, but if you leave it overnight or for a day or two, do not add the tomato until you serve it.

Chile ancho verde is the name given to poblano chiles in this area.

6 poblano chiles, charred, peeled, veins and seeds removed,
and cut into strips about ¼ inch (7 mm) wide

1 medium white onion, thinly sliced

1 garlic clove, finely chopped

½ teaspoon dried oregano, crumbled

¾ cup (188 ml) mild fruity vinegar or half rice vinegar
and half wine vinegar

salt to taste

6 ounces (180 g) tomatoes, skinned and thinly sliced (see note above)

2 tablespoons olive oil

Mix all the ingredients together and press down well into the vinegar, stirring from time to time so that it is seasoned evenly. Set aside (see note above).

REFRESCO DE TÍA MARIQUITA

WATERMELON AND RED WINE DRINK

María de Guadalupe de López Lara de Zorilla, Zacatecas

✸

[SERVES 8 TO 10]

I HAVE ADDED LIME JUICE TO THE ORIGINAL RECIPE TO ACCENTUATE THE FLAVOR.

3½ pounds (1.575 kg) watermelon

grated piloncillo or dark brown sugar to taste

1 teaspoon vanilla extract

¼ cup (63 ml) fresh lime juice or to taste

2 cups (500 ml) red wine

ice as necessary

½ cup (125 ml) roughly chopped pecans

Cut the watermelon into large pieces. Remove the center part, without seeds, and cut into small cubes—there should be about 1 cup (250 ml). Put the rest of the flesh that is dotted with the seeds into a blender and blend very briefly so that you don't break up the seeds. Pass through a fine strainer—you should have about 2 cups (500 ml). Stir in the sugar, vanilla, and lime juice. Just before serving add the red wine and watermelon cubes. Serve cold or over ice, with each glassful decorated with a few of the pecans.

SALSA MEXICANA ESTILO JEREZANO

FRESH MEXICAN SAUCE JERÉZ

❈

[MAKES APPROXIMATELY 1¾ CUPS (438 ML)]

WHEN I VISITED THE JERÉZ SUNDAY MARKET ONE DAY AT THE END OF THE CHILE HARVEST, THERE WERE PILES OF SHINY, MULTICOLORED CHILES OF ALL shapes and sizes mixed together in their various stages of ripeness. It was so different from the neat, separated piles seen in most Mexican markets.

I stopped to take a photograph just as a man was filling his large bag, scooping them up in handfuls. I asked how he was going to use them. He looked amazed that I should be asking such a question. "I am going to make a *salsa mexicana* of course." It's going to look spectacular, I thought, apart from all those crisp flavors and degrees of piquancy!

If your market carries a variety of colored chiles, or you grow them, this is just the sauce for you. You can vary it with what is available.

1 poblano chile, seeds and veins removed, finely chopped
1 red ripe jalapeño chile, seeds and veins removed, finely chopped
2 yellow chiles, seeds and veins removed, finely chopped
2 serrano chiles, finely chopped (do not attempt to remove seeds)
3 tablespoons finely chopped white onion
4 ounces (115 g) tomatoes, finely chopped, about ⅔ cup (164 ml)
½ cup (125 ml) water
3 tablespoons fresh lime juice
½ teaspoon dried oregano, crumbled
salt to taste

Mix all the ingredients together in a glass or nonreactive bowl and set aside to season for about 1 hour before serving.

CARNE CON CHILE GÜERO

PORK IN A GÜERO CHILE SAUCE

Restaurant Bar El Paraíso

※

[SERVES 4 TO 6]

THIS IS ONE OF THOSE SIMPLE BUT TASTY STEWS MADE WHEN THE SMALL YELLOW TRIANGULAR CHILES GROWN IN ZACATECAS ARE FRESH IN THE MARkets. The cooking method for the pork is like that of Michoacán: when partially cooked in water, most of the broth is drained off and the meat continues cooking with very little moisture until the fat renders out. It is then fried and the sauce added to the meat. This type of dish may be prepared ahead of time and, in fact, improves with standing a little before serving.

THE MEAT

2 pounds (900 g) stewing pork with some fat,
cut into 1-inch (2.5-cm) cubes

4 garlic cloves

salt to taste

THE SAUCE

12 güero chiles

12 ounces (340 g) tomatoes, broiled until soft (page 527)

6 garlic cloves, peeled

Put the pieces of pork into a heavy pan, add water to come just below the surface of the meat, the garlic, and salt, cover, and cook over medium heat for about 20 minutes. Drain off half of the broth and continue cooking uncovered until the pork is just tender—about 20 minutes. Continue cooking until the fat renders out and lightly fries the meat.

Meanwhile, char and peel the chiles, remove the veins and seeds, and chop roughly. Peel the tomatoes if you like (they do, I don't) and crush with the garlic and chiles to a textured sauce (this can be done in a food processor but not a blender, which would puree the mixture). Add the mixture to the meat in the pan and fry, adding a little more salt if necessary, until the moisture has reduced, about 5 minutes. Dilute with about 1 cup of the pork broth and continue cooking for another 5 minutes.

TAQUITOS DE CUERO

MINIATURE TACOS OF AVOCADO AND *CHICHARRÓN*

Restaurant Bar El Paraíso, Zacatecas

✸

[MAKES APPROXIMATELY 1¾ CUPS (438 ML), ENOUGH FOR 18 3-INCH (8-CM) TACOS]

THESE CRISP LITTLE TACOS FILLED WITH FRIED AVOCADO AND MADE EVEN RICHER WITH *CHICHARRÓN* ARE DELICIOUS—AND, I SUSPECT, DESIGNED TO shock the fat abstainers. You need eat only two, after all.

2 tablespoons vegetable oil
2 serrano chiles, finely chopped
2 tablespoons finely chopped white onion
salt to taste
1½ cups (375 ml) avocado pulp
1½ cups (375 ml) crushed chicharrón, *in very small pieces*
oil for frying
18 3-inch (8-cm) corn tortillas or larger ones cut into halves

Heat the oil in a skillet, add the chiles, onion, and a sprinkle of salt, and cook for a few seconds or until the onion is translucent. Add the avocado and crush it to a textured paste with a wooden bean masher. Cook, stirring well, for about 3 minutes. Just before preparing the tacos, stir in the *chicharrón*—if it is added too soon, it will become soft. It should remain crispy.

Heat about ¼ inch oil in a skillet. Put 1 heaped teaspoon of the filling in the middle of each tortilla, roll it up, and put seam side down into the hot oil. Fry until golden and crisp, drain on paper toweling, and serve immediately—this is pan-to-mouth food.

COAHUILA

The Journey North—Zacatecas to Torreón

WHEN I LEFT ZACATECAS EARLY ONE MORNING, I KNEW THAT MY JOURNEY WOULD BE RATHER A LONG ONE, ALTHOUGH SIX HOURS IS NOT THAT long when you are driving through an ever-changing landscape and picturesque villages—but for the most part these were semiarid areas. There were some lands under cultivation for chiles, corn, and beans, but they were under stress from years of drought, and it is hard to imagine that up until the first part of this century some of the largest and most prosperous cattle ranches in the whole country existed here, stretching up through Coahuila and even Chihuahua. A lot of the land was stripped bare during the heyday of mining in Zacatecas, not only for the mines but for the colonial houses where you can still see wooden beams of huge dimensions that must have come from local trees. A short treatise written in 1777 gives an extensive list of the great variety of trees growing then, which now have all virtually disappeared. Even as late as the twenties and thirties uncontrolled felling took place for very extensive charcoal production, and only a small valley area near Zacatecas covered with stunted oaks seems to have survived. ✷ I drove off the main highway for a few kilometers to look at Fresnillo, an important center for the isolated mines around the area. A well-kept *jardín*, a rococo church, and a few of what must have been elegant mansions during the nineteenth century told of better times than the homogenous present scene: the usual welter of traffic, blaring commercial announcements, and what appeared to be the majority of inhabitants, both young and not so young, jogging American style in the extensive, well-treed park. ✷ During my trips in recent years I have seen a lot of dried-up riverbeds, and not only through droughts but because of overuse of irrigation systems in unsustainable agricultural practices. The next town, Río Grande, despite its name, was no exception, and the riverbed snaking around part of the town was dead. ✷ Not surprisingly, the markets in the places I passed through were unexceptional, with predictable supplies of local crops—corn, chiles, and beans and none of the wonderful herbs and greens available farther south. ✷ Just as I was leaving Río Grande and feeling the midmorning pangs of hunger, I stopped for a late breakfast at a modern gas station complex with little stores catering to the needs of travelers, with a spanking clean restaurant—alas, without a name. The food was so fresh and excellently prepared: beans, eggs, tortillas, thick cream, milk, and cheese (goodness knows where the locals kept their cows) with the most efficient and thoughtful service. It reminded me that some of the best meals I have had on the road are these hearty *almuerzos* that last you well into the afternoon. I mentally gave them my three stars! ✷ Fairly soon I was on my way again, and on a toll road, expensive and devoid of traffic. As you whiz along in solitude, you can see an almost endless line of trucks and trailers cheek by jowl on the old two-lane highway that curves around the base of the mountain foothills. Gradually the land descends from this central plateau into the broad valley of Gómez Palacio and its twin city Torreón.

Torreón

I wish I could find something nice to say about Gómez Palacio in Durango and its twin city Torreón in Coahuila. The people I talked to were very friendly, open, and helpful, but even that did not convince me to stay more than two nights, so as to arrive on the appointed day at the appointed hour at the ranch in Chihuahua.

I remember that I was unimpressed with Torreón on my last visit over twenty years ago—it was a town without form or beauty, and I hurried away to Durango. Torreón grew in importance at the beginning of the century, when the cotton producers were enjoying prosperity, and later became an important dairying center. But there is very little to indicate that it has had a varied and cosmopolitan life, with people coming to live there from France, England, the Middle Eastern countries, and even China. The shops are garish, and the buildings, mostly ugly blocks, have nothing to recommend them. Only occasionally does one see a dignified old mansion or official building that has some style.

Wherever I go I take refuge in the markets, and that too was a surprise in Torreón. The fruits and vegetables are sold in a large alley some distance away, while the market itself houses, to begin with, the largest number of locksmiths I have ever seen cheek by jowl. I had the impression that the people of Torreón either change their locks every week or lose their keys by the dozens.

There are simple restaurants galore with white-capped cooks and waitresses imploring you to come in and try their specialties, but it was too early in the day. At one of the entrances a bad-tempered old man had a very interesting store selling all types of dried fruits and nuts, among them the fresh harvest of pink pine nuts that had just arrived from the Durango forests and, surprisingly, dates from a unique date palm area not far from Torreón. On the other side of the market the air was pleasantly musky with the abundance of dried herbs sold there. Every Mexican market has its herb stands, but here there were dozens—how could they make any money at all? And I suddenly remembered having read that in the late 1700s Padre Fray Juan Agustín Mori had appended a list of some 172 medicinal plants found in the northern part of Coahuila to his treatise on the province of Texas.

I was attracted, naturally, by a sizzling tray of fried fish marked *chicharrón de pescado*, next to an impressive array of varied types of fish. Fish in the middle of beef country and a beef-eating public! Immediately a conversation sprang up with the young salesman, who was soon joined by the owners of the stand. Conversation about food is always lively in Mexico, and we were soon exchanging recipes. They generously gave me three developed by their mother that they were serving in the restaurant opposite their fish stand (two of the recipes follow).

Later a very intelligent older lady in the Gómez Palacio tourist department (a rarity) told me all about the points of interest in and around the area, but even the Valley of Silence (that geographical and scientific phenomenon where radio signals, however strong, cannot be received) and the colorful *Festival de las Etnias* (Festival of Ethnic Groups) would not attract me back to Torreón.

CHICHARRÓN DE PESCADO

CRISP-FRIED FISH

Sra. Aurita Villela, Torreón

❂

[SERVES 6 AS A STARTER]

SMALL PIECES OF FISH SEASONED AND FRIED CRISP TO SERVE AS A SNACK ARE KNOWN AS CHICHARRÓN (CRISP-FRIED PORK RIND) DE PESCADO—A DISH VERY much of the north and northeast of Mexico. A friend recalls that in his youth in Tamaulipas he always looked forward to the visit of one of his uncles, who unfailingly turned up with a large bag of greasy and delicious *chicharrón de pescado*, fried, of course, in pork lard.

Actually, they make a delicious snack with tortillas and *guacamole* or seasoned with more lime juice. You may want to prepare this snack ahead of time and reheat it in a hot oven on trays lined with absorbent paper to soak up the excess oil.

Any type of fish, or fish trimmings, can be used.

12 ounces (340 g) fish fillets, skin and bones removed

3 garlic cloves, crushed

2 tablespoons fresh lime juice

2 teaspoons salt

1 teaspoon crushed peppercorns

¾ cup (188 ml) all-purpose flour

½ teaspoon powdered chile de árbol or very hot chile powder,
or to taste

1 tablespoon dried oregano, finely crumbled

vegetable oil for frying

Season the fish with the garlic, lime juice, salt, and pepper and set aside to season for 30 minutes.

Mix the flour with the chile and oregano and coat a few of the fish pieces—only those that you are going to fry in the first batch.

Heat about ½ inch of oil in a skillet and fry the fish, taking care not to crowd the pan, turning the fillets from time to time, until thoroughly crisp and a deep golden brown, about 10 minutes. Drain and prepare the next batch.

ESTOFADO DE RAYA

SKATE STEWED IN OLIVE OIL

Sra. Aurita Villela, Torreón

✳

[SERVES 4]

WHEN I WAS GROWING UP IN ENGLAND, SKATE, A FISH OF THE RAY FAMILY, WAS ABUNDANT AND MADE A VERY ECONOMICAL MEAL. FORMERLY IGNORED by the fashionable fish markets in Manhattan and other places, it is now acceptable (perhaps because New York's Le Bernardin introduced a skate salad on its menu some years ago). Other species of ray are very popular, both fresh and salt-dried, in Campeche, but it was a surprise to see a recipe for it in the center of northern Mexico.

This dish may be served as a main course with white rice or as a topping for *tostadas* or even as a filling for fish *empanadas*. If skate is not available, use any oily fish with flesh that can be shredded easily and withstand the longer-than-usual cooking. You need a good heavy olive oil for this recipe.

1½ pounds (675 g) skate

salt and freshly ground pepper to taste

3 tablespoons fresh lime juice

⅓ cup (83 ml) olive oil

⅓ medium white onion, finely chopped

2 small garlic cloves, finely chopped

6 ounces (180 g) tomatoes, finely chopped, about 1 cup (250 ml)

½ cup (125 ml) loosely packed roughly chopped cilantro

4 to 6 chipotle chiles en adobo, to taste,
roughly chopped with some of the sauce from the can

Season the fish with salt, pepper, and lime juice and set aside to season for about 30 minutes, turning once. Heat the oil in a shallow heavy pan. Add the fish with the onion and garlic and fry over medium heat, turning the fish once and shredding it with 2 forks—about 5 minutes or until the onion is translucent.

Add the tomatoes and *cilantro* and continue cooking over fairly high heat to reduce the juice—about 5 minutes. Add the chiles and cook for another 5 minutes. Adjust the seasoning.

Parras, Coahuila

Torreón may be one of my least favorite places in Mexico, but Parras, also in Coahuila, is one of my favorites. Parras de la Fuente, *"el oasis en el desierto"* (the oasis in the desert) as it is called, is a veritable oasis in the arid southern part of the state, almost equidistant from Torreón, the capital, and industrial Saltillo. I was invited to join some friends there one year for the *paleada* in October, when the pecan trees are shaken and beaten so that the ripe nuts fall off. It is one of the most important pecan-producing areas in northern Mexico.

When you see the scrubby land—although it produces a large variety of medicinal herbs and fragrant oregano—it is very difficult to realize that the first Spaniard to arrive there in 1572, Francisco de Urdinola, recognized the great potential of the area for cattle ranching, agriculture, and mining. In 1593 he was given vast holdings to form the largest *latifundio* (large land holdings by one owner) in New Spain. A few years later, since many vines had been planted and flourished there, it was given the official name of Santa María de las Parras (*parra* is Spanish for vine). The first looms were introduced as well as a mill for grain, powered by water from the numerous springs. Of course, later vines and olives were destroyed in New Spain so that wine and oil could not compete with those of the mother country.

At the end of the last century Don Everisto Madero, the grandfather of the ill-fated president Francisco Madero, bought vast tracts of land around Parras and introduced vines from all over Europe; he built up the most prestigious wine business in Mexico. Until about forty years ago the Madero winery was famous particularly for its sparkling and fortified wines, but, as the large family dispersed, interest in the winery waned and only vestiges of the vineyards remain today.

The weaving of fabric has persisted, and factories founded at the beginning of the century are now recognized as producing the finest denim for jeans; in fact, in the last year or so three more factories have opened. One can only hope that the very special ambience of this oasis will not be totally lost.

I began to feel in harmony with Parras a few kilometers away, as I drove through a broad avenue overhung with towering elms and native pecan trees. The narrow river meandered in rhythmic curves almost alongside, bordered by those most impressive of Mexican trees, *ahuehuetes* (*Taxodium mucronatum*). These members of the cypress family have a Náhuatl name meaning "old man of the water."

This time I was on my way back from my journey north for a very brief stopover; it was late October, and the fields on either side of the road were golden with flowers in the afternoon light. I wandered again through the older neighborhoods with their simple, traditional houses—and wanted there and then to buy one of them—guarded protectively by tall, grayish adobe walls and kept cool and shaded by the trees of the orchard: figs, pomegranates, quince, and pecans. They had such a secretive air of peace and isolation.

On my first visit I was invited in to see one of the old homes that had belonged to the Hacienda del Rosario and the Madero family. It was like stepping back into the past century: elegant European furniture, the filmiest of lace curtains, the family portraits, and fading photographs of family occasions under high-ceilinged rooms that stretched out in a leisurely fashion.

Stepping into the garden, I was briefly back in England, the England of my youth. The immense trees cast shadows over the lawn, lightly carpeting it with falling golden leaves. There were clumps of fading autumn flowers and the scent of roses. It took me a while to come back to the present.

Parras is famous not only for its *mezclilla*, the denim material from which jeans are made, but its luscious-looking and tasting sweetmeats: compressed candied figs, raisins, coconut, and fudge in all shapes and sizes, lavishly decorated with pecan halves. There are thin disks of the most delicious hard candy, *palenquetas* (dentists' delight) crammed with pecans, pepitas, or mixed nuts; you go to purchase two and come away with ten. You buy delicious cheeses, yogurt, and butter from the local technical school, and if you buy and scald the local milk you can eat the thick layer of richly colored cream, *natas*, with your yeast breads or even beans.

Food in Parras is fresh and simple, much of it produced locally: beef, beans much like pintos, unsophisticated but delicious sauces, flour tortillas, some made with excellent whole-wheat flour from Saltillo, and, of course, preserved fruits for dessert. On that first visit we sat in the garden for most of our meals, not always successfully dodging the ripe pecans that showered us as the tall trees swayed in the breeze.

On that first visit to Parras, my hostess suggested that we go and see Sra. Gregoria Flores, a renowned local cook who was particularly famous for the quality of her regional sweetmeats.

We walked to her house through narrow streets lined with small houses cheek by jowl, the rows broken occasionally by high adobe walls protecting overgrown orchards—they seemed mysterious and inviting with heavily laden boughs of vivid red pomegranates overhanging the walls.

Goyita, as she is known, is well into her eighties but still directs the production of her *dulces*, from her bed or rocking chair.

Two of her eight children were busying themselves over the huge vats set along the open gallery running along the back of the house. She told us about how she supported her young family after her husband's death by making *tamales* and snacks for the workers in the nearby factories. A particular favorite was *molletes*, round dark-colored rolls made with whole-wheat flour and raw sugar.

This is her recipe.

MOLLETES DE GOYITA, PARRAS

Sra. Gregoria Flores

❋

[MAKES APPROXIMATELY 20 3-INCH (8-CM) BREADS]

THESE *MOLLETES*, SEMISWEET BREADS WITH A FAIRLY DENSE CRUMB, ARE MADE OF HALF WHITE AND HALF WHOLE-WHEAT FLOUR. THE ANISE SEEDS are added whole and give a wonderful flavor to the dough. You can eat them either alone with *cafe con leche* or hot chocolate or with cream cheese. If you prefer them sweeter, sprinkle more brown sugar and some pecans on top before baking.

They stay fresh for several days but should be reheated. These *molletes* freeze well. Actually, I have kept some of them in a plastic bag in the refrigerator for two months—I forgot about them—and they were still good.

10½ ounces (300 g), grated piloncillo or dark brown sugar, 1¾ cups
(438 ml) loosely packed

3 cups (750 ml) water

1 tablespoon anise seeds

2 1-inch (2.5-cm) cinnamon sticks

THE DOUGH

1 pound (450 g) all-purpose flour, 4 cups (1 l)

1 pound (450 g) whole-wheat flour, stone-ground
if possible, 3½ cups (875 ml)

½ teaspoon ground sea salt

½ pound (225 g) vegetable shortening,
cut into small pieces, 1⅓ cups (333 ml)

2 ounces (60 g) cake yeast, roughly crumbled, a very scant
½ cup (120 ml) loosely packed, or 1 ounce (30 g) dried

1 tablespoon warm water

Have ready 2 large baking sheets, well greased, and 2 sheets of plastic wrap to cover completely, well greased.

Put the sugar and water into a saucepan along with the anise seeds and cinnamon. Bring to a boil, stirring to dissolve the sugar. Continue boiling until the liquid has reduced to 2 cups (500 ml). Set aside to cool to lukewarm, then remove the cinnamon.

Mix the flours and salt together. Rub the fat into the mixture until it resembles rough bread crumbs.

Cream the yeast with the warm water, pressing out the lumps with a wooden spoon. Add to the flour mixture and gradually stir in the syrup with the anise seeds. Mix to a stiff, rather sticky consistency, adding a little water if necessary to make a cohesive dough.

Turn the dough out onto a lightly floured board and knead for about 3 minutes. Form into a round cushion shape, place in a clean, greased bowl, and cover with plastic wrap and a towel. Set aside to rise—it should be spongy to the touch but will not rise spectacularly—about 6 hours.

Turn the dough out onto a lightly floured board, roll into a sausage shape about 2 inches (5 cm) in diameter, and cut into 20 pieces. Roll each piece into a smooth ball and press down until the dough is about ¾ inch (2 cm) thick. Place 2 inches apart on 2 well-greased large baking sheets, cover with greased plastic wrap, and set aside in a warm place—about 75°F (24°C)—until spongy to the touch and about 1½ times the original size, about 2 hours.

Meanwhile, heat the oven to 350°F (177°C) and bake—one tray at a time on the top shelf—until the *molletes* are firm and well browned, about 20 minutes. Remove and cool on a rack.

ASADO DE BODAS ESTILO PARRAS

PARRAS PORK AND CHILE WEDDING STEW

✺

[SERVES 6]

THIS VERSION OF *ASADO DE BODAS*, AS IT IS PREPARED IN PARRAS, IS SO DIF-
FERENT FROM THE OTHERS; IT IS A STRONGLY FLAVORED STEW OF PORK
popularly served for weddings and other family and ceremonial occasions. It is often accompanied by flour tortillas (or even whole-wheat flour tortillas) and beans that resemble
American pintos in color and flavor.

Rubbing the spices into the meat and setting it aside to season gives it a very good flavor.
Particularly noticeable is the flavor of the local oregano that grows wild in the arid hills
around.

The dish can be prepared ahead so that the sauce matures in flavor. In any case it is best
to let it cool off before serving, to skim off the excess fat that rises to the surface. Then it can
be reheated and served.

*2¼ pounds (1 generous kg) stewing pork with some fat,
cut into ¾-inch (2-cm) cubes*

1¼ tablespoons dried oregano

1 tablespoon cumin seeds

2 bay leaves, crumbled

2 cloves

5 garlic cloves, peeled

1 tablespoon salt or to taste

1 tablespoon mild vinegar

3 ancho chiles, veins and seeds removed

3 guajillo chiles, veins and seeds removed

approximately 3 cups (750 ml) water

3 tablespoons pork lard or vegetable oil

1 tablespoon sugar

½ orange, cut into slices

Put the meat into a bowl. Grind the oregano, cumin seeds, bay leaves, and cloves together to make a powder. Crush the garlic together with the salt and vinegar. Add the powdered herbs, mixing to a thick paste. Rub the paste into the meat with your hands and set aside to season —at least 1 hour or overnight in the refrigerator.

Cover the chiles with hot water and soak for about 20 minutes or until softened and reconstituted (do not leave too long in the water or they will lose their flavor). Drain, discarding the water. Transfer to a blender with 1½ cups (375 ml) of the water and blend as smoothly as possible.

In a heavy heatproof casserole, heat the lard, add the seasoned meat, and fry over medium heat until the meat is just starting to brown (take care: if the heat is too high, the spices will burn).

Add the blended chiles to the pan, pressing them through a fine strainer to remove the tough pieces of guajillo skin that stubbornly remain despite the blending. Fry the sauce for about 5 minutes, stirring and scraping the bottom of the pan to prevent sticking.

Add the remaining 1½ cups (375 ml) water, cover the pan, and cook over medium heat, stirring from time to time, for about 15 minutes. Add the sugar and orange and continue cooking until the meat is tender. Add a little more water if necessary to thin the sauce to medium consistency so it coats the back of a wooden spoon.

CHILAQUILES DE PARRAS

Sra. Bertha González de Morales

❁

[SERVES 6]

THE SAUCE

4 ancho chiles, seeds and veins removed

4 guajillo chiles, seeds and veins removed

1¼ cups (313 ml) water

1 small tomato, about 2 ounces (60 g), broiled until soft (page 527)

[CONTINUED]

3 garlic cloves, roughly chopped

2 tablespoons vegetable oil

1 teaspoon dried oregano, crumbled

salt to taste

approximately ½ cup (125 ml) vegetable oil

*8 5-inch (13-cm) corn tortillas, cut into 1-inch (2.5-cm)
squares and dried, preferably overnight*

½ cup (125 ml) finely chopped white onion

*approximately ⅓ cup (83 ml) grated queso añejo,
Chihuahua, Romano, or Muenster*

Cover the chiles with hot water and soak until soft and the flesh is reconstituted, about 20 minutes. Drain, discarding the soaking water. Put 1 cup (250 ml) of the water into a blender and add the drained chiles a few at a time, blending well after each addition.

Strain into a bowl through a fine strainer to remove the small pieces of guajillo skin. Rinse the jar and add the remaining ¼ cup (63 ml) water, the tomato, and the garlic and blend until smooth.

Heat the 2 tablespoons of oil in a skillet, add the tomato puree, and fry for a few seconds. Add the chile puree and fry over medium heat, stirring and scraping the bottom of the pan to prevent sticking. After 4 minutes, add the oregano and salt and cook for 1 minute more. The sauce should be of medium consistency, lightly coating the back of a wooden spoon. If too thick, add a little more water. Set aside and keep warm.

Heat the ½ cup oil in a skillet and fry the tortilla pieces, a few at a time, until crisp and golden. Drain each batch on paper toweling. Drain off all but 1 tablespoon of the oil. Return the tortilla pieces to the pan, sprinkle the onion over them, cover the pan, and cook over low heat, shaking the pan from time to time, until the onion is translucent, about 3 minutes. Stir in the chile sauce so that the tortilla pieces are as evenly covered as possible. Again, cover the pan and cook over medium heat, shaking the pan from time to time, for about 3 more minutes.

Sprinkle with the cheese and serve immediately.

CHILES RELLENOS EN SALSA VERDE

STUFFED CHILES IN GREEN TOMATO SAUCE

❀

[SERVES 6]

MY HOSTESS IN PARRAS, SRA. BERTHA DE MORALES, GAVE ME THIS RECIPE WHILE WE WERE THERE. IT WAS GIVEN TO HER ALMOST FORTY YEARS AGO when she was newly wed in Monterrey, by a lady of Lebanese descent who was an excellent cook.

This is an unusual and delicious variation on the theme of *chiles rellenos*, a welcome change from the more standard recipes. Instead of serving the chiles in a tomato broth, you pass the green sauce around separately at the table, so the batter remains crisper.

THE STUFFING

1 pound (450 g) stewing pork with some fat, cut into 1-inch (2.5-cm) cubes

½ small white onion, roughly sliced

2 garlic cloves, peeled

salt to taste

THE SAUCE

1 pound (450 g) tomates verdes, husks removed, rinsed

3 serrano chiles or to taste

½ small white onion, roughly chopped

4 small garlic cloves, roughly chopped

1 scant teaspoon cumin seeds

1½ teaspoons dried oregano

1 small bunch cilantro, thick stems removed, roughly chopped

3 tablespoons pork lard or vegetable oil

[CONTINUED]

*6 large poblano chiles, charred, peeled, veins and seeds removed
but kept whole with stalk attached*

3 eggs, separated

vegetable oil for frying

flour for dusting chiles

Put the meat, onion, garlic, and salt into a pan, barely cover with water, and cook over medium heat until the meat is tender—about 35 minutes. Drain the meat, reserving the broth. When it is cool enough to handle, shred it roughly and set aside.

Put the *tomates verdes* into a pan with the whole serranos, barely cover with water, and simmer until they are soft but not falling apart—about 10 minutes. Drain.

Put ½ cup (125 ml) of the reserved meat broth in a blender, add the onion, garlic, cumin, and oregano, and blend as smoothly as possible. Add another ½ cup of broth along with the *tomates verdes*, serranos, and *cilantro* and blend again to a textured puree.

Heat 1 tablespoon of the lard in a skillet, add the sauce, and fry over fairly high heat until reduced to about 3½ cups (875 ml). Add salt to taste and set aside.

In another pan, heat the remaining lard, then add the shredded meat and fry until it is just beginning to brown. Add 1½ cups (375 ml) of the sauce and continue cooking over a fairly high heat until the mixture is moist but not juicy. Adjust the salt.

Fill each chile with a scant ⅓ cup (81 ml) of the meat. Beat the egg whites until stiff but not dry, then gradually beat in the yolks with salt to taste. Meanwhile, heat oil about 1¼ inches (3 cm) deep in the pan. Pat flour over the surface of each chile just before frying, coat with the batter, and fry over medium heat in the hot oil, turning them over until they are an even deep golden color. Drain on paper towel.

Serve the chiles hot, passing the remaining green sauce, heated, separately.

NOTE: *This dish is not and should not be swimming with sauce.*

CHIHUAHUA

The Journey North — Torreón to Chihuahua

ESTIMATED MY TIME OF ARRIVAL AT THE RANCH IN CHIHUAHUA AS 1:30 ON OCTOBER 7, OR SO I HAD TOLD MY HOSTESS THREE WEEKS EARLIER IN MEXICO CITY. IT WAS A DISTANCE OF almost 400 kilometers from Torreón. I set off early as usual, anxious to keep my reputation for punctuality; *la hora inglesa* (English time) always elicits amused respect among the Mexicans. The first part of the journey was uneventful through flat agricultural land on a toll highway, so it was a relief to have another splendid breakfast in, again, a restaurant that could compete with the world's cleanest. The efficient and friendly waiter was proud of his immaculate appearance and displayed his short-cut nails scrubbed pink. ❋ Leaving Ciudad Jimenez, the true prairie begins: chaparral covered with a slight haze of green from a welcome rain, the first in many years of drought. It extends as far as the eye can see until it meets the foothills of the distant mountains, mountains you never seem to reach, no matter how far you drive. Turning north at Ciudad Camargo through the Prairie of the Giants you hardly see a soul, just groups of cattle gathering under the sparse shade or around a small patch of water. This is cattle country, producing some of the best Hereford beef, much of it exported to the United States.

There is a very special brilliance to the light here and a lingering scent of sagebrush on the air, and there are many hours of luxurious silence in which to listen to the sounds of nature without the intrusive noises of modern life: roaring trucks and cars and the ceaseless pounding of noise machines that follow men around like their shadows—noisy shadows!

It had been about twenty years since my last visit to Chihuahua and that was mainly to the capital, Chihuahua City, but also through the Barranca de Cobre in the western Sierra Madre, so I returned to this unknown part of the country with many expectations and my usual curiosity.

I was beginning to worry that I had passed the ranch, but there was no one to ask. Eighty-six kilometers had come and gone, at least according to my odometer, when I suddenly saw off to the right a gyrating wind pump and soon afterward a discreet sign saying Mesteñas. The ranch was named after the *Llanos de los Caballos Mesteños*, the plains or prairies of the mustangs, in which it was situated.

The wives of the ranch hands, who had lived there for many years, were ready and expecting me with their cooked dishes, recipes, and funds of information.

It was almost lunchtime, but some preparation had to be made for the next day. One of the men was called in to slice, very thinly, a substantial piece of freshly killed beef for *tasajo*; it was soon flapping and drying on the clothesline in the sun. Two of the children were sent off to collect *trompillos* (*Solanum eleagnifolium*), a small round berry about ¼ inch in diameter, pale green in color with lighter markings, that grows wild in Chihuahua. It is used either fresh or dried—when it turns yellow—to clabber the milk for *asadero* cheese. Socorro, who was to make the cheese, said it was not real *asadero* if it was made with any other type of rennet and showed me the milk that had already been set aside to sour, an important ingredient.

Flour tortillas were being made, and I was fascinated to see that each one was flattened with a heavy iron on the *comal* so that it would not bubble up. The long, skinny green chilaca chiles, like Anaheims, were being charred, sending off that distinctive and hunger-making aroma.

The nearest and only settlement for about eighty miles around is a mining community, now almost deserted. A few families stayed on after the mine closed, and there were a couple of little miscellaneous stores and the pride of the place: a small bakery turning out fresh bread twice a day, surprising in such a small and isolated place.

Our main reason for going there was to talk to one of the most dedicated traditional cooks, Sra. María Luisa Espinosa. After catching up on the goings-on of her numerous family, now spread out in many parts of Mexico, and reminiscing about the ups and downs of the mine, she gave us the simple local dishes to try: a *pipián*—it would be better with quail, she said—and an *asado* of pork (both of these recipes appear in this section).

The next day was no less hectic and started with a lesson from Socorro in cheesemaking. Half of the milk to be used had been soured for two or three days, and the other half had just arrived, still warm from the morning's milking. The *trompillos* were crushed with some warm water and strained into the milk, which was heated gently for about fifteen minutes. She took a little of the curd between her fingers and tested by stretching it; it was not smooth or flexible enough, so it was heated a little longer until the curds hung in thick, smooth skeins when Socorro dipped her wooden spoon into the curds and held it up high. Taking little balls of the curds, she flattened them out in oval forms about an eighth of an inch thick, six inches long, and three inches wide, salting them and setting them aside to drain. The children were forbidden to come near, or the whole production would have been eaten immediately. They like their cheese fresh, while everyone else prefers to let it mature and develop a pleasant acidity, which it does in a few hours.

Sra. Cruz demonstrated her dried beef and noodle dish before rolling out and frying *buñuelos* for dessert, while her daughter and daughter-in-law and their friends contributed to my knowledge of their food.

Beef, of course, is the main meat, prepared dried or fresh in different ways: there is *carne disco*, which conjures up the picture of preparing it for a discotheque. It is, in fact, a type of stir-fry carried out in a woklike discarded disk of a plow that has become too blunt to use. It is set up over a wood fire on a metal frame. Very roughly chopped onion and jalapeños are fried first, then the chopped meat, sometimes *chorizo* and bacon added with tomatoes. It is the favorite food for a *taquiza*, especially good for a large crowd, who make their own tacos with a pile of tortillas that are warmed up around the rim of the *disco*.

When a steer is killed, the men prefer to throw the mountain oysters, *criadillas*, straight onto a glowing fire, to eat with a sauce and tortillas, while the more refined way of preparing them is to boil, skin, chop, and fry this delicacy, also eaten with tortillas and a hot sauce.

Sometimes a goat is seasoned with chile paste and roasted, chicken is cooked in beer, a *salpicon* of shredded meats is mixed with many vegetables, lettuce, chiles, and mayonnaise and eaten with salt crackers and pork trotters in vinegar. Many of the dishes are accompanied by *frijoles borrachos*, beans cooked with beer and enriched with bacon and *chorizo*. It is hearty eating.

My stay was all too short, but it was time to continue to Ciudad Camargo, a thriving little agricultural town about one hundred kilometers away. Once more, my friend had prepared some of the local cooks, and I was whisked off as soon as we arrived to talk, to listen, and most important perhaps, to try some of the local food.

Chihuahua, like all the other northern Mexican states, has a climate of extremes: great heat, very cold and dry, with minimal rainfall. The crops grown during the summer rains are dried in the hot autumn sun: beans, squash, chiles, and corn. The squash is cut into rounds and dried for *orejones*, big ears, which can be used through the winter months. Part of the corn harvest is dedicated to make *chacales* (*chicales* in Coahuila, *chacuales* in Zacatecas). Mature but still tender corn kernels are cooked, dried in the sun, and then broken up roughly or ground to a slightly finer texture. They keep perfectly through the winter months, until the next harvest (and I have even kept some for about five years). *Chacales* are cooked as a vegetable or in soups (see the recipe that follows).

This part of Chihuahua is quite an important chile-growing area as well, and while the greatest part of the crop is dried, fresh chiles are also used: *chile de árbol, guajillo* (confusingly called *cascabel* there), *jalapeño*, and *chilaca* or Anaheim. The *chilaca*, or *chile verde*, the long, slender light green chile that ranges from mild to hot, is the one featured most commonly in the cooking of Chihuahua. While it is used fresh, or dried as *chile de la tierra* or *chile colorado*, there is an interesting variation: it is charred and peeled and then hung up to dry, whole, without removing seeds and veins. In this state it is known as *chile pasado*. I warn you, if you do this, 1 pound will reduce to 2 ounces. But it is well worth it because when rehydrated before cooking this chile has a delicious flavor and enhances the stews or *rellenos* or *chile con queso* in which it is used. In recent years mushroom cultivation has been introduced, and now the preferred filling for *chiles rellenos* is a mixture of mushrooms and cheese.

The crop of jalapeños, while still green, is mostly destined for the canning industry; once they ripen to red, their value is diminished. Not so many years ago they were simply thrown away in the latter stage, until Don Juventino Santos, an enterprising man from Tulancingo, Hidalgo, who was in the chile business, decided to smoke-dry them for *chipotle mora*.

When we were driving out from Camargo the following day to visit the Lago Toronto, the air was filled with the aroma of smoke and chiles, and there, a few yards from the roadside, were huge rectangular cement-block structures about twelve feet high. At intervals around the base were fire boxes filled with glowing, smoking logs. Spread out in a thin layer over the slatted surface were deep red, wrinkled jalapeños—the color darkens as the smoking process progresses. A man with a shovel was turning them over from time to time. The farther we drove out of town, the more small communities (*ejidos*) we saw and visited that were also dedicated to smoking chiles, and as we drove back that afternoon there were trucks tipping out their loads of the ripened jalapeños onto the newly vacated smoking beds.

This smoke-drying process takes several days in which time the weight of the chiles is reduced to one seventh that of the fresh. The smoked chiles are so cheap that one wonders how on earth anyone makes any money out of it at all. We bought sackfuls to support the local economy and distributed them lavishly to all the cooks we knew along the route back and in Michoacán.

They were extraordinarily picante, owing to the hot, dry summer. A recipe for them pickled *en escabeche* can be found in *The Art of Mexican Cooking*, and following is a recipe for chipotles *en adobo*.

CHIPOTLES EN ADOBO

✷

[MAKES ABOUT 3 CUPS (750 ML)]

PRESERVING CHILES BY SMOKE-DRYING DATES FROM PRE-COLUMBIAN TIMES, AND THE BASIC PROCESS, ALBEIT WITH SLIGHTLY DIFFERENT TECHNIQUES, IS still used today.

Jalapeño chiles—ripened, smoke-dried, and prepared in a pungent sauce for chipotles *en adobo*—have taken the American gastronomic world by storm. They are everywhere, the condiment of the decade, mixed with anything and everything: in sauces, seasoning pastes, soups, salads, breads, etc. (not yet, I sincerely hope, in ice cream). There are two types of *chipotles*: the larger, highly smoked, tobacco-colored one and the smaller mulberry-colored (as the name implies) *mora*—not to be confused with *moritas*, which are smaller. When I first came to Mexico many years ago, the larger light-colored chiles were more in evidence, canned in a light pickle, *escabeche*. Today the canning industry seems to favor the *mora*, possibly because its smaller size lends itself to the small cans.

Of the many brands exported from Mexico, my preference is for those packed in a darker-colored sauce, a real *adobo*, rather than those in a more acidic, tomato-based sauce. Of course, it is always interesting to make your own, without preservatives and fresh, for which I give a recipe here. This preparation is pungent; a milder version is given in the note that follows the recipe.

4 ounces (115 g) chipotle chiles (moras), about 60
3 ancho chiles, seeds and veins removed
1½ cups (375 ml) water
4 garlic cloves, roughly chopped
2 sprigs fresh marjoram or ⅛ teaspoon dried
2 sprigs fresh thyme or ⅛ teaspoon dried
pinch cumin seeds, crushed
1 bay leaf, torn into small pieces
2 tablespoons olive oil

¾ cup (188 ml) mild vinegar, pineapple in Mexico,
or half rice vinegar and half wine vinegar

¾ cup (188 ml) strong vinegar

2 ounces (60 g) dark brown sugar, about ⅓ cup (83 ml) firmly packed

1 tablespoon sea salt

Rinse the chipotle chiles and drain. Pierce each one right through with a sharp fork or skewer, put them into the pressure cooker with water to cover, and cook at low pressure for about 15 minutes—they should be soft but not mushy. (If you are not using a pressure cooker, cook over fairly low heat, tightly covered, for 30 to 40 minutes.)

Drain the chiles, remove the stems, and wipe off any stray seeds clinging to the outside. Set aside.

Meanwhile, cover the ancho chiles with hot water and simmer for 5 minutes. Drain and transfer to a blender. Add 1 cup (250 ml) of the water, the garlic, herbs, seeds, and bay leaf plus 4 of the cooked chipotles and blend until almost smooth.

Heat the oil in a shallow pan, add the blended ingredients, and fry for about 3 minutes, scraping the bottom of the pan to prevent sticking. Add the vinegars, the rest of the water, the sugar, and the salt and cook for 5 minutes more. Then add the rest of the cooked chiles and cook over low heat, scraping the bottom of the pan from time to time to prevent sticking, until the sauce has reduced and thickened—about 15 minutes.

Store in the refrigerator or sterilize and store in a cool place.

NOTE: *If you prefer a less pungent version of this recipe, cook the chiles first for about 5 minutes. Drain, slit them open, and remove the seeds and what remains of the veins. Discard the water and start at the beginning of the recipe, reducing the cooking time by about 5 minutes. If you wish to have a lighter sauce, add another 6 ounces (180 g) of tomatoes to the* adobo.

TORREJAS DE FRIJOL

BEAN FRITTERS IN CHILE SAUCE

Sra. Socorro Gracía de Sosa, Rancho Mesteñas

❊

[MAKES ABOUT 16 2-INCH (5-CM) FRITTERS]

THIS SIMPLE VEGETARIAN DISH IS PREPARED ON THE RANCH FOR THE MEATLESS DAYS OF LENT. IT IS PARTICULARLY DELICIOUS WHEN COOKED with the new season's crop of local beans for which the area and neighboring Zacatecas are famous.

The beans should not be cooked until they are soft; they should still be a little firm (but not *al dente*, please), drained well, and mashed to a stiff paste. If the paste is too loose, the *torrejas* will fall apart in the frying process.

Commenting on the onions, Socorro said they should be *"exquisitamente picada"* — exquisitely chopped.

Like all fritters and *chiles rellenos* covered with this light egg batter, they absorb a lot of oil. I suggest, as I have done many times before, preparing them a little ahead and reheating on a paper-lined tray in the oven so that the excess oil will seep out before putting them into the chile sauce.

8 ounces (225 g) bayo beans, flor de mayo, or pintos

salt to taste

3 tablespoons pork lard or vegetable oil

½ medium white onion, finely chopped

9 colorado de la tierra chiles, Californian, or
New Mexican chiles

2 garlic cloves, peeled

1 tablespoon vegetable oil

vegetable oil for frying

4 eggs, separated

Rinse the beans (do not soak overnight), drain, cover with hot water, and cook over low heat —or in a slow cooker—until fairly soft (see note above), about 2 hours, depending on the age of the beans. Add salt and cook for 5 minutes more. Drain well, reserving the broth for the sauce, and mash to a roughly textured paste.

Put the lard into a skillet, add the bean paste, and mash well into the lard. Cook for about 10 minutes, stirring and scraping the bottom of the pan to prevent sticking. Set aside to cool, then stir in the chopped onion and form into 16 patties about 2 inches (5 cm) in diameter. Slit the chiles open, remove the seeds and veins, cover with hot water, and soak for about 20 minutes.

Put 1 cup (250 ml) of the reserved broth into a blender, add the garlic and drained chiles a few at a time, and blend as smoothly as possible.

Heat the 1 tablespoon oil in a heavy pan and add the chile puree, pressing it through a fine strainer to extract tough pieces of the skin and as much of the juice and flesh of the chiles as possible. Cook over medium heat, stirring to prevent sticking, for about 5 minutes. Dilute 1½ cups (375 ml) bean broth and cook for 5 more minutes. Set aside and keep warm while you prepare the fritters.

Heat about ½ inch frying oil in a skillet. Beat the egg whites with a touch of salt until firm and then beat in the yolks one at a time. Coat the bean patties one by one in the beaten egg and carefully lower them into the hot oil.

Fry until well browned on the underside, turn very carefully (they tend to be rather soft), and fry on the second side. Drain on paper toweling. Place the fritters in layers in a casserole with some of the chile sauce in between the layers and reheat—either on top of the stove or, preferably, in the oven so that the ones at the bottom do not disintegrate—until the sauce starts to simmer and the fritters are well heated through (I stick a finger in to make sure). Serve immediately.

SALSA DE LOLA

LOLA'S SAUCE

Lola, Rancho Mesteñas

❋

[MAKES 1½ CUPS (375 ML)]

WHEN IT COMES TO SAUCES IN MEXICO, MY HEART DEFINITELY LIES SOUTH, BUT I HAVE TO ADMIT—AND WILLINGLY SO—THAT A SIMPLE NORTHERN sauce, made when the chiles are freshly picked, is crisp and enticing, especially with the simple meat dishes of the northern plains. In fact these are more like relishes. Lola does not aspire to be a great cook, but she prepared this sauce for us on a recent visit. It does, of course, depend on the freshness of ingredients, which are very finely chopped but not blended.

6 Anaheim peppers, charred, peeled, veins and seeds removed,
and finely chopped
6 ounces (180 g) tomato, finely chopped, 1 cup (250 ml)
1 garlic clove, finely chopped
3 tablespoons finely chopped white onion
salt to taste

Mix all the ingredients together well and leave to season in a cool place, not in the refrigerator, for about 1 hour before serving.

PUERCO EN PIPIÁN

PORK IN PEPITA SAUCE

Sra. Cruz Estela Ramos de Sosa

❋

[SERVES APPROXIMATELY 6]

ON THIS RECENT VISIT TO CHIHUAHUA AND THE RANCH, I HAD THE OPPORTUNITY TO TRY TWO RECIPES FOR *PIPIÁN*, ONE WITH THE INGREDIENTS FRIED and ground, and the other toasted and ground. I have opted for the toasted version, which has a more defined flavor. Although Señora Cruz said that either pork or beef could be used, she really preferred quail—a luxury these days—or beef tongue, cooked and sliced, or for Lent a well-cooked omelet cut into large pieces, which would make a good vegetarian dish.

The grinding process is always a problem—for non-Mexicans. On the ranch they grind the ingredients in a hand-cranked metal corn grinder, which is hard work in itself, or if there is a mill that grinds *nixtamal* for the tortillas, that is ideal. But failing those options I have evolved a method using the electric grinding devices most cooks now have in their kitchens to cut down on preparation time.

The local recipes for *pipián* also call for dried corn, toasted and ground, with corn tortillas as an alternative. I found it easier to use toasted tortillas, which are certainly easier to grind than toasted corn. But only as a very last resort should tortillas be made of those innocuous flours *minsa* or *masa harina*.

The local pumpkin seeds are the very slender, slightly yellowish ones with a thin husk—elsewhere in Mexico they are used as a *botana*, toasted and salted—but if they are not available, use those with a bulkier husk and substitute one quarter of the quantity with hulled raw pumpkin seeds. In all cases they should be raw.

THE MEAT

*2 pounds (900 g) stewing pork with some fat,
cut into ¾-inch (2-cm) cubes*

1 quart (1 l) water

salt to taste

½ medium white onion, roughly chopped

1 garlic clove, roughly chopped

THE SAUCE

*4 ounces (115 g) unhulled raw pumpkin seeds, 1⅓ cups (333 ml)
(see note above)*

4 5-inch (13-cm) corn tortillas, left out to dry the night before

1 guajillo chile

[CONTINUED]

1 seco, colorado de la tierra, or Californian chile

1 pasilla chile

heaped ¼ teaspoon cumin seeds

2 garlic cloves, roughly chopped

Put the pork in no more than 2 layers in a heavy pan, add the water, salt, onion, and garlic, and bring to a simmer. Cover the pan and continue cooking over low heat for about 30 minutes. The pork should be almost tender. Drain off and reserve all but ¾ cup (188 ml) of the broth and continue cooking, still covered, until the broth has been absorbed and the fat is rendering out. The pork should be tender but not too soft.

Toast the pumpkin seeds in an ungreased pan over low heat, turning them over from time to time so that they toast evenly—remember that the inside oily seeds cook faster than the husks. Set aside to cool.

Toast the dried tortillas until they are a deep golden color and crisp right through. Break into pieces.

Wipe the chiles thoroughly with a damp cloth, slit them open, and remove the seeds and veins. Toast them on a *comal* or griddle until the inside flesh is tobaccoey brown; when cool they should be quite crisp. Put the tortillas and chiles into a food processor and blend as much as possible. Taking a little at a time, grind to a powder in a coffee/spice grinder, adding the cumin with the last batch. Set aside. Put the pumpkin seeds into the food processor and grind as finely as possible, then, taking a little at a time, transfer to the coffee/spice grinder and grind to a slightly textured powder. Pass through a fine strainer and then grind the debris once more. Strain again and discard the debris of husks.

By this time the meat should be browning in its own fat, but add a little lard or oil if necessary. Add the ground ingredients and stir well, scraping the bottom of the pan thoroughly since the dried ingredients stick very quickly.

Put ½ cup (125 ml) of the reserved broth into the blender, add the garlic, and blend, then add to the pan with about 1 cup (250 ml) more of the broth. Cook over low heat, remembering to stir and scrape, for about 5 minutes. Add 4½ cups (1.125 l) more broth (adding water to make that much if neccesary) and cook over low heat until the sauce thickens slightly—it should coat the back of a wooden spoon just as the oil starts floating to the surface. The starch solids tend to sink to the bottom, so keep stirring. Adjust the salt and serve. If the sauce is left to stand, it will thicken considerably. Add more water or broth to dilute to the right consistency.

PAPA CUARTELERAS

GARRISON POTATOES

Sra. María Luisa Espinosa de Rodríguez, La Perla

❁

[SERVES 4]

WHEN SRA. ESPINOSA'S HUSBAND WAS HELD PRISONER IN THE BARRACKS FOR FAILING TO COMPLETE HIS MILITARY SERVICE, SHE VISITED HIM FAITHFULLY every day, bringing him food. One of the meals she prepared, and named after his predicament, was this nourishing potato dish.

I prefer to cook the potatoes unpeeled, but that is a matter of choice. The small, triangular yellow chiles pickled in vinegar or brine are called for, but you could substitute the more readily available jalapeño chiles *en escabeche*. Again I recommend letting the dish sit for a while before serving—it does improve the flavor.

2 to 3 tablespoons pork lard or vegetable oil, as needed
1 pound (450 g) potatoes, peeled and cut into ¾-inch (2-cm) cubes
salt to taste
½ medium white onion, thinly sliced
6 ounces (180 g) tomatoes, finely chopped, 1 cup (250 ml)
pickled yellow chiles to taste or jalapeño chiles en escabeche,
cut into quarters
approximately ½ cup (125 ml) water

Heat the lard, add the potatoes, sprinkle with salt, and fry over medium-high heat until just beginning to brown. Add the onion and fry until translucent, then add the tomatoes and cook for a few minutes more to reduce the juice.

[CONTINUED]

Add the chiles and water, cover, and cook over medium heat, shaking the pan from time to time to prevent sticking—about 15 minutes. The potatoes should be tender and moist but not too juicy. If they have too much liquid, remove the lid and reduce for a few moments. Cover and set aside for about 30 minutes before serving.

ASADO DE CHILE COLORADO

STEW OF PORK IN CHILE SAUCE

Sra. María Luisa Espinosa de Rodríguez, La Perla

❁

[SERVES 4]

THIS IS ONE OF THOSE SIMPLE BUT DELICIOUS STEWS TYPICAL OF THE COOK-ING OF THE NORTH OF MEXICO. EITHER PORK OR BEEF CAN BE USED, although the pork lends a fuller flavor to the dish. The local chile colorado in Chihuahua is akin to the Californian or New Mexican chiles. This stew develops flavor if cooked a few hours ahead.

1½ pounds (675 g) stewing pork with some fat,
cut into ¾-inch (2-cm) cubes
salt to taste
15 colorado de la tierra, Californian, or New Mexican chiles
approximately 2 cups (500 ml) water
1 bay leaf, Mexican if possible
1 heaped teaspoon dried oregano, crumbled
2 garlic cloves, roughly chopped
1 ½-inch (13-mm) cinnamon stick

Put the pork into a wide, heavy pan into which the meat will fit in no more than 2 layers. Barely cover with water, add salt, cover, and cook over medium heat until almost tender— about 30 minutes. Drain off most of the broth and reserve, adding enough water to make up to 2½ cups. Continue cooking uncovered until the fat has rendered out and the meat is slightly browned.

While the meat is cooking, slit the chiles open and remove the seeds and veins, cover with boiling water, and set aside to soak for 15 minutes. Drain well.

Put ⅓ cup of the reserved broth into a blender, add the bay leaf, oregano, garlic, and cinnamon, and blend as smoothly as possible. Add this to the meat in the pan and fry for a few seconds.

Add 1 cup of the broth to the blender and blend the drained chiles, adding a few at a time, to a smooth puree. Add the chiles to the meat in the pan, pressing them through a fine strainer to extract as much of the flesh and juice as possible from the debris of tough skins. Continue frying, scraping the bottom of the pan to prevent sticking—about 5 minutes. Add the rest of the reserved broth and continue cooking over low heat until the meat is tender and the sauce well seasoned. Adjust the salt. The sauce should now be of medium consistency and coat the back of a wooden spoon well.

CHILE PASADO CON CARNE SECA

DRIED MEAT WITH CHILE PASADO

Sra. Cruz Estela Ramos de Sosa

❂

[SERVES 4 GENEROUSLY]

THIS DISH EPITOMIZES THE FOOD OF THE DRY, SEMIARID LANDS OF THE NORTH, WITH THE CONCENTRATED FLAVORS OF THE BEEF AND CHILES. IT IS strong without being heavy.

I like to make this recipe ahead of time and let it season at least half an hour before serving. While it is not soupy, there should be plenty of broth. If too much is absorbed in the cooking, add a little more water.

Serve with refried beans and flour tortillas.

6 ounces (180 g) dried beef (recipe follows)
2 cups (500 ml) hot water
4 chiles pasados (page 179)

[CONTINUED]

3 tablespoons vegetable oil
½ medium white onion, finely chopped, heaped ⅓ cup (90 ml)
2 garlic cloves, finely chopped
8 ounces (225 g) tomatoes, finely chopped, 1⅓ cups (333 ml)

Rinse the beef in cold water. Cover with the hot water and leave to soak for 10 minutes. Drain and reserve the soaking water. Tear or cut the beef into small pieces.

Rinse the chiles in cold water. Slit them open and remove the seeds and veins. Tear or cut them into strips about ½ inch (13 mm) wide, cover with hot water, and soak for 5 minutes. Drain and reserve the soaking water.

Heat the oil in a heavy pan in which you are going to cook the stew. Add the beef and fry, turning over from time to time so that it cooks evenly, for about 3 minutes. Add the onion and garlic and continue frying until the onion is translucent but not browned—about 2 minutes more. Add the chile strips and fry for another 2 minutes, then add the tomato and cook, stirring from time to time until the juice has been absorbed.

Add water to the soaking water to make 1 quart (1 l). Add to the pan, stir well, cover, and cook over low heat until the meat is fairly soft (it will always be a little chewy) and well seasoned—about 40 minutes. Set aside to season for about 30 minutes.

CARNE SECA

DRIED BEEF

❁

[MAKES APPROXIMATELY 8 OUNCES (225 G)]

WHEN PROPERLY PREPARED, DRIED BEEF (NOT BEEF JERKY, WHICH IS USUALLY TOO CONCENTRATED AND CHEWY) CAN BE DELICIOUS, ALTHOUGH QUITE AN acquired taste. I have not seen many commercial brands in the Mexican markets, but two—if still available—I can recommend are La Fama brand, and La Parilla. If you want to do your own:

1½ pounds (675 g) steak, lean and without gristle

1 heaped teaspoon fine sea salt

1½ tablespoons fresh lime juice

Cut the steak, or have the butcher cut it, into paper-thin slices. Sprinkle on both sides with salt and lime juice and hang up to dry in the sun or in a dry, airy place. Depending, of course, on the strength of the sun and the amount of humidity in the air, it can take 3 days or more. It can then be stored for weeks, provided it is kept dry.

NOTE: *The good cooks of Chihuahua do not, of course, call the USDA food safety hotline to ask if it's okay to dry their uncooked beef on a clothesline, the way it's been done for generations. But if they did, they'd be informed that it's most definitely not okay from a microbiological point of view unless you're planning to cook the beef a long time, as you do in the preceding recipe. So only the intrepid should try this at home.*

CHILES PASADOS

DRIED GREEN CHILES

✹

[MAKES 4 OUNCES (115 G)]

CHILES PASADOS, GREEN CHILES, EITHER *POBLANOS* OR ANAHEIMS, CHARRED AND PEELED AND THEN DRIED, ARE VERY MUCH A THING OF THE CENTRAL northern states of Mexico. Of course, it is an ideal way of preserving them, apart from enhancing their flavor.

While they are sold commercially in the markets of Chihuahua and Durango, it is rare to find them elsewhere, although I have seen them on a couple of occasions in the United States. They can be reconstituted and stuffed for *chiles rellenos* or cooked with onion, tomatoes, and cheese for *chile con queso*, etc., and lend a delicious flavor to these dishes. They are easy to prepare.

2 pounds (900 g) poblano or Anaheim chiles, about 16 medium

Char the chiles whole, preferably directly over the flames of a gas stove, or right up under a gas or electric broiler—if you use other methods, such as blistering in the oven, you will cook

[CONTINUED]

the flesh too much. Immediately put them into a plastic bag and set them aside to "sweat"—which loosens the skin—for about 15 minutes. Slide your hands over the chiles, pulling off the charred skin.

Set them out on a rack or hang them up, if the stalk is still intact, in the sun or a very dry, airy place until completely dried, the time depending on the strength of the sun or the humidity in the air. Test by pulling up the stem to see if the flesh around it has completely dried out; that and the placenta holding the seeds take much longer because they are enclosed. Allow a week or so. If dried sufficiently and stored in a dry place, they can last for a year. Follow the recipe instructions for rehydrating and using.

CALDILLO DE CARNE SECA CON FIDEO GRUESO

DRIED BEEF AND NOODLE STEW

Sra. Cruz Estela Ramos de Sosa

❂

[SERVES 6]

CALDILLO IS A SOUPY STEW, A TRADITIONAL EVERYDAY DISH IN CHIHUAHUA. IT IS EATEN AS A MAIN COURSE WITH FLOUR TORTILLAS. I FIND THAT THIS IS best prepared a few hours ahead for the full flavor of the dried beef to permeate the broth. In Chihuahua a medium vermicelli is used, not angel hair, which would fall apart in the cooking. One of the local cooks told me that before frying dried beef she always soaks it for a short while in hot water so that it does not absorb so much oil.

8 ounces (225 g) dried beef (page 178)
¼ cup (63 ml) vegetable oil
6 ounces (180 g) vermicelli (see note above)
½ medium white onion, finely chopped, about heaped ⅓ cup (90 ml)
1 garlic clove, finely chopped
½ teaspoon peppercorns
¼ teaspoon cumin seeds
8 ounces (225 g) tomatoes, finely chopped, about 1⅓ cups (333 ml)

8 ounces (225 g) potatoes, peeled and cut into ½-inch (13-mm) dice

*5 cups (1.25 l) water or light beef broth (please, not canned!), including
the soaking water*

salt if necessary

jalapeño chiles en escabeche, *for serving*

Cover the beef with hot water and set it aside to soak for about 20 minutes. Drain well and tear into small pieces, reserving the soaking water.

In a heavy flameproof casserole, heat the oil, add half of the pasta, and fry, turning over from time to time to brown evenly. Drain and fry the remainder. In the same oil, fry the beef until it is just beginning to brown, add the onion, garlic, and the pepper and cumin crushed together, and fry for a few seconds without browning the onion.

Add the tomatoes and continue cooking over fairly high heat until some of the juice has been absorbed. Add the pasta, potatoes, and water and continue cooking over low heat—it should just simmer—until the potatoes are cooked, about 20 minutes. Adjust the seasoning. Set aside for about 1 hour before serving with the jalapeños.

CHACALES ESTILO CIUDAD CAMARGO

DRIED CORN SOUP

Srita. Rosa Hilda Nuñez

✲

[MAKES APPROXIMATELY 2 QUARTS (2 L)]

CHACALES IS THE NAME FOR COOKED, DRIED, BROKEN-UP PIECES OF CORN KERNELS LIKE *CHICOS*. THIS IS A VERY UNUSUAL AND DELICIOUS WAY OF preparing *chacales* in a soup, as it was served to us in Ciudad Camargo. You can use the New Mexican *chicos* in this recipe.

The *chacales* should be soaked overnight or at least 6 hours ahead of making this soup.

1 very heaped cup (265 ml) chacales or New Mexican chicos

7 cups (1.75 l) hot water

[CONTINUED]

2 teaspoons salt

1 cup (250 ml) water

8 ounces (225 g) tomatoes, roughly chopped, about 1½ cups (375 ml)

½ medium onion, roughly chopped, a scant ½ cup (125 ml)

2 large sprigs flat-leaf parsley

1 small celery rib, roughly chopped

1 tablespoon vegetable oil

½ teaspoon dried oregano, crumbled

TO SERVE

½ cup (125 ml) thinly sliced radishes

¾ cup (188 ml) grated Chihuahua cheese or Muenster

a picante sauce (recipe follows)

Put the *chacales* into a saucepan, cover with the hot water, add the salt, and leave to soak for at least 6 hours. Bring to a simmer and continue simmering, stirring from time to time to prevent sticking, until soft—about 1½ hours.

Meanwhile, put 1 cup (250 ml) of water into a small pan, add the tomatoes, onion, parsley, and celery, and cook over low heat until the tomatoes are soft, about 10 minutes. Transfer to a blender and blend until smooth.

Heat the oil in a skillet, add the blended ingredients, and fry over fairly high heat until reduced and seasoned—about 5 minutes. Add to the *chacales*—through a strainer if necessary—and continue cooking for 15 minutes.

Adjust the salt and add the oregano just before serving. Serve in deep bowls and pass the radishes, cheese, and sauce separately.

SALSA PARA CHACALES

SAUCE FOR DRIED CORN SOUP

Srita. Rosa Hilda Nuñez

❁

[MAKES APPROXIMATELY 1½ CUPS (375 ML)]

THIS IS A THIN, SHARP SAUCE OF DRIED CHILES TO BE SERVED WITH CHACALES.

3 ancho chiles, seeds and veins removed
2 chiles de árbol
2 chipotle moras
1 large tomate verde, husk removed, rinsed and quartered
1 garlic clove, finely chopped
dried oregano, crumbled, to taste

Wipe the chiles clean with a damp cloth. Remove the stalks and put into a small saucepan. Add the *tomate*, barely cover with water, and simmer for 10 minutes or until the *tomate* is soft. Strain and transfer to a blender, add the garlic and water to make 2 cups (500 ml), and blend as smooth as possible. Strain, discarding the debris of seeds, etc. Set aside for about 30 minutes. Just before serving, sprinkle the surface with oregano.

SALSA DE LILI

LILI'S SAUCE

Srita. Rosa Hilda Nuñez

❁

[MAKES APPROXIMATELY 1 CUP (250 ML)]

THIS IS VERY PICANTE, MORE A RELISH THAN A SAUCE.

4 large jalapeño chiles, charred, peeled, seeds and veins removed
6 ounces (180 g) tomatoes, charred until soft and peeled
1 very heaped tablespoon finely chopped white onion
approximately ⅓ cup (83 ml) water
salt to taste

[CONTINUED]

Finely chop the chiles and tomatoes. Be sure to catch all the juice that exudes and mix with the onion. Add enough water to make 1 cup (250 ml), then season with salt.

CALDO DE OSO

"BEAR BROTH" FISH SOUP

Sr. Jesús, Restaurant Los Cuatro Vientos, Lago Toronto

✹

[MAKES APPROXIMATELY 2 QUARTS (2 L)]

THE RESTAURANT CUATRO VIENTOS IS NEAR THE EDGE OF LA BOQUILLA DAM ON THE LAKE CALLED TORONTO BECAUSE IT WAS STOCKED WITH FISH FROM Toronto—or was, since the water has receded alarmingly with five consecutive years of drought. The owner, Don Jesús Casa, developed this soup using the catfish that stocked the dam. Although it is now known as *caldo de oso*, bear broth, it was originally *caldo odioso*, according to his very lively and intelligent daughter, Bertha Alicia, who now cooks and runs the place. The story goes that a fisherman, heartily sick of a daily diet of fish soup, called it odious.

The day we were there, Bertha Alicia prepared it especially for us with the preferred "blue" catfish that had been swimming around moments before. The fish were gutted and cleaned and cut into small steaks about 1½ inches (4 cm) wide with both head and tail included. In cooking the recipe I decided to give the broth a little more flavor and cooked an extra head and backbone right from the beginning.

This recipe is unusual because it is thickened with a seasoned roux.

THE ROUX

2 tablespoons olive oil

1 heaped tablespoon finely chopped white onion

1 small garlic clove, finely chopped

1 small tomato, finely chopped

⅓ cup (83 ml) all-purpose flour

¼ teaspoon dried oregano, crumbled

heaped ¼ teaspoon black peppercorns

⅛ teaspoon cumin seeds

¼ cup (63 ml) water

salt to taste

2 small catfish, gutted, about 1½ pounds (675 g) total

6 cups (1.5 l) water

1 extra fish head and backbone

salt to taste

12 ounces (340 g) tomatoes

4 sprigs fresh mint

2 tablespoons vinegar from pickled chiles
or juice from a can of jalapeño chiles en escabeche

1 ancho chile, wiped clean, seeds and veins removed,
and torn into small pieces

TO SERVE

roughly chopped cilantro

a hot chile sauce (page 85 or 183)

First prepare the roux: Heat the olive oil in a small pan, add the onion and garlic, and cook without browning until translucent. Add the tomato and continue cooking for a few seconds, then add the flour and fry until it is golden, taking care not to burn it. Add the oregano, the pepper and cumin crushed together, and the water and continue cooking, stirring all the time to prevent sticking, for about 3 minutes or until the mixture thickens. Add salt and set aside.

Rinse the fish and cut into slices about 1½ inches (4 cm) thick, including head and tail. Bring the 6 cups (1.5 l) water to a boil, add the extra head and backbone with the salt, and bring to a simmer. Add the whole tomatoes, and cook for about 10 minutes or until soft but not breaking open. Remove, drain, peel, and blend smooth. Set aside.

Continue simmering the broth for another 10 minutes. Mix 2 tablespoons of the roux with ½ cup (125 ml) of the fish broth—or blend—and return to the pan. Add the tomato puree with the mint, vinegar, and ancho chile and continue cooking for about 10 minutes. The

[CONTINUED]

broth should have thickened very slightly—if not, add a little more of the roux. Just before serving, add the fish slices and simmer until tender—about 5 minutes.

Serve with the *cilantro* and chile sauce on the side.

NOGADA

PECAN CANDY

Sra. Estela Romo, Ciudad Camargo

❋

[MAKES APPROXIMATELY 1½ POUNDS (675 G)]

IN THE NORTH OF MEXICO *NOGADA* IS A HARD CANDY MADE WITH *PILONCILLO*, CONES OF UNREFINED SUGAR, AND PECANS, WHICH GROW ABUNDANTLY THERE. (Of course, in and around Puebla, *nogada* is a sauce made of walnuts.)

I always look for a way to use the very-dark-colored *piloncillo* because of its wonderful flavor, but I found when testing this recipe that it never reached the hard-ball stage and the candy always remained a little sticky. This suspicion was confirmed by a friend of mine from Nuevo Leon, who said his mother always used the lighter *piloncillo* when making her *nogada*.

It is addictive.

> 1¼ pounds (565 g) light piloncillo or light brown sugar,
> about 3½ cups (875 ml)
>
> 3 cups (750 ml) water
>
> 2-inch (5-cm) cinnamon stick
>
> 4 ounces (115 g) pecans, roughly chopped,
> about a very heaped cup (265 ml)
>
> 6 ounces (180 g) whole pecan halves, about 1½ cups (375 ml)

Have ready a lightly oiled cookie sheet large enough to accommodate the candy in a thin layer.

Break the *piloncillo* up into small pieces and put into a large, heavy pan. Add the water and cinnamon and cook over low heat, stirring from time to time, until the sugar has dissolved.

Raise the heat and cook at a rolling boil until the syrup reaches the hard-ball stage on a candy thermometer—260°F (126°C). Immediately remove from the heat and stir in the nuts.

Continue stirring until the nuts are coated as evenly as possible. Spread the mixture out on the cookie sheet—as thin as possible given the thickness of the nuts—and set aside to cool and harden. Break into large pieces and store in an airtight container.

ROLLO DE NUEZ Y DATIL

DATE AND NUT ROLL

Sra. Estela Romo, Ciudad Camargo

✸

[MAKES 3 7-INCH (18-CM) ROLLS ABOUT 1½ INCHES (4 CM) IN DIAMETER]

I DON'T HAVE A SWEET TOOTH, BUT I FIND THIS ROLL DELICIOUS IN SMALL QUANTITIES. SRA. ROMO SERVED IT AS A TOUCH OF SWEET AFTER AN AMPLE lunch, and I was hooked. If stored in a dry place, well wrapped or in an airtight tin, it will last for many months. You do need whole milk, *not* 2 percent, and if you like, you could add a little half-and-half for added richness.

2 cups (500 ml) whole milk

1⅓ cups (333 ml) sugar

12 ounces (340 g) chopped dates,
about 2 very firmly packed cups (500 ml)

1 pound (450 g) pecans, roughly chopped,
about 4 very full cups (1 generous l)

Put the milk and sugar into a heavy pan and stir over low heat until the sugar has dissolved, then cook over high heat, stirring and scraping the bottom of the pan from time to time to prevent scorching, until reduced and thickened to the soft-ball stage—250°F (120°C) on a candy thermometer. Gradually stir in the dates and, when they are well incorporated, cook for about 2 minutes more.

Remove from the heat and stir in the nuts a little at a time. Continue turning the mixture over until the nuts are well coated, then set the mixture aside to season a little. When slightly warm and pliable, place the mixture on a piece of damp cheesecloth and roll out under your palms until it is about 1½ inches (4 cm) in diameter. Cut into the desired lengths and store.

RAJAS EN CERVEZA

CHILE STRIPS COOKED IN BEER

Sra. Olga B. de Baca, Chihuahua

✸

[SERVES 4 AS A FIRST COURSE, 6 AS A BOTANA (SNACK)]

FROM MICHOACÁN TO CHIHUAHUA AND BACK, EVERY RECIPE I KNOW THAT COMBINES CHILES WITH CHEESE MEETS WITH IMMEDIATE APPROVAL. GOING through my old files, I came across this delicious variation on the theme, given to me many years ago by Sra. de Baca. For a first course, I like to serve this in individual *gratin* dishes with corn tortillas.

3 tablespoons vegetable oil

1 cup (250 ml) finely sliced white onion

salt to taste

1 pound (450 g), poblano or Anaheim chiles, about 6 medium, charred, peeled, veins and seeds removed, and cut into strips, about 1¼ cups (313 ml) firmly packed

1 cup (250 ml) strong beer—none of that light stuff

6 ounces (180 g) Chihuahua, asadero cheese, medium Cheddar, or Muenster, thinly sliced

Heat the oil, add the onion and salt, and cook over low heat until translucent—about 1 minute. Add the chile strips, cover the pan, and continue cooking until the chiles are tender but not soft—about 3 minutes. Add the beer and continue cooking, uncovered, until it has been absorbed by the chiles. Spread the cheese over the top, cover, and heat through until melted. Serve immediately.

CHILE DULCE

SWEET CHILE RELISH

Sra. Lilia S. de Beck

✣

[MAKES APPROXIMATELY 2 CUPS (500 ML)]

ANOTHER RECIPE THAT CAUGHT MY EYE WHEN GOING BACK THROUGH MY OLD FILES WAS THIS NORTHERN MEXICAN "CHUTNEY." I SUSPECT THAT IT came from a local cookbook printed in 1975, *Cocinemos Mejor*. If so, I hope that they and Sra. Beck will forgive me for reprinting it. *Chile dulce* is very good with broiled or cold meats.

9 Italian plum tomatoes, peeled and roughly chopped

*4 poblano or Anaheim chiles, charred, peeled, veins and seeds
removed, and chopped, about rounded ½ cup (140 ml)*

½ cup (125 ml) mild vinegar

½ cup (125 ml) light brown sugar or piloncillo, crushed

½ teaspoon cloves, crushed

½ teaspoon allspice, crushed

1 ½-inch (13-mm) cinnamon stick, crushed

1 medium white onion, finely chopped

salt to taste

Put all the ingredients together in a heavy noncorrosible pan and cook over low heat for about 3 hours. The mixture should be moist and still slightly textured.

Store in the refrigerator.

THE CENTRAL HUB

Plátano (banana)

THE STATE OF HIDALGO, LYING DUE NORTH AND NORTH-EAST OF MEXICO CITY, IS MOSTLY MOUNTAINOUS, WITH ITS EASTERN REGION STRADDLING THE SIERRA MADRE Oriental. The only two main highways that transverse the state northward are among the most scenic and sinuous in Mexico. Much of the southern part is dry and semiarid but luxuriously dotted with mineral springs and pools frequented since pre-Columbian times by the indigenous Otomis of that area. ❁ The capital of the state, Pachuca, known as *La Bella Airosa* (The Beautiful Windy Place), is a mining center set in a bare, rocky mountain landscape. Curiously, one of its popular local foods is *pastes*, inherited from the Cornish miners who worked there in the nineteenth century. Although the originals were pastry turnovers filled with beef and vegetables, I have eaten them in a regional restaurant in Pachuquilla, not far from Pachuca, stuffed with ground pork and, of course, chiles. ❁ Some of my earliest recollections of journeys in Mexico took us up to the Texas border via the old Panamerican highway, which went through Pachuca and Tamazunchale in San Luis Potosí. It was always a fascinating drive, and when time permitted we always stopped on our way north to look at the elegant sixteenth-century Augustinian convent in Actópan and the rather wild paintings in the San Andrés monastery in Ixmiquilpan (also from the sixteenth century) and to take a refreshing dip in the thermal waters of a little *balneario* near Tasquillo, named for the Otomi goddess of water, Nicte-ha. There were spectacular views on either side of the highway and very few signs of life except for the occasional *ranchería*. ☀ As the road descended from the highlands, you drove through lush tropical vegetation; twenty years later it has practically all been cleared for intensive plantations of coffee and citrus. ☀ More recently a friend and I drove to Huejutla along the northeastern highway that goes to Veracruz. From Pachuca the highway climbs and curves through a stark landscape, planted sporadically with agaves and cacti, and the only greenery was in the gullies and ravines watered by springs; there you always found tall majestic walnut trees. The highway continues to climb up through sparse stands of oak and pine and across open grassland before descending the eastern slopes of the Sierra. There the road is narrow and hugs the sheer rock face —rather nerve-racking when long-distance buses come roaring along at an indecent speed. But this is cloud forest with lush undergrowth and huge tree-ferns almost dipping over the road, while at intervals water gushes out of the rocks and across the pavement in front of you. ☀ It happens so often that the journey itself is more attractive than the destination, and this was true of Huejutla. It is a nondescript little town, and the air was hot and sticky. There did not seem to be a great variety of local dishes even in the market, which was the most popular eating place. It was here that for the first time I tried the locally grown black beans, which were delicious, seasoned with a wild, creeping herb (I have talked about it in the Puebla section) of the *piper* family, with a strong flavor of *cilantro* (in fact it is called *cilantro de monte*) and eggs cooked with a delicate yellow flower of a climbing leguminous plant called *quebrachis*.

Apart from the journey itself, the most memorable part of that trip was a visit to a nearby indigenous Náhuatl village. The houses were constructed in traditional style with daub-and-wattle walls and palm-thatched roofs. Most of them were surrounded with flowering bushes or native fruit trees: I remember the fragrance of the *naranjillo*, a bush with a tiny white flower like a citrus blossom.

The people living there in Chililico devote themselves to making an unusual glazed pottery: bowls and water containers in graceful shapes—but not cooking vessels—highly decorated with leaf patterns in contrasting earth tones.

But most of the time I have spent in Hidalgo has been around Nopala and now Tula. I have published recipes from the Nopala area in *Mexican Regional Cooking*, mostly by Señora María Elena Lara, and I couldn't resist telling you about the unforgettable day I spent with the Angeles family near Tula.

Hidalgo Revisited

Some years ago, while I was living in Mexico City, I used to visit a friend's ranch in the nearby State of Hidalgo and enjoyed the earthy food that she prepared (some of her recipes are printed in *Mexican Regional Cooking*). Then I moved to Michoacán and my travels took me elsewhere, not difficult in this varied country. Not so long ago another friend came to visit me and brought some delicious little *gorditas* stuffed with *chicharrón prensado* that I had not tried before, made by her cook, who also comes from that part of Hidalgo. When I complimented her on them, she invited me to visit the family home there and see more of the local dishes.

Another year passed before I was free to go, so they took the opportunity to combine my visit with their yearly invitation to my friend's family. I was to go ahead to watch all the preparations, except for the barbecue of lamb, which would be snugly tucked up in the earth by the time I arrived.

Until Juanita, the cook, and her sisters came to work in Mexico City, they lived with their parents near Tula, in the Mezquital Valley in the eastern part of Hidalgo. The father and the sons who remained there live nearby and cultivate their lands, which with irrigation are in constant use, planted with corn, beans, chiles, squash, and alfalfa, among other crops, as well as keeping a few cows and sheep.

It was a hot May day, and the distant hills to the east were hazy and burnt to a golden brown, a sign that the dry spring months had taken their toll, while the irrigated valley spread out in front of us was a patchwork of different shades of green.

There were two kitchens in full action by the time we arrived, one inside the house where the beans and vegetables were cooking and another area set up for making tortillas and *antojitos* on a large scale. There were a couple of large burners set on the floor for the cooking of the *nixtamal* that had long since been sent to the local mill and converted into two types of *masa*: a finely ground smooth *masa* for the tortillas and *quesadillas* and a slightly textured one for the *tlacoyos* and *gorditas*.

I was fascinated by their improvised "stove": a large round zinc tub with a gas burner inside. It was covered with a sheet of metal that served as a *comal*, and the whole thing was set up on legs at working height.

Everyone had been called in to help. The daughters-in-law were making *quesadillas* of squash flowers collected that morning, *tlacoyos* to be filled with beans, and *gorditas* filled with *chicharrón prensado*. It was a constant, rhythmic production line as they patted out the *masa*, accompanied by the blending of delicious aromas. In the inside kitchen the dry fava beans had been cooked to a yellow mush, but the seasonings of chiles and onion had been held in abeyance so that I could see the amounts; nothing was measured. In the next pot the *frijoles quebrados* were being skimmed, but thoughtfully they had put some of the dried beans aside so that I could see just how roughly they were crushed on the *metate* before going into the pot. They would take about three hours to cook, and the loose, tough skins were constantly skimmed off. I looked at the clock. I was so hungry and thought longingly of a pressure cooker.

The daughters were setting the table and helping their mother prepare the food, while nieces and nephews, dressed in their party best, darted in and out, fetching and carrying, feeding the chickens in between their play and laughter.

As the afternoon wore on, the men came by, free from their farm chores and dressed neatly in their best shirts and trousers. They were carrying chairs and crates and speculating about how the barbecue, put into the ground five hours earlier, would turn out.

As the work progressed, hunger pangs grew and talk naturally revolved around food and the changes that had occurred over the years. Before roads connected them to Mexico City and Querétaro, when only a railroad some kilometers away served the community, and before the irrigation system had been installed, they lived mainly on what they could grow during the summer rains (scarce at the best of times) and what could be dried for the months ahead: corn, beans, and chiles. Tomatoes and *tomates verdes* were sliced and dried, even wild greens growing in the cornfields and the *huauzontle* (a member of the amaranth family), now cultivated, were dried in the shade. There were remnants of the natural plants, nopal cactus and fruit trees around the small farm that used to provide free food but was now devastated by the emissions of the local cement factory, while the fig trees laden with still-green fruit had somehow survived.

At three o'clock the rest of my friend's family arrived; lemonade and beer were offered, and the long-awaited *antojitos* were passed. It was difficult to hold back, even knowing what lay ahead, but we were distracted when it was announced that the barbecue pit was going to be uncovered.

We all filed out to watch. Three of the men picked up shovels and started to scrape the dirt back from the top of the pit—it always seems to take an age—then the layers of the protective sheeting, to expose the maguey leaves that lined the pit in a carefully overlapping sunburst pattern. Trays and tongs had been brought out for the meat, but the men insisted on using their hands, each time shaking their hands to relieve the pain inflicted by the hot meat. Then they were digging way down at the bottom corners of the pit and finally unearthed two large packages covered with maguey leaves held firmly with wire. These were the *ximbones*, chopped nopal cactus mixed with pork, onion, garlic, serrano chiles, and herbs. Finally it took two men to lift out the zinc tub containing the *consomé*, the juices from the lamb that had exuded during the long, slow cooking, enriching the water in which there were vegetables and chiles.

What a feast: the soups of dried fava beans and *frijoles quebrados,* the barbecued meats with piles of steaming tortillas and a sauce of sour tunas. The *consomé* was passed to those who could by then make room for yet another spoonful. Stewed guavas finished off the meal, but that was not all; a huge cake with lemon sauce appeared, and we were once again pressed to eat a final mouthful . . .

When the meal was finished, we took a leisurely walk as the sun was dropping. The air was fragrant with scents from the mountains where distant rains had begun to fall. We looked at the cattle bedded down for the night in a large hollow by the river and the black-faced sheep, obviously next in turn for the barbecue pit. We wandered on to the fields to pick the last of the squash and watch the fading rays of the sun cast their last brilliant light over the valley.

SALSA DE XOCONOSTLE

SOUR TUNA SAUCE

Sra. Paula Cruz de Angeles

⁂

[MAKES ABOUT 2½ CUPS (625 ML)]

XOCONOSTLE (OPUNTIA JOCONOSTLE) IS A SMALLISH, SQUAT CACTUS FRUIT THAT GROWS IN SEMIARID COUNTRY AND IS USED IN PART OF CENTRAL MEXICO — especially in Hidalgo, Guanajuato, and Aguascalientes—either in a table sauce like the following recipe, in a conserve, or to give an acidic touch to stews like *mole de olla.*

This fruit has a thin, light green skin with pinkish touches. The seeds are not dispersed through the flesh like those of the better known prickly pears but concentrated in the center of the fruit, encased in a layer of very acidy flesh about a quarter of an inch (7 mm) thick. There are no substitutes that I know of, but I have seen them in markets in Texas and from specialty distributors (like Frieda of California).

You can use either a blender or a *molcajete* for this sauce—purists will of course use the *molcajete* for better texture and flavor.

6 sour tunas (see note above)
⅓ cup (83 ml) morita chiles or the larger chipotle mora
1¼ cups (313 ml) water
2 garlic cloves
salt to taste

Put the tunas onto a *comal* or griddle over low heat and cook them slowly, turning them around and upending them so they are cooked thoroughly and slightly charred. This will take about 45 minutes if the tunas are large and firm. As you remove the tunas from the *comal*, place them in a plastic bag to "sweat" for about 10 minutes—as with chiles. This will facilitate the peeling process. Peel off the thin skin, cut them open, then scrape out all the seeds and discard. Chop the flesh well and remove any thin fibers.

Rinse the chiles briefly—they mustn't become too damp—pat dry, remove the stalks, and set on the *comal* to toast over low heat. Turn the chiles over frequently to prevent them from burning. They should be sufficiently toasted so they can be crumbled into a blender or *molcajete*.

BLENDER: Add 1 cup (250 ml) of water to the chiles along with the garlic and blend well. Gradually add the chopped tunas and blend briefly. This is a rustic sauce and should have a rather rough texture. Add salt and dilute with the rest of the water.

MOLCAJETE: Crush the garlic and salt with the dried chiles and gradually add ½ cup (125 ml) of the water and the chopped tunas, grinding to a rough texture. Add the rest of the water to dilute as desired.

SOPA DE HABA SECA

DRIED FAVA BEAN SOUP

Sra. Paula Cruz de Angeles

❁

[MAKES APPROXIMATELY 9 CUPS (2.25 L)]

THIS IS A PARTICULARLY DELICIOUS VERSION OF DRIED FAVA BEAN SOUP, WHICH IS TRADITIONALLY SERVED DURING LENT. YOU WILL NEED TO BUY THE peeled fava beans—yellow, not brown. I am afraid those sold in the United States, unless imported from Mexico, do not have quite such a good flavor, nor do they yield as much bulk; the cooking time is also much shorter.

Sra. Paula cooks her cactus pieces, *nopales*, by boiling them with baking soda and the husks of two *tomates verdes*, but I still prefer to cook mine *al vapor* to retain more nutrients, texture, etc. She says they should not be added to the soup until a few minutes before serving or they will spoil the yellow color, and I take the cook's word for it.

12 to 14 cups (3 to 3.5 l) water
1 pound (450 g) dried peeled fava beans
salt to taste
3 tablespoons vegetable oil
¼ medium white onion, sliced
4 serrano chiles, slit at the pointed ends
3 garlic cloves, roughly chopped
½ teaspoon cumin seeds, freshly ground (not powdered from a jar)
4 sprigs fresh mint or 1 tablespoon dried
3 cups (750 ml) cooked nopales *(page 18)*

Heat the water, add the fava beans, salt, and oil, and cook over low heat, stirring the beans from time to time since they tend to fall to the bottom of the pan and could easily stick and burn.

After 1 hour of cooking time, add the onion, chiles, garlic, and cumin. Continue cooking

[CONTINUED]

until the beans are completely soft and the soup has thickened slightly—it should have some texture from a portion of the beans that cook but do not disintegrate—1 to 1½ hours. Five minutes before serving, add the mint and cactus pieces and adjust the seasoning.

NOTE: *I like to prepare the soup well ahead and add the cactus and mint when reheating. The soup thickens as it sits, and you may have to dilute it with a little water.*

FRIJOLES QUEBRADOS

"BROKEN" BEANS

Sra. Paula Cruz de Angeles

❁

[MAKES ABOUT 10 CUPS (2.5 L)]

LOCALLY THIS WAY OF COOKING BEANS IS REFERRED TO AS "FRIJOLES DE FLOJA"—LAZY WOMAN'S BEANS—BUT IT STILL REQUIRES A LOT OF WORK. Sra. Paula crushes the dry beans on the *metate.* She does not soak them first because she says this detracts from the flavor. The *xoconostles* or sour tunas give this dish a distinctive acidity, but you could use *nopales* or even a sour apple in their place.

1 pound (450 g) flor de mayo or pinto beans

3 quarts (3 l) water

*3 xoconostles (see page 197) or 2 cactus paddles,
cleaned and cut into cubes, or 1 sour apple, cut into slices*

½ medium white onion, roughly sliced

11 guajillo chiles, about 4 ounces (115 g)

2 avocado leaves

salt to taste

1 small bunch cilantro, leaves and small stems, roughly chopped

Grind the dry beans roughly. Put into a large saucepan (or slow cooker), add 10 cups (2.5 l) of the water, and bring to a boil. Lower the heat and continue to cook until tender but not too soft (nor should they be al dente)—2 to 3 hours, depending on how fresh they are. Or cook them overnight at low heat in a slow cooker.

As the beans boil, the scum and skin particles should be skimmed off—this should be done very thoroughly. Halfway through the cooking time, add the *xoconostles* and onion.

Meanwhile, slit the chiles open, remove the seeds and veins, and lightly toast on the *comal*, taking care not to burn. Put into a small saucepan, cover with water, and simmer for 5 minutes. Set aside to soak for 10 more minutes.

Add the remaining 2 cups (500 ml) water to a blender, then the avocado leaves and drained chiles and blend as thoroughly as possible. Add the chile puree to the pan through a fine strainer, pressing out the debris of the skins well to extract all the flesh. Stir in salt and continue cooking for about 15 minutes more, adding the *cilantro* 5 minutes before the end of the cooking time. Serve with plenty of the broth.

GORDITAS HIDUALGUENSES

GORDITAS FROM HIDALGO

✺

[MAKES ABOUT 10 3-INCH (8-CM) GORDITAS]

I FIND THESE LITTLE *GORDITAS* TOTALLY ADDICTIVE; I CAN EVEN EAT THEM COLD. THEY ARE BEST EATEN WHEN THEY HAVE BEEN SITTING AROUND A little while to give the lard inside time to permeate and flavor the *masa*. This is one *antojito* that can be, and in fact is, better reheated. They could be made several days ahead and frozen.

> 1 pound (450 g) fairly coarse corn *masa for tamales (page 530)*,
> about 2 rounded cups (550 ml)
>
> 2 tablespoons pork lard
>
> 2 teaspoons anise seeds
>
> salt to taste
>
> ½ cup (125 ml) firmly packed filling, either beans *(page 202)* or
> chicharrón prensado

Mix the masa, lard, anise, and salt together well and divide the dough into 10 or more balls about 1½ inches (4 cm) in diameter. Cover them with a slightly damp cloth while you work.

Press one of the balls out to about 3½ inches (9 cm) on your palm or in a tortilla press—it

[CONTINUED]

should be just about ¼ inch (7 mm) thick. Spread 1½ teaspoons of the filling over the center, leaving a border of about ½ inch (13 mm). Fold the dough over the filling and flatten carefully, so that the filling does not break through the dough, to a circle about 2½ to 3 inches (6.5 to 8 cm) wide.

Warm an ungreased *comal* or griddle and cook the *gorditas* over low to medium heat for 5 to 7 minutes on each side, taking care they do not char. They should be very lightly browned in patches.

FRIJOLES PARA GORDITAS

BEAN FILLING FOR GORDITAS

Sra. Paula Cruz de Angeles

❁

[MAKES 5½ CUPS (1.375 L)]

THIS IS A SOMEWHAT RICH FILLING, BUT THE IDEA IS THAT THE EXTRA LARD ENRICHES THE *MASA* OF THE *GORDITA*. SRA. PAULA INSISTS ON GRINDING ON the *metate*—first the anise seeds and then the beans. It is worth making this amount because it is addictive and you can always freeze what you don't use for another batch of *gorditas*.

1 pound (450 g) flor de mayo or pinto beans
2 rounded tablespoons anise seeds
salt to taste
11 guajillo chiles
4 heaped tablespoons lard or vegetable oil

Rinse and drain the beans, cover with hot water, and cook over low heat until tender but not soft, about 2 hours, depending on the age of the beans. Strain and reserve the cooking water. Mash or process the beans to a textured puree. Grind the anise seeds in a spice grinder and add with salt to the beans.

Slit the chiles open, removing the veins and seeds. Lightly toast them on a *comal*, taking care not to burn them. Cover with hot water and simmer for 5 minutes, then set aside to soak for 10 more minutes.

Put 2 cups (500 ml) of the bean broth into a blender, add the drained chiles, and blend as thoroughly as possible.

Heat the lard in a skillet and add the chile puree through a fine strainer, pressing out the debris well to extract as much as possible of the flesh. Fry for about 1 minute, scraping the bottom of the pan to prevent sticking.

Stir in the beans and anise well and continue cooking the mixture, stirring and scraping the bottom of the pan, until it has reduced a little, looks nice and shiny, and just plops off the spoon, about 8 minutes.

MOLE DE OLLA HIDALGUENSE

POT *MOLE* FROM HIDALGO

Sra. María Elena Romero de Lara

✸

[SERVES 8]

THIS IS A BIG, COMFORTABLE STEW—FOR FAMILY OR FRIENDS WHO DON'T EXPECT YOU TO DO A LITTLE NUMBER WITH CHICKEN BREASTS (SKINNED OF course) in *cuitlacoche* sauce.

Sra. Lara prepared this *mole*, or soupy stew, when I was with the family on their ranch in Hidalgo many years ago. It was she who showed me the little brown *clavito* mushrooms (*Leophyllum decastes*) and collected wild anise (*Tagetes micrantha*) and *pericon* (*Tagetes florida*) in the fields to cook with the freshly picked corn. *Xoconostles* (*Opuntia joconostle*) or acidy tunas are used in some areas in a stew of this kind to bring out the flavor of the chiles; they are also made into a table sauce and even cooked in syrup as a dessert. Since they grow in central and northern Mexico, it is possible that they also occur in the southwestern desert areas of the United States. If not, I am sure that by now they are being imported to appease homesick Mexicans from those areas. They are round in shape, pinkish green in color, and do not have such fierce little thorns as the other types of tunas. If *xoconostles* are not available, use a peeled and finely sliced sour apple or leave it out altogether.

I always think it is better to make a substantial amount of a stew of this kind because it tastes better. Also, if you have a Mexican bean pot, cook it slowly in that.

2½ pounds (1.125 kg) short ribs with some fat,
cut into 1½-inch (4-cm) cubes

2 large scallions or several smaller ones,
roughly chopped with most of the greens

4 garlic cloves, roughly chopped

2 quarts (2 l) water

salt to taste

6 ancho chiles

6 pasilla chiles

1⅓ cups (333 ml) water

heaped ¼ teaspoon cumin seeds

heaped ¼ teaspoon black peppercorns

2 garlic cloves, roughly chopped

2 ears of corn (not too sweet), each cut into 6 pieces

12 ounces (340 g) chayote, peeled and cut into strips

12 ounces (340 g) green beans, trimmed and tied into
8 bundles of 5 or 6 each

8 ounces (225 g) zucchini, trimmed and cut into 8 pieces

3 sour tunas or 1 sour apple

1 small bunch cilantro

2 large sprigs epazote

TO SERVE
finely chopped white onion
roughly chopped cilantro
dried oregano
lime quarters

Put the meat into a large pot and add the scallions, 4 garlic cloves, and 2 quarts (2 l) water with plenty of salt. Bring to a simmer and continue simmering until the meat is half cooked —very approximately 40 minutes.

Meanwhile, slit the chiles open and remove the seeds and veins. Toast them lightly on a warm *comal* or griddle, taking care not to burn them, cover with hot water, and leave to soak for about 15 minutes.

Put ⅓ cup (83 ml) of the water into a blender, add the cumin, peppercorns, and 2 garlic cloves, and blend until smooth. Add the remaining cup (250 ml) of water and the drained chiles and blend to a smooth puree. Add this to the meat and bring to a simmer.

Add the corn, *chayote*, and beans, and cook for another 10 minutes. Then add the squash, sour tunas, and herbs, adjust the seasoning, and cook over very low heat for about 40 minutes. Serve in large bowls with plenty of the vegetables, meat, and at least 1 cup (250 ml) of broth and pass the additional ingredients separately.

Srita. Antonia Ortiz

For many years now my comings and goings between Zitácuaro, Mexico City, and points abroad—and either after or in anticipation of an arduous three-hour drive—have been cushioned by Antonia Ortiz, who comes from Hidalgo. She is the indomitable housekeeper of a very dear friend, whose house I use as a stopping point and in whose garage I leave my trusty truck.

Antonia is the salt of the earth; there is no other way of describing her. She runs a tight ship with the efficiency and good humor that many an executive would do well to emulate. There is not a maid or cook on the block who would not drop what she is doing to come to her aid, lend her a quart of milk or a few onions, and there is not a gardener, street sweeper, or local beat policeman who is not invited in for a coffee and sweet roll or a taco of whatever there was for lunch. I consider her the *grande dame* of the neighborhood.

On weekends Srita. Ortiz makes a long journey, three changes of buses, to go back to her *tierra* in the State of Hidalgo, to care for her aged and ailing mother. She returns laden with things to sell: delicious cheese from a small, local factory, large fat chickens that her brother-in-law raises, or samples of rich, fatty *chicharrón* and barbecued meat prepared that weekend for some family reunion.

She always has a new tip or recipe waiting for me and makes a sucking sound as she describes some new delight with shining eyes.

Nobody puts quite the same *sazón* as she does into a simple vegetable soup, enriched with a little chicken broth, or her bean soup: large navy beans cooked with a beef shin bone, vegetables, and seasoned with a lot of *cilantro*.

She beams as she helps me unload the truck with produce from my little ranch: *chayotes*, *nopales*, fresh eggs and fruits—whatever is in season—and immediately lays claim to the special crusty bread I bring her from my marketplace. But first she fills the kettle for my tea.

Here are three recipes that she recommends for a *taquiza* (taco party). In the last few years, as food prices have increased and money has become tight, there are many occasions when special entertaining means not a lavish buffet but *cazuelas* full of rice, beans, and *guacamole* and sauces with a pile of tortillas to be wrapped around many simple fillings. These can become a lesson in food economy: the chicken skin is not thrown away; she fries it crisp with lots of onions to make delicious tacos that are then doused in a very picante sauce. (I know some will shudder, but if you are on a strict diet or are a food snob, shut your eyes and just enjoy!)

CHICHARRÓN EN TOMATE VERDE

FRIED PORK SKIN IN GREEN TOMATO SAUCE

Srita. Antonia Ortiz

❀

[MAKES 2 ROUNDED CUPS (550 ML)]

THIS *TAQUIZA* RECIPE IS RUSTIC AND DELICIOUS AND QUITE MY FAVORITE WAY OF COOKING *CHICHARRÓN*, WHICH I DO ALLOW MYSELF ONCE IN A WHILE.

1 tablespoon pork lard

12 ounces (340 g) tomates verdes, *about 14 medium,*
husks removed, rinsed, and thinly sliced

½ small white onion, thinly sliced

3 garlic cloves, finely chopped

4 serrano chiles, finely chopped

4 ounces (115 g) thin chicharrón, broken into 1½-inch (4-cm) pieces

1 cup (250 ml) pork or chicken broth

salt as necessary

CHICHARRÓN

THERE ARE MANY *(probably far too many for some people)* delicious recipes for chicharrón *in this book. Chicharrón is the skin of the pig that is first dried, then stewed in hot lard, and then fried in even hotter lard that causes it to swell up, bubble, and become crisp. It is a popular foodstuff throughout Mexico. There are many Mexican markets in the United States that make their own, and quality varies, but there are a few excellent brands of commercial packaged "fried pork skins" that are in fact* chicharrón. *Avoid any that are tough and chewy; they have not been prepared properly. Although the very idea of chicharrón seems hopelessly fattening, in fact it's almost pure protein if it's cooked very crisp.*

Heat the lard in a wide skillet. Add the *tomates,* onion, garlic, and chiles and fry very gently, stirring and scraping the bottom of the pan to prevent sticking, for about 15 minutes. Add the *chicharrón* and broth, cover the pan, and continue cooking over a low heat for 20 more minutes . . . the *chicharrón* should be soft. Adjust the seasoning.

CHICHARRÓN EN GUAJILLO

FRIED PORK SKIN IN GUAJILLO SAUCE

Srita. Antonia Ortiz

❋

[MAKES 2½ CUPS (625 ML)]

YES, ANOTHER RECIPE OF ANTONIA'S FOR AFICIONADOS OF *CHICHARRÓN.* FOR THE UNINITIATED, THE SKIN ALWAYS SOFTENS IN THE SAUCE, AND IN FACT as it cooks it absorbs the sauce. It is even better several hours later or the next day. I like to sprinkle a little finely chopped white onion and roughly chopped *cilantro* on the filling before rolling up the taco.

6 guajillo chiles
6 puya chiles
1 cup (250 ml) water

[CONTINUED]

¼ white onion, roughly chopped

3 garlic cloves, roughly chopped

2 tablespoons pork lard

4 ounces (115 g) chicharrón, broken into 1½-inch (4-cm) pieces

2 cups (500 ml) chicken or pork broth

salt if necessary

Remove the stems, slit the chiles open, and remove the seeds and veins. Toast the chiles lightly on both sides on a warm *comal* or griddle, taking care not to burn them or the sauce will be bitter. Cover with hot water and simmer for 5 minutes. Set aside, off the heat, to soak for 10 more minutes.

Put the water in a blender, add the onion and garlic, and blend well. Gradually add the drained chiles and blend as thoroughly as possible.

Heat the lard in a large skillet and add the sauce, pressing it through a strainer to remove the tiny pieces of guajillo skin that never seem to blend away. Fry for 5 minutes, scraping the bottom of the pan from time to time to prevent sticking.

Add the *chicharrón* and broth (yes, the pan will look very crowded), cover the pan, and cook over low heat, stirring from time to time and scraping the bottom of the pan to prevent sticking, for 20 minutes. Set aside to season for at least 10 minutes before serving.

Add salt only if necessary. Some *chicharrón* comes already salted, and the broth may also be salted.

LONGANIZA CON PAPAS Y NOPALES

CHORIZO WITH POTATOES AND NOPAL CACTUS

Srita. Antonia Ortiz

❋

[MAKES 2½ CUPS (625 ML)]

THIS IS ONE OF ANTONIA'S PREFERRED RECIPES FOR A *TAQUIZA*. SHE USES *LONGANIZA*, A MORE ECONOMICAL TYPE OF *CHORIZO*, USUALLY MADE WITH odds and ends of meat and sometimes pork and beef mixed—each butcher has his own recipe—and stuffed into long lengths of pork casing. There is no onion, garlic, or chiles in this recipe because the *chorizo*—which can be used as a substitute—gives the necessary seasoning. Do not add salt until you taste at the end because many chorizos have an overabundance.

. I like to put some *salsa verde cruda* (page 223, without the optional avocado) in my taco with this filling.

1 tablespoon pork lard

*½ pound (225 g) nopal cactus, cleaned of its thorns
and cut into narrow strips*

½ pound (225 g) waxy potatoes, cut into medium-thick slices

4 ounces (115 g) longaniza or chorizo, cut into slices

salt as necessary

Heat the lard in a wide skillet, add the cactus pieces, and fry gently, uncovered, for about 30 seconds. All the juice will exude. Add the potatoes and *longaniza*, cover the pan, and cook over low heat for 30 minutes—but stir well and scrape the bottom of the pan from time to time to prevent sticking. The mixture will be fairly dry.

NOTE: *If the cactus pieces are not very fresh, you may need to add about ⅓ cup (83 ml) water to the pan.*
    I like to drain the filling of excess grease and even press it well in absorbent paper.

TAMALES DE NOPALITOS

CACTUS PADDLE TAMALES

☀

[SERVES 4]

THIS METHOD OF COOKING *NOPALES* WAS GIVEN TO ANTONIA BY A NEIGHBOR'S MAID. IT IS A DELICIOUS, UNUSUAL, AND HEALTHY WAY OF PREPARING *nopalitos* (except for the lard . . . but it does add great flavor, and most of it is absorbed by the corn husk). Surprisingly enough, the viscosity dries up in this method of cooking, and all the nutrients are retained. Although there is no *masa*, they are called *tamales* because they are wrapped in dried corn husks. Dried morita chiles or *moras* are used, but they are sometimes difficult to obtain, so canned chipotles can be substituted. Two large corn husks, one inside the other, must be used since they are cooked directly on the hot surface of the *comal* or griddle. It is better if they are slightly damp, but not soaked, before being used.

Serve these *tamales* as a surprise vegetable or even as a first course.

4 scant tablespoons pork lard or vegetable oil

3 medium cactus paddles (nopales), *cleaned of their tiny thorns and cut into thin strips*

¼ cup (63 ml) roughly chopped epazote, *leaves and thin stems*

4 morita chiles or moras (see note above), *wiped clean and torn into small pieces*

¼ cup (63 ml) finely chopped scallions with some of the greens

salt to taste

Have ready 8 large dried corn husks and 8 strings made by thinly shredding corn husks.

Divide the husks into pairs and place one inside the other. Spread the lard over the inside leaf. Mix all the ingredients together and divide into 4 parts.

Fill the prepared husks. Fold them over so that the filling is completely covered and secure at both ends.

Place the *tamales* on a warm griddle and cook over medium heat, turning them every 15 minutes so that they cook evenly. The husks will char slightly—no matter; it looks right and tastes even better.

THE STATE OF MEXICO

THE STATE OF MEXICO WRAPS ITSELF AROUND MEXICO CITY, ENGULFING MOST OF IT UNTIL IT MERGES WITH MORELOS IN THE SOUTH. A GREAT PART OF THE STATE IS densely populated until you get beyond the urban sprawl to the west and the magnificent forested Desierto de Los Leones (Desert of the Lions) and, to the south and west of Toluca, the capital city. ❀ The whole area around Toluca is unrecognizable from when I first knew it; it was a small town surrounded by *milpas* (cornfields) with a Friday market that truly reflected the foods, arts, and crafts of the countryside around. Now it is an urban mass practically swamping the neighboring villages like Metepec and San Felipe Tlalmimilolpan, where for years we enjoyed two very typical regional restaurants: El Caballo Blanco and Posada de San Felipe. ❀ Despite all this development, one of the great markets of Mexico, Santiago Tianguistenco, has so far withstood much of the homogenizing influences of urban Mexico. I invite you to make a tour with me.

These are among the oldest recorded markets in Mexico, dating back to pre-Columbian times. In just an hour's drive from Mexico City you can be transported to another world, one that is immensely colorful and bustling with the activity of rural life. And at the same time you will experience a great culinary adventure.

The name Tianguistenco derives from the Náhuatl words *tianquiztli*, meaning "the place of the market," and *tentli*, "on the edge of," and Metepec signifies "the hill of the magueys." They are both now satellite villages of Toluca, the capital of the state, which itself was once known for its picturesque market. When the Toluca market became too large and was moved farther out of town, it lost its identity and is no longer a mecca for tourists. Santiago and Metepec have grown too but have still managed to retain their unique characteristics.

If you happen to have a Tuesday free when staying in Mexico City, I suggest you visit the Santiago market. It is an easy drive out of Mexico City (due west on Highway 15) that winds as it climbs up along the edge of the Desierto de Los Leones, a national forest thickly wooded with conifers. From a high pass of about 9,000 feet the road drops down steeply into the valley of Toluca, which is dominated by the extinct volcano, El Nevado de Toluca. The slopes around the large crater are often covered with snow. Below, at La Marquesa, you turn off the main highway and drive south on a minor road that crosses rolling pastureland where traditional sheep raising has almost entirely given way to a vast recreational area. Amid the dozens of football fields and go-cart tracks, hundreds of small shacks serve simple local food to the thousands of *Capitalinos* who disgorge from the city each weekend.

There is only one road to Santiago, alternately marked Santiago, Chalma, or Mercedes Benz. Almost exactly at 22 kilometers you turn right, and in a few minutes you will see the first streets of Santiago. Park near the edge of town, or you might find yourself blocked in by buses and trucks. It is best to go early in the day, but remember the altitude is nearly 8,000 feet and the mornings are chilly. Most of all, go hungry and be adventurous about trying some of the interesting local foods.

As you enter the town, there is hardly room to walk along the streets, which are lined on both sides with makeshift stands constructed of wooden planks supported on trestles on which to display the produce. Above them is a patchwork of undulating canvas awnings—now gradually being changed to garishly colored plastics—all tilted at different angles, tenuously supported by thin poles and held steady (more or less) with a stout cord, to give shelter from the strong sun of these high-altitude plains or from the heavy summer rains.

The market activity starts the night before as trucks piled high with produce brought in from neighboring states start arriving to stake their claim for a good parking spot to unload at dawn. Very early on Tuesday morning the people from nearby villages arrive, crammed into local buses with crates and sacks of their produce and even live turkeys, chickens, and small pigs. The local police are out in full force, whistling frantically or standing at strategic points along the road, waiting for their dues from the truck drivers. "*Los mordilones*"—the "biters," as they are dubbed locally.

As you walk toward the center of the town you will probably be mesmerized by the piles of fresh produce: brilliant red tomatoes, shiny green chiles of many types and shades, and particularly an interesting variety of tomatillos—as they are known in the United States—large yellow and green, rather irregular in shape, they are known as *tomate verde manzano* (apple). I have rarely seen them elsewhere.

But don't forget to look down at the countrywomen sitting on the sidewalk, selling small bunches of herbs or wild greens that they have grown or gathered: lemongrass, a long, narrow-leafed wild sorrel (*vinagrera* or *lengua de vaca*), purslane, or a small-leafed plant that grows wild in tufts in the fields called *chivato* (*Calandrina micrantha*), which is eaten raw or as a salad or cooked with pork. There are the round-leaved *papaloquelite* and long-leaved *pepicha*, both pungent herbs eaten raw in tacos and especially with *guacamole*, and during the rainy season wild mushrooms.

I have never seen in any market in Mexico or elsewhere such piles of multicolored mushrooms gathered in the high pine forests and pastures in that part of the state. The much prized morels and cèpes are soon swept up by Mexico City restaurateurs, but who can complain when there are clusters of tender little donkey-brown *clavitos* (*Leophyllum decastes*), delicate, orange-colored chanterelles (*Cantharellus minor*), spongy *codorniz* or *palomas* (*Agaricus augustus*) with their creamy-brown speckled caps, and the spectacular blue (*azules*) *Lactarius indigo*, to name only a few. They are all juicy and delicious stewed with a little *epazote*, that most Mexican of herbs, onion, and chiles or added to a broth for soup or cooked with pork.

Just a little farther on you'll see an enormous pile of white rocks and powder. It is *cal* (calcium oxide), ready to be slaked or diluted for the corn that is to be made into tortillas. The stand has been in the same place as long as I can remember, along with the neighboring vendor of a large variety of dried chiles, rice, beans of all description, chickpeas, and lentils.

By the time you have reached the entrance to the covered market, you'll most certainly have built up an appetite. Right there is a woman selling *atole* (a corn gruel) with *tamales*. Probably not the best *tamales* in the world, but they go well with the hot *atole* and provide a good foundation for the rest of the eating you may be tempted to do. Farther along there are rows of small *fonditas*, little eating places, with rough benches and tables covered with brilliantly colored oil cloth and, to tempt you, out in front charcoal braziers heating large *cazuelas* (earthenware cooking pots) full of bubbling stews: pork rinds in green or red tomato sauce, pork again in a green sauce with fava beans and squash, chicken in a red *mole*. The most savory smell of all comes from the brick-red *menudo*, a beef tripe soup, seasoned with long stems of *epazote*.

Farther down are the cold foods: salads of fava beans and *nopales*, relishes of orangey-yellow *manzano chile*, fiercely hot, in a lime juice with onions, and lightly pickled pig's feet. As you turn the corner, look down again, for there is usually a young woman sitting on the floor, trying in vain to coax overactive frogs back into her plastic-lined basket. The frogs are cleaned and cooked in stews of chiles and tomatoes, and their embryos, *atepocates*, are seasoned with onion, chile, *nopales*, and tomatoes and cooked on a *comal*, well wrapped in several corn husks. You will most likely wonder what the small orange shrimplike animals are that are sold in small piles here and there in the market. They are *acociles*, small crustaceans (*Cambarellus montesumae*) from the streams and small lakes that still remain unpolluted. They have been cooked and are ready to eat as a snack with a squeeze of lime juice.

All of these and the little freshwater fowl, stewed with their heads still attached, represent the native foods of the area that have been eaten since pre-Columbian times. Up until the beginning of this century the whole valley of Toluca or, more precisely, the basin of the Río Lerma, was an area of lakes and causeways, lush in vegetation and rich in wildlife, and according to historian Javier Romero Quiróz, the local people who maneuvered their little craft along these waterways were referred to as the "Venetians of Mexico."

Most of the main hall of the market is given over to butchers, both local and from neighboring villages, selling freshly killed pork and the products they have prepared from it: blood sausage seasoned with mint and scallions, lard, thin sheets of *chicharrón* either porous or fatty, light, golden, or deep brown for every taste, head cheese flattened into small wheels in specially woven baskets called *tompiates*, and flattened meat seasoned with vinegar and ground chiles, *cecina*. As you walk around, you are aware of a delicious, spicy-vinegary smell of the freshly made red and green *chorizos*.

Chorizos are practically synonymous with the Toluca area. Cortés introduced cattle and pork into the valley, which was renowned for the quality of its corn, very early in the colonial period. Spanish techniques for sausage making and pork curing naturally followed, but they have long since taken on a truly Mexican character using readily available local ingredients. There are many types of *chorizo*, from luxurious ones, including almonds or pine nuts, for special customers, down to the inferior *longaniza*, which is not tied into links and usually includes cheaper cuts of pork and even beef.

About twenty-five years or so ago, green *chorizos* began to appear. There are some excellent ones, but because they are usually made in small quantities, they are more difficult to find. They are seasoned with herbs, greens, chiles, and sometimes *tomates verdes*. Many others are seasoned with commercially ground pumpkin seeds and spices, while those to be avoided at all costs are prepared in bulk in local packing houses, artificially colored and packed into plastic casings.

All over the market there is a brisk morning trade in *tacos de barbacoa*. The strong flavor and texture of the local lamb and mutton lends itself to the traditional cooking method in a pit barbecue. The unseasoned meat is wrapped in the thick, pointed leaves of the maguey—the century plant that produces *pulque*—first softened in the heat of the fire. The wrapped meat is then set into a metal pan in which the juices are collected, covered with earth, and cooked overnight. Succulent and delicious, the roughly chopped meat is generally wrapped into a flabby tortilla and seasoned with spicy red or green sauces, chopped onion, and *cilantro*. To accompany this taco you are offered a cup of *consomé*, the diluted juices of the meat spiked with hot chiles, *cilantro*, onion, and tomato. It all makes a wonderful pick-me-up, whatever the temperature.

If none of this hearty food appeals to you, it will not be long before you hear *"jugo de naranja,"* orange juice, as the vendor pushes his little cart through the crowds. Nothing could be fresher. He deftly cuts the oranges, squeezes them in a large metal press, and within seconds hands you a frothy glass of juice. His garbage is kept neatly in a large plastic bag hanging from the handles of his cart. Or, if breakfast cereal is your choice—this has come of late to the market as well—a young woman can be seen pushing her cart around slowly. It is packed with opened boxes of every imaginable type of cereal with milk, honey, sugar, or raisins to accompany them.

You can always tell where the *pulque* is being served by the fruity aroma that pervades the space around it. It is now brought to the market in plastic containers, but not long ago inflated pig skins, *cueros*, bouncing around in the breeze like enormous white balloons with legs, were quite a sight to see.

There are breads especially made for this market day in the small towns around. One young man brings quite a variety of semisweet breads: flavored with orange, *piloncillo* (raw sugar), enriched with *natas*—the thick creamy skin that forms on scalded milk. He learned from his grandmother and never fails to turn up here on a Tuesday. Another sells fancy breads for special occasions, including very large, highly glazed hearts, embellished with swirls and curlicues.

In the hot, dry months of spring the *capulines*, small, almost black wild cherries with an intense, sweet flavor, are in season. You can eat them raw, but they are also made into *atole* and *tamales*, cooked and mixed with cornstarch to thicken them and then wrapped in dried corn husks. But beware: all the pits are in there too! You will also see bags of *tortitas*, "rissoles" of dried, uncooked fava beans mixed to a paste and seasoned with onion, salt, and *epazote*. These nutritious little fried cakes are most common in the Lenten period, when they are added to stews or in chile/tomato sauces to provide protein on meatless days. Fava beans are grown year-round and are a staple food in that area, either fresh or dried.

My favorite of all the market's food are the *tlacoyos*. Dotted throughout the streets you will see women fashioning the intensely blue corn *masa* (dough) into fat oval cakes filled with the deep-yellow mashed dried beans. They are then baked on a *comal* until the dough is firm and flecked with brown. Some are then lightly fried in lard. I noticed a few women who were departing from tradition and adding crumbled *chicharrón* and ricotta to the filling (it makes me hungry to write about them). It makes you want to forget forever those boring, boneless, skinless chicken breast fad diets.

If you hear shouts of *"golpe, golpe"* ("blow" or "hit"), move out of the way in a hurry. The owners of the trolleys that transport goods all over the market are an impatient and aggressive lot. One of them was sporting a motor horn, and well he might—his trolley was piled high with a complete kitchen: stove, gas tank, tables, and chairs to boot!

If you don't share my passionate interest in regional foods, wander off down some farther streets where donkeys, mules, and pack horses are tethered and watch the quiet barter of bundles of wood for a kilo of flour or sugar. Or take a short ride out of town to the animal fair. You can spot it immediately by the number of shiny trucks and station wagons parked on a rise in the land. There business is taken very seriously as bargaining is carried on for the cows with the biggest udders, the most promising pedigree calves, or the strongest oxen for plowing, along with mules and horses. Groups of nervous lambs and pigs huddle to one side for the more modest buyers. Piles of sheep skins are unloaded to the nearby shoemaking town of Atenco, where they are used as shoe linings or vests. And there are colorful stands selling local leather goods: boots, belts, and saddles. But don't forget to stop for the best *tamales* and *atole* from the woman standing at the entranceway.

These scenes from the market of Santiago Tianguistenco tell a remarkable human story of the ingenious ways in which these mostly rural people carry on their lives with so little. You wonder just how long it can continue to exist as the inevitable urban sprawl of Toluca invades and overwhelms.

Metepec

HUEVOS ENCOBIJADAS

"BLANKETED" EGGS

Virginia Barrios

✺

[SERVES 1]

ON THE LONG DRIVE FROM MEXICO CITY I ALWAYS FIND IT COMFORTING TO STOP OFF AND CHAT WITH FRIENDS TO CUSHION MYSELF FOR THE CULTURAL shock—small but constant—between the social, urban life of the capital and the rusticity of my self-imposed isolation.

It is an easy leg of the journey from Mexico City to Metepec, a pottery village renowned for its fanciful and colorful figures of all shapes, themes, and sizes, as well as some of the most beautiful *cazuelas* and *ollas* in the whole of Mexico. (Monday is market day.)

It was once 5 kilometers south out of Toluca, the capital of the sprawling State of Mexico, but has now been almost completely engulfed by it. The village spreads out around the base of a sharp, conical rise in the land, and on the far side is the rambling, tree-shaded ranch house of my friends Virginia and Carlos Barrios. It is a cool, green oasis alongside the highway with its constant roar of heavy traffic.

Apart from publishing a delightful little series of books on Mexican themes, *Minutiae Mexicana*, American-born Virginia is a passionate cook. On many occasions, as I filter my morning coffee in her kitchen, I have been amazed at the number and variety of delectable little casseroles of local dishes that she provides for Carlos's breakfast: beans, corn, *quelites*, *chorizo*, and eggs in one form or another from her extensive repertoire.

One day I was particularly fascinated to see her carefully forming a "wall" of beans around a tortilla, inside of which she put an egg and a sprinkle of *cilantro*, garnishing the top with sauce and cheese. She explained that it was her version of a delicious and substantial breakfast dish, *huevos encobijadas*, blanketed eggs, served at Mi Ranchito, a renowned little hotel in the northern Sierra de Puebla. Although I have stayed at Mi Ranchito on many occasions, I have never seen it on the menu.

This is a recipe for a few, very few, special friends, intimate family or lovers, but not a crowd. The eggs could be fried in a very small pan or poached.

vegetable oil for frying

2 4-inch (10-cm) tortillas, left for a few hours to dry out a little

*⅓ cup (83 ml) refried black beans (rather dry and malleable),
kept warm (page 295 omitting the avocado leaves)*

1 fried or poached egg

salt to taste

heaped ¼ cup (70 ml) roughly chopped cilantro

⅓ to ½ cup (83 to 125 ml) tomato sauce (page 527), kept warm

2 tablespoons grated Chihuahua, Oaxaca, or Muenster cheese

1 tablespoon finely chopped white onion

Heat enough oil to form a very thin coating in a skillet and fry the tortillas on both sides until golden but not too crisp, adding a little more oil at a time as necessary. Drain well on paper toweling.

Put one of the tortillas onto a warmed plate. Form the bean paste into a "wall" around the edge, about ½ inch (13 mm) high. Place the egg inside, sprinkle with salt, and cover first with the *cilantro* and then with the second tortilla. Pour the sauce around and over it. Sprinkle the top with the cheese and onion, and put under the broiler until the cheese melts.

Serve immediately.

PASTEL DE ZAPOTE NEGRO

VIRGINIA'S ZAPOTE NEGRO CAKE

Virginia Barrios

❁

[MAKES 2 CAKES]

WINTER AND THE SEASONAL, HOT-COUNTRY CROP OF *ZAPOTE NEGRO* (*DIOSPYROS EBENASTER*) WAS JUST ABOUT TO END WHEN I LAST VISITED VIRGINIA BAR-rios. There was a delicious aroma floating around the kitchen as the cakes came out of the oven. We chatted as they cooled off, and soon I was dispatched on my way with a thick slice of *zapote negro* cake for my tea.

The recipe is her invention, a truly Mexican cake in that it utilizes indigenous ingredients very successfully. With the tremendous interest in new fruits and vegetables, I am sure there will be a widening market for *zapote negro*; in anticipation, I am including this recipe.

2½ cups (625 ml) pureed zapote negro (see box),
from about 2 pounds (900 g) fruit

¼ cup (63 ml) dark brown sugar

⅓ cup (83 ml) fresh orange juice

2 tablespoons fresh lime juice

1 ripe banana, mashed

1½ cups (375 ml) granulated sugar

3 cups (750 ml) all-purpose flour

¼ teaspoon salt

1½ teaspoons baking soda

1½ teaspoons ground cinnamon

4 eggs, well beaten

¾ cup (188 ml) vegetable oil

¾ cup (188 ml) golden raisins

⅔ cup (164 ml) hulled raw pumpkin seeds, lightly toasted

Have ready 2 cake pans, ideally 9 by 5 by 3 inches (23 by 13 by 8 cm), lined with well-greased and floured wax paper. Heat the oven to 350°F (177°C).

Mix the *zapote* puree with the brown sugar and juices, then stir in the banana and granulated sugar. In another bowl, mix together the flour, salt, baking soda, and cinnamon and add to the *zapote* mixture. Gradually incorporate the eggs, oil, and then the raisins and pumpkin seeds.

Divide the batter into the 2 pans and bake until firm and springy to the touch—about 1 hour. Cool on a rack.

PEPETO

PORK AND VEGETABLE STEW

Dr. Alfredo Garduño

❋

[SERVES 6]

I HAD ASKED MY FRIEND VIRGINIA, WHO LIVES IN METEPEC, WHAT SHE KNEW ABOUT A TYPE OF SAUSAGE OF THAT AREA CALLED *OBISPO*, BISHOP. YES, IT was always offered for sale in the market of Tenancingo some kilometers away, so we would go and find out.

The butchers' stands in the marketplace off Tenancingo were festooned with red and green *chorizos, longaniza,* and an extra-fat short sausage, the *obispo.* This is, in actual fact, the pig's stomach stuffed with the ground entrails of the animal and seasoned with chiles and herbs, the most important being *epazote.* It was tied very tightly in the middle so that it bulged on either side. I thought that it had acquired the name for its resemblance to a generously proportioned bishop of bygone days (and some today), but the expert on the subject of foods of the Toluca valley—Alfonso Sánchez García (nicknamed "el Profesor Mosquito"), who is the author of a little book called *Toluca del Chorizo*—says that it was named because of its color when cooked, a purplish red.

The butchers of Tenancingo seemed reluctant to give away their culinary secrets, so we did not press them and just bought some sausage to cook at home. Sad to say, it was interesting but by no means exciting. We continued on our way to explore other things, driving through the back roads toward Ixtapan de la Sal. We were nearing the late lunch hour and hungry when we saw a sign saying *"Comidas"* and an arrow pointing to a large *palapa*, palm-thatched roof, set back on a rise above the highway. In front of it was an orchard of sweet *limas*. (This *lima*, as opposed to the sour variety used in the cooking of Yucatán and Guerrero, is a small citrus fruit with a sort of pushed-up nipple at its tip, thus earning it the name *chichona*. While it has a thickly perfumed rind, the flesh is pale yellow, slightly sweet, and insipid. It is commonly used as one of the fruits in the Christmas piñata and said to have medicinal properties for those with high blood pressure.)

There were no other diners in the airy restaurant, and the only dish of the day was *pepeto*, with a pitcher of *lima* to drink. *Pepeto* turned out to be a light, brothy stew of pork with masses of fresh seasonal vegetables, served with freshly made corn tortillas. It was not difficult to work out the recipe.

The name *pepeto* is curious, and I was trying to find out its significance. Through Virginia I was put in contact with Dr. Alfredo Garduño, a great gourmet and connoisseur of the area's cooking. He told me that this dish is known only in a very small area of the State of Mexico, around Ixtapan de la Sal and Villa de Allende, with a completely different version that's in fact a soup, made farther away in the Zacualpan area (page 462), which I have mentioned before, Coatepec de Harenas.

Cheap cuts of meat are used: pork hock and backs and wings of chicken. I am giving his recipe, bearing in mind that substitutes can be made with stewing pork and other parts of chicken. The yellow, or green, or red manzano chile (known in other parts of Latin America as *rocoto*) can be replaced by any hot, fleshy chile like jalapeño and the *chilacayote* with zucchini or green squash. Don't skimp on the fava beans, even if they are starchy and past their best—they give a distinctive flavor to the stew. For best flavor, make it a little ahead and skim off the fat.

1½ pounds (675 g) pork knuckles, cut into 6 slices about ¾ inch (2 cm)
thick, or 1 pound (450 g) stewing pork (see note above)

1 medium white onion, roughly sliced

2 quarts (2 l) water

salt to taste

1½ pounds (675 g) chicken backs and wings or chicken pieces

1 pound (450 g) chilacayote or zucchini or green squash,
cut into large cubes

1 pound (450 g) fava beans, hulled and cleaned of inner skin

3 large ears of corn, one cut into rounds,
plus the shaved kernels of the other two

2 manzano or jalapeño chiles, cleaned of seeds and quartered

3 stems epazote

Put the pork knuckles into a large pot with the onion, water, and salt to taste, bring to a simmer, and continue simmering until partially cooked—about 40 minutes. Add the chicken pieces and cook for 30 minutes more. Add the *chilacayote* and fava beans and continue cooking for 10 more minutes, then add the corn and cook for another 10 minutes.

Add the *epazote*, adjust the seasoning, and continue simmering for another 5 minutes or until the meats and vegetables are very tender. The vegetables should not remain *al dente*—this is a stew.

SALSA DE TOMATE VERDE Y AGUACATE

MEXICAN GREEN SAUCE WITH AVOCADO

✹

[MAKES 2 CUPS (500 ML)]

ON MY ROUTE HOME TO ZITÁCUARO, ABOUT 20 KILOMETERS BEYOND TOLUCA ON A WIDE CURVE IN THE HIGHWAY, THERE IS A BIG SIGN ANNOUNCING EL Yukon Restauran (*sic*)—I must, sometime, ask them how they came by that name in such an unlikely spot. Several years ago I had a habit of stopping there for a very hearty breakfast of eggs with the most delicious locally made *chorizo*. Another few years passed, and for some reason—probably dietary—I would go straight on, trying not to think of that *chorizo*. On two occasions recently I happened to be driving past at about three o'clock in the afternoon and, feeling very hungry, decided to stop. Outwardly the place was the same, with the usual bevy of trucks and semiofficial cars parked in front, while inside their owners—highway police, telephone repairmen, and a few traveling salesmen—were heartily eating the freshly prepared, aromatic stews of meat and chiles. Obviously the same proprietors were still there.

On one of those occasions I ordered *mole de olla*, a soupy stew that came with the most succulent pork I had eaten in a long time. While I was waiting, a small, delicious homemade cheese and some pickled vegetables were put on the table for an unsolicited *botana*, with some thick handmade tortillas. On the second occasion I was all set to eat a plateful of mutton in pasilla sauce when a freshly made, very picante green sauce was put in front of me with some hot tortillas. I couldn't resist the many helpings that finally did away with my appetite and all thoughts of the main dish.

The raw, basic ingredients of the sauce had been blended together and then mixed with some mashed avocado (not much). It was not a *guacamole*, but there was enough avocado to lend richness and body to the sauce. It is a particularly good recipe when avocados are not at their best—unfortunately that seems to happen far too frequently these days in the United States.

½ pound (225 g) tomates verdes, about 10 medium
½ cup (125 ml) water
4 serrano chiles or to taste, roughly chopped
heaped ½ cup (135 ml) firmly packed roughly chopped cilantro
½ cup (125 ml) mashed avocado
salt to taste

Remove the husks from the *tomates verdes*, rinse well, and roughly chop.

Put the water into a blender, add the chiles and onion, and blend until fairly smooth. Add the *tomates verdes* and cilantro and blend to a textured consistency. Stir in (do not blend or the texture will be lost) the mashed avocado and salt. The sauce can be prepared an hour or two ahead but should be eaten the same day. Serve with corn tortillas.

MOLE DE OLLA CON TAMALES DE ELOTE

"POT MOLE" WITH FRESH CORN TAMALES

Sra. Yolanda de Suárez

✹

[SERVES 4]

THE FRIEND WITH WHOM I WENT TO ZACUALPAN, ESTADO DE MEXICO, HAD TOLD ME ABOUT THIS UNUSUAL DISH: A SOUPY *MOLE* POURED OVER FRESH corn *tamales*. It is so simple and tasty.

With so few ingredients, this dish requires an excellent chicken broth as a base and the freshest *epazote*.

The broth is sometimes cooked with meat, chicken, and/or vegetables or served with the *tamales*. I combined the two by putting 1½ cups (375 ml) of cooked vegetables—zucchini, beans, peas (almost anything you have on hand)—into the broth.

You will need about 1½ cups (375 ml) and 2 *tamales* per serving. The extra *tamales* can be frozen for some other occasion.

6 guajillo chiles
1 cup (250 ml) water
1 garlic clove, roughly chopped
⅛ teaspoon cumin seeds
1 tablespoon vegetable oil (I use chicken fat)
5 cups (1.25 l) strong chicken broth
salt to taste
1 large leafy stem epazote

Slit the chiles open, remove the seeds and veins, cover with hot water, and simmer for 5 minutes. Set aside to soak for 10 more minutes.

Pour ¼ cup (63 ml) of the water into a blender, add the garlic and cumin, and blend well. Add the remaining ¾ cup (188 ml) of water and the drained chiles; blend as thoroughly as possible.

[CONTINUED]

Heat the oil for frying, and when it is hot add the chile puree, pressing it through a fine strainer to extract the tough pieces of skin that never quite disappear. Fry for 5 minutes, scraping the bottom of the pan to prevent sticking. Add the chicken broth and simmer uncovered for 5 minutes, then test for salt. Add the *epazote* and simmer for 5 minutes more.

Put 2 heated *tamales* into the soup bowls and pour the hot broth over them.

TAMALES DE ELOTE

FRESH CORN *TAMALES*

Sra. Yolanda de Suárez

✴

[MAKES 16 3-INCH (8-CM) TAMALES]

THESE ARE THE SIMPLEST OF FRESH CORN *TAMALES*, NOT TO BE COMPARED WITH THE RICHER *UCHEPOS* OF MICHOACÁN. OF COURSE YOU WILL NEED CORN that is not sweet and has an adequate starch content—field corn, like that grown in Mexico. (A farmer's market or farm stand is your best source.) The corn needs to be mature but not too hard. Press your nail into a kernel; it should still be juicy.

In Zacualpan these *tamales* are cut up and put into a *mole de olla* (see preceding recipe). There the cooks add a few pieces of *tequesquite* (see note, page 257) into the water of the steamer and make a rack of the shaved corn cobs. Both steps, they say, give a better flavor to the *tamales*. I slavishly follow their instructions, but of course you can leave the *tequesquite* out.

When removing the husks, which will serve as *tamale* wrappers, from the ears of corn, take care to cut as close to the base as possible so that the leaf has a cup, which protects the end of the *tamale*. Then unfurl the leaves, without breaking them if possible. (See the illustrated instructions in *The Art of Mexican Cooking*, page 86.)

6 cups (1.5 l) corn kernels
1½ teaspoons baking powder
2 tablespoons sugar
1 teaspoon salt

Have ready at least 20 large fresh corn husks (the remaining ones can be used to line the steamer).

Prepare your *tamale* steamer (page 522) and don't forget to put coins in the water so that you can hear when it goes off the boil. (Detailed instructions on steamers are in *The Art of Mexican Cooking*, page 63.)

Pour the corn into a food processor and process until you have a textured puree. Mix in the rest of the ingredients. Don't begin to fill the leaves until you hear the coins rattling around in the steamer.

Put 2 tablespoons of the mixture down the center of the fresh corn husk, fold over firmly, but don't press it flat—the mixture has to have room to expand. Double over the pointed end of the leaf, on the side opposite the seam, and lay the *tamales* down horizontally in over-lapping layers in the top of the steamer. Cover with more leaves or a cloth, set the lid firmly onto the top of the steamer, weighing it down if necessary with a weight—I use a *molcajete*. Cook for 1¼ hours. When done, the *tamale* should roll easily away from the wrapping.

If storing for any length of time, keep them in the freezer once cooled. When reheating, remember not to defrost first.

POLLO EN SALSA DE CACAHUATE

CHICKEN IN PEANUT SAUCE

Sra. Yolanda de Suárez, Zacualpan

☀

[SERVES 6]

BOTH THIS RECIPE AND THE ONE FOR THE CANDIED PEANUTS THAT FOLLOWS WERE GIVEN TO ME BY A LIVELY YOUNG HOUSEWIFE/TEACHER WHO LOVES TO cook in between the hours of her work, writing her doctoral thesis on the history of this legendary mining town, and keeping house for her husband, the local baker, and their two children.

13 guajillo chiles or 10 guajillos and 6 puyas for more heat

3 tablespoons lard or rendered chicken fat

6 large pieces of chicken with skin

1½ cups (375 ml) raw peanuts with reddish papery skin still attached

1 garlic clove

approximately 1 quart (1 l) water

1 garlic clove, roughly chopped

¼ teaspoon cumin seeds

salt to taste

Remove the stems, if any, from the chiles, slit them open, and remove the seeds and veins. Cover with hot water and soak for about 20 minutes. Heat the lard in a skillet and add the chicken pieces in one layer so that they are not touching in the pan (you will probably have to do this in two batches). Fry the chicken pieces over medium heat, turning them around from time to time, until they are a deep golden color. Remove with a slotted spoon and set aside.

Add the peanuts and the unpeeled garlic to the pan and fry slowly until they are evenly toasted right through. Set aside.

Put 1 cup (250 ml) of the water into a blender and gradually add the drained chiles, blending well after each addition. Reheat the fat and add the chile puree, pressing it well through a fine strainer to extract as much of the juice and flesh of the chiles as possible from the debris of tough skins. Fry over medium heat, scraping the bottom of the pan to prevent sticking, for about 5 minutes.

Put ½ cup (125 ml) of the water into the blender, add the chopped garlic and cumin and blend well. Gradually add the toasted garlic and peanuts with another ½ cup (125 ml) water a little at a time and blend to a finely textured paste, adding a little more water if necessary to release the blender blade.

Add the mixture to the chile puree in the pan and cook for 5 minutes. Add the chicken pieces and the remaining water with salt as necessary and continue cooking uncovered over low heat, scraping the bottom of the pan from time to time to prevent sticking, until the chicken is tender and pools of oil form on the surface—about 20 minutes.

When finished, the sauce should be of medium consistency, lightly coating the back of a wooden spoon, and a brick-red color.

This dish can be prepared well ahead, even the day before serving.

CACAHUATES GARAPIÑADOS

CANDIED PEANUTS

Sra. Yolanda de Suárez, Zacualpan

✺

[MAKES 2 CUPS (500 ML)]

THERE WAS A HUGE BASKET FULL OF FRESHLY HARVESTED PEANUTS ON THE COUNTER WHEN WE WENT INTO SEÑORA YOLANDA'S GALLEY-SIZED KITCHEN to cook. I was curious about why she preferred to use them with the papery, reddish skin still attached; she replied that the skins not only helped the sugar adhere better but also provided a natural coloring (those who prepare them commercially add a chemical coloring agent) and iron supplement to the diet.

It is not worthwhile making less than this quantity; in fact you should make more while you are at it. They should be stored in an airtight container in a dry place—with the slightest moisture the caramel becomes sticky.

Warning: these candied peanuts tend to become addictive to sugar lovers.

2 cups (500 ml) raw peanuts with papery skin still attached
2 cups (500 ml) sugar
2 cups (500 ml) water
large pinch salt, optional (my addition)

Mix the ingredients together well in a heavy pan, heating through over medium heat. Stir until the sugar has melted. Raise the heat and keep stirring. When the water has evaporated, the sugar will quite suddenly form an uneven, thick coating around the peanuts. After about 10 minutes, lower the heat and keep stirring; the sugar will begin to melt and become trans-

[CONTINUED]

parent and gradually turn a caramel color. Keep stirring and scraping the bottom of the pan. The sugar, now syrup, will turn a darker brown and form a hard, uneven, and transparent coating around the peanuts (well, a few may remain exposed) after about 20 minutes. Quickly tip the peanuts out and spread in one (uneven) layer over a cookie sheet. Set aside to cool.

NOTE: *Do not, at any point in the cooking, or until completely cool, let the caramel come into contact with your skin: it will stick and burn ferociously.*

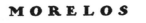

MORELOS

Guajes

THE STATE OF MORELOS AND ITS CAPITAL CITY, CUER-
NAVACA, LIE DUE SOUTH OF MEXICO CITY. I STILL HAVE
VIVID MEMORIES OF THOSE FIRST EVENING DRIVES TO
Cuernavaca in the late fifties with my husband, Paul. As the highway
descended into the valley of Morelos at sunset, we were met by one of the most
beautiful panoramas in the world. The setting sun cast a glow on the snowy tip of
Popocatépetl and transformed the whole valley and the mountains beyond into a
spectrum of diaphanous colors. We always stopped to take it all in, wondering why
other drivers rushed by unheeding and unmoved by the scene spread out before
them. ❂ It is still beautiful as you drive down the southern slopes of the mountains
that enclose Mexico City, but the beauty of that scene has faded, perhaps never to be
recaptured, diminished by smog from industry and uncontrolled growth and exacer-
bated in the winter by the burning off of the cane fields. ❂ To go to Zacualpan de
Amilpas, you turn off the main highway and drive through the spectacular valley

along the craggy, massive wall of deep red volcanic rocks of Tepoztzteco. The valley is alive with flowering trees in the spring and dotted with brilliant wildflowers after the summer rains. It opens out into flatter land planted with crops of tomatoes and chiles among other produce, gradually giving way to the cornfields. You pass Cuautla—once an attractive center of mineral baths and weekend houses surrounded by orchards but now overcome by ugly urban growth and lack of civic pride—and continue along the busy highway to Izucar de Matamoros, turning off after about thirty kilometers to Zacualpan.

I have included this story of my trip to Zacualpan de Amilpas and the recipes for *guajes*, because I found the experience fascinating. There are many wild, free foods in Mexico that are appreciated in areas where they occur, despite their strong flavors that would seem repugnant to outsiders: *jumiles*, caterpillars like *cuetlas (Erebus odoratus)* and *chimicuiles (Cossus redtenbachi)*, butterfly herb, *papaloquelite (Porophyllum macrocephallum)*, and *pepicha* or *pipitza (Porophyllum tagetoides)*. These recipes also provide some novel ideas for vegetarian dishes, substituting small lima or fava beans for the *guajes*.

With the enormous interest now in regional Mexican foods and the fact that Mexicans are fanning out all over the United States and bringing with them a demand for their native ingredients, it is little wonder that *guajes* were found recently by an aficionado of my books in a Mexican food store in Brooklyn.

A chance encounter and an idle remark led me to the home of artist/craftsman Roberto Falfan and his wife, Theresa Niño, in Zacualpan (Morelos), where their cook, Elpidia Tlacotla, showed me how to prepare the local dishes based on *guajes*. We met a short time before at the home of a mutual friend. It was midmorning, and so, not surprisingly, the subject of food came up and in particular the use of *guajes*, the flat beans, rather like the small limas, contained in long, flat mulberry-colored pods of a tree indigenous to the dry lands of central and southern Mexico, *Leucaena esculenta*, and spp. (*guaje* is the generic word in Spanish for pod). There is also a species that gives a green, edible pod, but the red ones are considered more flavorful by cooks in the area around Zacualpan.

On the day we arrived, the trees (normally growing wild, but here planted as if in an orchard) were festooned with bunches of shiny pods, but by the next afternoon they had been stripped off and packed into sacks, which were stacked by the roadside, waiting to be transported to the markets of Cuernavaca, Mexico City, and Izucar de Matamoras. Some of the locals said they would be shipped to Japan for the pharmaceutical industry, but I could never corroborate this or find out how they were to be used.

While the pods are still tender, they are opened up and the seeds that resemble immature lima beans eaten as a snack, their strong, pungent oils filling the mouth and sending off a slightly repugnant odor (for this reason they are said to be a cure for internal parasites). *Guajes* nevertheless provide an important supplement of minerals, proteins, and vitamins to the rather deficient, poor diet of the people living in the semiarid areas in which they grow.

A neighbor of mine in Michoacán says that they also benefit the lungs by oxygenating them. I am a true believer in local medicinal lore but have never tried this one out on a more sophisticated expert. It's a useful remedy since the pods form and are harvested during the winter months.

Not only are these seeds eaten raw, but they are cooked in local stews, toasted and crushed for a type of sauce, and dried out crisp to make a snack known as *cacalas*.

I have eaten *guajes* many times cooked in *guaxmole*, a dish typical of Puebla in October, when the dry, salty goat meat, *chito*, has been produced from the yearly *matanza*, or mass slaughter of goats. A thrifty neighbor of mine with a large family to provide for dries the pods and uses them in powder form in Lenten fritters, traditionally made of dried shrimp.

TORTITAS DE GUAJES EN SALSA DE JITOMATE

GUAJE FRITTERS IN TOMATO SAUCE

✺

[SERVES 4 TO 6]

SMALL FROZEN LIMA OR FAVA BEANS, DEFROSTED, CAN BE SUBSTITUTED FOR GUAJES.

THE SAUCE

1 small slice white onion, roughly chopped

1 garlic clove, roughly chopped

¼ teaspoon cumin seeds

¼ cup (63 ml) water

10 ounces (285 g) tomatoes, roughly chopped, about 1½ cups (375 ml)

1 tablespoon vegetable oil

2 to 3 cups (500 to 750 ml) water or chicken broth

salt to taste

THE FRITTERS

1 cup (250 ml) raw guaje beans or lima or small fava beans

¼ medium white onion, finely chopped

2½ ounces (75 g) queso añejo or Romano, finely grated,
about ⅔ cup (164 ml)

3 eggs, well beaten

salt to taste

vegetable oil for frying

Blend together the onion, garlic, and cumin with the water until smooth. Add the tomatoes a few at a time and blend until smooth. Heat the oil in a heavy pan, add the sauce, and fry until reduced and seasoned—about 8 minutes. Add the water or chicken broth with salt and cook for 5 more minutes. Keep warm while you prepare the fritters.

Put the whole *guaje* beans into a bowl, stir in the onion, cheese, and eggs—salt only if necessary, depending on the strength of the cheese. Heat the oil in a skillet—it should be about ½ inch deep—and fry large spoonfuls of the mixture over high heat until golden brown on both sides. Drain well. Add the fritters to the warm sauce and cook over low heat, turning them over once, until the *guajes* are cooked inside—about 30 minutes.

GUAXMOLE

A MOLE OF GUAJES

✸

[SERVES 4]

1½ pounds (675 g) stewing pork and pork ribs,
cut into small serving pieces
⅓ small white onion, roughly chopped
salt to taste
1 pound (450 g) tomatoes, roughly chopped
4 garlic cloves, roughly chopped
⅓ white onion, roughly chopped
2 tablespoons pork lard
1½ cups (375 ml) guajes or small lima beans
6 serrano chiles or to taste
6 large sprigs cilantro

In a saucepan, barely cover the meat with water, add the onion and salt, and simmer until half cooked—about 20 minutes. Strain, reserving the broth.

In a blender, puree the tomatoes with the garlic and chopped onion. Heat the lard in a casserole and fry the meat lightly. Add the tomato sauce and cook over fairly high heat until seasoned and partially reduced—about 10 minutes.

Put 1 cup (250 ml) of the reserved meat broth into the blender, add the chiles, and blend until smooth. Add the *guajes*, a little at a time, and blend to a textured consistency. Add this with another cup of the broth, the *cilantro*, and salt to taste and cook over low heat, stirring and scraping the bottom of the pan to prevent sticking, for about 45 minutes. The sauce should be of medium consistency—add more broth or water if necessary to dilute.

SALSA DE GUAJES

GUAJE SAUCE

✹

[MAKES APPROXIMATELY 1½ CUPS (375 ML)]

THIS IS A RUSTIC TABLE SAUCE, SO OF COURSE IT'S BETTER MADE IN THE *MOL-CAJETE*. IT SHOULD BE TEXTURED, NOT SMOOTH, AND SERVED WITH TACOS OR *tostadas*.

3 garlic cloves, peeled
4 (or to taste) serrano chiles, cooked on the comal
until fairly soft and slightly charred
1 cup (250 ml) guajes or lima or fava beans
approximately ½ cup (125 ml) water
salt to taste

Grind the garlic and chiles together to a paste. Gradually add the beans with a little of the water and grind to a textured, fairly rough consistency. Add salt and serve immediately.

CACALAS

TOASTED DRIED GUAJES

✹

[MAKES 1 CUP]

CACALAS ARE THE DRIED SEEDS OR BEANS OF THE *GUAJE* PODS AND RESEMBLE LARGE, FAT BROWN LENTILS AT FIRST GLANCE. I CAME ACROSS *CACALAS* FOR the first time in the market of Izucar de Matamoros and was told that they were eaten as a snack seasoned with lime juice and salt. They seemed very hard and not very interesting, so I stored them away and forgot about them. It wasn't until I visited Zacualpan de Amilpas that I learned how to prepare them correctly and to appreciate their crisp texture and pungent flavor.

I am afraid there is no substitute, but they are now available in Mexican grocery stores in the United States.

1 cup (250 ml) cacalas

1 tablespoon fresh lime juice

1 teaspoon ground sea salt

In an ungreased skillet, toast the *cacalas* over a low heat, moving them around from time to time so that they cook evenly and do not burn—15 to 20 minutes. When cool they should be quite crisp.

Transfer the *cacalas* to a small bowl, mix in the lime juice and salt, and return to the hot pan. Heat through once more, stirring constantly until the lime juice is absorbed and the salt forms a light coating over the surface of the seeds—5 to 10 minutes.

Tlacoyos

The Falfan family suggested I go and try Sra. Gosafat's very special *tlacoyos*, delicious little oval filled *masa* cakes. She erects her little stand every morning outside the local high school and does a brisk trade until midday, when there is nothing left. Although she had other fillings—potatoes cooked with strips of jalapeños and *chacales*, the little browned pieces from the bottom of the *chicharrón* vat (page 419), cooked with a guajillo sauce—those stuffed with ricotta and served with *gallitos* (page 239) were my favorites.

With something so simple, it is essential to have the best of ingredients: the corn *masa* (for tortillas) and ricotta that is not fat-free and slightly acidy.

Ricotta varies enormously. Try to get some from an Italian store and look for ricotta that's as natural as possible, which will be slightly lumpy. If it's moist and creamy, hang it overnight in a cheesecloth bag to drain.

Sra. Gosafat serves the *tlacoyos* straight off the *comal*, lifting up the top, thin layer of dough, spreading some of the *gallitos* over the ricotta, and then laying the flap back down again to cover the filling. Of course, she would think it absolutely ridiculous to give such arithmetic instructions, but it is necessary if you haven't actually seen it done. These are thinner and larger than most *tlacoyos*, but of course you can make them smaller and therefore easier to eat if you are passing them around as a *botana*.

TLACOYOS DE REQUESÓN

RICOTTA TLACOYOS

Sra. Gosafat Palacios de Coot

✸

[MAKES 8 TLACOYOS]

8 ounces (225 g) corn tortilla masa—*about 2 scant cups (480 ml)*
8 ounces (225 g) ricotta (see note, page 246) salted to taste
a little vegetable oil
gallitos (recipe follows)

Divide the *masa* into 8 balls about 1¾ inches (4.5 cm) in diameter. Take a ball of the dough and roll it into a cylinder shape. Flatten it gently in the tortilla press until you have an oval shape about 5½ inches (14.5 cm) long and 4 inches (10 cm) wide.

Put 1 very heaped tablespoon of the ricotta down the middle of the dough, close the sides to cover the ricotta completely, and form the dough into a bobbin shape about 5½ by 1½ inches (14.5 by 4 cm), rolling it between your palms. Press again to flatten lightly in the tortilla press or in your hands to form a flat, oval shape about 6 by 4 inches (15.5 by 10 cm). Brush a heated *comal* or griddle with a little oil and cook the *tlacoyos* over medium heat until the dough is cooked through but still soft and slightly browned in patches, about 10 minutes. Carefully lift up the top layer of the dough and spread the melting ricotta with some of the *gallitos*. Replace the layer of dough and serve immediately—this is pan-to-mouth food.

NOTE: *In most tortilla presses the dough will press out thinner on the handle side, especially when you are using a thicker dough for antojitos like* tlacoyos. *It is therefore necessary to press lightly on one side, then reverse the dough to obtain an even thickness.*

GALLITOS

JALAPEÑO CHILE RELISH

✻

[MAKES APPROXIMATELY 3 CUPS (750 ML)]

8 ounces (225 g) jalapeño chiles
1 cup (250 ml) finely chopped white onion
¾ cup (188 ml) fresh lime juice
½ cup (125 ml) water
salt to taste

Cut the stalks off the chiles and cut into diagonal slices about ⅛ inch (3 mm) thick. Cover with water, bring to a simmer, and continue cooking for about 2 minutes. Strain and remove the loose seeds only.

Put the chiles into a glass or noncorrosible bowl, add the rest of the ingredients, and set aside to season for at least 1 hour before serving.

Zacualpan de Amilpas

Although the trip to Zacualpan was ostensibly to research an article for a Mexican magazine on *guajes,* our host's mother had been forewarned of our visit and, being a passionate cook, had prepared the ingredients for other recipes. We had to try the local *mole de olla* made with *cecina*—thinly cut half-dried beef—from the neighboring villages of Tetela and Yecapixtla, well known for having the best *cecina* of grass-fed beef in the area. Indeed it had an excellent flavor and texture and was very lean. It was cooked with lots of vegetables in a broth seasoned with pasilla chiles—a favorite of the area—which made a very satisfying and flavorful dish. She made *tortitas* with bunches of *epazote,* stuffed with cheese, fried in an egg batter, and cooked in a simple sauce of pasilla chiles. (A botanist friend came across a similar dish in that area using wild sorrel, *vinagrera* or *lengua de vaca.*)

Sra. Falfan had lived in various regions of Mexico and talked about some unusual *chalupas* (canoes) as they are made in the Bajío region. One was hollowed-out cucumber filled with *queso añejo* and finely chopped onion, seasoned with vinegar and powdered *chile de árbol.* Another was *sopa de chilladora*—*chilladora* being the local name for blood sausage—and *lagrimas y risas*, tears and smiles, unfried pork rinds, *cueros*, in tomato sauce with hot chile. She reminisced about Lenten dishes prepared by her mother when the family budget was tight: oatmeal soup and these *tortas de arroz*, rice fritters, among others.

TORTAS DE ARROZ EN CHILE PASILLA

RICE FRITTERS IN PASILLA CHILE SAUCE

Sra. Carmen Vivanco de Falfan

❋

[SERVES 6, WITH 3 2-INCH (5-CM) FRITTERS PER SERVING]

I HAVE ADAPTED SRA. CARMEN'S RECIPE SLIGHTLY TO MAKE THE FRITTERS A LITTLE LIGHTER; OF COURSE, NOW THEY TEND TO ABSORB MORE OF THE sauce . . . no matter. I serve them with a little lime juice and some chopped onion or blend in a few cooked *tomates verdes* with the chiles. The touch of acidity enhances the chile sauce.

Start the evening before.

THE TORTAS

¾ cup (188 ml) long-grain white rice, not precooked or converted
¾ cup (188 ml) finely grated queso añejo or Romano
1 scant teaspoon salt
vegetable oil for frying
3 eggs, separated

THE SAUCE

10 pasilla chiles
approximately 7 cups (1.75 l) water
½ medium white onion, roughly chopped
2 garlic cloves, roughly chopped
4 tomates verdes simmered in water to cover for 8 to 10 minutes
(optional)
1½ tablespoons vegetable oil
salt to taste

THE EVENING BEFORE: Cover the rice with water and leave it to soak overnight. The following day, drain the rice well and grind in a food processor or blender to a finely textured consistency.

Mix the rice with the cheese and salt. Heat ½ inch oil in a skillet over low heat. Beat the egg whites until stiff but not dry. Beat in the yolks and gradually fold in the rice mixture. When the oil is hot, fry heaped tablespoons of the mixture to form fritters about 2 inches across until the surface of the mixture is just firm—about 4 minutes. Turn them over and fry on the second side until golden brown, about 3 minutes. Drain well on paper toweling.

THE SAUCE: Slit the chiles open, removing the seeds and veins. Toast them briefly on a warm *comal* or griddle, cover with hot water, and simmer for about 3 minutes. Set aside for another 10 minutes. Drain.

Put ½ cup (125 ml) of the water into a blender, add the onion, garlic, and *tomates verdes*, and blend until smooth. Add another cup (250 ml) of the water and the drained chiles and blend until smooth.

Heat the 1½ tablespoons of oil in a heavy pan and fry the sauce, stirring and scraping the bottom of the pan to prevent sticking, for about 5 minutes. Add the remaining water with salt to taste and simmer for another 5 minutes.

Add the fritters to the sauce and cook over low heat, uncovered, for 20 minutes. Carefully turn the fritters over and continue cooking for about 20 minutes or until the rice inside is tender (if you break one of them open, it should be spongy throughout). The sauce should be of medium consistency. Add a little more water if necessary to dilute.

Palpan

Palpan is a small village in a remote and less populated part of the State of Morelos where it shares its boundaries with Guerrero. It is set in a dry, semitropical landscape with majestic rocks towering above. It seems like a forgotten village; the road running through it is nothing more than a series of deep potholes. Nothing much goes on there; most families have some land where they grow corn and beans and a few head of cattle, but there is a predilection for the local, powerfully strong *mezcal*, which is addictive—as the friend who took me there can attest.

I had come to try a new and extraordinary dish, *pollo ahogado en natas*—chicken drowned in a chile cream sauce (the recipe follows)—in the home of Srita. Noemi Tello. It was truly delicious. The afternoon was calm enough until it was suggested that we should go to the *jaripeo* just a few miles away.

We took a precarious, unpaved road that hugged a steep rise with a dramatic falloff on the other side. A *jaripeo* is an exhibition of machismo if ever there was one, the men chatting with friends proudly showing off their mounts, drinking beer and *mezcal* until the next steer is brought into the ring. There were about thirty that evening, all trying to bring down the frightened and skittish animal with their lassos. They bring it down, and someone mounts it and hangs on while the bucking animal tries desperately to shake the rider off. It was a fascinating scene as the sun sank in the background, sent up flares of pink-red, and lingered in the sky until darkness fell.

It was a very drunken drive back that night with the Mexican music at full blast in the open car, our driver gesticulating and singing loudly to accompany it, in contrast to the soft, rhythmic patter of hooves on earth, the silence of the countryside around, and a sky that shone with stars.

A month or so later I was invited again to try *celosas* ("jealousies"), the specialty of another cook in Palpan. We arrived early one Sunday afternoon, well after the appointed time, and there was Sra. Maria Arriaga, cooking happily with an appreciative and hungry male audience downing innumerable *mezcals* and a lot of beer.

She was working with some of the finest white corn *masa* that I have ever seen except in Oaxaca: the secret, she says, is not to use too much lime and to wash the kernels thoroughly after the night's soaking and before taking it to the mill. She was making *gorditas de frijol* in the same oval form as *tlacoyos*. They were delicious, especially when smeared thickly with some of the dense, slightly soured cream. We tried but held back because we had come to eat *celosas*, a name only recently given to this simple snack by a neighbor, Manuel Tello.

She spread one of her thin tortillas with a thick layer of cream and then set it onto a hot skillet for the dough to crisp up and the cream to melt. She served the *celosa* with a green sauce. It was absurdly simple, but each ingredient was just perfect.

María had been brought up on a ranch nearby, and this enticing snack was something she remembers from her childhood. By now the men sitting around were well away in their cups, reminiscing about what they used to eat. There was no junk food then. It was all fresh and homegrown from the crops they remembered planting with their fathers: corn, beans, and small wild chiles; milk warm from the morning's milking, cheese, cream, and ricotta, everything prepared daily at home.

In the middle of this talk we were enticed away; another group of men had gathered to drink while several women were preparing food and snacks of fresh fava beans. The hulled but unskinned beans were put into a skillet over fairly high heat and shaken from time to time until they were lightly browned and the skins split open. They were then put into a plastic bowl with lime juice and salt. Tightly covered, they were shaken from time to time and left for 10 minutes before serving.

We passed up the *mole* they offered and returned for just one more *celosa*.

POLLO AHOGADO EN NATAS

CHICKEN DROWNED IN CREAM

Srita. Noemi Tello, Palpan

❀

[SERVES 6]

THIS DISH IS UNUSUAL IN THAT, UNLIKE MANY MEXICAN DISHES, THE AMOUNTS OF GARLIC AND SPICES ARE VERY LARGE BUT SURPRISINGLY balanced by the chiles and cream. Srita. Noemi used an enormous amount of cream, and I have reduced it by almost half.

In many parts of Mexico *natas* refers to the thick layer of cream that forms on the top of scalded raw milk, but here it is very thick soured cream, in fact crème fraîche, while *natitas* is used for the scalded version.

She advocates a free-range chicken flavor: the broth has to be strong, so to compensate somewhat I have cooked the chicken in a strong broth.

The sauce will be fairly thin, so you may want to serve it in shallow bowls with a lot of corn tortillas to sop it up. I use the fat skimmed off the broth to fry the chile puree.

5 cups (1.25 l) strong, well-salted chicken broth

1 small white onion, roughly sliced

3 garlic cloves, roughly chopped

1 4-pound (1.8-kg) chicken, cut into serving pieces

3 large sprigs fresh mint

THE SAUCE

5 ounces (140 g) guajillo chiles or half guajillo and half puyas for more heat, slit open and veins and seeds removed

14 garlic cloves, roughly chopped

20 allspice

20 cloves

12 ounces (340 g) tomatoes

2 cups (500 ml) crème fraîche

salt to taste

Simmer the broth with the onion and garlic for 5 minutes. Add the chicken pieces and mint and cook over very low heat until almost tender—about 25 minutes—depending on the quality of the chicken. Strain and degrease the broth, reserving the broth and the fat.

THE SAUCE: Cover the chiles with hot water and simmer for 5 minutes. Leave to soak for 10 minutes more. Drain and transfer to a blender with 1½ cups (375 ml) of the chicken broth. Blend as smoothly as possible and strain, pressing out as much flesh and juice as possible. Discard the chile debris.

Put ½ cup (125 ml) of the broth into the blender, add the garlic and spices, and blend until smooth. Gradually add the tomatoes and blend until smooth.

Heat 2 tablespoons of the chicken fat in a heavy pan, add the chile puree, and cook over low heat, scraping the bottom of the pan to prevent sticking, for about 10 minutes. Add the tomato puree and continue cooking over medium heat until reduced and seasoned, about 15 minutes. Add 2½ cups (625 ml) of the chicken broth and cook for 5 more minutes over fairly high heat.

Add the chicken pieces and cook for about 5 minutes, then gradually stir in the cream and cook over very low heat for about 10 minutes, adjusting salt toward the end of the cooking time.

CHILACAS RELLENAS EN NATAS

STUFFED CHILACAS IN A CHILE CREAM SAUCE

❋

[SERVES 4]

THE CHILE-CREAM SAUCE OF THE PRECEDING RECIPE IS SO DELICIOUS THAT YOU WILL WANT TO USE IT IN OTHER DISHES. SRITA. NOEMI IN PALPAN SAYS she often uses it with the black-green chilacas stuffed with a *picadillo*. I sometimes fill half the chiles with cheese and the rest with *picadillo*. But make sure the sauce is made only with guajillos and not puyas, which would make it too hot with chilacas.

I am sure that in the not-too-distant future chilacas (the chile pasilla in its fresh state) will be imported to the United States, but until then the dried pasillas (long, skinny black chiles, not the erroneously named anchos) can be used. Make sure that they are well cleaned of their veins, the hottest part, and of course the seeds.

8 chilaca or pasilla chiles (see note above)
1 heaped cup (275 ml) picadillo or 12 ounces queso fresco
or Muenster, cut into narrow strips
½ recipe for sauce from Pollo Ahogado en Natas (recipe precedes)

Have ready a baking dish into which the chiles will just fit in one layer. Heat the oven to 375°F (190°C). For chilacas, char, peel, and remove the veins and seeds, leaving the top intact. For pasillas, slit open and remove the seeds and veins. Cover with boiling water and leave to soak until reconstituted—about 15 minutes. Do not leave too long, or the flavor will seep out into the water.

[CONTINUED]

Drain the chiles well and pat dry. Fill each one with about 2 tablespoons of the *picadillo* or some strips of cheese. Fill them to bursting; it doesn't matter if the cut edges don't quite meet.

Set the stuffed chiles in one layer in the dish, pour the sauce around them, cover loosely with foil, and bake until they are well heated through and the sauce bubbling, about 10 minutes. Serve immediately with corn tortillas.

GORDAS DE REQUESÓN

GORDAS FILLED WITH RICOTTA

Sra. María Arriaga, Palpan

☀

[MAKES ENOUGH FILLING FOR ABOUT 10 GORDAS]

SRA. ARRIAGA MADE US SOME GORDAS IN THE FORM OF *TLACOYOS*, THICK OVALS MADE OF A VERY WHITE CORN MASA (PAGE 530)—WITH THIS FILLING. IT CAN also be used for tacos or *quesadillas*.

Commercial ricotta is often, not always, too moist. For this sort of recipe it is best to hang it up overnight in a cheesecloth bag to drain.

1½ cups (375 ml) drained ricotta, about 9 ounces
2 tablespoons roughly chopped epazote
1 heaped tablespoon finely chopped white onion
2 serrano chiles, finely chopped
salt to taste

Mix everything together well.

AT QUINTA DIANA

I. FLOWERS, KITCHEN TERRACE. 2. OUTSIDE OVEN ON KITCHEN TERRACE. 3-4. VIEW OF KITCHEN
TERRACE TO THE SOUTH. 5. THE ENTRANCE. 6. LOOKING DOWN MAIN ENTRANCE PATH.

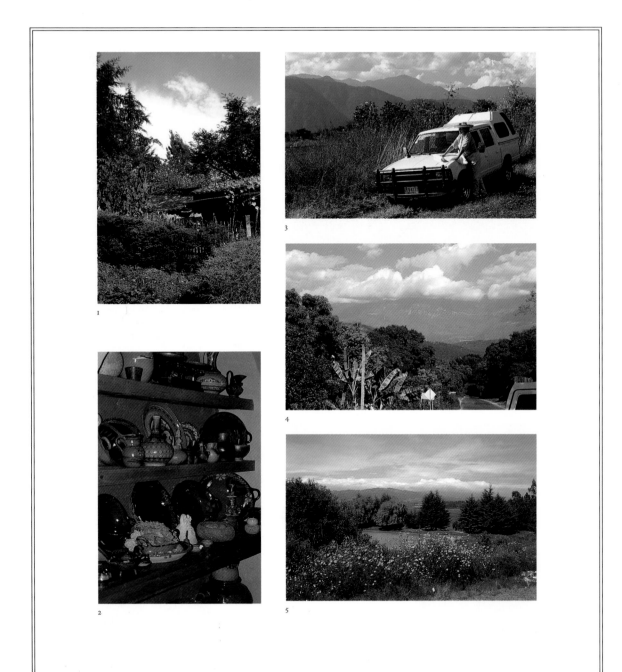

1. COWSHED AT QUINTA DIANA. 2. MY KITCHEN DRESSER. 3. STANDING BY MY TRUCK IN MICHOACÁN LANDSCAPE. 4. OAXACAN HIGHWAY — PINOTEPA NACIONAL TO TLAXIACO. 5. VIEW FROM HIGHWAY 15 — TOLUCA-ZITÁCUARO.

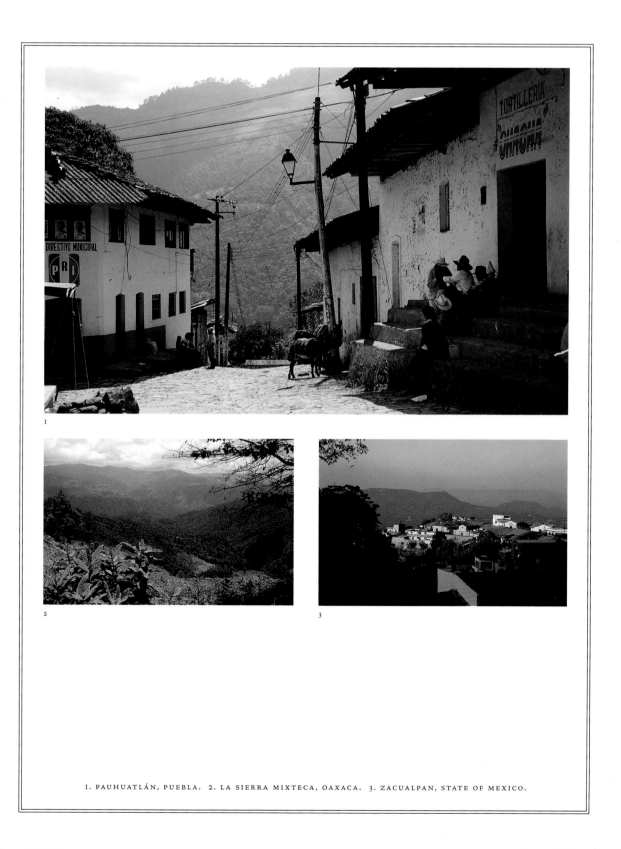

I. PAUHUATLÁN, PUEBLA. 2. LA SIERRA MIXTECA, OAXACA. 3. ZACUALPAN, STATE OF MEXICO.

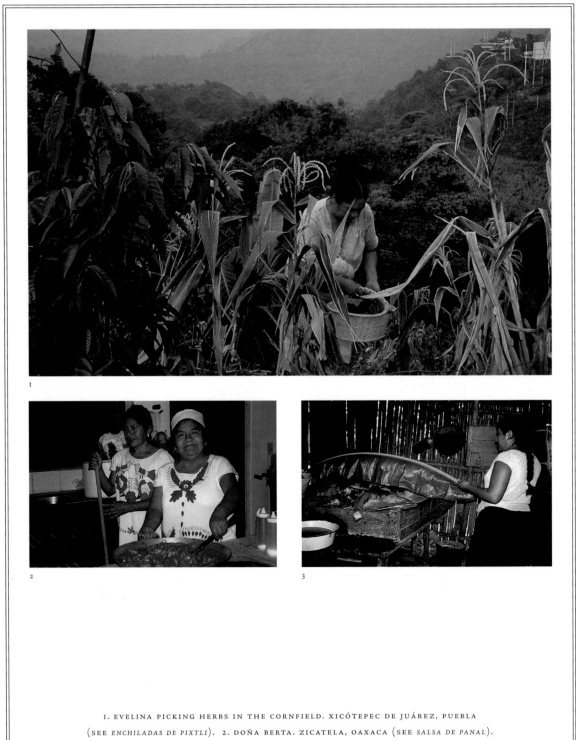

1. EVELINA PICKING HERBS IN THE CORNFIELD. XICÓTEPEC DE JUÁREZ, PUEBLA
(SEE *ENCHILADAS DE PIXTLI*). 2. DOÑA BERTA. ZICATELA, OAXACA (SEE *SALSA DE PANAL*).
3. WILTING A BANANA LEAF FOR *IXGUÁ*. TABASCO.

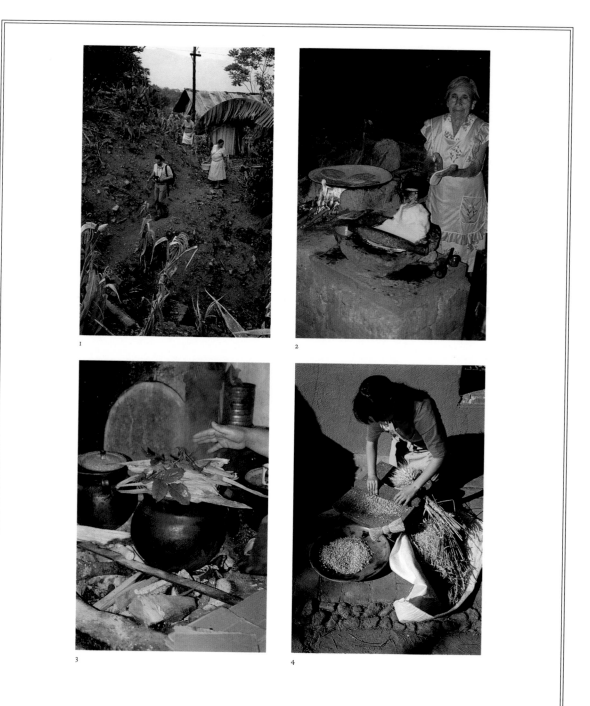

1. EVELINA AND ALAIN GOING TO PICK HERBS. 2. *LA ABUELA* (GRANDMOTHER) IN HER RUSTIC KITCHEN.
OAXACA. 3. SRA. BERNARDA BLESSING THE TAMALE POT. NEAR CUETZALAN, PUEBLA.
4. VERONICA GRINDING WHEAT. QUINTA DIANA.

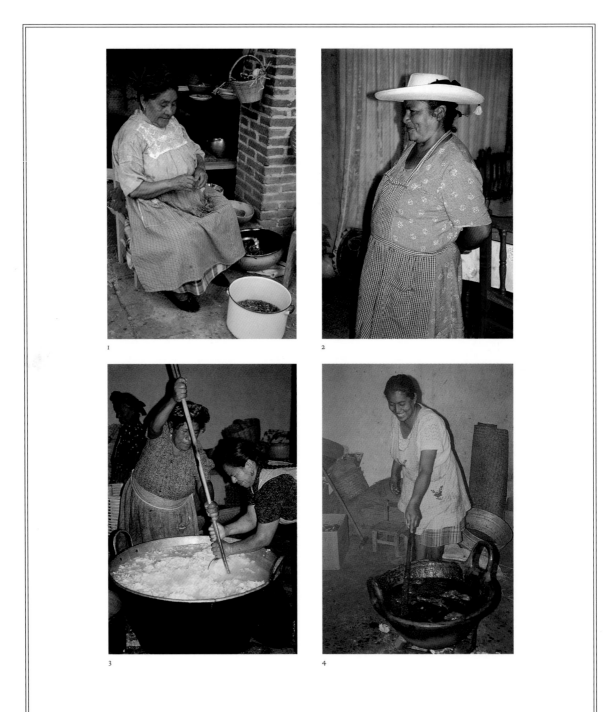

1. *LA MADRINA* (GODMOTHER) PICKING OVER THE HERBS. TEOTITLÁN, OAXACA. 2. EVELINA
MODELING MY GIFT OF A MICHOACÁN SOMBRERO. 3. STIRRING *LOS HIGADITOS DE FANDANGO*
(THE EGG DISH PREPARED FOR THE WEDDING CELEBRATIONS). TEOTITLÁN, OAXACA.
4. STIRRING THE MOLE MIAHUATECO, STATE OF PUEBLA.

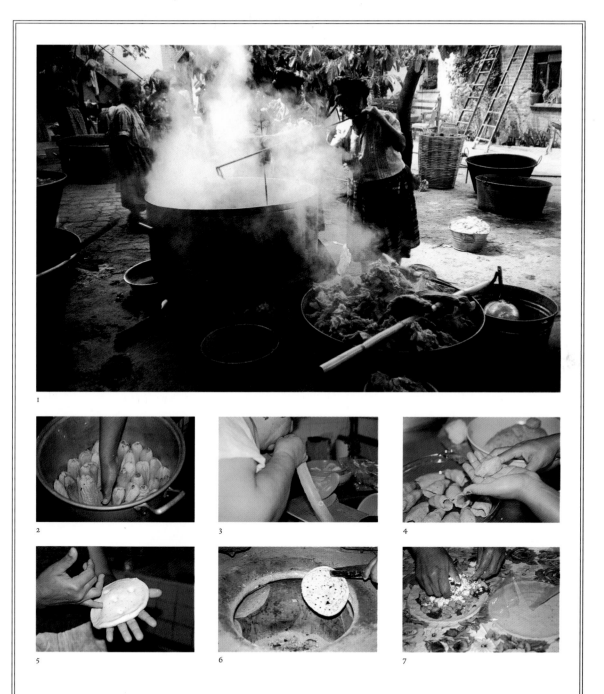

1. COOKING FOR THE FANDANGO. 2. STEAMING TAMALES. 3. INFLATING PORK CASINGS FOR MAKING LONGANIZA. EMILIANO ZAPATA, TABASCO. 4. FORMING *BOLITAS DE MASA*— NOTE THE UNUSUAL SHAPE. EMILIANO ZAPATA, TABASCO. 5. FORMING A TOTOPO. JUCHITÁN, OAXACA. 6. COOKING A TOTOPO IN A COMIZCAL, NEAR JUCHITÁN, OAXACA. 7. FILLING A *TORTILLA RELLENA* (STUFFED TORTILLA). FRONTERA, TABASCO.

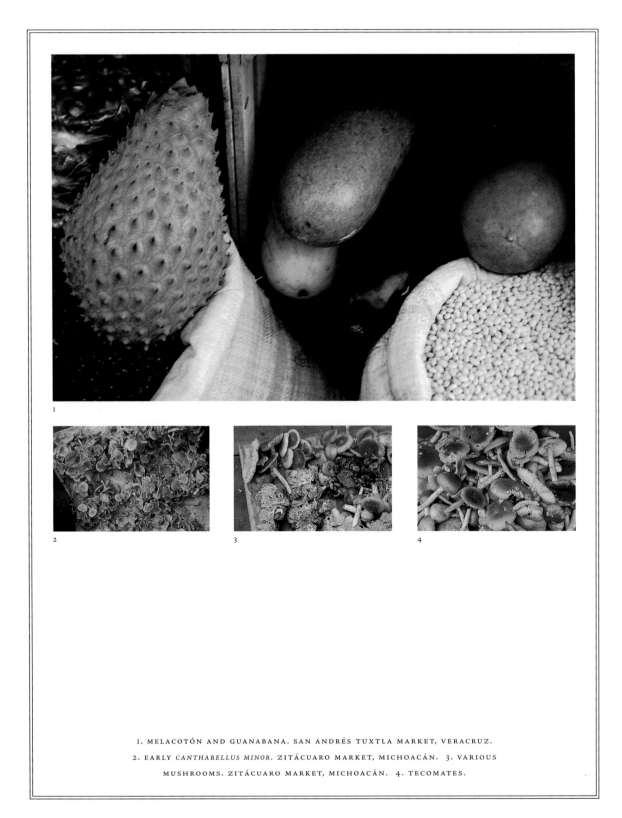

1. MELACOTÓN AND GUANABANA. SAN ANDRÉS TUXTLA MARKET, VERACRUZ.

2. EARLY *CANTHARELLUS MINOR*. ZITÁCUARO MARKET, MICHOACÁN. 3. VARIOUS
MUSHROOMS. ZITÁCUARO MARKET, MICHOACÁN. 4. TECOMATES.

1. YACA, OR JACK FRUIT, NAYARIT. 2. *MARAÑON* (CASHEW FRUIT). CAMPECHE MARKET.

3. DK'S SIGNATURE DISH — BLUE MUSHROOMS (*LACTARIUS INDIGO*) WITH BLUE CORN TORTILLAS.

4. PICKING THE *ESPIGA* (MALE FLOWER OF CORN PLANT). SAN PANCHO, MICHOACÁN.

5. *TIMBIRICHES* (FRUIT OF A SPECIES OF BROMELIAD). CHILAPA, GUERRERO.

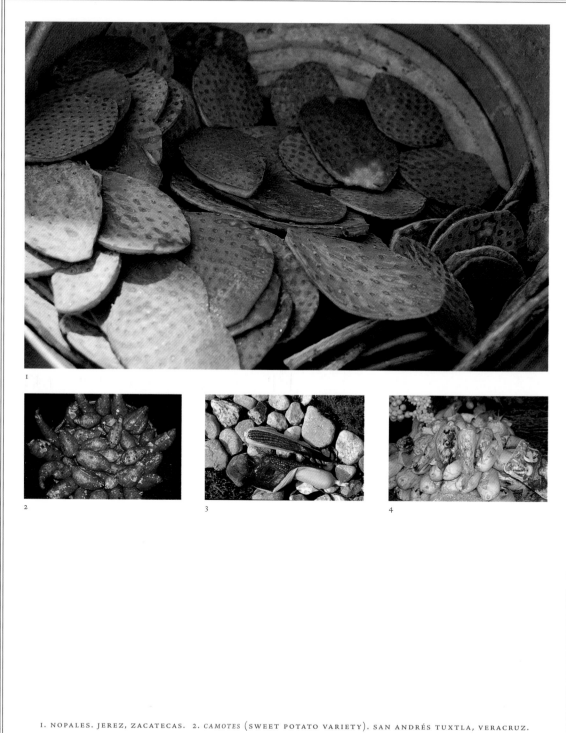

1. NOPALES. JEREZ, ZACATECAS. 2. CAMOTES (SWEET POTATO VARIETY). SAN ANDRÉS TUXTLA, VERACRUZ.
3. RED CORN. CHOLULA MARKET, PUEBLA. 4. CUITLACOCHE AND SOUP GREENS. CHOLULA MARKET, PUEBLA.

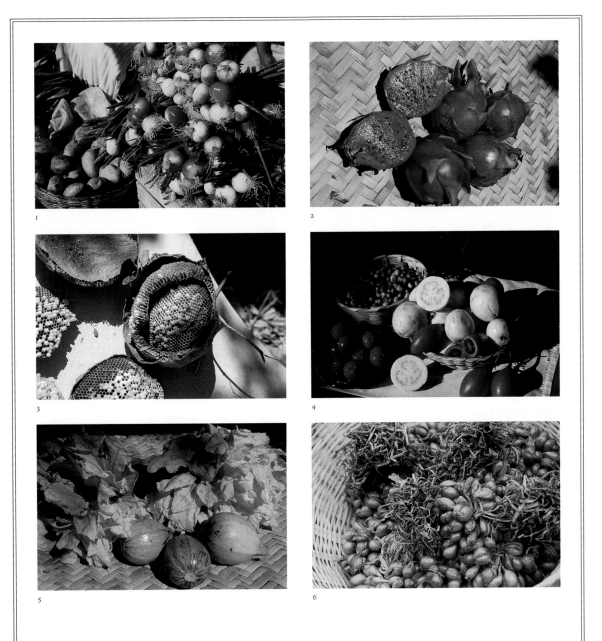

1. RED ONIONS AND MANGOS. VILLAHERMOSA MARKET, TABASCO. 2. PITAHAYAS. 3. WASPS' NEST FOR *SALSA DE PANAL*. PUERTO ESCONDIDO, OAXACA. 4. WINTER HARVEST—GUAVAS, TAMARILLOS, ETC. QUINTA DIANA. 5. SQUASH WITH FLOWERS. ZITÁCUARO, MICHOACÁN. 6. *CEBOLLITAS DE LA INDIA* (VARIETY OF SHALLOTS). SAN ANDRÉS TUXTLA MARKET, VERACRUZ.

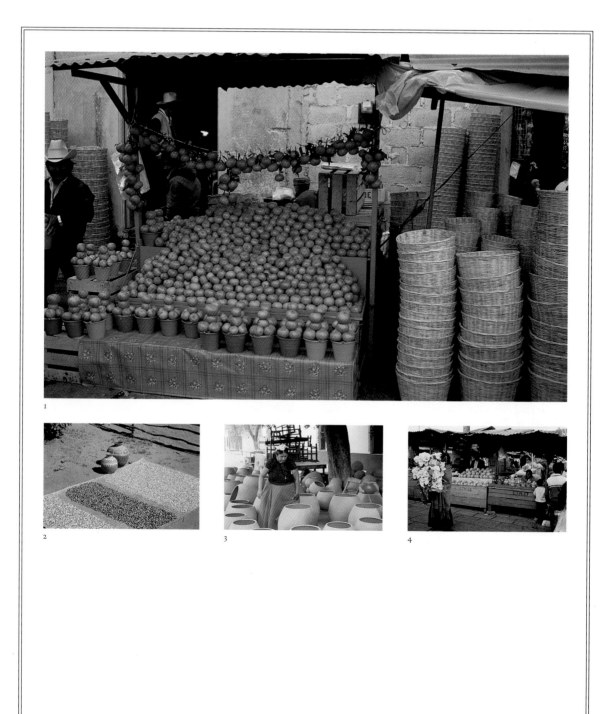

1. CHRISTMAS MARKET SCENE. SAN CHRISTOBAL, CHIAPAS. 2. DRYING CORN. PINOTEPA DON LUIS, OAXACA.

3. SELLING POTS AND COMIZCALES. JUCHITÁN, OAXACA. 4. MARKET SCENE. SAN CHRISTOBAL, CHIAPAS.

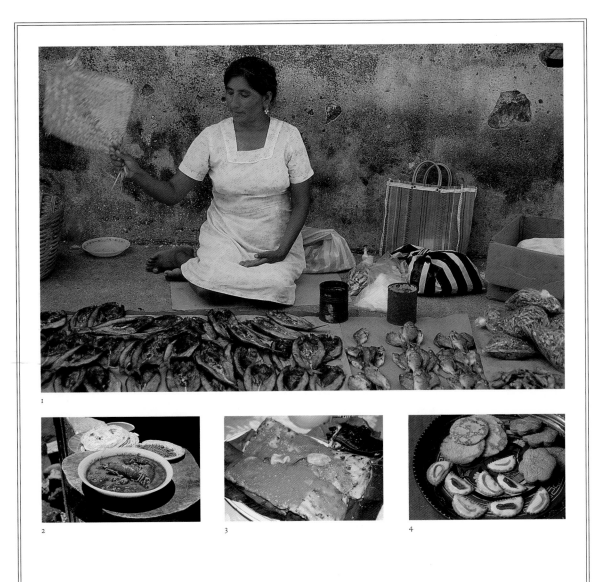

1. SELLING DRIED FISH. JAMILTEPEC, OAXACA. 2. *PIPIÁN DE ACAMAYAS.* APAZAPAM, VERACRUZ. 3. MAYAN

CHAYA TAMAL, *BRAZO DE INDIO.* CAMPECHE, CAMPECHE. 4. TRADITIONAL COOKIES. MASCOTA, JALISCO.

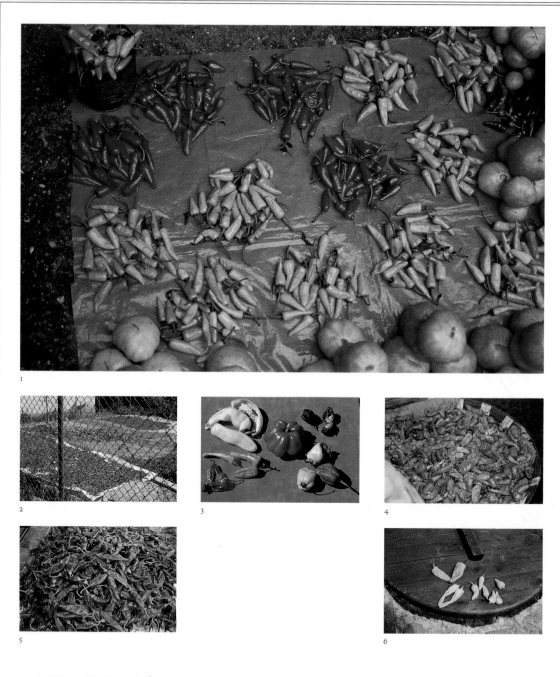

1. FRESH CHILES COSTEÑOS. JAMILTEPEC, OAXACA. 2. DRYING CHILES COSTEÑOS. PINOTEPA NACIONAL.
3. FRESH CHILES FROM CAMPECHE MARKET. X-CAT-IK, CHILE DE CUBA (EGGPLANT-COLORED HABANERO),
HABANEROS IN VARIOUS STAGES OF RIPENESS, FRESH CHILE VERDE AND DRIED, WHEN IT IS KNOWN AS
CHILE SECO. IN CENTER, CHILE DULCE, FRESH AND VERY RIPE. 4. FRESH CHILES CRILLOS. TEHUANTEPEC,
OAXACA. 5. CHILES GUAJILLOS (DRIED). JEREZ MARKET 6. TWO VARIETIES OF FRESH CHILES GÜEROS.

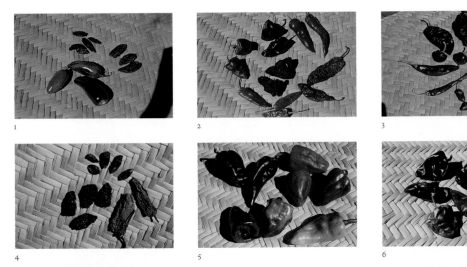

1. JALAPEÑOS FRESH AND DRIED, CHILE MORA, CHILE MORITA (DRIED SERRANO, LAST PICKING).
2. VARIOUS DRIED OAXACAN CHILES: CHILHAUCLE RED AND BLACK, CHILCOSTLE, COSTEÑO, PASILLA OAXAQUEÑA, OR CHILE MIJE (IN MIDDLE CHILE PASADO, NOT FROM OAXACA). 3. CORNER: PULLA, GUAJILLO, CASCABEL, ANCHO, MULATO, PASILLA, CATARINO OR CORA WITH CHILE DE ÁRBOL IN THE MIDDLE.
4. CHILPOCLES: MORA, MORITA, AND MECO. 5. FRESH CHILHUACLES: NEGRO, ROJO, AMARILLO (BLACK, RED, AND YELLOW) IN VARIOUS STAGES OF RIPENESS 6. CHILHAUCLES DRIED: BLACK, RED, AND YELLOW.
7. CHILACA FRESH, PASILLA DRIED . 8. CHILE POBLANO, DRIED AS ANCHO, PEELED AND DRIED AS PASADO.

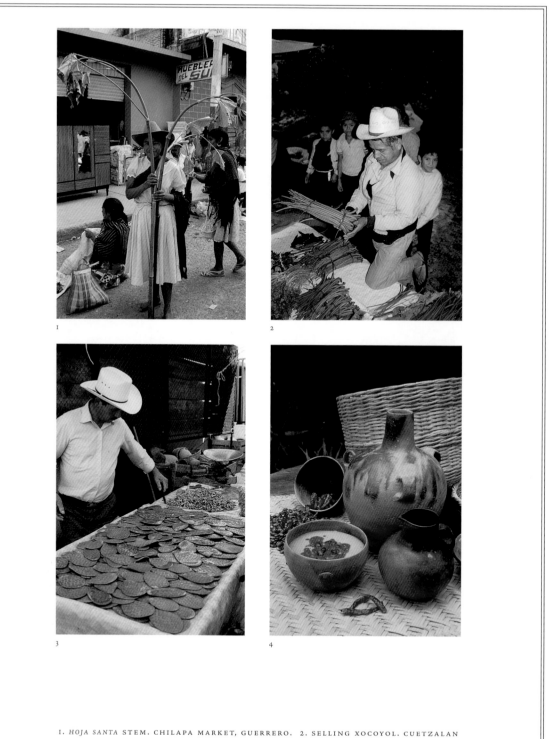

1. *HOJA SANTA* STEM. CHILAPA MARKET, GUERRERO. 2. SELLING XOCOYOL. CUETZALAN
MARKET, PUEBLA. 3. SELLING NOPALES. JEREZ MARKET, ZACATECAS. 4. POTTERY FROM SANTA ANA, PUEBLA.

THE STATE
OF PUEBLA

A S I SAT DOWN TO WRITE ABOUT PUEBLA, I TOOK OUT A
DOG-EARED AND RATHER CRUMPLED MAP THAT HAS AN
ALMOST PERMANENT PLACE AT THE BACK OF MY
truck. So many of my trips to the south of Mexico take me
through part of the state, and besides, I have crisscrossed it many times in search of
interesting cooks and their unique foods. I mentally retraced my steps to my favorite
places: Xicótepec de Juárez in the Sierra Norte de Puebla and Cuetzalan, across from
Xicótepec, the other side of an impassable ravine that divides the Sierra into two
parts, both accessible by different highways. ❁ On my way to Oaxaca I pass through
the southwestern part of the state, hot, lower country planted with sugarcane around
Izucar de Matamoros—where some of the most colorful pottery figures in Mexico
are made. En route to Santa Ana (page 267) I stopped at Tepejí de Rodríguez, to the
east of Izucar, to visit the little museum housing spectacularly beautiful pink fossils.
Many years ago I visited Tehuacán in the semiarid south to witness the almost

medieval scene of the *matanza* (page 465), the mass killing of goats, and years later went to eat *mole miahuateco* (page 275), made with the very special and delicious dried chiles grown in that area and nowhere else. I remembered a trip to a village on the lower slopes of Popocatépetl in search of special *molcajetes* decorated with elaborate designs or carved with the owner's name. It was on Sábado de Gloria, the Saturday before Easter, and as was the local custom, the children there doused us with water. From there we went on to Puebla to eat some of the first *escamoles*, large white ant's eggs, of the season. They were delicious and nutritious, fried lightly with a chile sauce.

On another occasion a friend and I traveled to Huaquechula, between Atlixco and Izucar, to see the highly ornate white satin altars prepared for All Saints and All Souls at the beginning of November, when the countryside was festooned with garlands of intensely blue morning glory, and then in August to Tezuitlán in search of huge orange mushrooms that I have never seen elsewhere. It is in this month that the markets in Puebla come into their own. A good example is Cholula, on the outskirts of Puebla de los Angeles, as the capital city is known. Apart from a profusion of wild green herbs, squash blossoms, and small red-cheeked pears and apples, there were huge piles of large, shiny dark green and red poblano chiles. Outside, along the sidewalks, vendors were selling their bags of whole and shelled walnuts, for this is the season for the renowned dish of *chiles en nogada*— poblano chiles stuffed with a chopped meat and fruit filling and smothered with a walnut sauce.

The city of Puebla is, without doubt, one of the most important centers of gastronomy in Mexico. In colonial times the convent kitchens there were the birthplaces of *criollo* (a mixture of Mexican and Spanish) dishes such as *mole poblano* and *chiles en nogada* and sweetmeats: *camotes* made with sweet potatoes and sugar and *palanquetas* of caramelized sugar and pumpkin seeds among many others, elaborate and often sophisticated dishes created by blending ingredients from both continents. With the introduction of cheese and cream, ways of preparing chiles and local vegetables were enhanced. Pork was used in stews and lard introduced.

There is one type of yeast bread that is practically synonymous with Puebla: round, flattish bread rolls known as *semitas* or *cemitas*. They have a crisp, light crust and a flattened topknot (made with a twist of the dough that is folded back on top) sprinkled with sesame seeds. When I first came across them they were earthier, with a thicker crust; now they are made with white flour, belying their name, which comes from *acemite*, meaning wheat flour with bran. Over the years I have published some of the better-known recipes from Puebla, and now it is time to explore some of the lesser-known but traditional foods that are prepared by local cooks in more remote places. Many of these recipes have never appeared in print before.

Xicótepec de Juárez

In my early days in Mexico, orchid-collecting friends were always talking about the lush country around Xicótepec de Juárez in the Sierra Norte de Puebla, where they went to collect wild orchids, but they never mentioned the food. The first trip that took me through Xicótepec en route to the pyramids of Tajín and the Veracruz coast was thirty years ago. The part of that drive I remember most was a stretch of road winding down the eastern slopes of the mountains toward Papantla through magnificent tropical cloud forest kept intensely green by the mists of damp, cool air rolling in from the Gulf of Mexico. (The forest has almost disappeared now, and in its place plantations of coffee are grown without shade.)

A friend and I had spent the night at the well-known, spotlessly clean little hotel (run by a family of German origin) Mi Ranchito. In a little rustic restaurant almost hidden from view among the trees we had eaten *tasajo de puerco enchilado*, thinly cut pork seasoned with a paste of ancho chile, fried, and served with a green tomato sauce and thick cream (page 257), some mushrooms cooked with chiles and *epazote*, and delicious *chorizos*. But even then I had no idea of the array of foods that I was later to learn about from Hortensia Cabrera, who was born and brought up in Xicótepec.

I have been back many times since then. I love the drive that takes you northeast out of Mexico City to a small village outside Pachuca, Pachuquilla, and the restaurant Mary Christy, where local foods are served in abundance. There were always freshly made *pastes*, meat pasties, a relic left behind by Cornish miners in the first part of this century. You can also eat *mixiotes* of lamb—more precisely mutton—seasoned with dried chiles and wrapped in the parchmentlike skin of the maguey leaves. Try the strong-tasting *chimicuiles*, pink worms that come out of the maguey plants after the summer rains.

More recently I have taken another route, passing Pachuca and driving by the pyramids of Teotihuacán and across extensive plains dominated here and there by low-lying haciendas. They are surrounded by maguey plantations at all stages of growth, the largest ones ready to be scraped out for the collection of *aguamiel*, eventually to be converted into *pulque*. And alongside the highway for miles around there are rows and rows of nopal cactus producing *nopales* year-round to supply the markets of Mexico City. Driving this way, I can arrive for a late breakfast at a little restaurant on the outskirts of Tulancingo, El Fuente. I still dream about those white corn tortillas made right there on the spot, orange juice squeezed while you wait, and thick, foaming milk with your coffee. It was there that I first tasted *tinga de pollo* (page 258).

After the flat agricultural lands around Tulancingo the scene changes to grasslands for dairy herds and apple orchards. I love to go there in the late summer, when trees are laden with deep-red apples sold in bins by the wayside with pears and preserves of peaches and plums alongside the fruit liquors and local honey.

The land is uneven, with sharp rises and deep ravines as you come to the little semitropical town of Huauchinango, with banana and coffee plantations around it and everywhere flowers of the most brilliant colors. From there the road passes high up along the eastern edge of the huge Necaxa dam, now bare of trees owing to indiscriminate logging, before descending once again into the lush landscape around Xicótepec.

The town of Xicótepec is not as attractive as it once was, the harmony of the traditional architecture in the main streets particularly broken by the ugly cement structures seen all over Mexico and, I suspect, all over the world.

I have not been there myself during Holy Week, but then and during fiestas the central plaza is filled with small stands selling the local *antojitos: molotes, tlacoyos, pintos, enchiladas de Santa Clara* (recipes to be found in *The Art of Mexican Cooking*), and *atoles*. There are two unique *atoles* made there: *chileatole*, served either hot or cold with fresh corn kernels, flavored with ancho chiles and *epazote*, and sweetened with *piloncillo* (raw sugar sold in cones), and yet another, with again a base of corn *masa* flavored with orange blossom and blended with balls of *masa* enriched with lard and filled with finely grated dry cheese. This one is also sweetened with *piloncillo*.

The tiniest of red tomatoes, *miltomates* as they are known there, that grow wild in the fields are used, crushed with garlic and green chiles, to make a sharp, strong sauce. The vines of the local elongated *chayotes* are cooked and used in soups or with scrambled eggs. In November you can find wild mushrooms growing under oak trees; these are known as *totolcozatl (Rhodophyllus abortivus)*, a type of puffball that is much sought after to be preserved in vinegar. This is just a sample of the wild foods gathered by the country people that are also cooked and eaten with relish in the more affluent homes.

Apart from the more common recipe for the local *adobo*, I will give accounts of my trips to the Xicótepec area for two unique local recipes—unpublished as far as I know.

ENCHILADAS DE PIXTLI

ENCHILADAS IN A MAMEY PIT SAUCE

✺

[MAKES 12 ENCHILADAS]

VISITORS TO THE MARKET OF XICÓTEPEC DE JUÁREZ IN THE SIERRA DE PUEBLA NORTE MAY BE TAKEN ABACK TO SEE A WOMAN SITTING ON THE sidewalk in front of her small piles of beans, squash, and herbs, offering *collares* (necklaces) for sale. As you look more closely, you can see, heaped together in a small pile, blackish brown (rather like very dark chocolate) cuneiformlike shapes, some glossy, some dull with occasional white patches on their surface. They are pieces of *pixtli* (the Náhuatl name for the mamey seed) strung together. They've undergone a rather elaborate process of boiling and smoking and are now ready to be toasted and ground to make a sauce for the unique local dish, *enchiladas de pixtli*.

I learned about this culinary curiosity from one of my most valued informants who was brought up in that area, my neighbor, Hortensia Cabrera de Fagoaga (she herself is an excellent cook, having a very special *sazón* that makes the simplest of dishes delicious). Through her sister, who still lives in the area of Xicótepec, I was put in touch with *the pixtli* expert, Señora Evelina Olvera, so that I could learn firsthand about this extraordinary use of the mamey pit.

Señora Evelina is a striking woman, tall, robust, white-haired, with the most beautiful face and smile. She works hard to support her family by making bread and preserves and preparing *pixtlis*. She insists on using her traditional, rustic kitchen, which is attached to a large, modern house, and cooking on a primitive but functional wood-burning *bracero* (type of stove) constructed of *adobe* bricks.

This area of the Sierra de Puebla is semitropical,* and the mameys are at their best here from about February through May. They have to be picked when perfectly ripe for the seeds to be at their best. The cinnamon-brown shell-like outer layer of the fruit is removed and the fragrant, red flesh cut away so that the elliptical, lustrous brown seed is left.

Señora Olvera had already accumulated dozens of the seeds at various stages of their preparation so that I could see the whole process. After rinsing they were put into a capacious earthenware pot (*ollo de barro*), which was then filled to the top with water. A handful of ash was added to the water, and the pot was set over a fairly lively wood fire. Once the water had come to a simmer, not a fast boil, it was held as near as possible to that temperature for the next two nights and days.

After years of experience, Señora Olvera knows just how much wood to put on the fire so that it will last from midnight until she rises at six in the morning. "They are ready," she told me, "*cuando ya no tienen vabito*" (when they are no longer slimy). At that point they are rinsed in fresh water and cleaned of the thin, rather slimy outer layer. This is a slow process; although it can easily be scraped off some of the seeds, others have to be scraped with your thumbnails (which means you have badly stained fingers when you have finished).

The seeds are now rinsed once again and put back into the pot with a change of water and this time, instead of lime thirteen different types of herbs and leaves are added to the pot and

*Although the usually benign climate with its almost constant mist-borne moisture is undergoing a change with the ruthless devastation of the ecology by de-forestation of native trees; this is done to plant a type of coffee that does not, alas, require the shade of the usual protective canopy of trees.

again the cooking is continued for two more days and nights. By this time the seeds should be tender enough to cut into edge-shaped pieces about 2 inches (5 cm) long and ⅜ inch (1 cm) wide. Each piece is pierced through the middle and strung onto a length of thread or fine string. The ends are joined so that they can be hung over the fire to dry out and be smoked. This step again takes about two days. The natural oils in the seeds exude in the heat, and as the pieces cool and dry out, irregular white patches are formed on their surface.

Some cooks fry the sauce with a little oil before immersing the tortillas, but the traditionalists say this takes away from the true flavor of the *pixtlis* and the herbs with which they are cooked. Others will add some toasted sesame seeds to the sauce, which is also frowned on by the purists.

Enchiladas de pixtli are traditionally served for *almuerzos*, the hearty midmorning breakfasts in Mexico, occasionally accompanied by a piece of grilled, smoked *tasajao* or *cecina* (thinly cut semidried and smoked meat typical of the area).

5 chipotle mora chiles or to taste
salt to taste
approximately 2 cups (500 ml) water
4 ounces (115 g) pixtlis
12 corn tortillas, freshly made and still warm

Remove the seeds from the chiles and toast them lightly on a *comal* or griddle for about 2 minutes, taking care not to burn them. Tear the chiles into small pieces and add them with the salt, water, and *pixtlis* to a blender. Blend to a slightly textured sauce (if grinding them on the *metate*, blend the *pixtlis* and chiles with a small quantity of water, adding more as necessary, and then transfer to a bowl and dilute with the rest of the water).

Transfer the sauce to a skillet or shallow *cazuela* and heat through until simmering. The sauce will thicken slightly, and it may be necessary to dilute it with a little more water. Dip the tortillas one by one into the sauce (it should cover the tortillas completely), double them over, and serve just as they are without any trimmings.

TAMALES DE VIGILIA

LENTEN TAMALES

✸

[MAKES APPROXIMATELY 30 4- BY 3-INCH (10- BY 8-CM) TAMALES]

JUST ABOUT TWO AND A HALF YEARS AGO, MY FRIEND AND NEIGHBOR IN ZITÁCUARO, HORTENSIA FAGOAGA, SERVED ME A *TAMAL* THAT WAS TO BECOME one of my absolute favorites. It was wrapped in a banana leaf and stuffed with black beans mixed with plenty of serrano chiles, *cilantro*, and *chayote*. These *tamales* were traditionally prepared for the Lenten period in her tierra, Xicótepec de Juárez, in the Sierra Norte de Puebla.

This past autumn I went to Xicótepec to record this extraordinary recipe. Her sister Yolanda Cabrera had arranged for us to visit a neighbor, Señora Concha López Garrido, who was famous for her *tamales* and the regional dishes of that area. Señora López was a vigorous black-haired woman in her late eighties (or so she thinks, because all records of this kind were destroyed during the Revolution). She remembers vividly the privations of those years, when whole families went into hiding in the sierras as their homes were ransacked and they were left without clothes or any personal possessions. She still cooks daily for friends and prepares orders of *tamales* for special occasions. Her assistant is her daughter Eva, who was grinding the corn, prepared the evening before, for our *tamales* when we arrived back from the market with the rest of the ingredients.

The beans typically used are the mature but still tender *ayacotes*, or fresh black beans from very long pods called *tapatlaxtlis*, and while they were cooking we went into the garden to pick *chayotes*, the smooth-skinned dark green variety with very compact flesh. (The *guias*, or tips of the vines, known as *espinosos*, are often cooked in soups or with eggs.) Señora Concha also cut the leaves that would be used for wrapping the *tamales*, known as *papatla*. This plant with its small red flowers is a species of the canna family, *Canna indica*. Another leaf that is used commonly and lends its fresh, fruity flavor to the *tamal* dough is called locally *frutilla* (*Renealmia* sp.). Although we had brought bunches of *causasa* from the market, Señora Concha showed us the plant, creeping along the ground at the base of a tree. Its fleshy leaf and stems have a pleasant, waxy, *cilantro* flavor and are used to flavor the beans.

For the *tamal* filling Señora Concha likes to use pumpkin seeds, although very often a native nut known as *chota (Jatropha curcas)*, is used instead.

We returned to the kitchen, where a spacious *bracero* constructed of compacted earth was covered with pots, some of which were boiling away on the hot red ashes. There was a gas stove in the next room, but the cooks insisted that tortillas and *tamales* must be cooked over a wood fire. The beans and *chayotes* had been cooked, the lard melted, and a pan of water in which *tequesquite* had been immersed overnight sat to one side.

Nixtamal of white corn had been prepared the evening before and rubbed clean of yellow skins, colored by the lime in which it had been soaking. By this time Eva had finished grinding the corn to a textured dough in the metal grinder and Concha was busy cutting the base of the *papatla* leaves into a triangular shape.

The preparation of the filling began in earnest. Toasted pumpkin seeds, garlic, and chiles were ground on the *metate* to a textured paste. This was added to the beans and the *chayote* and cooked for about 15 minutes. The lard was beaten with the *tequesquite* water to a thick, creamy consistency, and then the *masa* and chicken broth were added little by little. All this was hand-beaten until it became light and puffy and a small piece of the dough floated easily on the surface of a cup of cold water. A sign of the cross was traced in the dough before very large spoonfuls of it were smeared thinly over the inside of the leaves. An equally large amount of the filling was spread over the dough and the leaves neatly folded, so that the dough completely covered the filling.

By this time an earthenware pot with its improvised rack was heating and the *tamales* were stacked in crosswise layers so that the steam would penetrate easily and evenly. After about 50 minutes the first ones were taken out of the pot, still very tender and moist. As Señora Concha pronounced them ready, the joyful business of eating began. Delicious!

The following recipe is Sra. Tencha's, with a simpler way of preparing the *masa* and using ingredients more readily available for the filling.

She serves them alone or with some thick crème fraîche.

1 cup water (250 ml)

*6 ounces (180 g), chayote, peeled and cut into ¼-inch (7-mm) cubes,
about 1¼ rounded cups (320 ml)*

salt to taste

*8 ounces (225 g) zucchini, cut into ¼-inch (7-mm) cubes,
about 1¼ cups (313 ml)*

3 tablespoons pork lard

8 ounces (225 g) black beans, cooked until very soft and drained

14 serrano chiles, toasted and roughly chopped

*6 ounces (180 g) peanuts, about 1¼ cups (313 ml),
toasted and roughly chopped*

2 cups (500 ml) firmly packed roughly chopped cilantro

THE DOUGH

8 ounces (225 g) pork lard, about 1 heaped cup (270 ml)

2 pounds (900 g) masa for tortillas or masa for tamales (page 530)

1 tablespoon salt or to taste

Have ready a *tamale* steamer (page 522); 30 pieces (or more to be on the safe side) banana leaves, 8 by 7 inches (20 by 18 cm), softened over a flame, or 60 corn husks, soaked and dried (2 for each *tamale*).

THE FILLING: Bring the water to a boil in a saucepan, add the *chayote* and salt to taste, cover, and cook over medium heat for about 5 minutes. Add the zucchini, cover, and cook until both vegetables are just tender and soft—5 to 7 minutes. Drain and reserve the liquid.

Heat the lard in a heavy skillet and add the drained beans, mashing them roughly with the chiles over low heat for about 5 minutes. Add the cooked vegetables and peanuts and cook for 5 more minutes. The mixture should be moist, not juicy. If, on the other hand, it is too dry, add a little of the reserved vegetable broth. Stir in the *cilantro*, adjust the salt, and set aside to cool.

THE DOUGH: Beat the lard well until white and fluffy and gradually beat in the *masa* with plenty of salt to taste. If the mixture is very dry, add a little water or some vegetable broth; it should be of spreading consistency.

Spread 2 scant tablespoons of the *masa* about ¼ inch (7 mm) thick over a leaf rectangle roughly 4 by 3 inches (10 by 8 cm). Put 1 heaped tablespoon of the filling on one side of the dough. Double the leaf over so that the remaining dough covers the filling and fold the sides to make a waterproof package. If you are using corn husks, place the two of them together with the cut ends overlapping in the middle.

Lay the *tamales* horizontally in overlapping layers in the steamer, cover, and cook for 1 hour or until the dough separates easily from its wrapping.

TINGA DE POLLO

TINGA OF SEASONED, SHREDDED CHICKEN

Restaurant La Fuente, Tulancingo, Hidalgo

✻

[MAKES 3 ROUNDED CUPS (780 ML)]

THIS RECIPE IS AN INTERESTING VERSION OF THE BETTER-KNOWN PORK TINGA OF PUEBLA. I ALWAYS ORDER IT FOR A LATE BREAKFAST WHEN PASSING through Tulancingo on my way to the Sierra de Puebla. There it is served with excellent freshly made corn tortillas—but it is also used as a topping for *tostadas*, as a filling for tacos or bread rolls, or even as a main course with white rice.

6 ounces (180 g) chorizo, about 3 links
¼ cup (63 ml) finely chopped white onion
2 garlic cloves, finely chopped
2 cups (500 ml) finely shredded cabbage
4 small plum tomatoes, about 8 ounces, finely chopped
(1 rounded cup/265 ml)
3 canned chipotle chiles en adobo or to taste
2 tablespoons sauce from the can of chiles
2 scant cups (475 ml) poached and shredded chicken
⅓ cup (83 ml) chicken broth
1 avocado, sliced (optional)
salt to taste

Skin the *chorizos* and crumble into a large skillet. Cook over low heat so that the fat renders out, but do not let the meat brown. Strain off all but 3 tablespoons of the fat. Add the onion, garlic, and cabbage and fry over fairly low heat, stirring the mixture from time to time, until the vegetables are soft. Add the tomatoes and continue cooking over medium heat until most of the juice has been absorbed and the mixture is almost dry. Stir in the shredded chicken and broth and cook for another 5 minutes or until the mixture is moist but not juicy. Adjust the salt.

ADOBO

Sra. Hortensia Cabrera Fagoaga, Xicótepec de Juárez, Puebla

✸

[MAKES 2½ CUPS (625 ML)]

THIS SIMPLE *ADOBO*, OR PASTE OF ANCHO CHILES, IS TYPICAL OF THAT MADE IN AND AROUND XICÓTEPEC DE JUÁREZ. IT CAN BE USED IN VARIOUS WAYS: as a sauce with cooked pork, as a paste to spread over thinly cut pork, *tasajo de cerdo*, which is then dried or smoked and fried or grilled. With vinegar added it can be used to season *chorizos*.

It is better not to add salt until you decide how you are going to use it; if the pork is cooked with salt in a broth and the chiles are salted, for example, it will all be too much. Any extra can be frozen.

10 ancho chiles, veins and seeds removed
1 cup (250 ml) water
6 garlic cloves, peeled and slightly crushed
6 peppercorns, roughly crushed
½ teaspoon cumin seeds, roughly crushed

Flatten out the cleaned chiles as much as possible and toast on a griddle or *comal* over medium heat until the inside flesh turns a pale tobacco brown, just a few seconds. Take care not to burn the flesh, or the sauce will be bitter. Cover the chiles with hot water and leave to soak, for about 15 minutes—longer if the chiles were very tough and dry in the first place. Drain, discarding the soaking water.

Put ⅓ cup (83 ml) of the water into a blender, add the crushed garlic, peppercorns, and cumin seeds, and blend as smoothly as possible. Gradually add the chiles and the rest of the water and blend until almost smooth. Add more water only if necessary to release the blender blade. Remember, you want a paste, not a sauce.

TASAJO DE CERDO

※

[SERVES 4]

approximately ¾ cup (188 ml) adobo (recipe precedes)
salt to taste
1 pound (450 g) pork tenderloin or other cut from leg or shoulder,
butterflied out to about ¼ inch (7 mm) thick
melted lard or vegetable oil for basting

Mix the *adobo* and salt together and spread thickly over both sides of the meat. For best results, set aside on a rack for at least 6 hours or overnight to season. Brush the meat with a little of the lard or oil and grill slowly, for best flavor, over a charcoal fire until cooked through, about 20 minutes on each side.

Serve with a green tomato sauce and a little thick cream if you can bear it.

BRAISED PORK RIBS

※

[SERVES 4]

USE SPARERIBS FOR THIS RECIPE ONLY IF THEY ARE VERY MEATY AND HAVE A LITTLE FAT ON THEM.

2 scant cups (475 ml) adobo
salt to taste
2 pounds (900 g) pork chops, ½ inch (13 mm) thick, or 2½ pounds
(1.125 kg) country-style spareribs cut into 2-inch pieces
(see note above)
approximately ⅔ cup (164 ml) water

Mix the *adobo* with salt to taste and spread the meat thickly with it. Set aside to season for several hours or overnight.

Place the meat in no more than 2 layers in a heavy ovenproof pan, add the water, and cover tightly. Cook on top of the stove over very low heat, scraping the bottom of the pan from time to time to prevent sticking, or bake in a 250°F (120°C) oven, covered, until the meat is tender and the sauce reduced and thickened—about 1½ hours.

Serve with white rice and sliced white onion rings if desired.

PUERCO EN ADOBO

✺

[SERVES 4]

2 pounds (900 g) stewing pork with some fat, cut into 3-inch (8-cm) strips
¼ medium white onion
2 garlic cloves, roughly chopped
salt to taste
2 tablespoons pork lard or vegetable oil
2 cups (500 ml) adobo *(page 259)*

Put the pork into a saucepan along with the onion and garlic. Barely cover with water, add salt to taste, and bring to a simmer. Continue simmering until the pork is tender, about 20 minutes. Drain, reserving the broth; reduce or add water to the broth to make 2½ cups (625 ml).

In a heavy pan, melt the lard, add the *adobo*, and cook over medium heat, stirring and scraping the bottom of the pan from time to time to prevent sticking, for about 8 minutes. Adjust the salt, then add the meat and simmer for 10 more minutes. The sauce should be thick enough to cover the back of a wooden spoon without running off at the side.

Cuetzalan, Puebla

Cuetzalan is a magical place even in the worst weather. As the almost constant mists swirl around the tips of the sierras, envelop the town, and sink into the valleys, they reveal some of the most spectacular scenery in Mexico.

Situated in the southern fork of the Sierra de Puebla Norte, it is about a five-hour drive from Mexico City on a rather circuitous route, owing to the rugged terrain. Its rather somber highland, colonial architecture, and historical ambience have been preserved to a great extent because the highway ends there and only steep, sometimes impassable lanes connect it with the coastal plains of Veracruz below.

Narrow, cobbled streets wind up the slopes of the town from the central plaza with its Palacio Municipal, main church, and a few formal houses that were built at the beginning of the century.

The main commerce of the town is in the hands of Mexican families of Spanish descent, but on market days, Sunday and Thursday, the indigenous peoples, mainly Nahuas and Totonacs, from the small communities in the mountains around converge and fill the graded levels—like wide shelves—above the plaza in colorful array. The picturesque Sunday market, in particular, draws visitors from far and wide, and you hope it can withstand the usual onslaught—it has begun—of itinerant vendors who bring cheap plastics, shoes, clothing, and, worst of all, the raucous booming of cassettes that drown out the gentler noises of markets of this kind.

I have always found it a fascinating scene as vendors from the outlying communities, many in their native white costumes, spread before them small quantities of goods that they have cultivated, produced, or gathered wild from their small parcels of land: coffee roasted and ground, cakes of soft, very dark raw sugar with its rich, slightly smoky flavor, bunches of very long pods with tender black beans inside, bananas, pumpkin seeds, or small wild chiles. Others, mainly women, wander through the crowds offering embroidered mats or blouses, small weavings, simple basketry, or rustic clay cooking pots. Unique to this area are the primitive unglazed clay dogs, three in a set and sets of different sizes. They are used to support a *comal* over the smoldering wood of the kitchen fire.

The appointed place for selling flowers, herbs, and wild greens is around the bandstand in the center of the *jardin*. It was there that I found what I had been looking for: bunches of the fleshy stems of a wild begonia, *Begonia plebeja*, that is used as a vegetable.

On my last visit I came with a photographer, Alain Giberstein, especially to record the uses of that plant for an article I was writing for a Mexican magazine, *México Desconocido*, in a series on forgotten recipes. Although the vendors offered advice on how to cook this *xocoyol*—the name comes from Náhuatl words meaning sour stems, in one of the many interpretations—I was anxious to see just how it was prepared and in what type of dish. The local tourist delegate came to the rescue, and her mother, a shopkeeper and renowned local cook, agreed to give me a demonstration the following day.

I still wanted to see where and how the begonia grew, so that afternoon we drove about nine kilometers to a village we had passed on the way, promisingly named Xocoloyo. At the turnoff, marked with an almost invisible sign, we inquired in a modest little shack by the side of the road where we could find begonia plants growing. Señora Bernarda, the owner of the small general store, was short and plump with rosy cheeks. She wrapped herself in a heavy woolen *rebozo* (shawl), and we followed her over muddy fields between fierce-looking cows for about a mile before clambering down a steep slope with a fast-flowing, narrow river at the bottom. She pointed across to the other side, and there, hidden among the thick undergrowth, were the *xocoyol* plants, disappointingly not in flower. Although it is a native plant collected in the wild, people have now taken to propagating it to keep a constant supply coming into the market.

To cook the begonias, the stems, or petioles, are stripped of their leaves and stringy outside layer. They are cut into small lengths, cooked in a lye-type solution to remove some of the acidity, and then cooked in a light, dried chile sauce with scrambled eggs or added to cooked fresh beans in a sesame seed sauce flavored with *cilantro*.

Señora Bernarda was amazed at my interest in the simple things they ate and volunteered to make us some *tamales* with the brilliant red flowers of the *acayote* (a large fleshy bean that somewhat resembles a lima bean) vine that was spreading over the bushes in front of the house (the red flowers of a similar bean are used in the cooking of Oaxaca).

These simple recipes are delicious in their rusticity and make good vegetarian dishes. Of course, the frustrating part of these recipes is that no one seems to know how they evolved, why they became so popular, and what nutritional value they have.

While *xocoyol* do not have a predominating taste, they are pleasantly crisp and sharp in the recipes that follow. *Nopal* cactus makes a good substitute.

FRIJOLES GORDOS CON XOCOYOL

FRESH AYACOTE BEANS WITH XOCOYOL

Sra. Raquel Robles de Manzano

✴

[SERVES 4 AS A MAIN COURSE, 6 AS A SOUP COURSE]

IN CUETZALAN THIS RECIPE IS COOKED WITH THE LARGE AYACOTE BEAN AND XOCOYOL AND FLAVORED WITH *TEQUELITE,* A WILD, CREEPING PLANT WITH fleshy heart-shaped leaves that taste like *cilantro (Piper pseudoalpino),* but these substitutions work very well.

1¼ pounds (565 g) fresh or frozen lima beans

6 cups (1.5 l) boiling water

salt to taste

3 cups (750 ml) cooked xocoyol or nopal cactus strips (page 18)

scant ½ cup (120 ml) sesame seeds, about 2 ounces (60 g)

6 chiles de árbol or any small, very hot dried chiles

1 tablespoon vegetable oil

1 cup (250 ml) water

½ cup (125 ml) roughly chopped cilantro

Put the beans into a pot with the boiling water and salt, bring to a simmer, and continue cooking until tender—about 10 minutes. Add the cooked *nopales* and keep warm.

Toast the sesame seeds until golden in a small skillet and set aside to cool.

Toast the chiles on a warm griddle or *comal,* turning them from time to time and taking care not to burn them. Tear the chiles into small pieces and add to the seeds. Grind both to a textured powder in an electric coffee/spice grinder.

Heat the oil in a small, deep pan. Fry the ground mixture, stirring it well, for about 10 seconds. Add the cold water and boil for 2 minutes. Add to the beans. Cook over moderate heat, stirring from time to time since the seeds tend to collect at the bottom of the pan, until the mixture thickens slightly—about 10 minutes. It should now resemble a soup of medium consistency. Add the *cilantro* and cook for 3 minutes more. Serve in deep bowls with corn tortillas.

XOCOYOL TIPO CHORIZO

XOCOYOL COOKED LIKE CHORIZO

Sra. Raquel Robles de Manzano

❀

[SERVES 4]

SUBSTITUTING STRIPS OF NOPAL CACTUS FOR THE *XOCOYOL*, THIS RECIPE MAKES A DELICIOUS, VERY EARTHY BRUNCH DISH.

2 ancho chiles, seeds and veins removed

2 guajillo chiles, seeds and veins removed

1¾ cups (438 ml) water

2 garlic cloves, roughly chopped

3 cloves, slightly crushed

2 tablespoons vegetable oil or lard

1½ cups (375 ml) cooked strips nopal cactus (page 18)

1 sprig fresh thyme or ⅛ teaspoon dried

⅛ teaspoon dried oregano, crumbled

salt to taste

3 eggs

Toast the chiles lightly on a warm *comal* or griddle, taking care not to burn them. Cover with hot water and set aside to soak for about 15 minutes. Drain and set aside.

Put ¼ cup (63 ml) water into a blender, add the garlic and cloves, and blend as smoothly as possible. Gradually add the drained chiles and ¾ cup (188 ml) more water and blend until smooth.

Heat the oil or lard in a small flameproof dish (in which you could serve the dish) and add the sauce through a fine strainer, pressing the debris as firmly as possible to extract all the flesh of the chiles. Cook over medium heat, stirring from time to time to avoid sticking, until reduced and seasoned, about 5 minutes. Add the *nopales*, thyme, oregano, and remaining ¾ cup (188 ml) water with salt. Cook over medium heat for about 8 minutes more.

[CONTINUED]

Gradually stir in the eggs, lightly beaten with salt to taste, and continue stirring over low heat until they are set—about 5 minutes. The mixture will be concentrated. Serve in shallow bowls with corn tortillas and black, soupy beans, *de olla*.

After a good lunch of the dishes we had prepared, preceded by some of the much-touted local mushrooms—*sopitzas (Armillariella mellea)*, which resemble shiitakes in appearance and texture—Señora Raquel offered us a small glass of the local drink, *Yolispa*. It was green and fragrant and very much like the *Verde de Xico*, made with several different herbs steeped in sweetened alcohol. While the dishes in the Cuetzalan area are simple and fresh, many based on indigenous recipes, there is not the same variety as, say, in the Xicótepec area of the Sierra farther north.

We drove back through the pouring rain that had continued from the night before and left the road that winds down from the highest point at La Cumbre in a perilous condition. Part of the road had been washed away down the sheer ravine below.

When we reached Zacapoaxtla, the next town of any size, it was wreathed in clouds. It brought back memories of my very first trip in Mexico to the communities around Zacapoaxtla with Mary Elmendorf, who was distributing equipment donated by CARE. We were driven in a high truck over muddy tracks across riverbeds and through thick pine forests (now mostly vanished because of indiscriminate logging). She was the guest of honor, and we were regaled with *mole*, accompanied by rice, beans, and tortillas. This was my first real food experience outside the city, and I shall never forget the tastes of those simple foods cooked in large clay pots, *cazuelas*, over wood fires that were set on the mud-packed floors of a large thatch-roofed "kitchen." That was in 1957, and I still cherish the memory of it.

CHILATAS

Cuetzalan

✺

[MAKES 1½ CUPS (375 ML) LOOSELY PACKED]

CHILATAS IS A TEXTURED POWDER OF TOASTED AND GROUND SEEDS SEASONED WITH CHILE AND SALT. IT IS SPRINKLED OVER A FRESHLY MADE CORN TORTILLA or a dish of beans. I even use it on salads. It is delicious, healthy, crunchy, and addictive.

⅓ cup (83 ml) shelled peanuts
½ cup (125 ml) sesame seeds
½ cup (125 ml) hulled raw pumpkin seeds
⅛ teaspoon ground hot dried chiles
(not chile powder mixed with other condiments)
½ teaspoon medium-coarse sea salt or to taste

Toast each of the seeds separately in a heavy pan, taking care not to let them get too brown. Set aside to cool. Grind them separately in an electric coffee/spice grinder to a textured consistency. Mix together with the chile and salt and store in a dry place in an airtight container. It keeps indefinitely.

XOCOASTOLE—AN ATOLE OF SOURED MASA

In November two years ago I was finally able to accept a long-standing invitation from an archaeologist friend, Dr. Evelyn Rattray, to accompany her to a remote village in the State of Puebla (where, in her opinion, some of the most elegant pottery made in Mexico is to be found). Little did I guess that the trip would be so serendipitous and turn up a recipe for which I had been searching for some time.

After visiting a little museum in Tepejí de Rodríguez to see a small collection of spectacular local fossils, we headed off to Santa Ana, following the deep gorge of the Atoyac River. After several kilometers our track (for it was no more than that) branched off and seemed to wind incessantly through rocky scrubland; passing an occasional settlement of a few thatched-roof dwellings shaded by *guaje (Leucaena esculenta)* trees festooned with mulberry-colored pods.

We stopped briefly at one of these settlements to buy some extraordinary *comales*, each one marked on the underside with a bas-relief figure of a wild animal, but on another visit the women who had made them had disappeared without trace. For much of the journey it was as if we were driving through one continuous orchard, not of fruit trees but of *cazahuates* covered with large white blossoms.

After four hours of hard driving, with a friend acting as guide, we arrived at Santa Ana, a small village along the banks of a narrow river with irrigated strips of cultivated land on either side. As we drove in, the women immediately recognized my friend and came out to offer their latest handiwork: urns, water jugs, and bowls known as *cajetes*. I could see straight-away why my friend had come. The pottery was quite unlike any I had ever seen before: thin, beautifully crafted, predominantly orange hued with occasional dark patches of fire clouding. They were not glazed, but their surfaces were almost burnished with a finish, before firing, of a carefully applied and meticulously smoothed slip.

One of the women, more outgoing than the rest, called us over to her house, where a bunch of women were sitting drinking a hot liquid from *cajetes*. She invited us to join them in their *almuerzo*, a hearty midmorning breakfast. It was an *atole*, a gruel, of soured *masa*, *xocoastole* as they called it.

I had come across several regional recipes for *tamales* made of soured black *masa* but had only heard of the *atole*, and here it was. The steaming, slightly soured liquid, topped with a few beans and some chile sauce, was surprisingly refreshing in the hot midday sun.

It was a great disappointment to my friend that no one was actually making any pottery, and there were only two old ladies burnishing their pots while the rest of the women were out in the fields harvesting corn and pumpkins alongside the men.

The clay utensils in that remote village were made almost exclusively for their own needs, with a few more to sell at the main *ferias* of the few and distant neighboring towns. We could not stop buying, every shape and size: unusual-looking mortars with a delicate raised decoration inside, beautifully shaped pitchers, and three-handled bottles with long necks used for carrying hot drinks to the men working in the fields.

Quite suddenly there was no more room in our large station wagon. Reluctantly we sent some back with a neighbor's truck and sadly, as we had feared, some of the pieces were never to be seen again. Curiously, the pottery pieces we saw were in daily use in the kitchens, but the actual cooking was done in the more common, highly glazed clay pots with high-hooped handles that are made in the city of Puebla and the villages around.

There were many offers of hospitality as we wandered around the village, which spread out over about half a mile along the riverbank. But the moment we came across the compound of Fausta Hernández and her family, we knew that this was it. Entering through a roughly made gate of wooden slats was like walking into the past. The design and construction of the main house and its juxtaposition to the kitchen and the thatched, circular granary (*cuescomate*) formed a cohesive entity that emanated a sense of calm and security, while the courtyard gave a sense of simple bounty, spread with the newly harvested corn, beans, and multicolored pumpkins.

We politely refused our hostess's offer to stay in the adjoining cement-block house and set up our beds (yes, beds—after years of camping out near her digs, Evelyn had learned to make herself as comfortable as possible under difficult conditions) in the palm-thatched dwelling. It was typical of that region: a *vivienda campesina de dos aguas*, with a steeply pitched roof almost touching the ground on either side. The roof also served to protect the walls, which were made of closely placed stakes.

Not long after settling in, I began to ask about the local foods. Was there any chance that she could prepare some *xocoastole*? While agreeing, she pointed out that the early afternoon sun was not that strong—a requisite for the preparation of the corn—and set about gathering up some of the black-hued corn drying off in the courtyard. After shaving the kernels from the cobs, she began crushing it roughly (*una pasada, nomás*—only one grinding) on the *metate*, sprinkling it with water as she did so. It was then set out to be warmed in what was left of the sun.

As the sun was losing its strength, Fausta gathered up the corn into a large clay bowl, filled it with water, and set it on the earth floor of the kitchen. She then shoveled around it the still-glowing ashes of the cooking fire. She assured us that the ashes would continue to glow all night and give off sufficient warmth to ferment and sour the corn. Finally she covered the pot with an embroidered cloth.

What a night it turned out to be! A cold wind blew through the gaps in the wood, and it was impossible to get warm until I remembered that I had packed an electric pad—and in the center of the hut dangled one solitary outlet. Miraculously there was current. I pushed my bed into the middle of the room and managed to drop into sleep, with a comforting thought of morning coffee from my traveling pot.

When we got up early the next morning, the ashes were still glowing and the corn was indeed soured. It was strained once more into the soaking liquid that by this time had been transferred to a tall glazed *olla* (pot).

The fire was stoked up with another log, and as the *atole* cooked and thickened, salt was added and it was diluted with more water. The slow cooking continued until Señora Hernández was satisfied—it had the consistency of a thin gruel.

There were other small fires on the floor of the kitchen, and on one of them a pot of large beans, called *acayotes* (*Phaseolus coccineus*) were cooking with just salt, no other seasoning.

The chile sauce to accompany the *atole* was made from dried long orangey-red thin-skinned chiles of the area called *serranos* (not the common ones), simply ground with salt and water.

We were hungry by the time the *atole* was ready for our *almuerzo*. Fausta filled each bowl with steaming liquid, adding a spoonful of the beans in their broth and a swirl of chile sauce. Occasionally she would add a little of the chile sauce to the pot of *atole*, which was still cooking over a low fire. It was a warming and welcome breakfast after a cold night, just as it had been refreshing in the midday sun. She complained that it was not quite sour enough, it would have been better if she could have started it early in the day when the sun was hotter—but of course we hadn't even met her then. We continued to talk of the local food, consisting mostly of what they had on hand, grown or gathered. The nearest town was several hours away by car over rough ground, but they made a weekly trip to buy supplies. No wonder there was only a very little onion or garlic in the dishes that she would later prepare for us.

We were all in agreement that the main meal of the day should be a *pipián*, made with the newly harvested and dried pumpkin seeds. She sent the children out to pick *hoja santa* and avocado leaves for the *tamales*; luckily she had some fresh jalapeños on hand. She caught a protesting chicken that was wandering about near the table, and my heart sank. In all my years in Mexico I have had more than enough of those tough little chickens and turkeys. Of course, I was proved wrong. The chicken turned out to be tender and delicious. By now the menu had been extended to the local bean *tamales*. Many times I had eaten bean *tamales* in other areas, especially in the State of Puebla, but these were so different: layers of *masa* and beans rolled up and cut into small sausage shapes and each one covered with an avocado leaf.

The whole meal was a revelation in simplicity, with enormous flavor. By the time supper came, we couldn't believe that we were hungry again as Fausta produced an *atole* made of *masa* seasoned with *epazote* and green chile to accompany *tlaxcales*, small triangular cakes of blue textured corn cooked on the *comal*.

With a guide from the village we reluctantly left the next day soon after dawn, to begin another long ride, bouncing through rough country on a hardly discernible track through scrub and rocky riverbeds. Most of our new *comales* were, alas, broken, but there were enough pieces of that elegant pottery left to be in pride of place around the house, their beauty of form always reminding me of Santa Ana and the people who keep the tradition alive.

POLLO EN PIPIÁN VERDE

CHICKEN IN PUMPKIN SEED SAUCE

Sra. Fausta Hernández

❂

[SERVES 6]

SRA. FAUSTA, OF COURSE, HAS SPECIFIC INSTRUCTIONS ABOUT THE INGREDI-ENTS FOR THIS DISH AND THE WAY TO PREPARE THEM. THE UNHULLED PUMP-kin seeds she uses are thin with a narrow green border. She says they should be toasted on an earthenware, rather than a metal, *comal* because the metal will burn them without toasting right through . . . so toast them very slowly on whatever you have. For this simple *mole* there are no substitutes.

1 heaped tablespoon sea salt

approximately 7½ cups (1.75 l) water

9 ounces (250 g) unhulled raw pumpkin seeds,
about 2½ rounded cups (640 ml)

¼ cup (63 ml) melted lard or vegetable oil

1 large chicken, cut into serving pieces, plus 1 small breast, halved

6 jalapeño chiles, roughly chopped

2 ounces (60 g) tomates verdes, husks removed and roughly chopped

12 hoja santa leaves, stems removed and roughly chopped

4 large stalks epazote, roughly chopped

Stir the sea salt into 2 cups (500 ml) of the water until dissolved. Pour the salted water over the pumpkin seeds and massage them with your hands so that the salt impregnates the seeds. Drain well and discard the soaking water. Spread the seeds out in a thin layer on a cookie sheet to dry out. Toast lightly in a toaster oven or in a standard oven heated to 350°F (177°C) or place in a wide, heavy skillet and set over very low heat. The seeds should swell up, just begin to color, and start to pop around—be careful they do not become too dark brown or they will taste bitter and spoil the color of the sauce.

Set the seeds aside to cool and then grind in a spice grinder or *molcajete* to a finely textured powder. Mix with ½ cup (125 ml) of the water to a thick paste.

Heat the lard in a heavy casserole, add the seed paste, and fry over low heat, constantly scraping the bottom of the pan—the paste sticks very easily—for about 3 minutes. Add 4 cups of the water and stir well, add the chicken pieces and salt, cover the pan, and cook over low heat for about 15 minutes.

Meanwhile, blend the chiles, *tomates verdes*, *hoja santa*, and *epazote* with the remaining water, adding more if necessary to release the blender blade, until smooth. Stir into the pan and cook uncovered over low heat until the chicken is tender, about 35 minutes, testing for salt halfway through the cooking period. The sauce should be of medium consistency, lightly coating the back of a wooden spoon. Dilute if necessary with a little more water.

This dish can be cooked ahead of time but preferably the same day. Serve with corn tortillas and *tamales de frijol* (recipe follows).

AVOCADO LEAVES

IN SOME PARTS OF *Mexico these slightly anisey leaves are used whole or broken up as a seasoning, and you may sometimes see the powdered leaves for sale as well. Because there's been some concern about toxicity among some California aficionados, I think it's time to set the record straight.*

The toxicity reports relate back to a study done in 1984 at the University of California at Davis, which showed that dairy goats suffered some toxic effects from ingesting very large amounts of avocado leaves (the toxic agent remains unknown). The crucial point, according to Dr. Arthur L. Craigmill, toxicology specialist at Davis and one of the authors of the study, is that the toxic effects were traced to the Guatemalan avocado (Persea americana). When the goats were fed Mexican avocado leaves (Persea drymifolia), a different variety, there were no problems.

The Hass avocado, the best-tasting one grown in America, is a hybrid of indeterminate origin, though its DNA tests positive for a Guatemalan ancestor—hence the suspicions. No one has ever tested the Hass leaves for toxicity, but it seems unlikely that the small amounts used in cooking would cause any problems in any case.

When in doubt, choose based on taste, and that leads you to the aromatic Mexican leaves (though not all Mexican avocados have the fragrance), which are now available in the U.S. by mail order (see Sources).

TAMALES DE FRIJOL

BEAN TAMALES

❀

[MAKES APPROXIMATELY 40 3-INCH (8-CM) TAMALES]

THE BEAN FILLING

2 tablespoons lard

8 ounces (225 g) beans: flor de mayo, canarios, or pinto, cooked, about 3 cups (750 ml) drained

salt to taste

[CONTINUED]

THE MASA

1½ pounds (675 g) fairly dry tortilla masa, about 2⅔ cups (664 ml)
6 ounces (180 g) pork lard, about 1 scant cup (240 ml)
1 tablespoon salt or to taste

45 large avocado leaves, rinsed and dried

HAVE READY

toothpicks, if necessary
a large pastry cloth or piece of thin canvas or thick plastic
a tamale steamer (page 522)

THE FILLING: Melt the lard in a skillet, add the beans, and mash down to a textured puree. Cook over medium heat, scraping the bottom of the pan from time to time to prevent sticking, until the moisture has been absorbed and the mixture will barely plop off a spoon. Set aside to cool. Taste for salt.

THE DOUGH: Mix the *masa*, lard, and salt together with your hands. Smooth the dough onto a cloth or plastic sheet in the form of a rectangle about ¼ inch (7 mm) thick. Divide into 4 equal parts.

Divide the bean paste into 4 equal parts and spread each onto a piece of dough, leaving a border of about ¼ inch (.7 cm) uncovered. Carefully roll each piece, coaxing it off the cloth or plastic sheet into a roll of about 1¼ inches (3 cm) in diameter. Take one of the rolls and work gently into a thinner roll between ½ inch (13 mm) and ¾ inch (2 cm) in diameter. Cut into 3-inch (8-cm) lengths, wrap each with an avocado leaf, either securing it with a short toothpick or, as Fausta did, sticking the tough stem through the tip of the leaf. Proceed with the other pieces. Stack in the steamer, placing the *tamales* horizontally in overlapping layers.

Cook for about 1 hour. At the end of that time, test one to see if the *masa* has cooked through to the center.

Serve with *pipián* or alone with a tomato sauce.

MOLE MIAHAUTECO

※

[SERVES ABOUT 12]

A FEW YEARS AGO MY JOURNEY FROM JALAPA TO OAXACA TOOK ME THROUGH TEHUACÁN, PUEBLA. SOME OLD NEIGHBORS HAD MOVED THERE, SO I CALLED to say that I would be passing through. They raved about a *mole* from a nearby village made with some very special chiles, *miahuatecos*. The very mention of those chiles immediately transported me to a market I had visited there some years before when I was researching *Mexican Regional Cooking*. I remember piles of shiny, dark green chiles, some ripening to a deep red, being sold along the sidewalks: they were *miahuatecos*. They appeared to be large fresh mulatos and poblanos, but I was assured that these were different: the seeds of these *miahuatecos* had been planted elsewhere but never with the same results. There was something very special about the taste and texture of these chiles grown in the heat of the semiarid lands. (I also remember that market because just as I was about to buy a nice-looking *molcajete* a woman passing by hissed "Put water into it." I did, and the water filtered out through the legs as the annoyed vendor looked on.)

On that visit, Tehuacán looked the same as it had twenty-five years earlier: an almost forgotten dusty, sleepy little town, the streets lined with tamarisk trees. It was known only for its large spa hotel and the excellent mineral waters. But this last time I didn't recognize it as the same place. It had outgrown itself and was now flashy and noisy. My friends assured me that they had made all the arrangements for the following day and the ingredients would be on hand, ready for me to see all the elaborate preparations, and that we would be able to eat at a more or less reasonable hour.

We arrived the next morning to find the family still at breakfast, but one of the boys was sent off to bargain for the turkey. He came back with it under his arm, squirming and gobbling, nearly as big as its captor. Then the real action began as fires were started to heat water for plucking and cleaning the bird, another on the floor of the kitchen room with a metal tripod to hold the large *cazuela*, or *molera*, typical of Puebla with its high-hooped handles standing well above the rim. Another improvised firebox was made with some concrete bricks and the small gas top with two burners heated for toasting the cleaned chiles.

While the main cook, Sra. Sara de Jesús Robledo, fried the turkey, now in large pieces, together with the giblets, the feet, and the flabby flesh that hangs down below the beak, the older daughters each took one of the ingredients separately and fried it in what seemed to be endless melted lard. As the work gathered momentum and the chiles were toasted, I could see why it had been named *muy escandaloso*. The aroma wafted around us and was carried around the village by the dry breeze; it spread like gossip. This was no secret: Sra. Sara was making *mole miahuateco*.

The softer ingredients were mashed to a paste with a little water on the *metates*, while the crisp chiles were pulverized in the metal hand grinder (usually used for corn).

When it was finally finished in the late afternoon, it was a rather sweetish, but not cloyingly so, thinnish, very dark brown sauce, with large pools of fat on top. That is how it is preferred. However, I hasten to say that it was delicious and can be easily duplicated with far less fat—if you can't bear lard, then use chicken or turkey fat—and substitute *mulatos* for the *miahuateco* chiles.

When making *moles* or sauces that require ingredients to be fried, always strain them to remove any excess fat. But be sure to use enough fat to fry ingredients well. The pools of oil that form on the surface of the *mole* can always be skimmed off—I use it to fry the tortillas for *enchiladas de mole*.

1¼ pounds (565 g) mulato chiles

*2 6-pound (2.7-kg) turkeys, preferably, or
1 12-pound (5.4-kg) one, giblets included*

*approximately 1 pound (450 g) pork lard, 2 heaped
cups (550 ml), or rendered chicken or turkey fat*

salt to taste

2 pounds (900 g) plantains, peeled and cut into ½-inch (13-mm) rounds

12 ounces (340 g) raisins, about 2½ cups (625 ml)

4 semisweet rolls, sliced, or semisweet egg bread

4 ounces (115 g) almonds, about ¾ rounded cup (195 ml)

approximately 12 to 14 cups (3 to 3.5 l) water

12 ounces (340 g), sesame seeds, about a scant 2⅓ cups (580 ml)

8 garlic cloves, unpeeled

1 thick slice white onion

2 large avocado leaves

½ teaspoon anise seeds

1 teaspoon coriander seeds

10 cloves

1-inch (2.5-cm) cinnamon stick

1 2-ounce (60-g) tablet Mexican drinking chocolate

Wipe the chiles with a damp cloth to remove any dirt clinging to them. Remove the stems, slit open, and remove the veins and seeds. Reserve the seeds. Toast the chiles a few at a time on a warm *comal* or griddle, pressing them down so that they toast evenly, taking care not to burn them. The inside flesh will turn a dried tobacco color. Set aside to cool. (They should now be crisp.) Grind in a spice/coffee grinder to a textured powder and set aside.

Cut the turkey into serving pieces, rinse, and pat dry. Melt 1 cup (250 ml) of the lard in a large, deep pan in which you are going to cook the *mole*. Add the turkey pieces, one half at a time, sprinkle with salt, and brown slowly, partially cooking the meat, about 45 minutes. Remove the turkey pieces.

Meanwhile, in a large skillet, heat about 1 cup (250 ml) of the lard and fry the plantains,

[CONTINUED]

raisins, bread, and almonds separately, draining each ingredient well in a strainer to remove excess fat. Transfer to a food processor, add 1 cup (250 ml) of the water, and process to a thick paste, adding more water if necessary. Set aside.

In a an ungreased skillet over low heat, toast the sesame seeds for a few seconds, turning them over almost constantly until they are an even golden brown. Set aside to cool. Grind in a blender or electric spice/coffee grinder. Set aside.

Pierce the garlic skins with the tip of a knife so that the cloves do not explode and place them on an ungreased *comal* or griddle with the onion. Cook slowly until soft inside and slightly charred on the outside. Peel the garlic. On the same pan, toast the avocado leaves until crisp, taking care not to burn them. Set aside.

Put the remaining lard into a small skillet, add the spices, and fry them for a few seconds. Drain and add to the blender with the garlic, onion, and crumbled avocado leaves. Blend as smoothly as possible with ½ cup (125 ml) of the water.

First add the powdered chiles with 1 cup (250 ml) water to the fat and meat juices in the pan and fry, stirring almost constantly to prevent burning, for about 10 minutes. Add the raisin/plantain mixture and ground sesame and stir, cooking for about 10 minutes more. Add the ground spices and cook for 20 more minutes. Finally add the chocolate, broken into small pieces, the turkey, and 10 cups (2.5 l) water—the turkey pieces should be barely covered.

Cook the *mole* over medium heat for 1 hour, stirring from time to time and scraping the bottom of the pan well to prevent sticking. Add more salt as necessary and continue cooking until the sauce thickens, the oil floats to the top in pools, and the meat is tender, about 45 minutes more.

Serve with corn tortillas and *tamales de frijol* (page 273).

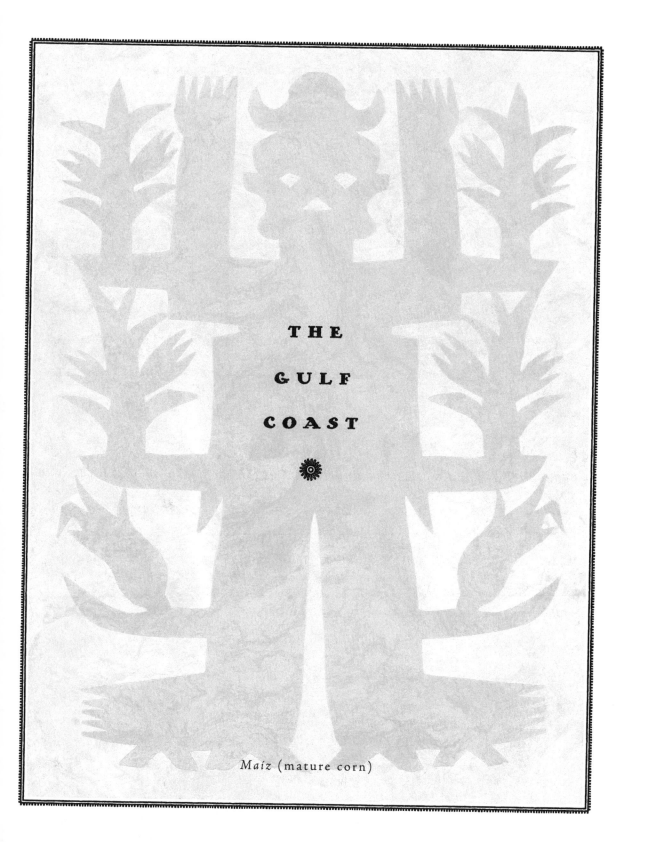

THE

GULF

COAST

❋

Maíz (mature corn)

VERACRUZ

VERACRUZ IS THE RICHEST STATE IN MEXICO. ITS COASTLINE EXTENDS FOR OVER FIVE HUNDRED MILES ALONG THE GULF OF MEXICO. MUCH OF THE LAND IS flat coastal plain with sharp incursions into the eastern slopes of the mountainous mass of central Mexico and the tail of the Sierra Madre Oriental in the northern part of the state. It has broad rivers, tropical forest, and fertile lands producing sugar cane, citrus fruits, pineapple, and mangoes among many others, and excellent coffee in the higher lands. It has petroleum in the south and extensive cattle ranching. Because of the diversity of its topography and historical and cultural influences—Spanish, Totonacs in the north, Popolocas in the south, and negroid groups nearer the port, among others—the cuisine, or rather cuisines, of Veracruz are rightly considered among the richest in Mexico. ❀ Sadly, because of this wealth, its natural resources have been pillaged: forests stripped of valuable hardwoods and left in devastating conditions, its rivers and land polluted, mostly by paper and sugar mills. There has been severe deforestation by cattle ranchers who are only just beginning to accept (of course not the old conservative machos) that cattle and trees are not incompatible. ❀ My last trip to the Isthmus through the southern part of Veracruz—Acayucan, Catemaco, and Orizaba—was admittedly in May, the hottest, driest time of year, but for practically the whole route the land was scorched or blackened. Earlier in the year the burning off in the cane fields sends black smoke over the countryside. Later the corn stubble is burned off by farmers wanting free potash for the next year's crop. Added to that are the fires set off by lazy roadworkers to clean the sides of the highway, fires that are usually left uncontrolled in the spring winds. ❀ I knew Catemaco twenty-five years ago. It was a cool, shady place and had a distinct air of mystery: no wonder it is considered the land of the witches. Now the hills around have been denuded, shaved clean of vegetation, mainly to plant corn or graze cattle. The valuable tropical forests around the Tuxtlas—supposedly nature reserves and protected by law—are gradually being eroded by timbermen, and even the famous Island of Monkeys is now in danger. ❀ I want to shout to the powers that be and the public in general: "Does anyone care?" And to all those responsible: "What legacy are you leaving for your grandchildren?" (Certainly not much, if any, of the natural beauty and bounty; in their place denuded countryside, theme parks, shopping malls, and ever more gigantic parking lots?) Of course, land resources have to be utilized, but surely without such destruction. Man must learn to live in harmony with his universe. ❀ Be that, sadly, as it may, I still love to go to Jalapa (and Catemaco), driving out from Mexico City up through magnificent pine forests along the Puebla highway, then branching off through Tlaxcala, Huamantla, and across the salt flats of the Laguna de Totolcingo. It is an amazing area: flat as far as the eye can see, it provides a vast treeless grazing ground for sheep and occasional groups of horses. I shall never forget the last time I drove that road one early morning in July and marveled at the brilliance of the light and colors of the land: gray and brown in winter and spring, with the rains it had taken on horizontal ribbons all shades of green and yellow. Billowing clouds had cast shadows deepening those colors and sharply etched the contours and ridges of the mountains beyond. Irate truck drivers tailgated unmercifully as I dared to slow down to take in more fully that unforgettable scene.

Soon you pass through foothills of the mountains where the soil is white and chalky—a rather dramatic scene—dotted with yuccas, cacti, and stunted black pines. Once again, you find yourself in a broad valley that stretches out to Perote and beyond, with desolate, barren slopes, stripped in recent years of their splendid pines (and no sign of reforestation). The soil is sadly poor through overintensive agriculture. I couldn't help thinking that, instead of using all those chemicals, they should have used compost made from the tremendous waste from the great markets of Mexico and Puebla.

This journey presents a fascinating and ever-changing scene, for now I am in an area of sober black volcanic rock, studded with tough grasses, thorny shrubs, and stunted pines. It too has an attraction and fragrance of its own. I always want to stop and wander but, of course, never do because the highway has its own peculiar magnetism and beckons, urging you to keep on going. At last the road begins to descend through steep, humpy hills, thickly covered with lush grass interspersed with small stands of trees. It is always surprising to see surefooted Fresian cattle grazing at vertical angles, a sight usually associated with primitive paintings. Not surprisingly there are stands and little farmhouses along the road selling cream and cheeses.

The town of Jalapa is a very special place—certainly not as beautiful as the surrounding country merits, but it is one of the liveliest cultural, political, and ecological centers in Mexico with its orchestra and splendid archaeological museum, the university, and even *un ejercito de los árboles*, a tree brigade.

Like many other towns in Mexico, or in the world for that matter, Jalapa has grown far beyond its original limits. As you enter from the north there is the usual plethora of small, messy workshops advertising mechanics and tire fixers, abandoned cars, and oil drums. The narrow streets in the center are crowded with people and cars. Always there is the pervading aroma of roasting coffee—and you buy the most delicious roasted peanuts in the same establishments.

There are still, however, enough quiet corners and picturesque old houses to give some notion of Jalapa's former life. People are friendly and helpful; they not only give explicit instructions when asked—I am always losing myself—but take the time to draw a little map of how to reach your destination. At one point I had a collection of them. And I have to mention the bus station, which I think says something about the personality of Jalapa—it is one of the most colorful and user friendly in the world, perhaps, thanks to a local enlightened architect.

The food too reflects the very personal feeling one gets in Jalapa. In the small *fondas* and family restaurants, even hotel restaurants like that of the Hotel Salmones (the recipe for *pollo en ajillo* is theirs), it is *comida casera*, family food, and you can always find well-cooked regional dishes. I am always drawn back to the two restaurants that epitomize this: La Fonda in the centrally situated Callejon del Diamante and La Churrería, adjacent to the Hotel Xalapa. They are owned and run by anthropologist Raquel Torres, whose dedication to preserving the local cuisine and culture is extraordinary. Elsewhere I have mentioned breakfast at La Fonda and often think longingly of the *tostadas* at La Churrería, heaped with a delicious mixture of shredded meats and vegetables, lavishly sprinkled with cheese, of the large succulent *tamales rancheros*, and the delicious chocolate and *atoles*. It is a very happy place besides.

For the main midday meal local restaurants serve stews of meats and vegetables, hearty soups, and always black beans. *Chileatole*—not a picante *atole* that would be served in other parts of Mexico under that name—is a stew slightly thickened with *masa* and spiced with *ancho* and *seco* chiles (*chipotle mora*). During Lent it would be made with vegetables, but more often with meats. The *mole verde* here (recipe in *The Cuisines of Mexico*) is distinctive too: a green tomato sauce with many types of vegetables and meat and enriched with small dumplings of *masa* and lard. At a special meal that Raquel prepared for a group of us, the emphasis was on vegetables: fritters of *chayote*, the bulbous root, a *pipián* of large fresh beans with *xoco*, meaning sour, *tamales* made of soured *masa* of black corn wrapped in a local leaf called *xoco* or *caballero* (*Oreopanax echinops*). When you refer to beans, *frijoles*, here, you mean black beans. They are used in every guise: in *tamales*, soups, stews, *antojitos*, refried to accompany breakfast eggs, or made into a sauce for *enfrijoladas*. In this damp and benign climate there are always wild greens, *quelites*, of many types that often take the place of meat in the indigenous communities and provide a healthy and nutritious meal. The variety seems endless, and the recipes given here are but a sampling of the richness of this cuisine.

I have to confess that I always look forward to escaping the bustle of Jalapa to stay in one of my favorite places in Mexico, Coatepec. Coatepec and neighboring Xico are in the heart of the coffee country. Coffee was introduced to the area in the eighteenth century by a Spanish entrepreneur, and it is the one crop that has had a stable history here and has survived the worldwide price fluctuations and the meddling of the now-defunct government-controlled Mexican Institute of Coffee. I was delighted to read in *La Cocina Veracruzana*—expertly researched by Maria Stoopen—that in 1875 Guillermo Prieto wrote of a visit to Coatepec, ". . . in Xalapa we tried and sipped the most sensual coffee of the land."

Coatepec and Xico both lie a few kilometers to the southeast of Jalapa and have miraculously maintained much of their picturesque architecture—houses on one level with thick, tiled roofs and wide porticoes through which you can occasionally glimpse a patio full of flowers and orchids, colorful year-round in this damp climate. The rains are very heavy during the summer—although last year there was a serious, almost-unheard-of drought—and for much of the remaining months a damp mist, locally called *chipi-chipi*, envelops the land and maintains the humidity in which these flowers and the coffee bushes flourish.

Small family businesses still exist here: creameries selling fresh, frothy milk from large churns in the morning, fresh cheeses, and yogurt. A few bakeries still exist where you can see the man kneading and forming the doughs into the complicated shapes called for in Mexican semisweet rolls—that goes on for most of the day. You don't need any directions to get there; you just follow your nose. There are saddlers making intricately decorated saddlery to order

—next door you can get any sort of old luggage repaired, which everyone else scorns—and naturally, coffee stores where local beans are roasted fresh each day. Most colorful are the liquor stores, not selling gin and whiskey, but the greatest selection of fruit liquors displayed with the precision of a parade ground. I suppose you could call it a "cottage industry," using liquor made with the product of the nearby sugarmills and locally grown fruits, both tropical and subtropical, many of which are grown among the coffee bushes—citrus, banana, passion fruit, *zapotes*, and many others. They are also flavored with mulberry, peanuts, and coffee. In Xico the most sought-after drink is *verde*, or green, flavored with lemongrass, lemon verbena, and fennel, among others, with rind of lime steeped in alcohol. There is a local saying: If you visit Xico and don't drink some *verde*, you haven't been to Xico.

Xico is only a short distance from Coatepec through coffee plantations shaded with towering trees. It has made a name for itself through the years, not only for its *verde* but also for a dish called *xonequi* (page 288): a soup of black beans with the herb of that name, *xonequi (Ipomea dumosa)*, a species of morning glory, and its very mild, fruity, black *mole*.

MOLE DE XICO

Sra. Rosario Flores, Xico

❋

[SERVES 10]

IF YOU TALK TO ANYONE ABOUT XICO, THEY INVARIABLY ASK IF YOU HAVE EATEN THE *MOLE*. IT IS FAMOUS—SURPRISING, SINCE IT IS SWEETISH AND very gentle, certainly not for those who like their food picante.

I have eaten and been given several recipes in Xico but finally agree with my friend Carmen Ramírez Degollado that the recipe for *mole de Xico* printed in *La Cocina Veracruzana* (sadly, an out-of-print limited edition printed privately under the sponsorship of an ex-governor of Veracruz) is the most representative: she serves it in her restaurant El Bajío in Mexico City.

Of course, it is a refined *mole* and only for those who can afford the expensive ingredients of pine nuts and hazelnuts. For those who can't, peanuts serve as a substitute.

When you go to the trouble of making *mole,* it is best to make more than you will use. It keeps for at least a month in the refrigerator and freezes for a much longer period.

12 mulato chiles, about 9 ounces (250 g)
8 pasilla chiles, about 2½ ounces (75 g)
pork lard or vegetable oil for frying
1 small white onion, sliced
6 garlic cloves, peeled
approximately 3 quarts (3 l) chicken or turkey broth
⅓ cup (83 ml) almonds
¼ cup (63 ml) hazelnuts
¼ cup (63 ml) pine nuts
⅓ cup (83 ml) pecans
3 tablespoons sesame seeds
¼ cup (63 ml) raisins
½ small plantain, sliced
8 prunes, pits removed
2 small rounds dried French bread
1 small corn tortilla, dried
1 large tomato, broiled until soft (page 527)
4 peppercorns, toasted and crushed
4 cloves, toasted and crushed
½-inch (13-mm) cinnamon stick, crushed
¼ cup (63 ml) grated piloncillo or soft brown sugar
1 ounce (30 g) Mexican drinking chocolate
10 large servings of young turkey or large chickens
salt as necessary

Remove the seeds and veins from the chiles, barely cover with water, and simmer for 5 minutes. Set aside to soak for 10 more minutes. Drain well.

Heat 2 tablespoons of the lard, add the onion and garlic, and fry without browning until translucent. Drain and add with ½ cup (125 ml) of the broth to a blender. Blend until smooth. Add another cup (250 ml) of the broth and blend a few chiles at a time to a very slightly textured puree. You will need to do this in 2 batches, using just enough broth to loosen the blender blades.

Add ¼ cup (63 ml) more lard to a deep, heavy pan in which you are going to cook the *mole*. Add the pureed chiles and fry gently, scraping the bottom of the pan from time to time because it will readily stick and scorch. Continue frying for about 10 minutes.

Add a little of the lard to a skillet and separately fry the rest of the ingredients up to and including the tortilla, adding only enough lard to coat the bottom of the pan and draining each ingredient in a strainer to remove excess fat. Crush the fried nuts, bread, and tortilla once to avoid overtaxing your blender. Add 2 cups (500 ml) of the broth to the blender, then blend the fried ingredients a little at a time, adding more broth as necessary to release the blender blade. Add the blended fried ingredients to the chile puree.

Blend together the tomato and spices, add to the mixture along with the sugar and chocolate, and continue cooking over low heat for about 10 minutes. Add another quart (1 l) of the broth and continue cooking, making sure the *mole* is not sticking to the bottom of the pan, for about 30 minutes. By now the *mole* should be thick, well seasoned, and have pools of oil forming on the surface. Either set aside to cool and store or continue as follows.

Heat about ¼ cup (63 ml) lard in a heavy pan and brown the pieces of turkey or chicken. Drain off the excess fat and add the meat to the *mole*. Continue cooking over slow heat for about 40 minutes, diluting with more broth and then adjusting the salt.

HUEVOS AL COMAL

EGGS COOKED WITH *HOJA SANTA* ON A GRIDDLE

Sra. Carmen Ramírez Degollado

✺

[SERVES 1]

ONE OF MY CLOSEST COOKING FRIENDS IN MEXICO IS CARMEN RAMÍREZ, THE ENERGETIC OWNER OF A LARGE RESTAURANT, EL BAJÍO, IN THE NORTH-eastern section of Mexico City. She was born and brought up in Jalapa, Veracruz, and I love to hear her talking about the recipes that her mother prepared for her young family.

Among them is this absolutely delicious and unique way of cooking an egg, which she often includes when preparing her spectacular Veracruzano breakfast for special occasions in the restaurant.

As the name implies, eggs were cooked on a *comal*, preferably of unglazed clay, on a lightly greased *hoja santa* leaf, and then served with a green or red sauce and hot corn tortillas.

Unless you have very fresh eggs that hold their shape when broken onto a plate, I suggest you use a very small skillet rather than a *comal* or griddle.

2 hoja santa *leaves, big enough to line a 6-inch (15.5-cm) skillet*
1 tablespoon soft lard or 1½ tablespoons vegetable oil
coarse sea salt to taste
2 eggs

Heat the pan well. Lightly grease the leaves on both sides and place in 2 layers in the very hot pan with the leaves extending over the edges. Sprinkle with salt and gently break 2 eggs side by side onto the leaves. Fold the leaves over lightly, put a lid over the pan, and cook until set, about 5 minutes—depending on how soft you like your eggs.

Serve immediately, still wrapped in the leaves, and top with a picante *salsa verde*.

XONEQUI

First published in Mexico Desconocido, *February 1992*

❀

[SERVES 6]

IT IS ALWAYS EXCITING TO SEE THE NAME OF AN UNKNOWN (TO ME) DISH ON A MENU, ESPECIALLY WHEN IT IS SUCH AN EXOTIC ONE. I WAS IN A SMALL regional restaurant in Xico, near Jalapa, in Veracruz, many years ago and saw the word X O N E Q U I, printed in capitals with double spacing—I suppose in case you should overlook it. I ordered it and was served a deep bowl of very brothy black beans with a slightly smoky piquancy, fortified with some type of greens and enriched with small balls of corn *masa* flavored with *epazote*. From then on I ordered it a number of times in different restaurants in that one area. (On inquiring in Jalapa and nearby Coatepec I was told disdainfully: "... *es otra clase de comida!*"—it's quite below their standard of fare!)

I asked a number of cooks about the recipe and found very little variation from one to the other: the chile may be blended and fried, the *masa* balls must have chopped onion in them —minor things that don't substantially change the flavor. I finally decided on the version printed here and given to me by Señora Dolores Guavichi de Galván (although she doesn't use onion in the *masa* balls, I use it, because I rather like the flavor).

When I asked where the *xonequi* leaves came from, she kindly offered to take me along to her parents' home. They live in a modest little house on the outskirts of town, at the back of which is a small garden area, a veritable "jungle" of edible wild plants, citrus, coffee and avocado trees, chiles and squash, all intertwined and thriving in the very rich soil and damp benign climate of that area. The thickly matted plant of *xonequi* was brilliant with magenta flowers in that November morning sun. (Her parents very kindly gave me a small root for my garden, and it is now taking over the frame destined for a reluctant kiwi vine.)

I asked the family if they had any idea how far back the recipe went: they remember their grandparents preparing *xonequi* for the midday meal, when they could not afford meat or fish, and that was probably four days a week at least. I also talked to Raquel Torres, a regional food expert and anthropologist in Jalapa (she has two delightful regional restaurants there) about *xonequi*. She told me that a similar dish was prepared in other villages but seasoned with a wild green, a species of *Peperomia pseudo-alpino*, with a strong *cilantro* flavor.

Since few people will be able to obtain *xonequi* leaves, I suggest substituting 2 cups of roughly chopped Swiss chard leaves with ribs and stalks removed.

> 8 ounces (225 g) black beans, rinsed and picked over, but not soaked
> approximately 3 quarts (3 l) hot water
> 2 garlic cloves, peeled
> 1 thick slice white onion
> 1 tablespoon pork lard (optional)

[CONTINUED]

salt to taste
1 large sprig epazote
2 chipotle mora *chiles*

THE BALLS OF CORN MASA
1 cup (250 ml) tortilla masa
salt to taste
1½ tablespoons pork lard
2 tablespoons finely chopped white onion (optional)
3 heaped tablespoons finely chopped epazote leaves

2 cups (500 ml) whole xonequi leaves or roughly chopped Swiss chard leaves

Put the beans into an earthenware pot or slow cooker. Cover with the hot water, add the garlic, onion, and lard, and cook over low heat until the beans are tender but not too soft, about 4 hours (or overnight in a slow cooker). Add the salt and *epazote* and continue cooking for 20 more minutes.

Cover the chiles with hot water and leave to soak until soft, about 30 minutes. Strain and add to a blender jar with ½ cup (125 ml) of the bean broth. Blend to a fine consistency and add to the beans.

Mix the ingredients for the *masa* balls together well and roll into balls about ¾ inch (2 cm) in diameter.

Add the *xonequi* leaves to the beans and cook over medium heat for another 15 minutes. Add the *masa* balls and cook over low heat for about 15 minutes. Test by breaking one open to see if it is cooked through to the center.

Serve the *xonequi* in bowls with plenty of broth and the ingredients distributed evenly.

SALSA DE CHILE SECO

DRIED CHIPOTLE MORA SAUCE

Xico, Veracruz

✸

[MAKES APPROXIMATELY 1¾ CUPS (438 ML)]

THIS VERY HOT, SMOKY-FLAVORED CHILE SAUCE IS THE ONE YOU ARE MOST LIKELY TO FIND ON THE DINNER TABLE IN THE CENTRAL AND NORTHERN parts of Veracruz. It is made of *chipotle mora*, called *chile seco* locally, which are smaller jalapeños ripened and smoke-dried.

I have included this recipe because I have found an abundant supply of these chiles in Mexican groceries, especially in the American Southwest. They are usually cheaper than other types of chiles, perhaps because of the large production now carried out in Chihuahua (see page 167).

The last few years, probably because of the heat and drought, have yielded bitingly hot crops, and when dried the chile is as picante as the *habanero*. In the markets of Puebla and Veracruz you may find this chile marked *capón*, because the placenta and seeds have been removed, presumably for the next season's plantings.

In northern Veracruz this sauce is mixed with mayonnaise and always served with shellfish. Many recipes given to me have called for the chiles to be fried, then ground with garlic and water, and for the sauce to be fried again; while a sauce made in this way has great flavor, it can burn your palate in earnest. I prefer to make the sauce using the following recipe and to include a couple of ancho chiles as they do in a little restaurant in Xico.

2 ancho chiles, veins and seeds removed
4 ounces (115 g) chipotle mora chiles, about 40
approximately 2 cups (500 ml) water
5 garlic cloves, roughly chopped
¼ cup (63 ml) vegetable oil
salt to taste

[CONTINUED]

Toast the chiles very lightly on a warm *comal* or griddle, taking care not to burn them. Cover with boiling water, bring to a simmer, and continue simmering for about 5 minutes. Set aside to soak until they are fleshy and soft, about 10 minutes more. Drain, slit them open, and remove the seeds and veins (wear rubber gloves for this).

Put ¼ cup (63 ml) of the water into a blender, add the garlic, and blend until smooth. Gradually add the chiles and another ¾ cup (188 ml) of the water and blend to a slightly textured consistency, adding more water only if necessary to release the blender blade.

Heat the oil in a medium skillet, add the blended chiles with salt to taste, and fry, stirring and scraping the bottom of the pan continuously to prevent scorching, for about 8 minutes. Dilute with more of the water, enough to make a fairly thick sauce. Set aside to cool. I prefer not to use this sauce right away but to let it ripen for a few hours.

CAMARONES VERDES

GREEN SHRIMP

❈

[SERVES 3 AS A MAIN COURSE, 4 AS A FIRST COURSE]

THIS RECIPE IS AN IRRESISTIBLE ONE CONTRIBUTED BY SRA. CARMELA DEL VALLE FOR *LA COCINA VERACRUZANA* AS IT IS PREPARED IN HER CÓRDOBA, Veracruz, restaurant.

This is one of the most delicious ways of cooking shrimp or crayfish and one that reflects the intense flavors so typical of the coastal areas of Veracruz. It is better to have very large shrimp, unpeeled and with heads if possible, which always add so much to the flavor.

This is not dainty eating: you really have to use your fingers and suck the wonderful juices and flavors from the heads and shells. You can, of course, serve the shrimp with white rice, although I prefer to have the rice first and then eat the shrimp with good corn tortillas. There will not be a lot of sauce, and it should have a rough texture.

1½ pounds (565 g) large shrimp with heads
(or 1¼ pounds without heads, 675 g)
5 garlic cloves, roughly chopped

salt to taste

*4 ounces (115 g) tomates verdes, husks removed,
rinsed, and cut into quarters*

1 large jalapeño chile, cut in half lengthwise

3 hoja santa leaves, stems and thick veins removed and torn up

1 large avocado leaf, stem removed and torn into pieces

¼ cup (63 ml) fruity olive oil plus a little extra for the final stages

Remove the legs and barbs of the shrimp. Cut along the back through the shell of each one and remove the digestive tract ("vein"). Set aside.

Crush the garlic together with the salt and mix to a paste with the water. Set aside.

Put the *tomates verdes*, chile, and leaves together in a small pan, barely cover with water, cover the pan, and cook for about 5 minutes over fairly low heat. Drain off all but ½ cup (125 ml) of the water and transfer to a blender. Blend to a fairly rough consistency. Set aside.

Heat the oil in a skillet large enough to hold the shrimp in one layer. Add the shrimp and stir over very high heat for about 1 minute. Add the garlic paste and cook, stir-frying for another minute. Add the blended ingredients and continue cooking, turning the shrimp constantly in the sauce, for about 3 minutes.

Set the pan aside to cool off slightly and allow the shrimp to absorb the flavors of the sauce.

Optional: sprinkle a little more olive oil over the top just before serving.

GORDITAS DE FRIJOL

MASA CAKES FILLED WITH BEANS

✦

[MAKES APPROXIMATELY 20 2½-INCH (6.5-CM) GORDITAS]

BREAKFAST IN JALAPA, VERACRUZ, IS SYNONYMOUS WITH A PLATE OF GORDI-TAS DE FRIJOL AND SOME TOMATO SAUCE AT LA FONDA, CALLEJON DEL DIA-mante, right in the center of Jalapa. The owner, anthropologist Raquel Torres, is dedicated to preserving local regional foods and customs, and La Fonda is a lively, inviting place in the early morning. A wonderful aroma emanating from the breakfast foods cooking in *cazuelas*, and *atoles* in earthenware pots, meets you in the narrow alleyway in which the restaurant is situated before you even enter the door. The cook whose job it is to make the *gorditas* forms them quickly and deftly, with a uniformity usually associated with machines. However, in other restaurants like El Parador Real near Xico, the *masa* is cut with a cookie cutter. I will give you two methods, but you will probably come up with your own.

1 pound (450 g) masa for tortillas (page 530), about 1¾ cups (438 ml)
3 scant tablespoons lard
salt to taste
2½ cups (625 ml) bean paste (recipe follows)
lard or oil for frying

Have ready a tortilla press (a standard metal one has a plate 6¼ inches [16 cm] in diameter) with 2 baggies and a 2½-inch (6.5-cm) cookie cutter.

Mix the *masa*, lard, and salt together. The dough will be slightly sticky and may be difficult to handle.

FIRST METHOD: Roll the dough into 16 balls, about 1½ inches (4 cm) in diameter. Press one of the balls out to a circle just over 5 inches (13 cm) in diameter. Carefully lift the top bag off; pick up the second bag and carefully loosen the dough. Do not remove it. Set the second bag down and cut out 2 circles with a cookie cutter 2½ inches (6.5 cm) in diameter. Put 2 teaspoons of the bean paste on one of the circles and fold the bag over with the second circle of dough so that it matches and covers the filling. Press the edge lightly to seal.

Repeat with the remaining balls and use the scraps of dough left over from the cutting to form 4 more balls.

SECOND METHOD: Divide the dough into balls of about 1¼ inches (3 cm). Press out in a tortilla press or on the palm of your hand to a circle about 3½ inches (9 cm) across. Put 1 scant tablespoon of the bean paste in the center and fold the dough over the filling. Pat out to form a circle about 2½ inches (6.5 cm) across and between ¼ and ½ inch (7 and 13 mm) thick.

TO COOK THE GORDITAS: Heat the lard or oil to a depth of about ½ inch in a small skillet over low heat. Carefully place the *gorditas* in the hot oil. Fry until the underside is crisp and golden, then turn the *gorditas* over and fry on the second side, about 4 minutes on each side.

Drain well and serve. This is pan-to-mouth food. The dough becomes leathery if reheated or left to hang around.

FRIJOLES NEGROS PARA GORDITAS

BLACK BEANS FOR *GORDITAS*

✻

[MAKES APPROXIMATELY 2½ CUPS (625 ML)]

ON MY FIRST VISIT TO JALAPA MANY YEARS AGO I WAS SURPRISED TO SEE VENDORS OUTSIDE THE MARKET SELLING A GREEN POWDER: ANISEY-FLAVORED toasted and ground avocado leaves, a typical seasoning for black beans. For this recipe you grind your own. The bean paste for *gorditas* should be quite dry; it is not fried as in many other similar recipes. Any leftovers can be frozen for the next batch or for *tamales*.

8 ounces (225 g) black beans
¼ medium white onion, roughly chopped
1 garlic clove, peeled
hot water
salt to taste
8 avocado leaves (page 270), toasted until crisp

Pick through the beans to remove anything that shouldn't be there. Rinse, drain, and put into a pot, add the onion, garlic, and hot water to come several inches above the surface of the beans, and bring to a simmer. Continue simmering until the beans are tender but not soft (not *al dente* either). Add salt and cook for 5 more minutes. Drain and use the broth for a vegetable soup.

Crumble the leaves, removing the tough stems, into an electric coffee grinder and blend to a powder.

Put the drained beans into a food processor and blend to a textured paste, adding the avocado powder. The paste should be quite dry.

POLLO EN AJILLO

CHICKEN IN GARLIC CHILE SAUCE

Hotel Salmones

✸

[SERVES 4 TO 6]

THIS IS A VERY ROBUST AND COLORFUL DISH, BUT ONLY FOR THOSE WHO LOVE GARLIC AND ARE NOT SURPRISED BY THE TOUGHISH TEXTURE OF THE *chile guajillo* rings. For this type of recipe a large, firm chicken (not the soft, rather slimy bagged supermarket chicken) will give the best results and not fall apart in the first step of the recipe. Pork or fish could also be used here.

The olive oil should be light to medium: extra-virgin is too heavy for this recipe.

The sauce should reduce considerably and cover the pieces of chicken rather thickly.

Although *pollo en ajillo* is traditionally served with corn tortillas, in my opinion the flavor is better balanced when it's surrounded by, or on a bed of, plain cooked rice, *morisqueta*.

3 pounds (1.35 kg) chicken, cut into serving pieces
salt to taste
water or light chicken broth
4 ancho chiles
14 garlic cloves, roughly chopped
6 guajillo chiles
⅓ cup (83 ml) olive oil (see note above)

Put the chicken pieces into a wide pan into which they will just fit in one layer. Sprinkle with salt and barely cover with water or light chicken broth (unsalted). Bring to a simmer and continue to simmer, turning the pieces over once until almost tender, just underdone— about 20 minutes. Drain and return to the pan. Reduce or add water to the broth to make 2 cups (500 ml). Set aside.

Meanwhile, slit the ancho chiles open and scrape out the seeds and veins. Cover with hot water and leave to soak until soft, about 15 minutes. Drain, discarding the soaking water.

Put the chiles into a blender jar with 1 cup (250 ml) of water and blend until almost smooth. Set aside.

Blend the garlic with ⅓ cup (83 ml) of water and set aside.

Wipe the guajillo chiles clean with a damp cloth. Slit open and scrape out the seeds and veins. Cut into thin rounds about ¼ inch (7 mm) thick.

Heat the oil in a skillet, add the guajillo rings, and fry for a few seconds, turning them over constantly until crisp—take care not to burn them. Add the pureed garlic and fry over high heat for about 10 seconds more or until the liquid has evaporated. Immediately add the ancho puree and fry once more, stirring and scraping the bottom of the pan constantly until slightly reduced—about 5 minutes. Add the broth, adjust the seasoning, and heat through.

Pour the sauce over the chicken pieces, cover the pan, and cook over medium heat, turning the pieces from time to time, for about 25 minutes.

NOTE: *This recipe may be cooked ahead of serving; it is even good the next day but does not freeze well.*

TAMAL DE CAZUELA

A VERACRUZ "POLENTA"

Sra. María Elena Romero

❂

[SERVES 4]

IN MANY PARTS OF MEXICO A *TAMAL DE CAZUELA* WILL CONSIST OF TWO LAYERS OF CORN *MASA* IN A CASSEROLE WITH A FILLING OF SEASONED SHREDDED pork or chicken with *mole*, etc., in the middle.

In this area of Veracruz a *tamal de cazuela* is a dish of thickened corn *masa* served like *polenta* with meat in a *mole* or fish with its sauce served on top. In this recipe, however, the chicken, chile, and *hoja santa* are all mixed in with the *masa*.

4 large servings of chicken—2 leg and thigh quarters and
1 large breast cut in half
water or chicken broth

[CONTINUED]

salt to taste
1 small white onion, roughly sliced (optional)
2 garlic cloves, peeled (optional)

1 ancho chile
1 pound (450 g) tortilla masa *(page 530), 2 scant cups (480 ml)*
5 ounces (140 g) pork lard, melted—1¼ cups (313 ml)
4 leaves hoja santa, *ribs removed and torn into large pieces*

Put the chicken pieces into a pan, cover with water or chicken broth with salt to taste, and add the onion and garlic. Bring to a simmer and cook until just tender, about 20 minutes. Remove and drain, reserving the broth and adding water as needed to make 3 cups (750 ml).

Slit the ancho chile open and remove the seeds and veins. Cover with hot water and leave to soak for 15 minutes or until soft and fleshy. Drain, transfer to a blender with ½ cup (125 ml) of the reserved chicken broth, and blend until smooth.

Mix the tortilla *masa* with most of a cup (250 ml) of water, reserving a little until you see how much the *masa* will absorb, to make a loose, smooth consistency. Transfer to a heavy pan and cook over low heat, gradually stirring in the lard and half of the remaining reserved broth. Continue cooking, stirring and scraping the bottom of the pan to prevent sticking.

When the lard has been completely absorbed, stir in the chile, *hoja santa*, and the rest of the broth to make a thin consistency. Cook over medium heat, again scraping almost continuously until the mixture thickens and thickly coats the back of a wooden spoon. Adjust the salt, add the chicken pieces, and cook until the mixture is thick enough and begins to shrink from the sides of the pan, about 20 minutes in all. Serve immediately.

PLÁTANOS RELLENOS

STUFFED PLANTAINS

Sra. María Elena Romero, Tlacotalpan

❋

[MAKES APPROXIMATELY 9 5-INCH (13-CM) *PLÁTANOS*]

PLÁTANOS RELLENOS, OR RATHER THE COOKED FLESH OF PLANTAINS STUFFED AND RE-FORMED INTO BANANA SHAPES, ARE A FAVORITE EVENING SNACK ON the Veracruz coast and especially in Tlacotalpan on the Paploapan River. It is important to choose plantains that have turned yellow but are still firm. They may also be stuffed with a *picadillo*, chopped beef seasoned with tomatoes, etc., but I prefer them stuffed with the dry, salty cheese that is traditionally used there and makes a good foil for the sweetish soft dough around it.

1½ pounds (675 g) ripe but not soft plantains
3 tablespoons all-purpose flour
salt to taste
½ cup (125 ml) finely grated queso añejo, cotija, Pecorino, or Romano
oil for frying

Slice off the ends of the plantains, but do not peel, then cut in half, lengthwise. Put into a saucepan, cover with water, and bring to a simmer. Lower the heat and cook very slowly until quite soft, about 1½ hours.

Drain the plantain pieces well. Peel and mash the flesh to a slightly textured consistency. Gradually work in the flour and salt and roll into balls about 2 inches (5 cm) in diameter.

Press one of the balls out onto a sheet of plastic with your hands (a rather sticky business, so slightly grease them if necessary) to a circle about 4½ inches (12 cm) in diameter and about ⅛ inch (3 mm) thick. Sprinkle 1 tablespoon of the cheese across the center and carefully coax the mixture off the plastic. Form it between your palms into a thin banana shape, completely sealing the cheese inside. Continue with the rest of the dough.

Put about 1 inch of oil in a skillet (it should just cover the "bananas") and heat to approxi-

[CONTINUED]

mately 275°F (135°C)—if the oil is too hot, the outside will brown too quickly and the inside will remain raw. Add the "bananas" and fry, rolling them over in the oil so they will cook and brown evenly, until they are a deep golden color, 10 to 12 minutes. Remove carefully with 2 spatulas and drain on paper toweling. Serve hot.

While they may be reheated (preferably in the oven on a paper-lined baking sheet so that excess oil will drain out), they are, of course, best eaten fresh.

ARROZ VERDE

GREEN RICE

Sra. María Elena Romero, Tlacotalpan

❁

[SERVES 6]

ALTHOUGH THE RICE DOES NOT TURN OUT A TRUE GREEN COLOR, IT HAS A VERY GOOD FLAVOR.

1 cup (250 ml) long-grain rice, not precooked or converted
¼ cup (63 ml) safflower oil
1 slice white onion, roughly chopped
3 garlic cloves, roughly chopped
4 jalapeño chiles
4 tomates verdes
1¼ cups (313 ml) water
salt to taste
½ cup (125 ml) peas or chopped green beans
2 sprigs cilantro
2 tablespoons fresh lime juice

Cover the rice with hot water and leave to soak for about 10 minutes (see note). Heat the oil in a skillet. Drain the rice and rinse in a heavy, deep pot, shake the rice once more to get rid of any extra water, and stir into the heated oil.

Fry the rice for about 5 minutes or until it is just beginning to change color or "dances in the pan," then add the onion and 1 clove of garlic. Fry for a few minutes more, taking care not to let the onion and garlic burn.

Puree the chiles, *tomates verdes*, and 2 cloves of garlic with ¼ cup (63 ml) of the water in a blender. Stir into the fried rice and fry for a few minutes more or until the mixture is almost dry. Add the remaining water, salt, peas, and *cilantro* and cook over medium heat until all the liquid has been absorbed and the rice is not mushy—about 15 minutes. Just before the end of the cooking time stir the lime juice into the rice, cover the pot, and continue cooking over very low heat until the rice has puffed up, about 10 minutes. Remove from the heat and set aside for about 15 minutes before serving to allow the rice to absorb any remaining liquid and become fluffy.

NOTE: *Every type of rice has a different absorption point, so the amount of liquid added may have to be adjusted to suit the brand you are using.*

BUÑUELOS DE ALMENDRA

ALMOND FRITTERS

✹

[MAKES APPROXIMATELY 30 1½-INCH (4-CM) BUÑUELOS]

WHEN GOING THROUGH MY NOTEBOOKS I CAME ACROSS THIS RECIPE. I HAD COLLECTED IT IN TLACOTALPAN IN 1976 BUT, ALAS, DID NOT NOTE THE cook's name . . . I hope she will forgive me. It is always better if you can use 1 ounce of bitter almonds to give more flavor, but if these are not available I have suggested a teaspoon of almond extract. I also like to add a little orange juice and the zest of lime.

It is better to fry the *buñuelos* in two or even three batches, straining the oil after each batch. I then put them onto a paper-lined tray and heat them in a 350°F (177°C) oven for about 10 minutes so that the excess oil will exude and be absorbed by the paper.

Start the night before.

> 4 ounces (115 g) almonds or 3 ounces (85 g) almonds and
> 1 ounce (30 g) bitter almonds
> ½ cup (125 ml) natas or thick cream

[CONTINUED]

⅓ cup (83 ml) granulated sugar
5 egg yolks, lightly beaten
approximately ½ cup (125 ml) all-purpose flour
pinch salt
1 teaspoon almond extract if bitter almonds are not available
2 tablespoons fresh orange juice (optional)
grated zest of ½ orange and ½ lime (optional)
2 egg whites
vegetable oil for frying
confectioners' sugar for dusting

The night before, cover the almonds with hot water and leave to soak until ready to use. Remove the skins and grind the almonds to a coarse texture in a coffee or spice grinder.

Mix together the almonds, *natas*, and granulated sugar and gradually add the yolks, flour, salt, and the optional flavorings. Beat the egg whites until stiff and fold them into the mixture. You should now have a soft but malleable paste. Add a little more flour if necessary to give the mixture more body.

Heat 2 inches (5 cm) oil in a deep pan and add the mixture in small spoonfuls. Fry until golden all over, about 4 minutes on each side, then dry on paper toweling—see note above. When thoroughly drained and cool, dust with the confectioners' sugar.

MINILLA VERACRUZANA

❂

[MAKES ABOUT 3½ CUPS (875 ML)]

A YOUNG CHEF FRIEND OF MINE, RICARDO MUÑOZ, IS DEVOTED TO THE TRADITIONAL FOODS OF MEXICO, UNLIKE MANY OF HIS PEERS, WHO IMMEDI-ately want to launch into the "nouvelle." He commented one day that he was not impressed with the recipe for *minilla* that I had contributed to a compiled Mexican cookbook. "I like mine much better, and I think you will too." I do, so I was given permission to publish his recipe.

Minilla is a Veracruzano word that I cannot find in any of my dictionaries. In essence it is a *"picadillo"* of fish, using leftovers, trimmings, and in the case of a restaurant in northern Veracruz, the pickings from a large fish head.

Ricardo says it may be served at room temperature or hot, as a topping for *tostadas*, as a filling for tacos, *empanadas*, and chiles, or served with white rice as a main dish.

While any fresh fish, crabmeat, etc., could be used, if not available (or if prices are pro-hibitive as they are in Mexico), you can use tuna canned in water, Ricardo's choice, breaking it up finely and squeezing in a piece of cheesecloth to extract all the liquid.

Thank you, Ricardo—delicious!

¼ cup (63 ml) olive oil, not extra-virgin

½ finely chopped white onion

1 teaspoon finely chopped garlic

2 heaped cups (550 ml) finely chopped tomatoes

1 tablespoon sugar

2 bay leaves, finely crumbled

2½ cups (625 ml) firmly packed drained water-packed tuna

2 tablespoons finely chopped flat-leaf parsley

¼ cup (63 ml) raisins, chopped

3 tablespoons chopped pitted green olives

1 tablespoon chopped large capers

½ teaspoon dried oregano, crumbled

salt to taste

Heat the oil in a skillet, add the onion and garlic, and fry without browning until translucent. Add the tomatoes and cook over fairly high heat until reduced to a fairly thick sauce—about 10 minutes. Add the sugar, bay leaves, and tuna and cook for 3 more minutes. Add the rest of the ingredients and cook over medium heat, stirring and scraping the bottom of the pan from time to time to prevent sticking until the mixture is fairly dry. Test for salt.

La Cocina de Doña Iris

On the several occasions that I have given classes to groups of visitors brought to Mexico by Marilyn Tausend, I have always included a visit to a friend, entomologist Martín Aluja, who lives in Coatepec, very near Jalapa. He has many talents, among those of a cook, and what's more, an appreciative eater. He always made my mouth water talking about the dishes prepared for him by Doña Iris of Apazapan while on his field trips to capture insects in the orchards nearby. He talked of her delicious smoked chicken, and a *pipián* of *acamayas*, large crayfish cooked in a *pepita* sauce, and her picturesque *cocina de humo* (traditional kitchen with a hole in the roof to carry the smoke out). So of course I had to go.

It took quite a while to set it all up; it had to be when we were both free midweek because weekends Doña Iris's extensive family congregated and there would be too much confusion and noise. And of course it had to be when the *acamayas* (*Atya scabra*) were not breeding.

There were many calls between Coatapec, Michoacán, where I live, and Coatepec, Veracruz, and messages carried to and from Doña Iris by fellow entomologists working in the area—there was no telephone in Apazapan—until everything seemed to be organized. Then a last-minute call from Martin apologizing because Doña Iris's son, who lived with her, had been elected *presidente municipal*, and one of the first things he did was to put a new facade on the house and modernize the kitchen, installing a new gas stove, more befitting his new status. A pity, but not crucial—the food was the most important thing!

The village of Apazapan lies about one hour's drive to the southeast of Coatepec on the northern bank of the Río de los Pescados. You get there along a narrow road that winds down from the coffee orchards of Coatepec into the lush and wide valley where the natural vegetation is broken occasionally along the roadside and on either side of the river with patches of sugarcane, fields planted with peanuts, corn with their accompanying beans and pumpkins, or orchards of mangoes, limes, and native plums, and, of course, bananas.

The house, with its newly cemented facade, was easily distinguishable from the more traditional ones in the long street that runs parallel with the riverbank. Doña Iris was waiting for us with a broad smile on her face, surrounded by a retinue of curious children and a few family helpers. Everything was prepared and ready to go except the chicken. The last *acamayas* of the season had been cleaned of their only inedible part, the black sac behind the head, and the pumpkin seeds had been husked by hand (never toast to open the husks, she said; that would impair the flavor of the *pepitas*). Once cleaned, they were toasted on a *comal* and ground to a textured powder in the hand corn grinder.

The *pipián de acamayas* that she was going to prepare was of special interest to me. The *pepitas* were crushed a second time on the *metate* with the chiles that had been soaked and the resulting paste sprinkled with the broth in which the *acamayas* had been cooked. Gradually, the greenish-hued oil was squeezed out and set aside to add later on, which would give the dish its unique flavor.

I had seen a similar method of extracting oil in Yucatán, to be added to a dish of *papadzules* (see the recipe in *The Art of Mexican Cooking*) or *pipián de venado*—venison cooked in a *pepita* sauce—just before serving to give a glossy green sheen to the surface. Here, however, curiously enough, it was added back into the sauce while the cooking was still in progress but was not absorbed.

She apologized that she had not been able to start smoking the chicken—it really needed many hours of slow cooking—and while she rubbed it with a mixture of garlic, salt, and vinegar, we were sent off to cut the green wood of *jobo*—the Veracruz name for the native plum, *Spondia mombin*—in a nearby orchard. When we returned, a wood fire had been started in a small *bracero*—firebox—on the back porch, the only remnant of her former traditional kitchen.

Now the cooking began in earnest. The *pipián* was bubbling away, and the chicken was turned from time to time over the smoking wood, and we were becoming very hungry. Sensing this, Doña Iris hastily asked her daughter to make some tortillas and set out a bowl of *pinole*—the name here applies to a textured powder of toasted *pepitas* ground with *piquín chile*, or the dried *chilpaya* that grows wild in the orchards and country around. In the hot ashes of the fire she charred tomatoes, jalapeño chiles, and some smaller—the size of a large shrimp—*acamayas*. They were ground to a paste in the *molcajete*. And there was one more thing to try with our tortillas: *salsa de cacahuate*—which is also used on top of white rice or diluted with broth and served with chicken. It was delicious but very picante.

At last the meal was ready. The family grew as we sat down to eat the fragrant and color-ful food. As the *pipián* was served, Doña Iris regretted not having smoked the *acamayas* for lack of time and for not being able to find *cruzeta* (a cactus with a cross-shaped leaf) to slice and cook for the *pipián*—never mind, it was extraordinary anyway. Conversation halted as we sucked away at the *acamaya* and chewed on the chicken bones; the silence was broken only by a request for more tortillas or a spoonful of black beans.

As we drove back through the silent valley at dusk, we recollected what a memorable day we had spent among these happy, generous people who were anxious to share their knowl-edge with us and the simple foods on which they lived from day to day: fish from the river, foods cultivated in their fields or collected in the wild.

PIPIÁN DE ACAMAYAS

LANGOSTINOS IN PUMPKIN SEED SAUCE

❀

[SERVES 4 TO 6]

I KNOW THIS IS HIGHLY ESOTERIC, BUT THERE WILL BE A FEW CURIOUS COOKS WHO WILL WANT TO TRY IT AND THEREFORE PRESERVE THE RECIPE from extinction.

The sauce will have a slightly lumpy and curdled appearance, but it is delicious. And don't take fright at the oil floating on the top; it is vegetable oil, and what's more, has a high vitamin E content.

Doña Iris uses the local pumpkin seed, elongated with a thin dark green rim.

You can use either jumbo shrimp or crayfish.

2 ancho chiles, veins and seeds removed
2 piquín chiles or chiles de árbol
1½ pounds (675 g) very large shrimp or crayfish, peeled and deveined
10 cups (2.5 l) water
salt to taste
8 ounces (225 g) hulled raw pumpkin seeds, about 1⅔ cups (414 ml)

3 large sprigs epazote, *stems and leaves*
2 cups (500 ml) diced cooked nopales *(page 18)*

Toast the ancho chiles lightly on an ungreased griddle or *comal*. Put the anchos and the whole, untoasted *piquín* chiles in a bowl, cover with hot water, and leave to soak for about 10 minutes. Drain.

Cover the shrimp or crayfish shells with the water, add salt to taste and boil for about 15 minutes. Drain, reserving the broth, and discard the shells.

Toast the pumpkin seeds in a heavy pan over low heat, shaking them and stirring them from time to time to toast evenly, until they begin to swell and pop around. Set aside to cool and then grind to a finely textured consistency in a coffee or spice grinder. Transfer to a dish with a slight rim.

Gradually mix in ¼ cup (63 ml) of the hot broth—holding back a little to see just how much the seeds will absorb—and start squeezing the seeds into a paste. Gradually the oil will start to exude; collect it in a small bowl. Keep squeezing and collecting as long as your patience holds out—there should be about ¼ cup (63 ml) of oil.

Put the *pepita* paste into a blender with 1½ cups (375 ml) of the remaining broth and the drained chiles and blend until smooth. Return to the remaining broth and cook over high heat, scraping the bottom of the pan to prevent sticking, until the seeds coagulate in lumps— about 15 minutes. Add the shrimp, *epazote*, *nopales*, and reserved oil, adjust the salt, and cook for about 10 minutes. Serve in a deep bowl with plenty of the broth and corn tortillas.

FRIJOLES NEGROS CON PEPITAS Y HOJA SANTA

BLACK BEANS WITH PUMPKIN SEEDS AND *HOJA SANTA*

❋

[MAKES APPROXIMATELY 6 CUPS (1.5 L)]

THIS MAKES A VERY NUTRITIOUS MEAL IN APAZAPAN, MADE WITH SIMPLE INGREDIENTS THAT THEY HAVE ON HAND—IN FACT, GROW THEMSELVES. I have added some serrano chiles, but they would use a very small local, wild *chilpaya*, either fresh or dried.

8 ounces (225 g) black beans

approximately 7 cups (1.75 l) water

¼ medium white onion, roughly sliced

1 large sprig epazote

salt to taste

1⅓ cups (333 ml) hulled raw pumpkin seeds, about 4 ounces (115 g)

2 hoja santa leaves, stalks removed and torn into large pieces,
or avocado leaves

2 serrano chiles, toasted

Run the beans through your fingers to catch any little stones or pieces of earth, rinse, and drain. Put into a bean pot, cover with the water, add the onion and *epazote*, and cook over very low heat (I like a slow cooker for this) until tender but not falling apart—3 to 4 hours, depending on the age of the beans. Add salt.

Put the pumpkin seeds into a heavy skillet over low heat and stir or shake them from time to time until they are evenly toasted and beginning to swell and pop around. Set aside to cool, then grind to a textured powder in a coffee or spice grinder and add to the beans.

Cook over low heat for about 15 minutes, stirring well from time to time since the seeds tend to stick to the bottom of the pot. Add the *hoja santa* and chiles and cook for 5 minutes more.

SALSA DE CAMARÓN

DOÑA IRIS'S SHRIMP SAUCE

✹

[MAKES 1 SCANT CUP (240 ML)]

DURING THEIR SEASON CRAYFISH ARE USED IN EVERY CONCEIVABLE WAY, PROVIDING FREE FOOD FOR THE PEOPLE WHO LIVE IN THE LITTLE RIVER VIL-lages. Large, unshelled shrimp can be substituted. I like to add a little olive oil and serve this as a spread, either with small corn tortillas or *tostadas*, etc.

4 large shrimp

2 medium tomatoes, broiled

2 jalapeño chiles, broiled

salt to taste

2 tablespoons olive oil (optional)

Broil the shrimp until just cooked inside. Peel, devein, and chop roughly.

Mash all the ingredients together well, adding salt and olive oil, either in the *molcajete* or in a blender.

Serve at room temperature.

SALSA DE CACAHUATE

PEANUT SAUCE

❋

[MAKES 2 CUPS (500 ML)]

THIS IS A PICANTE SAUCE USED TO SPREAD ON TORTILLAS, ON TOP OF WHITE RICE, OR DILUTED WITH BROTH FOR A CHICKEN STEW. AGAIN, THE PEANUTS would have been grown by the family. The chiles would be *chipotles moras*, the smaller, smoked ripened jalapeños; in that area and farther north in the Sierra de Puebla they are purchased already seasoned and called *capones*. If moras are not available, use canned chipotles *en adobo*.

When cooked, the sauce will be fairly thick but spreadable.

8 ounces (225 g) shelled raw peanuts, papery skin removed,
about 1½ cups (375 ml)

2½ tablespoons pork lard or vegetable oil

4 chipotle mora chiles, briefly rinsed and dried (not soaked)

2 cups (500 ml) water

2 garlic cloves, roughly chopped

2 black peppercorns

2 cloves

salt to taste

[CONTINUED]

In a heavy skillet or toaster oven, toast the peanuts over low heat until they're a pale golden color, about 15 minutes. Set aside to cool and then grind in a coffee or spice grinder to a medium-fine texture.

Heat the lard and fry the chiles, turning them over from time to time, for about 1½ minutes, being careful not to burn them. When they are cool enough to handle, tear them into pieces. Put ½ cup (125 ml) of the water into a blender, add the garlic and spices, and blend well. Add the chiles and blend to a puree.

In the same fat, fry the blended ingredients, stirring constantly to prevent sticking, for about 4 minutes. Gradually stir in the ground peanuts, cook for another 2 minutes, and then add the rest of the water with salt and continue cooking, stirring and scraping the bottom of the pan from time to time to prevent sticking—about 8 minutes.

Catemaco

One of the extraordinary gastronomic experiences in Mexico is eating in a waterside restaurant on the shores of Lake Catemaco. The lake is surrounded by volcanic mountains and until fairly recently was also surrounded by dense tropical growth. It has suffered through ruthless deforestation and pollution from the growing town of Catemaco, which attracts thousands of visitors on weekends and holidays—times to avoid if you want to enjoy the natural tranquillity of the place.

It's extraordinary because you can try a variety of dishes there unknown in other parts of Veracruz, let alone Mexico.

I often go to the restaurant *Los Sauces* and start off with several *botanas*, snacks or first courses: *togogolos*, shredded eel, and *topotes*. *Togogolos* are large snails from the muddy bottom of the lake: they are purged, cooked, and made into a salad with chopped tomato, onion, and chile or served hot in a tomato sauce. The preparation of the local eel in that restaurant is delicious, and I have included the recipe here.

Topotes are small, flat, oval fish that are absolutely delicious when fried crisp—so much better than the more usual little dried fish called *charales* that are served with drinks in many parts of Mexico. *Charales* always seem to have too much bone and too many scales for such small animals. *Topotes* abound in the lake during the early spring, when they are cooked fresh.

To preserve them for the next months and to stock local markets for Lenten dishes, they are dried and smoked in special ovens outside. It is a long, rectangular construction with an area for the wood fire on the ground and a simple structure holding up a canopy of slatted wood over which the fish are spread to dry and smoke over a very slow fire.

The most popular dish served there is without doubt *mojarra en tacho-gobi*, a small, whole tilapia, gutted, cleaned, and grilled over wood or charcoal. A brilliant red, rough-textured sauce of small wild tomatoes is then poured over the fish. These little tomatoes, with several names—*menudo, Zitlali, ojo de venado, tomate de monte (Lycopersicum pimpinellifolicum)*—are also found in the Sierra de Puebla Norte and usually made into a rustic table sauce textured by the rather tough skins. In this recipe they are crushed and fried with garlic and dried *chilpayas*; they are quite acidy and have a concentrated, delicious taste—in fact just how ordinary tomatoes used to taste!

Of course there are many other items on the menu—shrimp, octopus, oysters, and many other types of fish—but I generally stay with my old favorites.

Meals are served with either corn tortillas or, on request, *pellizcadas*, thickish corn tortillas about 6 inches in diameter. The surface dough is pinched up, or sometimes pressed up in "waves" with the back of a small spoon, and this uneven surface is spread with dark-colored lard from the bottom of the *chicharrón* vat and textured with crumbs of *chicharrón* called *mosmochos* in Catemaco.

Other *pellizcadas* are spread with a black bean paste and generously topped with strips of grilled, seasoned, and dried meat, either pork or beef.

To finish off the meal, rather than the very predictable flan or canned fruit, I like to buy those intensely sweet, crunchy coconut sweetmeats sold by little boys who wander from table to table or, more often, reach down into my capacious (and, by then in my travels, rather messy) bag for a ripe mango.

I always stay outside the town in a lakeshore hotel to watch the setting sun across the water and the lights of the village gradually coming on across the bay.

CHILE PASTOR

Sra. María Antonia Rabago de Bustamante, Santiago Tuxtla

✺

[MAKES I CUP (250 ML)]

THIS RECIPE WAS PRINTED IN *LA COCINA VERACRUZANA*. IT IS A SAUCE TYPICAL OF THE AREA THAT IS ALWAYS PUT ON THE TABLE AS A CONDIMENT OR REL-ish rather than a sauce. While particularly good with fish, it also goes with broiled meats, in soups, etc. I remember in Tapachula, Chiapas, being served very much the same dish, which was used as a dipping sauce for fried slivers of *malanga* (a delicious root grown in damp, tropical climates), so it could also be used with potato chips.

The recipe calls for red onions. In the Tuxtla market I saw rather large purple shallots, so I suggest you use shallots and chives for the flat-leaf chives used in Veracruz.

⅓ cup (83 ml) finely chopped shallots
¼ cup (63 ml) fresh lime juice
salt to taste
10 serrano chiles, charred until soft
2 garlic cloves, roughly chopped
⅓ cup (83 ml) water
⅓ cup (83 ml) finely chopped chives

Mix the shallots with the lime juice and salt.

Chop the charred serranos and mash to a paste with the garlic (or put them in a blender with the garlic and the water and blend smooth).

Mix all the ingredients together in a nonreactive bowl and set aside about 30 minutes to season before using.

ANGUILA GUISADA

SHREDDED EEL OR FISH

Los Sauces, Catemaco, Veracruz

☀

[MAKES 2 CUPS]

ALTHOUGH EEL IS CALLED FOR, ANY COOKED FISH OR SHELLFISH CAN BE SUB-
STITUTED. THE DISH IS SERVED AS A BOTANA WITH TOSTADAS OR TORTILLAS.

1⅓ cups (333 ml) cooked fish, crabmeat, eel, or shark,
cleaned of bones and skin and shredded
¼ cup (63 ml) mild olive oil, not extra-virgin
2 tablespoons finely chopped onion
2 garlic cloves, very finely chopped
4 black peppercorns
2 cloves
1 bay leaf, Mexican if possible
heaped ¼ teaspoon oregano
1 heaped tablespoon very finely chopped large capers
1 heaped tablespoon very finely chopped pitted green olives
2 jalapeño chiles en escabeche, very finely chopped
6 ounces (180 g) tomatoes, roughly chopped, about 1 heaped cup (260 ml)
⅛ teaspoon pure achiote or ½ teaspoon achiote paste
salt to taste

Squeeze as much moisture as possible from the fish.

Heat the oil in a heavy skillet, add the onion and garlic, and fry until translucent without browning. Add the fish and stir well. In a coffee grinder, grind together the peppercorns, cloves, bay leaf, and oregano and add to the fish, stirring well. Gradually add the capers, olives, and chiles.

Blend the tomatoes together with the *achiote* and add to the pan, stirring well over fairly high heat so that the sauce is reduced. Add salt and continue cooking for another 3 minutes or until well seasoned and dry.

CHILE-LIMÓN

CHILE AND LIME RELISH

Catemaco, Veracruz

✸

[MAKES APPROXIMATELY I CUP (250 ML)]

IN CATEMACO THIS *CHILE-LIMÓN* IS USED OVER BROILED TILAPIA. IT IS VERY SHARP AND HOT, MADE WITH THE VERY SMALL LOCAL WILD CHILE CALLED *chilpaya*. Many people use serrano chiles instead. The small *criollo* limes used are very fragrant and not quite as acidy as the larger ones usually used in the United States. I suggest you put in a very small amount of sugar to compensate.

8 serrano chiles, finely chopped
⅓ cup (83 ml) fresh lime juice
⅓ cup (83 ml) water
⅓ cup (83 ml) white onion, finely chopped
salt to taste
pinch sugar (optional)

Mix all the ingredients together in a nonreactive bowl and leave to season for about 10 minutes before using.

C ON EL AGUA A LA RODILLA VIVE TABASCO" (TABASCO LIVES KNEE-DEEP IN WATER) AND "MAS AGUA QUE TIERRA" (MORE WATER THAN EARTH) IS HOW ONE OF MEXICO'S most distinguished poets, Carlos Pellicer, describes his native state. ❁ Many of his other poems are eloquent in their praise of the exuberant vegetation and natural beauty of Tabasco. ❁ Tabasco lies around the bottom curve of the Gulf of Mexico with Veracruz to the north on its east side and Campeche northward on the west. It is an oddly shaped entity with incursions into Veracruz and Chiapas, even bordering on Guatemala. The Tabasco coast was one of the first places visited by the Spanish expedition in 1518 under the leadership of Juan de Grijalva, whose name was given to the immense river that flows from the highlands of Chiapas down through the coastal plains of Tabasco to the sea. His report on this fertile land where he traded beads for gold and information about the interior of Mexico prompted the expedition under Cortés a year later. At that time the lowlands were fairly densely populated with *Chontales*, an indigenous group related to the Mayas, who had been cultivating cacao for centuries before; it was at that time the most valuable commodity in Mesoamerica. Historical accounts of those times make Tabasco seem a very lively place! By the early part of this century the state was largely ignored when it came to development programs for roads and bridges, and later the capital, Villahermosa, and Teapa in particular were devastated by the Revolution.

My first visit to Tabasco was in the late fifties. My late husband, Paul, and I were traveling home from Yucatán, and the plane taking us back to Mexico City stopped in Villahermosa and, for a reason never explained, dumped us off unceremoniously. Paul was fuming since he had an assignment in Mexico City for his paper, the *New York Times*, but I was secretly pleased to stop and see a place I didn't know. We were assured that in six hours another plane would pick us up (it never materialized), so we had time to sightsee.

We wandered around this small and tranquil little town, visiting the museum and seeing for the first time the huge Olmec heads in La Venta park. I remember looking across at the far bank of the Grijalva River and seeing palm-thatched huts among dense tropical vegetation, wondering where on earth I was. It was a Mexico I hadn't seen before, so different from the altiplano around Mexico City or Yucatán for that matter. Just recently I was rereading *Terry's Guide to Mexico* by James Norman, published in 1963, five years after we had been there, and it said, ". . . State of Tabasco, a place of dense jungles, big game areas, sparse population and inadequate communications (we had an all-night drive back) . . . has little to offer touristically."

It is no longer like that. Much of the jungle has been cleared for fine timber, oil exploration, or to plant acres and acres of bananas. Acid rain is affecting fish and wildlife, let alone human beings, and even the age-old cacao plantations are now dying. Whenever I am driving there, roadside fires are the order of the day. But still, there are some beautiful and tranquil places as yet unspoiled.

It wasn't until seven years later that I returned with a friend to Villahermosa, staying there overnight before taking a little plane to Palenque—the road in those days was still unpaved and very rough—flying low over rich pastureland, lagoons, and rivers with cebu cattle grazing, followed by their retinue of white herons.

Although the archaeological site of Palenque is in the State of Chiapas, it is not far from the Tabasco border, and our journey on later to Bonampak, Yaxchilan, and finally Tenosique kept us in this geographical area. We ate our first *peje lagarto*, a gar, possibly a prehistoric fish with its tough skin and elongated jaw resembling those of an alligator. It was slowly grilled whole over a wood fire. Its flesh is very white with a delicate flavor, and there it was seasoned with a little *achiote* and *epazote*.

We had river snails cooked in a broth flavored with *hoja santa*, called *momo* there, and thickened with *masa*. On a picnic along the riverbank we charred the buds of a local palmlike plant, which open up into various strands with the heat. They were crisp and slightly bitter. Staying in river settlements along the Usumacinta River, we ate simply: fat, triangular bananas cooked in their skins over a smoldering wood fire, thick, coarsely textured tortillas and very tough little chickens in a broth seasoned with *achiote*. There were no other seasonings and no market for thirty miles or more. In the intense humid heat we refreshed ourselves with drinks of bitter orange or lime from trees growing in the clearings of the jungle. When we were clambering around the ruins of Yaxchilan, our guide cut *bejucos*, aerial tree roots full of delicious, cool water. It was an unforgettable experience.

Another five years passed before I visited Villahermosa again. I was by then widowed and living and working in New York and starting to give classes in Mexican cooking. For several months each year I traveled around Mexico gathering material for *The Cuisines of Mexico*. The town had hardly begun to grow by then, and life there was still quietly provincial; people had time to sit at their front doors in rocking chairs, gossiping, and were only too happy to talk to me for hours about their local food and customs. I filled notebooks of comments on the chiles, herbs, and foodstuffs I found in the markets of Villahermosa, but it was all too strange to publish in those days.

I ate turtle and crab in rich-flavored stews, *chirmoles* (page 336), drank refreshing *posol*, a drink made of dried corn, and breakfasted on black beans, rich, strong local cheeses, and grilled meat seasoned with garlic and bitter orange. For supper there were an amazing variety of *tamales*, and even the commercial ones sold in the streets were of very high quality. One of the most startling dishes was that of a small turtle, still in its shell and on its back, bathed in a green sauce flavored with *hoja santa*. It was a *pochitoque*, gelatinous and delicious. There were hearty meat stews of flavorful, grass-fed beef with an array of local root vegetables: *yucas*, sweet potatoes, *macals* or *malangas*, accompanied by the ubiquitous picante and acidy sauce: *salsa de chile* (page 349). It was a revelation in how simple food could be so flavorful.

I have become fascinated with Tabasco and in recent years have driven the length and breadth of it. One of the most memorable trips was to Tapijulapa up in the sierra shared with Chiapas, in fact very near the borderline. On the way I visited the little town of Teapa to see the dramatic grottos and waterfalls but most of all the botanical gardens nearby to see their collection of edible plants and tropical fruit trees, which provide free foods for the more isolated mountain communities. Tapijulapa is a charming little town that has miraculously maintained its colonial architecture and charm (owing, I am told, to the efforts of a local woman architect).

Not far off is another village, almost on the Chiapas border, Oxolotan, with the spectacular ruins of a sixteenth-century monastery. It is another Tabasco, so totally different from the main lowlands north of Villahermosa and along the coast. The land there is swampy, dotted with lakes and studded with little villages that are surrounded by cacao plantations. Most of the houses have their own banana groves and other tropical fruit trees and with brilliant flowers planted in front year-round. I like to pick up woven reed mats from small wayside stands outside Nacajuca or buy small goods made from the skins of fish or armadillos in the occasional artisan workshop. These indigenous communities are all en route to Comalcalco, a unique archaeological site with Chontal-Mayan pyramids made of bricks, since there was no stone in that whole area. But I must confess my mind always wanders to chocolate.

There are two charming cacao *fincas* in the area that I know of, both run by descendants of German families who started them several generations ago. Their houses are large, typical of the tropics, with high ceilings, cool corridors, and large, airy rooms full of brightly colored plants and surrounded by old trees. At the back of both are the cacao plantations. I don't think there is a more exotic fruit than the cacao; flowers at all stages of development sprout out of the rough bark of the trees and gradually grow into the bulky pods that hold the cacao beans. Production is small in both places; the disks of drinking chocolate, sweet or not so sweet, have a wonderfully intense flavor of pure cacao. Of course, you can also buy a chocolate powder or even wine made from the distilled white flesh that lines the huge pod.

A little farther along the road, going toward the coast, is a large *palapa* (palm-thatched shelter) housing a restaurant that serves regional dishes. I tried the duck in *chirmol* (see page 336), and it was the toughest duck I have ever encountered on a plate. But it had a delicious sauce that I mopped up with a very large corn tortilla *en mojo de ajo*; the tortilla is heated rather than fried in oil or rather strong-tasting ranch butter to which a lot of chopped garlic had been added.

From there it is a must to continue on to Paraíso and Puerto Ceiba.

My Tabascan neighbor here in San Pancho, and her husband, who many years ago commanded an army battalion in the region, insisted that I go to Puerto Ceiba to try the renowned *ostiones en escabeche*, oysters in a light pickle, for which a local expert, Don Tacho, was famous.

Carlos Franco, the general manager of the Hyatt Hotel in Villahermosa, who is a devoted fan (not only of my books but of the foods of Tabasco), paved the way for my visit by calling ahead to make sure that Don Tacho would be there and would talk to me. Puerto Ceiba is a little fishing community on the shores of the Laguna de Coapa that opens out into the sea. The mangrove swamps around the lagoon are a breeding ground for small oysters; just how many are harvested you can see by the mountains of shells stacked outside a large shed where the fishermen take their catch. Years ago, when he was already well known locally for his oyster preparations, Don Tacho decided to start a canning business and brought in a Japanese expert to advise him. Now his oysters, both in *escabeche* and smoked, are distributed in Mexico and abroad. As he was telling me the history of the place, his daughter brought in a *puntal*, a snack, a refreshing glass of cold *pozol*, and some deep-orangey-colored little fruits in syrup, *jicacos (Crysobalanus icaco)*, a regional specialty—alas without a really distinctive flavor, like many wild tropical fruits.

After inspecting his small but efficient factory, an extension of the house, we sat down at an enormous table—to accommodate his large extended family—to try the oysters of which he was so proud: first those *en escabeche*, with onion and carrot in a very light pickle—the vinegar was hardly discernible—and then, more to my taste, the smoked oysters, which had more character. The oysters themselves do not have too much taste after thorough rinsings in chlorinated water—alas, all the rivers that run into the *laguna* are contaminated, owing to the lack of sewage treatment plants in the villages and towns. But these small oysters are still one of the much-talked-of specialties of the area.

If you ask someone in Villahermosa where to eat oysters, you will most likely be directed to eat *ostiones tapescos* at the restaurant owned by Don Lacho's son, El Gran Ostion. With your drink you will be offered, free of charge, a *botana* of the famous *ostiones en escabeche*. Originally the *ostiones tapescos* were cooked at Puerto Ceiba on a trestle set above a fire of white mangrove wood. Several layers of oysters in their shells were placed over it and then covered with banana leaves. I suppose you could say they were steam smoked and had a very special flavor. A slightly modified cooking method takes place in the restaurant, but the oysters are light and delicious, especially when served with a *salsa de chile* (page 349).

The daily food in most homes in Tabasco, in either the towns or the countryside, is still very traditional. This was confirmed when I was reading the 1993 edition of *Libro de Cocina de la Mujer Tabasqueña*, edited by Edith V. Matus de Sumohano (no indication of who printed it), which was originally published in 1968 and has been revised several times. In it there is a chapter entitled: *"Pescados, Mariscos, Quelonios, and Reptiles"* (Fish, Shellfish, Turtles, and Reptiles). On the title page is a drawing of a turtle rearing out of a steaming pot and a very much alive snake draped on a serving platter with a smug smile on its face. Among others there were recipes for spider monkey, three different types of turtles (both forbidden because of dwindling stocks) *masacua*, a thick, long snake, and armadillo.

Many people who own ranches do, in fact, have a small water tank in their homes for the odd turtle that ventures out of the ponds or across the fields. They can still collect a dark, liquid honey deposited by wild bees in the hollow bark of trees or branches. They have bitter orange and *achiote* trees and can pick *perejil*; although that's the name for parsley, it is a spiky, tough-leaved plant, *Eryngium foetidum*, with a distinct taste of *cilantro* (in fact it is called *cilantro* in the Caribbean stores in New York). There are bushes of *hoja santa*, a creeping plant with a striped leaf called *matali* (*Tradescantia pendula*), which is infused to make a refreshing drink, and another with large leaves that have a downy white underside, called *to* or *hoja blanca* (*Calathea lutea*), used as a wrapper for *tamales*—and, until recently, commonly used in the markets to wrap food purchases. There are breadfruit and allspice trees (*Pimenta dioica*), edible roots and tropical wild fruits in abundance; it would be hard for anyone to go hungry in this extraordinary environment.

As I have mentioned elsewhere, chef Ricardo Muñoz has put me in touch through the years with various members of his mother's family so that I could experience firsthand family cooking in Tabasco. He had enthused about the cooking of a great-aunt who lived in very humble circumstances, despite their large land holdings, in the small village of Tierra Colorada, on the edge of the very long, skinny Laguna Matillas. Turning off the main highway going west out of Villahermosa, the road is unpaved, very roughly surfaced, and narrow. You get a special view of the marshy countryside, and the day that I went out there the *cocohite* trees (*Gliricidia sepium*) that formed live corrals were still showy with their pale pink blossoms. We stopped to pick *capulin* that were just ripening to deep purple (this is the cherrylike fruit of a tropical tree, *Muntingia calabura*, and not the tree of the same name that grows in the central highlands—*Prunus capuli*).

The village is strung out along a main unpaved track, each house surrounded by small family orchards, sometimes consisting of just a few fruit trees and edible plants, and in the small main *jardin* you get a view of the lake that almost wraps itself around the village. Before leaving that morning we had purchased a string of squirming *mojarras* and a slab of deep red grass-fed beef. Ricardo had insisted that Mamayé, his great-aunt, had a way of grilling meat and fish that was incomparable, and she willingly agreed to show us how she did it.

The fish were scaled and gutted, spread with sea salt, and set upright conveniently on the hood of my truck to dry out in the sun and breeze. It took about two hours. Meanwhile, Ricardo's mother, Patricia, and I walked around the village. It seemed like a homecoming for her; she stopped and visited along the way until it was time to cook the fish.

Mamayé prepared the seasoning of whole unpeeled garlic, crushed in the *molcajete*, salt, and bitter orange, spread it liberally over the fish, and grilled it, very near to the glowing wood, on both sides, brushing them from time to time with the dark, liquid lard that is used for practically everything in Tabasco. The meat was cut into thick slices and grilled, again close to the heat, briefly on both sides to seal in the juices. It was seasoned with a paste of garlic and salt, brushed with lard, and grilled once again. Extra seasoning was heated in a large frying pan, and strips of the steak were tossed in to heighten the flavor. It was all delicious, and both methods I shall introduce at home when I have an outside grill going. (Lime juice, or the substitute on page 529, can be used instead of the bitter orange.)

The most dramatic way of approaching Tabasco is from the east, crossing over the magnificent, newly constructed bridge connecting the Isla del Carmen with the rest of Campeche on the mainland. You then pass through small fishing communities strung out along the Laguna de Pom. Once you cross the bridge over the River of San Pedro and San Pablo, you are in the northeast corner of Tabasco. The first time I drove it was soon after the long bridge had been opened for traffic to Campeche, and the whole journey was a revelation, first driving four kilometers with the sea on one side and the Laguna de Términos on the other, and then over the two great rivers, San Pedro y San Pablo and the Grijalva, which delineates the border between Campeche and Tabasco.

The river Grijalva broadens out as it enters the gulf and was so spectacular a sight that I decided to turn around and go back over the bridge again. The journey from Campeche had been hot and sticky, and I was hungry, so I decided to eat something fast in Frontera, a sadly nondescript little port on the banks of the river, before driving on to Villahermosa. I remember on a previous visit there, Carlos Franco had made my mouth water describing a large, thick tortilla stuffed with shellfish, black beans, and cheese and then immersed in oil with lots of garlic, *en mojo de ajo* (actually he had tried it cooked with *mantequilla ranchera*, a rather strong-tasting but delicious butter). When I picked up the menu in the Palapa restaurant in Frontera, it was the first item on the menu that caught my eye. It seemed an enormous amount when it came, two 10-inch tortillas lightly colored with *achiote* and stuffed with cooked shrimp, a black bean paste, and a rather strong local cheese that was melting. It was getting late, so I couldn't stop and see how it was made. Just over a year later I returned for my lesson and just to make sure it was as good as I had remembered: it was (see recipe, page 350).

The cooking of Tabasco is unique and so little known, I suppose, because many of the ingredients are not available elsewhere, but I have picked out some of my favorite recipes (I hope as forerunners to a complete book on the subject in the future).

Despite the hot, clammy weather, which is debilitating, I know I will return there many times, especially in the spring, when the countryside is patterned with the pale pink blooms of the *cocohite* trees (*Gliricidia sepium*)—stakes that have taken root around parcels of pastureland—and the streets have a short spell of beauty when the *maculi* trees (*Tabebuia rosea*) are full of their luxurious pink blossoms.

IXGUÁ

SAVORY CORN CAKE

✹

[MAKES I 9-INCH (23-CM) CAKE, ABOUT I TO I½ INCHES (2.5 TO 4 CM) THICK]

THE NAME *IXGUÁ*, PRONOUNCED "*ISHWA*," IS IN ITSELF INTRIGUING. IT IS A MAYAN EXPRESSION (ACCORDING TO THE *DICCIONARIO DE MEJICANISMOS*) referring to a cake made with fresh corn and lard—although, of course, the pre-Columbian Mayas did not have lard.

It is much more difficult nowadays to find this sort of dish prepared in either restaurants or provincial homes, but I managed to track it down to Señora Evangelina, a woman who comes in from the country each morning with her savory and sweet *ixguás* and sells them outside the Town Hall in Emiliano Zapata. The next morning, she took me out to her home so that I could see the exact preparation.

The route took us along a narrow, dirt road, shaded with trees, that bordered the wide, impressive Usumacinta River. We passed some peaceful little river communities where the only signs of life were a few children sitting quietly on the riverbank dangling their fishing lines. We left the car in the care of a neighbor and started walking across extensive fields, thickly planted with corn. It was very hot and humid and seemed ages before we came to a patch of guava trees and stands of bananas in front of Señora Evangelina's house. It was typical of the area—one large room hung with hammocks, a tamped-earth floor, walls of narrow, straight branches, and a palm-thatched roof. There were the remains of a fire smoldering in the raised earth stove, and her husband, an invalid, was sitting silently weaving a fishing net to sell. Explaining to her daughter what we were going to do, she picked up her machete and sling and we went off to pick the corn.

She discarded many ears as unsuitable but finally selected twelve fat ones of mature, firm but still slightly juicy corn—young tender corn is not right for the *ixguá*. Back in the house, she began to husk and shave the kernels while her daughter cut large banana leaves and began wilting them over the fire that she had revived with a few pieces of guava wood. Then the grinding began in the hand-cranked metal corn grinder, and the textured paste was mixed with the very dark, liquid lard used in Tabasco, along with a little salt. (Some cooks like to grind fiery little *amashito* or paloma chiles in with the corn to give flavor, more than piquancy).

A deep, heavy pot was lined thickly with the softened banana leaves, then she poured in the batter and covered it with another layer of leaves. Then another layer of leaves went on, and she covered the pot with an inverted lid on which she shoveled a few hot embers to hurry the *ixguá* along. I am told that traditionally the *ixguá* is wrapped firmly in leaves and then cooked on top of a concave earthenware *comal*, but I imagine it is easier to control the cooking in a deep pot. The pot was set about 6 inches above the glowing wood fire and shaken from time to time to make sure that the *ixguá* was not sticking to the pan and burning on the bottom.

Halfway through the cooking time, she removed the top banana leaves, now dried, and replaced them with a fresh layer, then inverted the cake and cooked it on the second side. The earthy smell when it was cooking and finally done and unwrapped was unbelievable. The *ixguá* had a deep, golden brown crust on both sides and was about 1½ inches (4 cm) deep. It is often eaten as an evening snack, just as it is, but a neighbor of mine whom I have mentioned elsewhere, Señora Hilda Gómez, loves to douse the top with garlic, chopped and fried in olive oil.

Lard, especially this browned lard, always gives the corn a rich and wonderful flavor and texture, but for the anti-larders chicken fat or even duck fat, for that matter, can be substituted.

If you can find field corn, this is certainly a great dish to make when you have a charcoal grill going.

5½ cups (1.375 l) field corn kernels, cut as close to the cob as possible,
from 5 or more large ears
⅓ to ½ cup (83 to 125 ml) melted lard
1 habanero chile or other very hot small fresh green chile,
roughly chopped
salt to taste

Have ready a 10-inch (25-cm) heavy skillet lined thickly with wilted banana leaves that come up the sides of the pan and overlap completely over the top and a low charcoal fire with a rack set 6 inches above the coals.

Put the corn into a food processor with the lard and chile and process to a roughly textured consistency. (Or use a hand grinder,* and add the lard afterward.) Stir in the salt and pour into the prepared pan.

Cover the mixture completely with the overlapping banana leaves and a lid and cook, shaking the pan from time to time to make sure it is not sticking on the bottom, for about 45 minutes. The bottom crust should be thick and a dark golden brown. Remove the top leaves and replace with a layer of fresh leaves. Invert the pan on top of a plate and slide the *ixguá* back into the pan to cook on the second side, again well covered, for another 45 minutes. Serve hot, either alone or with broiled meats.

*For detailed instructions on using the hand grinder, see page 10 of *The Art of Mexican Cooking*.

ARROZ BLANCO TABASQUEÑO

WHITE RICE FROM TABASCO

✳

[SERVES 4]

IT IS VERY DIFFICULT FOR ME TO CHOOSE WHICH RICE DISHES I LIKE BEST OF ALL IN MEXICO, BUT I THINK THIS WAY OF COOKING RICE IN TABASCO HEADS the list. It has a very special flavor, from not only the fragrant *chile dulce* (page 361) and garlic

CHAYA

THE LEAVES OF THE chaya *bush* (Cnidoscolus chayamansa *and spp.) are used in the cooking of the Yucatecan peninsula, Tabasco and Chiapas, often mixed with masa or used as a wrapping for different types of tamales, cooked in meat stews or with eggs.*

Chaya often supplants meat in indigenous diets and in fact has nutritional qualities superior to it—including proteins, large quantities of calcium, significant amounts of phosphorus, and iron among others.

The leaves of chaya tend to be slightly tough. They are dark green with three pointed lobes, an average one measuring approximately 5 inches (13 cm) wide and 4 inches (10 cm) long.

Some species, especially those growing wild, have microscopic stinging hairs on the leaves, which can irritate the skin for several days. However, the latex in the stems can help alleviate the irritation.

Although spinach is often recommended as a substitute in most recipes, I prefer to use Swiss chard, which has more body when cooked.

but also the rice itself. It is a thin, short-grain variety that is grown in the South—Veracruz, Tabasco, and Campeche.

In most of Mexico rice is served as a separate course called a *sopa seca* (dry soup), and Tabasco is no exception. There it is often topped with strips of fried plantain or served with the ubiquitous *salsa de chile* (page 349).

Most cooks fry the garlic and then remove it or fry it with the rice. I prefer the method given, so that the flavor spreads evenly through the rice.

> *1 cup (250 ml) long-grain white rice such as Texmati,*
> *not precooked or converted*
> *¼ cup (63 ml) vegetable oil*
> *approximately 2 cups (500 ml) water*
> *2 small garlic cloves, roughly chopped*
> *½ green bell pepper, seeds removed and very thinly sliced*
> *salt to taste*

Rinse the rice well and drain, shaking the strainer well to get rid of any excess water.

Heat the oil in a heavy pan at least 3 inches (8 cm) deep. Add the rice and stir well so that the grains of rice are well impregnated with the oil.

Put ¼ cup (63 ml) of the water in a blender, add the garlic, and blend until smooth.

When the rice turns golden and it sounds brittle, add the blended garlic and bell pepper and continue frying, stirring from time to time to avoid sticking. Add the remaining water with salt, cover, and cook over medium heat until all the water has been absorbed and the rice is tender. Leave over very low heat for another 5 minutes, then set it aside, still covered, in a warm place to finish steaming in its own heat.

TAMALES DE CHAYA DE TÍA TONA

❀

[MAKES 36 TAMALES]

TÍA TONA IS THE GREAT-AUNT OF RICARDO MUÑOZ, MY VERY TALENTED CHEF FRIEND, AND LIVES WITH PART OF THE FAMILY ZURITA IN EMILIANO ZAPATA, Tabasco. Thanks to Ricardo, the family very kindly put me up and let me share their lives for a week or so, opening doors for me to meet the local cooks, learn, and eat. It was a great culinary experience!

Ricardo had drawn up a list of things I must not miss, and among them were Tía Tona's *tamales de chaya.* They are small and rectangular, wrapped firmly in a piece of banana leaf and boiled. I stood openmouthed as Tía Tona poured cold water over them after they had been stacked high in a deep pot in overlapping layers. They cooked perfectly in one hour, delicious and moist—not, as I expected them to be, soggy.

The preparation of the corn for these *tamales* is rather special, and I have given details in the recipe that follows. The dough, when prepared with the *chaya* (see the box, opposite), was more like a batter. Tía Tona told me that to test the consistency and balance you put the palm of your hand flat on the surface of the dough; nothing hard should stick to your hand. Well, that means quite a bit of lard; I have reduced it slightly.

As I have mentioned in other recipes, the lard used in Emiliano Zapata was brought to the house straight from the *chicharrón* vat, still hot and dark brown in color—it does give a marvelously earthy flavor to the dough!

I am sure that it will not be long before *chaya* is available in the United States—it is bound to be cultivated in Miami or Puerto Rico eventually, as the demand for more exotic ingredients grows. Meanwhile, I opt for white chard, which has a tougher leaf more akin to the *chaya*.

1 pound (450 g) chaya *leaves, stems removed,*
or 2 pounds (900 g) Swiss chard, stems and wide part of rib removed

boiling water

salt to taste

2¼ pounds (1 generous kg) tamal dough (recipe follows)
or masa for tortillas

11 ounces (315 g) lard, 1½ cups (375 ml) plus 2 tablespoons

Ricardo's additions (optional; page 329)

36 pieces banana leaf, roughly 8 by 10 inches (20 by 25 cm)

Cover the *chaya* with boiling water, add salt, and cook over high heat until almost tender— about 30 minutes (chard will need about half that time, depending on how tough it is). Strain, reserving the cooking water, and chop well. Set aside to cool a little.

Put the dough into a large mixing bowl, beat in the lard (with your hand is better, but if you shrink at the idea, then with an electric beater), and continue beating for about 5 minutes. Add about 3 cups (750 ml) of the cooking water ½ cup (125 ml) at a time until you have a loose dough. Stir in the *chaya* and optional additions. Adjust the salt.

Put 2 tablespoons of the dough in a rectangular shape on one half of a banana leaf, away from the edges. Fold the second side over to cover the dough completely. Make a double fold of the 2 edges, about ¼ inch (7 mm). Coax the dough back into place before folding the narrow sides to the back of the package to make it completely watertight. Set the *tamales* flat in overlapping layers in a deep, heavy pan, cover with cold water, bring to a boil, and continue cooking, covered, over medium heat until the dough is set and does not stick to the banana leaf—about 1¼ hours.

Serve in their leaves with some of the tomato sauce on page 330.

TAMALES DE CHAYA DE RICARDO

RICARDO'S *CHAYA TAMALES*

¾ cup (188 ml) chaya-cooking water
2 garlic cloves, roughly chopped
½ small white onion, roughly chopped
2 serrano chiles, roughly chopped
⅓ cup (83 ml) roughly chopped cilantro

Put the water into a blender, add the garlic, onion, and chiles, and blend until smooth. Add to the dough in the preceding recipe along with the *chaya* and *cilantro* and mix well.

MASA PARA TAMALES DE CHAYA

CORN MASA FOR *TAMALES DE CHAYA*

❋

[MAKES APPROXIMATELY 2¾ POUNDS (1.25 KG) DOUGH, ABOUT 6⅓ CUPS (1.6 L)]

IN TABASCO THE PREPARATION OF CORN FOR TORTILLA DOUGH OR FOR THIS TYPE OF *TAMAL* IS SLIGHTLY DIFFERENT FROM THAT OF, SAY, MICHOACÁN OR other parts of central Mexico. The corn is simply brought to a boil in the lime solution but not partially cooked. One cook I met, a professional tortilla maker, told me that she does not even leave the corn for her tortillas to soak overnight, or for any length of time for that matter, but has it ground as soon as it cools off. For these *tamales*, after the soaking, the kernels have to be rubbed very hard to loosen the papery skins and then ground, almost dry, to a textured consistency.

2 pounds (900 g) dried corn
approximately 6 cups (1.5 l) water
2 tablespoons powdered lime (page 530)

Rinse the corn and remove any debris that floats to the top of the water. Drain. Put the water on to boil, stir in the lime and then the corn, and bring to a rolling boil. Cover, remove from the heat, and set aside to soak overnight.

[CONTINUED]

Rinse the corn in several changes of water, rubbing the kernels between your palms to remove the slimy skins, drain, and grind or have ground, almost dry, to a dough of medium texture.

CHILE FRITO

TABASCAN TOMATO SAUCE

❈

[MAKES ABOUT ⅔ CUP (164 ML); IF FRIED, ½ CUP (125 ML)]

TRADITIONAL COOKS INSIST ON MAKING THE SAUCE IN A *MOLCAJETE*, BUT IF YOU ARE USING A BLENDER, BLEND A FEW OF THE TOMATOES WITH THE CHILES, garlic, and onion first and then add the rest of the tomatoes.

The local little wild chile is used in Tabasco, but any small and very picante green chile may be substituted.

This is the all-purpose tomato sauce of Tabasco that accompanies the local *antojitos*: *tostadas* and tacos, and *tamales* of *chaya* (Cnidoscolus chayamansa) and *chipilin* (Crotolaria may-purensis), both tropical herbs—or *manaitas, tamales* also typical of the region, with shredded pork and/or cabbage mixed in with the *masa*.

Although its name suggests that the sauce is fried, many cooks just mash the ingredients together in the *molcajete* like the *chiltomate* of the Yucatán peninsula. To fry the sauce, see the note below.

8 ounces (225 g) plum tomatoes, about 3 large
3 to 4 very hot small green chiles, to taste
1 small slice white onion
2 garlic cloves, roughly chopped
salt to taste
1 tablespoon vegetable or lard oil if frying

Put the whole tomatoes onto a hot griddle or *comal* and cook over medium heat, turning them over from time to time, until the skin is well browned and the flesh quite soft. Skin and roughly chop the tomatoes, taking care to save all the juice.

Cook the whole chiles in the same way over medium heat until the skin is blistered and the flesh is soft inside. Cook the onion slice in the same way. Chop both roughly.

Crush the garlic together with the chile, onion, and salt. Gradually add the tomatoes, mashing them or blending them to a textured sauce.

TO FRY THE SAUCE (OPTIONAL): Heat the oil in a small pan, add the sauce, and fry over fairly high heat until reduced to about ½ cup (125 ml).

Longaniza

I was curious about the *longaniza* of the area: I had tried this sausage and found it completely different from that of other regions of the country, strongly flavored with *achiote* and Seville orange juice. It was nevertheless delicious, and I wanted to know how it was made.

My hostess in Emiliano Zapata, Hilda, called Sra. Yudelia, a friend and neighbor who was the local expert and agreed to show me. Both women and many of their friends had been born and brought up on rather remote ranches, where everything had to be done by hand, and meals were made from ingredients that they either grew or found wild: their crops of corn, beans, and pumpkins, wild greens and herbs, their farm animals or wildfowl, venison, fish from the river, and turtles of many types from the fields and swampy land around.

Achiote trees, although native to the southern part of Mexico, are nevertheless planted, and every winter the laborious job begins of boiling the seeds until all the red pigment is concentrated in the water. The water is then boiled in large vats until it evaporates, leaving a concentrated red paste. No wonder the real thing is so expensive.

Bitter orange trees, a type of Seville introduced by the Spaniards centuries before, now also grow wild, and their juice is used lavishly in the cooking of meats and fish and fresh sauces throughout the whole Southeast of Mexico. They should always be peeled before juicing to avoid the bitterness contained in the oils of the peel. Sra. Hilda recounted how her mother, having no funnel for stuffing the sausages, would hold the mouth of the casing open by inserting the tough leaf of the orange tree.

Sra. Yudelia was using a rather intriguing-looking funnel, and when I commented how difficult sausage-stuffing funnels are to find in the United States now that everything is done with machines, she whisked me off to the edge of town along a muddy little track that led to the maestro's house: the man who had made hers. Under a roughly constructed palm-thatched shelter, amid a plethora of odd metal objects, he was working over a fire burning on the earth floor. It was urgent since I was to leave the next day: of course, the price went up accordingly for what must be one of the two most expensive sausage-stuffing funnels anywhere.

Both women take the utmost pains in preparing the pork casings. They are first washed in soapy water, then rubbed hard with the peel of Seville oranges and left to soak overnight in orange juice diluted with a lot of water. The next day they are scraped with the blunt side of a knife blade and rinsed once more. The casings were cut into lengths of about 20 inches (50 cm), tied firmly at one end, blown up to become completely inflated, tied again, and hung up in the sun to dry.

The *longaniza* itself is left to dry in the sun for three days before being stored and is usually grilled whole.

LONGANIZA TABASQUEÑA

LONG *CHORIZO* FROM TABASCO

Sra. Yudelia Abreu de Lara

✺

[MAKES 3 LONG SAUSAGES, ABOUT 11 INCHES (28 CM) EACH]

YOUR BUTCHER SHOULD BE ABLE TO PROCURE SOME SAUSAGE CASINGS FOR YOU WITH ADVANCE NOTICE.

2 pounds (900 g) tender pork with some fat
14 garlic cloves, roughly chopped
1 tablespoon salt
1 teaspoon black peppercorns
rounded ¼ teaspoon cumin seeds
1 teaspoon pure achiote or 1 tablespoon prepared achiote paste
½ cup (125 ml) plus 2 tablespoons bitter orange juice (page 529)
approximately 4 feet (1.2 m) small pork sausage casings,
cleaned and cut into 2 or 3 lengths

Trim the pork of any sinew or connective tissue and cut into small cubes. Grind, using the medium disk of a meat grinder (or have the butcher do it for you, but be sure the meat is trimmed first). Transfer to a large bowl.

Crush the garlic to a paste. Grind the salt, peppercorns, and cumin seeds, add to the garlic with the *achiote,* and dilute with the 2 tablespoons orange juice. Rub this mixture into the meat thoroughly (your hands will be stained, but it washes off in a day or so), adding the rest of the orange juice little by little. Cover and set aside overnight in the refrigerator.

Meanwhile, make a double knot at the end of the casings and run water through them or inflate to make sure there are no leaks. Rinse well and leave to soak in acidulated water for at least 30 minutes. Drain.

The next day, stir the meat well to distribute the juices evenly at the bottom of the bowl. Stuff the casings fairly loosely, tie up securely, and hang up to dry for about 3 days. They will keep well in the refrigerator for about 3 weeks, when they will continue to dry out. It would be best to give them a light coating of lard after the initial drying and store them in the freezer.

CHILAQUIL DE CHICHARRÓN

❀

[MAKES APPROXIMATELY 5½ CUPS (1.375 L)]

WHILE I WAS COOKING AND EATING WITH SRA. YUDELIA, SHE GENEROUSLY LENT ME HER MOTHER'S MANUSCRIPT COOKBOOK, SAYING THAT SHE USED IT as her cooking bible. Among others, this recipe caught my eye. If you permit yourself *chicharrón* once in a while, it is worth trying this delicious recipe.

Chilaquiles usually refers to a dish of stale tortillas cut or torn into pieces and cooked in a sauce. Instead of tortillas, this calls for *chicharrón* torn into pieces. The sauce itself could be used for other meats or fish.

It is rather substantial, so 1 cup is a sufficient serving for a snack or first course.

2 tablespoons lard or oil
1½ pounds (675 g) tomatoes, roughly chopped, about 4 cups (1 l)

[CONTINUED]

½ medium white onion, roughly chopped

3 garlic cloves, charred and peeled

3 or 4 amashito chiles or any small hot green chile, to taste

½ teaspoon peppercorns

⅛ teaspoon cumin seeds

½ teaspoon dried oregano

1 rounded tablespoon roughly chopped chives or scallion tops

2 rounded tablespoons roughly chopped epazote leaves

2 sprigs cilantro

1 pound (450 g) chicharrón—half thin and half fatty,
broken into pieces about 1½ inches (4 cm)

¼ teaspoon pure achiote or 1 teaspoon prepared paste

¼ cup bitter orange juice or substitute (page 529)

1½ to 2 cups (375 to 500 ml) water

salt to taste

Heat the lard in a wide pan. Puree the tomatoes, onion, garlic, and chiles in a blender, add to the pan, and fry for about 2 minutes. Grind together the pepper, cumin, and oregano in a coffee or spice grinder, add to the pan, and cook for 1 minute more. Add the chopped chives, epazote, and cilantro and cook for 1 minute more. Add the chicharrón. Dilute the achiote in the orange juice and add to the pan with the water. Check for salt (often the chicharrón has been presalted) and cook until the chicharrón is well seasoned—10 to 15 minutes. The sauce should be of medium consistency.

Serve with corn tortillas.

TOSTONES DE PLÁTANO

PLANTAIN *TOSTADAS*

Restaurant Los Tulipanes, Villahermosa

❁

[MAKES 6 5-INCH (13-CM) TOSTONES]

THERE ARE TWO TRADITIONAL, AND RELATED, RESTAURANTS IN VILLAHER-MOSA, THE CAPITAL OF THE STATE OF TABASCO, THAT SERVE THE BEST OF regional foods with a menu that helpfully provides a glossary of the indigenous names: Los Tulipanes and El Guaraguao.

One of the most impressive dishes is a fish salad made of the very white flesh of the *peje lagarto* (a gar), served in the hollowed shell of the fish, with the pointed head still attached.

Instead of bread, a basket of *tostones de plátano*, 7-inch (18-cm) disks of flattened plantain, crisp-fried and slightly sweet, appears on the table—they are addictive. To make them at home I use a normal-sized tortilla press with a 6-inch (15-cm) plate, but if you have a larger press you can make more impressive *tostones* that resemble those of Tabasco.

It is very important, when choosing the plantains, that while the skins are still green the flesh inside is just beginning to ripen and has a sweet flavor. The totally green ones are more starchy and bland.

Some cooks will dip the uncooked *tostones* into salted water before frying. But this breaks your oil down fast, so I have opted for the method used in Los Tulipanes' kitchen: salt is sprinkled on the plantain just after pressing down to flatten it.

Your press should be lined with pieces of heavy plastic—not those light ones recommended for making tortillas. I find a wok useful for the frying process; you can get the depth of oil without using too much of it.

You can reheat the *tostones* and make them crisp again by placing them on brown paper-lined trays in a 400°F (205°C) oven. The paper will absorb a lot of the excess oil. (I recommend the same method for *chiles rellenos*.)

2½ pounds (1.125 kg) plantains (see note above),
peeled weight about 1½ pounds (675 g)

[CONTINUED]

vegetable oil for frying
salt to taste

Cut the peeled plantains into lengths of 2½ inches (6.5 cm). Heat the oil—which should be at least 1½ inches (4 cm) deep in the pan—and add a few of the plantain pieces; be careful not to crowd the pan. Fry over medium heat, turning them over from time to time until they are an even golden brown, about 10 minutes. Remove and drain.

Place a piece of the plastic on each of the plates of the tortilla press. Put one length of the fried plantain upright on the bottom plate and smash it down with your hand to flatten slightly. Close the press and flatten the plantain out, turning the plastic around (because the plates are not always even) until you have an almost transparent even disk of about 5 inches (13 cm). The edge will not be perfectly even, but don't worry. Peel back the top plastic and sprinkle the plantain with salt, replace the plastic, and carefully transfer to the hot oil. Fry on both sides until crisp and a deep golden brown. Drain on brown paper and serve immediately.

POLLO EN CHIRMOL

Sra. Patricia Zurita de Muñoz

❋

[SERVES 6 GENEROUSLY]

THE NAME *CHIRMOL*, OR *CHIRMOLE*, IS DERIVED FROM THE *NÁHUATL* WORDS *CHILLI* (CHILE) AND *MOLLI* (A MIXTURE) AND, ACCORDING TO THE *DICCIONARIO de Mejicanismos*, means a very ordinary, or inferior, chile stew. I don't think devotees of the Tabasqueña kitchen take very kindly to that slight, and rightly so; I think it is delicious.

Sra. Patricia, who gave me the recipe, said that it is important to have a strong-fleshed bird: wild duck, a hen or rooster, to give authority to the broth and thus the sauce. Since this is impractical, if not impossible, for most cooks, I suggest substituting either a duck or even a small turkey, but, of course, cooking times will vary. This is a great dish to cook on an outside grill, but the meat and other ingredients should be charred over charcoal or hardwood, not charcoal briquettes.

Chirmol is served with small balls of tortilla dough, like dumplings.

1 4-pound (1.8-kg) chicken

salt to taste

12 ounces (340 g) tomatoes

1 small head garlic, papery outside skin removed

1½ medium white onions, cut into 6 pieces

5 4-inch (10-cm) corn tortillas

1 large ancho chile

8 ounces (225 g) unhulled raw pumpkin seeds, about 2⅓ cups (583 ml)

2 cups (500 ml) water

2 quarts (2 l) chicken broth

½ teaspoon pure achiote or 1 tablespoon prepared achiote paste

2 dried amashito chiles or 1 chile de árbol, crumbled

1 heaped teaspoon dried oregano, crumbled

24 small masa balls (recipe follows)

2 large sprigs epazote

Split the chicken open and flatten out a little. Sprinkle both sides with salt. Broil until well browned on both sides but still only barely cooked—15 to 20 minutes per side. Set aside to cool and then cut into serving pieces. Broil the tomatoes until soft and slightly charred. Broil the garlic whole along with the onion quarters. Toast the tortillas until crisp and very slightly charred.

Slit the ancho chile open, remove the veins and seeds, and toast briefly. Cover with hot water and soak for about 15 minutes. Drain. Toast the pumpkin seeds until just beginning to change color—they will swell up and pop around. Cool a little and grind as finely as possible in a coffee or spice grinder. Dilute with the water and stir well.

Put 1½ cups (375 ml) of the broth into a blender, gradually add the unpeeled garlic, onion, tomatoes, *achiote*, and ancho chile, and blend well. Break the tortillas up into small pieces and gradually add to the blender, blending well after each addition. Add a little more broth if necessary to obtain a slightly textured sauce.

Bring the remaining broth to a simmer in a saucepan and add the blended ingredients. Add

[CONTINUED]

the ground pumpkin seeds through a fine strainer, pressing down hard on the debris to extract as much of the liquid as possible. Add the dried chiles, oregano, and chicken pieces and cook over low heat until the chicken is tender and the sauce has thickened slightly, scraping the bottom of the pan from time to time to prevent sticking, about 20 minutes. Add the *masa* balls 10 minutes before the end of the cooking time with salt to taste, then add the *epazote* and cook for 2 minutes more. This dish may be prepared ahead up to the point of adding the chicken.

BOLITAS DE MASA

BALLS OF CORN TORTILLA DOUGH

✸

[MAKES 24 DUMPLINGS TO SERVE 6]

1 cup (250 ml) masa for tortillas, 9 ounces (250 g)
1½ tablespoons lard
salt to taste

Mix the ingredients together well. Divide the dough into 24 pieces and roll each one into a ball—they should be roughly ¾ inch (2 cm) in diameter. Roll the ball in the palm of your hand while you make a deep indentation with your index finger.

PESCADO AL VAPOR

STEAMED FISH

From 65 Recetas para Saborear Pescado, Gobierno de Tabasco

✸

[SERVES 4 TO 6]

THIS AGAIN IS ONE OF MY PREFERRED RECIPES FOR COOKING FISH. IT IS NOT STEAMED IN THE USUAL SENSE; IT IS REALLY STEWED.

I know it will go against the grain for most people to see lard, caramel-colored lard at that, from the *chicharrón* vat, but it does lend a wonderfully rich flavor to the fish. Those who can't stand the thought may, of course, use olive oil.

I usually serve this as a first course, but if you want to serve it as a main course, it should be accompanied by white rice and/or fried plantain.

The fish has to be very, very fresh, certainly not frozen and defrosted. Traditionally *robalo* (snook) is used, but red snapper, sea bass, striped bass, or white fish from the northern lakes can also be used.

6 small or 4 larger fish steaks, ¾ inch (2 cm) thick, with skin

salt to taste

2 tablespoons pork lard

2 tablespoons olive oil

1 medium white onion, thinly sliced

3 garlic cloves, finely chopped

*2 chiles dulces verdes or 1 large green bell pepper,
seeds and veins removed and cut into thin strips*

*1 habanero chile or other small hot green chile,
veins and seeds removed and cut into thin strips*

3 bay leaves, cut into strips

4 sprigs parsley, finely chopped

1 small bunch cilantro, roughly chopped

Rinse the fish, dry well, and season with salt. Heat the lard and oil in a heavy sauté pan in which the fish will just fit in one layer. Add the onion, garlic, chiles, bay leaves, and parsley, sprinkle with salt, and fry for about 3 minutes or until the onion is translucent—do not let it brown.

Add the fish steaks in one layer, sprinkle with the *cilantro*, cover the pan, and cook over low heat for about 5 minutes. Carefully turn the fish over and cook for 5 minutes more, uncovered. The fish should just be cooked through and the juice syrupy.

PESCADO EN MONE I

FISH WRAPPED IN *HOJA SANTA* AND BAKED WITH VEGETABLES

Sra. Hilda de Gomez Taglie

✺

[SERVES 4 TO 6]

FOR THOSE WHO LOVE THE FLAVOR OF *HOJA SANTA* (PAGE 526), CALLED *MOMO* OR *MONE* IN TABASCO, THIS IS THE ULTIMATE DISH. I KNOW THAT BY MODERN standards the fish will be a little overcooked, but that has to be sacrificed so that all the elements of flavors and textures merge. Add a little more oil if necessary to make the surface shiny and appetizing. Although in Tabasco many cooks make this dish on top of the stove, I prefer to bake it for better flavor and texture. There is no substitute for *hoja santa* leaves.

*5 snook, red snapper, or sea bass steaks, about 6 ounces (180 g) each
and about ¾ inch (2 cm) thick*

salt and freshly ground pepper to taste

¼ cup (63 ml) fresh lime juice

8 hoja santa leaves

¼ cup (63 ml) olive oil

1 medium white onion, thinly sliced

4 garlic cloves, thinly sliced

3 chiles dulces or 1 large green bell pepper, cleaned and thinly sliced

*2 pounds (900 g) tomatoes, very finely chopped,
about 4 rounded cups (1 l 60 ml)*

3 large carrots, sliced diagonally and cooked crisp

3 medium calabacitas or 2 zucchini, cubed and cooked crisp

Have ready an ovenproof dish about 2½ inches (6.5 cm) deep into which the fish can be placed in one layer. Heat the oven to 350°F (177°C). Season the fish with salt, pepper, and lime juice and place each on one of the leaves. Wrap the leaf around the fish. If it does not completely cover it, use the extra leaves. Place in one layer in the baking dish.

Heat 2 tablespoons of the olive oil in a skillet, add the onion, garlic, sweet pepper, and a liberal sprinkling of salt, and fry without browning for about 3 minutes. Add the tomatoes and cook over fairly high heat, scraping the bottom of the pan to prevent sticking, until some of the juice has been reduced—5 to 8 minutes. Spread the cooked vegetables over the fish layers, pour on the sauce and the rest of the olive oil, cover the surface with another layer of *hoja santa* leaves and then foil, and bake for about 1 hour.

MONE DE PESCADO II

FISH COOKED IN *HOJA SANTA* LEAVES WITH VEGETABLES

Ricardo Muñoz Zurita

✴

[SERVES 6]

THE TALENTED YOUNG CHEF RICARDO MUÑOZ HAS GENEROUSLY SHARED THIS FAMILY RECIPE WITH ME. I THINK IT IS A SENSATIONAL WAY OF PREPARING fish, with so many facets of flavor and texture. I think I prefer to steam rather than bake this recipe; it is a favorite of mine, and I tend to fluctuate between the two methods. *Robalo*, or snook, that most delicious fish from the gulf, is best for this dish, but use any nonoily fish available that can be cut into steaks—unskinned, of course.

For this recipe there is no substitute for *hoja santa* leaves—see page 526.

> *6 large or 12 small* hoja santa *leaves*
>
> *6 nonoily fish steaks, about 6 ounces (180 g) each*
> *and 1 inch (2.5 cm) thick*
>
> *salt and freshly ground pepper to taste*
>
> *¼ cup melted pork lard or olive oil*
>
> *vegetable oil for frying*
>
> *1½ pounds (675 g) ripe plantains,*
> *peeled and cut lengthwise into thin slices*
>
> *12 ounces (340 g) tomatoes, thinly sliced*
>
> *1½ medium white onions, thinly sliced*

[CONTINUED]

3 garlic cloves, thinly sliced

2 x-cat-ik chiles* or 1 large hot yellow pepper plus 1 red chile dulce and
½ green bell pepper, seeds removed and thinly sliced

⅓ cup (83 ml) roughly chopped cilantro

Have ready 6 pieces of banana leaf about 12 by 12 inches (30 by 30 cm), softened over a flame, and 6 strips for tying.

Set out the banana leaves with a *hoja santa* leaf in the middle. Season the fish with salt and pepper and brush with some of the melted lard.

Heat a little of the vegetable oil in a skillet, add a layer of the plantain slices, and fry until a deep golden color on each side, about 8 minutes. Drain well and add the next layer, adding a little more oil as necessary.

Heat water in a steamer over low heat or heat the oven to 350°F (177°C).

Divide the plantain slices into 6 and place in one layer across each of the *hoja santa* leaves. Spread the tomato slices in another layer. Place a portion of fish on each.

Heat 2 tablespoons of the lard in a skillet, add the onions, garlic, and chiles, and fry, without browning, for about 3 minutes. Sprinkle well with salt and mix in the *cilantro*. Spread on top of each piece of fish. Fold the *hoja santa* leaf over the top of the fish and vegetables; if it does not cover them completely, use 2 leaves, then fold the banana leaf over to make a waterproof package. Tie firmly but not too tightly.

Place the packages in the steamer and cook over medium heat for 20 to 25 minutes. Set the packages aside, but keep warm, for about 10 minutes before serving so that the juices and flavors are concentrated.

*See The Art of Mexican Cooking, page 465.

TAMALES COLADOS

Sra. Hilda Zurita, Emiliano Zapata

✸

[MAKES APPROXIMATELY 25 TAMALES ABOUT 3½ BY 2½ INCHES (9 BY 6.5 CM) WRAPPED]

FOR MANY YEARS I HAD INSISTED THAT THE *TAMALES COLADOS* MADE BY MY FRIEND'S MAYAN COOKS IN MÉRIDA WERE THE FINEST IN MEXICO—BUT suddenly, overnight, my loyalties switched to those made in the southern part of Tabasco. The almost transparent *masa* was whitish and literally trembled at the touch, a requisite for the most exacting cooks. Many cooks in Yucatán now use *masa* for their *colados*, with corn that has been cooked with lime, but in Tabasco and Campeche they still use the locally grown thin-kerneled pale yellow *criollo* corn, and it is cooked without lime. The corn is put into boiling water, brought just to a boil, and then left to soak overnight. The next day it is rinsed and then ground to a dryish textured meal rather than a damp *masa*.

I had called my hostess ahead to say that I was coming on a certain day and that I would like to take her offer to make the *colados* and be initiated into that culinary mystique. The evening I arrived she dropped her work—making the most exquisite wedding dresses with all hand-worked appliqués of laces and pearls—and we rushed around gathering up the ingredients: first the corn harvested by a neighbor, then to the almost closed shop on the corner that sold pumpkin seeds. The next morning she was reprimanded by the rather severe-looking housekeeper that she had bought the wrong variety, and a little boy from the neighbor's house across the way was dispatched for the correct ones (small, fat *menudos*). Once again he was dispatched for lard, which came still hot and brown from the *chicharrón* vat of the neighboring butcher. Miraculously the next morning on the breakfast table were locally raised chickens, again *criollos*, not high-bred ones, for better flavor and texture—for no self-respecting cook would dream of using a commercial chicken for such luxurious *tamales*.

I suspect that Tía Tona, the grandmother—who had been up since the crack of dawn—had already plucked, drawn, and cut them up, ready for the *tamale* making. Each portion of chicken had been cut again, bone included, into smaller pieces to fit the size of the *tamal*, along with the feet, gizzards, and livers (sometimes the *tamales* are made with just those and no extra meat). The new *achiote* of the season was there too, pure and brilliantly colored. Many of the longtime residents of Emiliano Zapata work and live there but have small cattle ranches where they plant—although it is a native tree—the *annatto* (*Bixa orellana*) to have a supply of *achiote* year-round, since it is used liberally in many dishes.

Three kilos of corn had been prepared the night before and ground that morning. The meticulous work of straining began, first through an ordinary metal strainer and then through a double layer of cheesecloth. It requires two people holding a corner of the cheese-cloth in each hand and gently swishing the "sling" from side to side until as much of the milky liquid as possible is extracted. Then comes the long cooking of that liquid with a lot of lard until it thickens. When cold it sets to an opaque jelly. It seemed an age, especially in the heat of the day, before the *tamales* were finally filled and wrapped and safely cooking in the pot. Then work on the *socucos* began. This was an apprenticeship I shall never forget.

When we finally tried the *tamales* that afternoon, I could honestly say that they were the finest I had ever tasted: the strong-looking sauce was (surprisingly) gently flavored with the toasted ground pumpkin seeds, garlic, and habanero chiles (grown in abundance about 30 kilometers away).

It perhaps goes without saying that this recipe is for the dyed-in-the-wool aficionado.

Start the day before.

THE MASA

*2¼ pounds (1 generous kg) dried corn, approximately 5½ cups (1.375 l),
or 2¾ pounds (1.24 kg) textured* masa *from a tortillería*

11 cups cold water (2.75 l)

1¼ cups (313 ml) melted lard

filling for tamales colados *(recipe follows)*

Have ready about 50 pieces of banana leaf about 10 by 8 inches (25 by 20 cm) and about 30 (allow extra) 15-inch (38-cm) lengths of string.

To make your own *masa*, rinse the corn well in cold water, removing any flotsam on the surface of the water. Strain. Cover the corn with boiling water, bring to a rolling boil, boil for 1 minute only, remove from the heat, and set aside to soak overnight. The following morning, grind, almost dry, to a textured *masa*. You should have about 2¾ pounds (1.24 kg).

Put the cold water into a large pot. Gradually add the *masa*, dispersing it and pressing out the lumps with your hands. Strain through a colander into another pot, pressing out the debris or wringing it out in a piece of cheesecloth—to extract as much as possible of the opaque liquid. Reserve the debris for *socuco*, the recipe that follows.

With 2 large pieces of cheesecloth forming a double layer, strain the liquid again so that no solids pass into the final liquid. Heat the lard in a wide, heavy pan. When it's just beginning to bubble, add the strained liquid and begin stirring and scraping the bottom of the pan to prevent the starches from sticking and burning. Now you need a lot of patience! Keep stirring and scraping until the mixture thickens to the point that you can see the bottom of the pan and it starts to sizzle around the edge. This will take from 45 minutes to 1 hour.

Turn the mixture out into a mold so that it is about—not more than—¾ inch (2 cm) thick (I use a roasting pan 13 by 8½ inches (33 by 21.5 cm) and set aside to cool and set. It should resemble a blancmange and shudder at a touch.

Meanwhile, prepare the banana leaves by passing them over a flame or an electric burner on high until they become pliable. Set aside in a double layer to cool. (Each *tamal* will be wrapped in a double layer.)

Divide the *masa* roughly into 25 pieces about 2½ by 2½ inches (6.5 by 6.5 cm). Place a piece on each of the double layers of banana leaf; add a piece of chicken and just less than ¼ cup (63 ml) of the sauce. Wrap securely by putting the 2 long sides together and giving them a small double fold. Press the sides of the leaf a little to make sure that the loose sauce is not trying to escape and fold the sides back under the *tamal*. Tie securely but not too tightly— remember, there is a very delicate *masa* inside.

Place the *tamales* horizontally in overlapping layers in a heavy pan, pour cold water over them with 1 tablespoon of salt, cover, and cook over medium heat, once they come to a boil, for about 2 hours. If in doubt, remove one of the *tamales*, do not unwrap, but set aside in a

[CONTINUED]

cool place or in the refrigerator for about 15 minutes to see if the *masa* sets (local cooks can tell by touching the leaf to see if it is cooked and the contents are firm to the touch).

NOTES: *This is the local method of cooking tamales, but they must be wrapped securely. If in doubt, steam them in the normal manner, covering the top of the steamer with plastic wrap so that none of the moisture can escape. Some cooks insist that all tamales boiled in this way should be wrapped in leaves of hoja de to (Calathea lutea), which is completely waterproof. These are often served with a salsa de chile (page 349), but that is a matter of taste. I think it detracts from the surprisingly delicate flavors, of both the masa and the filling. Colados cannot be made with masa harina, etc. The only substitute would be masa for tamales from a local tortillería. Don't serve these tamales right away. In Tabasco the traditional cooks hang them up in a large basket to cool off and allow the masa to set. These tamales should not be stored for more than about 3 days in the refrigerator, but they can be frozen.*

FILLING FOR TAMALES COLADOS

[ENOUGH FILLING FOR 25 TAMALES]

THE CHICKEN

3 pounds (1.35 kg) chicken, cut into serving pieces

6 cups (1.5 l) chicken broth or water

3 garlic cloves, unpeeled and crushed

salt to taste

THE SAUCE

5 garlic cloves, roughly chopped

3 habanero or other very hot green chiles, roughly chopped

2 teaspoons pure achiote or 1½ tablespoons prepared paste

1¼ cups (313 ml) masa for tortillas (page 530)

6 ounces (180 g) small unhulled raw pumpkin seeds, 1½ cups (375 ml)

2 cups (500 ml) cold water

1 scant tablespoon Mexican oregano, Yucatecan if possible, crumbled

salt to taste

3 large sprigs epazote

Cut the chicken pieces again to make 25 small portions. Heat the broth, add the garlic with salt to taste, add the chicken pieces, and cook over low heat for about 20 minutes—it should not be completely cooked. Drain, reserving the broth, and set aside.

Add 1½ cups (375 ml) broth to a blender, gradually add the garlic, chiles, *achiote*, and *masa*, and blend until smooth. Stir into the warm broth. Toast the pumpkin seeds over low heat, stirring them from time to time until the husks begin to change color, swell, and pop around. Set aside to cool a little, then grind as finely as possible in a coffee/spice grinder.

Dilute the pumpkin seeds with the cold water and add through a fine strainer to the broth mixture, pressing out the debris to extract as much liquid as possible. (Or put the water into the blender and add the seeds little by little and blend as finely as possible. The result will not be quite as finely textured as that produced by the former method.)

Bring the remaining broth to a simmer, add the chicken pieces and oregano, and simmer, scraping the bottom of the pan from time to time to prevent sticking until the sauce begins to thicken, 10 to 15 minutes. Add salt as necessary and the *epazote*, then simmer for about 3 minutes more. The sauce should resemble a gravy that just covers the back of a wooden spoon. It should also be a very bright red color. Set aside to cool a little.

SOCUCO

Sra. Hilda Captedon, Emiliano Zapata

❊

[SERVES 6 OR MORE]

SOCUCO IS THE "COMPANION" TAMAL TO THE PRECEDING *COLADOS*, UTILIZING THE DEBRIS, *SHISH*, LEFT AFTER THE GROUND CORN HAS BEEN STRAINED OF its starchy juice and typical of the area around Emiliano Zapata.

Less than one hour away in Tierra Colorado, the *shish* is used in a different manner—ground to a firmer consistency and used to thicken the sauce for fillings of their *tamales colados*.

Socuco is generally made into a large elongated form, a giant *tamal*, but of course it can also be made into smaller *tamales*. Traditionally it is wrapped into a large, ribbed leaf sometimes referred to as *hoja blanca* for the whitish film on the underside of the leaf. In fact it is *hoja de to* (*Calathea lutea*), a plant native to the marshy areas of Tabasco.

Before the age of plastics, *hoja de to* was used as a wrapping (*to* is the Mayan word for wrapping)—and still is in some parts—for the balls of ground corn used in the regional drink *pozol*, for wrapping meat in the markets, or for carrying food to the workers in the field. When I was making *socuco* with Sra. Hilda, she lined the *to* with a piece of banana leaf. When making it at home with no *to* on hand, I use a double thickness of banana leaf. If it is not available—but it does lend a good flavor—use foil.

This *tamal*, like others made in the same area, is boiled, starting with cold water, but I have modified the cooking process by setting a shallow rack in a heavy pot to support the *socuco* and then pouring on enough boiling water to come halfway up the side of the *tamal* and not entirely cover it.

We ate the *socuco* cut into thick slices and grilled on an ungreased *comal*—it literally fries in its own fat—accompanied by a *salsa de chile*. It was textured and delicious and, surprisingly, not too greasy.

> 2 *cups (500 ml)* masa *for tortillas (page 530)*
> 1¼ *cups (313 ml) corn debris (see preceding recipe)*
> 1½ *cups (375 ml) light chicken broth*
> 2 *habanero*, pico de paloma, *or any hot fresh chile, or to taste*
> 1 *teaspoon pure achiote or 1 tablespoon prepared* achiote *paste*
> ½ *cup (125 ml) melted dark lard*
> *salt to taste*
> 4 *ounces (115 g)* chicharrón, *roughly crumbled*

Have ready 2 large pieces of banana leaves about 20 by 16 inches (50 by 40 cm), softened over a flame, and 4 strings for tying, about 2 feet (60 cm) long.

Mix the *masas* well together. Put ½ cup (125 ml) of the broth into a blender, add the chiles and *achiote*, and blend until smooth. Add to the *masa* together with the lard and salt. Mix well, then stir in the *chicharrón* pieces until well distributed throughout the dough, which should be an intense orangey-red and almost runny. Add more liquid if necessary.

Spread the dough in the middle of a double layer of the prepared leaves in a rough rectangle. Fold the long sides of the leaves together and double them over securely. Press the *masa* at both ends—it tries to escape—and fold back the overlapping leaves at the side. Tie securely.

Place in a pot with a shallow rack, pour on boiling water to come at least halfway up the sides of the *tamal,* cover the pot, and cook over lively heat for about 1½ hours. Have boiling water ready to replenish as the steaming water boils away. The dough should come cleanly away from the wrapping leaves.

SALSA DE CHILE

CHILE SAUCE

❋

[MAKES ABOUT ¾ CUP (188 ML)]

SALSA DE CHILE IS AN EVERYDAY TABLE SAUCE, ACTUALLY MORE OF A CONDIMENT IN TABASCO. IT IS THIN, VERY HOT, AND HAS THE PUNGENT GREEN flavor of the little wild *amashito* chile (*Capsicum annuum* spp.). This chile is oval, an average one measuring about ⅜ inch (1 cm) long. The leaves are also used in the cooked green sauces of the region.

Traditionally this sauce is made with the juice of bitter oranges or, if not available, mild vinegar or lime juice. The bitter oranges of the hot coastal plains and southeastern region have a slight sweetness that is found in those grown at a higher, cooler altitude, so if those you buy are very acidy, or you are using lime juice, add about ⅛ teaspoon sugar.

My neighbor Hilda chops the onion very finely, but chef Ricardo prefers to crush it so as to bring out the flavor more.

Of course this type of sauce is best made in the *molcajete,* but if you are using a blender, be careful not to overblend; it should have a roughish texture.

15 amashito *chiles or 8 serrano or other hot green chiles*
¼ *cup (63 ml) finely chopped white onion*
salt to taste
⅔ *cup (164 ml) bitter orange juice or substitute*
(see note above and page 529)

[CONTINUED]

Place the whole chiles onto a hot *comal* or griddle and toast over medium heat, rolling them over from time to time so that they cook evenly. They are done when the skin is blistered and partially browned and they are soft right through. Chop roughly.

Crush the chiles, onion, and salt together to a rough paste, gradually adding the juice.

This sauce will obviously not freeze well, but it keeps for several days in the refrigerator.

TORTILLAS RELLENAS EN MOJO DE AJO

TORTILLAS FILLED WITH SHRIMP AND FRIED IN GARLIC OIL

✳

[SERVES 6]

THIS RECIPE IS BASED ON ONE FROM LA PALAPA RESTAURANT IN FRONTERA, TABASCO (PAGE 322). I AM TOLD THAT ORIGINALLY THESE TORTILLAS WERE filled with shrimp or crabmeat and octopus, so the recipe lends itself to many variations, depending on what is available.

For this recipe you will need a standard 6-inch (15.5-cm) tortilla press and at least 3 baggies.

THE MASA

1 pound (450 g) masa for tortillas (page 530), 2 scant cups (480 ml),
for 12 5½-inch (14.5-cm) tortillas

2 tablespoons all-purpose flour

scant ⅛ teaspoon pure achiote or
heaped ¼ teaspoon commercial achiote paste

salt to taste

THE FILLING

½ cup (125 ml) black bean paste (page 295, without the avocado leaf)
the shrimp filling (recipe follows)
⅓ cup (83 ml) crumbled queso fresco or Muenster, grated

vegetable oil
6 garlic cloves, roughly chopped

Mix the tortilla *masa* with the flour, *achiote*, and salt and divide into 12 equal parts. Roll into balls about 1½ inches (4 cm) in diameter. If you can't make the tortillas right away, cover with a damp towel or plastic wrap.

Line the tortilla press with 2 baggies and press one of the balls of *masa* out to a 5½-inch (14.5-cm) disk. Remove from the press, still on the baggie. Spread with about 1 heaped tablespoon of the bean paste, 1 very heaped tablespoon of the shrimp filling, and 1 heaped tablespoon of the cheese. Press out another tortilla and carefully lay it over the first to cover the filling completely. Seal the edges together firmly.

Heat ½ inch oil in a small skillet with a little of the chopped garlic, add one of the tortilla "sandwiches," and fry for about 2½ minutes on each side—it should not be very crisp, just slightly golden. Drain and serve with the garlic pieces sprinkled over the top.

Then proceed with the rest of the tortillas.

THE SHRIMP FILLING

[MAKES 1 CUP (250 ML)]

2 tablespoons vegetable or olive oil
2 tablespoons finely chopped white onion
3 tablespoons finely chopped green bell pepper
salt to taste
½ cup (125 ml) finely chopped tomato
1 cup (250 ml) roughly chopped peeled raw shrimp

Heat the oil in a small skillet, add the onion and pepper with a sprinkle of salt, and fry for a few seconds without browning. Add the tomato and fry over high heat, scraping the bottom of the pan until the mixture is moist but not juicy. Stir in the shrimp, adjust the seasoning, and cook over fairly high heat until the shrimp is just cooked crisp—about 3 minutes.

CAMPECHE

PROVINCIA AZUL, DONDE ES AZUL EL CIELO, DONDE ES AZUL EL MAR." "BLUE REGION, WHERE THE SKY IS BLUE, WHERE THE SEA IS BLUE." I THOUGHT OF THIS QUOTE (FROM CARLOS PELLICER) the other day as I was driving across the long bridge that links La Isla de Carmen to the mainland of Campeche. The sea and sky, both a pale lustrous blue, seem to converge at a hardly discernible line. There was nothing else to be seen but a few seabirds and an occasional fish jumping in the still water. I wondered if I dared stop on the bridge to take a photograph, but the trailers and trucks were coming up behind at a fast lick. When I come back, I thought. ☀ On the journey back a storm had blown in and all was gray with silvery-green reflections of the mounting clouds in the water. Again it was impossible to stop as I watched the oncoming traffic in the rearview mirror—and besides, I would need a wide-angle lens to do justice to the beauty of that turbulent scene. ☀ Campeche, the town, has always been a very special place for me. My first extended stay there to study the food was in the summer of

1969. The *Malecón* (promenade) stretched for several kilometers along the rim of gulf, and the landfill between that and the town itself was dotted with a few buildings of hideous design and construction (I cannot use the word *architecture*). The *baluartes,* fortifications, built to defend the town against the most daring of pirates in the eighteenth century stood back partially crumbling with neglect, the still elegant, whitish stone mottled with grays and blacks. Behind those walls lay the town itself; it was white and clean with immaculate small plazas overhung with flowering trees and shrubs surrounded by houses of simple but beautiful design that I have come to associate with that of the southern ports: Tlacotalpan, which is almost intact, and Veracruz, Alvarado, and Ciudad del Carmen, as they used to be. ✹ In those days the market was small and compact, full of locally grown produce and fruits, and the eating stands served well-made regional specialties. I shall always remember the fish market. It stood on its own near the water's edge; it was light and cooled with breezes from the gulf. In the early morning fishermen brought their enormous catches of shrimp, shark, dogfish (*cazón*) of all sizes, and baskets of multicolored fish still squirming and shiny, fresh out of the water. ✹ The outdoor cafés were always busy with local businessmen in white *guayaberas* passing the day gossiping and playing dominoes over numerous cups of coffee. Family life took place behind closed doors until the evening Mass, when the women folk sauntered through the *jardín* in front of the cathedral. And, of all the trivial things that I remember, there were no curtains at the bedroom windows of that ugly (and still ugly) hotel that faced the gulf. The lower half of the glass was only frosted and still not sufficiently opaque. As the sun dropped and the lights came on in the room, the local lads indulged in their favorite pastime of sitting on the promenade benches watching the unsuspecting visitors undress for bed or change to go out to supper.

When I visited some local cooks, mostly in restaurants, I noted over and over again through the years: "the freshest of fish, but grossly overcooked. Tasteless and watery." It was a little more difficult to ruin the solid-fleshed Morro crab claws, the specialty of Campeche at that time. (Some of those recipes are to be found in *The Cuisines of Mexico* and *Regional Mexican Cooking.*)

Ten years ago I happened to be driving back to Tabasco from Yucatán and stopped for the night in Campeche. I was dismayed; some of the lovely old houses had been replaced by modern monstrosities and the little plazas either destroyed or neglected. (I once again stayed at that ugly hotel, but this time the windows were curtained.) I stayed only through part of the morning and made this trivial observation in my notebook: "Is this the start of the Campeche health movement? Stout matrons, hardly seen in the streets before, their hair still wrapped up in curlers, were walking in clutches in the early morning light, but nevertheless taking the opportunity of their newly acquired habit to catch up on the local gossip."

Recently I visited Campeche again, this time to stay longer and learn more about this very special place, not only from the point of view of its food but to see the countryside and the lesser-known (than those in Yucatán, for example) Mayan sites of Edzná, Calakmul, Chicanna, Becan, and Xpujil. Their magnificent tall structures, many with elaborate stone carvings, are awe-inspiring and especially impressive in their splendid isolation, surrounded as far as the eye can see by thickly wooded, untamed land.

By now the city had grown, spreading out over the surrounding hills, while the Malecón now extended even farther by landfill stretch along the water for many more kilometers. Today Campeche, ever noisy, is even more so, and the commercial streets bustle with life. The decay of the ramparts has been halted by a conservation order, which also includes the restoration of the elegant old homes and derelict buildings, bringing them back to a useful existence and restoring the architectural harmony of the past.

The *baluarte* of Santiago, for instance, has been transformed into a botanical garden for native plants, and the main thoroughfares have been planted with flowering trees. When I was there in May, the flame trees, *tabachín*, were ablaze with color alternating with the delicate *lluvia de oro* and their cascading bunches of yellow flowers and the pale pink *macuilis*.

At first glance the market seemed to have changed little; the small eateries were doing a brisk trade in the morning with *panuchos*, *pan de cazón*, and *negritos* (traditional specialties based on inflated tortillas stuffed with bean paste, etc. (see *Regional Cooks*, page 14). The freshly killed grass-fed beef still looked horribly red and tough (although, in fact, it has an excellent flavor), and you can still buy very large, fat white fowl for local dishes.

The fish market that used to be so colorful has been incorporated into the main market building and isn't as picturesque as it used to be. Most of the fishermen now sell their catch where their boats come in and are moored, on the *malecon*. All complain that stocks of fish are diminishing. Undoubtedly overfishing, illegal catching in the closed seasons, and the natural foods of the fish being destroyed by contamination of the waters nearer the shore all play their part. However, most of the blame belongs to the government-owned petroleum industry, Pemex, which has flagrantly disregarded the preventive measures against polluting the sea while giving lip service to them.

One long counter in the market is devoted to *cazón asado*, grilled dogfish (page 362), sold alongside the herbs and condiments with which it is cooked: flat-leaf parsley, chives, *epazote*, *chiles habaneros* and *güeros*, called here *x-cat-ik*.

Outside the main market building is a covered area where mountains of fresh chiles are sold, all colors at all stages of ripeness: habaneros, dulces, verdes, rosados, *x-cat-ikes*. There are *chaya* leaves, dark green squash formed like pattypan, and fresh *ibes*—light green flecked with black, shucked then and there from their long, skinny green pods.

At last I was here in May for the *marañon* season—the brilliantly colored fruits of the cashew nut. The sidewalks around the market were perfumed by these exotic fruits, smelling and tasting like strong, very ripe strawberries. A few days earlier I had seen them growing, hanging down from the trees like small, shiny red lanterns terminating with that curious formation resembling a parrot's beak in a shiny gray casing, the cashew nut. Some of the fruits were a deep salmon-pink color, and others, from a different tree, were yellow. For the whole of my stay, *agua de marañon (Anacardium occidentale)* was served with every midday meal. One of the traditional cooks told me that on no account must the flesh of the fruit be put into the blender; it had to be mashed by hand. I can vouch for it that this is the best method. It is the most exotically perfumed drink of any I know.

The home cooks that I visited and cooked with still prepare daily their traditional recipes and take great pride in them; it is their "soul food." Strong Mayan influences can be seen in the preparation and ingredients of many of the local dishes, while others show a complete melding of Mayan and Spanish, and still others have a distinctive Lebanese influence—there are large Lebanese communities of long standing in the Yucatecan peninsula.

For those families who still follow traditional eating patterns, there is a predictable weekly sequence to the dishes prepared: on Mondays it is *comida de floja* (the lazy woman's meal—although it still requires a lot of preparation), *frijol con puerco*, beans and pork (recipe in *Regional Mexican Cooking*). On Tuesdays beef is served in some form or other, often thin steaks in a tomato sauce, breaded, or stewed with charred onion and garlic, seasoned with oregano, and served with plain white rice. To digress: I am very partial to the rice grown in this state—it has a very satisfying, earthy flavor that reminds me of the rice from Guayana that I remember eating years ago on the Caribbean islands. Sadly, as with many other good things, production is dwindling because of the low prices paid to the producers.

Wednesday is the day for preparing a simple *puchero*, or stew, with chicken or beef with vegetables, and Thursday for *cazón* (dogfish) in any one of its various preparations. On Friday my friends and their cooks like to choose a whole fish, or fish steaks, often seasoned with tomato and chile dulce and cooked in a banana leaf.

Every Saturday cattle are slaughtered to ensure an abundance of beef for the Sunday *puchero de tres carnes* (stew of three meats). The fresh offal is immediately bought up for *chocolomo*, a hearty soup/stew served only on Saturdays.

In spite of the hot climate freshened somewhat by breezes from the sea, Sunday is a day of heavy eating. In the early morning there was a steady stream of people going to their favorite cook, usually a man, of *cochinita pibil*. A small, but not suckling, pig is seasoned with a paste of *achiote* and spices dissolved in bitter orange juice, wrapped in banana leaves, and cooked in a pit barbecue. The stomach and large intestines are stuffed with and cooked with the meat. A slice of this *buche* and the roughly shredded pork is stuffed into the Campeche-style French bread roll, for breakfast.

The main meal of the day is a *puchero de las tres carnes*, the most substantial of stews with pork, beef, and a fat hen (the hen is very important for flavor). The meat is served with the vegetables, a bowl of the broth on the side along with a helping of rice and the typical relishes of the region: chopped onion in Seville orange juice, a *salpicón*, radishes chopped with *cilantro* and chile, again in orange juice, and (another relish) *chile habanero* charred and crushed. Now, I like my food piping hot, so I never know where to start first; picking at this and that at random, I am full far too early in the game, to my annoyance. A Sunday *puchero* is an excellent prelude to a long siesta. If there is meat left over, it is shredded and added to mashed vegetables for tacos.

Eating patterns are always more likely to change in the larger urban centers, while in the more isolated rural areas there has to be much more reliance on ingredients readily available. One family I know that lives in Campeche, but also has a ranch about ninety kilometers away, remembers being brought up on what it cultivated: corn, beans, squash, roots, vegetables in various guises, and wild game, especially venison—before the shooting of it was forbidden to conserve rapidly dwindling stocks.

Sra. Concepción told me about the preparation of the ritual food for the *comida de milpa* (food of the cornfield), *El han-li-cool*, which she still prepares under the guidance of her father, who was a strong believer that the gods of the mountain have to be appeased to ensure a good harvest, to pray for rain, or to give thanks for a good harvest. She remembers as a young woman how the corn flourished in the field where the offering was made, while other fields that had been planted were not nearly so lush and productive.

After the ritual killing of turkeys and chickens with prayers chanted in Mayan, the food was cooked in a pit in the ground, *pib*, dug in the field to be blessed. There was *pan de milpa* or *gordas*, nine or thirteen layers of corn *masa* between alternate layers of pureed beans and toasted ground pumpkin seeds, the whole wrapped in banana leaves. When the meal was served, part of it was crumbled into the broth from the meats. There were also *bolillitos*, indeed like small, round *bolillos* (bobbin-shaped bread rolls), also filled. These are eaten together with the fat skimmed off the meat broth.

Without doubt, one of the most important foods in Campeche is *cazón* or dogfish. There are at least five species: *cagüay*, *t'uc t'un*, *cornua*, *pech*, and *jaquetón*. These are much preferred over shark, a near relative, for having firmer and less watery meat. Of course, everyone has a preference and will argue hotly in favor of one or the other. Another strong preference is between fresh *cazón* and *asado*, the latter grilled until it is slightly charred. The *cazón asado* in the market was not prepared by the vendors but principally by one man. I thought it would be interesting to see just how it was prepared and, directed by neighbors, went to see him. No, he made all sorts of excuses, including the fact that he did the grilling at four in the morning. Nobody believed him. Perhaps he thought I would set up in competition until someone pointed out that I did arrive in a black police car (lent by a friend in the Justice Department) with a burly escort/chauffeur—that was enough to make anyone suspicious.

After a little scouting around farther up the coast to what was once a prosperous little fishing village, but now invaded by Pemex, we found a man who was semiretired but who had agreed to grill some for us if we brought them to him early the next day.

Soon after eight o'clock I was bargaining for two healthy-looking *tuctunes* and hurried along to Sr. Gregorio. He told us to find a fisherman to clean them, and for a few pesos they were gutted and washed and laid flat with the head, tail, and backbone still intact. But first they had to dry a little in the hot morning sun, a good time to have a typical breakfast of *panuchos*, filled with cooked *cazón* and black beans, with beer. By the time we finished, he had the charcoal fire smoldering with a simple metal rack about 6 inches (15.5 cm) above the heat. Grasping the fish by the tail, he threw them one by one, skin side down, onto the grill. From time to time he lifted them up to look at the color, and in about ten minutes (this depends, of course, on how thick the flesh is) he threw them over onto the flesh side and again left them for about eight minutes—the flesh was about 1 inch (2.5 cm) thick and each *cazón* was about 3 feet long.

I stayed chatting with Sr. Gregorio. He told me that times were bad. Up until a few years ago he was kept busy grilling between 100 and 120 *cazón* every day. Now he did only a few occasionally but kept himself busy helping his daughter in her small shop, where she also prepared and sold snacks, when he wasn't preparing and salting ray (fish). It takes an expert hand to cut, with geometrical precision, vertical slits through the skin and flesh to expose the bone so that the fish is, in essence "butterflied" out to flatten like a fan. *Abanicos de raya* cooked with potatoes is a traditional local dish. Most of the cooks I met prefer the species with a shiny gray skin and eye-catching polka dots to the *blanca* or white species.

At one time he had thirty-six people working for him and, apart from the time spent fishing, used to cut and salt more than a hundred fans in twelve hours. It is important, he says, to wash the fish in *agua de lluvia* (rainwater, an expression I was to hear time and time again; at one time everyone used to collect rainwater, and many still do). Once cut, they are salted, but with sea salt only, and left overnight piled one on top of the other to drain. As soon as the sun was hot enough the next morning, the *abanicos* were set out to dry for about six hours, depending on the seasonal strength of the sun. The morning I was there, huge boxes were piled high with these fans, all spoken for, except for a few that he let me buy and take to all my new cook friends. Sr. Gregorio lamented that the young men of today do not want to do this work and carry on the tradition: "*Se tira mucho suero*"—you lose too much sweat, he said.

When not working, he was dressed neatly, sitting in a low chair by the door of the house to catch the sea breeze. He was slow of movement but had skin that many a woman would envy—due, said his daughter, to his healthy diet of fish and fruit.

When the car came back for me, we wrapped the *cazón* up in several layers of newspaper, but, he warned, if the fish was to travel, it had to be packed with thick layers of *epazote* in between—I forgot to ask why. The grilled fish was packed again most carefully, but from the curious glances it was quite evident by the time I reached Mexico City airport that I had come straight from Campeche.

Among traditional cooks in Campeche, there is consensus about how to prepare these regional dishes and the ingredients that go into them, with very little variation from one to another. As I have mentioned before, some hotly argue for *cazón asado*, others prefer fresh *cazón*, some use *chile dulce* (a small, wrinkled variety of sweet pepper) in their *miniestra*—a basic mixture employed in many dishes using tomatoes, onion, chiles, and often *epazote* leaves—some like it hot and use *chile seco*; others don't.

Although shark has a rather watery flesh, it could be used by increasing the amount and squeezing the flesh well before seasoning, or use any firm-fleshed fish such as cod, groupers, etc. While it need not be grilled, purists like me, who try to duplicate as faithfully as possible the traditional methods, will want to do so. To my mind, it does enhance the flavor. One cook I know cooks the *cazón* and then mixes it with a lot of pounded *epazote* until it is an appetizing green color.

Campeche's Regional Ingredients

When I was planning to visit Campeche and stay for the first time, I remembered the reminiscences of Juan O'Gorman, the distinguished Mexican artist and architect, over dinner one night. Years earlier he was carrying out a project on the building of new schools in Campeche and, if my memory is correct, accepting a very low fee. The grateful governor, to express his appreciation, promised to have his cooks prepare a different seafood dish every day of his long sojourn. I am afraid I can't remember the food that he described with such relish; a pity, but how could I have known that my life would become so very much involved with Mexican food?

The variety of seafood in Campeche is enormous—the lighter-fleshed fish being much preferred over those with darker flesh—while the ingredients that season or accompany them are not as varied as those of, say, Veracruz or Oaxaca. But because of the different methods of cooking meats and fish and the numerous ways in which the spices and vegetables are combined, the cuisine appears to be more extensive than it really is. Nevertheless, outside of Mexico, it has never received the attention that it deserves.

As neighboring states, Campeche and Yucatán have much in common with their Mayan roots, much the same culinary traditions and ingredients and, therefore, built-in rivalries. I have even heard cooks in Campeche insisting that their dishes are more authentic because they have preserved those traditions more assiduously. (Of course, to enter into an argument of this kind would be tantamount to instant ostracism by one or the other for daring to enter into a partisan debate in which there would never be a resolution.)

Some of the regional ingredients will obviously not be available in some parts of the United States, but there are reasonable substitutes. For instance: the *chile dulce* is a small, thin-fleshed green pepper gathered into an undulating top. It has a more delicate flavor than the green pepper and, of course, is not picante. Substitute half the amount of ordinary green pepper.

The oregano used in its dried state is a species with a larger leaf than the ordinary oregano and a pronounced aroma. Of course, the ordinary Mexican oregano may be substituted for it.

In Campeche you will hear them mention *oregano fresco*, or fresh oregano. This is not true oregano at all but a large, fleshy stemmed plant with an average leaf of about 2½ inches (6.5 cm) long and 2 inches (5 cm) wide, pointed and slightly serrated: *Plectranthus (Coleus) aboinicus*. There is no real substitute, so I suggest using the ordinary fresh or dried oregano.

The *cebolla verde* is a small very white onion with thin, flat leaves. Usually the leaves only are used. It is also referred to as *cebollina*.

The *calabacita*, or little squash, is the same as that used in Yucatán: it has a dark green skin and yellow flesh, appears round or slightly elongated with an undulating surface like that of a pattypan squash. When fully mature and dry, it turns a deep yellow color and its seeds are the *pepita menuda* or *chinchilla* used unhulled, always toasted to a golden brown. Use any green squash for this when called for in the vegetable and meat stews that abound despite the hot weather.

No substitute can really come up to the complex flavor of the Seville-like or bitter orange. (While they are grown in California and Arizona, there is also a bitter one that does not have the aroma or flavor of the Seville.) As a substitute, use a fruity, mild vinegar or use half rice vinegar and half good-quality wine vinegar. (Perhaps we can start a campaign with growers in California, Texas, Florida, and Puerto Rico to produce and send us more. After all, the bitter orange grows at many altitudes and is used as an ornamental tree in Sacramento Park, for example.)

Here are some of the recipes given to me by some of the cooks in Campeche.

CAZÓN ASADO FRITO

GRILLED AND SEASONED DOGFISH MEAT

Sra. Manuela Chuc

✸

[MAKES 3¼ CUPS (813 ML) TIGHTLY PACKED]

2 large sprigs epazote

2 teaspoons salt

1 pound (450 g) cazón asado, *cut into large pieces,
or charcoal-grilled shark*

¼ cup lard or oil

½ medium white onion, finely chopped

1 tablespoon finely chopped epazote leaves

*1 pound (450 g) tomatoes, about 7 large plum tomatoes,
finely chopped, 2 rounded cups (550 ml)*

1 habanero chile, charred and finely chopped

1 teaspoon powdered seco chile or powdered chile de árbol

1 tablespoon bitter orange juice or substitute (page 529)

Barely cover the *epazote* with water, add salt and bring to a boil. Lower the heat, and when simmering add the *cazón*. Cook over low heat for about 10 minutes (for fillets about 1 inch/2.5 cm thick). Set aside to cool in the broth and drain well. When the fish is cool enough to handle, remove the skin and bones and any dry pieces around the edges and mash the flesh with your hands.

Heat the lard in a skillet, add the onion and chopped *epazote*, and fry without browning for about 1 minute. Add the tomatoes and habanero chile and continue cooking for about 5 minutes or until almost dry. Add the mashed *cazón*, salt to taste, and chile powder and continue frying and stirring to prevent sticking for 5 more minutes. Finally, stir in the orange juice and set aside to cool.

TORTITAS DE CAZÓN GUISADOS

CAZÓN FRITTERS IN BROTH

✸

[MAKES APPROXIMATELY 18 2-INCH (5-CM) FRITTERS]

AMONG THE MANY RECIPES THAT SRA. CASTRO SHARED WITH ME, THIS ONE
WAS PASSED DOWN FROM HER GRANDMOTHER.

THE BROTH
6 cups (1.5 l) water

10 peppercorns

5 garlic cloves, peeled

1 rounded tablespoon achiote paste

salt to taste

1 tablespoon vegetable oil or melted lard

1 chile dulce or ½ green bell pepper, finely chopped

½ small white onion, finely chopped

2 tablespoons all-purpose flour

¼ cup (63 ml) water

1 large sprig epazote

2 x-cat-ik chiles or a mild yellow pepper

THE FRITTERS
melted pork lard or vegetable oil for frying

3 eggs, separated

2 tablespoons all-purpose flour

1 cup cazón asado frito (recipe precedes)

Heat the water in a wide saucepan. Crush together the peppercorns, garlic, and *achiote* paste
with salt. Add this to the pan and continue cooking over low heat.

Heat the oil in a skillet, add the chile dulce and onion, and fry until the onion is translucent. Add to the pan.

Mix the flour with the water to make a smooth paste. Add some of the hot broth to dilute

[CONTINUED]

and smooth out any lumps. Stir this into the broth and cook for about 10 minutes. Add the *epazote* and x-cat-ik. Set aside and keep warm.

Heat the lard or oil in a skillet over low heat while you prepare the fritters.

Beat the egg whites until stiff but not dry, gradually add the yolks, and continue beating. Gradually add the flour and stir in the *cazón*. Add salt only if necessary.

Carefully add the mixture in tablespoonfuls to the hot oil and fry until golden brown underneath, about 4 minutes, then turn over and fry on the other side. Drain on paper toweling. Keep stirring the mixture while you're cooking, because the *cazón* tends to drop to the bottom of the beaten eggs.

TO SERVE: Carefully transfer the *tortitas* to the broth and heat through for about 5 minutes. Serve in deep bowls.

JAROCHITOS EN FORMA DE TAMALES

Sra. Manuela Chuc

❀

[MAKES 24 TAMALES]

JAROCHITOS ARE EATEN HOT AND JUST AS THEY ARE, FOR BREAKFAST OR SUP-PER. THEY CAN ALSO BE SERVED IN A LIGHT CALDO OR A SOUP OF BLACK BEANS as a midday meal (recipe follows).

2¼ *pounds (1 generous kg)* masa *for tortillas or tamales (page 530)*
11 *ounces (315 g) dark pork lard, melted, about a scant 1½ cups (350 ml)*
salt to taste
1¼ *cups (313 ml) firmly packed* cazón asado frito *(page 362)*

Have ready 48 dried corn husks (2 per *tamal*) and 48 strips of dried corn husks (2 for each *tamal*), plus extra for lining the steamer, *or* 24 pieces of banana leaf 5 by 8 inches (13 by 20 cm) and 24 ties. Prepare the *tamale* steamer by putting coins in the water of the bottom section. Line the rack with more leaves and set over low heat.

Beat the *masa*, lard, and salt together for about 5 minutes. Take a ball of the dough about

1¾ inches (4.5 cm) in diameter and flatten it out to a circle about 3½ inches (9 cm) across and ½ inch (13 mm) thick. Put 1 heaped teaspoon of the *cazón* filling in the center, fold the dough over the filling, and roll the dough between your palms into a bobbin shape, like an elongated cylinder. Place 2 of the husks together, broad ends in the middle, points at the ends, place the *tamal* in the center, fold the leaves over to cover the *tamal* (don't flatten it), and secure both ends with the ties.

When the water is boiling and the coins jingling, place the *tamales* horizontally in the top of the steamer and cook over lively heat for about 1½ hours or until the *masa* can be rolled easily away from the corn husk. It is always worthwhile to break one open to see if this rather dense *masa* is cooked all the way through.

JAROCHITOS EN CALDO DE FRIJOL

JAROCHOS IN BLACK BEAN BROTH

Sra. María Esther Pérez Campos

❀

[SERVES 4 TO 6]

JAROCHO IS THE NAME FOR A NATIVE OF THE SOUTHERN VERACRUZ COAST, BUT CAN ALSO REFER TO SOMETHING NATIVE AND ROBUST, WHICH THIS DISH definitely is.

8 ounces (225 g) black beans, cleaned and rinsed
1 large sprig epazote
½ medium white onion, roughly chopped
salt to taste
2 tablespoons pork lard, melted
½ small onion, thinly sliced
2 sprigs epazote
1 habanero chile
12 uncooked jarochos *(recipe precedes)*

[CONTINUED]

Put the beans, large *epazote* sprig, chopped onion, and salt into a pan with water that comes about 4 inches (10 cm) above the surface of the beans. Cook over low heat until the skins of the beans are soft. Add salt to taste and cook for 10 minutes more—about 2½ hours, depending on the freshness of the beans. Or cook overnight in a slow cooker.

Puree the contents of the pot in a blender. If the beans are old and the skins extra tough, pass the puree through a fine strainer and discard the debris.

Heat the lard in a skillet, add the sliced onion, 2 *epazote* sprigs, and chile, and fry gently until the onion is translucent. Add the bean puree and cook for about 5 minutes.

Dilute the beans with enough water to make 5 cups (1.25 l), adjust the seasoning, and bring to a simmer. Carefully add the uncooked *jarochos*, cover the pan, and continue cooking over low heat until the *jarochos* float to the top—about 10 minutes. Carefully roll them over to cook on the other side and continue cooking for another 10 minutes.

Serve 2 or 3 *jarochos* in a deep bowl with about ¾ cup (188 ml) of the bean soup.

CHERNA EN SU JUGO

GROUPER COOKED IN ITS JUICE

Sra. María Dolores Cel

❂

[SERVES 6]

THE NAME OF THIS RECIPE IS CERTAINLY AN UNDERSTATEMENT. IT IS ONE OF THE MOST DELICIOUS WAYS TO COOK FISH I HAVE COME ACROSS IN MEXICO.

Sra. Cel is one of those passionately traditional cooks who happily spent hours reeling off a string of her everyday recipes from memory. She then invited me to go and cook with her and, of course, eat with her and the family—a huge one that congregated from all over town when they heard of the incredible number of dishes she was going to prepare.

For this recipe she uses a whole, large fish or two smaller ones and slashes the skin on both sides so that the seasoning will penetrate the flesh. Of course, the sauce is richer with the gelatinous quality of the bones and head.

As if it needed any more flavor, this dish is served with *salsa de chile*, page 349.

heaped ½ teaspoon cumin seeds

12 peppercorns

1 tablespoon dried oregano

5 garlic cloves, peeled

2 teaspoons achiote paste

2 teaspoons salt or to taste

*2 groupers, about 2½ pounds (1.125 kg) each, or 2¼ pounds
(1 generous kg) fish steaks about 1 inch (2.5 cm) thick*

6 tablespoons bitter orange juice or substitute (page 529)

¼ cup (63 ml) olive oil

1 small bunch flat-leaf parsley with stems, roughly chopped

1 medium white onion, broiled

2 chiles dulces or 1 green bell pepper, broiled, seeded, and thinly sliced

1 pound (450 g) tomatoes, thinly sliced

4 x-cat-ik chiles or a mild yellow pepper, broiled and left whole

Grind the cumin, peppercorns, and oregano together in a coffee or spice grinder. Crush the garlic, add the ground spices, *achiote*, and salt, and mix to a paste. Spread this paste on both sides of the fish, pour on the orange juice, and set aside to season for a minimum of 30 minutes.

Heat the oil in a skillet, add the parsley, onion, and chiles dulces, and fry without browning, for about 3 minutes. Add the sliced tomatoes and continue cooking for about 5 minutes. The mixture should still be juicy. Place the fish in a shallow pan and spread with the tomato mixture. Add the whole x-cat-ik chiles, cover, and cook over medium heat, shaking the pan from time to time, until the fish is just cooked—about 15 minutes, depending on the thickness of the fish, weight of the pan, heat, etc. Set aside to season, off the heat, for about 10 minutes before serving.

IBES GUISADOS

STEWED WHITE BEANS

Sra. Concepción Gala

❂

[SERVES 6 TO 8]

SRA. CONCEPCIÓN GALA HAS A RANCH ON THE ROAD TO CHETUMAL AND IS USED TO COOKING GAME SHOT ON THE RANCH. AS IT BECOMES SCARCE AND AT TIMES illegal, she falls back on the traditional food of her childhood.

This is an unusual way of cooking dried white beans and makes for an excellent vegetarian dish. *Ibes*, dried white beans, together with small black beans are those most commonly used in the cooking of this region.

1 pound (450 g) dried small white beans
1 medium white onion, roughly sliced
2 large sprigs epazote
salt to taste
8 ounces (225 g) cabbage, finely shredded, about 4 cups (1 l)
1 heaped teaspoon achiote seasoning paste (recado rojo)*
8 eggs

Run your hands through the beans, picking out any little bits of earth or stray debris. Rinse, put into a pan with the onion and *epazote,* and add water to come 4 inches (10 cm) above the surface of the beans. Cook over low heat—or in a slow cooker—until they are tender but not falling apart (about 3 to 4 hours, depending on the age of the beans). Add more water if necessary to make about 7 cups (1.75 l). Bring the beans to a simmer again, add the salt, cabbage, and *achiote,* and bring to a simmer.

Continue cooking until the cabbage is almost tender—about 5 minutes. Carefully add the eggs one at a time—it is best to break each egg over a saucer first and then slide it into the broth. Cover the pot and cook until the eggs are firmly set. Serve in deep bowls with 1 egg per person and plenty of the cabbage and broth.

*See *The Art of Mexican Cooking,* page 427.

PESCADO EN MACUM

Sra. Socorro Castro

✷

[SERVES 6]

IT IS MUCH MORE COMMON FOR A HOUSEWIFE TO USE A WHOLE FISH THAN
FILLETS. YOU COULD USE A WHOLE GROUPER OR SNAPPER OR THICK FILLETS
from either of these fish. They should be cooked in one layer.

*2½ pounds (1.125 kg) fillets of fish about 1 inch (2.5 cm) thick,
cut into 6 serving pieces*

½ cup (125 ml) fresh lime juice mixed with 1 cup (250 ml) water

½ teaspoon cumin seeds

12 peppercorns

1 tablespoon dried oregano

6 garlic cloves, peeled

2 teaspoons achiote paste

salt to taste

4 to 6 tablespoons bitter orange juice or substitute (page 529)

6 tablespoons olive oil

1 medium white onion, thinly sliced

1 pound (450 g) tomatoes, thinly sliced

2 x-cat-ik chiles, grilled

banana leaves to cover (optional)

Rinse the fish with the lime juice and water and pat dry. In a coffee or spice grinder, grind
together the cumin, peppercorns, and oregano. Crush 2 cloves of the garlic, add the ground
spices and *achiote* paste with salt, and mix well. Dilute to spreading consistency with the
orange juice. Spread this on both sides of the fish and set aside to season for at least 30
minutes.

Heat the oil in a skillet that will hold the fish in one layer. Fry the remaining 4 cloves of
garlic for about 30 seconds or until golden, remove from the oil, and discard. Add the fish and

[CONTINUED]

fry for about 3 minutes on each side. Remove and set aside. Add the onion to the pan and fry for a few seconds—they should not brown—add the tomatoes, and fry over fairly high heat for 3 minutes. Put the fish back into the pan, add the x-cat-ik chiles, and cook, covered, over gentle heat for about 15 minutes or until the fish is just tender. I like to set it aside for about 10 minutes before serving to develop flavor.

BISTECK EN VIRE VIRA

STEAK AND ONIONS CAMPECHANA

Sra. Concepción Gala

❋

[SERVES 6]

THIS IS A VERY SIMPLE, QUICK RECIPE FOR SMALL STEAKS, USUALLY SERVED WITH FRIED PLANTAIN, PLAIN POTATOES, AND A SALAD OF LETTUCE, TOMATOES, and radishes. Always leave some fat on the steaks for flavor—you don't have to eat it.

½ teaspoon black peppercorns
heaped ½ teaspoon dried oregano
3 garlic cloves
salt to taste
5 tablespoons bitter orange juice or substitute (page 529)
6 small steaks about ½ inch (13 mm) thick, lightly pounded
2 tablespoons pork lard or oil
1 medium white onion, thinly sliced

Crush the peppercorns, oregano, and garlic together with salt. Dilute with the orange juice. Season the steaks on both sides. Stack on top of one another and set aside to season for at least 30 minutes.

Heat the lard and when very hot sear 3 of the steaks on both sides. Remove and continue with the rest of the steaks. Return to the pan in one layer. Add the onion and fry until browned, then pile on top of the steaks. Cook only until tender.

THE SOUTHERN PACIFIC COAST

Ejotes (green beans)

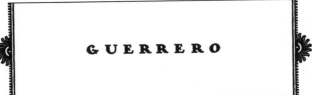

GUERRERO

Chilapa

CHILAPA LIES IN THE FOLDS OF THE NORTHERN SLOPES OF THE SIERRA MADRE DEL SUR AT THE HEAD OF A WIDE VALLEY SURROUNDED BY RUTHLESSLY DEFORESTED RANGES, just over fifty kilometers due east of the state capital, Chilpancingo. It is reached by a narrow highway, paved only in recent years, that winds through passes still mercifully forested with pine and oak (and, unfortunately, with piles of garbage desecrating the landscape; a sad reflection on the mismanagement of the seat of the state government). Without a doubt, its Sunday market is one of the most colorful in all Mexico, despite the crass invasion of stalls that sell imported goods and noise boxes of ridiculous dimensions contaminating the otherwise peaceful flurry of activity. ❀ Chilapa on a Sunday provides a fascinating showcase for the handicrafts and produce of the indigenous peoples who converge there from the surrounding villages and for the remarkable culinary talents of the local women. ❀ The town was founded in 1533—or '63, by the Augustinians, depending on which source of information you choose; the Augustinian version is according to the *Augustine Chronicle* by Padre Grijalva. The high standards of culture and learning during the centuries has earned it the name "La Atenas del Sur, cuna de las artes y letras" (The Athens of the South, cradle of arts and letters), but its Sunday market offers such a variety of delicious foods and breads, both sophisticated and simple, that I would also dub it the "Lyons of Mexico." ☀ I first became aware of the cooking of Chilapa when my dear friend Maria Dolores gave me a little book on the subject in 1984, the year it was published. I have visited Chilapa many times since, and it was with considerable amusement that I read the comments at the beginning of *Cocina Tradicional de Chilapa* by "The Researcher." He says getting the women to divulge their recipes amounted to a "heroic feat." "There was always one person who considered herself the expert on a certain dish and guarded her secrets like a veritable treasure. Another cook would ask: What did she tell you? And she gave you pure rubbish; *que barbaridad*, she said two onions, I only use a half." ☀ His experience in staying in one of those dreadful hotels was exactly the same as mine. "Ah, that hotel I will never forget! The patio had been rented for a *quinceaños* (coming-of-age party) that finished at dawn with music *sui generis*, very Americanized. I was kept awake by alcoholic brawling. The second time in the same hotel I had brought a fighting cock for a friend. There was nowhere else to keep it but in my room. At one o'clock in the morning, it started crowing—I shot up in my bed. It continued every hour, on the hour. On another occasion, it was the 12th of December, and at four o'clock in the morning a thunderous noise awoke me. In my comatose state I thought that the ghosts of General Zapata had returned to take the town: it was the sound of rockets. I started to doze off again when the loudspeakers of the Cathedral blared out an invitation to the devout to take part in the Celebration of the Virgin of Guadalupe, whose day it was. And on another day, it was a group of Evangelists who started singing their religious hymns at 11 o'clock at night. I had better not go on."

I could add to that: a cow lowing all night in a makeshift stable behind my room and a fractious baby to boot. Staying in those out-of-the-way places with their so-called hotels is not a comfortable business, and Chilapa can boast three of the worst. Food research at this level can be a very tiring business as I have found out to my detriment, I am sorry to say, over the many years that I have been traveling in Mexico.

Chilapa, alas, is not today a beautiful place, despite its fascinating Sunday market. Through the years earthquakes have taken their toll, the cathedral has burned, and in its place is a tasteless cement structure. It is a very devout town—it even has a seminary—and I cannot help wishing that the aesthetic education of recent generations of priests could equal that of their early predecessors.

For the market, the very first *marchantes* from the more remote villages start arriving on Friday afternoon to stake out their claims for places along the sidewalks to display their simple produce: miniature pineapples and watermelons, elongated avocados, starchy triangular bananas, all securely packed in hand-woven *tolcopetes* lined and covered with banana leaves. There are cakes of raw sugar (*panocha*) cunningly packaged and neatly tied with the *bagazo* leaf of the sugarcane.

The pace quickens Saturday morning as the trucks adapted for traversing rough terrain disgorge their passengers, laden with bundles of all shapes and sizes—live chickens and turkeys, even gas tanks from villages with enchanting names such as Atzacoaloya, Ayahualco, Pantitlán, and Ayahualulco!

Outside the main covered market a brisk trade has already started in *atole blanco, tamales dulces, tamales con rajas y salsa*, and the most delicious, *tacos de chivo*, goat. Meanwhile vendors in the streets are displaying their fruits, vegetables, and herbs. I always head for the main street that leads into town from the highway. There, sitting on the sidewalks, are the countrywomen with actually very little to sell, just what they've been able to gather from the wild or grow: small piles of *colorín* (coral) flowers, *pitos*, sweet, acid, and juicy *piñuelas*, or *timbiriches* from the plant *Bromelia karatas*. There are live black *chumilines* (a species of beetle) for the aficionados of their peppery liquid, a *frijol silvestre* (wild bean) known as *epatlaxtli*—a staple food of the rural areas prepared with eggs and tomatoes *en especia* or *en adobo* for the Lenten period. The bean's red flowers are also cooked and mixed with eggs for *tortitas*, or fritters. There often is a young woman wandering around with a bundle of tall stalks of *tlanipan*—*clanipan* as they say (*hoja santa*)—with just a few leaves left on top. Stripped of their stringy exterior, the stems are cut up and either chewed raw or cooked with eggs or perhaps put in a stew.

There are many little piles of small, very shiny red onions—the preferred onion for accompanying many of the local dishes, *camotes*, or sweet potatoes, of many different colors, shiny red dried beans called *montañeros* that are particularly delicious, and brilliant red misshapen tomatoes, bulbous and gathered in at the top. These really taste and smell like the tomatoes of old, before the tasteless *jitomates guajes* (plum tomatoes) were genetically engineered.

With the summer rains come other foods, many of them gathered growing wild: delicate *guias* called simply *enredadores* from Villa Flores, the sweet "*pepinos*," a cucumberlike fruit called *cuajilotes* (*Parmentiera edulis*) to be eaten raw or prepared as a *remedio*, cure, for the stomach, a cure from the town of Tepatlazingo.

A woman from Zacualapa was selling small bunches of cooked bulbs that she called *cebollín*, or *cebolleta*. Surprisingly, the flesh was layered but starchy, reminiscent of the texture of a chestnut. There were long *hojas de milpa*, leaves of the cornstalk for wrapping bean *tamales*, and a few huge green-hued *toronjas* (grapefruit). After peeling off the thick outer layer of the flesh, they are coarse textured but sweet and juicy. There were some herbs that were new to me, and the vendor very patiently answered my questions and repeated the unfamiliar names: a wide-leafed *pepicha* called *escobeta* and *cocolache*, a small serrated leaf with an even more pungent flavor. And *copanquelite*, a variation of *papaloquelite*, and this same better-known *papaloquelite* was also named *tepelcacho*—all of these herbs are eaten raw in tacos.

There were bunches of wild anise, *anís de campo*, with the enchanting name of *tlalahuacate*, used for flavoring *atoles* or for giving flavor to a simple variation of *pozole* using fresh corn with *calabacitas* and guajillo chiles. Each area has its own chile, or so it seems. One could find tiny *acatlecos*, *mochitecos*, and *joyeños*, both fresh and dried, depending on the time of year. There could be found the larger dried varieties also from La Joya, confusingly called *ancho* (a small smooth-skinned chile that rather resembles the *taviche* of Oaxaca), and the fuller *chilaca* that resembles a thin-skinned smaller *ancho*, both of which are used for the local *mole rojo*.

But apart from the foods, it is mandatory to visit the street where crafts are sold. Fine and colorful basketry is a specialty as well as the delightful *artesanias* from neighboring villages: delicate *"torres"* of fireworks, *tigrillo* (tiger) masks of all sizes, painted wooden figures, and a variety of toys, fantasies in wood or straw demonstrating the neverending wit and creativity of the native artisans.

The traditional Sunday morning breakfast for Chilapeños and visitors alike is *pozole blanco*. One of the renowned *pozole* makers of the town, Cenaida Rodríguez, arrives with her husband before dawn with their *pozole* that has been cooking slowly overnight to serve to the very early morning risers or those who have spent the night sleeping on the sidewalks or under the *portales* of the Palacio Municipal to shelter from the rain. *Pozole blanco* is almost mandatory Monday and Sunday mornings while *pozole verde* (see *The Art of Mexican Cooking*) is served from 11:00 A.M. to 3:00 P.M. on Thursdays. Local legend has it that *pozole* was created in Chilapa, and I am sure this boast has created some heated discussions among the dedicated evening *pozole* eaters from the state of Jalisco.

It is said that before the diocese of Chilapa existed, the church was administered from Puebla. On the occasion of a visit from a church dignitary, women from all over the area got together to organize an appropriate welcome for him. They knew a lot of people would be attending, so they prepared a very large quantity of food and in particular corn for tortillas, but had forgotten that there were not enough women to prepare said tortillas. After a fruitless search for tortilla makers, somebody suggested that they should add pork and seasonings to the corn and serve it as is, along with onion, lime, and chile, and call it *pozole*. When everyone applauded, they realized how much people, including the prelate, had enjoyed the food.

It was so tasty that the idea of *pozole* spread to other parts of Mexico to become the national dish—although Chilapa can still boast of the greater number of variations. According to Father Salazar, this legend dates from the eighteenth century, and the word *pozole* comes from the *Náhuatl* word for "edible mixture": *pozolli*.

The long table of Cenaida's food stand is set with toasted and ground chile guajillos (they can also be *de árbol* or *piquín*), oregano, lime halves, and red onion, all finely chopped but kept separate. Meanwhile, *tostaditas*, *chicharrón*, and avocado can be added on request at an extra charge. Occasionally someone will ask for canned sardines to be mashed into a serving of *pozole* or request a raw, whole egg to be cooked in the heat of the sturdy broth. You pay for the amount of meat that is put into your serving, and many of the humbler *comensales* will order just corn and broth. That morning conversation was scarce; everyone was concentrating on eating, to be interrupted only by a polite exchange of condiments from one side of the table to the other.

In the meantime the central plaza had been transformed overnight, the ground covered with commodities of all kinds: dried fish of all sizes, large orange-colored dried shrimps, sacks of beans, and rows of clay-colored, rather austere but functional *jarras* of *barro* with brick red rims, almost all of them devoid of any decoration, *comales*, perforated *ollas*, *pichanchas* for rinsing the *nixtamal* and *pozoleras*. I was told that the original bowls for *pozole* had rounded bottoms and stood on a ring of woven palm, and while they are still made this way, they have now been given three legs to support them.

Along one side of the *jardín* large trestle tables were set up for the large baskets of luscious-looking sweet rolls of all shapes and sizes: *viudas*, *sobados*, *caracoles*, *rellenos*, *volcanes*, and *hojaldras*, all baked to a rich, dark brown. There was *pan de requeson* (ricotta) and flat *panocheras* filled with the locally produced natural sugar. As I was leaving, I caught sight of a very large flat bread filled with that excruciating pink-colored paste so loved by the village bakers. The vendors laughingly called them "americanos."

As the day progressed and the *pozole* supplies ran out, they were replaced by another wave of regional dishes, the variety and quality of which I have rarely seen in Mexican markets. The women who prepare them have devoted much of their lives to cooking their local dishes for the Sunday market and for the interminable rounds of *compromisos* in which the large, well-to-do families are constantly involved. I sadly pass up the little round *chalupas* typical of the area—sold ready-made in large plastic bags—and head for the delicious *quesadillas de verduras* (recipe on page 382) served with a *salsa verde* and crumbled cheese. If, while you're eating, an old lady passes with *tamales*, stop her and try one—they are exquisite!—but then again maybe I was just lucky. They were unforgettable.

Even if you think you can't manage it, try at least a piece of *tostada* spread with *frijoles adobados*, shredded pork and chicken, and lots of trimmings before moving on to the more substantial dishes. María Gutíerrez's *mole verde* is quite simple but absolutely delicious (recipe on page 380) served with corn tortillas into which you wrap a piece of raw purple onion, and sprinkle a little juice from a *lima agria*. Another specialty of hers is the local *mole rojo* made of chiles from La Joya accompanied by *sopa de pan*—a savory bread pudding made with chicken livers and hard-cooked eggs seasoned with saffron and bitter orange juice.

Another of the Sunday cooks selling their very special foods is María de Jesús Sánchez, famous for her *gallina rellena*, a very complicated version of a stuffed hen that is always served at weddings. Equally complex is *fiambre*—pig's feet, chicken, and shredded beef, each with its own flavorings and *agrito*, an acidy dressing used both on beef and with the vegetables that adorn the dish.

You may be lucky enough to try the barbecued pig's head or some of Aida Mendoza's *marrano relleno*—stuffed pig, a preparation typical of the Guerrero coast. In her book, apart from these rather elaborate recipes, Señora Casarrubias records simple but very tasty and healthy recipes. For example, *panile*, a mix of *epazote* and green chiles ground together with salt for seasoning freshly roasted or boiled corn-on-the-cob. And *tlanipal*, the stalk of the *hoja santa* that I have mentioned before, but served raw with green chiles, the juice of *lima agria*, and *salsa de dedos*, finger sauce—the ingredients are mashed between the fingers rather than cut up and mixed beforehand.

There is *chacualole*, a sauce made of the local grapefruit, which is sour and rather coarse, and the simplest of soups, using the inside fleshy part of a pumpkin with *guajillo chiles* and *epazote*. And *mole de pimienta*, a pepper *mole* that is meatless, also made with *chiles guajillos*, *tomates verdes*, and spices. If you have a sweet tooth, there are plenty of *helados*, ices, and small plates of *bien me sabe*, a type of custard decorated with raisins. You can have a turnover of purple-hued sweet potato. But do try to find the elusive lady renowned for her delicate *empanadas de arroz*—rice turnovers, that is. The variety of foods in this market seems infinite and the hours you spend there on a Sunday far too few.

PAN DE HUEVO CORRIENTE

ORDINARY EGG BREAD

❂

[MAKES 4 ROUND LOAVES ABOUT 6 INCHES (15.5 CM) IN DIAMETER, 10 OUNCES (285 G) EACH]

ALTHOUGH THE NAME *PAN CORRIENTE* SOUNDS DEPRECATING, THE RECIPE DOES IN FACT PRODUCE A DELICIOUS *PAN DULCE*, SEMISWEET YEAST BREAD, suitable for making the *capirotada* (bread pudding) recipe in this book (page 64). Please don't try to hurry with this dough; the slow rising does give a wonderful flavor, as does the lard. But if you really balk at using lard, substitute vegetable shortening.

1¾ ounces (52 g) or a very heaped ⅓ cup crumbled cake yeast

4½ ounces (130 g) (½ cup plus 2 tablespoons) sugar

approximately ¼ cup (63 ml) warmed whole milk

1 pound (450 g) all-purpose flour, about 4 rounded cups (1.1 ml),
plus a little extra for dusting, warmed and sifted

3 ounces (85 g) or a rounded ⅓ cup pork lard, softened,
with extra for greasing

1½ teaspoons finely ground sea salt

4 eggs, lightly beaten

brown sugar to sprinkle the breads (optional)

Have ready 2 large oven trays, lightly greased.

Cream the yeast with the sugar and warmed milk and put into the bowl of an electric mixer. Gradually beat in the flour, lard, and salt along with the eggs and continue beating until you have a smooth, sticky mass—about 5 minutes. Throw some of the extra flour

[CONTINUED]

around the bowl and beat again until the dough pulls away from the side of the bowl and clings to the dough hook.

Cover the bowl with plastic wrap and a towel (it is not necessary to turn the dough out into a clean bowl) and leave it to rise in a warm place—about 70°F (20°C)—until it has doubled in volume, about 6 hours.

Turn the dough out onto a lightly floured board and cut into 4 equal pieces. Roll each piece into a large, smooth ball and lightly grease the outside. Flatten them into disks about ½ inch (13 mm) thick and place 2 on each tray. Cover with greased plastic wrap and again set out in a warm place to rise to 1½ times its present size—about 1½ hours.

Meanwhile, heat the oven to 400°F (205°C). Bake one tray at a time until the bread is a deep brown color. After 15 to 20 minutes it will begin to rise quite a bit in the oven. *Optional:* Sprinkle the top with brown sugar just before baking.

MOLE VERDE

GREEN MOLE

Sra. María Gutierrez, Chilapa

✸

[SERVES 6]

THIS IS A SIMPLE BUT DELICIOUS *MOLE VERDE* TYPICAL OF THE REGION USING SIMPLE INGREDIENTS THAT ARE FOUND THERE, WITH A PREDOMINATING FLAVOR of *hoja santa, epazote,* and the sharp acid flavor of the *lengua de vaca*—a wild sorrel. The crisp accompaniments are unique: a layer of red onion—like a spoon—containing the juice of a tart *lima,* wrapped inside a corn tortilla.

THE MEAT

1½ pounds (675 g) stewing pork with some fat, cut into cubes of about 1½ inches (4 cm), or 2¼ pounds (1 generous kg) country-style pork spareribs

¼ medium white onion, coarsely chopped

2 garlic cloves, peeled

salt to taste

6 ounces (180 g) unhulled raw pumpkin seeds, about 2 cups (500 ml)

6 ounces (180 g) tomates verdes, *husks removed, rinsed,*
and coarsely chopped

6 large leaves lengua de vaca *or sorrel, rinsed, stems removed,*
and coarsely chopped

4 leaves hoja santa, *stems and veins removed, coarsely chopped*

8 large sprigs epazote, *5 coarsely chopped, 3 left whole*

4 jalapeño or 6 serrano chiles, coarsely chopped, or to taste

approximately ¼ cup (63 ml) pork lard or vegetable oil

Cover the meat with water in a heavy pan and add the onion, garlic, and salt. Bring to a simmer and let simmer until tender but not too soft, about 40 minutes. Drain the meat, reserving the broth. Measure the broth and make more with water or reduce over high heat to about 5 cups (1.25 l). Set aside.

Toast the pumpkin seeds in an ungreased pan, turning them over and shaking the pan from time to time to prevent them from burning. Set them aside to cool and then grind them in an electric grinder to a fine powder. Put 1½ cups (375 ml) of the broth in a blender, gradually adding the *tomates verdes, lengua de vaca, hoja santa,* chopped *epazote,* and chiles, blending as smooth as possible.

Heat the lard in a flameproof casserole in which you are going to serve the *mole* and fry the blended ingredients, stirring and scraping the bottom of the pan to prevent sticking; cook for about 25 minutes. Add the rest of the *epazote.*

Stir ½ cup (125 ml) of the broth into the pumpkin seeds until you have a smooth consistency and gradually stir into the cooked ingredients. Continue cooking over low heat, stirring constantly for 10 more minutes. Take care that the pumpkin seed mixture does not form into lumps; if this happens, put the sauce back into the blender and blend until smooth. Add the remaining broth and the meat, adjust the salt, and cook over low heat until well seasoned, about 15 minutes. If the sauce is too thick, add a little water to dilute.

QUESADILLAS DE VERDURAS

VEGETABLE QUESADILLAS

Chilapa

✺

[MAKES FROM 18 TO 20 3½-INCH (9-CM) QUESADILLAS]

I LOVE THESE QUESADILLAS AND COULD MAKE A WHOLE MEAL FROM THEM. FRY THEM EVEN IF YOU CAN'T NORMALLY BEAR FRIED FOODS. THE LOCAL COOKS boil the vegetables separately, but I prefer to stew them together to retain flavor and nutrients. These *quesadillas* are served in the morning in the Chilapa market on a bed of lettuce leaves, with a green tomato sauce and crumbled *queso fresco*.

2 tablespoons vegetable oil
1 cup (250 ml) ¼-inch (7-mm) diced carrot
1 cup (250 ml) ¼-inch (7-mm) diced chayote
¼ medium white onion, finely chopped
salt to taste
1½ cups (375 ml) water
1 cup (250 ml) chopped green beans
1 cup (250 ml) diced zucchini
1 cup (250 ml) corn kernels, not too sweet
4 serrano chiles, finely chopped
18 ounces (510 g) masa for tortillas (page 530), 2 cups (500 ml)
vegetable oil for frying
romaine lettuce leaves
approximately 1½ cups (375 ml) cooked salsa verde
approximately ¾ cup (188 ml) crumbled queso fresco

Heat the 2 tablespoons oil in a shallow pan, add the carrot, *chayote*, onion, salt, and ½ cup (125 ml) of the water, cover, and cook over medium heat for about 8 minutes. Add the vegetables, chiles, and remaining water, cover the pan, and cook over low heat, shaking the pan now and again to prevent the contents from sticking. Cook until the vegetables are tender but not soft.

Set aside to cool a bit. The mixture should be moist but not too juicy—strain off any extra liquid and drink it.

Divide the *masa* into balls of about ¾ inch (2 cm) in diameter and cover them with a damp cloth while you work with the first ones. Put about ½ inch vegetable oil in a skillet and heat well. Using a tortilla press and plastic bags, press out a ball of the dough to about 3½ inches (9 cm) in diameter and proceed making *quesadillas*, filling the raw dough with a heaped tablespoon of the vegetable filling. Carefully fold the dough over the filling and fry in the hot oil until crisp and golden on both sides. Drain on paper toweling. Serve immediately on a bed of lettuce with some of the green sauce and a generous sprinkling of cheese.

ADOBO

Sra. María de Jesús Sánchez

❋

[MAKES ABOUT 3 CUPS (750 ML)]

THIS ADOBO MAY BE SERVED EITHER AS A SEPARATE DISH OR MIXED INTO BEANS FOR *FRIJOLES DE NOVIA* (RECIPE FOLLOWS). ANY LEFTOVERS CAN, OF course, be frozen.

> 1 pound (450 g) stewing pork with a little fat,
> cut into ¾-inch (2-cm) cubes
>
> salt to taste
>
> 9 guajillo chiles, seeds and veins removed
>
> 2 tablespoons pork lard
>
> 6 peppercorns
>
> 4 cloves
>
> ⅛ teaspoon cumin seeds
>
> ½-inch (13-mm) cinnamon stick
>
> ¼ teaspoon dried oregano, crumbled
>
> 2 garlic cloves, peeled
>
> 1 small tomato, roughly chopped
>
> 2 bay leaves

[CONTINUED]

Cover the meat with water in a saucepan, add salt, and cook over low heat until tender—about 45 minutes. Drain, reserving the broth.

Cover the chiles with hot water and leave to soak for about 15 minutes. Heat the lard in a skillet and fry the meat lightly, pressing it down to shred it coarsely. Remove with a slotted spoon and set it aside.

Put ½ cup (125 ml) of the broth into a blender, add the spices, oregano, garlic, tomato, and bay leaves, and blend as smoothly as possible. Add this to the heated lard in the skillet and fry for about 1 minute. Add the drained chiles to the blender along with another cup of broth and blend until smooth. Add this to the pan while pressing it through a fine-mesh strainer to extract as much as possible of the juice and flesh. Discard the debris. Continue frying for about 5 minutes while continually scraping the bottom of the pan to prevent sticking. Add the meat with salt to taste and continue cooking for 10 more minutes. The mixture should be on the dry side.

FRIJOLES DE NOVIA

BRIDE'S BEANS

Casa Pilli Restaurant

❂

[MAKES APPROXIMATELY 3½ CUPS (875 ML)]

ACCORDING TO THE NEWLY PUBLISHED LITTLE BOOK *EL ARTE CULINARIO DE CHILAPA* COORDINATED BY THE OWNER OF THE MOST TRADITIONAL RESTAU-rant in Chilapa, Señora Magdalena Casarrubias Guzman, these beans, also called *frijoles adobados,* were so named because they were always served at weddings. Nowadays they are served almost daily either as a spread for *tostadas* or to accompany a *mole.* They are elaborately decorated with radish flowers, strips of a fresh cheese, jalapeño chiles *en escabeche,* and lettuce leaves.

The delicious local red beans, *montañeros,* or *ayocotes* are the beans usually used for this dish, but others such as *canarios,* pintos, or *flor de mayo* can also be used. These beans have a strong flavor, and a little goes a long way. You can always freeze the leftovers.

8 ounces (225 g) red, canario, or pinto beans
½ medium white onion, coarsely chopped
2 bay leaves
3 garlic cloves, peeled
salt to taste
1 tablespoon lard
½ medium white onion, sliced
4 ounces (115 g) chorizo
1 cup (250 ml) adobo (recipe precedes)
¼ teaspoon dried oregano, crumbled

Rinse and pick over the beans. Cover them with hot water, add the chopped onion, bay leaves, and garlic, and bring to a simmer. Continue cooking until the skins of the beans are soft. Add salt and continue cooking for about 10 minutes more. Strain the beans, reserving the broth for a soup—or drink it. Blend the beans into a textured puree and set aside.

Heat the lard in a skillet, add the sliced onion, and fry for a few seconds without browning. Remove them and set them aside. Remove the casing from the *chorizo* and crumble into the pan, cooking it gently over low heat until the fat has been rendered out and is just beginning to brown. Add the *adobo* and fry, stirring and scraping the bottom of the pan to prevent any food from sticking—about 8 minutes. Add the pureed beans and mix well. Continue cooking and stirring for about 10 more minutes—the mixture should almost dry out. Stir in the oregano and heat it all through before serving.

CHALUPAS DE CHILAPA

❁

[MAKES ABOUT 18 2½-INCH (6.5-CM) CHALUPAS]

FOR ANYONE LIVING IN MEXICO CITY, A *CHALUPA* IS A SMALL CANOE-SHAPED ANTOJITO OF CORN MASA NAMED AFTER THE SMALL BOATS THAT PLIED THE canals of the floating gardens of Xochimilco. In Puebla, just over 100 kilometers to the southeast, they are round and pinched up around the edge. In Guerrero, many more kilometers to the southwest, they are crisp concave disks of very thin *masa*. Traditionally the *masa* should be of the wide white corn kernels called *cacahuazintle*, or *maiz pozolero*. The kernels are cooked in a solution of water and lime, a bit longer than if they were being prepared for tortilla dough and left to soak overnight. All the outer skin-shells are rubbed off and the corn ground to a very smooth *masa*. It is delicious! However, for those enthusiasts who will take the time to make *chalupas* but can't go through the trouble, use a really good corn tortilla *masa* (but not the prepared flours like Quaker masa harina or any of their equivalents in Mexico).

The instructions tell you to make a small ball and press it out to a thin, concave disk, which takes some doing! I press the *masa* over the curved base of an individual egg poacher, which works quite well. I then put the whole thing into the hot oil until it is crisp and a deep golden color on the outside. It will then come away easily from the mold, and now you must fry it on the other side. The *chalupa* has to be deep to hold the brothy sauce that moistens the meat. It is then trimmed with a slice of raw onion and a small piece of chipotle *en adobo*. The first time I came across these *chalupas* was in a little *cenaduría* in Chilpancingo, where they were served with a pineapple *atole*. I ate six but could have eaten more because I can't resist crispy things.

> 8 to 10 ounces (225 to 285 g) masa *for tortillas*
> *(about 1 rounded cup/275 ml)*
> *vegetable oil for frying*
> *meat for* chalupas *(recipe follows)*
> *sauce for* chalupas *(recipe follows)*
> *18 thin slices white onion*
> *about 9 chipotle chiles* en adobo

Roll the *masa* into evenly round spheres of about 1 inch (2.5 cm) in diameter. Form them concavely as suggested above or flatten them out in a tortilla press to a size roughly 2½ inches (6.5 cm) in diameter and shape them into concave disks. Heat about ½ inch vegetable oil in a skillet and fry the *chalupas* over high heat until quite crisp. Drain them well and trim them with a few strips of meat, 1 tablespoon of the brothy sauce, a little piece of onion, and half a *chipotle*. Serve immediately.

MEAT FOR CHALUPAS

[MAKES APPROXIMATELY 1 HEAPED CUP (265 ML)]

1 pound (450 g) boneless stewing pork, cut into 1-inch (2.5-cm) cubes
salt to taste

Put the pork, water just to cover, and salt in a pan and cook over low heat until tender, about 45 minutes. Leave the meat to cool off in the broth. Drain, reserving the broth. Shred the meat, discarding the fat and sinew. Set aside and keep it warm (some cooks fry the meat, but I think it is better just as it is).

SAUCE FOR CHALUPAS

[MAKES APPROXIMATELY 2 CUPS (500 ML)]

8 ounces (225 ml) small tomates verdes
2 serrano chiles
2 guajillo chiles, seeds and veins removed
1 tablespoon lard
1 tablespoon piloncillo or dark brown sugar
salt to taste

Put the *tomates verdes*, serranos, and guajillos into a small pan. Barely cover with water, put a lid on, and cook over medium heat until the *tomates verdes* are soft. Strain off most of the liquid, then transfer it together with 1 cup (250 ml) of the broth reserved from cooking the pork for the *chalupas* to a blender. Blend until smooth.

Heat the lard in a skillet and add the blended ingredients, pressing them through a fine-mesh strainer. Cook over medium heat. Add the sugar and salt and continue cooking, never forgetting to stir well and to scrape the bottom of the pan so that nothing scorches and sticks to it. Cook until the mixture reduces and thickens—about 5 minutes. Set aside and keep warm.

OAXACA

To EVEN BEGIN TO WRITE ABOUT THE FOODS OF OAXACA IS A FORMIDABLE TASK. THIS IS BY FAR THE MOST COMPLEX AREA IN MEXICO TO KNOW AND UNDERSTAND. THE DIFFIcult terrain, some of it still without paved roads, the many cultural groups, and the microclimates that produce the different types of chiles, herbs, and wild edible plants and how they are used could be the study of a lifetime. In my other books over the years I have published many recipes from Oaxaca that only begin to scratch the surface of these diverse cuisines. Here I would like to give more of an overview and tell you a little more about my travels in this fascinating state. ☀ My first trip to Oaxaca, and on to Chiapas, was just over thirty years ago. My friend Irene Nicholson, a stringer for the *Times* of London and poetess, and I decided to go and see the ceremonies in Zinacantán and the city of Oaxaca as we passed through. With much trepidation, my foreign correspondent husband, Paul, agreed to let me drive the *New York Times'* Triumph Mark II. It was the longest journey I had made by car, but I was confident after my weeks of instruction about the mechanics of it by a former British army mechanic and fellow owner of a Triumph. In those days the route from Mexico City was more circuitous, through Tehuacán, and then there was the long, lonely stretch of road to Huajuapan de León through bare country with the occasional spectacular cacti and palms. You also had to ford a small but fast-flowing river—it was the rainy season. The road then climbs up through bare hills until its serpentine descent into the valley below. ❈ There is a final long rise, and then, as the road descends on the other side, the land falls away steeply to a valley with serried rows of peaks and sharp drops, the sheer rock faces and soil a brilliant orange-red in contrast to their fresh green capping of new growth. And there below, standing alone majestically with the treeless eroded land as a backdrop, is the sixteenth-century Dominican monastery of Yanhuitlán. It is, without doubt, one of the most spectacular sights in Mexico. There follows a long, straight stretch of road through rocky land, white with limestone, where only palms and cactus thrive (the palms are woven into the baskets for which Oaxaca is so famous, with simple but brilliant-colored designs called *tenates*). On either side of the road are thin strips of cultivation: corn, pumpkins, or wheat where there is a spring of water to irrigate, and the occasional small village or settlement. Later on in the fall you can see the dried cornstalks or other fodder held high above the earth and protected from marauders in the outstretched thick limbs of the trees. The highway rises again and winds along a ridge with the land dropping off steeply on either side, giving distant views of the mountainous country of the *alta mixteca*, much of it bare of trees or thinly covered with tall, dark pines. As the road begins to descend once more for the final stage of the drive, the vegetation is a little more lush with scrubby oaks, pines, and richer undergrowth as the road finally winds down into the extensive valley of Oaxaca.

I have been back many times during the years and think back with nostalgia about tranquil Oaxaca; the air cool and scented, the sky limpid, and the old buildings of moss-green mottled stone standing serene before the senseless modernization that was at first unchecked. It was a magical place and in many ways still is. But now buses roar along, belching out their smoke and fumes, and every driver (certainly every taxi driver) is allowed to zoom loudly through the streets with *macho* exhausts designed to attract attention to the driver.

No writing on the foods of Oaxaca should be without its mention and appreciation of those outstanding regional cooks who (however unwittingly) are devoted to the preservation of their traditional foods using the authentic ingredients and their painstaking preparation: Abigail Mendoza in Teotitlán del Valle, Señoras Esmirna and Juanita of Tlaxiaco, Señora Armandina of Pinotepa, Señoras Oralia Pineda and Amelia Castillo in Juchitán, and my first teachers—the late Micaela of Tezoatlán and Señora Domitila Morales in Oaxaca itself, among many others.

Abigail is *the* star of the Zapotec kitchen. She is immensely capable, and intelligent, with always a smile on her wonderfully expressive face. She and her galaxy of sisters prepare the local traditional foods at her restaurant, Tlalmanalli, in the weaving village of Teotitlán del Valle using age-old methods. It may seem like hard labor to an outsider, but years of practice from an early age allow them to make light work of it. Their late father was much respected in the village and on different occasions was *mayordomo* of church festivities. Owing to her mother's illness, Abigail took over the onerous and responsible task of preparing the food that is ritually served on those occasions, as well as the feast served at the *fandangos*—elaborate weddings—of her brothers. This year, in May, I was invited to attend a *fandango* to mark the wedding of one of the brothers and stood mesmerized for the three days I was there—it lasts five—at the incredible amount of organization that goes into receiving and feeding five hundred guests and fifty helpers, the latter mostly relatives and godmothers. The preparations took over not only the large patio of the house—where two enormous cebu bulls were slaughtered—but an empty field opposite where the tortilla makers were set out under an improvised shelter, kneeling beside their *metates* to give one final grinding to the *masa* before making their individual large tortillas and *tlayudas* on earthenware *comals* over a wood fire.

Eight of the largest pigs were killed the day before, and every part of the animal was used—the skin for *chicharrón*, the entrails fried for *viuces*, the blood for *moronga* sausage, and the meat cut up into hunks and hung up to air in an open area of a neighbor's house. Fifty turkeys, sixty hens, kilos of dried chiles, and what seemed like tons of vegetables were deftly dealt with. Surprisingly the men were sorting the beans and dealing with the turkeys, while the older and more experienced women were directing the others in making the stews, *moles*, *atoles*, and sauces. There was a continual low hum of activity accentuated by the rhythmic grinding of the ingredients for the *tejate*, or *chocolate atole*, in the patio, accompanied by the quiet gossiping and giggling of the young women who were allotted the task. They were kneeling in front of their *metates*—kept exclusively for this use—in two long lines facing each other. They worked for hours, rocking to and fro with the motion and only very occasionally would you see one of them resting. The women of the family hardly slept and by the third day looked tired and disheveled (I quietly thanked the powers that control the universe for not having been born a Zapotec maiden). At every stage of the proceedings there were blessings—over the animals to be sacrificed, for the exchange of gifts between the parents of the couple and the godparents of the wedding,* and distribution of food, and for those who had come to help. There were the ceremonial dances and processions to the family altar with brightly painted *jícaras* full of sugar-flowers. I will leave Abigail to give you the details of the food in a cookbook that I have urged her to write for several years now and which is still in its embryonic stage. Here are two of her recipes, which I use often: *arroz con camarón seco* and *salsa de chile pasilla (de Oaxaca)*.

*The sponsors who agree to take on the expenses of the celebration

ARROZ CON CAMARÓN SECO

RICE WITH DRIED SHRIMP

Srita. Abigail Mendoza

✺

[SERVES 4 TO 6]

ALTHOUGH THIS IS A TYPICAL LENTEN DISH, A MAIN COURSE FOR ABIGAIL, I
LIKE TO SERVE IT AS A FIRST COURSE ANY TIME OF THE YEAR SINCE IT IS A
delicious and different way of cooking rice. Of course there are many variations of this recipe.
In Juchitán it tends to be simpler with the addition of a little pure *achiote* for color and flavor.
In other areas they use the large fleshy-leaved "oregano" (*Plectranthus amboinicus*) instead of
the dried oregano.

*3 ounces (85 g) small dried shrimp,
about 1½ rounded cups (375 ml), firmly packed*

1 cup (250 ml) long-grain white rice, not precooked or converted

2 tablespoons vegetable or olive oil

1 large scallion, including some of the green leaves, chopped

6 serrano chiles

1½ cups (375 ml) water

3 garlic cloves, coarsely chopped

scant ¼ teaspoon cumin seeds

2 cloves

4 ounces (115 g) tomatoes, coarsely chopped, about ¾ cup (188 ml)

¼ teaspoon dried oregano

salt to taste

Rinse the shrimp in cold water to remove the excess salt. Remove the heads and legs and
reserve. Immerse the shrimp in fresh water and leave to soak for 5 minutes. Rinse the rice
twice in cold water and drain well. Heat the oil in a flameproof casserole and stir in the rice
so that the grains get coated evenly with the oil. Cook over medium heat for about 3 minutes,
then add the scallion and serrano chiles and continue cooking, taking care not to let the
onion burn, for a few minutes longer or until the rice begins to take on a pale golden color.

DRIED SHRIMP

DRIED SHRIMP PLAY AN *important part in the diet of Oaxacans—not surprisingly since the main source for them is the waters of the Isthmus at the extreme south of the state. They are caught in abundance in the waters off San Mateo del Mar, and after a brief cooking they are salted and dried in the sun—the drying process is aided greatly by the constant high winds for which that area is renowned. Dried shrimp make a durable source of protein that can withstand the heat and can be transported to remote areas in the sierra without fear of spoiling.*

The concentrated flavor of dried shrimp enhances soups, rice, tamales, beans, and table sauces, and once you acquire a taste for it (it is too strong for many visitors) it becomes quite addictive. In Oaxacan markets dried shrimp are sorted and priced according to size from the large 2½-inch (6.5-cm) ones to the smallest of about ¾ inch (2 cm)—not forgetting the minuscule ones, ¼ inch (7 mm), found along the Pacific coast.

Good-quality dried shrimp are now to be found in Mexican food markets and in the Mexican food section of some supermarket chains in the United States, but take care in choosing them. Do not buy the small packages of bright-orange-colored shrimp bodies, peeled and headed; they have no flavor. Nor should you buy the packages marked "dried shrimp powder," a great proportion of which is pure salt. Try to find whole unpeeled dried shrimp.

Most dishes in Oaxaca call for shrimp that have had their head and legs removed. The head is very flavorful and—without the black eyes—should be stored for making shrimp fritters. They are very salty at best. Rinse in cold water, drain them, and cover with fresh cold water. Leave them to soak for about 10 minutes, no longer, or they will lose a lot of flavor. Store in a dry place for up to several months.

Meanwhile, put ½ cup (125 ml) of the water in a blender, add the garlic, cumin seeds, and cloves, then blend until smooth. Gradually add the tomatoes and the reserved heads and legs of the shrimp, blending until almost smooth. Add the puree to the rice and cook over medium heat, stirring and scraping the bottom of the pan until the juice has been absorbed —about 15 minutes. Add the shrimp, oregano, and salt if necessary with the remaining cup

[CONTINUED]

of water, cover, and cook over low heat until all the water has been absorbed—about 15 minutes. Season well and set aside off the heat for the rice to expand for 10 to 15 more minutes before serving. Serve each portion with one of the chiles. Serve with chile pasilla sauce if desired (recipe follows).

SALSA DE CHILE PASILLA (DE OAXACA)

CHILE PASILLA (OAXACAN) SAUCE

Srita. Abigail Mendoza

✺

[MAKES APPROXIMATELY 1 CUP (250 ML)]

ONE OF THE MOST INTRIGUING SAUCES OF MEXICO IS THIS ONE FROM ABIGAIL MENDOZA, THE STAR OF ZAPOTEC COOKING. SHE SAYS THIS SAUCE may be made with either the smoky, fruity dried *chile pasilla* from Oaxaca or the dried *chile de agua*, which is very picante but not so flavorful. I suggest you use *chipotles moras* if *pasillas* are not available. There is an interesting difference here because the *hoja santa* is *asado*, toasted until almost crisp, which gives a spicier flavor. You do need the pale-colored Mexican dried shrimp—be sure the heads are still attached (use the meaty body part for the rice in the preceding recipe). This sauce would traditionally be ground on the *metate* (not in the *molcajete*) and served as a table sauce, to be eaten with just a tortilla, on top of the rice cooked with the rest of the shrimp, or on top of a bowl of *frijoles de olla*.

6 large chiles pasillas de Oaxaca *or* 12 chipotle mora *chiles*

*⅓ cup (83 ml) loosely packed dried shrimp heads
(see note above) with the eyes removed*

4 hoja santa leaves, toasted on a comal or griddle until crisp

3 garlic cloves, peeled

1 cup (250 ml) water

salt to taste

Rinse the chiles rapidly in cold water and wipe clean and dry. Lightly toast the chiles (in warm wood ash, if possible) on a *comal* or griddle; remove the seeds and tear into pieces.

Toast the shrimp heads on the *comal,* turning them over frequently so they do not burn. Crumble them into a blender, add the chiles, *hoja santa,* garlic, and water, then blend to a textured consistency. Stir in salt to taste. Add more water if necessary to bring the sauce to a medium consistency.

COLORADITO

Sra. Soledad Díaz

✳

[SERVES ABOUT 10]

COLORADITO, LITERALLY "LITTLE COLORED ONE," IS ONE OF THE FAMOUS SEVEN MOLES OF OAXACA. RECIPES, OF COURSE, VARY IN QUANTITIES AND BALANCE of flavors but always within certain parameters. Soledad Díaz uses this *coloradito* for her *enchiladas de bautizo* (recipe follows) as well as for a main dish with chicken or pork. The recipe was handed down to her from her grandmother, but she has made certain modifications over the years to suit her taste.

1 medium white onion, coarsely chopped

3 garlic cloves, peeled

salt to taste

10 large servings of chicken

8 ancho chiles

18 guajillo chiles

1½ pounds (675 g) tomatoes

⅓ cup (83 ml) sesame seeds

6 garlic cloves, unpeeled

1 medium white onion, cut into quarters

4 sprigs fresh thyme or ¼ teaspoon dried

4 sprigs fresh marjoram or ¼ teaspoon dried

4 cloves

4 peppercorns

[CONTINUED]

1-inch (2.5-cm) cinnamon stick
lard for frying
¾ cup (188 ml) pecans
heaped ½ cup (130 ml) unskinned almonds
heaped ½ cup (130 ml) raisins
6 ½-inch-thick (13-mm-thick) slices sweet yeast roll, dried
1 1½-ounce (45-g) tablet of Mexican drinking chocolate

In a large pot, boil enough water to cover the chicken. Add the chopped onion and peeled garlic with salt to taste and boil for about 10 minutes. Lower the heat, add the chicken pieces, cover, and simmer until almost cooked, about 20 minutes. Drain and set aside, reserving the broth for the *mole*.

Slit the chiles open, removing the seeds and veins. Toast lightly on a *comal* or griddle, rinse in cold water, and soak in warm water for about 10 minutes. Drain, keeping the *anchos* separated from the *guajillos*.

Cover the tomatoes with water and simmer until soft but not falling apart, about 5 minutes. Drain and set aside. Toast the sesame seeds in an ungreased pan over medium heat, stirring from time to time so that they brown evenly. Take care not to burn them! Set aside to cool and grind to a textured powder in a coffee/spice grinder. Set aside.

Put the unpeeled garlic and quartered onion onto an ungreased *comal* or griddle and cook over medium heat, turning the pieces from time to time, until translucent and slightly charred. Peel the garlic and put into a blender with ¾ cup (188 ml) of the chicken broth. Add the onion, herbs, and spices and blend as smooth as possible. Add the *anchos* little by little, blending after each addition and adding more broth only if needed to release the blender blade.

Heat 3 tablespoons of lard in a heavy pot in which you are going to cook the *mole*. Add the blended ingredients and fry, scraping the bottom of the pan to prevent sticking, over low heat. Meanwhile, add another ¾ cup (188 ml) of the broth to the blender and blend the *guajillos* a few at a time until they are as smooth as possible. Add them to the pan, pressing the puree through a fine strainer to extract as much of the juice and flesh as possible. Discard the debris. Continue cooking the mixture while preparing the rest of the ingredients.

Heat a little more of the lard in a skillet and fry the pecans, almonds, and raisins separately, transferring each of them to a strainer to drain off the excess lard. Finally, fry the bread slices. Crush all the ingredients together so that you do not strain your blender to its limits. Add 1 cup of broth to the blender, add the crushed ingredients, and blend to a textured paste. Add the paste to the pan. Stir well and cook over low heat.

Add the tomatoes to the blender and blend until almost smooth. Add to the pan together with the chocolate and 2 more cups (500 ml) of the broth and cook over medium heat, stirring and scraping the bottom of the pan, for about 15 minutes. When the *mole* is well seasoned, adjust the salt, add the chicken pieces, and cook for 10 more minutes.

ENCHILADAS DE BAUTIZO DE TRES CARNES

ENCHILADAS FOR A BAPTISM WITH THREE MEATS

Srita. Soledad Díaz

✸

[MAKES 12 ENCHILADAS]

THESE *ENCHILADAS* ARE A SPECIALTY OF THAT UNPRETENTIOUS AND CHARM-ING LITTLE RESTAURANT IN OAXACA, EL TOPIL. THEY ARE A FAVORITE OF mine. The owner, Soledad Díaz, who gave me the recipe, said that it was passed down to her by her grandmother, Paula Ríos. The filling can also be used for *chiles rellenos* or even *tamales*. This is an excellent way to use any leftover *mole*.

HAVE READY

vegetable oil for frying
12 6-inch (15.5-cm) corn tortillas
approximately 3 cups Coloradito (recipe precedes)
approximately 4 cups (1 l) filling
a serving dish that will hold the enchiladas in 1 layer
½ cup (125 ml) queso fresco
1 white onion, thinly sliced into half-moons

[CONTINUED]

Heat a little of the oil in a skillet and fry the tortillas lightly on both sides. They should just heat through well and wilt, not be fried crisp. Blot well. To keep the tortillas from becoming too greasy, add only a little oil at a time as needed. Dip the tortillas into the *coloradito* to coat them well. Put some of the filling across the center, roll them up loosely, and set in one layer in the serving dish. Pour on the remaining sauce. Sprinkle with the cheese and onion slices and serve immediately.

THE FILLING

[MAKES APPROXIMATELY 4½ CUPS (1.125 L)]

3 tablespoons lard or vegetable oil

1 medium onion, finely chopped, 1 cup (250 ml)

4 garlic cloves, finely chopped

salt to taste

1¼ pounds (565 g) tomatoes, peeled and finely chopped

3 peppercorns, crushed

3 cloves, crushed

3 sprigs fresh thyme, finely chopped, or ¼ teaspoon dried

3 sprigs fresh marjoram, finely chopped, or ¼ teaspoon dried

1 teaspoon dried oregano, crumbled

1 small bay leaf, crumbled

½ cup (125 ml) coarsely chopped raisins

⅓ cup (83 ml) coarsely chopped blanched almonds

10 large capers, coarsely chopped

8 pitted green olives, coarsely chopped

1 cup (250 ml) cooked, shredded, and chopped pork

1 cup (250 ml) cooked, shredded, and chopped beef

1 cup (250 ml) cooked, shredded, and chopped chicken breast

½ cup (125 ml) broth in which the meats were cooked

1 tablespoon brown or granulated sugar

Heat the lard, add the onion and garlic with a sprinkle of salt, and fry without browning until translucent. Add the tomatoes and continue cooking until the juice is reduced—about

5 minutes. Add the rest of the ingredients except the meats, broth, and sugar and cook over medium heat, stirring and scraping the bottom of the pan until the mixture is well seasoned, about 5 minutes. Add the meats, broth, and sugar, and cook again until the mixture is well seasoned and almost dry but still shiny and appetizing in appearance, 5 to 8 minutes.

POLLO ALMENDRADO

CHICKEN IN ALMOND SAUCE

Sra. Beatríz Alonso, La Casa de la Abuela, Oaxaca

✦

[SERVES 6]

LA CASA DE LA ABUELA, FORMERLY MI CASITA, IS A LIVELY RESTAURANT ON THE SECOND FLOOR OF A BUILDING ON THE MAIN *JARDÍN* OF OAXACA. Sra. Alonso generously gave me this recipe from her menu. It is a delicious version of this classic Oaxacan dish and is especially good for those who do not like to eat chiles.

⅓ medium white onion, coarsely sliced
3 garlic cloves, crushed
salt to taste
6 large servings of chicken, skinned

THE SAUCE
1 pound (450 g) tomatoes
pork lard or vegetable oil for frying
1½ cups (375 ml) raisins
1 cup (250 ml) slivered almonds
3 garlic cloves, unpeeled but with skin slit (so that they won't explode)
1 thick slice white onion
¼ medium ripe plantain, peeled and sliced
1 slice rich bread, such as challah
⅓ cup (83 ml) sesame seeds
1-inch (2.5-cm) cinnamon stick

[CONTINUED]

2 cloves

2 peppercorns

1 large sprig flat-leaf parsley

TO SERVE

approximately 20 green olives

¼ cup (63 ml) whole almonds

strips of jalapeño chiles en escabeche

Put 2 quarts (2 l) water into a pan, add the onion, garlic, and salt, bring to a boil, and simmer for 5 minutes. Add the chicken pieces and continue simmering until *just* tender, not soft, about 25 minutes. Drain the chicken, reserving the broth. Measure the broth and reduce or add water to make 7 cups (1.75 l).

Cover the tomatoes with water in a saucepan, bring to a simmer, and cook about 10 minutes until soft, taking care not to let them burst open. Drain, puree in a blender, and set aside.

Heat a little of the lard in a skillet and fry the raisins, almonds, garlic, onion, plantain, and challah one by one, until browned, draining each one in a strainer to rid it of excess fat. Add a little more lard or oil only when necessary. Toss the sesame seeds in the hot pan until a deep golden brown (sprinkle them with salt if they begin to pop around too much or jump out of the pan).

Put 1 cup of the chicken broth into a blender, add the cinnamon, cloves, peppercorns, and parsley, and blend, adding the sesame seeds little by little. The mixture should be fairly smooth. Add a second cup of the broth and continue blending the fried ingredients, stopping the blender from time to time to loosen the ingredients that tend to form a solid mass at the bottom of the blender. Add another 2½ to 3 cups (625 to 750 ml) of broth, which will probably be necessary to prevent your blender from burning out. Blend until fairly smooth; you do not want it to look like gruel.

Heat 3 tablespoons of lard or oil in a heavy flameproof pan in which you are going to cook the *almendrado*. Add the blended ingredients, then stir and scrape the bottom of the pan immediately, since the raisins in the mixture tend to scorch very quickly. Cook for 5 minutes, adding a little more fat if necessary. Add the tomato puree and continue cooking and scraping the bottom of the pan until the mixture has reduced and thickened and is well seasoned, about 8 minutes. Add the remaining broth and cook for another 10 minutes. By then the sauce should be of medium thickness and lightly coat the back of a wooden spoon. Decorate with the olives and almonds and serve the chiles separately.

SOPA DE GUIAS

SQUASH VINE SOUP

❋

[SERVES 8 TO 10]

IT MAY SEEM ABSURD TO INCLUDE A RECIPE FOR THIS SOUP WHEN FEW IF ANY OF THE INGREDIENTS ARE AVAILABLE OUTSIDE OAXACA, BUT IT MUST BE recorded in detail because it not only reflects so perfectly the healthy, earthy foods of the valley of Oaxaca, but it's also simply a culinary curiosity. Many visitors, both foreigners and tourists from different parts of Mexico, are curious about it. The *guias* are the wandering vines of a species of squash that is light green in color and roughly pear shaped. The vines are cultivated year-round in the valley of Oaxaca, although they're less prolific in the dry season. The other herbs, or *quelites* (wild greens), are indigenous and grow wild in the rainy season, although they too are now cultivated year-round.

You will find these ingredients for sale in the Mercado Juárez at the center of Oaxaca, by countrywomen sitting on the ground, while in the Mercado de Abastos (the wholesale market) farther out they are at least given the dignity of space on some of the vegetable stands. I only hope this recipe will tempt you to try *sopa de guias* next time you visit Oaxaca or to try making a version of it, especially if you live in a country with wild edibles around or if you have an incredibly varied garden like California cook/gardener Sylvia Thompson's. In the Union Square Greenmarket in New York City, they have, in late summer, *tenerumi*, a similar squash vine much beloved by Sicilians, as well as some *quelites*. Some California farmer's markets have them as well.

For the best flavor this soup should be made in this fairly large quantity. It is served in deep soup bowls, often with little dumplings, *chochoyotes* (see *The Art of Mexican Cooking*) floating in it, or with limes and a *chile pasilla* sauce with toasted, ground worms in it! I find that the last two garnishes detract from the delicate flavor of the herbs. Of course it makes a great vegetarian dish if you don't add the dumplings, which have lard and *asiento* in them.

approximately 10 cups (2.5 l) water
1 small head garlic, cut in half horizontally
1 medium white onion, coarsely chopped
salt to taste
2 corncobs, preferably field corn, not the sweet variety
2 tender zucchini or green squash
8 large guias, squash vines
1 small bunch piojito (Galinsoga parviflora)
1 large bunch chepil (Crotolaria longirostrata)
1 small bunch chepiche (Porophyllum tagetioides)
1 small bunch squash flowers

Put the water into a large pot, add the garlic, onion, and salt, and bring to a boil, boiling for about 5 minutes.

Remove the husks from the corn. Cut 1 of them into slices about 1¼ inches (3 cm) thick. Shave the kernels from the other cob. Rinse and trim the squash and cut into strips or ¾-inch (2-cm) cubes. Rinse the *guias* well and shake dry. Remove the tendrils and any tough parts. Strip off the stringy outer part of the stems. Snap the stems into 2-inch (5-cm) pieces. If parts of the stem are tough, discard them. Leave the leaves attached. Rinse the *piojitos* well and shake dry. Discard the lower stems and tear into pieces. Rinse the *chepil* well and shake dry. Remove the rosettes of the leaves and discard the stems. Rinse the *chepiche* well and shake dry. Remove and discard the bare stems and tear the rest into small pieces. Remove all but 1 inch (2.5 cm) from the stems of the squash flowers. Strip off the stringy outside of the stems and the sepals. Leave the base of the flower and the pistils; they do not make the soup bitter. Coarsely chop the flowers.

Blend the corn kernels with about ½ cup (125 ml) of the cooking water, return to the pot with the corn slices, and continue cooking for 10 minutes or until the corn is tender. Add the squash and *guias* and continue cooking for about 10 minutes. Add the rest of the greens and squash flowers and cook for 10 more minutes or until all the vegetables are tender. Remember always to have the broth boiling when adding the greens to preserve the color as much as possible. Serve as suggested above. If you are adding *chochoyotes*, they should go in just after the final herbs when the water comes up to a simmer again. If the water boils too hard, they will disintegrate.

Isthmus of Tehuantepec

When you come to the Isthmus of Tehuantepec, it seems like another world, so different is it from the valley towns of Oaxaca—and the rest of Mexico for that matter. Although it is only a three-and-a-half-hour drive, it seems endless in parts where the bare sierras seem to close in on you, one range after another, and hardly any signs of life appear except the occasional settlement of houses with a restaurant and a shack announcing that they mend tires or do all sorts of mechanical repairs. It is a lonely road too, except for the occasional truck or trailer. It was even more so when I first drove it that summer in 1965 and wrote in my notebook about the surprising number of brilliantly colored birds and one in particular with a long tail and shimmering green-gold feathers—it could only have been a quetzal.

Finally the road does descend and you may catch a glimpse of the great Juárez dam on the left. From then on there are a few villages surrounded with tropical vegetation. Thick stands of palm, mango trees, and patches of corn—which grows year-round there—announce the proximity of Tehuantepec. It is still a fairly small, compact town with dark red tiled roofs, and many of the old houses of typical, hot-country architecture still exist. The small central garden is fairly well kept and always colorful with tropical flowers. It is not as noisy as some towns since the most popular form of transport is still the tricycle with a small cart on the back. It is always an imposing sight to see a handsome, erect Tehuana dressed in a flowing skirt and brightly embroidered *huipil* standing in the cart with her purchases piled alongside. It is stiflingly hot and humid in summer, but refreshing winds whip up to gales on some of the roads toward Juchitán and beyond. The market itself is dark and cluttered with stands selling homemade cheeses, flowers, dried fish and shrimp, rather unappetizing-looking cooked chickens or hens with their eggs, and piles of rice. In the evening the fare is either *garnachas* from a street stand or *tamales* of dried fish or iguana. The *tamales* of that area can be delicious, but I have yet to bite into one without getting a mouthful of skin and bones—I always seem to get the tip of the iguana's tail.

I prefer to wander outside in the streets around the market where the most serious eating takes place throughout the morning on the improvised tables set along the sidewalk. On the other side of the road the women, wearing regional skirts and *huipils*, line up selling their produce: many types of mangoes, misshapen tomatoes, small pineapples, round green *guayas* (*Talisia olivaeformis*), the dried white corn of the area with flat kernels, and banana leaves for making *tamales*. At one side of the street a woman is selling what appears to be tall paper funnels. They are in fact stacks of *totopos* sold in bulk, many of them to be transported to villages around the coast or to the Oaxaca markets. *Totopos* are unique to the Isthmus. They are crisp disks of corn *masa*—they say you can make them only with the locally grown corn—dotted with small perforations. This is food that can be carried to the fields or on a journey without spoiling in the humid, hot climate.

I was curious to see how they were made and was directed to San Blas, a small village on the edge of Tehuantepec that has seen much better days. Many of the streets are unpaved and impassable in a low-slung car, while the older houses are neglected and crumbling. It was behind one of these disintegrating walls that I found some women who were willing to show me how these *totopos* are made. Under the dingy shelter several of the women were engaged in different stages of *totopos* making; from the cooking of the corn to the working of the *masa* to forming the *totopos* either on a piece of plastic or in their hands while the woman who places them on the sides of the oven was perforating them with two small sticks. These ovens are in fact bulbous, earthenware shapes that are set into the ground or in a special built-up area at a convenient working height. The base is often made of stone or some other hard material that will not crack from the heat of the fire. When the sides of the oven are hot enough, the *totopos* are slapped onto them, the mouth of the oven is closed, and they are cooked until crisp and only slightly browned. The ones they were making were of the white corn, but later I bought some that were a grayish brown from the black bean paste mixed with the *masa*.

On one of my trips to the Isthmus I went with a friend to San Mateo del Mar, a

Huave (indigenous group) village way out on a narrow peninsula jutting into the Gulf of Tehuantepec. There was no paved road: most of the way the track was well defined but sandy and irregular. This was like a journey into the past. For the most part it was desert, and quite unexpectedly there was a patch of green pasture with sheep grazing and green patches of coconut palms. The streets of the village were very broad, and many of the houses quite primitive with woven palm fencing to protect them from the sands blown up by the strong, steady wind. The women in the market were surprised to see us and reluctant to talk very much about how they prepared the dried fish and shrimp, the chief source of livelihood of the families living there. As the women left the market from the opening at the far side, it was a beautiful sight to see them with baskets on their heads, their brightly colored skirts swaying in the wind with every rhythmic step they took. It is a drive of only twenty-six kilometers on to Juchitán over a very windy stretch of road whose only saving grace is a line of *palo verde* bending in the wind, their yellow flowers adding some colors to the otherwise drab landscape.

Juchitán is a very unattractive town, raucous and vibrant; you are nevertheless attracted back to it like a magnet. I have been lucky enough to have been initiated into its delicious and very different food by Señora Pineda and Señora Oralia Castillo, whose recipes I am giving here. Efficient and organized, they had many of the local dishes ready for me. Apart from the recipes here, Sra. Amelia fried some of the *tasajo* with onions. One never expects that dark, fatless grass-fed beef to taste anything but strong, but it has a most delicious flavor and is tender to boot—or at least that cut tended to be. The meat there is cut about ½ inch thick, seasoned with salt and lime juice, and then hung up to dry. It takes only three to four hours in the heat and wind to dry sufficiently to be stored (in an airy place, of course). It is traditionally served with beans.

In these recipes the cooks use jalapeño chiles. They are left whole so that they do not make the dish hot, but the person who wants piquancy can then eat the chiles. Time and time again I have heard that people in this area are generally very discerning and don't like hot food. I was curious about why they did not use the local chiles *criollos*: "too hot," they would say, "and the skin is rather tough. We prefer to use serranos or jalapeños."

Besides the usual pork, beef, and chicken, wild game meats such as venison, iguana, and armadillo are very much sought after; certainly there were a lot of green iguanas tied up in the market. The *achiote* used here is concentrated like that of Tabasco State; a little goes a long way, and it is expensive compared to *achiote* seasoning paste—with other spices ground into it—from the Yucatán Peninsula.

The dried shrimp here are often rubbed with a little *achiote*, I suppose to make them look more appetizing, as they are in the Tuxtla Gutiérrez market. Food stands almost clog the streets, but nobody seems to mind, and one wide street off to the side is devoted to the local pottery—a lot of it garishly painted, while the large water containers and ovens for the *totopos* are still unadorned. The women here are dominant; they control the commerce and the festivities. The *velas* or fiestas have their roots in the pantheistic celebrations in pre-Columbian times of the Zapotecs who came south from the Oaxaca Valley to the Isthmus. At that time the *velas* were invocations to their gods for the flowers, corn, trees—especially fruit trees—fish, and alligators that were important symbols in their lives. During the centuries that followed the focus of the *velas* was modified by the church—a perfect example of syncretism—so that the spring celebrations became those of San Clemente, of the rains and the abundance they bring to San Juan, and of corn to San Isidro Labrador.

I was there last for a *vela* honoring one of the patron saints of a church in a barrio almost on the edge of town. People began to arrive quite late in the evening, the young folk in their best outfits, the older women carrying trays of food, bedecked in their gala costumes with their gold necklaces, bracelets, and earrings—it is the custom to display their wealth (nowadays many of them have cheap copies made, since robberies have become commonplace and on this occasion there were guards at the entrance to the square in front of the church where an awning had been set up for the occasion). As the music began, it was these beautifully dressed ladies who got up to dance with each other, holding up their skirts on either side and swaying gracefully. The queen of the evening and her consort entered to the march from *Aida* played at a painfully slow pace as they stepped forward and then backward—which made the going rather slow. The next day it was time to leave and drive across the Isthmus to Veracruz.

GUETAVINGUI

CAKES OF *MASA* AND DRIED SHRIMP

Sra. Amelia Castillo, Juchitán, Oaxaca

❋

[MAKES 18 2½- TO 3-INCH (6.5- TO 8-CM) CAKES]

GUETAVINGUI ARE SMALL CAKES OF TEXTURED CORN *MASA*, AS FOR *TAMALES*, FILLED WITH A DRIED SHRIMP AND A *MOLITO* (LITTLE *MOLE*) THAT IS NOT cooked, made of toasted unhulled pumpkin seeds, tomato, a little green chile, very lightly flavored with *achiote*. They are baked in the oven.

THE FILLING OR MOLITO

18 large or 36 small dried shrimp (page 393)
½ cup (125 ml) unhulled raw pumpkin seeds
3 tablespoons water
1½ pounds (675 g) Italian plum tomatoes, coarsely chopped, 4 cups (1 l)
1 jalapeño chile, coarsely chopped
1 scant tablespoon masa for tortillas (page 530)
¼ teaspoon pure achiote or ½ teaspoon achiote paste
salt to taste

THE MASA

¼ cup (63 ml) water
½ cup (125 ml) firmly packed coarsely chopped epazote
3 ounces (85 g) pork lard, a rounded ⅓ cup (about 87 ml)
3 ounces (85 g) asiento (page 419), ½ cup (125 ml)
1½ pounds (680 g) masa for tamales (page 530), as dry as possible
salt to taste

Rinse off the shrimp in water to wash off the excess salt then soak in water for 10 minutes. Drain. Remove the heads, legs, and tails and reserve. Set the bodies aside.

Toast the pumpkin seeds in an ungreased pan until the husks turn a dark golden color (take care not to burn them since the seed inside cooks first). Set aside to cool and then

[CONTINUED]

grind to a textured powder in a coffee/spice grinder. Put the water in a blender, add the tomatoes, and blend. Then add the chile, shrimp debris, *masa*, and *achiote*. Blend to a slightly textured puree. Add more water only if necessary to release the blender blade. The puree should be fairly thick. Add salt if necessary.

Heat the oven to 350°F (177°C). Put the water into a blender, add the *epazote*, and blend until smooth.

Beat the lard and *asiento* together in a bowl and gradually beat in the *masa*, *epazote* water, and salt. Continue beating for a few minutes more (without burning out the motor of your beater) until you have a fairly stiff, rather sticky dough. Divide the dough into 18 portions and roll into balls of about 1¾ inches (4.5 cm) in diameter.

Make a deep well in one of the balls. Put one shrimp into the bottom with 1 heaped teaspoon of *molito* on top. Cover, if possible, with the dough (it doesn't matter if some of the *mole* is still exposed). Flatten slightly and place on an ungreased baking sheet. Repeat with the remainder of the balls, setting them about 1½ inches (4 cm) apart on the baking sheet. Put another dab of *mole* on top of each *guetavingui* and bake for about 30 minutes—you'll have to sacrifice one by opening it up to see if the dough has been cooked thoroughly. Eat them warm.

POLLO GARNACHERO

Sra. Amelia Castillo

❀

[SERVES 6]

AS THE NAME SUGGESTS, THIS DISH OF CHICKEN IS SEASONED AND ACCOM-PANIED BY THE SAUCE AND A *CHILITO* PREPARED FOR *GARNACHAS*. IT IS A MEAL in itself, a delicious combination of flavors and textures. Traditionally lard is used for frying the chicken and potatoes, but I often use melted chicken fat. Those who abhor frying and would like to reduce fat content can brush the chicken and potatoes on all sides first with some of the fat, then liberally brush on the sauce, and grill until well browned.

1 3½- to 4-pound (1.6- to 1.8-kg) chicken, cut into serving pieces, the
breast cut into quarters

½ medium white onion, coarsely sliced

3 garlic cloves, coarsely chopped

salt to taste

3 large potatoes, peeled and cut into ¼-inch (7-mm) slices

approximately ⅓ cup (83 ml) pork lard or chicken fat

approximately ⅓ cup (83 ml) salsa para garnachas (page 411)

3 cups (750 ml) chilito (page 412)

Barely cover the chicken with water, add the onion, garlic, and salt, and bring to a simmer. Continue cooking slowly until the chicken is almost tender, about 20 minutes. Add the potato slices and continue cooking until they are still somewhat firm and the chicken is tender—about 10 minutes. Drain, reserving the broth for the sauce.

Heat some of the lard in a wide skillet. Add some of chicken pieces in one layer, sprinkle liberally with the sauce, and fry on both sides until slightly crispy. Remove and keep them warm while you continue with the rest of the chicken. Repeat the process with the potato slices. Serve the chicken and the potato slices nearly smothered in the *chilito*.

GARNACHAS JUCHITECAS

Sra. Amelia Castillo

❀

[MAKES 12 3-INCH (8-CM) GARNACHAS]

EVERY REGION HAS AT LEAST ONE POPULAR EVENING *ANTOJITO*—USUALLY BASED ON CORN *MASA*—AND THE ISTHMUS OF TEHUANTEPEC IS NO EXCEPtion, with its *garnachas* quite unlike any others I have come across. Those served on the street stands in the evening are not to be compared with the ones prepared in the homes of Tehuantepec or Juchitán. I was fortunate enough to have them prepared for me by a friend's cook, a distinguished-looking lady wearing the traditional dress—her *huipil* was a royal purple color with a long billowing skirt. These *garnachas* are like a small thickish tortilla, spread with beef mixed with onion, topped with a little chile sauce and a fine sprinkling of crumbled dried cheese. They were assembled on a platter; to the side was a mound of *chilito*, a picante vegetable relish, for each person to serve himself as a final flourish atop this very tasty snack of many surprising textures.

THE MEAT

12 ounces (340 g) boneless steak, trimmed of fat and cubed
½ medium white onion, roughly sliced
2 garlic cloves, coarsely chopped
salt to taste
heaped ¼ cup (70 ml) finely chopped white onion

THE GARNACHAS

1 rounded cup (260 g) masa for tortillas (page 530)
approximately ¼ cup (63 ml) pork lard or oil for frying
approximately ½ cup (125 ml) salsa para garnacha (recipe follows)
½ cup (125 ml) finely grated queso añejo or Romano
1 heaped cup (265 ml) chilito (page 412)

In a saucepan, barely cover the meat with water, add the sliced onion, garlic, and salt to taste, and cook gently until the meat is tender, about 50 minutes. Set aside to cool off in the broth, then drain and chop. Mix with the ¼ cup onion.

Divide the *masa* into 12 small balls and cover them with a cloth while you make the *garnachas*. Press one of the balls into a thickish circle about 3 inches (8 cm) in diameter and cook as you would a tortilla on an ungreased *comal* or griddle. Cover each cooked *garnacha* with a cloth while you cook the rest.

Melt half of the lard in a large skillet, place the *garnachas* in one layer in the pan, top each with a tablespoon of the meat mixture and a good teaspoon of the sauce, and cook, gently flipping the lard over the surface of the *garnachas* from time to time for about 5 minutes. They should be *slightly* crispy on the bottom.

Set aside, cover, and keep warm while you cook the rest. Sprinkle very lightly with the cheese and serve with the *chilito* on the side.

SALSA PARA GARNACHAS

SAUCE FOR GARNACHAS

✺

[MAKES 2½ CUPS (625 ML)]

14 small Oaxacan pasilla *chiles* or 25 chipotle mora *chiles*

2 pasilla chiles de Mexico, negros

2½ cups (625 ml) chicken broth

12 ounces (340 g) tomatoes, cooked whole in the broth
for about 10 minutes to soften

2 tablespoons lard or melted chicken fat

4 garlic cloves, chopped

salt to taste

Slit the chiles open, remove the seeds and veins, douse quickly in hot water, and wipe dry. Tear into several pieces. Put into a blender and cover with 1½ cups (375 ml) of the chicken broth. Leave to soak for about 15 minutes. Add the tomatoes and blend until smooth.

Heat the lard in a skillet, add the garlic, and fry without browning for 3 seconds. Add the sauce and cook over medium heat, scraping the bottom of the pan to prevent sticking, for about 8 minutes. Add the rest of the broth and salt if necessary and continue cooking for about 3 more minutes. The sauce should be rather thin but should lightly coat the back of a wooden spoon. Add more water or broth if necessary or reduce to that consistency. Set aside and keep warm. If you don't use all the sauce for the *garnachas*, or the chicken dish on page 408, freeze it for another occasion.

CHILITO

❋

[MAKES 4 CUPS (1 L)]

THIS IS MORE *CHILITO* THAN YOU'LL NEED FOR THE *GARNACHAS* BUT ABOUT RIGHT FOR THE CHICKEN ON PAGE 408. IT IS WORTH MAKING THIS QUANTITY —this is a delicious relish for cold meats or in sandwiches.

2 Oaxacan pasilla *chiles* or 6 chipotle mora *chiles*
3 fresh jalapeño *chiles*
1 large carrot
3 cups (750 ml) finely shredded cabbage
3 garlic cloves, thinly sliced
¼ medium white onion, thinly sliced
2 teaspoons dried oregano
⅓ cup pineapple vinegar or mild, fruity vinegar (see page 524)
salt to taste

Slit the *pasilla* chiles open and remove the seeds and veins. Douse quickly in hot water, wipe dry, and clean. Tear them into several pieces. Slice the jalapeños crosswise without removing the seeds. Shave the carrot into thin, broad ribbons with a potato peeler. Mix all of the ingredients together—the vinegar should just moisten, not drown, the ingredients. Set aside to season for about 1 hour.

MOLE DE GUINADOOXHUBA

A MOLE OF TOASTED AND CRUSHED CORN

Sra. Amelia Castillo Romero

❋

[SERVES 6]

MANY TIMES I HAVE SEEN ABIGAIL MENDOZA IN TEOTITLÁN DEL VALLE PREPARING HER *CEQUEZA*, A SIMPLE BUT VERY TASTY DISH WITH A BASE OF toasted and ground dried corn in a chile/tomato sauce. In the Isthmus of Tehuantepec a similar dish is prepared, *guinadooxhuba* (impossible to pronounce). I have tried several versions but prefer this one, shown to me by Doña Amelia, the very dignified cook of a friend in Juchitán. Beef may be used instead of pork, or even beans for a vegetarian version. The pork Doña Amelia used was *costillitas*, small pieces of very meaty ribs. Ribs in the U.S. seem to have been shorn of all their meat, so I have called for country-style spareribs cut into ½-inch cubes. The sauce will be brick red and textured, rather like a thickish soup. It should be served in shallow bowls, and the recipe should yield enough sauce to serve each person 1½ cups, plus some of the meat of course.

2 pounds (900 g) country-style spareribs, cut into 1½-inch (4-cm) cubes
approximately 6 cups (1.5 l) water
⅓ medium white onion, roughly sliced
3 garlic cloves, coarsely chopped
salt to taste
2 pounds (900 g) tomatoes
1 fresh jalapeño chile
⅛ teaspoon pure achiote or ½ teaspoon commercial achiote *paste*
8 ounces (225 g) dried corn kernels
2 large sprigs epazote

Cover the meat with 1 quart (1 l) of the water in a large pan, add the onion, garlic, and salt, and bring to a simmer. Simmer until almost tender, about 25 minutes. Add the whole tomatoes and cook for about 10 minutes. Transfer the tomatoes to a blender and add the chile and *achiote*, blending until smooth. Strain the tomato mixture into a saucepan, bring to a boil, and cook for about 8 minutes, scraping the bottom of the pan from time to time to prevent sticking.

Meanwhile, put the corn into an ungreased wide skillet in one layer (divide the corn into 2 batches if necessary). Toast over medium heat, stirring from time to time until the kernels turn a shiny, even brown. When cooled, use a grain mill or Kitchen-Aid attachment to grind them down into a roughish texture, like steel-cut oats. Cover with the remaining

[CONTINUED]

water and stir well. When the grains have settled, skim off the skins that float to the top. Add this to the tomato mixture with 1 cup (250 ml) of the meat broth and cook over fairly low heat, stirring from time to time to prevent sticking, about 10 minutes. Add the rest of the broth and meat and cook for 10 minutes more. Add the *epazote* and adjust the salt, then cook for 5 more minutes. The ground corn will have softened by now but it will still be textured to the palate.

MOLITO DE CAMARÓN SECO

"LITTLE" MOLE OF DRIED SHRIMP

Sra. Amelia Castillo

❁

[SERVES 4 TO 6]

THIS IS A VERY UNUSUAL TYPE OF *PIPIÁN* BECAUSE IT INCLUDES CREAM. IT IS USUALLY PREPARED DURING THE LENTEN SEASON AS A MAIN COURSE. THE pumpkin seed used in the Juchitán area is small, with a lightish brown border, named *corriente* (commonplace).

4 ounces (115 g) Mexican dried shrimp, about 1¾ rounded cups (440 ml)
1½ rounded cups (400 ml) unhulled raw pumpkin seeds
1 cup (250 ml) crème fraîche
8 ounces (225 g) tomatoes, coarsely chopped, about 1½ cups (375 ml)
1 scant teaspoon pure achiote or 2 teaspoons achiote paste
3 tablespoons masa for tortillas
2 jalapeño chiles (optional)
salt to taste
3 large sprigs epazote
5 eggs, lightly beaten

Rinse the shrimp in cold water and drain. Remove the heads, tails, and legs of the shrimp, but don't peel. Put the bodies and debris into separate bowls, cover with warm water, and soak for 15 minutes. Meanwhile, toast the pumpkin seeds in a large ungreased skillet until the husks have turned a deep golden color and the seeds start to pop around (be careful and mind your eyes). Set aside to cool and then grind in a coffee or spice grinder to a finely textured powder. Mix with 1 cup (250 ml) of the water in which the shrimp have been soaking.

Put the crème fraîche into a heavy pan and bring to a simmer; simmer for 3 minutes. Add the ground seeds, pressing them through a strainer and pressing the debris hard so that all the moisture and seed particles are extracted—there should be about 2 tablespoons of the debris left in the strainer. By this time the mixture may look curdled, so don't forget to either lower the heat a lot or remove it from the heat altogether. If it curdles, just put it into a blender and blend until smooth. Cook over very low heat for 5 minutes, stirring and scraping the bottom of the pan to prevent sticking.

Put the shrimp debris and 1 cup (250 ml) of the shrimp water into a blender, add the tomatoes, *achiote*, and *masa*, and blend until smooth. Add this to the pan through the strainer and cook for another 10 minutes, taking care that the seeds and the *masa* do not stick to the bottom of the pan. Add water if necessary to bring the mixture up to 5 cups (1.25 l). Add the shrimp bodies and the chiles and cook for 10 more minutes. Adjust the salt. Add the *epazote*, gradually stir in the eggs, and cook over low heat until set.

Serve with corn tortillas.

TAMALES DE PESCADO SECO

TAMALES FILLED WITH DRIED FISH OR SHRIMP FROM TEHUANTEPEC

❂

[MAKES APPROXIMATELY 24 4- BY 3-INCH (10- BY 8-CM) TAMALES]

THESE ARE THE MOST DELICIOUS *TAMALES* AND QUITE UNUSUAL COMPARED WITH THE REST OF THOSE PREPARED IN DIFFERENT REGIONS OF OAXACA. While they are often filled with dry *lisa*, a fish abundant in the water around the Isthmus, dried shrimp can also be used, and I much prefer them. The textured *tamal* dough is beaten with lard and with *zorape* or *asiento* (the dark brown lard with very crisp "crumbs" of fat and skin that comes from the bottom of the *chicharrón* vat, page 419) and also flavored with *epazote*. The *tamal* dough must be rather dry to absorb the blended *epazote*.

The lady who gave me the recipe—I lost the notebook in which I had her name—makes them to sell commercially, but unlike many other vendors she does not skimp on quality. The lost notebook is another story. I was so distressed to lose it. I must have left it in the *jardín* of Tehuantepec when I sat down to eat a *tamal* of iguana. I went to the local radio station to announce the loss and offer a reward. The announcer noticed my yellow truck outside with the words *Casa Ecológica* on the side, so I was immediately put on the air to describe my house and ranch and how I apply my ecological ideas to the way I live . . . but I never recovered my book.

THE MASA

about ¼ cup (63 ml) water

½ cup (125 ml) tightly packed roughly chopped epazote leaves

1¼ pounds (565 g) masa for tamales (page 530), as dry as possible

3 ounces (85 g) lard, about ⅓ rounded cup (87 ml)

3 ounces (85 g) asiento, about ½ cup (125 ml)

salt to taste

THE MOLITO

1¼ cups (313 ml) unhulled raw pumpkin seeds

2 cups (500 ml) water

1 large tomato, coarsely chopped, about ¾ cup (188 ml)

½ medium white onion, coarsely chopped

½ teaspoon pure achiote or 1 teaspoon achiote paste

2 tablespoons masa for tortillas (page 530)

1 tablespoon lard

salt to taste

HAVE READY: a *tamale* steamer, 24 pieces of banana leaf, about 9 by 7 inches (23 by 18 cm), softened over a hot flame or burner, and 3 large dried shrimp per *tamal*, around 72 shrimp, or 24 2-inch (5-cm) square pieces dried fish—but allow for more in case of extra *masa* or left-over *molito*.

Rinse the excess salt from the shrimp, then remove the heads and legs only. Do not soak. If you're using dried fish, rinse the pieces of excess salt and soak for 15 minutes. Drain well.

Put the ¼ cup (63 ml) water into a blender, add the *epazote*, and blend until smooth. Mix well into the *masa* and then beat in the lard and *asiento*. Add salt. Set aside to season.

Put the seeds into an ungreased skillet and toast over low heat, stirring them from time to time so that they toast evenly. They should be a deep golden brown, and some should begin to pop around. Set aside to cool, and then grind in an electric spice grinder to a medium texture.

Put 1 cup (250 ml) of water into a blender, add the tomato, onion, *achiote*, and *masa*, and blend until smooth.

Heat the tablespoon of lard in a skillet, add the blended ingredients, and then stir in the ground pumpkin seeds with salt to taste. Add the second cup (250 ml) of water and cook over medium heat, scraping the bottom of the pan to prevent sticking. The starch content of the seeds will expand in the heat, and the sauce will thicken to a medium consistency that will coat the back of a wooden spoon. Cook for about 5 minutes. Set aside to cool.

Put the steamer on to heat the water at the bottom, and don't forget to add coins so their rattle will let you know if it goes off the boil or if the water level falls below the danger point. Set out the pieces of banana leaf.

Give the *masa* a final beating of about 3 minutes. Spread 2 scant tablespoons of the *masa* about ⅛ inch (3 mm) thick over the center of the banana leaf—it should cover an area of about 4 by 3 inches (10 by 8 cm). Place the 3 shrimp, or the piece of fish on one side of the *masa*, then cover with 1 large tablespoon of the seed mixture. Fold half of the leaf over so that the *masa* almost covers the filling. Secure the edges and fold up the sides. Set in overlapping horizontal layers in the steamer. Cover well and steam for about 1¼ hours or until the *masa* is cooked through and comes cleanly away from the leaf.

TAMALES DE FRIJOL

BEAN TAMALES FROM TEHUANTEPEC

✸

[MAKES APPROXIMATELY 24 4-INCH (10-CM) TAMALES]

THESE *TAMALES* ARE MOST UNUSUAL IN HAVING THE *MASA* MIXED WITH EPA-ZOTE AND CHILE SERRANO. I FIND THEM DELICIOUS AND ALWAYS EAT MORE OF them than I should. The careful preparation of a textured *masa* is all important; it should be as dry as possible so that the lards and blended ingredients will be absorbed. In Juchitán as in Tabasco the dark lard from the bottom of the *chicharrón* vat, with little crisp pieces of skin and fat, are used in the dough—it is called *asiento* in Oaxaca, *zorape* in Juchitán. Some people serve them with a sauce, although I don't think they need it. A light tomato sauce would be most suitable; anything stronger will detract from the taste.

THE FILLING

[MAKES ABOUT 2½ CUPS (625 ML)]

½ pound (225 g) black beans, 1 very heaped cup (265 ml)

6 garlic cloves, unpeeled

¼ medium white onion, coarsely sliced

salt to taste

2 tablespoons lard

THE DOUGH

¾ cup (188 ml) coarsely chopped epazote leaves

4 serrano chiles, coarsely chopped

4 ounces (115 g) lard, about ⅓ cup plus 3 tablespoons (100 ml)

4 ounces (115 g) asiento (page 419), about ⅔ cup (164 ml)

salt to taste

1½ pounds (675 g) masa for tamales (page 530)

Have ready a *tamale* steamer with coins in the bottom and approximately 30 dried corn husks, soaked in hot water until soft and pliable, shaken dry, and drained in a towel.

THE FILLING: Rinse and pick over the beans. Cover with hot water and add the garlic and onion. Cook over low heat in a bean pot or slow cooker until quite soft, 2½ to 3½ hours, depending on how old the beans are. Add salt and simmer for a few hours more.

Drain the beans, saving the broth. Put ½ cup (125 ml) of this broth into a food processor and process to a textured puree. Heat the lard in a skillet, add the bean paste, and fry, stirring and scraping to prevent sticking. Cook for about 8 minutes or until fairly dry. Set aside to cool.

THE DOUGH: Put ½ cup (125 ml) bean broth or water into a blender, add the *epazote* and chiles, and blend until smooth. Set aside. Put the lard and *asiento* into the bowl of a mixer and beat for about a minute or so with 1 tablespoon salt. Gradually add the *masa* and the blended ingredients and beat well. Taste for salt.

Heat the steamer over low heat. Give a final shake to the soaked corn husks.

Spread 2 heaped tablespoons of the dough over the upper part of the leaf. Put 1 heaped tablespoon of the bean paste down the middle of the dough and fold the husk so that the dough covers the bean filling. Fold back the tip of the husks. Set the finished *tamales* on a tray while you assemble the rest. By this time the water in the steamer should be boiling.

Stand the *tamales* upright in the steamer, cover them with any extra leaves or a towel, and cover with a tight lid. Steam over fairly high heat until, when tested, the dough is spongy and rolls easily away from the husk, about 1¼ hours.

PASTEL DE VERDURAS

VEGETABLE "CAKE"

✳

[SERVES 6]

THIS *PASTEL DE VERDURAS*, OR *ENSALADA* AS IT IS ALSO CALLED, WAS SERVED AS PART OF A BUFFET SUPPER IN OAXACA. IT HAD BEEN PREPARED BY A GUEST who came from Ixtepec, a small town on the Isthmus de Tehuantepec.

Although it is usually served at room temperature, it can also be served as a hot first course. The vegetables should be a little tender more than al dente to absorb the flavors and meld with the cream and eggs.

This dish is more often cooked in a *cazuela* over slow heat on top of the stove but can also be cooked in the oven. I find the latter easier since it cooks more evenly.

The cheese used there is a rather pungent dryish one from Chiapas, but a finely grated Romano can be used as a substitute.

Of course, this recipe lends itself to many variations, depending on tastes and what is on hand. For instance, it could be served with a sauce of *rajas* (narrow strips of poblano chiles) and cream or tomato, etc.

I cook this in a 6-inch soufflé dish about 2½ inches deep and carefully turn it out onto a serving dish when cold.

> ½ pound (225 g) waxy potatoes, peeled and cut into ¼-inch (7-mm)
> cubes, about 1½ cups (375 ml)
>
> ½ pound (225 g) carrots, cut into ¼-inch (7-mm) cubes,
> about 1½ cups (375 ml)
>
> ½ pound (225 g) green beans, cut into very small pieces,
> about 1¾ cups (438 ml)
>
> 1 tablespoon vegetable oil
>
> ⅓ medium white onion, finely chopped, scant ⅓ cup (about 80 ml)
>
> 4 serrano chiles, finely chopped
>
> ½ pound (225 g) tomatoes, finely chopped, about 1 heaped cup (260 ml)
>
> ¾ cup (188 ml) crème fraîche

¾ cup (188 ml) finely grated Chiapas or Romano cheese
4 eggs, lightly beaten
salt and freshly ground pepper to taste

Have ready a 6-cup (1.5-l) ovenproof dish, well buttered, and enough boiling salted water to barley cover each of the vegetables.

Put the potatoes into the boiling salted water and cook for about 5 minutes. Bring the water back to a boil, add the carrots, cook for 5 or 6 minutes, and drain. Repeat with the green beans. Reserve the cooking water. Heat the oven to 350°F (177°C).

Meanwhile, heat the oil in a skillet, add the onion and chiles, and cook over medium heat for about 1 minute without browning. Add the tomatoes and continue cooking over fairly high heat, scraping the bottom of the pan from time to time to prevent sticking, until the juice is reduced—about 5 minutes. Stir into the cooked vegetables.

Beat the cream and cheese into the eggs and stir into the vegetable mixture. Adjust the seasoning (the cheese is very salty, so it may not need any extra salt). Turn the mixture into the mold and cover. Bake on the top rack of the oven until the *pastel* is set and firm to the touch, about 25 minutes. Set aside to cool off before turning it out onto a serving dish—or serve hot like a soufflé.

The Pacific Coast of Oaxaca

When you drive along the Pacific highway of Oaxaca, you are inland for most of the way, with rare glimpses of the sea and those long and beautiful beaches. You cross many dry riverbeds, which are dry for most of the year until the rains come and carry the floodwaters down from the Sierra Madre to the sea. The land is scrubby for much of the time, impoverished by the clearing of trees and undergrowth for cattle. There are occasional villages marked by small plantations of mango, papaya, and bananas, with sadly yellowing coconut palms sheltering orchards of lime trees. But through the years I have stopped off at the local markets and talked to cooks who have introduced me to some really remarkable new tastes.

At the beginning of the rains I want to dash off and try once more that delectable sauce of *chicatanas*, flying ants. Señora Armandina, who has taught me a lot about the regional foods, says that at the first rains they emerge from the loamy soil in her patio and gather around the lightbulbs; she and her family are ready and waiting to trap them. The *chicatanas* are first cooked in salted water, then toasted and ground with garlic and *chiles costeños* to a loose paste or sauce—it makes my mouth water even writing about them. It is almost impossible to try to describe the tastes of wild things, but I always have the impression that I have just eaten hazelnuts. The same sauce is also used in *tamales* and unmistakably perfumes the rather heavy *masa*.

Another gastronomic rarity is a sauce made with the nest containing the eggs of a black wasp in Puerto Escondido. The taste is stronger and more earthy than that of the *chicatanas* but still delectable and bursting with protein besides.

There are tiny mussels, *tichindas*, from the lagoons along the coast. They are either cooked in a sauce or stuffed into *tamales*, shell and all—there were actually ten stuffed into the *tamal* I had the other summer—and as they open up the juice is absorbed by and flavors the *masa*.

In the Pochutla market you can find bags of miniature dried shrimp no more than 6 millimeters long, and narrow, dried fish about ½ inch long; they are used in rice or in fritters and are very popular during Lent.

Fish smoked in Puerto Angel, cooked in a tomato broth or *pipián*, also contribute to the regional dishes of the Pochutla area. Oysters, small and briny, are sold for a mere song along the beaches of Puerto Escondido, but it is becoming harder all the time to persuade the fishermen to leave them in the shell—alas, it is always easier to carry them in plastic bags! You can eat crisp, raw *lengua de perro* (a small elongated monkfish) if you order them ahead in Playa Roca Blanca. There is a great variety of fish, but it is mostly grilled or cooked in a sauce of tomatoes; it is all very fresh and unpretentious, but there are no notable dishes as there are, for instance, in Campeche, Tabasco, and Veracruz. In the small local markets there are always freshly killed locally produced pork, beef, and rather skinny chickens, but at certain seasons they are supplemented by iguana, armadillo, and venison.

These meats are cooked in light *moles* or stews seasoned with *chiles costeños*, both red and yellow, that are grown in the area around Pinotepa Nacional. They are either orangey-red or a brilliant yellow, thin skinned, between 2 and 3 inches long, and very picante. The red one is more commonly used toasted and ground for table sauces or soaked and blended with other ingredients for the cooked sauces. A small triangular chile, *tuxta,* is popular in Puerto Escondido. It too is very hot and very colorful, starting out a pale yellow, often smudged with mauve and ripening to an orange-red. It is used mostly for table sauces, either fresh or dried. There are *tamales* of pumpkin and *tamales* of seven layers with beans and pumpkin. The excellent yeast breads in Juquila are made rich with plenty of lard. Finally there are huge sweet *tostadas* of *masa* and sesame or coconut ground together to eat with coffee or *atole.* Señoras Bertha, Aura, and Armandina all shared their recipes with me and cooked for me and were patient with all my questions.

MOLE DE IGUANA NEGRA

MOLE OF BLACK IGUANA

Sra. Galván, Puerto Escondido

✵

[SERVES 4 GENEROUSLY]

THE RECIPE WAS GIVEN TO ME FOR BLACK IGUANA, BUT TAKE HEART, YOU CAN ALSO USE PORK—THEN YOU SUBSTITUTE THE ORIGINAL TOMATOES FOR *tomates verdes.* While they would use neck and spine bones of pork, as usual I recommend country-style spareribs. While I have seen *chiles costeños* in U.S. markets (orangey-red chiles about 3 inches long, thin skinned, and very hot) I suggest you substitute *pulla,* although they do not have the same sharp, rustic flavor. (Bring a lot back with you when you go to Oaxaca.)

Like so many other *moles,* the sauce is best if left for 30 minutes or so before being eaten to develop flavor.

1½ pounds (675 g) country-style pork spareribs

salt to taste

4 ounces (115 g) costeño *chiles, about 40, cleaned of stems, veins, and seeds*

3 garlic cloves, roughly chopped

[CONTINUED]

¼ medium white onion, roughly chopped
¼ teaspoon dried oregano, crumbled
3 hoja santa or avocado leaves, toasted until crisp
2 peppercorns
2 cloves
8 ounces (225 g) tomates verdes, husks removed and rinsed
2 tablespoons pork lard or vegetable oil
2 tablespoons masa for tortillas (page 530)

Cover the pork with water, add salt to taste, bring to a simmer, and continue simmering until tender, about 40 minutes. Drain, reserving the broth.

Toast the chiles lightly, taking care not to burn the skins. Cover with hot water and leave to soak until soft and the flesh is reconstituted—about 15 minutes. Drain.

Put ½ cup (125 ml) of the broth into a blender, add the garlic, onion, oregano, *hoja santa*, peppercorns, and cloves, then blend as smooth as possible.

Cut the *tomates* into pieces, barely cover with water, and cook until tender, about 8 minutes. Drain off half the water and set aside. Heat the lard in a flameproof casserole dish, add the blended ingredients, and fry over medium heat for about 1 minute.

Put 2 cups (500 ml) of broth into the blender, add the drained chiles, and blend as smooth as possible. Add to the pan by pressing through a fine strainer to extract as much as possible of the juice and flesh. Cook, stirring from time to time, for about 5 minutes.

Blend the *tomates verdes* together with the tortilla *masa* until smooth and keep adding it to the pan, stirring from time to time to prevent sticking. Cook for about 5 minutes or until the sauce thickens slightly. Add the meat, salt as necessary, and continue cooking and stirring for another 10 minutes. The sauce should be of medium consistency. Dilute if necessary. For the best flavor, set it aside for about 30 minutes before serving.

MOLE DE VENADO

MOLE WITH VENISON

Sra. Galván, Puerto Escondido

✸

[SERVES 4]

WILD MEATS ARE OFTEN USED IN PICANTE *MOLES* ALONG THE PACIFIC COAST:
THE STRONG FLAVORS STAND UP WELL TO THE SHARP COSTEÑOS. THE METHOD
of cooking the mole is virtually the same as in the previous recipe. You will notice that in
many parts of Oaxaca the tomatoes or *tomates verdes* are added *after* the chile/spice base has
been cooked and seasoned.

You could substitute lamb (mutton would be better) if you don't have venison or beef.
When toasting the unpeeled garlic, always make a small slit in the skin so that it does not
explode and you won't have to pick it up off the counter or floor.

*1½ pounds (675 g) stewing meat (see note above) with
some bone and a little fat, cut into serving pieces*

salt to taste

4 ounces (115 g) costeño chiles, about 40, stems, seeds, and veins removed

2 guajillo chiles, stems, seeds, and veins removed

3 garlic cloves, toasted

¼ medium white onion, toasted

2 cloves

2 peppercorns

3 avocado leaves, toasted until crisp

¼ teaspoon dried oregano, crumbled

2 tablespoons lard or vegetable oil

½ pound (225 g) tomatoes, roughly chopped, about 1¼ cups (313 ml)

salt to taste

Cover the meat with water and salt to taste, bring to a simmer, and continue cooking until
tender but not soft—about 40 minutes, depending on the cut used. Drain, reserving the
broth.

[CONTINUED]

Toast the chiles lightly on a *comal* or griddle, cover with hot water, and leave to soak until soft and the flesh is reconstituted—about 15 minutes. Drain.

Put ½ cup (125 ml) of the reserved broth into a blender, add the garlic, onion, cloves, peppercorns, avocado leaves, and oregano, and blend as smooth as possible.

Heat the lard in a flameproof casserole and fry the blended ingredients for about 1 minute.

Put the drained chiles into the blender, add 2 cups (500 ml) of the reserved broth, and blend as smooth as possible. Add to the pan, pressing them through a fine strainer to extract as much as possible of the juice and flesh. Continue cooking, stirring and scraping the bottom of the pan to prevent sticking, for about 5 minutes. Put the tomatoes into the blender, blend as smooth as possible, and add to the pan, stirring well.

Cook the *mole* for about 10 minutes. Add salt and the meat and simmer for 10 minutes more. Set aside for about 30 minutes before serving for the flavors to mature. The sauce should be fairly loose, not quite as thick as that of the *mole de iguana* (preceding recipe). Dilute with more broth if necessary.

TORTA DE MASA

MASA AND EGG PANCAKE

Doña Bertha Ortíz

❋

[SERVES 3]

DOÑA BERTHA, WHO RUNS THE KITCHEN FOR A GROUP OF HOMES ON THE PUNTA DE ZICATELA NEAR PUERTO ESCONDIDO, COOKED THIS TORTA ONE morning for me when I couldn't decide what I really wanted to eat apart from the predictable *tamal* or egg dishes she had already prepared.

It is a recipe from her childhood on a ranch in the sierra near Putla de Guerrero. Presumably it was an economical way of eking out the eggs for a large family. Doña Bertha served it with a very strong sauce of *chiles costeños*; it was delicious.

Of course it can also be considered a basic idea on which there is no end of variations: add finely chopped onion and *chiles serranos*; top with chile strips and cheese or tomato sauces.

The pan size is important because you don't want it too thin or too thick. Ideally a pan 7½ inches in diameter should be used.

⅓ cup (83 ml) masa for tortillas (page 530)
½ cup (125 ml) water
2 large eggs
salt to taste
2 tablespoons finely chopped white onion (optional)
3 tablespoons melted lard or vegetable oil

Put the *masa* and water into a blender and blend until completely smooth. Add the eggs and salt and blend again. Stir in the onion if you're using it.

Heat the lard or oil in a skillet (see above) and pour in the egg mixture. Cook over medium heat, covered, until the top of the mixture is just set—about 15 minutes. Slide onto a plate and then reverse to cook on the other side, uncovered, for 5 more minutes.

TAMALES DE CHILEAJO

Doña Bertha Ortíz, Puerto Escondido

❋

[MAKES 30 TAMALES]

THESE ARE SPICY LITTLE *TAMALES* THAT ARE COOKED FOR A LONGER TIME BECAUSE THE FILLING INGREDIENTS ARE RAW. AN ALMOST IDENTICAL RECIPE was given to me in Pinotepa Nacional with the name of *tamales de carne cruda, tamales* of raw meat.

Doña Bertha insists that the meat must be on the bone and can be either pork or chicken. Actually, pork gives a better flavor, especially when reheated.

The *masa* should be spread thinly over the banana leaves, which makes these *tamales* all the more delectable. I like to beat the lard with water in which *tequesquite* has been soaked overnight (*agua asentada de tequesquite*, page 257), but of course it is not always available, so baking powder may have to be substituted.

THE MEAT

1 pound (450 g) meaty flattish pork ribs cut into 32 1-inch (2.5-cm)
squares (not cubes)

¼ cup (63 ml) fresh lime juice

1 teaspoon salt

THE SAUCE

½ cup (125 ml) water or meat broth

4 garlic cloves, roughly chopped

⅛ teaspoon cumin seeds

2 cloves

4 peppercorns

1 teaspoon dried oregano

1 small onion, roughly chopped

12 ounces (340 g) tomatoes, roughly chopped,
about 2 rounded cups (550 ml)

15 guajillo chiles, seeds removed and soaked for 10 minutes

40 costeño chiles, seeds removed and rinsed

⅔ cup (164 ml) water

salt to taste

THE MASA

6 ounces (180 g) pork lard, about 1 scant cup (240 ml)

1 teaspoon salt or to taste

½ cup (125 ml) tequesquite water (page 257)
or ½ cup (125 ml) water mixed with 2 teaspoons baking powder

1¼ pounds (565 g) masa for tamales, roughly ground (see page 530)

Have ready at least 30 pieces of banana leaf about 9 by 8 inches (23 by 20 cm), passed over a flame or burner to soften, and a *tamale* steamer with water and coins in the bottom.

THE MEAT: Mix the meat with the lime juice and salt and set aside for 30 minutes.

THE SAUCE: Put the ½ cup (125 ml) water into a blender, add the garlic, cumin, cloves, peppercorns, and oregano, and blend until smooth. Gradually add the onion and tomatoes and blend again until almost smooth. Separately, drain the *guajillos*, tear into pieces, and put into a blender with the *costeños* and about ⅔ cup (164 ml) water. Blend as smooth as possible. Add to the other blended ingredients, pressing through a fine strainer to extract any hard bits of skin. Add salt and mix well.

THE MASA: Beat the lard for about 3 minutes or until thickened and fluffy. Gradually add the salt and *tequesquite* water and continue beating for 3 more minutes. Add the *masa*, a little at a time, beating well after each addition, until all the *masa* is incorporated. Continue beating for a minute or so more; the dough should be moist and porous but fairly stiff.

Grease your hands, take a ball of the dough about 1½ inches (4 cm) in diameter, and flatten it into a very thin circle in the center of a piece of banana leaf. Put a piece of the meat and a very full tablespoon of the sauce onto one side of the dough. Fold the leaf over so that the other side of the *masa* covers the filling. Fold the 2 sides together and fold back the 2 ends. Continue with the rest of the *tamales*.

Meanwhile, set the steamer over low heat so that the water is boiling and the coins jiggling around by the time you have assembled all the *tamales*. Put one layer of the *tamales* into the steamer, cover, and cook for 8 minutes (so that the bottom layer does not get completely flattened) and place the remaining *tamales* in overlapping layers into the steamer. Cover with more leaves or a towel and steam for 2 hours. Always keep some water boiling on the side in case you need to replenish the water in the steamer—test in the usual way: the *masa* should separate from the leaf easily, but make sure that the meat is thoroughly cooked through.

CUITLACOCHE ESTILO COSTEÑO

CORN FUNGUS FROM THE OAXACAN COAST

✺

[MAKES 1 CUP (250 ML) FIRMLY PACKED FILLING FOR 14 TO 16 SMALL EMPANADAS]

THE LOCAL WAY OF PREPARING THE CORN FUNGUS IS TO BLEND IT WITH THE OTHER INGREDIENTS TO A LOOSE PASTE AND THEN PUT IT RAW INTO AN *empanada* of raw tortilla *masa* and either cook it on a *comal* or fry it. I prefer to cook the filling first, which makes for a better flavor; the fungus will be reduced by about half prepared in this way.

1 pound (450 g) cuitlacoche *when shaved from
corn cob, roughly chopped, about 4 cups (1 l)*
2 garlic cloves, *roughly chopped*
3 costeño *chiles or chiles de árbol, toasted whole and crumbled*
2 tablespoons roughly chopped *epazote leaves*
2 tablespoons *vegetable oil*
salt to taste

Put the *cuitlacoche*, garlic, chiles, and *epazote* into a food processor and process to a finely textured paste. Heat the oil in a skillet and cook the mixture until it is moist but not juicy—10 to 15 minutes. Add salt. Set aside to cool a little before making the *empanadas*.

EMPANADAS DE HONGOS

MUSHROOM TURNOVERS, OAXACA

✺

[MAKES APPROXIMATELY 2 CUPS (500 ML) FILLING, FOR 12 TO 15 QUESADILLAS OR TACOS]

A COUPLE OF SUMMERS AGO, I WAS DRIVING ALONG THE OAXACAN COAST, AS USUAL STOPPING IN AT THE VILLAGES EN ROUTE TO LOOK FOR ANY NOVEL-ties their markets could provide. In one, near Pinotepa Nacional, there were the usual vegetables—carrots, tomatoes, and onions—and small piles of dried fish, which provides the main source of protein in that rather poor area. Then a basket of very tiny, grayish-brown mushrooms caught my eye. They were most appropriately called mouse ears, *orejitas de raton*, or *honguitos de palo*. The old lady, the only one selling them, was reluctant to tell me how she prepared them or allow me to take a photograph without my agreeing to buy a large quantity at a greatly inflated price. Of course I did, and hurriedly and hopefully took them to a small food stand that had just opened for breakfast and seemed to specialize in *empanadas*.

The woman cook did finally agree to prepare them for me in the local fashion. To my surprise she put all the ingredients raw and roughly chopped into a blender. She then pressed a very large, thin tortilla, covering half of it with the raw filling and a sprinkle of dry, salty cheese, then, folding the tortilla over to make a large *empanada*, she cooked it very slowly with a smear of lard on the *comal*. I could hardly wait. Despite her warning, I bit into it right away; I burned my tongue, and the hot juice ran down my arm, but what a delicious breakfast, just compensation for a very early morning start from Puerto Escondido.

When trying the recipe at home, I used tender little field mushrooms and juicy chanterelles, but you could use any small juicy mushrooms, preferably wild, either gathered or sold in your area.

I have tried the filling both raw and slightly cooked and prefer the latter, frying it in a little oil for a few minutes to heighten the flavors and reduce the juice. I also prefer to chop the mushrooms rather than blend them. The filling is delicious in *quesadillas* and tacos.

1 pound (450 g) mushrooms (see note above)

10 costeño *chiles or any small, hot, dried chiles, or 8 chiles de árbol*

2 hoja santa *leaves*

¼ *cup (63 ml) water*

6 small garlic cloves, roughly chopped

2 tablespoons vegetable oil

salt to taste

¼ cup (63 ml) finely grated salty cheese, Romano or pecorino

Wipe the mushrooms clean and chop fine. Wipe the chiles clean, slit open, remove the seeds and veins, toast lightly on a *comal* or griddle, and tear into pieces. Wipe the *hoja santa* clean, cut out the main rib, and chop roughly. Put the water into a blender, add the garlic, leaves, and chiles, and blend until smooth.

Heat the oil in a skillet, add the blended ingredients, and fry over medium heat for 1 minute. Add the mushrooms and salt and cook over medium heat, stirring from time to time, until well seasoned and some of the juice has evaporated—5 to 8 minutes.

Spoon the filling into tortillas to make tacos or *quesadillas*—or, if you have the large local tortillas, use them to make the *empanadas* (see above.) Sprinkle a little salty cheese on top.

TAMALES DE RAJAS

TAMALES FILLED WITH CHILE STRIPS

Sra. Armandine, Pinotepa Nacional

✸

[MAKES APPROXIMATELY 24 SMALL TAMALES]

THE FILLING

1 pound (450 g) tomatoes, broiled (page 527)

4 garlic cloves, coarsely chopped

salt to taste

THE MASA

6 ounces (180 g) lard

½ cup (125 ml) tequesquite water (page 257)
or warm broth mixed with ½ teaspoon baking powder

1½ pounds (675 g) masa for tamales (page 530)

salt to taste

12 ounces (340 g) queso fresco or Muenster, cut into strips
about ½ inch (13 mm) wide

48 epazote leaves

12 serrano chiles, each cut into quarters,
seeds and veins removed if you like

Have ready a steamer for *tamales* and approximately 30 dried corn husks, soaked and shaken dry, with a few extra for the steamer.

Blend the unskinned tomatoes, garlic, and salt to a rough texture. Set aside. Beat the lard until fluffy, gradually beat in the *tequesquite* water or substitute, and beat again for about 3 minutes. Gradually add the *masa* and salt, beating after each addition. Finally, continue beating for 3 more minutes.

Spread 1 very heaped tablespoon of the *masa* in a thin layer over the inside top part of a corn husk. Add 1 tablespoon of the tomato sauce, a strip of cheese, 2 *epazote* leaves, and 2 strips of chile. Fold in the sides of the husk so that the dough covers the filling, then fold the pointed end up and in to join with the sides of the husk.

When all the *tamales* have been assembled and folded, stack them vertically in the steamer. Cover them well with the extra unused husks and a towel and steam for 1 hour.

MOLE COSTEÑO

MOLE AS PREPARED ON THE COAST

Sra. Armandine, Pinotepa Nacional

❁

[SERVES 8]

THIS *MOLE* IS MOST TYPICALLY PREPARED WITH IGUANA, THOUGH CHICKEN IS MORE COMMONLY USED THESE DAYS. BUT I WAS WARNED THAT WHILE THE black iguana is preferred, the green ones can be used, and so much the better if they have formed eggs—ecologically very unsound with today's population growth. A typical meal for this *mole* would start with rice cooked with tomato, etc., and after the *mole* the beans are served.

THE MEAT

8 large servings of chicken

½ medium white onion, roughly chopped

3 garlic cloves, peeled

salt to taste

THE SAUCE

9 ancho chiles

*30 costeño chiles, about 3 ounces (85 g), or 10 chiles de árbol
and 20 puyas*

8 guajillo chiles

12 small garlic cloves, unpeeled, lightly charred in a dry skillet

10 cloves

10 peppercorns

1-inch (2.5-cm) cinnamon stick

1 tablespoon dried oregano

[CONTINUED]

pork lard for frying
10 unskinned almonds
⅓ cup (83 ml) raisins
4 ounces (115 g) peeled ripe plantain, cut into thick slices
2 pounds (900 g) tomatoes, broiled until soft (page 527)

Put the chicken, onion, garlic, and salt into a pan with water to cover, bring to a simmer, and continue simmering until just tender. Leave in the broth for 15 minutes, then drain, reserving the broth and adding water if necessary to make 5 cups (1.25 l).

Slit the chiles open, removing the seeds and veins. Toast lightly on a *comal* or griddle, rinse in cold water twice, and drain. Keep the *guajillos* apart from the other 2 chiles.

Put ½ cup (125 ml) of the broth into a blender. Add the roasted garlic, spices, and oregano and blend until smooth. Add another ⅔ cup (164 ml) of the broth and gradually add the *anchos* and *costeños*, blending well after each addition. Add more broth only if necessary to release the blender blade.

Heat about 3 tablespoons lard in a heavy pan in which you are going to cook the *mole*. Add the blended ingredients and cook over low heat, scraping the bottom of the pan to prevent sticking. Put another ½ cup (125 ml) of the broth into the blender, add the *guajillos*, and blend as thoroughly as possible. Add to the pan, pressing through a fine strainer to extract as much of the flesh and juice as possible. Continue cooking over low heat while you prepare the rest of the ingredients.

Heat a little more of the lard and fry the almonds until well browned, then the raisins, followed by the plantain. Transfer to the blender and blend with ½ cup (125 ml) of the broth, adding a little more if necessary to release the blender blade. When the mixture is almost smooth, add it to the pot and continue cooking. Blend the broiled tomatoes and finally add them to the pot. Continue cooking the *mole* for about 20 minutes over medium heat, making sure it does not stick in places and scorch.

Stir in the rest of the broth, add the chicken pieces, test for salt, and cook over medium heat for 10 to 15 minutes more.

ESTOFADO PARA BODAS

CHICKEN FOR A WEDDING

Sra. Armandine, Pinotepa Nacional

✶

[SERVES 6]

6 large servings of chicken
½ small white onion, roughly sliced
3 garlic cloves, peeled
salt to taste

THE SAUCE

about 6 tablespoons pork lard, vegetable oil, or chicken fat
1 small onion, finely chopped
4 garlic cloves, finely chopped
2 pounds (900 g) tomatoes, thinly sliced
½ cup (125 ml) raisins
¼ cup (63 ml) slivered almonds
12 pitted green olives, halved
3 whole jalapeño chiles en escabeche, quartered
2 tablespoons juice from the can of chiles
1 tablespoon sugar
1 teaspoon dried oregano, crumbled
3 peppercorns
3 cloves
¼-inch (7-mm) cinnamon stick
12 ounces (340 g) potatoes, peeled and thickly sliced
8 ounces (225 g) peeled plantain, sliced lengthwise
2 thick slices pineapple, peeled, cored, and quartered

Cover the chicken, onion, and garlic with water, add salt, and bring to a simmer. Continue simmering until the chicken is just tender, about 30 minutes. Set aside to season in the broth while you prepare the sauce.

[CONTINUED]

Heat 3 tablespoons of the lard in a skillet, add the onion and garlic, sprinkle with salt to taste, and fry without browning for about 1 minute. Add the tomatoes and cook over fairly high heat for about 5 minutes. Add the raisins, almonds, olives, chiles, chile juice, sugar, and oregano and continue simmering. Crush or grind the spices together and add to the pan. Add 2 cups (500 ml) of the broth in which the chicken was cooked and continue cooking for about 5 minutes more.

Shortly before serving, heat about 3 tablespoons lard in a skillet and fry the potatoes, covered, turning them over from time to time, until tender and well browned. Drain. In the same fat (add a little more if necessary), add the plantain and fry until well browned. Drain.

Ten minutes before serving, add the chicken pieces to the sauce and a little more broth if necessary to dilute it to medium consistency. Add the pineapple and cook over low heat for about 10 minutes. Test for salt. Top the dish with the fried potato and plantain and serve.

Tlaxiaco

Tlaxiaco had always been a glamorous name to me—"El Paris Chiquito" (the little Paris) of the Mixtec region, as it was known in its heyday. The name derives from the Náhuatl word *Tlchqiaco* (given to it by the conquering Aztecs in the fifteenth century), which means a watchtower from which to observe the surrounding country.

Even in pre-Columbian times it was a center of culture and commerce, situated as it was strategically on the main route from the Pacific to the center of the country. Little is known about the colonial history of Tlaxiaco, but it came into being as an important *mestizo* (mixture of Spanish and Mixtec) town during the early part of the nineteenth century and had a brilliant, if not lasting, golden age that was to be diminished with the ravages of the Revolution.

I had read about that golden age, when innovative impresarios started small industries to provide the necessities for the large haciendas, ranches, and Mixtec settlements in the surrounding sierra—who, in turn, brought their produce and animals to sell in Tlaxiaco. It became once again an important center of culture and commerce.

It is fascinating to conjure up the life of the rich families who imported luxuries from Europe through the ports of the Pacific, the latest fashions from France in clothes, furniture, and draperies, even grand pianos—thus earning its name of Little Paris. I had all this in mind when Tlaxiaco finally came into view after a rather arduous journey from Puerto Escondido, 360 kilometers away.

A friend and I had set out early that morning, stopping to eat breakfast in our favorite food stand in the busy market of Pinotepa Nacional and continuing along the narrow road, hardly a highway, that goes north to Tlaxiaco. At the first village the recently harvested *chiles costeños* were set out in a symmetrical pattern to dry in the sun, making strikingly colorful bands of bright red and yellow.

We stopped again to buy some of the attractive *huipiles* for which San Pedro Amusgos is so famous, sold in small stores along the road. Much of the countryside had been cleared for cattle with the occasional fields of withering chile plants and, where there are small rivers, patches of tropical vegetation and fruits: bananas and papayas. Just before the land drops down into Putla, the only town of size between the coast and the mountains, you get a magnificent view of the Sierra Madre towering over the landscape. We were to go over those heights.

After eating lunch in Putla and a brief look at the town, we set off with some trepidation in the direction of Tlaxiaco. It was quite a perilous highway of abrupt curves and unguarded edges with the occasional long trailer descending unnervingly on the other side. As far as the eye could see, the orange-colored earth and rocks were bare of vegetation, with deep crevices made deeper every year by the unchecked rainfall. This is the worst erosion I have ever seen —a shocking reminder of how this country has been raped from the time of the Conquest on ... and still is today. This land could have produced food, trees, and shelter for wild animals and birds, to say nothing of edible plants.

At the highest point in the ascent there is a narrow valley of poor soil, dotted occasionally with pines. You see unexpected flashes of color and suddenly realize that this is the land of the Triques, who wear the brilliantly embroidered *huipiles*. They have lived in this remote area since pre-Columbian times with a different language, culture, and customs from those of the surrounding Mixtecs. Desperately poor, they either eke out a living off the land or migrate to Oaxaca to sell their embroideries, again living in miserable conditions. From there it is a long, steep, and winding descent into the almost bare valleys that surround Tlaxiaco.

Of course, I was disappointed in the town, which is run-down; on the outskirts many of the *adobe* houses are disintegrating. Only a few buildings have been cared for as a reminder of its former days.

But Tlaxiaco comes alive on Saturday evenings when the vendors start arriving from the areas around to set up their stands or arrange piles of produce on the ground, and from early the next day other villagers arrive with their earthenware pots and simple kitchen equipment, wooden tortilla presses, and earthenware *comals*.

The *Casa de Cultura* is very active and has some lively programs to encourage some of the traditional arts: dances in particular and gastronomy. It was there that I met Señora Esmirna Cruz Rojas, who with Sra. Juanita has generously given me recipes for this part of my book, including the very complicated meal comprising *mole negro* and its accompaniments. There it is served on the same plate with a *picadillo* of lamb entrails, seasoned tomatoes, and spices; it can also be fried with beaten eggs and a *salsa* that more resembles a casserole of layered tomatoes and onions, also with spices, herbs, almonds, and raisins. I am afraid the *mole* is one I dislike, with *chile ancho* and a lot of chocolate, and that is why I am not repeating the recipe here.

RELLENO PARA CHILES PASILLAS DE OAXACA

STUFFING FOR *CHILES PASILLAS DE OAXACA*

❁

[MAKES APPROXIMATELY 3½ CUPS (875 ML)]

SRA. JUANITA IS FAMOUS IN AND AROUND TLAXIACO NOT ONLY FOR THE EXCELLENCE OF THE REGIONAL FOOD SHE SERVES IN HER RESTAURANT, Juanita, but also for her high standard of catering for fiestas or wandering dignitaries and *politicos*. A recipe of hers that I particularly like is for a filling of *chiles pasillas*, the smoky-flavored chiles of the Mije area in Oaxaca, or the fresh *chiles de agua* from the valley of Oaxaca. I know another cook in the Mixteca Alta, the region around Tlaxiaco, who uses a similar filling for *chiles anchos*, and, of course, it goes very well with *poblanos*.

1 pound (450 g) stewing pork with some fat,
cut into 1-inch (2.5-cm) cubes

salt to taste

3 tablespoons pork lard

5 garlic cloves, finely chopped

⅓ medium white onion, finely chopped

3 tomates verdes, husk removed and finely chopped

8 ounces (225 g) tomatoes, finely chopped, about 1 cup (250 ml)

½ small plantain, peeled and cut into small cubes

½ cup (125 ml) raisins

⅓ cup (83 ml) slivered almonds

¼ cup (63 ml) finely chopped pitted green olives

½ thick slice pineapple, peeled and cut into small cubes

4 stems flat-leaf parsley, finely chopped, 1 heaped cup (265 ml)

sugar to taste

Put the meat into a pan, cover with water, add salt, and bring to a simmer. Simmer until the meat is tender, about 40 minutes. Leave to cool off in the broth. Drain and chop.

Heat the lard in a heavy skillet, add the garlic and onion, and fry for a few seconds until transparent but not brown. Add the *tomates verdes* and tomatoes and cook over fairly high heat until the juice has been absorbed, about 8 minutes. Add the rest of the ingredients with salt to taste.

Cook over medium heat, stirring and scraping the bottom of the pan to prevent sticking, for about 5 minutes. Add the meat and cook for 5 minutes more or until well seasoned. Set aside to cool before stuffing the chiles.

TO STUFF THE CHILES: Use the largest *pasilla* chiles, about 3½ inches (9 cm) long. You will need about 1½ tablespoons of the filling for each chile.

Carefully slit the chiles open down one side and remove the seeds and veins (if the chiles are very dry you may need to soak them in warm water for about 10 minutes or longer to rehydrate them). Drain well and stuff them with the filling, being sure the cut edges meet. Coat with beaten egg and fry as for *chiles rellenos* (for fuller instructions, see *The Art of Mexican Cooking*, pages 138 and 140 to 142). Serve with a cooked tomato sauce such as the one on page 528, made with pork broth.

AMARILLO DE PUERCO CON FRIJOL BLANCO

YELLOW *MOLE* OF PORK WITH WHITE BEANS

Sra. Esmirna Cruz Rojas, Tlaxiaco

☀

[SERVES 6 TO 8]

8 ounces (225 g) small white beans, 1 very heaped cup (300 ml)

3 unpeeled garlic cloves, roughly chopped

½ small white onion, roughly chopped

salt to taste

approximately 2 quarts (2 l) water

2½ pounds (1.125 kg) country-style pork spareribs

4 ounces (115 g) guajillo chiles, about 24

3 garlic cloves, peeled

2 tablespoons pork lard or vegetable oil

2 large hoja santa leaves, stems and large ribs removed

Pick over the beans, rinse well, and put into a pot with the chopped garlic, onion, and salt. Cover with the water and cook over low heat until tender but not mushy (not *al dente*)—3 to 5 hours, depending on how old the beans are. Remove the onion and garlic.

Put the meat into a separate pot with salt to taste and water to cover, bring to a simmer, and continue simmering until the meat is just tender—about 35 minutes. Drain, reserving the broth. There should be about 3 cups (750 ml); if not, reduce over high heat or add water to make that amount.

Remove the stems from the chiles, slit them open, and remove the seeds and veins. Lightly toast the chiles on a *comal* or griddle, cover with hot water, and soak for about 20 minutes. Drain and transfer to a blender with the peeled garlic and 1½ cups (375 ml) of the meat broth. Blend until completely smooth.

Heat the lard in a skillet and add the sauce, pressing it firmly through a fine strainer to extract as much of the flesh and juice as possible. Discard the debris. Cook the sauce over fairly high heat, for about 5 minutes, stirring and scraping the bottom of the pan to prevent sticking.

Put the cooked pork into a heavy pan in which you are going to cook the final *mole* and cook over medium heat so that any fat renders out. Continue cooking until the meat browns lightly in its own fat—about 15 minutes.

Add the chile sauce and fry, scraping and stirring as usual (the chile sticks very easily), for about 5 minutes or until the sauce has reduced around the meat. Add the beans and their broth and heat through for about 10 minutes. Just before the end of the cooking time, tear the *hoja santa* into large pieces and add to the stew.

Serve with corn tortillas.

CHILATE DE RES

BEEF STEW WITH CHILES COSTEÑOS

✵

[SERVES 6]

CHILATE IS A SIMPLE DISH FROM THE ERODED NORTHEASTERN PART OF OAXACA KNOWN AS LA MIXTECA ALTA. IT IS A SLIGHTLY PICANTE SOUP/STEW served in deep bowls with lime quarters and chopped onion to give the final seasoning. Many families use chicken, but I prefer this beef recipe from Tlaxiaco. The different cuts of meat, much of it on the bone, add great flavor to the broth.

2½ pounds (1.125 kg) stewing beef, short ribs, shin,
and a small proportion of boneless meat

salt to taste

5 garlic cloves, unpeeled

½ medium white onion, thickly sliced

3 plum tomatoes, about 7 ounces (200 g)

3 tomates verdes, about 3 ounces (85 g), husks removed and rinsed

10 costeño chiles or 6 puyas and 4 chiles de árbol

½ cup (125 ml) masa for tortillas (page 530)

2 large sprigs epazote

[CONTINUED]

finely chopped white onion
lime quarters

Put the meat into a heavy pot with water to cover and salt. Cover and cook over medium heat until tender—about 1½ hours, depending on the quality of the meat. Reduce the broth over high heat or add water to make 6 cups (1.5 l). Put 1 cup (250 ml) aside for the *masa*.

Put the unpeeled garlic and the onion onto an ungreased *comal* or griddle and cook until the garlic is soft and the onion slightly charred but translucent. Peel the garlic and set aside.

Put the tomatoes and *tomates verdes* onto the *comal* or griddle or under the broiler and cook until soft and slightly charred. Transfer to a blender.

Lightly toast the whole chiles on a *comal* or griddle, rinse briefly, tear into pieces, and add to the blender with the peeled garlic and onion, then blend until smooth. (If you're using *puyas*, remove the seeds and veins before toasting and soak for about 10 minutes, then blend separately and pass through a strainer before adding to the rest of the ingredients.) Add the blended ingredients to the 5 cups (1.25 l) of broth.

Put the separate cup (250 ml) of broth into the blender, add the *masa*, and blend until smooth. Stir into the other broth mixture. Cook over low heat until the sauce thickens slightly, taking care not to let it stick to the bottom of the pan. Add the meat and *epazote* and cook, still over low heat, for about 5 minutes. Serve in warm bowls, passing the onion and lime quarters separately.

JINÁ EN ESCABECHE

SOUTHWESTERN CAESAR'S AMANITAS IN A LIGHT PICKLE

Sra. Esmirna Cruz Rojas, Tlaxiaco

✺

[MAKES 2½ CUPS (625 ML)]

THE MUSHROOM WITH THE DELIGHTFUL NAME JINÁ (PRONOUNCED "SHINA") IS THAT SPLENDID ORANGEY-RED CAPPED AMANITA CESAREA WITH SPONGY yellow gills. It grows prolifically in many parts of Mexico and up to a very large size.

En escabeche here is rather a misnomer, since only 1 tablespoon of vinegar goes into the dish. But it is also called *en su jugo*, in its own juice, which refers to the first part of the cooking. Before cooking, that brilliant skin has to be peeled off; both caps and stems are used.

Any tender mushroom can be used for this recipe.

Chiles are not cooked with the mushrooms, but the dish is served with a sauce of *chile pasilla de Oaxaca* and tortillas to accompany it. The dish is served either as a *botana* or as a first course.

2 tablespoons lard or vegetable oil
¼ white medium onion, thinly sliced
2 small garlic cloves, finely chopped
½ pound (225 g) tender mushrooms, peeled and sliced
salt to taste
1 tablespoon mild vinegar
4 ounces (115 g) queso fresco, quesillo de Oaxaca,
or Muenster, cut into slices

TO SERVE
salsa de chile pasilla (see The Art of Mexican Cooking)
corn tortillas

Heat the lard in a skillet, add the onion and garlic, and fry gently without browning for a few minutes. Add the mushrooms with salt, cover, and cook over low heat until tender, about 5 minutes.

Add the vinegar and cook for 1 minute more. Spread the cheese over the surface of the mushrooms, cover, and heat through until it melts.

Serve as suggested above.

JINÁ ASADO

GRILLED CAESAR'S AMANITAS

Sra. Esmirna Cruz Rojas

✺

[SERVES 1]

THIS IS A VERY SIMPLE AND UNUSUAL WAY IN WHICH CAESAR'S MUSHROOMS
ARE PREPARED IN TLAXIACO. HOWEVER, THEY ARE VERY JUICY; WHEN I TRIED
the recipe, the moisture ran off the edge of the *comal*, and the cheese melted and stuck to it. I
have come up with this method, which could be applied to any large field mushroom—less
messy!

Señora Esmirna insisted that the mushrooms should not be eaten with a sauce but
"dry"—in her words, just with a corn tortilla. Actually it is very good on a whole-wheat bread
crouton too.

butter or vegetable oil to grease the pan
2 large Caesar's amanitas or large field mushrooms
salt to taste
1 thick slice very cold queso fresco, quesillo de Oaxaca,
or Muenster, large enough to cover the surface of a mushroom
2 thin slices garlic
3 large epazote leaves

Heat a small, heavy skillet and grease well with butter. Season the gill sides of the mushrooms with salt.

With the gills inside, make a mushroom "sandwich" with the cheese, garlic, and *epazote*
leaves. Secure the mushrooms together with a toothpick.

Make sure that the pan is sizzling hot and cook the mushrooms on one side until well
browned—about 5 minutes. Carefully turn the "sandwich" over and cook on the second side
for another 5 minutes or until the mushrooms are cooked and the cheese melted. Serve
immediately as suggested above.

MUSHROOMS IN CHILE GUAJILLO

Sra. Esmirna Cruz Rojas, Tlaxiaco

✳

[MAKES 2 HEAPED CUPS (600 ML)]

THE WILD MUSHROOMS THAT ARE GATHERED IN THE PINE FORESTS AROUND TLAXIACO IN THE RAINY SEASON ARE PREPARED SLIGHTLY DIFFERENTLY from those of, say, Michoacán or the state of Mexico. The following recipe is for *oreja de venado* (*Hypomyces lactifluorum*), which is an orangey-red trumpet-shaped mushroom with stem and fluted cap of the same crisp texture. The flesh inside is white and without any strong discernible texture. My instructions were to tear them into strips, though you could of course julienne them—but not too finely, or the texture will be lost in the chile sauce. You can use any firm, crisp mushroom as a substitute.

This recipe is served either as a *botana* or as a first course with corn tortillas.

> *7 guajillo chiles, veins and seeds removed*
> *8 ounces (225 g) mushrooms (see note above)*
> *1½ tablespoons pork lard or oil*
> *¼ medium white onion, thinly sliced*
> *⅓ cup (83 ml) water*
> *2 garlic cloves, roughly chopped*
> *salt to taste*
> *1 tablespoon fresh lime juice*

Cover the chiles with hot water and set aside to soak for about 15 minutes on a skillet.

Clean the mushrooms with a damp cloth and tear or cut into strips. Heat the lard, add the onion, and cook for a few minutes without browning. Add the mushrooms and cook over medium heat, stirring them from time to time, for about 8 minutes. If they are very dry, cover with a lid.

Drain the chiles. Put the water into a blender, add the garlic, and blend gradually. Add the

[CONTINUED]

drained chiles and blend as smooth as possible. Add the chile puree to the mushrooms in the pan, pressing it through a strainer to extract the tough pieces of skin. Stir well, add salt, and continue cooking and scraping the bottom of the pan to prevent sticking. Add the lime juice and cook for about 8 more minutes, until well seasoned.

Sierra Juárez

Among the many memorable journeys I made during those early days in search of cooks and recipes, one particularly stands out in my mind: from Tuxtepec over the Sierra Juárez to Oaxaca.

The highway runs almost parallel to the river Papaloapan, and on either side were fields of sugarcane with their white plume, like pampas grass, swaying in the breeze (I am told that they were past their best at this stage). The area around *ingenios*, sugar mills, is always depressing—rivers are polluted and often dead, the workers' houses are squalid and poorly constructed, and the sides of the roads leading from the fields to the mill, scorched or blackened with fire and layered with the trampled and smelly *bazago*, the pulp left after the processing. Passing the huge mill of San Cristobal was just like that: a no-man's-land.

Tuxtepec was much smaller then, a small tropical town, sultry but clean, shaded by hundreds of mango trees. The mangoes are so prolific that nobody bothers to collect them. The delicious manilas (to my mind still the most luscious of them all) were going to waste, though in markets farther north they were fetching considerable prices. The market was nondescript except for, as usual, the marginalized indigenous peoples from the sierra who had come, dressed in their colorful native clothes, selling intriguing herbs and greens collected wild in the botanically rich cloud forests.

The night's stay was rather uncomfortable, since the best rooms had been taken over by an American film crew (I never did find out which film they were shooting). But I was up at dawn to catch the first *camioneta* for Oaxaca: the *camioneta* turned out to be a short, sturdy fat old bus with about thirty seats and a huge rack on top, piled high with snacks and small animals—so typical a cargo in out-of-the-way places.

In less than one hour we stopped in Valle Nacional at a small rustic restaurant for a hearty *almuerzo* of eggs, tortillas, and the most delicious black beans. I also insisted on trying the *pomelos,* a type of grapefruit that had fallen off the laden trees around the resaturant and were rotting on the ground. Nobody seemed to use them!

What was supposed to have been a stop of twenty minutes extended comfortably while the food was served slowly, and lively conversations were struck up among the other passengers, the driver, and anybody else sitting around.

The countryside around Valle Nacional is highly cultivated with chiles jalapeños, tobacco, corn, and bananas, with the abundance of water flowing down in rushing streams from the sierra towering above. We finally set off again at a lumbering pace, the land steadily rising with every twist and turn in the road through a thick jungle of luxuriant palm trees and lush undergrowth, sheltered by many types of tropical trees that fanned out protectively over the rest.

The road, narrow in parts, had been carved out of the rock face that towers above it. The rock was richly covered with vegetation and deeply ridged here and there with cascading water, which flows across and eats away at the unguarded, exposed side of the road. The land below falls steeply away into narrow valleys cultivated with bananas, corn, and coffee, in between seemingly neverending rows of soft green mountains. How could anybody not be moved by sights like these?

Looking back at one point, we could see the peaks of three snow-capped volcanoes, dramatic against the brilliant blue sky with wispy clouds hovering around them.

As the road climbed higher, the vegetation began to change. There were forests of oak and pine, and the sides of the road were brightened with large red thistles, lupines, and Indian paintbrush. The brilliance of the light defined every pine needle so that it seemed as though it was made of silk, shining in the morning sun, while the trunks emanated their strong, resinous perfume.

When we finally reached the highest point of the road, the views were breathtaking: the luxuriant lands to the north, through which we had come, and to the south, as far as the eye could see, an endless landscape of bare or badly eroded mountains. There were very few patches of crops and scattered, dark splashes of pines where the road drops down into Ixtlán and finally into the valley of Oaxaca. But the incandescent light of that valley shed a a glow that makes even the barest of lands seem magical. Little did I know then that I would be back again in the years ahead, many times, to visit the Sierra Juárez.

It was through ethnobotanist friends Gary Martin and Alejandro de Ávila, who provided me with some typewritten recipes from the Chinantec area, that I began to realize the wealth of wild foodstuffs that were available and that formed a great part of the local diet. I spent one unforgettable day with Gary collecting plants in the rain forest, picking the wild *chayote*, and finally distinguishing the Mexican bay leaf, *Litsea glaucescens*, a tree growing in the higher pine and oak forests.

We spent most of the day with a Chinantec aquaintance who showed me the edible wild plants and flowers among the exuberant undergrowth: tall stands of *hoja santa* (*Piper auritum*), the heart-shaped leaf of the *cilantro silvestre* (*Peperomia pseudo-alpino*), named for its unmistakable *cilantro* flavor, the young shoots of *taro*, and *tepejilotes* (*Chamaedorea tepejilote*), flower buds from a small palm. We roasted them over an open wood fire until the sheath gradually opened to reveal the long strands of cream-colored flowers. They are crisp and slightly bitter, eaten either alone or in a yellow *mole*. There was also stir-fried watercress fresh from the nearby streams. The food is simple and nutritious: corn, pumpkins, beans, *chayotes*, and several types of bananas that are cultivated, many types of wild greens, flowers, and mushrooms, fish and aquatic animals from the many streams, seasoned with the wild *cilantro*, *hoja santa*, and avocado leaves.

Beef and chicken are still somewhat of a luxury, but there is wild game of many types, often preserved by salting and smoking over the wood-burning stove. They drink *atoles*, dried corn–based gruels, mixed with unripe green bananas, amaranth, and wheat berries or fresh corn. The sick and elderly are given *atoles* made with broken-up tortillas or enriched with eggs. There are stews of many types of wild green, often flavored with chile guajillo brought in from Tuxtepec or Oaxaca, as is the dried, salted fish for *tamales*.

I was fascinated and made the journey several times, vowing never to repeat my first experience of staying there. It was without doubt the most uncomfortable night of my life. My bed was a thin mattress on planks of wood, and despite four heavy blankets tied round me like a cocoon—I had forgotten my sleeping bag—I shivered all night as the clouds came down, clammy and cold, bringing rains that pounded the tin roof ceaselessly. A hen was clucking in one corner of the small cement-block room, and the toilet facilities made those in the Third World seem clean and luxurious. I there and then rescheduled my research from three days to one and a half and panicked the next day when my car's sodden carburetor refused to kick in. It took all the ingenuity of some traveling salesmen, who happened to pass and heed my pleas for help, to get the engine started.

Suffering from vertigo in the mountains, I had asked a driver to come and pick me up for the return journey, but that was for two days hence. There was no way out; I had to drive myself. I shall never forget the horror of that return journey, much of it on the outside edge of the road with steep, vertiginous drops below. I inched my way at a snail's pace around the blind, unguarded bends, hooting desperately to warn oncoming traffic that I was well over on their side. The fast-traveling empty timber trucks bore down on me, their drivers cursing me roundly. The hours stretched out endlessly, and I sighed with relief and slackened my grip on the wheel rounding the last bend when Oaxaca finally came into sight.

Cuicatlán

Many years ago I became fascinated with a chile unique to Oaxaca, the *chilhuacle*. When I can, I make a yearly pilgrimage to Cuicatlán, where they are grown, either driving from Tehuacán—although the highway is very lonely and has a deplorably pitted surface—or from Oaxaca, the capital of the state, 140 kilometers away. Cuicatlán is a peaceful little agricultural town dramatically situated below the towering rocks of burnt umber at the head of the Cañada, as the valley of Oaxaca's Río Grande is known. The first part of the journey goes through the extreme north of the central valley until the highway veers off to the northeast and starts to climb through lands with occasional stands of oaks and pine.

The views across the rift valley are spectacular as the road begins its descent, winding through a semiarid landscape of cacti and shrubs, which in themselves are so beautiful in the early spring when they are in flower. The road then follows the river valley, with strips of cultivation on either side in places no more than a kilometer wide of groves of lime trees, mangoes, papayas, *chicozapotes*, bananas, and avocados. As you approach Cuicatlán, the fields of cultivation are more extensive, with corn, tomatoes, eggplants, okra, and, of course, the *chiles criollos*, native chiles, as the *chilhuacles* are known. Every region in Mexico, sometimes every small settlement, has its *chile criollo*, and they are all very different in size and character.

Nobody could tell me exactly how long these chiles have been grown here, but they say that their characteristic flavor changes if grown under other climatic and soil conditions, so they can be considered unique, just as the large, very special *poblanos* grown in Miahuatlán, Puebla, are unique.

The crop of *chilhuacles*, black, red, and yellow, is grown principally for drying and selling to the markets of Oaxaca and Puebla, but during the latter part of the rainy season they can be found fresh in those markets, either green or when they are just beginning to ripen. When fully ripe they're charred, peeled, and cooked as *rajas* (chile strips with onion) with cheese or in broths. They are deliciously fruity but startlingly hot—and brilliantly colored (see photo in color insert). The ripened ones are used whole for *chile caldo* (recipe follows), the seasonal harvest dish of the area.

When dried they are typically squat and very light in weight with a matte surface. Their cost soars with every passing year, but even so growers find that it is hardly profitable to plant them. It is a vicious circle, of course. Typically they are used for the *moles* and stews unique to Oaxaca, but cooks prefer to adapt the cheaper guajillo chile—although, alas, it does not have the same sharp flavor and distinctive color (see the recipes *Chichilo Negro* and *Mole Negro Oaxaqueño* in *The Art of Mexican Cooking*).

CHILE CALDO

CHILE BROTH

Sra. María de Jesús Mata

❁

[SERVES 6 TO 8]

PREPARING A *CHILE CALDO* IN THE FIELDS AT HARVEST IS A CUSTOM THAT IS FAST DYING OUT IN CUICATLÁN. IT IS A GREAT PITY; THE TASTE OF THIS type of country food cooked over a wood fire in the open air is unmatched, not to mention the enhancing freshness of the ingredients. This recipe is unusual because the freshly picked ripened red *chilhuacles* are added to the *caldo* almost at the last moment and add a very special flavor to it. The ripened *chilhuacle* is a bright red. It is thin skinned, very picante, and squat, almost square, about 2 inches (5 cm) long and wide.

As a substitute for the *chilhuacles* I suggest using either ripened *poblanos* or half green *poblanos* and half red bell peppers.

On a recent visit to Cuicatlán with one of the leading chile growers, a *chile caldo* was prepared for me. There was a frantic search in the morning for the wild, broad-podded beans that are traditionally cooked in this stew, tender pod and all. Finally some were found, and although a little past their best owing to harsh weather, the pods and beans were tender and delicious. I suggest using either very tender fava beans or very young lima beans in their pods.

3 quarts (3 l) water

½ medium onion, roughly sliced

3 garlic cloves, unpeeled

salt to taste

1½ pounds (675 g) beef short ribs, cut into small pieces

1½ pounds (675 g) pork knuckles, cut into small pieces

8 small pieces of chicken

1 pound (450 g) tomatoes, roughly chopped

6 garlic cloves, roughly chopped

*6 thick slices pumpkin or squash (large acorn squash, unpeeled,
including the center strands and seeds)*

*2 large ears fresh corn (please, not that sweet soft stuff),
each cut into 6 pieces*

2 chayotes, about 1½ pounds (675 g), peeled and cut into strips

*8 ounces (225 g) fresh limas in their pods or shelled fava beans
(see note above)*

1 large scallion, roughly chopped

7 ripe chihuacles (see note above)

1 large bunch cilantro

[CONTINUED]

Put the water into a large pot with the onion, garlic, and salt and bring to a boil; lower the heat and simmer for 10 minutes. Add the beef and pork and continue cooking for about 40 minutes. Add the chicken and cook for 10 more minutes.

Meanwhile, put the tomatoes and chopped garlic into a blender and blend until smooth. Add to the pan. Add the pumpkin, corn, *chayotes*, lima beans, and scallion and cook until they are almost tender, about 30 minutes. Adjust the salt, then add the chiles and *cilantro* and continue cooking until all the ingredients are tender and the broth is well flavored.

Serve in deep bowls with plenty of the broth and corn tortillas.

NOTE: *Time will vary depending on the quality of meats and vegetables.*

RAJAS DE CHILES CRIOLLOS DE CUICATLÁN

FRESH CHILE STRIPS FROM CUICATLÁN

❀

[MAKES 1½ CUPS (375 ML)]

CHILES POBLANOS OR, EVEN BETTER, CHILES CHILACAS CAN, OF COURSE, BE SUBSTITUTED FOR THE *CRIOLLOS* OF CUICATLÁN, ALTHOUGH THEY LACK THE intensity of flavor and heat.

The fresh chiles cooked in this way during the harvest of local chiles are used as a filling for tortillas, *un taco campestre*, a rustic taco, or to be eaten with cheese or broiled meats. These are the most colorful and hot-fruity tasting *rajas* I have ever eaten.

2 tablespoons oil
½ medium white onion or 1 large scallion, thinly sliced
3 garlic cloves, sliced
salt to taste
12 ounces (340 g) tomatoes, finely chopped, about 2 cups (500 ml)
4 poblano chiles or 8 chilacas, charred, peeled, veins and seeds removed, and cut into narrow strips, about 1 scant cup (240 ml)
2 large sprigs epazote

Heat the oil in a skillet, add the onion and garlic with a sprinkle of salt, and fry over medium heat without browning until translucent. Add the tomatoes and continue cooking over fairly high heat, stirring and scraping the bottom of the pan to prevent sticking, until the juice has been absorbed—about 8 minutes. Stir in the chile strips and *epazote* and cook for another 5 minutes. The mixture should be moist but not juicy.

A MISCELLANY

OF CULINARY

EXPERIENCES

❋

Mango

MOLE PRIETO

BLACK *MOLE*

María Luisa Mendez, Tetla, Puebla

❂

[SERVES 6 TO 8]

IT WAS ONE OF THOSE STORMY NIGHTS HERE IN SAN PANCHO WHEN THE LIGHTS GO OUT JUST AS I PREPARE TO TYPE AND THE TELEPHONE WORKS IN fits and starts. To my surprise the telephone *did* ring, and I noted the urgency in the voice of my great friend and accomplished cook and teacher, María Dolores Torres Yzabal. I knew it meant a culinary surprise of some sort. Her daughter Miranda had called her to say that her secretary, Luisa, had returned from her *tierra*, Tetla, in the State of Tlaxcala, with some very special *mole* made of dried *cuitlacoche*, or *hongo de maíz* as they refer to it there (so as not to confuse it with the bird of the same name). Miranda said that her mother must try it because it had an extraordinary aroma and great taste and, she added, "Please call Diana and tell her about it."

Almost six months has gone by since then, because we had to wait until the corn and its fungus, *cuitlacoche*, had dried out completely in the fields. This happened at the beginning of November, when we received a call from Luisa's mother inviting us to come and try this extraordinary dish at her home a few kilometers beyond Apizaco.

We were anxious to collect some of the dried *cuitlacoche* ourselves, so first we went into the *milpa*, cornfield. The dried leaves were rustling in the breeze, and the sad and drooping cornstalks were surrounded and enlivened by yellow, pink, and purple flowers that flourish after the rains in this most colorful time of the year.

We were not very successful since it was hard to distinguish at first between the dried, blackish corn tassles and the shriveled and disintegrating fungus. However, we were relieved to find that Doña María Luisa, anticipating our visit, had already set aside a supply of it. She had also saved some from the year before, but that was crawling with weevils (*gorgojos*)—all the more protein, I thought—because, according to local lore, the corn was planted when the moon was new and as a result the corn and fungus would most certainly be attacked by the insects. Now, had the corn been planted when the moon was fuller, this would not have occurred, she explained.

Doña María Luisa showed us how to prepare these sad-looking remnants of what was once a delicious, juicy fungus and convert them into a unique and delicious *mole*.

She carefully removed the corncob from its sheath of dried husks and separated the already crumbling, fibrous mass encasing a fine, black powder.

By then the meat was cooked, so she began to prepare the sauce for the *mole*. As far as she knew, it was prepared only in the villages of that area and just at the time of the *pisca*, when the dried corncobs are harvested and stored for the year ahead. It was, in my opinion, a regional recipe par excellence! The preferred meat, or rather bones, for this dish is the spinal column of the pig, *espinazo*, and although the spine contains very little meat, it's delicious—and besides, the bones give flavor and density to the sauce.

A simple brazier filled with charcoal (wood would enhance the flavor of the dish) was set alight, and as the fire began to glow the cooking began in an earthenware *cazuela*. A delicate aroma of *cuitlacoche* was soon wafting around us while we hungrily watched as these simple ingredients, blended and simmered together, were converted into a unique and delicious culinary surprise.

2½ pounds (1.125 kg) pork neck bones or country-style spareribs
or 1 large chicken

½ medium white onion

1 large garlic clove, peeled

salt to taste

THE MOLE

4 large guajillo chiles

4 light brown chipotle chiles or or 6 mulberry-colored moras

1½ cups (375 ml) water

1 large garlic clove, peeled

1 heaped tablespoon chopped white onion

1½-inch (about 1.5-cm) cinnamon stick

2 cloves

1⅓ cups (333 ml) dried cuitlacoche (corn fungus; see note above)

2 tablespoons pork lard, melted

¾ cup (188 ml) masa for tortillas (page 530)

2 small bay leaves

Cover the meat with water, add the onion, garlic, and salt, and cook over medium heat until tender—about 40 minutes, depending on the quality of the meat. Drain, reserving the broth.

Meanwhile, tear the chiles into pieces without removing the veins and seeds, cover with hot water, and soak for about 10 minutes. Rinse and transfer to a blender with the seeds still attached to them. Add 1 cup (250 ml) of the water along with the garlic, onion, cinnamon, cloves, and dried fungus and blend until smooth.

Heat the lard in a *cazuela* or fireproof casserole, preferably over a charcoal or wood fire. Add the sauce through a fine strainer, pressing the debris down well to extract as much of the sauce as possible. Stir well.

Put the *masa* into a blender, add ½ cup (125 ml) water, and blend until smooth. Add to the sauce and stir well. Cook over moderate heat for about 15 minutes, stirring and scraping the bottom of the pan to prevent sticking.

When it is well seasoned, add the meat and about 2 cups (500 ml) of the meat broth, stir well, and cook over fairly high heat until the *mole* thickens a little. Add salt to taste and the bay leaves and cook for 5 more minutes.

The sauce for this *mole* should not be too thick, but lightly cover the back of a wooden spoon. Serve the *mole* accompanied only by corn tortillas.

Ahuautli—A Pre-Hispanic Food as It Is Prepared Today

Ahuautli, the microscopic eggs of the *Ephydra hians* species of aquatic flies from the *Corixidae* and *Notonectidae* families that abound in the lakes of the valley of Mexico, have provided free and highly nutritious food for the indigenous people of the area for centuries. They still do today and, moreover, provide a valuable commodity for barter or sale in the local markets as well as the large Mexico City markets like La Merced.

I was recently urged by an archaeologist surveying the area around Chimalhuacán—a village near Lake Texcoco, or what remains of the lake, which diminishes yearly with uncontrolled pollution—to go and record some of the present-day preparations and uses of these remarkable foods. *Ahuautli* was first called the "caviar of Mexico" by the Spaniards, and rightly so because of its delicate flavor, the meticulous care with which it is harvested and prepared, and, thus, its high price. These aquatic flies lay their eggs on the sedge grasses or on rushes that are fast disappearing now. Strands of these grasses, *polotes*, are knotted and then secured in the shallow water.

I was put in touch with a family living in Chimalhuacán whose forebears for generations have supported their families on the different foods that the lake produces: *charales* (little fish), edible insects, frogs, *ajolotes* (*Ambystoma trigrinum*), and various migrant fowl (now illegal) and *espirulina*, an algae that forms on the water. After the winter frosts, whole families go out to collect *tequesquite* (chloride and sodium carbonate), a salt that forms a thin gray crust over the soil around these lake areas. *Tequesquite* was used as salt in pre-Columbian times and still is, as a raising and softening agent for beans, corn, *tamales*, etc. (see page 257). The preparation of these foods has undoubtedly undergone modifications over the centuries, especially with the introduction of ingredients from the Old World: onion, garlic, *cilantro*, the last used in abundance in the recipes given to me.

The Escalante family and their eleven children, living in miserable conditions, have a wealth of information about the life and activities, past and present, of the area around Chimalhuacán. The lake area is now densely populated and highly contaminated with garbage and untreated sewage, which threatens the very existence of the remaining small bodies of water and the wealth of foods that they still—amazingly—produce.

Sr. Escalante offered to go on a brief fishing trip with the photographer who had accompanied me, but this was delayed while his energetic wife whisked out of the kitchen, drying her hands on her apron. She hurriedly and roughly mended a disintegrating net hanging from the rectangular frame of his gear, the end of which was a patchwork of old rags—these too had to be sewn together. To excuse its condition, they said that a new, good-looking net would immediately be stolen!

About two hours later the men returned with a bucket half full of two types of aquatic flies, *moscas de pájaro* and *cuatecones* or *pintos*, the latter distinguished by their lighter color and longer, slimmer bodies. They had also uprooted some of the grasses covered with the small, grayish eggs of the flies, the *ahuautli*. The grasses were laid out very carefully on a cloth in the sun for the eggs to dry. It took one hour, the grasses turned once very carefully. During the hour they anxiously watched the fleeting clouds, praying that the threatening storm would not break or the *ahuautli* would *chiquear* (an unusual use of the word, here meaning to hatch out).

Shooing off the hens who were eyeing our lunch greedily, Sra. Gloria and one of her daughters began to rub the grasses very gently between their hands so that the eggs were separated from their host and fell onto the cloth below. Then the tedious job began of picking out from the eggs any stray piece of grass, followed by rolling their palms over the eggs with a circular motion so that any particles of dust would be loosened and fall through the cloth and onto the ground below. This slow process required great patience and throughout the handling of the *ahuautli*, we were told, an even temper. Any show of impatience and speed would again cause the eggs to hatch out.

The *metate* was brought out into the patio, where the earth had been trodden flat and bare by so many feet, and only a few *nopal* cactus and surprisingly some exuberantly fruiting fig trees survived the harsh conditions. The *mano*, muller, had been broken that morning so another daughter was dispatched to borrow one from the neighbor . . . all this took time, and everyone, it seemed, had time on his hands. The workers were far outnumbered by the spectators.

The *ahuautli*, now dried and cleaned, was crushed—one roll of the muller, no more—and mixed to a thick paste with water. As the oil was heating in a large skillet on the kitchen stove, the paste was mixed into beaten eggs until smooth. The leisurely pace now quickened. Someone was dispatched for tortillas, and a sauce of *pasilla* chile was hurriedly made in the *molcajete*. Large spoonfuls of the mixture were dropped and flattened out in the hot oil. Suddenly the mixture seemed to come to life, thickening and crinkling up around the edges of what were now "*tortas*," large fritters.

They were not, I must admit, appetizing to the eye, but the delicious aroma that permeated the air heralded the delicious flavor of the *ahuautli*, which was not in any way diminished in its tortilla wrapping and topped by some of the pasilla sauce.

It was indeed a caviar!

The *ahuautli* has a slightly grainy texture and flavor reminiscent of a fine fish roe, and like roe it is highly nutritive. In her book, *Los Insectos Como Fuente de Proteinas en el Futuro*, Dra. Julieta Ramos Elorduy de Conconi lists *ahuautli* as one of the indigenous foods of Mexico that contain a high percentage of nutritious elements.

Apart from eating it in *tortas*, *ahuautli* can be prepared in *albóndigas* or added to a Lenten dish of *romeritos*. When in short supply for a more substantial dish, a thick paste can be smeared onto the uncooked side of a *gordita* of *masa* and then browned on the *comal*. The rest of what we prepared that day was reserved and later put into a green sauce with *nopalitos*.

While *ahuautli* is more abundant during the rainy season, it can be stored year-round, and naturally the price rises considerably (in July of several years ago it cost 100 new pesos for *un cuartillo*, the equivalent of four oval sardine cans).

It is interesting to note that the eggs of the *cuatecón*, or *pinto* variety of the fly—the fly itself is cooked in tamales—are larger, a slightly different color, and are considered to have a better flavor.

Jumiles — A Visit to Zacualpan, State of Mexico

I had made a casual remark to a friend who lives in Metepec that the year before I had eaten some *jumiles* (small, triangular brown beetles, *Atizies taxcoensis*, vulgarly called "bedbugs of the mountains") in Cuautla, Morelos. I had always wanted to go back and see how they were caught and used—other than in the notorious local tacos of live *jumiles*, where the more fleet-footed ones have to be swept back into the mouth and firmly crunched to prevent them from escaping. Virginia, who is as fascinated as I am with the curiosities and delicacies of indigenous Mexico, told me that Taxco, in the State of Guerrero, holds a yearly *Fería de Jumil* in November. If I couldn't make it, I could accompany her later on a trip to Zacualpan in the southern part of the state, where she goes regularly to donate books to the more remote schools. There *jumiles* provide the gastronomic highlight of the year. We fixed a date, and she called ahead to make sure we could occupy the hotel owner's suite of rooms, since the plumbing in the other guest rooms was, to say the least, unpredictable. At the same time, she alerted some of her traditional cook friends that we were coming.

The drive took us just over two hours at a brisk lick. We set out along the small toll road that first skirts the lower slopes of the extinct volcano, El Nevado de Toluca, which dominates the vast plains around Toluca and the base of the Lerma River. Several kilometers before Ixtapan de la Sal the road narrows. Farther on, beyond the town, it begins to wind down alongside the sheer rock face of the canyon and crosses deep ravines, where the only patches of color among the dry, brittle bushes and undergrowth were remnants of lingering autumn flowers, so brilliant just a few weeks before.

After curving and undulating through the foothills, the road finally levels out and enters a broad plain, watered by small streams fed from springs in the surrounding mountain range. The landscape is dotted with a few *rancherías*, small groups of houses, with their accompanying corn patches—by now almost bare, except for the yellowing stalks, which were rustling in the breeze.

Massive, smooth, gray stone boulders stuck out of the ground like huge phallic symbols as we entered the valley, and the land beyond was scattered with sharp, conical peaks. Off in the far distance, wrapped around a steep rise in the land was Zacualpan, a small, isolated mining town almost on the Guerrero border. It was founded as early as 1528 by the Spaniards, the very first *Real de Minas* in the whole of the New World. Gold and silver, among other metals, have been mined there throughout the centuries, and the town has suffered the fluctuations of fortune just like any other mining area.

As you drive up the steep, cobbled streets, it is rather like taking a step back into the past. The houses along these streets or those huddled on the sharp inclines around the center have retained much of their traditional architectural features, with the wide eaves of their tiled roofs hanging protectively over the sidewalks.

When we arrived, the center was crowded with people and their trucks from the countryside around, but they quickly dispersed as soon as the mayor had finished his *informe*, an account of the municipality's work that past year. I had the strange feeling that I was on a film set: the small plaza seemed overwhelmed by the buildings around, the closeness of the large church, the bandstand, the squat hotel that occupied one whole side of the square, the market stalls, and the row of stores and houses set up on a higher level. They dwarfed the sixteenth-century architectural gem, the town hall, which was tucked away in a side street.

Only a few people remained, sitting or kneeling on the ground with their modest piles of produce for sale in front of them—fat-shelled peanuts, corn, and a great variety of beans: large fawn ones called *gordos* (fat ones) and purply mottled ones, *criollos*, a local variety, and what's more, *nuevos*, newly harvested and dried, which would ensure that the skins would not be tough. There were also a few bright red tubers known as *papas de agua* (*Sagitaria maerophylla*), or water potatoes—rather misleading, since they are not grown in water. Inside they are white fleshed and taste somewhat akin to jícama. There were the usual tropical fruits trucked in from the hot country: pineapples, bananas, guavas, and small lengths of sugarcane for the Christmas piñatas. All this bounty but no *jumiles*. "Those who bring them down from the hills don't come until Saturday." It was the usual story!

Jumiles are collected from the dead leaves of small oak trees and around their base by people living up on the slopes of the sierra. They're hurriedly carried to market before they die—and have an even stronger smell. Since they appear for only three months, November through January, they are considered a seasonal delicacy (and probably an aphrodisiac) and provide a free source of protein as well as healthy omega-3 oil for the indigenous people.

Of course, we need not have worried. As we entered the portal of the hotel, a neatly dressed, round-faced little woman assured us that she had laid in a supply and, what's more, had some of the local bean *tamales* for us to try on the orders of El Capitán, the owner of the hotel. (I was amazed. I didn't think managers like her still existed in provincial Mexico. In my experience, you are met at the receptionist's desk by some gum-chewing young person who is more intent on watching the soap opera on television than attending to a would-be client.)

The friends who were to give us recipes were teachers at the exemplary local secondary school. It was the day of their Christmas party, and they were feverishly making last-minute purchases and arrangements for the meal. Since they were so busy, we sought out the part-time cook at the hotel, who turned out to be a great source of information. Born and brought up in a remote village down the valley, she was an enthusiastic cook. She preferred to eat her *jumiles* toasted whole, sprinkled with lime juice and salt, and wrapped up inside a tortilla. She also makes a sauce of them, toasted whole and mixed with finely chopped onion, chile manzano, and lime juice, to be eaten with cooked beans or, again, in tacos.

At that point one of the teachers arrived and gave *her* version of a sauce: grind together the uncooked *jumiles* with either raw tomato or *tomate verde* and fresh serrano chile. No onion or garlic is allowed in the sauce, for that would detract from their flavor! For me nothing could detract from or cover that flavor—it is so pungent and lingers in the mouth. We were then whisked off—the pace of our visit had quickened—to another teacher/sister-in-law, who immediately started cooking several dishes (see recipes in the chapter on the State of Mexico).

We were starving by the time we arrived for the party at the engineer's house by the old mine and made light work of the delicious *chorizos* grilled over charcoal and even the rich, fatty *chicharrón*, the pride of the local butcher who made them (husband of our teacher friend) and who was well away in his cups before we sat down to eat.

Some of the group watched intently as we were served the local delicacy, pork cooked in a sauce of *jumiles*. I took one bite. I thought of the delicious sauce of wasp grubs in their comb and of flying ants that tasted like hazelnuts on the coast of Oaxaca—and decided that I really could live without another taste of *jumiles*. My sentiments must have escaped our hosts, who presented us with some live beetles to take home.

As we turned out the light that night, we heard what we thought was a mouse scratching to get in, but when I turned the beam of my flashlight in the direction of the noise, there they were, a hundred frantic little *jumiles*, struggling to get out of their plastic bags.

Las Matanzas de Puebla

More than twenty years ago in a remote hacienda in central Mexico I witnessed a macabre scene that is enacted every year. Beginning in the last week of October, hundreds of goats are primitively (but painlessly) slaughtered and butchered daily for three weeks with unerring efficiency and speed. Within the space of three hours the scene that passes before your eyes seems at times like some ritualistic dance of death, with roots reaching back into thirteenth-century Spain.

These *matanzas*, mass killings, were most certainly linked to the Mexican *Mesta* (the *Mesta* was a stockmen's association established in Spain in 1273 to control and regulate the trans-humant movement) created in Mexico by ordinances from Spain in 1537. This was a logical conclusion to the transhumance, when pastures in the central plateau were exhausted. They continued on a wide scale down through the centuries until recent years, when such large herds of goats are fast declining. Possibly only two significant *matanzas* are still in existence today, and time alone will tell just how long these will continue.

The impresarios are the *patron* and his wife, of predominantly Spanish background, who come from a small town in Oaxaca. Each year in spring they send out *compradores*, buyers, to inspect and buy whole herds of goats for slaughter. In May, when the summer rains start and bring fresh pasture to the central plateau, the goats are driven slowly, grazing as they go, toward the hacienda where the slaughter is to take place. At its best, pasture is sparse and water scarce, but the texture and strong flavor of the flesh and the amount of fat produced are all said to be improved when the goats are fed salt at intervals. They're also given no water to drink, deriving their only liquid from the juicy tissues of the succulents and cacti that abound in the semiarid landscape.

Each year the *patron* rents one of the few remaining haciendas designed especially for the *matanzas.* These provide the working space necessary for this specialized industry—for an industry it is—providing hides, bones, dried meat, and fat for tallow and soap, in great quantities. Each year he contracts through the *mayordomo.* Accounts differ as to how the *mayordomo* is appointed, but it is most probably an office handed down through families from generation to generation. At least this was the case with a woman I met whose father had been a *mayordomo.* She had always accompanied him to help during the *matanzas,* and when he relinquished the work she became the *mayordoma,* in charge of the women workers, while her husband became the *mayordomo.* He in turn contracts for the *matanceros,* who kill and butcher the goats, and for the women who cook and do the chores during their temporary encampment at the hacienda. They all came from Chilac, a village about ten miles from the hacienda. For generations the peasant farmers have left their fields at the end of the harvest and dedicated themselves to this work.

It was eleven o' clock in the morning when we drove into the courtyard of the hacienda. It was deserted except for a few children who stopped in their play to look at us with curiosity and some emaciated dogs scavenging for scraps of meat. A few late blooms on the jacarandas, the red berries on the *pirule* trees, and the grayish green of the tamarisks were the only patches of color to relieve the monotony of the dun-colored adobe walls. Through an opening in the wall at one side of the drive came four boys carrying a litter—a straw mat tied around two roughly hewn poles—piled with a slithering ochre-colored mass of goats' stomachs. They were carrying them down to be washed in the small river that was rushing along the outer limit of the hacienda, serving as both bathhouse and laundry. We retraced their steps through the opening and found ourselves in an encampment, set up between the outer wall of the hacienda and the tall cornstalks of a neighboring field. There were lean-to shelters of dried palms and long grasses interwoven with thin, vertical wooden stakes. This was where the *matonceros* lived and ate during the *matanza* period. Looking around, it seemed to be an almost complete microcosm of village life that has hardly changed at all through the centuries.

The women had improvised their kitchens; on small fires set between large river stones they were preparing and serving the midday meal before the work began. Some of the women were kneeling on the ground, grinding the corn for tortillas in traditional fashion on *metates*, the rectangular, volcanic rock grinding stones. Others were patting the dough between their hands and cooking the tortillas on the *comal*, a large, thin disk of unglazed earthenware.

There were beans simmering in large, earthenware pots, and in front of the seated men were small bowls of simple, local indigenous foods: very hot chile sauces, the long, thin red pods called *guajes* that contain an edible bean with a fiercely pungent flavor, and small, green olivelike berries cooked with tomatoes, garlic, and *cilantro*, called *tempesquixtles (Bumelia laetevirens)*—they have a very delicate perfumed flavor, and it is said that once you have eaten them you will always return to Tehuacán.

A young girl was sitting there braiding dried strips of palm for baskets, while in another part of the camp some old crones were more seriously at work singeing the fur off the goats' feet from the previous day's slaughter. Hundreds of these small, cloven feet, strung closely together in huge clusters, had been tied up in the trees around the camp to save them from the prowling dogs. There was even a small stand selling soft drinks, although many of the older men had brought along with them their own supply of *aguardiente*, a strong liquor made of fermented juice from sugarcane. A woman was seated on the ground with her children around her, selling small piles of peanuts, pumpkin seeds, chewing gum, and dried, roasted fava beans, a sight common to any street corner throughout Mexico.

Strung out over this scene and flapping overhead like a laundry line were the flattened stomachs and intestines of the goats from the previous day's slaughter—part of the perquisites of the *matanceros* (butchers), along with the feet and ears. Under the shelters were the sleeping quarters of the men. The bare earth floor had been swept clean. Blankets, clothes, and flight bags were neatly slung over lines or hung onto pegs stuck in the wall, while the *petates* (coarse woven straw mats used for practically everything in village life) for sleeping were rolled up and stacked to one side. To add to the scene there was the incongruous sight of windpipes, still fresh and bloody, hanging up to dry.

We continued our tour of the main part of the hacienda. Off to the right of the entrance drive was a large corral, *toril*, where hundreds of goats were awaiting the day's business. In the building to one side was a primitively equipped kitchen with long trestle tables where the rest of the workers ate their meals. And next to it another room, bare except for a double bed, chair, and night table where the *patron* and his wife, unheeding (or perhaps enjoying) the odor of the fried bones that were piled up in one corner, taking up at least half the space. Across the driveway was the office, dominated by huge scales, where the *patron's* wife was weighing some of the "merchandise" and calculating the price with the help of an electronic pocket calculator.

Through the office window one could see a large, open patio area with an overhanging roof forming a shelter along the far side. At right angles to it was another building, and as we came in from the strong sunlight we could just make out through the eerie, smoky atmosphere men stirring big cauldrons of fat with long hand-hewn wooden paddles. From time to time they would dredge up some fried livers with a crude metal strainer and carry them out to cool off on straw mats in the patio.

Others were pressing crispy little bits of fat from the cauldrons in a stout wooden press until every drop of lard had been extracted and a solid block of *chicharrón prensado* was ready to be sent to the local markets.

The rendered lard was strained through a straw mat tied onto two rough pieces of wood and poured through a funnel into an inflated goat's stomach. The stomach was tied securely at the top and thrown onto the bizarre-looking pile at one end of the room: hundreds of goats' stomachs, taut with solidified fat and alive with hungry flies. It was a Goyaesque scene as the *fritangueros* (men who were frying) finished off their work from the previous day's killing. There was a speck of light high up at the far end. It was a candle flickering in front of a replica of the Virgin of Guadalupe. Dangling from a rough iron peg at one side was an offering: the fried liver of the first goat slaughtered that year.

Just before one o'clock that afternoon, the goats were driven into the main patio, and they huddled together nervously as the *matanceros*, all clean and neatly dressed, filed in carrying their baskets, bottles of refreshments, and very small chairs that looked as though they belonged in the nursery. With hardly a word to each other they stripped to their underwear and, hanging their belongings neatly on the pegs under the shelter at one end of the patio, began methodically to distribute huge baskets at intervals of a few meters, then spread out before them the indispensable *petates*.

Some of the men were sporting their favorite baseball caps with peaks turned jauntily towards the back, others wearing wildly decorated T-shirts, while some appeared to be wearing loincloths, and at least one man had on a natty pair of checked bermuda shorts. They all had long-bladed, fearsome-looking knives stuck in their belts.

In times gone by it was customary for the *mayordomo* to lead the men in singing a prayer of blessing every day before the killing began, but now it is usually sung once only, on the first day of the *matanzas*.

At a signal from the *mayordomo*—an immense, broad-shouldered, bandy-legged man dressed in white and wearing a wide-brimmed straw hat—groups of the men rushed forward and, each grabbing a goat, sometimes two, by the horns, dragged them toward the *picadores*, who were brandishing their long-bladed knives like dervishes. With one thrust at the goat's throat they expertly hit the jugular. An occasional onlooker rushed forward with a bucket to catch the blood spouting out of the dying animal. Through a haze of dust, the incredible scene unfolded in uncanny silence, broken only by the scuffle of feet, some low-toned bleats, and a gush of urine from a terrified little goat as it hit the ground. The onlookers, a few smartly dressed businessmen from the nearby town, some peasant women with children in their arms, stood by silently and seemingly unmoved. One little girl started to cry and hid her face in her mother's skirt. But to most it was just a routine daily occurrence during the weeks of the *matanzas*. It was all over in twenty minutes. Fifteen hundred goats, perhaps more, had been slaughtered. The mats were stained a brilliant red with the congealing blood, and there was a sickening smell of goat.

It was now the *mayordomo*'s business to see that the carcasses were distributed evenly among the groups of men—*ranchitos*, as they are called—and then began a frenzy of orderly butchering. The brawniest of the men slit the skins from neck to abdomen and, with their knives held between their teeth and steadying the carcass with their feet, ripped it off with one continuous motion. The heads came off next; the animals were cut open, the entrails scooped out, and the carcass dismembered. After each hacking the cut pieces were thrown onto growing piles of haunches, ribs, shoulders, and stomachs; so quickly were they butchered that the haunches at the bottom of the pile were still quivering like fish taken from the water.

The men were now squatting or sitting on their little chairs. Their arms and legs grotesquely covered with blood, they weilded their knives with uncanny speed. Not one word was exchanged. The sound of hacking and the metallic ring of knives constantly being sharpened filled the patio. We could have been in some medieval marketplace.

They stripped the meat of the pelvic bones and spine, which were stacked ready to be sold for the local specialty, *mole de cadera* (a soupy stew of goat bones and chiles), and flown to aficionados all over Mexico. A young man was hacking off the horns on a small wooden block and throwing the heads into a tall basket from which a hundred eyes stared accusingly at us. The very small boys were cleaning out the ears with great care. The entrails were separated and the intestines carried on a litter over to two incongruously respectable young men from Mexico City who were carefully washing and skeining them as though they were of the finest silk. There were growing piles of brilliant red spleens, green bile ducts, and bloody vocal cords; even the unspent turds were collected in neat piles to go back to the fields. Nothing went to waste. By now some of the men were working under the shelter using the goat skins to keep the meat off the dirt floor, while others were using them as slings to carry bones to some other part of the patio. As the work progressed, tensions began to relax and the men started to chat, smoke, or take swigs of *aguardiente*, while the youngest boys giggled uncontrollably as they squirted each other with milk from the udders.

By now there was a steady stream of men coming and going through an archway at one end of the patio carrying the meat to another group of men (*tasajeros*), who would do the final stripping and sorting. They were sitting in a line under a tiled shelter, expertly and rapidly cutting every scrap of meat from the bones into long strips and carefully removing every ounce of fat. No sooner was there a pile of meat in front of them than it was carried off and thrown into a large concrete pit filled with strong brine. Three boys trampled it unceremoniously with their bare feet and, scooping it up in armfuls, slung it onto the waiting litter.

At this point we were in a walled area of about two acres, almost completely covered with straw mats on which the meat was spread out to dry in the hot November sun. There was a constant rhythm of movement as the men spread the fresh meat out to dry and systematically turned the partially dried meat from the previous day. Some of it had already dried out enough and was ready for packing. It was carried back under the shelter, where it was rolled into huge bales and wrapped into one of those indispensable *petates*. A lid of the same material was sewn on with a rough cord, and it was ready for the marketplace, where it would be sold as *chito*.

We returned to the main patio to find the *matanceros* carefully dressed up again, despite their blood-caked limbs, as though they were commuting some distance instead of just walking two hundred yards back to their camp. The patio was immaculate in its way, baskets stacked, *petates* rolled up, and the ground swept clean with the besoms that had been stowed back onto the roof where they belonged. One by one the leader of each group was called to the office to account for the number of goats butchered, and as soon as this was done they lined up, chatting and happy. These expert killers who had looked so tough a short time before relaxed and joked with us as they waited to leave through the large wooden entrance doors that had been closed as soon as the *matanza* began. They were guarded by the *patron's* bodyguards, two tough, unsmiling men with guns on their hips who neither changed expression nor spoke as they frisked each man, even lifting up their caps, to search for any scraps of concealed meat. One man was caught with a very small piece tucked under a sack he was carrying over his arm, but it was all taken in good humor and part of the day's work. The next morning they would be up again at the crack of dawn, cleaning the hides, rendering the fat, and frying the bones.

MUSHROOMS

I ALWAYS KNOW WHEN THE MUSHROOM SEASON HAS JUST STARTED. ONE MORNING AT ABOUT FOUR O'CLOCK SOMEWHERE IN THE FIRST PART OF JUNE, THE DOGS START UP THEIR nervous, sporadic barking, uncertain whether neighbors or strangers are about. We had had first tentative rains and the little field mushrooms, *hongos de llano* or *San Juaneros*—named for San Juan's day on June 24—must be pushing their way up through the grass on the long mesa to the south of my house. For the next two weeks there will be a constant flow of people of all ages from nearby San Miguel and San Pancho in the early hours, hurrying along in the dark, flashing their lamps and chatting animatedly in expectation of arriving first for this free harvest. This year the mushrooms were prolific as the communal land has laid fallow for several years and been used for grazing the cattle, but next year, who knows? There is talk that it will all be tilled and planted with corn! ☀ These little mushrooms herald the beginning of the most colorful season of the year, when masses of large fragrant squash flowers, baskets piled with the last of the wild blackberries, and piles of multicolored mushrooms are sold along the sidewalks outside the market, lighting up the drab streets. From the early hours well on into the morning the country folk from the surrounding mountains unload their baskets brimming with a variety of mushrooms. Stepping off the local buses and walking the streets, they distribute them to the vendors sitting on small stools or squatting along the sidewalks while selling small piles of fruits they themselves have grown or selling wild greens they have gathered. ✸ There is almost a predictable order in which the mushrooms will appear with, of course, a few surprises now and then: the first *hongos de llano*, little donkey-brown and cream-colored *clavitos*, an elusive pile of orange *enchilados*, or *coxales* (named for the pine needles among which they are found), coral mushrooms of all shades called *pata de pájaro* or *escobetillas*, the brilliant orange *tecomates*, creamy brown *tejamaniles*. There are also black *gachupines* with their cream-colored relatives followed by a plethora of blue, mauve, orange, red, and mahogany varieties with morels, called *elotes* here, until the end of the season in September. ✸ This tremendous variety of mushrooms provides the townspeople with a seasonal gastronomic treat, but more important, it represents a source of free food and modest income for the country people, who often live in very poor conditions in the surrounding mountain settlements. From a very early age children start collecting edible mushrooms, which they learn to identify by oral tradition passed along by older generations. Very rarely does one hear of an incidence of mushroom poisoning. Centuries before the scientific classification of mushrooms by mycologists and botanists, the Aztec and other cultural groups were able to distinguish the differences between the edible and the inedible, poisonous, or hallucinogenic species of mushroom; it was essential to know, not only because of their importance as a food source but also for their role in religious ceremony. And to this day Mexicans add a whole peeled garlic clove to the wild mushrooms as they cook; if it turns color, there's a poisonous mushroom in the pan.

Although I am more familiar with the range of mushrooms to be found in the high pine forests in the neighboring states of Michoacán and Mexico, I have come across lesser-known mushrooms in Sierra de Puebla Norte, *totocozcatl (Rhodophyllus abortivus)*, which are considered a delicacy when preserved in vinegar with herbs. Farther to the south are the immense orange *chiltascas (Lactiporus sulphureus)*. There is also the *xopitza (Armilliella tabescens)* from the Cuetzalan area and the tiniest grayish brown "mouse ears" from the coast of Oaxaca. Curiously the latter are often blended with other ingredients and stuffed, uncooked, into large *quesadillas* or *empanadas* (page 430).

Last but not least is the fungus that grows on corn, *cuitlacoche*, one of the "newly discovered foods" now a rage in the United States. When fresh and juicy it is delicious, but it deteriorates in flavor as it begins to disintegrate and become starchy. However, in Tlaxcala it is left to dry on the stalk and then used as the fragrant black base of a simple *mole*. I have already dealt with *cuitlacoche*, its preparation and recipes, at length in *The Art of Mexican Cooking*, so I have intentionally left it out of this chapter.

Note: Traditional cooks with whom I have worked have repeatedly told me that they prefer to use lard for most of their mushroom dishes. But of course for vegetarians and those afraid of lard, vegetable oil can be substituted.

A Mushroom Hunt in the Shadow of Monte Tlaloc

The whole thing started when my friend Josie told me about a trip she'd made to the Monte Tlaloc area to scout a route for trekking horses the following weekend. All my friends have been warned that whenever they travel they should ask about the local foods, so she dutifully discovered that the specialty of the area was a *hongo enterrado*, a buried mushroom. We both immediately thought it might be a type of truffle and decided to go out and find it.

Early in August, in the middle of the rainy season when mushrooms are prolific, we drove to the village, just off the Puebla road. We soon found Luis, her guide of the previous visit, who volunteered to take us to his mother's house after promising that she was a great mushroom cook. The house was poor, but very neat and clean and surprisingly warm despite the high altitude and the dampness of the earth around the house from the rains of the night before. What a valiant old lady—yet not so old, but worn down by a hard life: a cruel husband and sixteen children, eight of whom had since died. It was she who had to support them, grinding 15 kilos of corn daily on the *metate* to sell in the market and embroidering by candlelight until she was nearly blind. But she is still feisty, and that is what has saved her.

Several of her sons gathered around—"*canijos todos,*" she hissed (loosely translated, "all no-good bastards")—as we asked her questions about the mushrooms and how they were prepared. One of her sons appeared with a huge *porcino*, and without further ado she hacked it into six pieces, put an abundance of pork lard (enough to make a few *toques* fall askew) into a pan, fried lots of onion, garlic, and strips of jalapeño, and then proceeded to fry the porcino. She thought she should add even more lard just to make sure, but we demurred: enough was enough.

Stuffed into a thick, freshly made tortilla, the mushroom was delicious, and reluctantly we had to agree that really the lard was just right. We asked about the *hongos enterrados.* This was the wrong season; they generally appear at Easter time. But if we could come back that evening, a few may have been brought in. As the morning wore on, they all talked about the mushrooms of that area with their local names: *pechugas*—they have to be cooked in two changes of water because they are bitter; the delicate *mantecadas*; the *amarillos* that are even better when dried and cooked on the *comal.* We were asked if we had sampled *elotes* (morels) stuffed with cheese and fried in batter or *pata de pollo,* coral mushrooms cooked and stuffed with a *picadillo* (meat stuffing), batter dipped, and fried (I have tried all these recipes, but the tastes and textures of the mushrooms had been lost, so I prefer the cooking methods in her recipes that follow this text). She said the little *tejamaniles* are the most delicious of all, baked in the hot ashes of the fires lit for heating their breakfast foods in the cold morning hours. She made a sucking noise that signified her appreciation for the taste of those particular mushrooms.

We asked about local wild greens. She promptly gave us two recipes for salads of *chivitos* (*Calandrinia micrantha*). I had often bought these delicate little oval leaves in the market of Santiago Tianguistengo and had been told that they grew along the riverbanks during the rainy season. But no, they were growing in the fields above the village, we were told. Another son had joined us—no *canijo*, this one. He was fat and jolly and offered to take us up to pick some. Several grandsons joined as we all piled into his old van that until recently had been used to transport a musical show around the country. The faded fringed curtains and peeling paint bespoke better days—he had exchanged it for an old minibus that was no longer permitted to transport people into Mexico City. The van lurched and grunted as it lumbered up the steep, winding track through pine forests and the occasional patches of cultivated land, until it stopped dead. We got out and searched the barley field with no luck. But in an adjoining grassy patch there were the clumps of *chivito* amid brilliantly colored little wildflowers and white blooming thistles. The pines were now glistening in the brilliant sunlight, and we felt we could reach out and touch the tree-clad slopes of Monte Tlaloc, so clear was the air. As we inched back down the hill, some of the first mushroom gatherers were returning with their finds. They had been up since the early morning hours, but most of them would be returning later that afternoon. We were again advised to come back in the evening when the main sorting would take place just in case some *hongos enterrados* had been found.

We returned to Mexico City and went back that night through pouring rain. The sorting and cleaning of the mushrooms had been under way for some hours as it turned out, and tall baskets of each variety were piled high, some already covered with plastic and tamped down, ready for the early morning drive the next day to the main wholesale markets in Mexico City. The real business was managed by Señora Lascano's hard-nosed daughter, who bought the mushrooms from the gatherers and sold them to the markets; she was the entrepreneur of the family. It was with some difficulty that we persuaded her to let us watch and take photographs and perhaps find one of the *enterrados*. As we talked, she softened noticeably and even allowed us to buy some of the huge *porcini* (mine was for my lawyer, a dedicated gourmet, whom I was to see the next morning) and a wide variety of mushrooms to try out the recipes and discover new textures and flavors. Again we asked about the *enterrados*, and yes, there were just two that had been found amid the piles of mushrooms on the sorting tables. They were not, however, the expected truffles, just bulbous white affairs with root/ stems supporting a nest of miniature mushrooms.

It had been a long day. The rain had stopped, and the air was clear and fragrant as we headed back. The whole valley of Mexico, stretched out before us, was a mass of sparkling light, its edges like massive tentacles reaching into the narrow valleys between the surrounding mountains.

OREJA DE PUERCO GUISADA PARA QUESADILLAS

LOBSTER MUSHROOMS COOKED FOR *QUESADILLAS*

Sra. Hortensia Fagoaga, Sierra de Puebla Norte

❀

[MAKES APPROXIMATELY 2 CUPS (500 ML)]

THIS MUSHROOM IS LIKE A ROUGHLY SHAPED TRUMPET, WITH FIRM WHITE FLESH COVERED WITH A THIN, DEEP-ORANGE SKIN—IT'S KNOWN IN THE United States as lobster mushroom (*Hypomyces lactifluorum*). There is also a totally white variety called *oreja de borrego* that can be used equally well in this recipe. It was in fact this recipe that encouraged me to use this mushroom more often. It makes a delicious and rather delicate filling for fried *quesadillas* or tacos. This same mushroom, thinly sliced and cooked with pork in a sauce of *chile ancho,* is also used in the sierra as a filling for *tamales.* Traditionally all the ingredients were ground together to a textured paste on the *metate,* but now the food processor has all but eliminated all that hard work (although it gives it a slightly different texture).

Any firm-textured mushroom with compact flesh can be substituted.

1 pound (450 g) lobster mushrooms, wiped clean and coarsely chopped
(leave skins intact)—about 2½ cups (625 ml)
1 cup (250 ml) finely chopped white onion
¼ cup (63 ml) coarsely chopped epazote leaves

[CONTINUED]

4 serrano chiles or to taste, coarsely chopped
¼ cup (63 ml) lard or vegetable oil
salt to taste

Put the mushrooms, onion, *epazote*, and chiles in a food processor and blend to a textured paste.

Heat the lard in a skillet, add the mushroom mixture with salt, and cook over medium heat, stirring well and scraping the bottom of the pan to prevent sticking, until the mixture is almost dry and shiny—about 15 minutes.

HONGOS DE LLANO GUISADOS

FIELD MUSHROOMS COOKED WITH CHILE AND *EPAZOTE*

❖

[MAKES APPROXIMATELY 1½ CUPS (375 ML)]

THESE LITTLE MUSHROOMS (*AGARICUS CAMPESTRIS*), CALLED FIELD MUSHROOMS IN THE UNITED STATES, ARE DELICIOUS JUST GRILLED OR SAUTÉED. THIS IS my favorite way of cooking them—Mexican duxelles, if you will—as a filling for tacos, *quesadillas*, or *empanadas*.

1 pound (450 g) field mushrooms
3 tablespoons vegetable oil
⅓ cup (83 ml) finely chopped white onion
2 garlic cloves, very finely chopped
2 serrano chiles, very finely chopped
salt to taste
2 tablespoons roughly chopped epazote *leaves*

Wipe the mushrooms with a damp cloth and chop both heads and stems very finely. Heat the oil in a skillet and add the onion, garlic, and chiles. Sprinkle with salt and cook over low heat for about 2 minutes without browning. Add the mushrooms and cook over fairly high heat until the juice that exudes has evaporated—about 10 minutes—adjusting salt and adding the *epazote* just before the end of the cooking time.

PATA DE PÁJARO EN MOLITO

CORAL MUSHROOMS IN A CHILE SAUCE

Sra. Augustina Vásquez de Lascaño

✸

[SERVES 6]

THIS IS A VERY SIMPLE COUNTRY RECIPE GIVEN TO ME BY A FAMILY LIVING IN A *RANCHERÍA* SURROUNDED BY PINE FORESTS IN THE WESTERN PART OF THE State of Mexico. Every morning shortly after dawn the whole family goes out to collect this free harvest provided by the summer rains. Although locally mushrooms of many types are cooked together with pork in a stew, they also provide a substitute for meat much of the time and are considered a delicacy. This recipe calls for *pata de pájaro* (bird's foot) or *escobetilla* (little scrubbing brush), but you can substitute any firm mushroom. There are several species of these coral mushrooms (*Ramaria* spp.) of many different colors: cream, brown, orange, yellow, and even a mauve, most of which are edible. Most local cooks will advise cooking these mushrooms in water first, but they tend to lose their crisp texture, and I have come to no harm eating them simply sautéed. They are also delicious lightly pickled and served as a snack with drinks (a recipe is also given in *The Art of Mexican Cooking*).

1 pound (450 g) coral mushrooms
salt to taste

THE SAUCE
6 guajillo *chiles*
6 pasilla *chiles*
1½ cups (375 ml) of the mushroom-cooking water or light chicken broth
2 garlic cloves, coarsely chopped
2 cloves
6 peppercorns
⅛ teaspoon cumin seeds
3 tablespoons lard or vegetable oil
2 large sprigs epazote

[CONTINUED]

Divide the mushrooms into smaller clumps and wash off any soil by dipping them quickly into hot water. Cover with boiling water, add salt to taste, and cook over high heat for about 10 minutes. Drain and reserve the cooking water.

Slit open the chiles, remove any stems, veins, and seeds, and toast them lightly, taking care not to burn them. Cover the chiles with hot water and let them soak and reconstitute for 15 to 20 minutes. Put ½ cup (125 ml) of the mushroom-cooking water into a blender, add the garlic and spices, and blend until smooth. Gradually add the *pasilla* chiles and blend again.

Heat the lard in a skillet, add the puree, and fry over low heat while you blend the *guajillos*. Add the *guajillo* puree to the pan, pressing it out through a fine strainer (there are always little pieces of tough skin that resist blending). Continue frying over medium heat, scraping the pan from time to time to prevent sticking, for about 5 minutes. Add the remaining water or broth and cook for another 10 minutes. Add the *epazote* and salt to taste, then continue to cook for 5 more minutes.

HONGOS TROMPETAS PARA TACOS

LOBSTER MUSHROOMS FOR TACOS

Sra. Hortensia Cabrera de Fagoaga

✵

[MAKES APPROXIMATELY 2⅔ CUPS (664 ML)]

ALTHOUGH COOKED WITH THE SAME INGREDIENTS AS THE PRECEDING RECIPE, THESE TROMPETAS—OREJAS DE PUERCO (*HYPOMYCES LACTIFLUORUM*)—ARE a different mushroom from the Río Frío area; the texture and therefore flavors are different. Of course, any firm mushroom with compact flesh may be substituted. For this recipe the orange-red skin is scraped off before cooking.

1 pound (450 g) lobster mushrooms
¼ cup (63 ml) pork lard or vegetable oil
½ medium white onion, thinly sliced
2 garlic cloves, finely chopped
3 to 4 jalapeño chiles, cut into thin strips

salt to taste

3 tablespoons coarsely chopped epazote

Scrape or peel the orange-hued skin from the stalks and caps of the mushrooms and cut into thin strips. Heat the lard in a skillet, add the onion, garlic, and chiles with a sprinkle of salt, and cook over medium heat without browning for about 1 minute. Add the mushrooms, cover the pan, and cook over medium heat, shaking the pan from time to time to prevent sticking. Remove the lid, taste for salt, add the *epazote*, and cook over fairly high heat until the mushrooms are tender-crisp, the mixture fairly dry and beginning to fry, about 10 minutes.

HONGOS AMARILLOS EN SALSA VERDE

CAESAR'S AMANITAS IN GREEN SAUCE

Sra. Augustina Vásquez de Lascaño

❀

[MAKES 3 CUPS (750 ML), SERVING 3]

THE SPECTACULAR-LOOKING *AMANITA CAESAREA* WITH ITS ORANGE-RED CAPS AND SOFT YELLOW GILLS IS PROLIFIC IN THE HIGHLANDS OF CENTRAL MEX-ico. In the Río Frío area they are known as *amarillos*—while in other areas they are *tecomates*, or *yemas*—and while mostly cooked in their fresh state, I am told they are also dried to be used in nonmushroom seasons. It is important to cook this dish at least 1 hour ahead of time for the flavors to blend and intensify. It makes a delicious and interesting first-course dish.

12 ounces (340 g) tender mushrooms

2 tablespoons pork lard or vegetable oil

½ medium white onion, thinly sliced

1 garlic clove, finely chopped

2 fresh jalapeño chiles, 1 cut into narrow strips, 1 coarsely chopped

salt to taste

½ pound (225 g) tomates verdes, husks removed, rinsed,
and coarsely chopped

[CONTINUED]

2 cups (500 ml) light chicken broth

2 large sprigs epazote

Cut off the soiled tips of the mushroom stems and rinse briefly only if there is loose dirt adhering to the mushrooms. Peel off the orange-colored skins and discard. Cut the caps into quarters and slice the stems into narrow strips. Heat the lard in a skillet, add the onion, garlic, chile strips, and salt, and cook over medium heat without browning for about 2 minutes. Add the mushrooms and cook over fairly high heat, shaking the pan to prevent sticking, for about 5 minutes to reduce some of the juice that exudes from the mushrooms.

Puree the *tomates verdes* with the chile and ⅓ cup (83 ml) of the chicken broth in a blender. Add to the pan and cook over high heat until the sauce has reduced and seasoned—about 10 minutes. Add the remaining broth and *epazote*, adjust the seasoning, and cook for 10 minutes more. The sauce should now be of medium consistency. Serve the mushrooms with plenty of the sauce and corn tortillas.

HONGOS AZULES CON CREMA

INDIGO MILKCAPS IN CREAM

❂

[MAKES APPROXIMATELY 4 CUPS (1 L)]

I ALWAYS WAIT ANXIOUSLY FOR THE BLUE MUSHROOMS, AÑILES (*LACTARIUS INDIGO*), THAT BEGIN TO APPEAR IN THE MARKETS IN THE EASTERN PART OF Michoacán and the State of Mexico at about the middle of July. Grayish blue on the outside, when cut the flesh is a brilliant blue, which unfortunately changes to a dull bluish green in the cooking. As the mushrooms age they become slightly discolored, but they are still good to eat. They do not have that very earthy taste of some wild mushrooms, but unlike the latter they retain a crisp quality when cooked.

Of course you may cook them without the cream, but I do think that, like morels, their flavor is enhanced by it. I like to serve them as a first course in small ramekins with deep blue corn tortillas . . . my signature dish, you might say, although I heartily dislike the phrase. As a matter of fact, because of their crisp quality, they freeze well after being cooked in this way, which is certainly a boon when the season is so short. This recipe was inspired by Sra. Hortensia Cabrera de Fagoaga.

1¼ pounds (565 g) blue mushrooms
2 to 3 tablespoons vegetable oil
2 garlic cloves, finely chopped
2 heaped tablespoons finely chopped white onion
4 chilaca or poblano chiles, charred, peeled,
seeds and veins removed, and torn into narrow strips
salt to taste
¾ cup (188 ml) crème fraîche or to taste
2 tablespoons coarsely chopped epazote

Cut off the soiled mushroom stem tips. Wipe the mushrooms with a damp cloth and cut into slices about ⅛ inch (3 mm) thick. Heat the oil in a wide skillet. Add the garlic, onion, and chile strips with a sprinkle of salt and fry for about 3 minutes without browning. Add the mushrooms, cover the pan, and cook for about 5 minutes. They should be just cooked but still crisp. Stir in the cream, *epazote,* and salt if necessary and continue cooking for about 3 minutes, uncovered, over medium heat, stirring to prevent sticking. Set them aside to season for at least 15 minutes before serving.

CALABACITAS CON HONGOS

SQUASH WITH MUSHROOMS

Sra. Dominga Maldonado de Jiménez

❁

[SERVES 4 TO 6]

THIS IS MY ALL-OUT FAVORITE DISH. EVEN WITHOUT THE CREAM AND CHEESE IT MAKES A DELICIOUS VEGETABLE SIDE DISH; IF YOU INCLUDE ALL the rich things and serve it in individual gratin dishes, it makes a wonderful first course or main vegetarian course. I have modified the traditional recipe by cooking the mushrooms separately so that the flavor is intensified. The small tender *clavitos (Leophyllum decastes*), literally "little nails," known as fried chicken mushrooms in the United States, are my preferred mushroom for this recipe, but any small, juicy mushroom can be substituted.

3½ tablespoons vegetable oil

2 heaped tablespoons finely chopped white onion

1 large poblano chile, charred, peeled,
seeds and veins removed,
and cut into narrow strips

salt to taste

1 pound (450 g) zucchini or other green squash, cut into ¼-inch
(7-mm) cubes, about 3 cups plus ½ rounded cup (890 ml)

½ pound (225 g) mushrooms (see note above), rinsed and shaken dry

½ cup (125 ml) loosely packed coarsely chopped cilantro

4 ounces (115 g) queso fresco or Muenster, thinly sliced

½ to ¾ cup (125 to 188 ml) crème fraîche

Heat 2 tablespoons of the oil in a skillet, add the onion and chile strips with a sprinkle of salt, and cook without browning for about 1 minute. Add the squash, cover the pan, and cook over medium heat, shaking the pan from time to time to prevent sticking, until the squash is almost tender—about 10 minutes.

Meanwhile, toss the mushrooms in the remaining 1½ tablespoons of oil, sprinkle with salt, and stir-fry in another pan for about 5 minutes or until the juice that exudes has become almost gelatinous. Stir the mushrooms into the squash. Sprinkle the *cilantro* over the vegetables, then cover with the cheese and cream. Cover the pan and cook over gentle heat for about 5 minutes, or until the cheese has melted.

PATAS DE POLLO CON RAJAS

CORAL MUSHROOMS WITH CHILE STRIPS

Sra. Augustina Vásquez Lascaño

❋

[MAKES ABOUT 2 CUPS (500 ML)—ENOUGH FOR 12 TO 14 TACOS OR *QUESADILLAS*]

THIS IS ANOTHER RECIPE FROM THE RÍO FRÍO AREA, WHERE CORAL MUSH-ROOMS ARE CALLED *PATAS DE POLLO*—CHICKEN FEET. IT MAKES A DELICIOUS textured filling for tacos or *quesadillas*. By adding eggs to the mushrooms you could serve it as a light first course or even as a brunch dish.

> 12 ounces (340 g) coral mushrooms
> 3 tablespoons lard or vegetable oil
> ½ medium white onion, thinly sliced
> 1 garlic clove, finely chopped
> 2 poblano *chiles, charred, peeled, seeds and veins removed,*
> *and cut into narrow strips*
> salt to taste
> 3 or 4 eggs, lightly beaten (optional)

Cut off the soiled bases of the mushrooms. Shake in hot water to loosen any dirt still adhering to them and drain. Cut the mushrooms into strips. Heat the lard in a skillet, add the onion, garlic, and chile strips, sprinkle with salt, and fry for about 15 minutes, shaking the pan from time to time to prevent sticking. Remove the lid and continue cooking until most of the juice has evaporated, adding more salt if necessary.

If you're using eggs, stir them in well and cook over low heat until set. Serve immediately.

I HAVE A MODEST COLLECTION OF OLD MEXICAN COOKBOOKS, MOST OF THEM PUBLISHED IN THE LAST CENTURY, AND I LOVE TO DELVE INTO THEM TO SAVOR AND REVIVE SOME OF THE tastes and textures of a bygone age. I often hide away and cook from them after one of my brief immersions in the current culinary scene. It is true, the latter has spawned some truly great books, but, alas, far too many have been hyped beyond their worth or written with terse and rigid formulas: no fat, no salt (but what of flavor? food is meant to be enjoyed, not only to nourish), and cooked in as short a time as possible—no joy in that! ❀ The most complete first record of what people grew, hunted, and ate in pre-Columbian times is contained in the Florentine Codex: pictographs of the daily life of the Azteca transcribed shortly after the Conquest by Fray Bernadino de Sahagun in his *Historia de la Nueva España*. The novelty of the food surprised the first invaders; even Cortés mentions it in his *Cartas de Relación* to Carlos V. The Anonymous Conquerer (who has never been identified and whose original document has been lost) mentions food along with religion, customs, and buildings. And a Captain in Cortés's army, Bernal Díaz del Castillo, wrote a lively account of his first impressions of the marketplace of Tenochtitlán and the meals of Moctezuma. ✹ Hernández, the king's physician who was sent to catalog plants and their uses—as both medicine and food—left an invaluable record. ✹ Many other mentions of food occurred in clerical documents, and one of the most amusing accounts is that of an English monk, Thomas Gage, who, instead of allowing himself to be transshipped to the Philippines, defected and traveled through the south of Mexico and Guatemala. There is a small recipe book consisting mostly of sweetmeats that is purported to have been written by the nun/poetess Sor Juana Inés de la Cruz before her death in 1695, but some scholars dispute this. Some years ago I came across an eighteenth-century manuscript from a convent listing all the dishes and meals served during Lent. There must exist many such documents. ✹ From the early part of the nineteenth century, printed recipe books began to appear, and while many of the recipes were of Spanish origin, they included many integrating Mexican ingredients and dishes like *moles*, *pipiáns*, *tamales*, etc., as they had been used in convents at the beginning of the colonial period. But these elegantly bound books were for the well-to-do. Some had been compiled for worthy church charities, and they shamelessly "borrowed" from each other. ✹ After the Independence in 1810, Mexico was opened up to foreigners for the first time: scientists, diplomats, miners, engineers, and adventurers, in dispatches or diaries, always commented on some aspect of the food they found there. They were surprised and often expressed strong views, especially on chiles, beans, and tortillas, of which they came across plenty. The earliest book I have is dated 1828, followed by two published in 1831, but by far the most important was *El Cocinero Mexicano*, published by Galván in Mexico City in 1845. It was written in the form of a dictionary. The contents were described on the title page in the form of a wide goblet. Facing is an engraving depicting a kitchen of the times with a rotund chef cooking while his assistants, a man and a woman, are preparing and chopping foods. Underneath are two decorative plates of salads or rather how they should be presented—surprisingly in color. There are pages of menus at the back with diagrams, very precise ones, of how to carve meats, poultry, and fish.

Apart from some very doable recipes—and I include here a delicious sauce or relish and a squash stuffed with squash flowers, much like the innovations of today—it makes wonderful reading. This is the sort of book you pick up time and time again and always find extraordinary bits of information. Would you believe that when an ox has done its ten-year service to agriculture the meat is at its most nutritive—that is, after a six-month fattening period? In fact, there are ten pages and fifty-four recipes devoted to *buey*, or ox. When corn was brought to Europe for the first time, the book says, "it was cultivated by the poor farmers and was known to them as Turkish wheat."

In Mexico, with minor exceptions, a hearty breakfast is called *almuerzo*. Here the dictionary makes the distinciton between a formal *almuerzo* and one for friends and intimates with dishes like *mole, pipián, chiles rellenos, enchiladas,* refried beans, etc., to be accompanied by wine, beer, and *pulque*. For more formal occasions, when entertaining visitors, the dishes prepared are European: pies, roasts, and salads. For those who elect to have a breakfast in bed, the book suggests chocolate, coffee, milk, or tea, breads and pastries of many types, hot fried foods, hard-cooked eggs, and, apart from generous amounts of white wine, a bottle of *aguardiente* to lace your coffee!

After one of those hearty meals—to nourish them until after evening Mass—the writer says: "Replete, our illustrious and modern Midases return to their businesses and dedicate themselves all the more energetically to their gold mines, fully aware that they must do so if they are to keep up this sumptuous way of eating to which they have become accustomed. . . . but this opulent regime does not apply to the humble pensioner or the modest student of the muses."

When it comes to supper, our writer waxes positively lyrical: "If breakfast is the meal for friends and lunch more formal, supper is the meal of love. It is the hour of repose; the end of business and duties. The soft light of evening is more favorable to lovers. Women are more charming at suppertime than any other time of day. As the time approaches when they rule over their sweet domain they become more tender and seductive. The night is theirs to reign over with irresistible seduction." That should put ardent feminists on the warpath!

CALABACITAS RELLENAS DE FLOR

ZUCCHINI OR ROUND SQUASH STUFFED WITH SQUASH FLOWERS

❁

[SERVES 6]

I FOUND THIS RECIPE IN *EL COCINERO MEXICANO EN FORMA DE DICCIONARIO* AND THOUGHT IT APPROPRIATE FOR MODERN EATING; BESIDES, IT IS VERY COLOR-ful. It is better if you can find small, round squash. I have added the cream and cheese to the recipe, which adds richness and makes it a perfect vegetarian (except for the very strict ones) dish.

THE FILLING

[MAKES ABOUT 2 CUPS (500 ML)]

1 pound (450 g) squash flowers, about 5 cups (1.25 l) tightly packed

3 tablespoons vegetable oil or butter

½ medium white onion, finely chopped

2 garlic cloves, finely chopped

8 ounces (225 g) tomatoes, finely chopped, about 1 heaped cup (265 ml)

salt to taste

1¼ pounds (565 g) zucchini (see note above)

½ cup (125 ml) crème fraîche

⅓ cup (83 ml) finely grated Chihuahua cheese or Muenster

[CONTINUED]

Remove the stalks and stringy green sepals from the flowers, rinse briefly, shake dry, and chop roughly.

Heat the oil in a skillet and fry the onion and garlic until translucent.

Add the tomatoes and salt and cook over medium heat until almost dry—about 4 minutes. Add the chopped flowers, cover the pan, and continue cooking until the mixture is almost moist but not juicy. Set aside.

Cut the squash in half lengthwise and set in one layer, cut side down, in a wide pan. Cover with boiling salted water and cook over low heat for about 10 minutes. Turn them over and continue cooking until they are just tender. Drain and cool. Heat the oven to 375°F (190°C). Scrape out the flesh and seeds and again set cut side down to drain for about 10 minutes.

Stuff the squash with plenty of the flowers and place in one layer in an ovenproof dish. Loosely cover and cook for about 15 minutes or until well heated through. Pour the cream around the squash, sprinkle the tops with the cheese, and return to the oven until the cheese has melted and the cream is bubbling, about 10 minutes. Spoon the cream over the top when serving.

SALSA MACHO

VIRILE SAUCE

❃

[MAKES APPROXIMATELY 2 CUPS (500 ML)]

MANY REGIONS OF MEXICO HAVE THEIR *MACHO* SAUCE. THIS VERSION COMES FROM *DICCIONARIO DE COCINA* AND MORE RESEMBLES A RELISH OR SOME OF THE *salsas borrachas*. It should be left to season for at least 2 hours before serving or made the day before. It will keep in the refrigerator for at least 2 weeks and gets better every day.

2 ancho *chiles*
4 pasilla *chiles*
1 tablespoon lard or vegetable oil
½ cup (125 ml) finely chopped white onion
2 garlic cloves, finely chopped

1 cup (250 ml) pulque (page 12) or light beer

salt to taste

TOPPING

approximately ¼ cup (63 ml) finely grated queso añejo or Romano

2 tablespoons olive oil (optional)

Douse the chiles quickly in hot water—do not soak—and wipe dry and clean with a cloth. Slit the chiles open and remove the seeds and veins, reserving the seeds.

Flatten the chiles as much as possible and toast on a warm *comal* or griddle, turning them over from time to time until they become crisp when cooled—about 5 minutes. Crumble the chiles into a small, deep dish.

Heat the lard in a skillet and fry the chile seeds until crisp and brown.

Drain and add to the crumbled chiles. Add the rest of the ingredients and stir well.

To serve, sprinkle with the cheese and oil.

Cooking et al. as They Did in 1877

I hope it will always give me as much pleasure to have a "new" Mexican cookbook in my possession as it did when *La Cocinera Poblana* came my way and was added to my collection. It was published in Puebla in 1877 and has a richly tooled red leather binding stamped with gold. It is dedicated in a most elegant hand: *"Emiliano Colladoe, to my beloved aunt Amada Guiao, September 13th, 1879."*

It has always rather amused me to read the comments on the jackets of cookbooks—often written by well-known food writers or chefs—extolling their contents in rather extravagant terms. In 1877, however, it was the custom to point out these virtues on the title page. Here, for instance, is *La Cocinera Poblana, Practical Manual of Spanish, French, English and Mexican Cuisines*—in that order. "It contains more than two thousand recipes, simple and easy to prepare with special sections on pastrymaking, confectionery, and desserts." But this is not all. We are also promised ". . . secrets of the dressing table and domestic medicine to preserve good health and prolong life." On the following page the *Advertencia* tells us: "This book which we are offering the public is undoubtedly very useful and fills a gap in family knowledge. Cookery books with which we are familiar generally contain many recipes that have no application here." It goes on to admit that it is a revised version of Spanish publication edited by "... a practical cook who has omitted irrelevant recipes and added some exquisite dishes that have been tried over the years with great success ... and we believe that *La Cocinera Poblana* will be very much sought after." Extravagant claims perhaps, but frank.

The first chapter, as usual, is dedicated to soups. Not the most inspiring of soups and many, it would seem, intended for invalids. I immediately turned to the back of the book— where I normally start anyway—and found a mine of information under the title *Miscelanea*. There you are told how to varnish or paint a floor red, engrave on crystal, or make a paste for cleaning silver. Sandwiched rather unexpectedly between the latter and *"How to Clean Gloves Without Wetting Them"* (rub the gloves well with bread crumbs mixed with a powder of burnt bones and finish off by wiping them with a cloth impregnated with powdered alum and earth) is *"How to Clear and Beautify the Skin."* (Simmer some rose petals or rosemary flowers in white wine and rub the liquid well into the skin.)

I shuddered slightly to read that you should apply a decoction of lead ore, with other ingredients, if you want your hair dyed black or smear a bald pate with beef marrow or chicken fat to make the hair grow again (recent studies, however, indicate that chicken manure is more effective, since it has a powerful hormonal content). There is *"Water of the Angels"* made of myrtle flowers, *"Water of the Sultanas"* perfumed with balsam, vanilla, and a bouquet of flowers, and an infusion of common cooking herbs to strengthen the teeth, next to the repairing of porcelain and the washing of silk dresses.

I continued reading, fascinated by the *"Higiene Doméstica."* It includes a brief pharmacopia of homemade ingredients: unguents, infusions, poultices, and even *"How to Apply Leeches,"* followed by descriptions of palliatives and cures for ills such as measles, yellow fever, gangrene, bad breath, and rabies and instructions for recognizing the signs of death. I also learned something I didn't know about old age: "While the faculties and senses are generally weakened in old age [there is fortunately a *mas o menos* inserted here] the palate is strengthened and becomes more sensitive. Because of this, old people tend to lean towards gastronomy. But they should control their propensity for eating too much, especially when their economic situation permits them to put on a good spread. . . . Sobriety is not only advisable for hygienic considerations dicated by prudence, but a necessity." Authoritative words indeed!

> "Dicen que los viejos mueren   They say that old men die
> por comida o por caida.   by overeating or falling down.
> Ande, pues, con tiento el viejo   Then go easy old man,
> Y modere la comida."   and eat moderately.

I turned back to the recipes. There was a mutton stew with a sauce made of hazelnuts and the juices of cooked pomegranates, how to cook a hen in twenty-five different ways, and *vaca prensada.* The thought of a whole pressed cow was amusing but not exactly appetizing. There was also a recipe telling how to preserve fish *"de la corrupción"*—intriguing.

The order of the recipes becomes rather haphazard. We are informed by the editor that the fish recipes are being inserted after the veal and before the pork because at that particular moment in the preparation of the book fish was cheap and plentiful! There is a table of standard cooking times and miscellaneous information such as what to do about tough poultry. According to this, feathers and all, the bird is left to soak in a solution of wood ash and water for twenty-four hours. It is then plucked and cleaned—rather a messy job, I would think, and then soaked again for twenty-four hours. After boiling for fifteen minutes it is ready to be roasted. And the flavor?

Browsing on through the book I came across a recipe for English boiled pudding—boiled in a cloth as we used to at home. Two and a half pounds of beef marrow is suggested as the fat with suet as an alternative. There was a *"Pastel Inglés Llamado Liverpool."* From the vague descriptions it seemed to be a type of choux pastry with thin layers of Gruyère cheese (perhaps a Liverpudlian would like to throw some light on this).

This book is possibly more complete than Mrs. Beeton's. There are explicit directions about how to carve and serve. They are more or less normal except for the fact that you are advised to put the carving knife or serving spoon back onto the platter and not to wield it in the air or lay it on the cloth. The pages devoted to *"Urbanidad en la Mesa"* are full of good advice. There are the usual admonitions: "Don't talk with your mouth full, don't put your elbows on the table or dig your neighbor in the ribs with the spoon, don't pour your coffee into the saucer to cool off," etc., etc. But one does begin to wonder about the readership when one reads: "during dessert do not stuff your pockets full of fruits and sweets; only those lacking in culture throw pellets of bread at their fellow diners; only badly brought up people break their glass in exuberance after giving a toast—this smacks of barracks-room behavior; don't roll up the sleeves of your evening jacket as if you were going to wash your hands."

There are a few delicious items such as "Don't take the dog when you go visiting or out to dine; only coach drivers throw wine in their soup; if you should find something dirty on your plate, return it to the serving maid without saying anything and mention it to the cook only if you find something dangerous, like a pin, in the food."

I finally got around to the Mexican recipes: *moles, pipiáns, tamales,* and *tinga escandalosa.* It was almost a letdown, but I decided to cook some of them. The tripe and onions of my youth had almost put me off tripe forever until I cooked it with *chiles pasillas* and chickpeas—it is gutsy stuff (recipe follows) and a really economical dish. I stuffed *chiles poblanos* with chard and young peas, which makes a good vegetarian dish or interesting first course. A *guisado de chiles en vinagre* sounded interesting enough: chicken, ham, *chorizos,* spices, almonds, capers, and olives in a sauce of blended, pickled jalapeños. But it was fierce and disappointing. And then two desserts caught my eye: an almond sponge flavored with the grated rind of limes and a rice pudding with a difference (both recipes published in *The Art of Mexican Cooking*).

La Cocina Poblana did indeed live up to its promise!

CHILES RELLENOS DE ACELGAS Y CHICHAROS

CHILES STUFFED WITH CHARD AND PEAS

❁

[SERVES 6]

6 large poblano *chiles*

2 tablespoons unsalted butter

5 ounces (140 g) crumbled queso fresco,
Chihuahua *cheese, or Muenster, grated*

8 ounces (225 g) Swiss chard
8 ounces (225 g) shelled peas, about 1½ cups (375 ml)
salt to taste
pinch of sugar
2 to 3 tablespoons vegetable oil
¼ medium white onion, finely chopped
2 garlic cloves, finely chopped
12 ounces (340 g) tomatoes, chopped, about 2 cups (500 ml)

Place the chiles, whole with stems attached, over a flame, turning them from time to time so that the flesh does not burn, until the skin is blistered and slightly charred. Remove from the flame and immediately place them in a plastic bag. Set them aside for about 15 minutes to steam—the skin should then easily slip off (I advise you to do this by placing a large strainer over the sink drain to avoid some of the mess).

Carefully slit each chile open lengthwise and cut out the center core to which the seeds are attached, taking care to leave the stem base that forms the top of the chile intact. Carefully remove the veins that are attached to the flesh, taking care not to shred the flesh, and rinse the chile "shells" in cold water. They are now ready to stuff. Set them aside (see note below).

THE STUFFING: Rinse the chard well in cold water and trim off the tough stalk ends (which are often sandy), but leave the white stalks intact. Have a saucepan ready with lightly salted boiling water about 1½ inches (4 cm) deep. Add the chard and cook, uncovered, turning the leaves over frequently, until they are just tender—about 5 minutes, depending on how tough they were, etc. Drain in a colander (reserving the liquid for the stockpot or drinking it), chop well, and set aside.

Meanwhile, cover the peas with boiling water, add the salt and sugar, and cook until tender but not soft—about 5 minutes, depending on age and quality. Drain and set aside.

Heat the oil in a heavy skillet and fry the onion and garlic gently, without browning, until translucent. Add the chopped tomatoes and cook over fairly high heat, stirring from time to

[CONTINUED]

time, until the mixture has been reduced to a thickish sauce—about 8 minutes, depending on how juicy the tomatoes are, etc. Stir in the cooked chard and peas, adjust the seasoning, and cook over medium heat for about 3 minutes longer—the mixture should be fairly dry. If there is too much juice, reduce quickly over high heat.

Heat the oven to 375°F (190°C). Have ready an ovenproof dish into which the chiles will just fit in one layer. Smear it thickly with the butter.

Stuff the chiles with the vegetable mixture and set them in the prepared dish. Cover with foil and bake until well heated through, about 20 minutes.

Sprinkle liberally with the cheese, cover the dish again, and bake until the cheese has melted but not browned, about 20 minutes.

NOTES: *The chiles can be prepared ahead of time or the day before. I do not recommend freezing them since they lose their delicious flavor and texture. Do not stuff the chiles until the last minute. The filling tends to become rather watery with the juice that exudes from the flesh of the chiles. If you prefer a richer dish, pour on ⅔ cup (164 ml) slightly salted thick cream when the dish first goes into the oven. When the cream is bubbling, sprinkle with the cheese. The vegetables could be steamed if you prefer.*

PANCITA EN MOLE

TRIPE IN MOLE

❁

[SERVES 6]

6 ounces (180 g) dried chickpeas, about 1 cup (250 ml)
2¼ pounds (1 generous kg) tripe, callo de res (see note below)
¼ medium white onion, roughly chopped
2 garlic cloves, chopped
1 tablespoon salt or to taste
5 mulato chiles
3 garlic cloves, roughly chopped
5 peppercorns, crushed
approximately 1¼ cups (313 ml) water
1½ tablespoons pork lard

Start the day before. Cover the chickpeas with hot water and soak overnight.

Scrub the tripe well and cut into 2-inch (5-cm) squares. Cover with water in a large pot, add the onion, garlic, and salt, and bring to a boil. Lower the heat and simmer for about 4 hours or until tender.

Add the chickpeas and the water in which they were soaked to the tripe and cook until they are tender but not too soft. (Mexican cooks have a great tendency to overcook things until they lose all texture—it makes a very unappetizing dish.) Strain the meat and chickpeas and set in a warm place, reserving the broth—you should have about 1 quart (1 l) of broth. If there is more than that, reduce quickly over high heat.

Remove the stems from the chiles, slit them open, remove the veins and seeds and flatten them as much as possible. Heat a *comal* or griddle and toast the chiles lightly on both sides, taking care not to burn them. Cover the chiles with boiling water and leave them to soak for 15 to 20 minutes. Strain and transfer to a blender. Add the garlic, peppercorns, and water and blend until smooth, adding a little more water if necessary only to release the blender blade —the puree must be thick.

Heat the lard in a *cazuela* or heavy flameproof pan. Add the chile puree and fry over fairly high heat, stirring and scraping the bottom of the pan to prevent sticking, for about 8 minutes.

Add the tripe, chickpeas, and about 2½ to 3 cups (625 to 750 ml) of the broth in which they were cooked. Adjust the seasoning and simmer over medium heat until the ingredients are well seasoned and the sauce is thickened. Add more broth if necessary.

NOTES: *For best results, don't take shortcuts and buy precooked tripe or precooked chickpeas. There will be no good broth, and the flavor of the dish will be lost. Buy the beef tripe that looks like a towel, callo (in fact in Yucatán it is called toalla), and buy it only if it has been scrubbed white. If it is a messy-looking brown color, it will be a problem to clean and have a very strong odor. You could, of course, cook this in a pressure cooker. I would allow about 40 minutes for the tripe, then add the chickpeas and cook them together for 20 to 30 minutes more. Time will vary slightly with the quality of the ingredients.*

ARROZ CON CHILE ANCHO

RICE COOKED WITH ANCHO CHILE

La Cocinera Poblana, *1877*

✺

[SERVES 4]

APART FROM BEING SOMEWHAT OF A RICE ADDICT, I WAS FASCINATED BY THE UNUSUAL COMBINATION OF FLAVORS OF *CHILE ANCHO* WITH SAFFRON. Although the original recipe was rather vague, it does say to add the chiles whole, but I prefer to tear them into pieces to distribute the flavor and texture throughout the rice.

I sometimes serve this rice to accompany a fish dish, which I think it does very well.

¾ cup (188 ml) long-grain unconverted white rice
a few saffron threads
1½ cups (375 ml) water
2 ancho chiles, seeds and veins removed
3 tablespoons vegetable oil
salt to taste
2 heaped tablespoons finely chopped white onion

Cover the rice with hot water and soak for 5 minutes. Rinse well and set aside to drain.

Soak the saffron threads in ½ cup (125 ml) of the water for about 15 minutes. Lightly toast the chiles on an ungreased *comal* or griddle, then cover with hot water and soak for 15 minutes.

Heat the oil in a flameproof dish. Give the rice a final shake to get rid of excess water and add to the oil. Stir well to cover the grains evenly, sprinkle with salt, and fry for about 5 minutes, stirring the rice from time to time. Add the onion and continue frying until the rice is just beginning to change color—about 5 minutes.

Add the saffron water with the remainder of the plain water, together with the chiles torn into strips, and cook, covered, over low heat until all the liquid has been absorbed—about 15 minutes. Set aside off the heat, still covered, for at least 10 minutes before serving.

PAPAS CON CHILE

POTATOES WITH CHILE POBLANO

La Cocinera Poblana, 1877

❈

[SERVES 4]

I AM ALWAYS LOOKING FOR NEW WAYS OF PREPARING POTATOES, WHICH ARE, WITHOUT DOUBT, A HIGH FAVORITE IN ANY FOOD POLL. THERE ARE SOME excellent varieties of potatoes grown in the higher lands around where I live, and for part of the year I can buy the small light brown ones with a flaking skin more akin to the new potatoes to be found in England in the spring.

I suggest you use waxy new potatoes for this recipe. It can, of course, be made ahead and in fact improves in flavor. To make a more substantial dish, I often add cheese at the last moment.

12 ounces (340 g) small waxy potatoes, cubed or thickly sliced

salt to taste

3 garlic cloves, roughly chopped

*4 poblano chiles, charred, peeled, seeds and veins removed,
and roughly chopped*

3 tablespoons vegetable oil

3 ounces (85 g) Oaxaca cheese or Muenster, cut into thin slices

In a saucepan, cover the potatoes with hot water, add salt, and cook over medium heat until just tender, still a little *al dente*, about 10 minutes. Drain, reserving the cooking water, cool, and peel.

Put 1 cup (250 ml) of the cooking water, the garlic, and the chiles into a blender and blend to a slightly textured sauce.

Heat the oil in a skillet, add the blended ingredients, and fry over fairly high heat, scraping the bottom of the pan to prevent sticking, for about 5 minutes. Add the potatoes and cook over low heat until well seasoned—about 8 minutes. Just before serving, stir in the cheese, and just heat through to melt. Serve immediately.

Libro de Cocina, Toluca 1895

My friend Virginia Barrios, who has contributed to my understanding of the food of her area, lent me two manuscript cookbooks a few years ago. They belonged to a friend who was from an old Toluca family. I gathered that nobody had paid them much attention until I once again asked to consult them, since I had made the *tamales de San Luís* with such success—despite the very vague instructions. There were in fact two volumes, one slimmer than the other, both bound in green cloth with a maroon leather spine bearing the laconic word *cocina*.

What obviously started out as a series of recipes were bound at a later date, since Volume I commences with page 134, followed by page 2. Most of the recipes were recorded in the most exquisite handwriting with the finest of nibs in pale brown ink.

There is a recipe for cookies from the sisters Josefina and Dolores that bears the date "Toluca 1895," but presumably it was a collection that had been added to over the years. It had obviously been kept in the kitchen: there is an unfinished cookie recipe in a child's rough handwriting, and two pages are taken up with large drawings of mustachioed men in sombreros. At the end of the second volume, faded newspaper clippings of recipes are stuck on the pages, followed by typewritten transcriptions of the recipes: clearer to read but lacking the flavor and magic of 100 years.

There is a *mole verde* recipe decorated with a garland of flowers held up by two little birds, *haz me pronto* (do me quickly) little cakes, *pan Inglés* (English bread) raised with *pulque*, turkey cooked in a puree of pineapple—I tried it, but it was not to my taste—an overly rich dessert of pineapple and *natas*, another named *basura* (garbage) of pineapple and coconut. However, the recipes I have given here I found irresistible and, what's more, delicious.

CHILE DE JARAL EN FRÍO

STUFFED ANCHO CHILES SERVED COLD

✴

[SERVES 6]

JARAL IS THE NAME GIVEN TO ANCHO CHILES IN THE AREA AROUND TOLUCA.

While this is not a recipe that you will want to stick to slavishly, despite reverence to its seventy-five years of age, the dish has many interesting flavors and textures and lends itself to many innovations and interpretations. This is an asset in these days with the current, fevered search for new tastes.

It is just as well to make plenty of the filling, which can be used as a *salpicón* for tacos.

6 large ancho chiles
2 tablespoons red wine vinegar
salt to taste

THE FILLING
1 pound (450 g) skirt steak, cut into 2-inch (5-cm) cubes
¼ medium white onion, roughly sliced
salt to taste
2 tablespoons vegetable oil
⅓ cup (83 ml) finely chopped white onion
2 garlic cloves, finely chopped
12 ounces (340 g) tomatoes, finely chopped, about 2 cups (500 ml)
½-inch (1.5-cm) thin cinnamon stick
2 cloves
2 peppercorns
⅓ cup (83 ml) raisins
2 tablespoons roughly chopped flat-leaf parsley

THE DRESSING
1 pound (450 g) zucchini, thickly sliced, cooked, and drained
1 cup mashed avocado

[CONTINUED]

2 tablespoons vinegar
2 tablespoons olive oil
¼ cup (63 ml) roughly chopped cilantro (optional)
salt to taste

Slit the chiles open and carefully remove the seeds and veins, leaving the chiles intact for stuffing. Barely cover the chiles with water and bring to a simmer. Simmer for about 5 minutes and leave to soak for another 10 minutes or until the skins are soft. Drain well. Sprinkle the inside of each chile with 1 teaspoon of vinegar and a little salt and set aside to season for about 1 hour while you prepare the stuffing.

THE FILLING: Cover the steak with water, add the sliced onion and salt, and bring to a simmer. Continue simmering until the meat is tender—35 to 40 minutes. Drain and set aside to cool. When cool enough to handle, shred the meat.

Heat the oil in a skillet, add the ⅓ cup onion and the garlic, sprinkle with salt to taste, and fry over medium heat for 1 minute. Add the tomatoes and continue cooking for 5 more minutes to reduce the liquid. Crush the spices together, add them to the pan with the raisins and parsley, and cook together for 5 minutes. Add the shredded meat and cook until well seasoned, moist, and shiny—about 5 more minutes. Taste for salt and set aside to cool.

Drain the chiles well, stuff each one with the meat mixture, and set on a serving platter. Put the zucchini, avocado, and the rest of the dressing ingredients into a food processor and blend until smooth. Pour the dressing over the chiles and serve at room temperature with corn tortillas.

ENTOMATADO

PORK CHOPS IN GREEN TOMATO SAUCE

❁

[SERVES 6]

THE FLAVOR OF THIS DISH IMPROVES IF IT IS PREPARED AN HOUR OR SO AHEAD OF TIME AND REHEATED. *TOMATES VERDES VARY IN ACIDITY. IF THEY* are very acid, add a little brown sugar to the sauce to counterbalance the flavor.

I like to serve this dish with plain rice, although the book suggests serving it with chile strips and hard-cooked eggs.

Thick shoulder chops are better than the dry center loin chops for this type of recipe.

*6 large pork chops, about ¾ inch (2 cm) thick,
with some fat, about 1¾ pounds (800 g)*

salt to taste

THE SAUCE

3 tablespoons vegetable oil

¾ cup (188 ml) finely chopped white onion

*1 pound (450 g) tomates verdes, husks removed,
rinsed and finely chopped, 3¼ cups (813 ml)*

½-inch (13-mm) cinnamon stick

scant ¼ teaspoon caraway seeds

3 peppercorns

3 cloves

3 sprigs fresh marjoram or ¼ teaspoon dried

3 sprigs fresh thyme or ¼ teaspoon dried

*1 large ancho chile, wiped clean, veins and seeds removed,
and torn into narrow strips*

Put the meat into a saucepan, cover with water, and add salt. Bring to a simmer and continue cooking over low heat until the meat is just tender—about 40 minutes. Drain and reserve the broth.

Heat the oil in a flameproof casserole, add the onion, and fry for a few seconds without browning. Add the *tomates verdes* and salt to taste and continue cooking over fairly high heat until some of the juice has evaporated. Grind the spices together and add with the herbs and *ancho* chile to the sauce. Continue cooking over medium heat, stirring and scraping the bottom of the pan to prevent sticking, for about 10 minutes. Add 2½ cups (625 ml) reserved broth and the meat, adjust the seasoning, and continue cooking over low heat for about 10 minutes more.

Set aside to season for about 1 hour before serving.

CHILES POBLANOS RELLENOS EN SALSA DE AGUACATE

STUFFED POBLANO CHILES IN AVOCADO SAUCE

❋

[SERVES 6]

*6 medium poblano chiles, charred, peeled, veins and seeds removed,
but kept whole*

½ cup (125 ml) mild vinegar

¾ cup (188 ml) water

2 bay leaves, Mexican if possible

5 garlic cloves, finely chopped

2 cloves

3 peppercorns

½-inch (13-mm) cinnamon stick

½ teaspoon salt

THE STUFFING

2 cups (500 ml) cooked peas

2 tablespoons vegetable oil

⅓ cup (83 ml) finely grated queso añejo, cotija, or Romano

2 tablespoons drained large capers

salt to taste

THE SAUCE

2 cups (500 ml) avocado pulp

2 tablespoons vegetable oil

THE DECORATION

lettuce leaves

large capers, drained

sliced radishes

Start 3 days ahead. Put the cleaned chiles into a glass or nonreactive container and cover with the vinegar, water, spices, and salt. Press the chiles down well so that they are covered by the marinade and leave at the bottom of the refrigerator for 3 days, turning them over occasionally. Drain well, reserving the marinade.

THE STUFFING: Put the peas and 2 tablespoons of the marinade into a food processor and blend to a textured paste. Heat the oil in a skillet and fry the puree over low heat, stirring from time to time, for about 5 minutes. Remove from the heat and stir in the cheese and capers. Adjust the seasoning. When the mixture is cool, stuff each of the chiles with about ⅓ cup (83 ml) of the mixture and arrange them on a serving platter.

THE SAUCE AND DECORATION: Just before serving, put the avocado pulp, oil, and salt to taste in a blender or food processor and blend until smooth. Spread over the stuffed chiles and decorate with the remaining ingredients.

TORTA DE FLOR DE CALABAZA

SQUASH FLOWER TORTE

❋

[SERVES 4 TO 6]

I AM SURE THIS HAS HAPPENED TO YOU AS WELL: YOU LEAF THROUGH A NEW OR UNFAMILIAR OLD COOKBOOK AND MARK RECIPES YOU WANT TO TRY. SOME turn out to be very nice, others very good and tasty, and just a few of them are gems that almost blow your culinary mind. When you first try one of these, you want to rush around to friends, hot plate in hand, so that they may enjoy it with you right at that moment. A lot of good that wish would do me, living as I do in my "splendid isolation" (and sometimes not so splendid).

I do hope this recipe turns out as well for you as it did for me. A lot, however, will depend on the quality of the squash flowers—they should be very fresh and fragrant—and the excellence of the corn tortillas, which should be neither too thick nor too thin.

A 2-quart (2-l) French soufflé mold is ideal, one around 7½ inches (19 cm) in diameter and at least 3 inches (8 cm) high.

This is a substantial dish and can make six small first courses (which I serve with a light tomato sauce and crème fraîche), or four main courses—which you could serve in the same way, although I prefer to accompany it with a plain tomato salad.

vegetable oil for frying

8 5-inch (13-cm) corn tortillas, cut into quarters and partially dried

5 poblano chiles, charred, peeled, seeds and veins removed,
and roughly chopped

1 cup (250 ml) thick crème fraîche

salt to taste

2 cups (500 ml) cooked squash flowers,
drained at the last minute before using (recipe follows)

6 ounces (180 g) queso fresco or Muenster,
cut into thin slices and divided into 3 parts

Heat the oven to 350°F (177°C).

In a skillet, heat oil about ⅛ inch deep and fry the tortilla pieces, a few at a time in one layer, until they start to puff up but do not become crisp. Drain well on paper toweling and divide into 4. Blend the chiles with the crème fraîche and salt—it may look curdled, but don't worry.

Start layering the ingredients in the mold: ¾ cup (188 ml) of the chile cream, a layer of tortillas, 1 cup (250 ml) of the flowers, with a layer of a third of the cheese over the top, another layer of tortillas and ¾ cup (188 ml) chile cream, a third layer of tortillas, a second layer of flowers and cheese, finishing off with a fourth layer of tortillas and the last of the chile cream on top with the remaining cheese crumbled over it.

Cook on the top rack of the oven for 45 minutes or until bubbling from the bottom. Set aside for at least 10 minutes before serving. Serve as suggested above.

COOKED SQUASH FLOWERS

FOR DIAGRAMS AND DETAILED INFORMATION ON THE MALE AND FEMALE FLOWERS, SEE *THE ART OF MEXICAN COOKING*, PAGE 150.

2 tablespoons vegetable oil

¼ cup (63 ml) finely chopped white onion

1 garlic clove, finely chopped

1 serrano chile, finely chopped

salt to taste

1¼ pounds (565 g) cleaned squash flowers
(stalks and stringy green sepals removed), roughly chopped
2 tablespoons roughly chopped epazote leaves

Heat the oil in a skillet, add the onion, garlic, and chile, sprinkle with salt, and fry without browning until translucent. Add the chopped flowers, cover the pan, and cook over low heat until quite tender—about 10 minutes. Add the *epazote* and cook for a few seconds more.

NOTE: *If the flowers tend to be dry, you may need to add about ⅓ cup (83 ml) water. If, on the other hand, they have plenty of moisture, you will have to reduce the juice by cooking them uncovered for the last few minutes.*

TAMALES DE SAN LUÍS

Toluca cookbook, 1895

✸

[MAKES 36 MEDIUM TAMALES]

I CAN NEVER QUITE DECIDE FROM AMONG SO MANY EXACTLY WHICH ARE MY FAVORITE TAMALES, BUT THESE CERTAINLY RUN NECK AND NECK WITH VERY few others at the top of my list.

As I have mentioned in the opening comments to this section, the instructions for making these *tamales* were very vague, so it meant reconstructing the recipe. I did make one change: instead of using ordinary tortilla *masa*, I have used a slightly textured one and leavened it with the traditional *tequesquite* water (see page 257), a trick I learned from a cook in the Sierra de Puebla. However, if you use baking powder, the effect will be almost the same.

Be sure to let the filling cool off before attempting to assemble the *tamales*.

Any leftover *tamales* may be frozen and will keep for about 1 month, but remember, do not defrost them before reheating. Place the frozen *tamales* into a hot steamer and heat through for 15 to 20 minutes.

THE FILLING
2 tablespoons vegetable oil
¾ cup (188 ml) thinly sliced white onion

[CONTINUED]

5 *large* poblano *chiles, charred, peeled,*
seeds and veins removed, and cut into narrow strips

salt to taste

1½ *pounds (675 g) tomatoes, roughly chopped, about 4 cups (1 l)*

1 *garlic clove, roughly chopped*

10 *ounces (285 g) Chihuahua cheese or Muenster, cut into narrow strips*

THE DOUGH

8 *ounces (225 g) pork lard*

¼ *cup (63 ml)* tequesquite *water (page 257)*
or 1 teaspoon baking powder

3 *ancho* chiles, *veins and seeds removed*
and soaked in hot water for 15 minutes

1¾ *pounds (800 g) masa for tamales*
or tortillas (page 530), about 6 cups (1.5 l)

salt to taste

about ⅓ cup (83 ml) chicken broth or water

Have ready a steamer assembled for the *tamales* (page 522) with coins in the water, about 40 dried corn husks, and 40 ties of shredded husk, soaked to soften and drained.

THE FILLING: Heat the oil in a skillet, add the onion, chile strips, and salt, and fry over medium heat until the onion is translucent but not browned—about 5 minutes.

Puree the tomatoes with the garlic in a blender and add to the chiles in the pan. Continue cooking over high heat until some of the juice has been absorbed and the sauce thickened a little around the strips of chile—about 8 minutes. Adjust the salt and set aside to cool.

THE DOUGH: Beat the lard together with the *tequesquite* water or baking powder until white and fluffy.

Meanwhile, add the drained *ancho* chiles and liquid to a blender and blend until smooth. Gradually beat into the lard.

Add the *masa* to the lard mixture a little at a time, beating well after each addition. Continue beating until the mixture is well aerated and a small dollop of the *masa* will float on the surface of a glass of water—about 10 minutes. The mixture should just plop off the spoon. If it is too stiff, add some of the chicken broth.

ASSEMBLING THE TAMALES: Spread 2 tablespoons of the dough inside a corn husk, leaving plenty of room at the top and bottom for folding over. Place 2 chile strips, some sauce, and a strip of the cheese in the center and fold the edges of the husk over so that the dough almost covers the filling. Fold the ends over toward the middle and tie firmly but not tightly, leaving enough room for the dough to expand.

When the water in the steamer is boiling and the coins rattling, stack the *tamales* vertically, packing them firmly but not tightly in the top of the steamer. Cover the steamer with a tight lid and cook over high heat until the dough, when tested, comes cleanly away from the husk —about 1 to 1¼ hours.

NOTE: *Try to obtain dried corn husks that come with the cupped end intact; the folding will be easier, and you need not tie them.*

Novisimo Arte de Cocina, 1831—Newest Art of Cooking

This slim little volume was also published in 1831, and no doubt there was some competition between it and the newly published *El Cocinero Mexicano*. It is bound in brown mottled leather with the title stamped in gold on a strip of red and a simple flower design stamped along the spine. *El Novisimo Arte de Cocina* was printed in Mexico City and is dedicated to "*Las Señoritas Mexicanas.*" It doesn't mince words over the description of the contents, written as a subtitle: "An excellent collection of the best recipes . . . that can be prepared at the lowest possible cost and as easily as possible."

I have included here two recipes that caught my eye, one for Lenten beans and the other for cabbage salad. They sound rather mundane beside those named *Angel, The Magic Wand, Friars and Nuns,* and *Take off your Hat* . . .

ENSALADA DE COL

CABBAGE SALAD

Novísimo Arte de Cocina, 1831

✸

[MAKES APPROXIMATELY 4 CUPS (1 L)]

THIS IS THE FIRST RECIPE IN THE SALAD SECTION, ALTHOUGH SOME OF THE INGREDIENTS, INCLUDING THE CABBAGE, ARE COOKED. THEY MUST HAVE hated the taste of cabbage, because the instructions are to soak it overnight, wash in two or three waters, and then cook with a head of garlic . . . *then* rinse well!

The day I had some fresh cabbage from the garden I decided to make this dish. I serve it either at room temperature or lukewarm and find this better if left to sit for an hour or so for the flavors to marry. It is very good the next day.

1 small cabbage, about 1½ pounds (675 g), washed well and thinly sliced
1 teaspoon salt
4 unpeeled garlic cloves, crushed
1 quart (1 l) boiling water
3 tablespoons mild olive oil
¼ cup (63 ml) finely chopped white onion
¼ cup (63 ml) loosely packed, roughly chopped parsley
¼ cup (63 ml) loosely packed roughly chopped pitted green olives
1½ tablespoons wine vinegar
strips of jalapeño chiles en escabeche *to taste*

Add the cabbage, salt, and garlic to the boiling water and cook for a few minutes, until just tender but still slightly al dente. Drain well.

Heat the oil in a large skillet, add the onion, parsley, and a sprinkling of salt, and fry slowly until the onion is translucent. Add the cabbage and stir-fry until slightly wilted—about 3 minutes. Transfer the cabbage to a bowl, stir in the olives, vinegar, and chile strips, adjust the seasoning, and set aside as suggested above.

FRIJOLES PARA VIGILIA

LENTEN BEANS

❋

THIS IS ONE OF THE MANY MEXICAN RECIPES FOR LENT AND MEATLESS DAYS. I THINK IT IS AN INTERESTING VARIATION ON COOKING BEANS AND A VEGE-tarian dish to boot. No, pork lard was never ruled out in Lenten dishes and *tamales*, but of course you can substitute vegetable oil.

I suggest two ways of serving these beans: as a puree to cover eggs set on a crouton or diluted and served with croutons and egg on top as a soup.

8 ounces (225 g) beans, Mexican negros or canarios, black or pinto,
cooked, and their broth, about 3½ to 4 cups (875 ml to 1 l)

2 cloves, roughly crushed

scant ¼-inch (7-mm) cinnamon stick, roughly crushed

3 peppercorns, roughly crushed

rounded ¼ teaspoon dried oregano

3 large sprigs thyme or ⅛ teaspoon dried

3 tablespoons pork lard or vegetable oil

½ medium white onion, finely chopped

1 cup (250 ml) water

salt to taste

FOR THE EGG DISH

8 slices French or sourdough bread, fried crisp

8 poached or fried eggs

5 to 6 tablespoons finely grated queso fresco, añejo, or Romano

FOR THE SOUP

2 cups (500 ml) water

6 slices French or sourdough bread, fried crisp

6 poached or fried eggs

5 to 6 tablespoons finely grated queso fresco, añejo, or Romano

[CONTINUED]

Put ½ cup (125 ml) beans and their broth into a blender, add the cloves, cinnamon, peppercorns, oregano, and thyme, and blend until smooth.

Heat the lard in a skillet, add the onion, and fry gently until translucent. Add the pureed beans and cook over medium heat, stirring from time to time to prevent sticking, for about 5 minutes.

Puree the rest of the beans and gradually add them to the pan with the water. Cook over medium heat, scraping the bottom of the pan from time to time to prevent sticking, for 5 more minutes. Adjust the salt.

TO SERVE (EGG DISH): Put a fried crouton in each ramekin. Cover with the egg and ½ cup (125 ml) of the bean puree. Sprinkle with the cheese and serve immediately.

TO SERVE (SOUP): Dilute the bean puree with the water and bring to a simmer. Pour 1 cup (250 ml) of the beans into each soup bowl, place a crouton on the surface, and cover with an egg and cheese. Alternatively, you could put the egg into the beans and sprinkle small croutons on top. I like to serve this bean dish with some green sauce passed separately.

Nuevo y Sencillo Arte de Cocina—*New and Simple Art of Cooking*

This fat little volume, attractively printed on fine paper now yellowed with age, is the third edition, printed in 1865 and compiled by a Doctora Antonia Carrillo de Madrid. On her death a note inside informs us, "the rights and permissions passed to her daughter." It was written "for a Mexican lady" and the recipes tried by "intelligent people before it was handed to the printers." The preface states that the purpose of the book was "to enable cooks to prepare the recipes perfectly without any difficulty at all. The author has concentrated on explaining each recipe, as clearly as possible without unnecessary words." It is amusing to see that she has adapted them for Mexican palates "without European stimulants."

I always turn to the vegetables first because the meats and poultry are usually cooked in an elaborate way with lots of spices and sausages a la Española. Here you are apt to find more Mexican ingredients used.

I tried a stuffed green squash recipe: she is precise about their being "small and round" and tells us exactly how to clean them out for stuffing with a vegetable mixture of beets, cauliflower, carrot, lettuce, almonds, and raisins and then cover them with a walnut sauce (avocados were treated in the same manner). All too much, I thought when I tasted it. But I did find two bean recipes that I liked very much and give later on.

The chapter on preserves is very practical. Two whole pages are dedicated to candying pineapple (I shall try it one day soon), the test for the right consistency of the syrup (without a thermometer, of course) being "take a spoonful of the syrup, blow on it and then let it drip from the spoon. It should not run, but form a thick thread." Alternatively, you can take some between your thumb and index finger (ouch), and as you open them up a string of syrup is formed. In another recipe she warns that "butter should neither be discolored nor rancid."

FRIJOLES BLANCOS GUISADOS

WHITE BEANS WITH *CILANTRO* AND CHILE ANCHO

❀

[SERVES 6]

I COULDN'T RESIST THIS RECIPE, WHICH PRODUCES A THICK SOUP ENRICHED WITH CHEESE. IT IS ESPECIALLY GOOD AS A WINTER DISH WITH A SALAD AND is suitable for all but the strictest of vegetarians.

8 ounces (225 g) white beans
6 cups (1.5 l) water
¼ medium white onion, roughly sliced
3 garlic cloves, roughly chopped
4 large sprigs cilantro
salt to taste
2 ancho chiles, veins and seeds removed,
lightly toasted and soaked for 15 minutes
2 tablespoons lard or vegetable oil
2 tablespoons finely chopped white onion
3 ounces (85 g) queso fresco, crumbled, or Muenster, finely diced

TO SERVE
4 serrano chiles, charred and roughly chopped
finely chopped cilantro

[CONTINUED]

Pick over the beans, rinse well, and put into a large saucepan with the water, sliced onion, garlic, and *cilantro*. Cook over low heat until tender, about 2½ hours, depending on the age of the beans; they could also be left to cook overnight in the slow cooker. Add the salt and cook for about 10 minutes more.

Put 1 cup (250 ml) of the bean liquid plus ½ cup (125 ml) of the beans into a blender, add the chiles, torn into pieces, and blend until smooth.

Heat the lard in a skillet, add the chopped onion, and cook without browning until translucent. Add the chile puree and cook over fairly high heat for about 2 minutes, scraping the bottom of the pan to prevent sticking. Add this mixture to the beans and cook over medium heat until well seasoned, about 15 minutes.

Stir in the cheese and, when melted, serve immediately. Top with chiles and *cilantro al gusto*.

FRIJOLES CON PULQUE

BEANS COOKED WITH *PULQUE*

❈

[MAKES APPROXIMATELY 3½ CUPS (875 ML)]

THIS RECIPE IS RICH AND DELICIOUS. BEANS COOKED IN THIS WAY MAKE AN EXCELLENT FILLING FOR TACOS ACCOMPANIED BY A GREEN TOMATO SAUCE.

8 ounces (225 g) bayo, canario, or pinto beans
salt to taste
1 large ancho chile, seeds and veins removed
1 cup (250 ml) pulque (page 12) or light beer
2 tablespoons lard
2 tablespoons vegetable oil
3 rounded tablespoons finely chopped white onion
6 ounces (180 g) queso fresco, crumbled

Pick over the beans, rinse, drain, cover with water, and cook over low heat until the skins are soft, about 3½ hours. Add the salt and continue cooking for 10 more minutes. Reduce over high heat to 3½ cups (875 ml).

Lightly toast the chile, cover with hot water, and set aside to soak for about 15 minutes or until soft. Drain. Put ½ cup (125 ml) of the *pulque* into a blender, add the chile, and blend until almost smooth.

Heat the lard and oil in a skillet, add the onion, and fry without browning until translucent. Add the beans and chile mixture and cook until reduced and shiny. Add the rest of the *pulque* and continue cooking for about 15 minutes. When the mixture has reduced to a thick paste, stir in the cheese. When it has melted, serve immediately.

ARROZ CON CAMARONES

RICE WITH SHRIMP

❈

[SERVES APPROXIMATELY 6 AS A FIRST COURSE]

THIS DELICIOUS WAY OF COOKING RICE CAME UNDER THE HEADING "SOPAS," OR SOUPS—ACTUALLY IT'S A DRY SOUP AND A TYPICAL DISH TO BE SERVED during Lent.

If you can buy fresh shrimp with the heads intact, so much the better. The heads add to the flavor of the broth. You could also boost the flavor with some dried shrimp ground and added to the rice. Traditionally it is served alone, and it's best that way to appreciate the flavors, but I know some will want to put a sauce on it—make it a green sauce if you do.

8 ounces (225 g) medium shrimp
a few saffron threads
salt to taste
1½ cups (375 ml) long-grain white rice, not precooked or converted
½ cup (125 ml) vegetable oil or half lard and half oil
½ medium white onion, finely chopped
3 garlic cloves, finely chopped
2 jalapeño chiles, seeds and veins removed and cut into strips
8 ounces (225 g) tomatoes, finely chopped, about 1 heaped cup (265 ml)
4 large sprigs flat-leaf parsley, roughly chopped

[CONTINUED]

3 cloves, crushed

4 peppercorns, crushed

⅛ teaspoon cumin seeds, crushed

Peel and devein the shrimp. Put the shells and saffron into a pan, cover with water, add salt, and simmer for about 20 minutes. Strain, pressing down well on the shells to extract as much of the flavor as possible. Reduce or add water to the broth to make 2½ cups (625 ml). Discard the debris.

Cover the rice with hot water and soak for 10 minutes. Strain well and rinse once more in cold water. Drain well again.

Heat the oil in a heavy pan (a *cazuela* or Le Creuset casserole is ideal for this recipe). Give the rice a final shake in the strainer and stir it into the oil with a sprinkle of salt. Fry over medium heat, stirring from time to time so that it cooks evenly. When it sounds brittle as you stir it and is just about to turn a golden brown color, add the onion, garlic, and chile strips and fry for 2 minutes. Add the tomatoes, parsley, and spices and cook for 3 minutes or more until some of the juice has been absorbed.

Add the broth and cook over medium heat until it has been almost completely absorbed—10 to 15 minutes.

Stir in the shrimp, quickly and briefly, so as not to break up the rice, cover the pan, and cook for 5 minutes more, until the rice is tender and swollen.

Set aside, still covered, for 10 more minutes before serving.

Recetas Prácticas para la Señora de Casa
Practical Recipes for the Housewife, 1893 and 1895

There are two volumes with this title, published in Guadalajara in 1893 and 1895 to raise funds for the hospital of La Santísima Trinidad. They are not books that I have used very much, except as references, but some years ago I came across a recipe for *cajeta de piña*, a paste of pineapple and banana, almost identical to one given to me many years earlier by the very first maid I had when I came to Mexico in 1957. She couldn't remember how she had come by the recipe since she was unable to read or write. I published her recipe in *The Cuisines of Mexico* in 1972.

The preface to these two volumes has always amused me: "The majority of cookbooks that have been published to date have contained a great number of recipes which the compilers have gathered from here and there without taking care to see whether they are good or not, or whether they work or not. The recipes that we have printed in this volume, to the contrary, are all well-known and well tried . . . we have taken care not to include those that are more suitable for kitchens of inns, hotels or guest houses!"

One recipe that I particularly like, for a *salsa de chile pasilla*, follows.

SALSA DE CHILE PASILLA

PASILLA CHILE SAUCE

❁

[MAKES JUST OVER 1 CUP (260 ML)]

THIS IS A PASILLA CHILE SAUCE WITH SLIGHTLY DIFFERENT FLAVORS, EXCELLENT WITH BROILED OR COLD MEATS.

4 large pasilla chiles, seeds and veins removed
3 garlic cloves, roughly chopped
1 ⅛-inch (3-mm) cinnamon stick, crushed
4 peppercorns, crushed
2 tablespoons mild, fruity vinegar
1 cup (250 ml) water
salt to taste
finely chopped white onion

Heat a *comal* or griddle over low heat. Flatten the chiles out and toast carefully for about 1 minute on each side—the inside flesh should turn a tobacco color. Take care not to burn them, or the sauce will be bitter.

Douse, do not soak, the chiles in cold water and tear into pieces. Crush the garlic together with the cinnamon and peppercorns and dilute to a paste with the vinegar.

[CONTINUED]

Put the water into a blender, add the chile pieces and the garlic mixture, and blend to a textured sauce. Add salt. Just before serving, sprinkle the onion on top of the sauce.

Apendice al Libro de Cocina, *Jules Gouffe, 1893*

This is a slim volume with a decorative tooled red leather spine. The subtitle states that it is a "formula of Mexican and Spanish Cuisines" and by a Frenchman, no less. I can only assume that the main volume is dedicated to French cuisine.

This *Apendice* has no introduction, and while many of the recipes are of decidedly Spanish origin, there are also several typically Mexican dishes, like *mole, pipián,* etc. But what I found more interesting were those recipes of European origin that incorporated Mexican ingredients. *Jamón en vino tinto,* ham in red wine, was immediately followed by *Jamón a la mexicana,* ham Mexican style, substituting *pulque* for the red wine. Some cakes and cookies included ground hominy flour.

There are no fewer than sixty-two sauces; those that particularly caught my attention while browsing through the book were *salsa de gitomate con chile a la italiana,* tomato sauce with chile Italian style; one made with *tomate verde* and white wine—a *mestizo* sauce if ever there was one; and a relish, more than a sauce, of *chile poblano.* There were *aceitunas en adobo*—olives in a *chile ancho* sauce, and *sopa de fideos con chile*—pasta or dry soup of vermicelli and *chile ancho,* neither of which I had ever come across before.

The last recipe follows, along with the irresistible *calabacitas divinas.*

SOPA SECA DE FIDEO CON CHILE ANCHO

ANGEL HAIR PASTA WITH ANCHO CHILE

✳

[SERVES 4]

SOPA SECA, OR DRY SOUP, IS SERVED AS A PASTA COURSE WOULD BE IN ITALY.

I like to serve this dish as a separate course or lunch dish, with slices of avocado and sprinkled with a finely grated strong cheese and, of course, quartered limes.

4 ancho *chiles, veins and seeds removed*

2½ *cups (625 ml) chicken broth or water*

2 *cloves*

1 *garlic clove, roughly chopped*

⅛ *teaspoon cumin seeds*

¼ *cup (63 ml) vegetable oil*

4 *ounces (115 g) very fine vermicelli or angel hair pasta,*
preferably in skeins or nests

salt to taste

approximately ⅓ cup (83 ml) finely grated queso añejo *or* Romano

avocado slices

quartered limes

Cover the chiles with water and simmer for 5 minutes. Leave to soak for another 5 minutes or until soft and reconstituted. Strain.

Put ¼ cup (63 ml) of the broth into a blender, add the cloves, garlic, and cumin seeds, and blend until smooth. Add another cup of the broth, add the strained chiles a few at a time, and blend until smooth, adding more broth only if necessary to release the blender blade.

Heat the oil in a heavy pan, add the pasta, and fry, turning it over from time to time, until it has turned a deep golden color, about 5 minutes. Strain off the excess oil. Add the blended sauce to the pasta and fry over medium heat, scraping the bottom of the pan to prevent sticking, for about 3 minutes. Add the remaining broth with salt as necessary and cook, covered, over low heat until the pasta is just cooked (neither al dente nor mushy)—5 to 8 minutes.

Serve as suggested above or with crumbled fried *chorizo* and crème fraîche.

CALABACITAS DIVINAS

DIVINE SQUASH

✸

[SERVES 4 TO 6]

THIS RECIPE IS DIVINE ONLY IF YOU HAVE TOP-QUALITY *CHORIZO*, EITHER COMMERCIAL OR HOMEMADE. IN THE ORIGINAL RECIPE THE CHILES AND *EPAzote* were blended, but I think this method gives a better flavor.

2 tablespoons lard or vegetable oil
1½ pounds (675 g) zucchini, finely diced
4 heaped tablespoons finely chopped white onion
salt to taste
5 chorizos, each about 3 inches (8 cm) long, skinned and crumbled
*3 poblano chiles, charred, peeled, veins and seeds removed,
and cut into narrow strips*
4 sprigs epazote leaves, roughly chopped

Heat the lard, add the zucchini, onion, and salt, cover the pan, and cook over low heat until the squash is just tender, not soft—about 10 minutes. Shake the pan from time to time to prevent sticking. If the squash is rather dry, add a few tablespoons of water.

Put the *chorizos* into a small pan over low heat and cook until the fat renders out. Strain and add the *chorizo* to the squash together with the chile strips and *epazote*. Cook, uncovered, until all the flavors have blended—about 5 minutes.

SALSA DE CHILE POBLANO

POBLANO CHILE SAUCE

✸

[MAKES APPROXIMATELY ⅔ CUP (164 ML)]

THIS IS REALLY A RELISH MORE THAN A *SALSA*. THE FLAVOR IS CONCENTRATED, AND A LITTLE GOES A LONG WAY. I LIKE TO SERVE IT WITH BROILED fish or in chicken tacos.

3 poblano *chiles, charred, peeled, and veins and seeds removed*

2 tablespoons finely chopped white onion

2 to 3 tablespoons light olive oil

salt to taste

Cut the chiles into very fine dice; do not crush them, or they will lose their crisp texture. Mix in the rest of the ingredients and set aside to season for about 1 hour before serving. (It is better the next day.)

SALSA DE TOMATE Y VINO

MEXICAN GREEN TOMATO AND WHITE WINE SAUCE

❀

[MAKES APPROXIMATELY 2 CUPS (500 ML)]

ANOTHER RELISH, THIS TIME VERY SHARP. THE AUTHOR RECOMMENDS SERVING IT WITH ROASTED PORK LOIN OR PIGEONS.

2 tablespoons lard or vegetable oil

1 pound (450 g) tomatoes verdes, husks removed and very finely chopped,
about 2 rounded cups (550 ml)

salt to taste

3 cloves

4 peppercorns

4 sprigs thyme or heaped ¼ teaspoon dried

1 cup (250 ml) sweet white wine

Heat the lard in a skillet, add the *tomates verdes* and salt, and fry, covered, over low heat until very soft, about 5 minutes. Crush the cloves, peppercorns, and thyme together, add to the pan, and fry, uncovered, for a few seconds more. Add the wine and cook for about 5 minutes or until the sauce has reduced a little and is well seasoned.

BASIC
INFORMATION

The following notes are meant only as a useful guide to the uncommon ingredients that are called for in these recipes, basic cooking utensils, and measurements. More detailed information on other ingredients, including chiles, cooking methods, etc., can be found in *The Art of Mexican Cooking* (Bantam Books, 1989).

Cooking Equipment

In Mexico one cannot visualize a kitchen without a *comal* (the traditional mortar and pestle made of volcanic rock), *molcajete*, or *cazuelas* and a *tamale* steamer.

· A *comal* is a disk of thin metal or unglazed clay that goes over a stovetop burner or fire for cooking tortillas or char-roasting ingredients, mainly for table sauces. Use a heavy cast-iron griddle if you have no *comal*.

· *Cazuelas* are wide-topped glazed clay pots for cooking on a gas flame or over wood or charcoal. They are not suitable for an electric burner. Heavy casseroles, such as Le Creuset, or heavy skillets of different sizes can be substituted.

· A blender, preferably with two jars, is endlessly useful.

· A food processor is useful for only a few recipes, where stated. It will never blend a chile or other sauce as efficiently as a blender.

· *Tamale* steamer or how to improvise one: The ideal, of course, is to find a simple metal Mexican *tamale* steamer with four parts: a straight-sided, deep metal container with a per-

[522]

forated rack that sits just above the water level, an upright divider to support the *tamales* in three sections, and a tight lid (illustrated in *The Art of Mexican Cooking*). This type of steamer can often be found in a Mexican or Latin American grocery along with the *molcajetes* and tortilla presses. Failing that, any steamer can be used as long as the part holding the *tamales* is set deep down near the concentration of steam—*tamales* must cook as fast as possible so that the beaten *masa* firms up and the filling doesn't leak into it, a messy affair! A couscous steamer is not suitable for that reason.

I have had to improvise on many occasions: I think the most successful was a perforated spaghetti or vegetable holder, which normally sits down into the water, set onto four upturned custard cups so as to hold it just above the level of the water—which should be about 3 inches deep. To hold in as much steam and heat as possible, cover the top of the pot with tightly stretched plastic wrap. (But remember to prick and deflate it before inspecting the *tamales*.)

Measures and Equivalents

I have attempted to give both weights and cup measures where feasible.

For liquid measures I use a standard 8-ounce (250-ml) glass cup, and *for solids* an 8-ounce (250-ml) metal cup. Preferably measuring cups should be the standard ones with straight sides and not those plastic ones in fancy shapes.

When I refer to 8 ounces (225 g), I mean weight, not the 8-ounce liquid measure. For example, 1 cup (250 ml) of corn *masa* weighs about 9 to 9½ ounces (250 to 262 g) and may even weigh a little more if it is very damp. A cup (250 ml) of dry *tamal masa* weighs about 6 ounces (180 g).

I always try to persuade cooks to buy a good heavy-duty scale, not the light ones that hang from a wall and bounce around or those that have a container that slips off its base with the slightest movement. Not only will you weigh more accurately but you've spared the messy business of forcing fat into cups and then having to scrape it out and deal with a greasy sink.

Ingredients

See the Index for ingredients that are featured in boxes throughout the book: *pulque*, *chilacayote*, *pozole*, *chicharrón*, *zapote negro*, *chaya*, dried shrimp, avocado leaves, and *asiento*.

FATS AND OILS

PORK LARD is still used in many areas for cooking: it's either a pale cream color or a much darker stronger lard that comes from the bottom of the *chicharrón* vat. The latter is often used with the little bits of *chicharrón* still in it and called *asiento*.

The taste lard gives to these traditional dishes is simply incomparable, and it actually has less saturated fat and cholesterol than butter. If you don't have access to good fresh lard (from a Mexican or German butcher, not the overprocessed blocks at the supermarket, which are often beef fat), it's very easy to make your own.

HOMEMADE LARD

Preheat the oven to 325°F (165°C).

Chop a pound or two of pork fat into small cubes, discarding any bits of tough skin. A handful at a time, mince that fat in a food processor.

Place it in one or two heavy ovenproof skillets on the top rack of the oven for 20 to 25 minutes or until the fat has rendered out. Strain out the crunchy little bits and give them to the birds.

Store the lard, tightly sealed, in the refrigerator, where it will keep for several months.

Vegetable oil of several types is available in Mexico, but I still prefer safflower oil, called *cártamo* or *alazor*. Corn oil tends to be too heavy.

Olive oil is occasionally used for recipes that are more Spanish in origin.

VINEGAR

If not otherwise stated in the recipe, any commercial vinegar will do. To make a mild vinegar it is best to mix half rice vinegar with a good-quality wine vinegar.

Many Mexican cooks, especially those living in the provinces, make and use a mild pineapple vinegar (see recipes in *Cuisines of Mexico* and *The Art of Mexican Cooking*). In Colima the vinegar is pale and honey colored, made of fermented *tuba*, the sap from a local palm tree. In Tabasco and Veracruz a delicious vinegar is made from overripe bananas.

BANANA VINEGAR

✹

[MAKES I PINT]

4 pounds overripe bananas

You will need 2 containers: one with a perforated bottom that sits firmly into a second non-reactive container. Slit the skins of the bananas, but do not remove them, and press them into the top container. Cover with cheesecloth and a lid and set in a warm, damp place. A pale orange-colored liquid will exude and collect in the bottom container. Little flies will invade, and there will be a rich brewing smell. Foamy cream-colored flecks will appear in the liquid —don't worry. From time to time, press down on the rotting bananas. Given the right amount of heat and humidity, this first process can take about 2 weeks and up to 1 month. When you see that the bananas will yield no more juice you are ready to proceed.

Have ready a sterilized glass container and strain the liquid into it through cheesecloth. Cover the jar and set in a warm place. As the days go by, a thick skin will form on the surface. Don't worry, this will gradually turn into the "mother," a gelatinous substance that makes for good vinegar. After 2 weeks the vinegar should have attained full strength and a pleasant acidity. Remove the top layer and rinse so that you have an almost transparent gelatinous mother. Put this back into the jar. I have kept this type of vinegar for several years.

CHEESE

The most difficult cheese to find a substitute for is *queso fresco*. In Mexico it is traditionally sold in small round cakes about 2 inches (5 cm) thick. When made correctly, it is an unso-phisticated but delicious cheese that is crumbled on top of *antojitos* (*masa* snacks), *enchiladas*, etc., or used for stuffing chiles and *quesadillas*.

To make *queso fresco*, whole milk is clabbered, the curds are drained, and then they are ground to fine crumbs. They are then pressed into wooden hoops and left to drain off the excess whey. The cheese should be creamy colored, pleasantly acidy, and melt readily when heated. Very few commercial copies of *queso fresco* in the United States fulfill those requirements, with one notable exception that I know of (I hope now I shall hear of others), made by the Mozzarella Cheese Company in Dallas (2944 Elm Street, Dallas, TX 75226; 214-741-4072). Once you find a good one, always buy extra and freeze it for up to 3 months.

For many *antojitos* the dry, salty *cotija* or *añejo* cheese may be used, but it will not—and should not—melt easily. Several good ones are distributed in the United States, but alas, they are cut into pieces from a large wheel and often no brand name is put on the package.

For stuffing chiles, etc., use my standby, Muenster (domestic, not imported) that melts easily.

EPAZOTE

Epazote, Teloxys (formerly *Chenopodium*) *ambrosioides,* is a North American herb that grows wild in poor soil. It has pointed, serrated leaves and a clean pungent taste—a little like creosote. It is an essential flavor in the cooking of central and southern Mexico. Tortilla soup is not a real tortilla soup without it! You may find it in a Mexican grocery or at the farmer's market, but it's easy to grow (see Sources).

ACHIOTE

Achiote paste—annatto seeds ground with other spices and mixed with crushed garlic and vinegar or bitter orange juice—is a popular seasoning in recipes from the Yucatecan peninsula. However, in Tabasco and the Isthmus of Tehuantepec they use pure *achiote*, which is just the coloring boiled from the seeds and reduced to a paste. The pure paste is hard to come by elsewhere, but the Yucatecan paste is distributed widely in Mexico and the United States under different brand names, the most popular of which is La Anita.

To make the paste at home, see *The Art of Mexican Cooking,* pages 427 to 428.

HOJA SANTA

This large heart-shaped leaf of a tropical shrub, *Piper auritum,* with a pronounced anisey flavor is used to season foods in the southern part of Mexico. It also grows wild along Texas riverbanks, I am told; it is often referred to as the rootbeer plant and the flavor likened to sarsaparilla.

In some recipes the flavor may be replaced by avocado leaves, but for others there is no substitute.

I have seen plants for sale in many nurseries throughout the Southwest, and occasionally Mexican markets will sell packages of the dried leaves, but they tend to crumble to dust. Fresh leaves can be mail ordered either from: Lucinda Hutson (who wrote a charming and informative book on tequila) at 4612 Rosedale, Austin, TX 78756, (512) 454-8905, or Brookside Farms, 13110 Roy Road, Pearland, TX 77581, (713) 997-2291 and 771-3314.

BROILING TOMATOES

This technique gives tomatoes a very special depth of flavor; it's used for a lot of cooked and fresh sauces, and it's a great way to preserve a large harvest for the winter months—just broil the tomatoes and store them in the freezer.

For just one or two tomatoes, roast them on an ungreased *comal* over medium heat, turning from time to time, until they're blistered and brown all over. For a bumper crop, choose a baking sheet just large enough to hold the tomatoes, line it with foil, and place the tomatoes on it. Broil them 2 inches from the heat, turning frequently until they're blistered and brown and soft inside. Scoop them up, including the juices, and use them in recipes or store in 1-pound batches in the freezer.

SALSA DE JITOMATE

COOKED TOMATO SAUCE

✺

[MAKES ABOUT 2¼ CUPS (563 ML)]

A GOOD BASIC TOMATO SAUCE WITH ITS ORIGINS IN THE SIERRA DE PUEBLA. YOU NEED DELICIOUS RIPE TOMATOES FOR THIS SAUCE; CANNED OR OUT-OF-season tomatoes just won't deliver the flavor.

1½ pounds (about 3 large) tomatoes (675 g)
4 chiles serranos, or more to taste
2 garlic cloves, peeled and roughly chopped
3 tablespoons safflower oil
sea salt to taste

[CONTINUED]

Put the tomatoes in a saucepan with the chiles, cover with water, and bring to a simmer. Continue to cook at a fast simmer until the tomatoes are fairly soft but not falling apart—about 5 minutes. Set aside.

Put the garlic and ⅓ cup (83 ml) of the cooking water into a blender jar and blend until you have a textured consistency—about 5 seconds. Add the tomatoes and blend for a few seconds; the sauce should have a roughish texture.

Heat the oil in a frying pan or *cazuela*, add the sauce, and cook over high heat, stirring from time to time and scraping the bottom of the dish, until reduced and the raw taste of garlic has disappeared—about 6 to 8 minutes. Add salt to taste.

CALDO DE JITOMATE

A SIMPLE TOMATO BROTH

❉

[MAKES ENOUGH BROTH FOR 4 LARGE CHILES]

CHILES RELLENOS ARE USUALLY REHEATED IN A SIMPLE TOMATO BROTH SUCH AS THIS ONE. YOU COULD ALSO ADD A BAY LEAF, ¼ TEASPOON DRIED THYME, a ¼-inch (7-mm) piece of cinnamon stick, and a clove.

*¾ pounds (about 2 medium) tomatoes,
roughly chopped, unpeeled (340 g)*
2 tablespoons finely chopped white onion
1 garlic clove, peeled and roughly chopped
½ cup (125 ml) water
1½ tablespoons safflower oil
2½ cups (625 ml) chicken broth or pork broth
sea salt to taste

Put the tomatoes, onion, and garlic with the water in a blender jar; blend until fairly smooth.

Heat the oil in a heavy pan, add the blended ingredients, and cook over fairly high heat until reduced and thickened—about 10 minutes. Add the broth, adjust seasoning, and cook for 5 minutes more.

Add the stuffed and fried chiles and cook gently, turning them over very carefully, for about 10 minutes.

BITTER ORANGE SUBSTITUTE

❀

[MAKES ABOUT ½ CUP (125 ML)]

2 tablespoons fresh grapefruit juice
2 tablespoons fresh orange juice
1 teaspoon finely grated grapefruit rind
¼ cup (63 ml) fresh lime juice

Mix everything together thoroughly about 1 hour before using. Keep in the refrigerator, tightly sealed, no more than 3 or 4 days.

POACHED AND SHREDDED CHICKEN

❀

[MAKES ABOUT 2 CUPS (500 ML)]

1 large chicken breast, about 1½ pounds (675 g), with skin and bone
3 cups (750 ml) chicken broth
salt as necessary

Cut the chicken breast in half and put into a pan with the chicken broth. Bring to a simmer and continue simmering until the meat is tender—about 20 minutes. Set aside to cool off in the broth. Remove skin and bone and shred the meat coarsely. (If it is shredded too finely, the meat loses flavor.) Add salt. Reserve the chicken broth for another dish.

MASA OR DOUGH FOR
CORN TORTILLAS AND TAMALES

✼

[MAKES 1¾ POUNDS (800 G) — 3¼ CUPS (813 ML)]

I HAVE ALWAYS SLAVISHLY FOLLOWED THE METHOD OF PREPARING DRIED CORN FOR TORTILLA *MASA* THAT MOST OF MY NEIGHBORS AND MY EARLY teachers employed. But one day Señora Catalina, who comes to care for the masses of flower pots I have dotted around the terraces, told me of another method. "It will give you the most delicious *masa*," she said. Here is her method:

1 quart (1 l) water
2 tablespoons powdered (slaked) lime
1 pound (450 g) dried corn, about 2¾ cups (688 ml)

Heat the water in a large nonreactive pan. Stir in the lime and bring to a rolling boil. Add the corn, stir well, cover, and again bring to a rolling boil. Set aside, still covered, until the following day, a minimum of 12 hours. Then rinse the corn well, strain, and grind it, or send to the mill to be ground to the required consistency: either very smooth for tortillas or *martajada* or more rough-textured for some types of *antojitos* or *tamales*.

LIME (CAL)

In Mexico slaked lime (calcium oxide) is always used to prepare *masa* dough. The lime comes in small rocks, which you can see for sale in Mexican marketplaces. In America, your best source is a garden supply store, and you may have to buy a lifetime supply, since it usually comes in very large bags.

Once you have the lime, it needs to be slaked. Take a piece about the size of a golf ball and crush it as completely as you can. Put it in a noncorrosible bowl (and be careful not to get any near your eyes). Sprinkle the lime well with cold water; it will hiss impressively and send up a little vapor. Once the action subsides, your lime is slaked. Dilute with water, and then pour the milky liquid through a strainer into the corn water for the masa.

Take a taste before you cook it: there should be a slightly acrid burn; if it seems really strong and bitter, dilute it a little; if it's weak, add a little more lime.

Store any remaining lime in a tightly sealed jar. Over time it will slake on its own, as it draws moisture from the air—you can still use it, though it won't fizz up in the same way.

DRIED CHILES REFERRED TO IN THIS BOOK

NAME	AVG. SIZE	SHAPE	COLOR	SURFACE	FLAVOR	HEAT
ancho (dried poblano)	4.5 x 3 in. 12 x 8 cm	triangular	raisin	wrinkled	fruity	generally mild with exceptions
árbol, used fresh locally	2.5 x .25 in. 6.5 cm x 7 mm	long, skinny	brick red	smooth shiny	sharp	very, very hot
cascabel, fresh bola, local	1.25 x 1 in. 3 x 2.5 cm	roundish	raisin	smooth shiny	fairly sharp	hot
chilcostle	5 x 1 in. 13 x 2.5 cm	long, skinny, often curved at the end	raisin with lighter patches	matte undulating	sharp	hot
cora, used fresh locally	1 x .5 in. 2.5 cm x 13 mm	elongated oval	raisin	smooth shiny	fairly sharp	hot
guajillo, used fresh locally	5 x 1.25 in. 13 x 3 cm	elongated triangular	raisin	smooth shiny	fairly sharp	fairly hot
mora (smoke-dried jalapeño)	2 x .75 in. 5 x 2 cm	triangular blunt	mulberry	wrinkled matte	fruity, sharp smoky	very, very hot
pasado (peeled dried poblano or Anaheim)	2.5 x 1.25 in. 6.5 x 3 cm	1. triangular 2. long, narrow	blackish	fairly smooth matte	fruity	1. slightly hot 2. mild
pasilla (dried chilaca)	6 x 1 in. 15.5 x 2.5 cm	long, skinny blunt	black	shiny, vertical wrinkles	fruity, sharp smoky	medium to hot
pasilla de Oaxaca	3.5 x 1.25 in. 9 x 3 cm	long, narrow	mulberry	wrinkled matte	fruity smoky	very hot
seco del norte de la tierra (dried Anaheim type)		long, narrow		smooth matte	fruity	hot to mild

FRESH CHILES REFERRED TO IN THIS BOOK

NAME	AVG. SIZE	SHAPE	COLOR	SURFACE	FLAVOR	HEAT
Anaheim, verde del norte, etc.	5.5 x 1.25 in. 14.5 x 3 cm	long, thin, often blunt	light green	smooth, shiny	mild	mild to hot
chilaca (dried, pasilla)	7 x 1 in. 18 x 2.5 cm	long, skinny	blackish green	shiny, ridged vertically	sweetish, fruity	mild to hot
güero, not dried, also caribe	2.5 x 1 in. 6.5 x 2.5 cm	short, triangular	yellow	smooth, shiny	sharp	hot
habanero, not dried in Mexico	1.75 x 1.25 in. 4.5 x 3 cm	lantern-shaped	light green orange when ripe	shiny, smooth undulating	sharply perfumed	extremely hot
jalapeño (smoke-dried, chipotle)	2.5 x 1 in. 6.5 x 2.5 cm	long, fat, blunt	mid to dark green	smooth, shiny	fruity green	very hot
manzano, not dried	2 x 1.75 in. 5 x 4.5 cm	squat	green to yellow (var. red)	smooth, shiny	sharp, fruity	extremely hot
poblano (dried, ancho)	4.5 x 2.5 in. 12 x 6.5 cm	triangular fat, pointed	very dark green	shiny, slightly undulating	fruity, rich	medium to hot
serrano (dried, serrano)	2 x .5 in. 5 cm x 13 mm	bullet-shaped	mid to dark green	shiny, smooth	sharp, almost bitter	very hot
x-cat-ik, not dried	4.5 x .75 in. 12 x 2 cm	long, thin pointed	pale yellow	smooth, shiny, slightly undulating	sharp but fruity	hot

SOURCES

With the deluge of foods coming in from Mexico and the steady stream of workers coming back and forth across the border, we may soon see the day when a sources section in a Mexican cookbook is unnecessary, at least for city dwellers. Meanwhile, here are a few suggestions for mail-order foods, plants, and equipment. Other sources are mentioned with discussion of specific ingredients.

The CMC Company

800-262-2780

PO Box 322

Avalon, NJ 08202

Stocks dried chiles (including *chipotle morita* and *pasilla de Oaxaca*), Mexican avocado leaves, *chorizo*, *masa* (Masteca brand from Texas), *pozole*, *piloncillo*, and equipment such as tortilla presses, *comales*, and *molcajetes*. No fresh foods.

Shepherd's Garden Seeds

860-482-3638

30 Irene Street

Torrington, CT 06790-6658

Sells seeds for many chiles, *tomates verdes* (tomatillos), and several Mexican herbs, including *epazote*.

King Arthur Flour

800-827-6836

PO Box 876

Norwich, VT 05055-0876

Stocks Nielsen-Massey's real Mexican vanilla.

RECIPE INDEX

GENERAL INDEX